Dynamic Capabilities Between Firm Organization and Local Systems of Production

Changes in technology and demand require firms to learn how to continuously reshape unique and non-imitable resources and competences. A firm's capacity to achieve this is captured by the concept of dynamic capabilities. This book offers an analysis of how firms manage to reconfigure their pool of idiosyncratic resources, skills and competencies to deal with the highly turbulent environments in which they are embedded, thus tackling the issue of how dynamic capabilities must be defined and conceptualized.

This book brings together several contributions aimed at showing how firms' differential exploitation of their dynamic capabilities comes to be highly dependent on the role of socio-territorial entities and on the institutional set up. Thus, different formal and informal types of organization are observed at different levels of analysis. In so doing, the book aims at conveying a transversal perspective to the analysis of firms' dynamics, calling for a multidisciplinary and multilayer approach.

This book will be fascinating reading for researchers and policy-makers looking to improve their understanding of the concepts underlining dynamic capabilities. It will also be of interest to students engaged with the theory of the firm, industrial districts and clusters and business groups.

Riccardo Leoncini and **Sandro Montresor** are both Professors of Economics at the University of Bologna.

Routledge studies in global competition
Edited by John Cantwell
University of Reading, UK
and
David Mowery
University of California, Berkeley, USA

14 **The Economics of Innovation, New Technologies and Structural Change**
Cristiano Antonelli

15 **European Union Direct Investment in China**
Characteristics, challenges and perspectives
Daniel Van Den Bulcke, Haiyan Zhang and Maria do Céu Esteves

16 **Biotechnology in Comparative Perspective**
Edited by Gerhard Fuchs

17 **Technological Change and Economic Performance**
Albert L. Link and Donald S. Siegel

18 **Multinational Corporations and European Regional Systems of Innovation**
John Cantwell and Simona Iammarino

19 **Knowledge and Innovation in Regional Industry**
An entrepreneurial coalition
Roel Rutten

20 **Local Industrial Clusters**
Existence, emergence and evolution
Thomas Brenner

21 **The Emerging Industrial Structure of the Wider Europe**
Edited by Francis McGowen, Slavo Radosevic and Nick Von Tunzelmann

22 **Entrepreneurship**
A new perspective
Thomas Grebel

23 **Evaluating Public Research Institutions**
The U.S. Advanced Technology Program's Intramural Research Initiative
Albert N. Link and John T. Scott

24 **Location and Competition**
Edited by Steven Brakman and Harry Garretsen

25 **Entrepreneurship and Dynamics in the Knowledge Economy**
Edited by Charlie Karlsson, Börje Johansson and Roger R. Stough

26 **Evolution and Design of Institutions**
Edited by Christian Schubert and Georg von Wangenheim

27 **The Changing Economic Geography of Globalization**
Reinventing space
Edited by Giovanna Vertova

28 **Economics of the Firm**
Analysis, evolution and history
Edited by Michael Dietrich

29 **Innovation, Technology and Hypercompetition**
Hans Gottinger

30 **Mergers and Acquisitions in Asia**
A global perspective
Roger Y. W. Tang and Ali M. Metwalli

31 **Competitiveness of New Industries**
Institutional framework and learning in information technology in Japan, the U.S. and Germany
Edited by Cornelia Storz and Andreas Moerke

32 **Entry and Post-Entry Performance of Newborn Firms**
Marco Vivarelli

33 **Changes in Regional Firm Founding Activities**
A theoretical explanation and empirical evidence
Dirk Fornahl

34 **Risk Appraisal and Venture Capital in High Technology New Ventures**
Gavin C. Reid and Julia A. Smith

35 **Competing for Knowledge**
Creating, connecting and growing
Robert Huggins and Hiro Izushi

36 **Corporate Governance, Finance and the Technological Advantage of Nations**
Andrew Tylecote and Francesca Visintin

37 **Dynamic Capabilities Between Firm Organization and Local Systems of Production**
Edited by Riccardo Leoncini and Sandro Montresor

Dynamic Capabilities Between Firm Organization and Local Systems of Production

Edited by Riccardo Leoncini and Sandro Montresor

Routledge
Taylor & Francis Group
LONDON AND NEW YORK

First published 2008
by Routledge
2 Park Square, Milton Park, Abingdon, Oxfordshire OX14 4RN

Simultaneously published in the USA and Canada
by Routledge
711 Third Avenue, New York, NY 10017

First issued in paperback 2014

Routledge is an imprint of the Taylor & Francis Group, an informa business

Typeset in Times by Wearset Ltd, Boldon, Tyne and Wear

British Library Cataloguing in Publication Data
A catalogue record for this book is available from the British Library

Library of Congress Cataloging in Publication Data
A catalogue record for this book has been requested

ISBN 978-0-415-40000-8 (hbk)

ISBN 978-1-138-01048-2 (pbk)

ISBN 978-0-203-93739-6 (ebk)

R.L.
To Sabrina, Davide, Lorenzo, again and again and again . . .

S.M.
To Betty, indelible mother of my soul

Contents

Figures

Tables

Contributors

Antonelli, Gilberto, Department of Economics, University of Bologna, Italy.

Belussi, Fiorenza, Department of Economics, University of Padua, Italy.

Cainelli, Giulio, Department of Mediterranean Societies, University of Bari, Italy; CERIS-CNR, Milan, Italy.

Ciravegna, Luciano, DESTIN, The London School of Economics and Political Sciences, London, UK; INCAE Business School, Costa Rica; Department of Economics and Quantitative Methods (SEMEQ), University of Piemonte Orientale, Novara, Italy.

De Liso, Nicola, Faculty of Law and Department of Law, University of Lecce, Italy.

Gabrisch, Hubert, Halle Institute for Economic Research, Halle, Saale, Denmark.

Giuliani, Elisa, Department of Business Economics, University of Pisa, Italy; Science and Policy Research Unit (SPRU), University of Sussex, UK.

Iacobucci, Donato, Department of Informatic, Business and Automation Engineering, Marche Politechnic University, Ancona, Italy.

Leoncini, Riccardo, Department of Economics, University of Bologna, Italy; CERIS-CNR, Milan, Italy.

Lombardi, Mauro, Department of Economics, University of Florence, Italy.

Marangoni, GianDemetrio, Department of Economics, University of Padua, Italy.

Mollo, Maria de Lourdes, Department of Economics, University of Brasilia, Brazil.

Montresor, Sandro, Department of Economics, University of Bologna, Italy.

Morrison, Andrea, Department of Economics and Quantitative Methods (SEMEQ), University of Piemonte Orientale, Novara, Italy; CESPRI, Bocconi University of Milan, Italy.

Nosvelli, Mario, CERIS-CNR, Milan, Italy.

Pegoretti, Giovanni, Department of Economics, University of Trento, Italy.

Pietrobelli, Carlo, CREI, University of Rome 3, Italy.

Pilotti, Luciano, Department of Economics and Management, University of Milan, Italy.

Rabellotti, Roberta, Department of Economics and Quantitative Methods (SEMEQ), University of Piemonte Orientale, Novara, Italy.

Sedita, Silvia Rita, Department of Economics, University of Padua, Italy.

Segnana, Maria Luigia, Department of Economics, University of Trento, Italy.

Solari, Stefano, Department of Economics, University of Padua, Italy.

Teixeira, Joanilio Rodolpho, Department of Economics, University of Brasilia, Brazil.

Vergori, Anna Serena, Faculty of Law, University of Lecce, Italy.

Zamparini, Luca, Faculty of Social, Political and Territorial Sciences, University of Lecce, Italy.

Acknowledgements

We warmly thank, first of all, the authors of all chapters for their work for this book, including careful revisions of their contributions. We also thank the other researchers who participated in the PRIN Project 2003–2005 on "Dynamic capabilities, firm organization and local systems of production", within which this book germinated, and all those who attended the workshops where preliminary versions of the chapters have been discussed, for their useful comments and discussions, in particular: Antonio Accetturo, Alessia Amighini, Roberto Antonietti, Mauro Baranzini, Leonardo Bargigli, Stefano Breschi, Ferruccio Bresolin, Stefano Brusoni, Tommaso Ciarli, Luciano Ciravegna, Giorgio Colacchio, Lucia Cusmano, Bruno Dallago, Annunziata De Felice, Andrea De Panizza, Giuditta De Prato, Laura Ehrlic, Giovanni Filatrella, Dimitri Gagliardi, Rishab Ghosh, Antonella Guerrieri, Giovanni Guidetti, Alessandro Iacopini, Sandrine Labory, Francesco Lissoni, Alessandro Lomi, Marilene Lorizio, Isabella Martucci, Andrea Masini, Massimiliano Mazzanti, Maureen McKelvey, Stanley Metcalfe, Anna Montini, Fabio Montobbio, Enrica Moranti, Pier Carlo Padoan, Ivana Paniccia, Paolo Pini, Marco Rangone, Francesco Rentocchini, Alessandro Romagnoli, Stefania Rossetti, Federica Saliola, Alessia Sammara, Paolo Seri, Giuseppe Tattara, Marco Valente, Giovanna Vertova, Giuseppe Vittucci Marzetti, Roberto Zoboli.

Finally, we want to thank Nicola Grassano, Luisa Mengoni, Francesco Rentocchini of the Routledge Project Management Team and, above all, Kelly Alderson of Wearset Publishing Services, for their careful, patient and passionate editorial assistance.

Introduction

Riccardo Leoncini and Sandro Montresor

The origins of the book

This book hosts a selection of the numerous papers produced within the 2003 PRIN Project (Project of Research of National Relevance) on "*Dynamic Capabilities Between Firm Organization and Local Systems of Production*".[1] The Project involved, for two years (2003–2005), a large number of Italian researchers located in six research units, based in the following Universities[2]: Polytechnic University of "Le Marche" (Ancona), University of Bologna, University of Lecce, University of Eastern Piedmont "Amedeo Avogadro" (Novara), University of Padua and University of Trento. The research units carried out their activity with the co-financing of the Italian Minister of University and Research (MIUR) under the coordination of the Research Unit of Bologna, of which the two editors of this book have been, respectively, director (Riccardo Leoncini) and assistant director (Sandro Montresor).

The starting point of the Project was the need, perceived by its components on the basis of their research experience and competences, to develop a new interpretative framework of such a crucial issue as *the firms' dynamics*. On the one hand, it was evident that, at the beginning of the twenty-first century, the advent of the so called "learning-economy" had brought to the fore, in the debate and of the policy agenda, the firms' capacity to deal with faster technological changes, shorter product life-cycles, more frequent job shifts and a more lively industrial demography (David and Foray, 1995, p. 14). On the other hand, the economists' toolbox to deal with this issue, although quite packed, did not appear completely equipped. In particular, it seemed to lack a conceptual framework that could help disentangling the manifold and complex nature of the dynamics of the firms' as *organizations* embedded in *local production systems*.

In analysing firms' dynamics, internal organizational factors (such as, for example, labour division, routines and governance structures) are as important as external environmental ones (such as, for example, market structure, institutional set-up and infrastructures), and as important are their mutual relationships, given that the former co-evolve with the latter. However, the economic research on the issue appears to have mainly treated these two sets of factors separately, by focusing either on the former or on the latter, depending on the specific line of analysis. A conceptual bridge between the two sets of determinants of the firm's dynamics appeared to the Project's components still missing and urgent to be developed.

In trying to fill this gap, the research team identified the notion of "dynamic capabilities" – the keyword of the title – as a useful starting point to derive a broad analytical framework of the firms' dynamics. Once meant in a general, economic sense, the concept of dynamic capabilities can actually be used to link consistently the main research strands on the issue. A concise review of the theoretical background of the Project, and of the book, can be useful in illustrating this point.

The relevant literature

Since its appearance in strategic management (Teece and Pisano, 1994; Teece *et al.*, 1997),[3] the concept of "dynamic capabilities" has progressively flourished in industrial organization as an extremely useful concept to investigate the firms' dynamics. In particular, it has turned out to be very fruitful in addressing the way organizations deal with technological challenges (Dosi *et al.*, 2000, p. 15) and, in general, in accounting for the different dynamic performances firms show in front of highly turbulent business environments (e.g. Iansiti and Clark, 1994).

The inspiring rationale of the concept is apparently straightforward. If technological breakthroughs and other sources of change – such as the increasing volatility of consumers' preferences and the competitive pressure induced by globalization and liberalization – "select" some firms rather than others, as the empirical evidence suggests,[4] this is not only because firms adopt and implement different deliberated strategies, especially in terms of time response to change (Reinganum, 1989; Christensen, 1997). This occurs also and above all because firms have a different capacity to deal with change or, in brief, different "dynamic capabilities" (Teece *et al.*, 1997; Jones, 2001).

While this seems to be a reasonable starting point, its rigorous conceptualization within the domain of strategic management and industrial organization has raised some problems. On the one hand, it has been argued that, having significant common properties across firms, and being "equi-final", dynamic capabilities are not inimitable and unique, and thus do not represent a secure source of competitive advantage for them (Eisenhardt and Martin, 2000). On the other hand, dynamic capabilities have been questioned to be a necessary organizational means to deal effectively with change, giving firms the alternative chance to rely on "*ad hoc* problem solving" (Winter, 2003). These and other problems one can identify by surveying the "organizational" approaches to the issue (Leoncini *et al.*, 2006), mainly related to the lack of distinguishable organizational "attributes", apparently represent an obstacle to the "operationalization" of the concept, which thus runs the risk of remaining a "would-be" one (Williamson, 2003).[5]

As a way out from these problems, the 2003 PRIN Project suggested to take on a broader perspective and to look at dynamic capabilities with a "system approach". This amounts to recognizing that dynamic capabilities are what make firms capable to co-evolve with their hosting environments, and running a process which depends, not only on their internal organization – and organizational learning in particular – but also on their hosting environment – especially the territorial one – and their constituting resources – especially the human ones. In so doing, the approach to dynamic capabilities developed within the book tries to consistently integrate the organizational approach, from which it has originated, with two other approaches which, although not always explicitly, have addressed the firm's capacity to deal with change. A sketch of these three approaches, on which the contributions of the present book draw at different extents, is thus opportune at this point.[6]

The organizational literature: knowledge and learning

The first body of literature that contributes to the scientific background of the book is represented by what can be called the "organizational route" to dynamic capabilities. We here refer to a wide range of studies that, in spite of relevant differences, all focus on the "internal organization" of the firm as a key aspect in understanding its dynamics. Indeed, these studies maintain that the dynamics of the firms is mainly linked to the evolution of their organizational knowledge and to their organizational learning. Putting it simply, in adapting their existing capabilities over time, or in acquiring, if not even developing new ones, firms are actually learning something new (Loasby, 1996; Dosi *et al.*, 2000).[7]

This route of analysis encompasses contributions of heterogeneous extraction such as strategic management (e.g. Teece *et al.*, 1997; Eisenhardt and Martin, 2000), economics of innovation and technology management (e.g. Tushman and Anderson, 1986; Henderson and Clark, 1990), organization studies (e.g. Nonaka, 1994; Garud and Rappa, 1994) and evolutionary economics (e.g. Zollo and Winter, 2002; Zott, 2003).[8]

The numerous insights provided by these studies, and those emerging from their complementary reading, have made the dynamic capabilities issue less "black-boxed" than it appeared at the beginning. The investigation of the process of "organizational knowledge creation" (Nonaka, 1994, p. 15) and of "managerial cognition" (Garud and Rappa, 1994), for example, has cast new light on the role that organizational "learning-traps" and "managerial myopia", respectively, have in explaining the different ways and effectiveness firms deal with their changing environment. Furthermore, the same route of analysis has also arisen the question of the social elements intervening in the process of knowledge creation and that of the boundaries between private and social costs/benefits in it (Antonelli and Pegoretti, 1995). Last, but not least, dealing with dynamic capabilities from an organizational perspective has contributed to detect and tackle some crucial problems with the role of knowledge in explaining the firm's dynamics, the actual storability and transferability of knowledge being one of the most important (Michellone and Zollo, 2000; De Liso, 2001).

Following the organizational route, however, the studies on firms' dynamics that have incurred in a certain focalization-bias, if not even a problem of defocalization, with respect to the "external", relational and contextual aspects which affect the dynamic capabilities of the firm. Indeed, while concepts hinting at the external relationships of the firm float around quite often in the organizational accounts of dynamic capabilities, their actual relevance is hidden by setting them at work in "aseptic" competitive environments in which relationships are mainly of a formal nature. In the technology-related literature, for example, the firm's environment is simply portrayed as an "industry" populated by "established organizations" (incumbents) and "new entrants", interacting through competitive relationships (Tushman and Anderson, 1986, pp. 445–446). Non-competitive relationships among firms, and relationships with other institutions and organizations of different nature, are instead given a marginal role in shaping organizational learning and the capabilities dynamics (Iansiti and Clark, 1994).

In order to overcome this bias, a bridge needs to be laid towards other research lines: the two that follows in particular.

The literature on "local systems of production": the socio-economic context and the institutional set-up

The scientific background of the book finds in the literature on "local systems of production" a second important ingredient. This literature actually represents a second, possibly less direct,[9] route towards the dynamic capabilities of the firms, in which it is their "external environment" to play a crucial role in driving their dynamics. Once more in simple terms, the basic idea is that the geographical space links the "software" of the firms – that is, their organization – to their "hardware" – made up of the social community, the formal and informal institutions, and the tangible and intangible infrastructures that insist on its territory. Accordingly, the firm's dynamics is also, and above all, a process which involves the local system in which the firm produces its goods and services, and whose outcome depends on how the relative socio-economic context and institutional set-up are actually configured (Rullani, 1993).

As for the organizational route, also the present one is extremely variegated, encompassing such different approaches as the "standard" (e.g. Becattini, 1987, 1990; Bellandi, 2001) and "new" (e.g. Ferrucci and Varaldo, 1993; Belussi and Gottardi, 2000) "industrial district" approach, that of the so-called "milieu innovateur" (e.g. Aydalot, 1986; Camagni, 1991), the research stream on the "regional system of innovation" (e.g. Howells, 1999; Cooke, 2002) and on the "new industrial spaces" (e.g. Storper and Walker, 1983; Scott, 1988).[10]

Benefiting from different degrees of complementarities and synergies, these studies have further illuminated the complexity of the firm's dynamics process. The most recent literature on industrial districts, for example, has highlighted how the districts themselves represent "cognitive systems" which, by networking the cognition processes of the individual firms, crucially affect their capabilities of recognizing and dealing with change and innovation (Belussi and Gottardi, 2000, p. 17). The idea of the regional system of innovation, instead, has emphasized the role that the "institutional fabrics" and the "informal links" in which the firms of a certain region are "embedded" have in explaining their capacity to innovate and evolve competitively (Cooke, 2002).

The "environmental route" has, however, taken the scholars of the field towards another focalization-bias, somehow symmetric to that we have identified in the previous section, with respect to the "internal organization" of the firms, which are part of local systems of production. Indeed, while it catches important contextual/relational issues, the lens of local production systems takes some focus out of the firm as a knowledge-creating organization, and even more as an organization that manages the dynamics of its capabilities. Dynamic capabilities in fact tend to degenerate into social and system-specific capabilities. And firms have different abilities to benefit from them, rather than to build them up. This is most evident, for example, in the literature on the "milieu innovateur", where the firm appears nearly undistinguishable from the environment. The milieu actually determines the innovative behaviour of firms to the point that it is not the firm who innovates, but the territory itself (Gay and Picard, 2001).

Such a focalization-bias represents an obstacle to an accurate understanding of dynamic capabilities as serious as that we have detected in the previous section. The symmetry of the biases renders the integration of the two bodies of literature even more urgent. While integrating the organizational route with more attention for external aspects, the environmental one actually benefits from its focus on the firms' organization. What is more, both can benefit from the integration of a third route of analysis that recognizes the crucial role of human resources and skills for the firms' dynamics.

The literature on labour skills and competencies: individual, organizational and social capabilities

A third route of analysis, somehow independent from the previous two, but still converging on the same issue, focuses on the role that individual agents play in the learning processes of the firm and in its dynamics: that is, on the "individual" skills and capabilities of the firm's workers and managers. The basic idea is quite straightforward: as they are forged in the socio-economic context of the firm and as they get integrated in the firm's organizational competences, skills and individual competencies represent a sort of *trait d'union* between the firm's internal organization and the firm's external environment, the other two routes towards dynamic capabilities. Accordingly, firm's dynamics also depends on how "on-the-job" training complements and/or substitutes the "off-the-job" one provided by the relevant educational system, and on how far the latter is supported by the presence of adequate socio-economic elements at the macro- and at the meso-economic levels.

Also, this third route of analysis combines different streams of research: on the one hand, the literature on the demand for, and supply of, skilled labour services (Ashton and Green, 1996), and on the related notion of "learning function" (e.g. Green, 1998; Green *et al.*, 2001); on the other hand, that on the "social" factors (active elements) and constraints (passive elements) affecting the ability of an economic system to increase its potential for growth at an aggregate level – i.e. its "social capabilities" (e.g. Abramovitz, 1986; Temple and Johnson, 1998) – and its development at the local level – i.e. its "social capital" (e.g. Trigilia, 2001; Mazzanti *et al.*, 2005).

In addition to several more specific results, the most important contribution of these studies to the dynamic capabilities issue is that of showing how their analysis requires us to combine, not only the organizational and the local levels of analysis discussed in the previous sections, but also the macro-economic level: that of the labour market and of the educational system in particular. Indeed, as we will see, following this third route of analysis, dynamic capabilities can be conceived also as "macro-capabilities", very much affected by the external relations of an economic system, that is by its internationalization processes, and by the sectoral structure of its production system.

Once more, however, also this third route of analysis runs the risk, if left alone, of leading to biased analyses. Unless combined with the organizational route, for example, organizational competencies might be thought to be the simple sum of individual skills, while their relationships are rather holistic and non-additive. The same holds true with respect to the relationship between individual and social capabilities, a proper account of which requires us to make the second route, based on local production systems, intervene.

By combining these three strands of literature, the approach to dynamic capabilities, developed in the book might appear, at first sight, excessively eclectic. On the other hand, although drawing on the three pieces of the scientific background to different extents, all the contributions of the present book coherently share the common idea that dynamic capabilities should be conceived of as *capabilities to undertake a "truly complex" process of change*. On the one side, dynamic capabilities could be referred to the homeostatic capacity of the firm to fine-tune its capabilities set and its organizational structure with respect to the outer environment, if the environmental signals do not exceed a certain threshold level, specific to it. On the other side, dynamic capabilities refer to the (truly dynamic) capacity of the firm to shifting its boundaries, in order not to be overwhelmed when the environmental pressure becomes excessive.[11]

Of course, this complex process of change can occur at different levels of analysis, according to which the book is actually structured.

The content of the book

The book is made up of three parts. Part I – Firm and organizational level – in which the firm is the unit of analysis, and the relationships, either formal or informal, are investigated from several viewpoints.

In Chapter 1, Leoncini and Montresor approach the relationships between learning and change at the firm level. In the *learning economy* it is crucial to understand how firms try to cope with the twin layer of relationships upon which learning processes are based: the internal level, and the external ones. Firms are thus conceived as a complex (adaptive) system of resources, capabilities and competencies. Results are then corroborated by the empirical analysis based on a non-standard factorial technique, i.e. multiple correspondence analysis. Results confirm that firms with high dynamic capabilities in terms of innovation are associated to a pervasive use of ICT and to limited outsourcing activities, while firms with low innovative dynamic capabilities are characterized by a lower use of ICT that is limited to auxiliary activities and to a certain resort to outsourcing.

In Chapter 2, the role of entrepreneurial teams is analysed by Iacobucci, according to a classification of dynamic capabilities based on the degree of change in organizational routines, and the nature (either passive or proactive) of the relationships with the external environment. The analysis focuses on detecting the factors affecting the ability of small- and medium-sized firms to innovate and grow, in particular as far as the role of the entrepreneur is concerned in spurring innovation and growth by exploiting new business opportunities. The empirical evidence furnished by this Charter, is derived from in-depth case studies of medium-sized business groups. The evidence supports the important role of the entrepreneurs involved in the development of new ventures, and that differences are related to the nature of the entrepreneur, or more precisely to the model of entrepreneurial specialization.

In Chapter 3, Marangoni and Solari explore another important element, the group, which has assumed increasing importance in the formation, management and improvement of the firms' dynamic capabilities. The group is important in this respect, as it introduces a set of formal relationships aimed at increasing firms' competence, on top of those, typically informal, already highlighted in the previous contributions. This Charter analyses the role of group formation from the viewpoint of the competence of the firm, focusing on its dynamic capabilities. In this context, business group formation is driven by the accumulation of "flexible" organizational capabilities as core competences of firms. This thesis is then evaluated, and confirmed, by the empirical evidence derived from an investigation of formal business groups in the northeast regions of Italy.

The first part of the book is then closed by Antonelli and Nosvelli in Chapter 4, in which it is claimed that when the focus is upon how informal knowledge transfer is seen from an informal point of view, then it becomes crucial to tackle the way knowledge flows are organized and dealt with by heterogeneous agents that transfer more or less formalized kinds of skills. A "learning function" is defined and empirically applied to the analysis of the learning paths adopted for transferring the skills demanded by firms. This function makes it possible to detect some relevant aspects that the literature points out as crucial for a better understanding of the dynamics of learning processes. In general complementarities among education and training components emerge, although what is true for the whole industry, comes to be more differentiated when small and large firms are differentiated: fragmented in the former case, more integrated in the latter.

Part II – Local and meso-economic level – is aimed at highlighting the meso level at which several different aspects determine different paths in how dynamic capabilities and external relationships are generated and dealt with.

In Chapter 5 Lombardi tackles the very relevant theoretical point of how dispersed knowledge among agents is built in such a way as to determine emergent patterns of ordered behaviour. The chapter aims at building a theoretical framework and a research programme for the analysis of the evolution of competencies and capabilities, based on the morphogenetic approach. The analysis focuses on the evolution of knowledge through the combination and re-combination of pieces of information into rules. The structure of interactions supplies an explanation of the formation of constraints at different levels of complex entities, which are the ultimate elements behind the formation of technical regimes and socio-technical systems.

Also at the meso level, it is crucial to focus on the importance of Global Value Chains. In Chapter 6, Morrison, Pietrobelli and Rabellotti stress that this approach has, in fact, recently shown that international linkages play a crucial role to access technological knowledge and enhance learning and innovation. This form of industrial organization may be particularly beneficial for firms located in developing countries, which are bound to source technology internationally. However, the issues of learning, technological efforts and investments to create and improve technological capabilities at the firm-level remain largely uncovered. These issues may importantly contribute to explain why and how developing countries' firms benefit, to different degrees, from participating in Global Value Chains.

The issue of formal and informal knowledge flows is again tackled in Chapter 7 by Belussi, Pilotti and Sedita, where the issue of how knowledge is developed in localized systems of specialized firms (i.e. in industrial districts) is tackled from the viewpoint of the development of informal social networks (called communities of practice), and firms networks. This determines an osmotic process between the internal and the external levels of the district knowledge. The functioning of the modern industrial district is then described, emphasizing the elements of "learning at the boundaries", where local actors mix sources of knowledge located inside with external sources. Empirical evidence is then presented to show the different patterns with which knowledge flows are organized within local systems.

Also business groups are re-examined from this different viewpoint. In Chapter 8, Cainelli and Iacobucci show how the creation of business groups is not only specific to large firms but, in Italy, it is also widespread among small- and medium-sized firms and in industrial districts. The presence of business groups poses, from a theoretical point of view, the question of whether the business group or the single legal unit should be considered as the unit of the economic analysis. The analysis focuses on the role of structural variables, such as spatial agglomeration and technology, in determining some features of business group organization. The empirical evidence gathered confirms that more business groups are more present in industrial districts than in non-district areas.

Moreover, belonging to an industrial district is not the only determinant, but the "size" of the local system and also the strength of agglomeration forces are crucial.

Chapter 9, by Ciravegna and Giuliani, analyzes the role of multinationals in creating clusters exploring whether both productive and knowledge linkages are formed between multinational corporations (MNC) and domestic suppliers in Costa Rica. The analysis reveals that MNCs have established increasingly more productive linkages with domestic firms over time, although the vast majority of these linkages are with domestic firms that trade imported goods, whereas only a small percentage of the domestically procured goods is manufactured in the country. Finally, although MNCs have provided, and still provide, the incentives for suppliers to increase their knowledge, they rarely provide financial support or other forms of direct assistance.

Part III – Sectoral and macro-economic level – supplies a view from both a macro and sectoral perspective of the concept of dynamic capabilities, as we are aware of the existence of a third level where capabilities formation gets guided and co-determined in a non-linear process of interaction with the institutional interface.

In Chapter 10, Mollo and Teixeira furnish a theoretical setting for a macro-economic approach to the concept of dynamic capabilities. Indeed, the chapter stresses the importance of a macro-economic perspective in order for the economic system to trigger structural change. This requires a proper macro-dynamic environment, as well as social and economic progress. Therefore, the concept of macro-dynamic capability is thoroughly analysed in order to confer it an heterodox content whose analytical foundation is derived from a number of scholars of diverse ideological conceptions. In particular, the chapter deals with the monetary and financial conditions needed to sustain productive investment and economic development.

In Chapter 11, Antonelli and Pegoretti tackle the difficult question of how knowledge and competence are affected by the structural economic dynamics and by the business cycle. The resulting dynamics is heavily dependent on the intertwining of internal-to-the-firm micro-economic factors (such as organizational capacity) and external macro-economic factors related to social capital (such as the education and the training systems). As a result of this relationship, the degree of competitiveness of firms within an economic system, comes as the final outcome of the degree of flexibility and/or rigidity of the single firms, matched to the level of social capabilities that the system is able to generate and to make available for them.

Chapter 12, by Gabrisch and Segnana, is focused on the relationships between trade and capabilities as internal determinants of specialization and in particular of vertical intra-industry trade flows. This particular structure is shown by the decomposition of intra-industry shares in trade between EU and candidate countries. This chapter focuses on relative wage differences, country size and income distribution as determinants of the increasing share of vertical intra-industry trade. The chapter concludes that EU firms have been able to increase their product quality and to shift low-quality segments to candidate countries, thus hinting to a product-quality cycle in these regions.

Finally, Chapters 13 and 14 offer a sectoral analysis, by focusing on very different topics, as ICT and tourism. In Chapter 13, De Liso analyses how the role of digital information and communication technologies has evolved through time to become fundamental in production – both in manufacturing and services – and, at an increasing rate, in consumption. In order to cope with their diffusion (both horizontal and vertical) it is necessary to revise the Smithian principle of the division of labour, and to precede it by the adjective digital. Digital technologies contributed to the re-definition of sectors and their relative importance. It has also been an impetus for the modification of the international division of labour, with regards to both software (as a growing proportion of program writing is performed outside the perimeter of the mostly industrialized countries), and hardware (as Japan, and more recently the Asian Tigers, have become the world's biggest producers of key computer components).

Chapter 14, by Vergori and Zamparini, is aimed at exploring the way in which the economic issues related to seasonality of demand can be tackled by the administrative authorities, by exerting their role and displaying their dynamic capabilities. Indeed, persistent seasonality can be viewed as an indicator of the fact that local administrative authorities and institutions are not able to establish good relations with tourist firms to help them to exploit their competitive potential. The econometric analysis performed, seems to confirm that there is room for intervention by local administrations and institutions in order to help the development of dynamic capabilities that might actively contribute to the creation of a complementary markets in the off-peak season months.

Notes

1 Previous versions of some of these papers, along with others which are not hosted in this book, have been published in the series of electronic Working Papers of the Project at the web-site http://www2.dse.unibo.it/prin (following the appropriate link).
2 In all the cases, the research units were made up of members of specific faculties and departments of these universities, whose indication is provided in the list of contributors.
3 Dynamic capabilities have been originally defined as "the firm's ability to integrate, build and reconfigure internal and external competences to address rapidly changing environments" (Teece *et al.*, 1997, p. 577).
4 On this point, the seminal works are among those by Henderson and Clark (1990), Tushman and Anderson (1986) and Iansiti and Clark (1994).
5 These problems are currently stimulating serious attempts at building up a new research agenda for the issue. See Zahra *et al.* (2006).
6 For a deeper discussion of the relevant literature see Leoncini *et al.* (2006).
7 The theory of the firm which underpins this organizational route is actually one in which resources, capabilities and competences (RCC) are as important as contracts in accounting for the firms' nature (the existence issue), the different ways they integrate within markets (the boundaries issue), and the structures they choose to organize themselves internally (the organization issue) (Langlois and Foss, 1999; Montresor, 2004).

8 For each of the four streams of studies, the references indicated are purely exemplificative and possibly non-fully representative. For a deeper and more refined analysis see Leoncini *et al.* (2006).
9 The explicit use of the term "dynamic capabilities'' is actually rare in this literature, although dynamics and the capacity to deal with it are retained crucial in the analysis of local systems of production (Quadrio-Curzio and Fortis, 2002).
10 Also in the present case, the references provided are merely illustrative of the seminal ones. For a broader discussion see Leoncini *et al.* (2006).
11 For a deeper discussion of this point see Leoncini *et al.* (2006).

Bibliographical references

Abramovitz, M. (1986), "Catching up, forging ahead, and falling behind", in Wolff, E.N. (ed.), *The Economics of Productivity*, vol. 2, Cheltenham: Edward Elgar.

Antonelli, G. and Pegoretti, G. (1995), "Paths of technological change, markets for production factors and the social cost of knowledge", *Dynamis – Quaderni IDSE*, no. 6.

Ashton, D. and Green, F. (1996), *Education, Training and the Global Economy*, Cheltenham: Edward Elgar.

Aydalot, P. (1986), "The location of new firm creation: the French case", in Keeble, D. and Wever, E. (eds), *New Firms and Regional Development in Europe*, London, Sydney and Dover, NH: Croom Helm, pp. 105–123.

Becattini, G. (ed.) (1981), *Marshall. Antologia di Scritti Economici*, Bologna: Il Mulino.

Becattini, G. (1987), *Mercato e Forze Locali. Il Distretto Industriale*, Bologna: Il Mulino.

Becattini, G. (1990), "The Marshallian industrial district as a socio-economic notion", in Pyke, F., Becattini G. and Sengenberger, W. (eds) *Industrial Districts and Inter-Firm Co-operation in Italy*, Geneva: ILO.

Bellandi, M. (2001), "Local development and embedded large firms", *Entrepreneurship and Regional Development*, vol. 13, pp. 189–210.

Belussi, F. and Gottardi, G. (2000), "Models of localised technological change", in Belussi, F. and Gottardi, G. (eds), *Evolutionary Patterns of Local Industrial Systems. Towards a Cognitive Approach to the Industrial District*, Aldershot: Ashgate, pp. 13–48.

Camagni, R. (ed.) (1991), *Innovation Networks. Spatial Perspectives*, London: Belhaven Press.

Camagni, R. (1999), "La ville comme Milieu: de l'application de l'approche GREMI à l'évolution urbaine", *Revue d'Economie Régionale et Urbaine*, no. 3, 591–606.

Christensen, C.M. (1997), *The Innovator's Dilemma: When New Technologies Cause Great Firms to Fail*, Boston: Harvard Business School Press.

Cooke, P. (2002), "Regional innovation systems: general findings and some new evidence from biotechnology clusters", *Journal of Technology Transfer*, vol. 27, no. 1, pp. 133–145.

David, P. and Foray, D. (1995), "Assessing and expanding the science and technology knowledge vase", *STI Review*, vol. 16, pp. 14–68.

De Liso N. (2001), "Tecnologie dell'informazione e della comunicazione, terziarizzazione e nuova divisione del lavoro digitale" *Moneta e Credito*, vol. 54, no. 216, pp. 425–459.

Dosi, G., Nelson, R.R. and Winter, S.G. (2000), "Introduction", in Dosi, G., Nelson, R.R. and Winter, S.G. (eds), *The Nature and Dynamics of Organizational Capabilities*, Oxford: Oxford University Press, pp. 1–22.

Eisenhardt, K.M. and Martin, J.A. (2000), "Dynamic capabilities: What are they?", *Strategic Management Journal*, vol. 21, pp. 1105–1121.

Ferrucci, L. and Varaldo, R. (1993), "La natura e la dinamica dell'impresa distrettuale", *Economia e Politica Industriale*, vol. 80, pp. 73–97.

Garud, R. and Rappa, M.A. (1994), "A socio-cognitive model of technology evolution: the case of cochlear implants", *Organization Science*, vol. 5, pp. 344–362.

Gay, C. and Picard, F. (2001), "Innovation, agglomération et espace. Une mise en perspective de la literature", *Économie et Sociétés*, vol. 35, pp. 679–716.

Green, F. (1998), "The value of skills", University of Kent at Canterbury, Department of Economics, Discussion Paper no. 19.

Green, F., Ashton, D. and Felstead, A. (2001), "Estimating the determinants of supply of computing, problem-solving, communication, social and teamworking skills", *Oxford Economic Papers*, vol. 53, no. 3, pp. 406–433.

Henderson, R.M. and Clark, K.B. (1990), "Architectural innovation: the reconfiguration of existing product technologies and the failure of established firms", *Administrative Science Quarterly*, no. 35, pp. 9–30.

Howells, J. (1999), "Regional systems of innovation?", in Archibugi, D., Howells, J. and Michie, J. (eds) *Innovation Policy in a Global Economy*, Cambridge: Cambridge University Press, pp. 67–93.

Iacobucci, D. (2002), "Explaining business groups started by habitual entrepreneurs in the Italian manufacturing sector", *Entrepreneurship and Regional Development*, vol. 14, no. 1, pp. 31–48.

Iansiti, M. and Clark, K.B. (1994), "Integration and dynamic capability: evidence from product development in automobiles and mainframe computers", *Industrial and Corporate Change*, vol. 3, no. 3, pp. 557–606.

Jones, N. (2001), "Exploring dynamic capability: a longer-term study of product development following radical technological change", INSEAD R&D Working Papers, 2001/20/TM.

Langlois, R.N. and Foss, N.J. (1999), "Capabilities and governance: the rebirth of production in the theory of economic organization", *Kyklos*, vol. 52, no. 2, pp. 201–218.

Leoncini, R. Montresor, S., Vertova, G. (2006), "Dynamic capabilities between firm organization and local development: a critical survey", *Economia Politica*, no. 3, pp. 475–502.

Lipparini, A. and Lorenzoni, G. (1996), "Le organizzazioni ad alta intensità relazionale. Riflessioni sui meccanismi di 'learning-by-interacting' nelle areee ad alta concentrazione di imprese", *L'Industria*, vol. 4, pp. 111–119.

Loasby, B.J. (1996), "On the definition and the organisation of capabilities", mimeo, presented at the IDSE-CNR seminar, Milan, June.

Marangoni, G., Colombo, G. and Fezzi, G. (2002), "Modelling intra-group relationships", Paper presented at the 14th International Conference on Input-Output Techniques, Montreal, Canada.

Marshall, A. (1920), *Principle of Economics: An Introductory Volume*, 8th edn, London: Macmillan.

Mazzanti, M., Cainelli G. and Mancinelli, S. (2005), "Social Capital, R&D and Industrial Districts", FEEM Working Paper no. 84.05.

Michellone, G.C. and Zollo, G. (2000), "Competencies management in knowledge-based firms", *International Journal of Manufacturing, Technology and Management*, vol. 1, no. 1, pp. 20–41.

Montresor, S. (2004), "Resources, capabilities, competences and the theory of the firm", *Journal of Economic Studies*, vol. 31, no. 5, pp. 409–434.

Nonaka, I. (1994), "A dynamic theory of organizational knowledge creation", *Organization Science*, vol. 5, no. 1, pp. 14–37.

Quadrio-Curzio A. and Fortis, M. (2002), (eds), *Complessità e Distretti Industriali*, Bologna: Il Mulino.

Rabellotti, R. (2001), "The effect of globalisation on industrial districts in Italy: the case of Brenta", Working Paper no. 144, Institute of Development Studies, University of Sussex, available at www.ids.ac.uk/ids/bookshop/wp/wp144.pdf), mimeo.

Reinganum, J.F. (1989), "The timing of innovation: research, development and diffusion", in Schmalensee, R. and Willig, R. (eds), *Handbook of Industrial Organization*, vol. I, Amsterdam, North-Holland, pp. 849–908.

Rullani, E. (1993), "Networks and internationalization: managing complexity through knowledge", in Zan, A., Zambon, S. and Pettigrew, A.M. (eds), *Perspectives on Strategic Change*, Norwell, Mass. and Dordrecht: Kluwer Academic, pp. 107–142.

Scott, A. (1988), *New Industrial Spaces*, London: Pion Limited.

Storper, M. and Walker, R. (1983), "The theory of labour and the theory of location", *International Journal of Urban and Regional Research*, vol. 7, pp. 1–43.

Teece, D.J. and Pisano, G. (1994), "The dynamic capabilities of the firms: an introduction", *Industrial and Corporate Change*, vol. 3, pp. 537–556.

Teece, D.J., Pisano, G. and Shuen, A. (1997), "Dynamic capabilities and strategic management", *Strategic Management Journal*, vol. 18, no. 7, pp. 509–533.

Temple, J. and Johnson, P.A. (1998), "Social capability and economic growth", *The Quarterly Journal of Economics*, August, pp. 965–990.

Trigilia, C. (2001), "Capitale sociale e sviluppo locale", in Bagnasco, A., Piselli, F., Pizzorno, A. and Trigilia, C., *Il Capitale Sociale*, Bologna: Il Mulino.

Tushman, M.L. and Anderson, P. (1986), "Technological discontinuities and organizational environments", *Administrative Science Quarterly*, no. 31, pp. 439–465.

Williamson, O.E. (2003), "Examining economic organization through the lens of contracts", *Industrial and Corporate Change*, no. 4, pp. 917–942.

Winter, S.J. (2003), "Understanding dynamic capabilities", *Strategic Management Journal*, vol. 24, pp. 991–995.

Zahra, S.A., Sapienza, H.J. and Davidsson, P. (2006), "Entrepreneurship and dynamic capabilities: a review, model and research agenda", *Journal of Management Studies*, vol. 43, no. 4, pp. 917–955.

Zollo, M. and Winter, S.J. (2002), "Deliberate learning and the evolution of dynamic capabilities", *Organization Science*, vol. 13, pp. 339–351.

Zott, C. (2003), "Dynamic capabilities and the emergence of intraindustry differential firm performance: insights from a simulation study", *Strategic Management Journal*, vol. 24, pp. 97–125.

Part I

Firm and organizational level

1 Learning and firm dynamics

Theoretical approaches and empirical analysis of dynamic capabilities

Riccardo Leoncini and Sandro Montresor

1.1 Introduction

The aim of this chapter is to investigate the relationships between learning and change at the firm level. In the *learning economy*, this relationship has become crucial for the firm, spurring an upsurge of interest in both its theoretical conceptualization and empirical measurement. Faster technological change, shorter product life-cycles, more frequent job shifts and a lively firm demography have made learning – a flow kind of concept – rather than knowledge – a stock kind of concept – the key determinant of the economic success of the firm. Increasingly more, firm competitiveness and growth are dependent on innovation, whose successful development relies on the building-up of new competencies and skills, rather than on a large amount of economically useful knowledge.

How firms define their problem-solving strategies, shape their cognitive models and develop their organizational capabilities to learn has attracted the attention of several streams of research in organizational economics and in the economics of the firm. Either explicitly or implicitly, each of them addresses an aspect of what can be called the *dynamic capabilities* of the firm. Dynamic capabilities can in fact be seen as an important bridging concept between the firm learning and the firm dynamics.

The first part of the chapter is devoted to a critical survey of these contributions, where a certain organizational bias is detected. Indeed, the advent of the learning economy has made the relationship between learning and change increasingly more dialectic. Not only does learning enhance the capabilities of the firm to innovate, but it also triggers and imposes change on other firms, which are in turn required to learn. The learning economy has actually increased the *transformation pressure* the firm is subject to, favouring those organizations which are change-oriented to the expenses of the slow-learners. In this last respect, the specific organizational and geographical environment such a transformation pressure originates from identifies a selection mechanism, which concurs to identify those firms whose capabilities to learn are relatively higher. While only marginally retained by the organizational accounts, this insight pervades a different strand of literature, which focuses on the firm dynamics within geographically delimited production and innovation systems. The analysis of this research programme is thus inescapable for a proper understanding of the relationship between learning and change.

Moving from these premises, in the central part of the chapter an original methodology is suggested to develop a comprehensive analysis of the dynamic capabilities of the firm. The dialectic link between learning and change is addressed by looking at the firm as a complex (adaptive) system of resources, capabilities and competencies. Although serious work is still needed in the attempt to translate the language of complexity into that of the economics of the firm, its conceptual pillars turn out to be extremely useful to overcome a reductive analysis of the firm dynamics. In particular, both organizational and environmental factors can be set at work once it has been realized that also in the firm, as in other complex systems, homeostatic processes differently intertwine with structural adjustments depending on the relative speed of change and learning themselves.

The last part of the chapter addresses the delicate issue of the empirical analysis of the relationship between learning and change at the firm level. At the outset, the firm dynamic capabilities are difficult to measure with more or less articulated proxies. Conversely, they must be somehow 'elicited' by observing the actual learning processes and performances of the firms (typically in terms of innovative projects). Furthermore, direct questions that control for possible self-evaluations biases have to be posed. These needs make a case-study methodology almost natural for the identification of the determinants of dynamic capabilities, with both *pros* and *cons*. Indeed, case studies allow for detailed and specific results but at the expense of important losses of generality and replicability, not to mention the risk of a certain ex-post rationalization. For these reasons, statistical and econometric analysis are as well important to accomplish more robust results and have to be carried out, although the nature of the data often imposes the researcher to use non-standard techniques of analysis.

In this vein, the chapter concludes by illustrating the results of the application of a 'mixed methodology'. The case study of a specific local system of production – Treviso (northern Italy) – is investigated by resorting to a non-standard factorial technique, that is multiple correspondence analysis. Interesting correspondences are identified between the dynamic capabilities of the firm and both their organizational and environmental features. Some of them were expected: 'pro-active' firms – i.e. with high dynamic capabilities in terms of innovation – for example, are associated to a pervasive use of ICT and to limited outsourcing activities, while 'reactive' firms – i.e. with low innovative dynamic capabilities are associated to a use of ICT which is limited to auxiliary activities and to a certain resort to outsourcing. Some other results instead add new elements to the understanding of the dynamic capabilities issue: 'pro-active' firms, for example, are not those with the closest associations to local relationships with suppliers and customers, while international arm's-length relationships appear more conducive in terms of dynamic capabilities. Useful insights are also obtained in the attempt at linking dynamic capabilities with the firm structure: pro-activeness, for example, is positively associated to the firm size in terms of sales and employment, as well as with a specialization in specialized suppliers sectors.

1.2 The firm in the learning economy: dealing with dynamics

'X-economy' like concepts – with X equal to 'new', 'net', 'ICT', 'knowledge-based' and 'learning', just to mention a few – are increasingly more popular in the scientific community. Although with differences, all of them are used to 'catch' the changes that, from the late 1980s onward, have radically transformed the fundamentals of financial and real markets, in both developed and developing economies.

In general, these concepts are quite fuzzy, as they lack a systematic definition, a sound conceptual substance and, what is more, the empirical crystallization attributed by original statistical indicators. Their diffusion is not free from the conditioning of the institutional contexts in which they have been generated (OECD being a notable example).[1] However, it is also true that some of these concepts have worked as useful guideposts in identifying new priorities in both research investigations and, eventually, in policy making.

This appears to be the case of the 'learning-economy'. Although not yet accompanied by a battery of consistent statistical indicators (such as, instead, for the knowledge-based economy), the reference to the learning economy is at least legitimated by some new facts on which evidence is building (Lundvall and Johnson, 1994; Lundvall, 1996; Lundvall and Borras, 1997; Lundvall, 1998; Lundvall and Nielsen, 1999). Faster technological change, shorter product life-cycles, more frequent job shifts and a lively firm demography, along with other dynamic shifts, all point to an economy in which learning, rather than 'knowledge access and distribution' (David and Foray, 1995, p. 14) is the crucial factor in determining the performance of individuals, firms, regions and countries.

Obviously, the distinction between *knowledge-economy* and *learning-economy* draws on a qualified idea of learning, as something more than pure information/knowledge acquisition. Indeed, once the limits to the codification of knowledge are recognized, along with the relevance of tacit knowledge and the complementarity between the two (Polanyi, 1958/1978; Foray and Lundvall, 1996), learning turns out to be a complex process with very special features: interactive (Lundvall, 1992), organizational (Nonaka, 1994), institutional (Johnson, 1992; Foray, 1997) and 'infrastuctural' (Smith, 1997), just to mention a few. In this qualified meaning, *forgetting* becomes a necessary pre-requisite for learning, rather than an impediment to it (Lundvall and Borras, 1997), while new competencies and skills in turn add to the stock of new knowledge (Lundvall, 1997).

The fact that learning has become the crucial competitive factor appears particularly evident for firms, with respect to which the above-mentioned dynamic shifts translate into an increase in the 'transformation pressure' and in the need to 'innovate and adapt to change' (Lundvall and Nielsen, 1999). Indeed, in a typical evolutionary process, firms are urged to develop a twofold ability. On the one hand, they are asked to learn to introduce change, in order to increase the variety of exploitable technological opportunities. On the other hand, they need to learn to adapt to change, in order to be positively selected. Learning and dynamics thus become a unique and intertwined process, while the capabilities to innovate and those to absorb innovations become the two facets of what we could call the 'dynamic capabilities' of the firm.

As is well-known, economists of heterogeneous extraction have approached the concept of dynamic capabilities for a long time, providing different definitions and conceptualizations for it. In order to proceed further in our argument, and illustrate in which sense the dynamic capabilities of the firm could be deemed the firm capabilities to stand the learning-economy (section 1.4), a concise recognition of the state of art is therefore necessary (section 1.3).

1.3 Firm dynamics and dynamic capabilities:[2] the state of art

The concept of dynamic capabilities has been put forward to account for the different ways and effectiveness with which firms face the 'turbulence' of the environment. In particular, to explain why firms show different dynamic performances once their sector has been shaken by some kind of pervasive technological change. Its inspiring rational lies in the problems that the neoclassical theory encounters in reducing the issue to a pure question of strategic incentives to invest in innovation. Even once the nature of the technological shake – i.e. incremental rather than radical – has been disentangled, predictions based on strategic arguments are not empirically robust (Henderson, 1993; Jones, 2001). Non-strategic-matching empirical results require to investigate the impact of technological change on the firm organization (i.e. communication channels, information filters, routines, procedures and the like) and to consider the different research capabilities of the firms.

The notion of dynamic capabilities tries to respond to such a need, that is '[the] need [of] much better models of heterogeneous capability – its evolution and its role in competition – [...] to fully understand the competitive implications of technological change' (Henderson, 1993, p. 268). Indeed, the concept and its rationale have attracted researchers of the firm from diverse disciplines, both in economics and in other social sciences. However, the contributions on these issues are just apparently uniform. In spite of substantial conceptual and terminological overlapping, relevant differences emerge among them with respect to the inner nature and functioning of dynamic capabilities. In disentangling such differences an original taxonomy of four approaches seems applicable. As will be shown (see Table 1.1), the four approaches present some elements of complementarity. Yet they endorse differences that lead to non-entirely aligned predictions.

1.3.1 The strategic management approach

The first item of such a taxonomy is the definition provided by the forerunners of the concept (Teece and Pisano, 1994; Teece *et al.*, 1997). As it was introduced as an alternative explanation of competitive advantage, in the following, this position will be referred to as the 'strategic management approach' to

Table 1.1 The main approaches to dynamic capabilities

	Strategic management	*Technology*	*Organization*	*Evolutionary*
What are dynamic capabilities?	Higher-level strategic capabilities (competitive advantage)	Technological capabilities (organizational competences to overcome inertia)	Capabilities to create organizational knowledge (renew managerial cognition)	A learned collective activity (intentional routines)
What do they apply to?	Lower-level strategic capabilities/resources (competitive advantage)	Technology (i.e. technological knowledge, skills, know-how, recursive activities)	Organizational knowledge (managerial cognition)	Operational routines (quasi-automatic routines)
Which is their core element?	Organizational learning from a strategic point of view (competitive advantage)	Organizational learning combined with strategic considerations	Organizational learning from an organization theory perspective	Cognitive learning from an evolutionary viewpoint (variation-selection-retention)
How is the firm conceived?	A set of resources and capabilities whose integration/combination is a static factor	A technical system of resources with respect to which technological integration is dominant	An organization in which individual and collective knowledge interact	A set of organizational routines and capabilities
How is the firm environment dealt with?	An aseptic (strategic like) diamond with which the firm is integrated in formal terms (competitors, suppliers and consumers)	An industry characterized by competitive relationship and with a special focus on external (formal) technology integration and consumer integration	A set of organizations interacting (mainly) on a formal basis (inter-organizational learning)	A system of institutions which operate in a socio-political context with a territorial specification

dynamic capabilities. According to it, dynamic capabilities are conceived as a particular 'firm's ability' to manage its 'internal and external competencies' in order to face its 'changing environment' more competitively than its rivals (Teece *et al.*, 1997, p. 516).

Apparently, the definition is purely a functional one. Dynamic capabilities are just 'higher-order' capabilities, which differ from 'lower-order' ones because of their function. Indeed, they would serve dynamic firms to break out the rents and the path dependency guaranteed to the rivals by their having rare, valuable and inimitable lower-order capabilities (Collis, 1994, p. 149). The inner nature of dynamic capabilities is thus still that of 'capabilities', although of a special kind. In this last respect, the present approach draws on some previous works in the field of strategic management, in particular on the seminal paper by Leonard-Barton (1992). According to her 'dynamic paradox', the 'core capabilities' of the firm can turn into 'core rigidities' if the firm itself is unable to renew them.

It should be stressed that, in the present approach strategic capabilities, both static and dynamic, are not always clearly distinguished from 'individual' resources, i.e. resources that are separable from the firm context and thus able to carry a market price. Indeed, dynamic capabilities take on the nature of a very special kind of resource – i.e. organizational and non-price-carrying – only when they are related to processes of organizational learning (Dierickx and Cool, 1989). Dynamic capabilities are in fact directly connected to the 'organizational processes' of the firm. Their 'dynamic role' is precisely that of allowing the firm to learn through 'communication codes and search procedures, which are rooted in specific organizational settings' (Teece *et al.*, 1997, p. 518).

Although the emphasis is on the firm competitive advantage, its internal organization is crucial for dynamic capabilities. Two peculiarities should, however, be remarked. First of all, learning is indicated as the only truly 'dynamic concept'. As such, it is clearly distinguished from the 'coordination/ integration' of the firm competencies – instead treated as a 'static concept' – and from their 'reconfiguration' – retained as a 'transformational concept' (Teece *et al.*, 1997, pp. 518–512). In so doing, the way in which the integration and the coordination of the firm capabilities actually help firms learn is not explored. Second, integration and coordination capabilities are mainly conceived as internal, that is relating tasks and activities within the boundaries of the firm. The role of external integration is simply sketched, and always by referring to those formal kinds of relationships (Teece *et al.*, 1997, p. 519) which feed up processes of 'inter-organizational learning'. That kind of knowledge (mainly tacit) firms acquire, often unintentionally, through less formal techno-economic relationships with other firms and organizations, instead, is not addressed. This last peculiarity is typical of contributions in the field of strategic management. Although by placing knowledge at the basis of a sound theory of the firm (e.g. Grant, 1996), they still consider the 'environment' in which the firms operate in a quite aseptic way: that is as a set of competitive relationships among competitors, suppliers and customers.

1.3.2 The technology approach

A second approach to dynamic capabilities can be identified around those contributions, mainly of an empirical nature, which have focused on the different capabilities that different firms have to implement and/or use new technologies. This could be actually considered one of the most fruitful fields of application of the dynamic capabilities rational. Indeed, its two constitutive elements – 'the shifting character of the environment' and 'the role of strategic management' in dealing with it (Teece and Pisano, 1994, p. 557) – find an immediate specification in, respectively: (i) the 'technological discontinuities' which destroy (rather than enhance) the firm's existing competence (Tushman and Anderson, 1986); (ii) the change in the communication channels, interpretative filters and organizational routines (in brief, in the 'architectural knowledge') the firm needs to implement in front of these discontinuities (Henderson and Clark, 1990). Nonetheless, the focus on technological aspects is so dominant that the concept of dynamic capabilities as such is only rarely used in an explicit way (e.g. Iansiti and Clark, 1994).

In what can be termed the 'technology approach', dynamic capabilities are identified with research and technological capabilities. That is, capabilities which apply to a certain technological element, such as: the 'knowledge' the firm masters in setting a new product dominant-design (Henderson and Clark, 1990); the 'skills and know-how' the firm uses to deal with new products and processes (Tushman and Anderson, 1986); the recursive chain of 'activities' through which the firm engages in technological problem-solving (Iansiti and Clark, 1994).

While the application to technology makes dynamic capabilities more concrete, in this approach their inner nature is conceptually more diffuse. On the one hand, organizational learning still seems at the core of their explanation (Iansiti and Clark, 1994, p. 17). On the other hand, a certain connection remains with the 'problem-solving' strategies of the firm. In particular, how much to invest in the new technology and when to adopt it. This strategic influence, which reveals a certain overlapping between the present and the previous approach, crucially affects the way the firm environment is depicted. First of all, the firm is described in 'technical' terms, as a community of engineers and strategies designers trying to tackle the firm technological complexity. This implies that, with respect to its external environment, the firm just needs to have a 'technology integration capacity' (Iansiti and Clark, 1994, p. 565). Picking-up that external, codifiable knowledge, which is more suitable to be linked with its existing knowledge base, is the most crucial capability. The same capacity does not apply, instead, to other forms of knowledge integration, of a more tacit nature, which calls for some kind of physical proximity between the firm and its interacting organizations. A second strategic influence on the present technological approach concerns the characterization of the firm environment. In general, it is depicted as an 'industry' populated by 'established organizations' (incumbents) and 'new entrants', among which the relevant relationships are mainly of a competitive nature (Tushman and Anderson, 1986, pp. 445–446). Non-competitive relationships among firms, and relationships with other institutions and organizations of a different nature, are instead just given a marginal role in shaping organizational learning and the capabilities dynamics. Furthermore, out of the manifold set of relationships that the firm establishes beyond its boundaries, only those with customers are deemed relevant for the capability-building process (Iansiti and Clark, 1994).

Definitively richer are the accounts provided for both the firm and its environment by those contributions which explain the dynamics of technology by resorting to system thinking. That is, by referring to the variety generation and selection mechanisms which apply to the technical, organizational and social components inter-related in large technological and socio-technical systems (e.g. Vincenti, 1994; Hughes, 1987; Tushman and Rosenkopf, 1990). Relationships and integration channels within and between firms are in fact addressed more satisfactorily. However, the encapsulation of firm capabilities in this framework of analysis is less advanced and less explicit than in the strategic analysis of technology.

In spite of these influences, the strategic management and the technology approach provide quite different predictions on which would be the 'superior' firm in terms of dynamic capabilities. The former points out those firms which manage to reconfigure their resources and capabilities to make them rent yielding in a new competitive equilibrium scenario. The latter, instead, favours those firms that are able to drive the 'creative destruction' of such an equilibrium through the successful adoption of a new technology. Although, to the authors' knowledge, empirical tests have not been provided yet, the two predictions lead to the identification of the same firms appears at least theoretically implausible.

1.3.3 The organization approach

Although organizational learning is crucial also in the previous approaches, organization theory enters more pervasively in a third approach which makes the firm's reaction and pro-reaction to change mainly dependent on the structure and composition of the relative organization. As in the previous technological approach, and also in the present 'organization approach', the explicit use of the dynamic capabilities concept is infrequent. However, there is no doubt that its inner logic is at work, although to a different extent depending on the specific contributions.

At the outset, important seeds can be found in the literature on the patterns the firm follows in 'creating' new knowledge (Nonaka, 1994; Nonaka and Takeuchi, 1997). These patterns are actually modelled as driven by the capability of the firm to create further knowledge, i.e. to learn. The creation of organizational knowledge, in turn, depends on a 'spiral' of events through which knowledge is transformed into further knowledge. Dynamic capabilities thus apply to knowledge itself. What is more, they are crucially affected by its availability. Organizational learning in fact tends to be dominated by local processes of search (March and Simon, 1958). Accordingly, when a technological discontinuity shakes the firm environment and urges the firm to learn distantly from what it knows, core competencies become 'core rigidities' (Leonard-Barton, 1992). In such a framework, therefore, dynamic capabilities are thought to be used in contrasting the organizational inertia and the path dependency associated with the learning process.

In these and other similar organizational accounts (e.g. Levitt and March, 1988; March, 1991), the attention to interactive kinds of aspects among firm/organization members, as well as to organization-wide conditions and management models is higher than in the previous two approaches (Nonaka, 1994). Furthermore, such a relational dimension also spans beyond the boundaries of the firm, and makes external interactions extremely relevant in driving organizational learning. However, these relational considerations are only partially encapsulated. First of all, although both formal and informal external communication channels are considered (Nonaka, 1994), the latter are simply treated as an extension of the standard intra-organizational case, rather than a constituent part of it. Accordingly, they are not given any special attention. Furthermore, following a typical strategic management approach, the 'environment' within which firms operate is often reduced to an aseptic triad (customers–suppliers–competitors), affecting individual rather than organizational learning.

Similar stylizations of the firm environment can also be found in a more recent strand of organization studies linking the dynamic capabilities of the firm to the role of managerial cognition (Garud and Rappa, 1994). This is the case, for example, of those contributions which point to the reconfiguration of the different modules of the firm's organization induced by a change in the architecture of its product modules, and to the implications of their matching in terms of flexibility (e.g. Sanchez and Mahoney, 1996). Similarly, organizational change is maintained as driven by knowledge change also by those contributions which draw on system theory the idea of the firm as a set of 'loosely coupled systems' (e.g. Orton and Weick, 1990).

The capacity of the firm to adapt successfully to radical new technology would depend on the mental models and strategic beliefs that boundedly rational managers develop in driving firm decisions, rather than on organizational learning or the firm's capability set. Indeed, the shaping of these cognitive representations by the historical environment – either through the shared 'dominant logic' of working together (Prahalad and Bettis, 1986) or through the 'imprint' of the firm founders (Baron *et al.*, 1999) – makes it difficult for the top managers to adapt their mental models in rapidly changing environments (Barr *et al.*, 1992). Dynamic capabilities should therefore be related to how beliefs evolve within organizations, to the role of hierarchy in cognition and, first and above all, to how capabilities and cognition relate (Tripsas and Gavetti, 2000).

In this last respect it should be stressed that the empirical tests of this cognitive hypothesis seem to provide different predictions from those one could associate to the technology approach. In both case studies (e.g. Tripsas and Gavetti, 2000) and systematic analysis (e.g. Kaplan *et al.*, 2003), cognitive arguments seem to explain both the firm inertia and the firm pro-action in front of technological discontinuities also after having controlled for alternative explanations (among which there is the availability of relevant technological capabilities).

1.3.4 The evolutionary approach

The theoretical background on which dynamic capabilities draw is in general evolutionary. With the partial exception of strategic management, this holds true for all the approaches analysed so far. Indeed, they all link the advent of new technological paradigms to the evolution of the firm knowledge base (Dosi *et al.*, 2000). On the other hand, it is possible to distinguish a group of studies which settle dynamic capabilities more explicitly in the variation–selection–retention model at the core of evolutionary theorizing (Cyert and March, 1963; Nelson and Winter, 1982).

In what can be accordingly termed the 'evolutionary approach', dynamic capabilities are related to the minimum ontological element of the evolutionary firm, i.e. to its organizational routines. On the one hand, dynamic capabilities directly apply to 'operational routines' – rather than to generic competencies or capabilities – allowing the firm to generate and modify them whenever it is necessary (Zollo and Winter, 2002, Zott, 2002). On the other hand, dynamic capabilities are distinguished from the routines they apply to, on the basis of their intentional and deliberated character. In other words, while operational routines are conceived as automatic or quasi-automatic responses to environmental changes, capabilities and dynamic capabilities are instead related to those 'constant dispositions and strategic heuristics that shape the approach of a firm to the non-routine problems it faces' (Nelson and Winter, 1982, p. 15).

Also in this approach organizational learning is crucial in determining the dynamic capabilities of the firm. Dynamic capability is, in fact, conceived as a 'learned, regular pattern of collective activity' (Zollo and Winter, 1999, p. 17). Here, however, organizational learning is fitted within an evolutionary model, which enlarges the scope of 'attributes' on which dynamic capabilities depend. The focus on variation, for example, recovers in the analysis the nature (e.g. exploratory vs. exploitative, cognitive vs. experiential) and the direction (i.e. imitative vs. experimental) of organizational search, whose choice also depends on the costs of deploying the relative resources (Zott, 2003). The retention of the routines that the firm has learnt to select, instead, recovers the delicate issue of the timing of their actual implementation (Zott, 2003). What is more, the map which connects dynamic capabilities to organizational learning is widened by addressing those routines that standard organization theory relegates to 'off-line' activities: knowledge 'articulation' and 'codification'. Conversely, the latter two are here pointed out as important forms of learning, through which the firm actually develops its dynamic capabilities.

On the basis of these considerations, the added value of the evolutionary approach appears extremely important. First of all, it adds an important evolutionary qualification to the relevance of organizational learning for dynamic capabilities. While it is involved in the 'selection' of a new set of ideas, mainly through articulation and codification processes, the firm also gets engaged in the 'generative variation' of further knowledge. Accordingly, the 'exploration' of new knowledge does not necessarily prime its 'exploitation', as it is instead suggested by some accounts of the organization approach (e.g. March, 1991). Further qualifications are added by simulating the evolutionary model in the attempt at suggesting propositions to be empirically tested. Quite interestingly, the predictions the evolutionary approach would suggest do not purely reduce to that of the previous approaches.

On the other hand, it must be noted that the evolutionary model is set in a framework (a typical 'knowledge-cycle') which occurs entirely within the boundaries of the firm, and with respect to which the firm environment does not play a direct dynamic role. Environmental factors are just 'viewed [...] as inputs to the dynamic capability building process, rather than part of the process itself' (Zollo and Winter, 1999, p. 11). However, once fitted in a broader evolutionary framework, this view appears a contingent simplification rather than a general hypothesis. Given the importance that evolutionary economics has traditionally attributed to the institutions making up the surrounding environment of the firm (Hodgson, 1988), their role in shaping the dynamic capabilities of the firm is another evolutionary qualification of the issue. The introduction and the subsequent development of innovation system kinds of concepts (Lundvall, 1992; Nelson, 1993) actually implement the idea that institutional and policy contexts, with their spatial and territorial characterizations, crucially shape the dynamic capabilities of the firm, thus introducing important policy implications (Metcalfe, 1995).

The survey of the literature on dynamic capabilities clearly shows how 'complex' the relationship between organizational learning and firm dynamics is. In the four approaches we have identified such a complexity is mainly due to the complexity of the firm organization itself. What is outside of its boundaries, and could be termed the 'firm environment', is instead differently retained, but never as crucial as the firm organization. Indeed, a certain focalization-bias seems to us apparent in the analysis of dynamic capabilities. By focusing on the internal organization of the firm, the relational and contextual aspects, affecting the creation and development of dynamic capabilities, have been somehow neglected.

In trying to recover the role of relations and context in shaping firms' learning processes one might turn to a different strand of literature, focusing on a geographical, rather than an organizational kind of environment. Although without an explicit reference to dynamic capabilities, the literature on the so-called 'local systems of production' in fact stresses the relevance, in adjusting and building up firms' capabilities and learning, of factors such as, for example, the localization in a Marshallian 'industrial district' (Marshall, 1890; Becattini, 1979, 1987), the embeddedness in an 'innovative milieu' (Aydalot, 1986; Camagni, 1991a), and the firm setting in a 'regional system of innovation' (Braczyk *et al.*, 1998; Cooke *et al.*, 1998). However, a critical survey of this kind of literature with respect to dynamic capabilities shows a bias somehow symmetric to that implied by organizational learning (Leoncini *et al.*, 2006). Indeed, such 'environmental' accounts inevitably take some focus out of the firm as a knowledge creating organization, and even more as an organization managing the dynamics of its capabilities. Thus, dynamic capabilities tend to degenerate into geographically delimited, system-specific capabilities: firms have different individual (rather than organizational) abilities to benefit from, rather than to build up.

In the light of this argument, rather than overcoming the bias coming from the organizational side, this kind of literature provides a different environmental bias of the relationships between the learning of firms settled in local systems of production and their dynamics.

Evidently, both 'organizational' and 'environmental' factors play a crucial role in shaping the dynamic capabilities of the firm. What is more important, they are strictly interconnected. Accordingly, laying a bridge between the two correspondent theoretical perspectives becomes an essential task. How to accomplish it is however not unquestionable.

1.4 Firm organization and firm environment: towards a synthesis

While sticking to either the organizational or the environmental account inevitably entails a partial view of dynamic capabilities, and of the process of learning and firm dynamics, one might think that, somehow overlapping them, would enable us to capture the same capabilities more accurately. A similar exercise is somehow implicit in an interesting research programme which has recently tried to extend to spatial systems of firms a relational approach of inter-organizational nature (Lipparini, 1995; Lipparini and Lorenzoni, 1996). The starting point of this last stream of studies is the role played by the firms' relational set-ups. According to this 'relational view', setting-up firm networks, signing-up partnership agreements with other organizations, managing the ensuing relationships, or simply involving (also informally) customers and suppliers in business operations, would increase the learning capabilities of the firms involved. The dynamic capability of the firm is in fact retained, nothing but a 'relational capability'.

The relevance of a relational argument has emerged both from a theoretical (Ferrucci and Varaldo, 1993; Lipparini and Lorenzoni, 1996) and an empirical (Brioschi *et al.*, 2002, 2004) point of view. However, this kind of combined perspective does not allow the biased-views we are dealing with to overcome. Indeed, the retrieval of organizational aspects in the analysis of local production systems seems to occur at the expenses of those tacit and informal elements which are typical of the environmental side, and which get therefore somehow hidden, if not even lost.

Therefore, it seems to us that a more fruitful research line might be that of analysing the dynamic capabilities of the firm by drawing on complex sciences.

Although, not free from methodological problems, looking at the firm as a *complex system* seems a promising research line to capture the manifold nature of the firm (e.g. Montresor and Romagnoli, 2004) and the evolutionary dynamics of its environment (Fuller and Moran, 2000, 2001). On the other hand, complexity appears also somehow abused so that some instructions on how we intend to relate it to dynamic capabilities is necessary at the outset.

1.4.1 Some hints and concepts about complexity

The theory of complexity constitutes an interdisciplinary field of inquiry, where several approaches find a sort of convergence path. Indeed, complexity theory is made up of several separated contributions from fields as different as biology, chemistry, physics, computer science, etc. Although they all refer to the same set of core propositions, there are wide differences among them, as far as both the theoretical and the methodological backgrounds are concerned. This has to do with the fact that, although they all deal with the same classes of non-linear problems, all these different approaches have been developed independently and for differently specified kinds of problems. Thus, it is not surprising to find in the literature on the topic a certain kind of methodological pluralism which so far has somehow conditioned the spreading of this discipline, with regard to the more 'compact' and 'cohesive' reductionist approach. Many have pointed out to the lack of an integrated model, to some ambiguities in the definition of what precisely holism means and implies, the lack of unified methodological guidance for empirical analysis. And this is even truer when complex science is applied to social science.

The first set of concepts we will refer to in dealing with complexity, is about *connectivity*. Indeed, the main characteristic of a complex system is that each unit cannot determine its state unless it interacts with the others. Hence, the degree of connectivity among agents becomes a crucial element for understanding complexity. In fact, we can talk about complex systems only if there are some connections between the constituents units.[3] And connecting units means that there must be some exchange between them, and that the state of one unit cannot be independent from that of at least another one. This has many implications. Starting from the impossibility of using a comparative statics approach, to the realization that dynamic patterns only emerge as result of several linked dynamics of the units, to the fact that every unit has a different impact upon the system dynamics (hierarchy), to the fact that if a system of relationships can be defined, separated from others, then there will be a set of relationships with other systems (what is defined as an ecosystem), and that the final state of a system results from the co-evolution of several related systems.

Moreover, connectivity implies that there are *signals* (quantities of energy or matter[4]) which flow among the connected units. Thus, the higher the connectivity, the greater the exchange of signals among the units. This has the implication that the greater the flow of energy and matter between units, the higher the signal overload that the unit involved has to manage. This in turn implies that the higher the flows of signals that a unit has to deal with, the more 'organized' it must be. Therefore, unless the degree of organization of a unit increases with the increasing degree of connectivity, increasing connectivity implies greater pushes towards instability. As a corollary, we could say that the degree of connectivity per se is not at all an asset of an ecosystem, but rather it can constitute a serious constraint to its performance (whatever performance is meant to be).

Another set of concepts is related to the notion of *feedback*. It must be preliminarily noted that feedbacks are not a peculiarity of complex systems, but they are a crucial elements in orthodox (Newtonian) systems too. However, what differentiates the two is that in the latter case the predominant element is constituted by negative feedback. Indeed, based on the working of negative feedback, a system can be shown to be stable. Negative feedback is one of the most important elements in determining the level of (either local or global) stability. Once positive feedback is considered, disequilibrium points will exhibit the 'undesired' behaviour of exploding away from equilibrium.[5] Positive feedback has the implication that more than one equilibrium point comes to be determined, which has implications upon predictability. But, there is more to this, since, if this notion is coupled with that of sensitivity to initial conditions, we are left with two elements calling for unpredictability: one quantitative (positive feedbacks) and one qualitative (dependence on small events). Hence, it must be kept in mind that two mechanisms are at work when diverging paths are observed: one related to the effect of positive feedbacks, another one related to sensitivity to initial conditions.

Another set of concepts relate to the work of Ilia Prigogine on *far from equilibrium dissipative structures*. If a system is forced in a state that is far from equilibrium, it is possible to show that the resulting dynamics determines what Prigogine (1976) defined as 'order through fluctuations'. The system reconfigures itself in order to maintain a stationary dynamic state that is defined by the balance of dynamic exchange of energy with the environment, and that since it requires an inflow of energy to be maintained it is 'dissipative'. The system can maintain its state by continually exporting 'disorder' and importing 'order' from outside. This process has the quite interesting peculiarity that for the system to stay far from equilibrium, it has to explore the surrounding space of possibilities and to discover how to create new ways to link their constituent units (i.e. to innovate). Indeed, this state is quite interesting if applied to social sciences. In fact, when an agent is forced away from equilibrium (i.e. away from well established patterns of behaviour) it becomes crucial to start a process of exploration of the possible alternatives. The agent is therefore pushed towards an innovative behaviour in order to search for alternative ways to reach a certain target.[6]

Another appealing result for socio-economic systems is that this approach allows for the description of *deterministic and subsequent stochastic behaviour*. Indeed, this is quite an interesting result, since it can serve the purpose of describing the rational (Newtonian) behaviour of economic agents (along a single deterministic trajectory), and the relevance of small historical events in the neighbourhood of bifurcation points. In this way it is possible to describe both the consolidated patterns of behaviour followed for long periods by agents, and the subsequent willingness of single agents to deviate from this consolidated type of behaviour (or the crucial role of small casual events of limited quantitative relevance). From a Schumpeterian (evolutionary) perspective, the two components can describe both average and deviant behaviour.

We can thus analyse in depth the problem of *predictability* within this particular framework. The problem of predictability has to be seen from the multi-layered perspective that complex system theory encompasses. Indeed, under certain conditions the behaviour of a highly non-linear system is characterized by deterministic patterns. This means that, in these cases, there are bi-univocal relationships between the variables, which determine completely regular and 'linear' relationships. Within this first set of conditions, the system exhibits predictability and reversibility: the system moves along a stable trajectory and it can move in either direction. At this stage it can be said that negative feedback is at work. If a certain threshold is overcome, completely different patterns are put in motion. In this case the system is unstable, and unpredictable. Positive feedback contributes to make the path further diverge from the starting point.

However, for certain values of the parameters' set the system could operate on the edge between these two states. It is therefore called the 'edge of chaos' or 'phase transition'. The behaviour at the edge of chaos is characterized by bounded instability, which means that the specific behavioural pattern is unpredictable, but this unpredictable pattern is confined within a certain predictable general framework that delimits the set of likely behavioural patterns.

Therefore, predictability means in this case that what we have is a range within which we can exercise our predictions. Attractors constitute equilibria of the system dynamics, and some of their characteristics, which are known, circumscribe the behaviour of the system, which in this way is predictable, obviously not in the way reductionism has taught us. Moreover, it can well be said that strange attractors are the elements that guarantee the presence of *variety* within the system. Indeed, since it is possible to converge towards a set of possible organizational forms, rather than one only, this implies that the system will continuously feed itself from the variety generated by the process of convergence, if, and only if, this process converges to an attractor rather than to a point.

An important element to deal with in this sketch of complexity is related to the unit of analysis. Indeed, especially in dealing with social sciences, the proper definition of the unit of analysis is an extremely important issue. Since complex systems are characterized by the emergence of 'macro aggregates' that are qualitatively different from their constituent elements, there is the problem of determining which is the level to which the analysis is carried out, and thus the choice of the unit of analysis. At this regard we can set out two propositions: a strong and a mild one. The strong proposition argues that, although human beings are definitely different from other (natural) elements constituting examples of complex systems (mainly because they are conscious individuals with purposeful actions), there is no difference between the two at aggregate level. If we consider the aggregate human actions we can safely discard the fact that single behaviour can influence the whole system behaviour.

A milder explanation takes into consideration the system itself as composed by many interlinked agents. By definition, one agent's action is influenced by and influences that of all the other agents of the system. But as one agent's behaviour depends on that of others, we can safely say that it is a process of co-evolution deriving from responses from all the elements of the system. Thus, if, on the one side, the particular structure of this social ecosystem cannot be separated from the strategic behaviour of its constituents, on the other, complexity is generated, not by the raising level of interconnections, but by the fact that these interactions create structures which have properties radically different from those of the elements that generated it. This is the generally accepted (and widely debated) concept of *emergence*: the system needs to be evaluated as an interacting entity, irreducible to the behaviour of its micro aggregates.

A final word about the role of signals exchanged among agents. We will refer in the course of the chapter to information exchange as the (maybe only) way with which organizations communicate and establish relationships, and as the central element through which the process of co-evolutionary growth is fuelled. We do not have the space to elaborate further this point (see, for instance, Clark, 1991, for a useful recap), but to simply put forward some useful elements. Information in general is central to all the literature that relates to innovation. Information is useful in this context since it is relational, it can to a certain extent be measured and stored, and as it increases, it needs increasing levels of organization. The contextualization of information passes through a double process of cognitive and institutional coding which, for example, can be referred, depending on the level of analysis chosen, to technological paradigms, routines or dynamic capabilities.

1.4.2 A 'system approach' to dynamic capabilities

Drawing on complexity sciences in interpreting the firm dynamics is for the sake of the present chapter extremely fruitful. It is in fact suggested that the inner determinants of this dynamic process can be directly related to the dynamic capabilities of the firm, and in a way that allows one to consider both organizational and environmental factors in a consistent way. Firm dynamics can be sketched as a process triggered and fuelled by the intertwining of two factors: (1) the threshold level in the firm response mechanisms to environmental flows; (2) the relative balance between environmental 'turbulence' and inner 'entropy'.

(1) The first factor is the 'usual' homeostatic mechanism which, in this case, applies to whichever of the firm-system 'functional layers' (Fuller and Moran, 2001): in particular, to the legal, the organizational, the capabilities and the institutional layers (Montresor and Romagnoli, 2004). The elements and relationships of these layers are indeed subject to structural change once the relevant environmental signals overcome a certain threshold level. In the case of the legal

layer, a relevant example is provided by the change intervened in the firm governance models following the historical diffusion of sparse stockholders without any interest in the management and control of the firms. Once it had reached a certain level, this process actually determined the famous divorce between property and control (Berle and Means, 1932). With respect to the organizational layer, instead, a homeostatic mechanism can be seen at work in the changes that the organizational structures of the large companies have undergone over time as a consequence, for example, of the overcoming of a certain level of diversification: the notable transformation of U-firms into M-firms can be read in this way (Chandler, 1962). As far as the capabilities layer is concerned, organizational routines are the structural component subject to homeostatic kinds of pressure, maybe the most known since the works of Nelson and Winter (1982) and Simon (1955). In this case, the element (the routine) delimiting the search patterns remains stable (i.e. is not subject to structural change) unless it consistently fails to deliver its pre-determined goal. Finally, homeostatic elements can be seen at work also by referring to the institutional layer of the firm, in the sense indicated, for instance, by the transformation of 'networked firms' into 'networks of firms' (Antonelli, 1987). In this last case, as the institutional context changes (and, for instance, intermediate institutions start appearing and diffusing on the firm territory), it might become profitable for firms to be part of a network rather than being only internally networked: it is when the 'signal' from the institutional set-up overcomes a certain threshold that the profitability of 'being outside' becomes larger than that of 'being inside'.

(2) As far as the second factor is concerned, the process of evolution that firms undergo depends on the 'relative' dimension of the environment, rather than on its absolute dimension. Hence, the relative dimension of the relationships firm/environment can assume quite different specifications. Indeed, it is possible to consider the environment firms face from both a functional and a territorial point of view, and both of them allow for an active role of firms (i.e. a bi-univocal causal relationship): they can actively work to co-define their environment, either by clustering spatially with others, or by 'tuning' their dimension with respect to the sector/technological regime they are part of, in order to try and smooth out to a certain degree the environmental turbulence.

It is fairly obvious that differences in sectoral specificity, technological regimes and spatial clustering provide completely different environmental set-ups, with completely different needs and possibilities for the firms to survive and prosper. If these patterns are referred to the evolution in the natural world, it becomes easy to understand the importance of this difference, and the relevance for the final result of allowing units of selection to interact with the 'global' environment, rather than with its neighbourhood.[7]

In general terms, although the resulting dynamic process cannot be merely decomposed in factors (1) and (2) identified above – i.e. the firm response threshold level and the relative turbulence/entropy balance – as it rather results from their mutual interaction, they play different roles. The former determines the actual degree of the firm-system response to the signals coming from the environment. This allows the firm-system structure to remain qualitatively unchanged unless the signals overcome the threshold, thus spurring an 'innovative passage' through the edge of chaos, which can result in the emergence of a novel system structure. The latter, instead, informs about the way the threshold level of the system itself changes subject to the dynamics of its 'relative' environment. Indeed, on the one side, the firm-system tends to smoothe out the degree of volatility of its relationships with a turbulent environment through the progressive incorporation of fractions of the environment itself, thus expanding the system's boundaries. On the other side, as the balance between the system and its environment dynamically shifts, the latter decreases in size relative to the firm's. Thus, as the relative dimension of the environment decreases, in turn its degree of 'overall' stability progressively decreases to cause increasing fluctuations in the entropy exchange.

The previous dynamic process can be described more concretely by referring to the firm as a set of interrelated capabilities, whose degree of entropy is so-to-say fine-tuned by a two-tiered mechanism. On the one side, inner mechanisms of organizational learning define certain levels for the firm capabilities, within which the firm performances are retained to be satisfactory with respect to its goals. Indeed, this is actually what happens when the firm is capable of accommodating the environmental turbulence (mainly, but not only, of technological nature) by resorting to specific integration/combinatory principles, Lamarckian routines, and problem-solving algorithms. On the other side, but simultaneously, a co-evolution process is set into motion in which the firm interacts with its environment, in order to reach a dynamic balance between turbulence and entropy. Again, this is what actually happens when the firm implements different kinds of integration strategies, or sets up some kind of institutional network (both formally and informally) with the other actors, which make up its environment and provokes its turbulence.

Once the firm dynamics is figured out in this way, its dynamic capabilities assume a twofold nature. On the one side, they refer to the capacity of the firm to fine-tuning its capabilities set and its organizational structure in order to fit its competitive relationships with the outer environment. On the other side, dynamic capabilities also refer to the capacity of the firm to (strategically) shift its boundaries typically, but not exclusively, through the integration channel, in order not to be overwhelmed when the environmental pressure becomes excessive. The two sides have a different nature, since the first represents the so-called 'static component' of dynamic capabilities, and the second is instead the most inherently dynamic, referring to the firm capacity to suitably stretch its boundaries to redistribute the pressure between several internal components, and between the inner and outer environment. However, these two components of dynamic capabilities are strictly interrelated, as the firm boundaries, which somehow separate them, are intrinsically dynamic. Indeed, the firm boundaries are not simply a 'red line' between the inner and the outer firm environment, while they are defined, consistently with the system approach here embraced, on a functional basis. By adopting a functional criterion, the firm can, in fact, be identified as a set of 'functions', in turn related to its own resources and capabilities, to keep the level of entropy under 'control', in order not to make it dissolve within the environment (for instance, as a bundle of contracts), or to make it enlarge to the point of comprehending (for instance, as a result of deep integration/conglomeration) the whole environment. The actual organizational setting of a firm is thus defined as a sort of 'indifference' dynamic state, emerging at the edge of chaos. Similarly, the firm variety turns out to be the result of a push-and-pull process. In such a twofold process, on the one side, firms are constantly trying to cope with a turbulent outer environment by moving their boundaries out, e.g. by extending their functions, thus expanding the dimension of their technical system with respect to the outer environment. On the other side, firms face a turbulent inner environment calling for entropy export in order to dynamically balance the degree of internal order, by outsourcing some of their functions.

The capabilities of the firm to undertake this complex process of change are in fact its dynamic capabilities. Their nature is evidently quite different from that of the approaches reviewed in the first part of the chapter. Indeed, following the present approach dynamic capabilities apply to the firm as a system of capabilities, rather than to one or another of its constitutive elements (be they routines, competencies or technology). Their core element is the firm capacity to undertake a complex adaptive process, rather than its ability to implement an organizational kind of learning. In fact, such a capacity is not purely organizational, and merely consisting of an evolution process of its organization in response to changing patterns of the selection mechanism. On the contrary, once the firm dynamics is conceived as a co-evolutionary process, environmental factors become as relevant as organizational ones in explaining dynamic capabilities, thus actually laying a bridge between the two perspectives that have been reviewed. Indeed, dynamic capabilities come to depend on: (i) the relative extension of the firm with respect to the environment; (ii) the relative speed of entropy exchange; (iii) the role of the relevant technological system, and of the correspondent institutional set-up, within which a particular firm (or a set of firms) operates.

(i) As far as the first point is concerned, the system approach here proposed suggests that dynamic capabilities do not simply depend on the absolute size of the firm, but rather on its relative extension with respect to the hosting environment, being the sectoral or the territorial environment of the firm. A large, vertically integrated firm, operating within a narrow 'technological regime' (Breschi *et al.*, 2000; Malerba and Orsenigo, 1997) – for example in terms of 'technological opportunities' (Breschi and Malerba, 1997) – will possibly have different dynamic capabilities from a firm as large as the previous one but operating within a more pervasive techno-economic environment. Similarly, the dynamic capabilities that are necessary to a small firm will differ depending on the firm having to face the turbulence originating in a quite localized industrial district, rather than that of a more territorially diffused system of production. Looking for a correlation, possibly positive, between firm size and dynamic capabilities would, therefore, be misleading. On the contrary, the relative firm dimension could well be detrimental to the firm's capability to keep its entropy within a certain balance. This occurs, for example, if the environment, being relatively 'small', cannot absorb relevant flows 'coming out' from the firm: such as for a highly innovative firm operating in a technological regime in which appropriability is extremely difficult to obtain, or for a firm of an expanding business group which is 'forced' within a certain territorial partition. Also in these cases, however, the degree of turbulence of the outer environment could be so low, with respect to the relative dimension of the firm, that it might never overcome the firm's threshold level to force a qualitative leap. In the previous examples, appropriating innovations or even implementing them might not be so necessary if the relevant technological regime is not marked by diffuse opportunities. Similarly, extending control and ownership relationships over the territory might not be so crucial if the competitive process remains mainly played at the local level.

(ii) The relative speed of the entropy exchange is obviously another crucial element in affecting dynamic capabilities. In fact, a relatively stable environment, in which the flow of, for instance, information is easily predictable, has completely different implications on the firm dynamic capabilities with respect to an environment where overloading of information prevails. In the first case, the high (if not even total) predictability of the environment dynamics tends to make the 'static' side of dynamic capabilities more relevant than its inherently dynamic one. The relative instability induced by an incremental innovation occurring in the firm sector is a typical example of this first case, to face which the firm just needs to be capable to fine-tuning its 'ordinary' learning mechanisms (though they still are dynamic capabilities). In the second case, instead, unpredictable changes in the firm environment force heavy re-configurations of its organizational learning procedures, thus reversing the relevance of the two dynamic capabilities components. The relevant example of this second case is that of a quite dramatic technological breakthrough in the firm sector: if the firm capabilities thresholds are overcome, the firm needs to re-design its entropy balance, and possibly extend or change its organizational boundaries and its administrative procedures. Of course, in-between these two polar cases – which can well have a territorial rather than a purely sectoral specification – a continuum of environmental turbulence can be envisaged, the response to which determines different degrees of combination of the two dynamic capabilities factors. This argument naturally extends the relevance of the dynamic capabilities concept per se, as drawing on such capabilities is necessary, although to a different extent, not only in front of paradigmatic technological changes but, more in general, also in dealing with minor (incremental) changes, and not only of a technological nature.

In more general terms, we could say that if the environment is mainly characterized by the presence of negative feedback, this environment can be said to be stable, in the sense that endogenous forces are acting in order to maintain the system close to its equilibrium state, and to prevent it from 'explosive' exponential departure from it. Thus, when an agent is active within a stable environment, all the tools of conventional planning/optimization can be used effectively in order to gain a certain level of desired performance. The negative feedback that is at work (i.e. the usual equilibrating market forces) allow for a relatively high degree of precision in forecasting the results of a certain course of action. The usual planning approaches are thus applicable with efficacy.

Organizations acting within this stable (or slowly moving) and predictable environment have strong incentives to incorporate larger and larger portions of the environment in order to smooth any kind of perturbation coming from outside. In this way, they can both deal effectively with a relatively less turbulent environment and reduce uncertainty in their transactions by advocating to hierarchies in managing contracts about very specialized kinds of inputs. In this way, organizations progressively move their boundaries out through a process of incorporation of the environment. In so doing the capacity of organizations to export entropy towards the environment progressively decreases, thus creating a balance which comes to be less and less favourable to the organization. However, from complex system theory we know that this is possible only insofar as the balance of the entropy exchange with the environment is not too unfavourable to the organization. In other words, in front of a quite stable environment (or with very few and predictable turbulences), it is possible for the organization to encompass further portions of environment in order to gain the implied gains in efficiency due to a reduction in transaction costs. From this point of view, it is quite straightforward to explain how organizations are so-to-say deemed to grow (e.g. by vertical integration), that is by benefiting from the ensuing economies of scale in order to face the increasing levels of competition pressure. However, we are now equipped to understand why the process of growth comes to a stop, and hence why small firms do exist. In fact, this process would imply that the level of information (the signal) necessary to its functioning increases to the point that it would be impossible to manage. The increasing number of linkages is an element of instability for an open system, since the information load for each unit increases exponentially. Thus a system with a high level of information exchange would be unstable. This explains why firms do not grow as we might expect. Or, better to say, this explains that within the system there are no (institutional) elements to help manage the information overload.[8]

(iii) Coming to the third determinant of dynamic capabilities, following a complex system perspective, the 'environment' in which the firm operates is in turn conceived as a system too. This naturally follows from the extension of the view we have applied to the firm, to all the other institutions and organizations, which make up the firm's environment (Monks, 1998). Once the firm environment is considered as a system, of which the system-firm is also part, drawing on the literature on innovation and technological systems in investigating its dynamics becomes unavoidable (for a review see Edquist, 1997). In particular, it becomes possible to qualify the different sub-systems of a technological system (Leoncini, 1998; Leoncini and Montresor, 2003) to which the dynamic capabilities of the firm apply according to the twofold dynamical mechanism previously described. A co-evolutionary process of that kind can, in fact, be envisaged by looking at the firm as an organization involved, respectively, in the introduction or adaptation of new technological ideas and knowledge, and thus co-evolving within the scientific-core (sub-system) of a technological system; in the actual implementation of its innovative outcomes (or of those of others) into new products or processes, and thus co-evolving within specific technical sub-systems; in the interaction with those agents which acquire the outcome of their economic activity, and thus co-evolving within the market sub-system; in the interplay with those formal (such as patent offices or chambers of commerce) and informal (such as social norms or standards) institutional arrangements which make the previous co-evolutionary processes possible, and thus the co-evolving within a specific institutional set-up. In each of these four dynamical processes the firm threshold levels refer to different kinds of response mechanisms: for example, to a change in the consumers tastes (in the market sub-system), rather than to the introduction of a new scientific breakthrough (in the scientific core), or to a new law on patenting (in the institutional set-up). And also, the entailed entropy-turbulence balances and the 'firm layers' (Montresor and Romagnoli, 2004) are different with respect to which the firm boundaries get repositioned: for example, the legal layer (such as in the extension of the so called corporate control), rather than the organizational layer (such as in the case of a vertical integration process), or that of its capabilities (such as in the case of a de-focusing, differentiation strategy). Referring to the hosting environment of the firm as a technological system is thus extremely helpful in better qualifying the functioning of its dynamic capabilities, as well as in retaining the crucial role that institutions have in allowing them to turn from capabilities to running a dynamic process into an actual pattern of change. What the firms learn is in fact inevitably shaped by the relations, typically of an informal nature, they develop with the social and institutional environment underpinning the system, by which their cognitive structures are also affected.

1.5 How to measure dynamic capabilities? Case studies and beyond

The idea that organizational and environmental accounts of the firm's dynamic capabilities have to be properly combined is not only a theoretically based recommendation, but also a requirement suggested by empirical evidence. On the one hand, some applied studies on the organizational nature of dynamic capabilities also point to the relevance of so to say 'external factors'.[9] On the other hand, an increasing number of empirical studies on local systems of production has captured the role of the firm organization and organizational settlements in driving their collective dynamics.[10]

Although highly instructive, these kinds of studies are affected by some problems. First of all, they are usually carried out on the basis of few selected units of analysis, which are retained to have experienced a certain dynamic process (in Iansiti and Clark, 1994, for example, a certain number of development projects): ex-post rationalizations thus hamper wider generalizations, not to say systematic predictions. Second, although these studies recognize the relevance of both kinds of factors, they remain anchored in either the organizational or environmental approach and they do not try to compare their relevance, not even their relationships.

In trying to remedy these two problems, in the last part of the paper we aim at carrying out an empirical analysis of dynamic capabilities which considers them as simultaneously and interactively driven by the firm organizational structure and relationships and by the distinguishing features of the environment in which they operate. Such a kind of analysis is extremely demanding in terms of proxies, as the nature of the aspects under investigation is quite specific. Accordingly, in order to be as specific as possible, we have resorted to a direct kind of analysis, in which firms have been directly asked to answer detailed questions about their dynamic capabilities, organizational and environmental factors, and to pick-up from a list of 'closed' answers the most appropriate category for each question. As we will see, this choice has affected both our field of analysis – a set of firms of the province of Treviso – and our tools of investigation – based on a multiple correspondence analysis.

1.5.1 A multiple correspondence analysis of dynamic capabilities for the province of Treviso

Although the system kind of analysis of dynamic capabilities we propose is quite general, in order to make its added value and rational more visible we have chosen to start setting it at work in a case study with a certain degree of '*ad hoc*ness'. Indeed, the interpretive power of an analysis of dynamic capabilities which considers both organizational and environmental aspects appears more evident by focusing on a geographical area where both aspects are known to be relevant: on the one hand, the presence of idiosyncratic local systems of production, for example, of a district nature; on the other hand, a certain variety of typical organizational structures and arrangements such as, for example, vertically integrated or quasi-integrated companies with diffused delocalization policies. Searching for such an area, and crossing these search criteria with data availability, we have ended up with focusing on the province of Treviso, one of the most dynamic areas of the northeast of Italy, where the tradition of the industrial districts has recently been coupled with a certain organizational turmoil (Anastasia and Corò, 1993; Bresolin and Biscaro, 2001; Osservatorio Unioncamere di Treviso, 2004).

The set of firms used for the empirical analysis is taken from a survey recently undertaken at the University of Padua (Italy) (Marangoni *et al.*, 2003). The coverage of the survey, although extremely detailed, is not that large: 89 firms, which represent almost 8 per cent of the total firms of the province. On the other hand, the dataset of the survey is based on an extensive questionnaire which contains many questions on the organizational and environmental aspects we are interested in. What is more, a couple of these questions are directed to 'elicitate' the dynamic capabilities of the firm, with respect to different sources of dynamics: and this of course has made the questionnaire an important starting point for our analysis. Apart from very few cardinal variables, the questionnaire is entirely made up of multiple-choice questions. In the vast majority of cases, the answer amounts to a 'modality' and this has affected the analytical tool chosen: the multiple correspondence analysis.

As is well-known, multiple correspondence analysis (MCA) is a special version of the more popular principal component analysis (PCA), introduced to deal with nominal variables, rather than cardinal ones, made up of an appreciable number of categories (Benzécri, 1973). Their rational is basically the same. Its final objective is that of identifying a limited number of 'factors' (the equivalent of the PCA 'components') which are able to reproduce as much as possible of the 'inertia' (the equivalent of the PCA 'variance') revealed by a 'bunch' of points in a vector space. Once the factors are identified, the variables/categories and/or the observations can be projected on a limited number of factoral spaces, which result from their orthogonal combination. Two kinds of analysis can thus be carried out on them: (i) a 'factorial analysis' which, through a set of indicators (of mass, distortion, absolute and relative contributions[11]), aims at attaching to the axes a semantic meaning, re-interpreting the original observations on their basis and carrying out further econometric analysis; (ii) a 'structural analysis', which investigates the shape of the projections and the distances among the points, in order to detect clusters and possible associations between the variables. Before moving to the results of these two bits of analysis, let us look more in depth at the structure of the dataset.

1.5.2 The structure of the dataset

In order to run a MCA which was both 'sound' and functional to our investigation of dynamic capabilities the questionnaire of the University of Padua has been substantially re-elaborated (Appendix 1). First of all, given that the 'noise' of the results is the higher, the larger is the size of the (Burt) matrix to implement the MCA, we have substantially reduced the number of variables, from the original 67 to 42. Only few of the original questions that were not directly relevant for our analysis have been directly dropped (for example, the breakdown of the firm machinery by typology). In the majority of cases, instead, two or more questions have been condensed into one by amending the set of the correspondent answers.[12] Second, in order to reduce the bias introduced by an unbalanced dataset, the few continuous variables of the original questionnaire have been transformed into nominal ones.[13] For the same reason, the number of available categories for each variable has been made more homogeneous, ranging from a minimum of 3 to a maximum of 5.[14] Finally, even the categories of the original dataset that were not so unbalanced have been rearranged in order to eliminate categories with nil or very low frequencies, while missing answers have been recovered as an extra category.[15]

For the scope of our investigation, the variables have been collected into several broad groups, reflecting the various characteristics along which the analysis has been performed (Appendix 1). The groups describe, besides to the most usual set of variables (e.g. of structure, production efficiency, innovation, etc.), other key aspects of this analysis (such as organization, relationships with customers/suppliers, relationships with the environment, existence of capabilities). Indeed, we have rearranged the dataset in order to get useful information about the patterns of vertical (INTV) and horizontal (INTH) dis/integration, outsourcing (OUTS) and delocalization (LOCD). Also all the different activities related to the linkages with suppliers and customers are quite important for our analysis, as well as cooperation with competitors (see the group 'relationships'). To them we have added two other important variables on how the firms perceive their placement within both the material infrastructural (MIFR) and the immaterial infrastructural (IFR) set-up.[16] This information is necessary for at least two reasons. First, because of our framework, which is mainly focused upon the relationships between inner and outer environment. Second, because of the particular industrial structure of this part of Italy, characterized by the heavy presence of industrial districts, for which these variables all contribute to building up the 'industrial atmosphere'.

A final remark must be made about the crucial variables of the present application, those related to the firm capabilities. First of all, the high level of detail of the questionnaire has allowed us to distinguish two kinds of dynamic capabilities variables related to, respectively, the innovative and the market side. In this way we have been able to take into account the firm capabilities in front of two sources of change: one due to technological change (CDIN), the other due to a change in the market fundamentals (CDMK). The two variables refer to the ability of the firms to anticipate or not the future evolution of, respectively, technology and market, and have been built up by investigating whether they have had 'difficulties or not' in doing that. In both cases, the choices are among four alternatives: (i) 'yes, there are difficulties' (CDIN and CDMK=10); (ii) 'no, we anticipate it' (CDIN and CDMK = 40); (iii) 'no, we can adapt quickly' (CDIN and CDMK=30); (iiii) 'no, we adapt only when necessary' (CDIN and CDMK= 20). It is thus clear that we have both different types and different combinations of abilities to respond/adapt to external stimulus, either from the technical or from the market side.

1.5.3 Significance and semantic interpretation of the axes

The first set of results that we present is based on a MCA run with respect to 26 active variables (Appendix 2). The application does not include five structural variables, which will be used as supplementary ones in the following, and another 11 non-structural variables, which in previous attempts have turned out to introduce either relevant distortions or irrelevant explanations of the total inertia of the data.

With as many as 26 active variables and 106 categories, we have decided to focus our attention on the first four axes which explain, on average, more than 4 per cent of the total inertia of the observations each (the average eigen-value is 3.8 per cent=1/26) and, altogether, nearly 20 per cent (Table 1.2).[17]

Table 1.2 Histogram of the 80 eigen-values

No.	*Eigen value*	*Percentage of explained inertia*	*Cumulated percentage of explained inertia*	
1	0.1783	5.79	5.79	**
2	0.1359	4.42	10.21	***
3	0.1297	4.22	14.43	***
4	0.1284	4.17	18.6	**
5	0.1214	3.94	22.54	***
6	0.1114	3.62	26.16	**
7	0.1057	3.43	29.6	**
8	0.0971	3.15	32.75	**
9	0.094	3.06	35.81	***
10	0.0919	2.99	38.79	**
11	0.0868	2.82	41.61	***************************************
12	0.0844	2.74	44.36	**************************************
13	0.0813	2.64	47	*************************************
14	0.0796	2.59	49.59	************************************
15	0.0741	2.41	52	**********************************
16	0.0712	2.31	54.31	********************************
17	0.0691	2.24	56.56	*******************************
18	0.0645	2.1	58.65	*****************************
19	0.0583	1.89	60.55	***************************
20	0.0565	1.83	62.38	**************************
21	0.055	1.79	64.17	*************************
22	0.0536	1.74	65.91	*************************
23	0.0519	1.69	67.6	************************
24	0.0508	1.65	69.25	***********************
25	0.0499	1.62	70.87	***********************

26	0.0484	1.57	72.44	**********************
27	0.045	1.46	73.9	*********************
28	0.0449	1.46	75.36	*********************
29	0.0433	1.41	76.77	********************
30	0.0422	1.37	78.14	*******************
31	0.0403	1.31	79.45	*******************
32	0.0381	1.24	80.69	******************
33	0.0359	1.17	81.85	*****************
34	0.0348	1.13	82.99	****************
35	0.0335	1.09	84.07	****************
36	0.0325	1.06	85.13	***************
37	0.0295	0.96	86.09	**************
38	0.0283	0.92	87.01	*************
39	0.0272	0.89	87.9	*************
40	0.0256	0.83	88.73	************
41	0.0237	0.77	89.5	***********
42	0.0234	0.76	90.26	***********
43	0.0222	0.72	90.98	**********
44	0.0203	0.66	91.64	**********
45	0.0189	0.61	92.25	*********
46	0.0185	0.6	92.85	*********
47	0.018	0.59	93.44	*********
48	0.0167	0.54	93.98	********
49	0.0157	0.51	94.49	********
50	0.0144	0.47	94.96	*******
51	0.014	0.45	95.41	*******
52	0.0135	0.44	95.85	*******
53	0.0115	0.37	96.23	******
54	0.0111	0.36	96.59	*****

continued

Table 1.2 continued

No.	*Eigen value*	*Percentage of explained inertia*	*Cumulated percentage of explained inertia*	
55	0.0105	0.34	96.93	*****
56	0.0095	0.31	97.24	*****
57	0.0093	0.3	97.54	*****
58	0.0088	0.29	97.82	****
59	0.0073	0.24	98.06	****
60	0.0067	0.22	98.28	****
61	0.006	0.2	98.47	***
62	0.0058	0.19	98.66	***
63	0.0053	0.17	98.83	***
64	0.0047	0.15	98.99	***
65	0.0044	0.14	99.13	**
66	0.0039	0.13	99.26	**
67	0.0037	0.12	99.38	**
68	0.0034	0.11	99.49	**
69	0.0031	0.1	99.59	**

The cross-analysis of the absolute and relative contributions of the active variables/categories (Table 1.3) shows that CDIN is relatively well explained (i.e. with a high cumulated contribution) by the first factor, along which only two of the four correspondent categories are significant (CDIN=20 and CDIN=40).[18] In other words, the first axis discriminates between a group of firms which perceive themselves as pro-active, and thus revealing dynamic capabilities in front of innovations (CDIN=40), and another one which instead just reacts to innovations by substituting the old technology with no adaptive effort (CDIN=20). In the following, we will briefly refer to the two groups as, respectively, the 'pro-active' and the 'reactive' group. Let us observe that 'non reactive' (CDIN=10) and 'adaptive' firms (CDIN=30) have instead a negligible explanatory power: in other words, the firms of the sample are always alert to innovation turbulences, either to the minimum (CDIN=20) or to the maximum (CDIN=40) extent, with no intermediate solutions.

Searching for those active categories which can be more directly associated to the two groups of firms, we have at first checked the absolute contribution and the mass of those whose inertia is accounted by the first axis to a greater extent. In so doing we have identified: the location of the firm competitors (COMS) and of their customers (CUSS), the diffusion of information technologies (DINF and WEB), the introduction of technological innovations (INNO) and the firm location into a group (GRUP). Considering also the location of the firm suppliers (SUPS), and the recent trend in the international commercial relationships of the firm (DEXP), the first axis can be taken as a proxy of a combination of variables whose nature is to a certain degree homogeneous. Indeed, nearly all refer to the extension of the main firm relationships, according to a broad idea of both distance – geographical (COMS, CUSS, SUPS and DEXP) and organizational (GRUP) – and relationships – i.e. by considering the role of information technologies in allowing for and managing them (DINF and WEB). Once it has been considered that innovations are often the outcome of sound user–producer and producer–producer relationships, also the remaining variable (INNO) can be related to this semantic meaning of the axis. Accordingly, it identifies the meta-variable of the 'relationships extension' along which the original observations could be redistributed.

As far as the second factor is concerned, the greatest contributor to its inertia is a variable of environmental placement, which captures the effect of the intangible infrastructures of the firm environment (e.g. business services, universities, etc.) on the firm itself (IFR). The contribution of the variable referring to MIFR is less appreciable, but still among the greatest of the second factor. If we observe that the remaining contributing variables are, so to say, proxies of the static (CAPR and COST) and dynamic (INTV and DINV) efficiency of the firm, an important conclusion can be reached: the second axis refers to the firm capacity to set its production activities at work efficiently in its system of local infrastructures. Accordingly, it can be taken as a meta-variable for the 'settling capacity' of the firms in their business environment.

The inertia of the third factor is mainly explained by a set of heterogeneous variables. Among them, three accounts for the employment dynamics of the firm:

Table 1.3 Coordinates, absolute and relative contributions of the active categories on the first five axes

Categories	*Mass*	*Distortion*	*Coordinates*					*Absolute contribution*					*Relative contribution*				
			1	2	3	4	5	*1*	2	3	4	5	*1*	2	3	4	5
4, GRUP		[AD]															
AD10 – GRUP=10	2.59	0.48	0.27	−0.01	−0.15	−0.02	0.03	1.10	0.00	0.50	0.00	0.00	0.15	0.00	0.05	0.00	0.00
AD20 – GRUP=20	0.69	4.56	−0.86	0.16	0.45	−0.26	0.05	2.90	0.10	1.10	0.40	0.00	0.16	0.01	0.04	0.02	0.00
AD30 – GRUP=30	0.48	7.09	−0.23	−0.19	−0.09	0.31	−0.34	0.10	0.10	0.00	0.40	0.40	0.01	0.00	0.00	0.01	0.02
AD40 – GRUP=40	0.09	43.50	−0.06	0.00	1.52	0.88	0.60	0.00	0.00	1.50	0.50	0.30	0.00	0.00	0.05	0.02	0.01
Cumulated								4.10	0.20	3.10	1.30	0.70					
7, DEXP		[AG]															
AG20 – DEXP=20	0.22	16.80	−0.57	0.49	−0.90	−1.74	−1.42	0.40	0.40	1.40	5.10	3.60	0.02	0.01	0.05	0.18	0.12
AG30 – DEXP=30	2.33	0.65	0.44	0.07	0.12	−0.04	0.27	2.50	0.10	0.30	0.00	1.40	0.30	0.01	0.02	0.00	0.11
AG40 – DEXP=40	1.08	2.56	−0.69	−0.15	0.22	0.40	−0.29	2.80	0.20	0.40	1.30	0.70	0.18	0.01	0.02	0.06	0.03
AG50 – DEXP=50	0.22	16.80	−0.75	−0.47	−1.53	0.16	−0.05	0.70	0.30	3.90	0.00	0.00	0.03	0.01	0.14	0.00	0.00
Cumulated								6.50	1.00	5.90	6.50	5.70					
8, DEMP		[AH]															
AH10 – DEMP=10	0.13	28.67	−0.48	1.64	−0.70	−1.24	−1.60	0.20	2.60	0.50	1.60	2.70	0.01	0.09	0.02	0.05	0.09
AH20 – DEMP=20	0.26	13.83	−0.48	−1.01	−0.61	0.64	−0.61	0.30	1.90	0.70	0.80	0.80	0.02	0.07	0.03	0.03	0.03
AH30 – DEMP=30	2.07	0.85	0.41	0.10	0.13	0.17	−0.20	2.00	0.10	0.30	0.40	0.70	0.20	0.01	0.02	0.03	0.05
AH40 – DEMP=40	1.12	2.42	−0.56	−0.09	0.31	−0.15	0.41	2.00	0.10	0.80	0.20	1.60	0.13	0.00	0.04	0.01	0.07
AH50 – DEMP=50	0.26	13.83	−0.12	−0.20	−1.41	−0.70	1.23	0.00	0.10	4.00	1.00	3.20	0.00	0.00	0.14	0.04	0.11
Cumulated								4.50	4.80	6.30	4.00	9.00					
9, DINV		[AI]															
AI20 – DINV=20	0.39	8.89	0.15	0.84	−0.80	−0.14	−0.83	0.10	2.00	1.90	0.10	2.20	0.00	0.08	0.07	0.00	0.08
AI30 – DINV=30	0.99	2.87	0.68	0.40	0.32	0.27	−0.18	2.60	1.20	0.80	0.60	0.30	0.16	0.06	0.04	0.02	0.01
AI40 – DINV=40	1.43	1.70	−0.03	−0.57	0.20	0.19	−0.11	0.00	3.40	0.40	0.40	0.10	0.00	0.19	0.02	0.02	0.01
AI50 – DINV=50	1.04	2.71	−0.67	0.08	−0.28	−0.46	0.64	2.60	0.10	0.60	1.70	3.50	0.17	0.00	0.03	0.08	0.15
Cumulated								5.20	6.60	3.80	2.70	6.20					
10, COST		[AJ]															
AJ10 – COST=10	0.09	43.50	1.60	−0.58	0.50	0.98	−2.00	1.20	0.20	0.20	0.70	2.90	0.06	0.01	0.01	0.02	0.09

AJ20 – COST=20	0.26	13.83	−0.33	−1.95	0.09	−1.35	−0.99	0.20	7.20	0.00	3.70	2.10	0.01	0.27	0.00	0.13	0.07
AJ30 – COST=30	0.82	3.68	0.15	−0.40	0.28	0.32	0.26	0.10	1.00	0.50	0.60	0.50	0.01	0.04	0.02	0.03	0.02
AJ40 – COST=40	2.51	0.53	−0.11	0.38	0.03	−0.02	0.04	0.20	2.70	0.00	0.00	0.00	0.02	0.28	0.00	0.00	0.00
AJ50 – COST=50	0.17	21.25	0.51	−0.44	−2.13	0.25	0.61	0.30	0.20	6.00	0.10	0.50	0.01	0.01	0.21	0.00	0.02
Cumulated								1.90	11.40	6.70	5.10	6.00					
11, EMPS		[AK]															
AK10 – EMPS=10	1.34	1.87	0.29	0.08	0.11	−0.34	−0.08	0.60	0.10	0.10	1.20	0.10	0.04	0.00	0.01	0.06	0.00
AK20 – EMPS=20	0.13	28.67	−0.36	−2.07	−2.06	−1.00	−0.04	0.10	4.10	4.30	1.00	0.00	0.00	0.15	0.15	0.03	0.00
AK30 – EMPS=30	2.38	0.62	−0.14	0.07	0.05	0.24	0.05	0.30	0.10	0.10	1.10	0.00	0.03	0.01	0.00	0.10	0.00
Cumulated								1.00	4.20	4.40	3.30	0.10					
12, CAPR		[AL]															
AL10 – CAPR=10	0.69	4.56	0.36	−0.32	0.74	−0.18	0.40	0.50	0.50	2.90	0.20	0.90	0.03	0.02	0.12	0.01	0.04
AL20 – CAPR=20	0.78	3.94	−0.63	0.15	−0.37	−0.50	0.14	1.70	0.10	0.80	1.50	0.10	0.10	0.01	0.04	0.06	0.00
AL30 – CAPR=30	1.56	1.47	0.10	0.40	−0.04	0.18	−0.11	0.10	1.80	0.00	0.40	0.20	0.01	0.11	0.00	0.02	0.01
AL40 – CAPR=40	0.82	3.68	0.11	−0.63	−0.19	0.28	−0.26	0.10	2.40	0.20	0.50	0.40	0.00	0.11	0.01	0.02	0.02
Cumulated								2.30	4.80	4.00	2.60	1.60					
18, YINF		[AR]															
AR10 – YINF=10	0.95	3.05	−0.21	−0.20	0.43	0.38	0.34	0.20	0.30	1.40	1.10	0.90	0.01	0.01	0.06	0.05	0.04
AR20 – YINF=20	1.77	1.17	−0.10	−0.01	−0.15	−0.09	−0.31	0.10	0.00	0.30	0.10	1.40	0.01	0.00	0.02	0.01	0.08
AR30 – YINF=30	0.39	8.89	0.27	0.80	0.07	−0.07	0.62	0.20	1.80	0.00	0.00	1.20	0.01	0.07	0.00	0.00	0.04
AR40 – YINF=40	0.65	4.93	0.36	−0.17	−0.41	−0.27	−0.10	0.50	0.10	0.80	0.40	0.10	0.03	0.01	0.03	0.01	0.00
AR50 – YINF=50	0.09	43.50	0.45	0.11	1.05	−0.09	0.69	0.10	0.00	0.70	0.00	0.30	0.00	0.00	0.03	0.00	0.01
Cumulated								1.10	2.30	3.20	1.60	4.00					
19, DINF		[AS]															
AS10 – DINF=10	1.56	1.47	−0.73	−0.05	0.14	0.14	−0.16	4.60	0.00	0.20	0.20	0.30	0.36	0.00	0.01	0.01	0.02
AS20 – DINF=20	0.78	3.94	0.72	−0.26	0.45	−0.05	−0.22	2.30	0.40	1.20	0.00	0.30	0.13	0.02	0.05	0.00	0.01
AS30 – DINF=30	0.30	11.71	0.30	0.08	0.20	0.34	0.77	0.20	0.00	0.10	0.30	1.50	0.01	0.00	0.00	0.01	0.05
AS40 – DINF=40	1.21	2.18	0.40	0.20	−0.52	−0.24	0.15	1.10	0.40	2.50	0.50	0.20	0.07	0.02	0.12	0.03	0.01
Cumulated								8.10	0.80	4.10	1.10	2.30					
20, WEB		[AT]															
AT10 – WEB=10	0.22	16.80	1.64	−0.15	1.02	−0.85	−0.72	3.20	0.00	1.70	1.20	0.90	0.16	0.00	0.06	0.04	0.03

continued

Table 1.3 continued

Categories	*Mass*	*Distortion*	*Coordinates*					*Absolute contribution*					*Relative contribution*				
			1	*2*	*3*	*4*	*5*	*1*	*2*	*3*	*4*	*5*	*1*	*2*	*3*	*4*	*5*
AT20 – WEB=20	1.69	1.28	0.19	0.15	–0.28	0.07	–0.25	0.40	0.30	1.00	0.10	0.90	0.03	0.02	0.06	0.00	0.05
AT30 – WEB=30	1.94	0.98	–0.35	–0.11	0.13	0.03	0.30	1.30	0.20	0.30	0.00	1.40	0.12	0.01	0.02	0.00	0.09
Cumulated								4.90	0.50	3.00	1.30	3.20					
24, INNO		[AX]															
AX10 – INNO=10	0.43	7.90	–0.36	0.01	1.04	–0.68	0.29	0.30	0.00	3.60	1.60	0.30	0.02	0.00	0.14	0.06	0.01
AX20 – INNO=20	1.73	1.22	–0.05	–0.30	–0.11	0.20	–0.05	0.00	1.20	0.20	0.50	0.00	0.00	0.08	0.01	0.03	0.00
AX30 – INNO=30	0.91	3.24	–0.15	0.08	–0.37	0.02	0.08	0.10	0.00	1.00	0.00	0.00	0.01	0.00	0.04	0.00	0.00
AX40 – INNO=40	0.65	4.93	0.07	0.75	–0.04	–0.06	0.08	0.00	2.70	0.00	0.00	0.00	0.00	0.11	0.00	0.00	0.00
AX50 – INNO=50	0.13	28.67	2.62	–0.31	0.78	–0.23	–1.28	5.00	0.10	0.60	0.10	1.80	0.24	0.00	0.02	0.00	0.06
Cumulated								5.50	4.00	5.30	2.20	2.20					
26, INTV		[AZ]															
AZ10 – INTV=10	0.39	8.89	–0.56	0.92	–0.07	–0.46	0.18	0.70	2.40	0.00	0.60	0.10	0.04	0.09	0.00	0.02	0.00
AZ20 – INTV=20	0.13	28.67	–0.42	–1.04	–1.90	0.83	–0.34	0.10	1.00	3.60	0.70	0.10	0.01	0.04	0.13	0.02	0.00
AZ30 – INTV=30	2.98	0.29	0.00	0.04	0.10	–0.05	–0.02	0.00	0.00	0.20	0.10	0.00	0.00	0.01	0.03	0.01	0.00
AZ40 – INTV=40	0.35	10.12	0.80	–0.99	–0.05	0.62	0.12	1.30	2.50	0.00	1.00	0.00	0.06	0.10	0.00	0.04	0.00
Cumulated								2.10	6.00	3.90	2.40	0.30					
27, INTH		[BA]															
BA10 – INTH=10	1.60	1.41	–0.15	–0.14	0.29	0.00	0.12	0.20	0.20	1.00	0.00	0.20	0.02	0.01	0.06	0.00	0.01
BA20 – INTH=20	0.17	21.25	0.47	–1.37	1.67	–0.85	–0.52	0.20	2.40	3.70	1.00	0.40	0.01	0.09	0.13	0.03	0.01
BA30 – INTH=30	0.22	16.80	–0.41	0.85	0.31	0.03	–0.51	0.20	1.20	0.20	0.00	0.50	0.01	0.04	0.01	0.00	0.02
BA40 – INTH=40	1.86	1.07	0.13	0.15	–0.44	0.08	0.01	0.20	0.30	2.70	0.10	0.00	0.02	0.02	0.18	0.01	0.00
Cumulated								0.80	4.10	7.60	1.10	1.00					
28, OUTS		[BB]															
BB10 – OUTS=10	0.26	13.83	–0.26	–0.03	0.57	0.51	–0.12	0.10	0.00	0.60	0.50	0.00	0.00	0.00	0.02	0.02	0.00
BB20 – OUTS=20	1.34	1.87	0.26	0.17	0.33	–0.45	0.11	0.50	0.30	1.10	2.10	0.10	0.04	0.01	0.06	0.11	0.01
BB30 – OUTS=30	1.17	2.30	–0.01	0.12	–0.05	0.53	0.04	0.00	0.10	0.00	2.50	0.00	0.00	0.01	0.00	0.12	0.00
BB40 – OUTS=40	0.99	2.87	–0.37	–0.31	–0.44	–0.22	–0.27	0.80	0.70	1.50	0.40	0.60	0.05	0.03	0.07	0.02	0.03

BB50 – OUTS=50	0.09	43.50	1.08	–0.52	–1.11	0.96	1.18	0.60	0.20	0.80	0.60	1.00	0.03	0.01	0.03	0.02	0.03
Cumulated								1.90	1.30	4.10	6.20	1.80					
29, LOCD		[BC]															
BC10 – LOCD=10	1.04	2.71	–0.50	0.10	0.37	0.21	0.10	1.40	0.10	1.10	0.30	0.10	0.09	0.00	0.05	0.02	0.00
BC20 – LOCD=20	0.22	16.80	–0.74	0.56	–0.51	–0.84	–0.09	0.70	0.50	0.40	1.20	0.00	0.03	0.02	0.02	0.04	0.00
BC30 – LOCD=30	0.43	7.90	–0.78	–0.59	–0.01	1.26	–0.87	1.50	1.10	0.00	5.30	2.70	0.08	0.04	0.00	0.20	0.10
BC40 – LOCD=40	2.16	0.78	0.47	0.02	–0.12	–0.27	0.13	2.70	0.00	0.30	1.20	0.30	0.28	0.00	0.02	0.09	0.02
Cumulated								6.20	1.70	1.80	8.00	3.10					
30, SPIN		[BD]															
BD10 – SPIN=10	0.43	7.90	–0.53	–0.30	0.90	–0.72	–0.63	0.70	0.30	2.70	1.70	1.40	0.04	0.01	0.10	0.07	0.05
BD20 – SPIN=20	0.65	4.93	0.63	0.62	–0.18	0.12	0.24	1.50	1.90	0.20	0.10	0.30	0.08	0.08	0.01	0.00	0.01
BD40 – SPIN=40	2.77	0.39	–0.07	–0.10	–0.10	0.08	0.04	0.10	0.20	0.20	0.20	0.00	0.01	0.02	0.02	0.02	0.00
Cumulated								2.20	2.40	3.10	2.00	1.70					
32, SUPK		[BF]															
BF10 – SUPK=10	3.41	0.13	0.06	–0.03	–0.08	0.16	0.07	0.10	0.00	0.20	0.70	0.10	0.02	0.01	0.05	0.21	0.04
BF20 – SUPK=20	0.26	13.83	–0.19	1.07	0.66	–0.44	–0.83	0.10	2.20	0.90	0.40	1.50	0.00	0.08	0.03	0.01	0.05
BF30 – SUPK=30	0.09	43.50	0.25	–2.70	0.73	–3.43	–1.55	0.00	4.60	0.40	7.90	1.70	0.00	0.17	0.01	0.27	0.06
BF40 – SUPK=40	0.09	43.50	–1.88	0.50	0.49	–1.64	1.15	1.70	0.20	0.20	1.80	0.90	0.08	0.01	0.01	0.06	0.03
Cumulated								1.90	7.00	1.60	10.80	4.30					
33, SUPS		[BG]															
BG10 – SUPS=10	0.82	3.68	0.87	–0.02	–0.18	–0.47	–0.33	3.50	0.00	0.20	1.40	0.70	0.21	0.00	0.01	0.06	0.03
BG20 – SUPS=20	2.33	0.65	–0.11	0.10	0.21	–0.01	0.31	0.20	0.20	0.80	0.00	1.90	0.02	0.02	0.07	0.00	0.15
BG30 – SUPS=30	0.69	4.56	–0.65	–0.32	–0.50	0.58	–0.66	1.70	0.50	1.30	1.80	2.50	0.09	0.02	0.05	0.07	0.09
Cumulated								5.30	0.70	2.30	3.20	5.10					
35, CUSK		[BI]															
BI10 – CUSK=10	2.81	0.37	–0.12	–0.22	0.04	0.28	0.19	0.20	1.00	0.00	1.70	0.90	0.04	0.13	0.00	0.21	0.10
BI20 – CUSK=20	0.86	3.45	0.43	0.62	–0.39	–0.67	–0.52	0.90	2.40	1.00	3.00	1.90	0.05	0.11	0.04	0.13	0.08
BI30 – CUSK=30	0.09	43.50	0.63	1.65	0.74	0.33	–0.74	0.20	1.70	0.40	0.10	0.40	0.01	0.06	0.01	0.00	0.01
BI40 – CUSK=40	0.09	43.50	–0.93	–0.82	2.00	–2.65	0.34	0.40	0.40	2.70	4.70	0.10	0.02	0.02	0.09	0.16	0.00
Cumulated								1.70	5.50	4.10	9.60	3.20					

continued

Table 1.3 continued

Categories	*Mass*	*Distortion*	*Coordinates*					*Absolute contribution*					*Relative contribution*				
			1	*2*	*3*	*4*	*5*	*1*	*2*	*3*	*4*	*5*	*1*	*2*	*3*	*4*	*5*
36, CUSS		[BJ]															
BJ10 – CUSS=10	0.61	5.36	0.83	−0.36	−0.48	−0.20	0.26	2.40	0.60	1.10	0.20	0.30	0.13	0.02	0.04	0.01	0.01
BJ20 – CUSS=20	2.20	0.75	0.11	−0.10	0.13	0.18	0.21	0.20	0.20	0.30	0.50	0.80	0.02	0.01	0.02	0.04	0.06
BJ30 – CUSS=30	1.04	2.71	−0.73	0.42	0.00	−0.26	−0.61	3.10	1.30	0.00	0.50	3.20	0.20	0.06	0.00	0.02	0.14
Cumulated								5.60	2.10	1.40	1.30	4.40					
38, COMS		[BL]															
BL10 – COMS=10	0.17	21.25	0.35	−0.26	−1.31	−0.09	0.74	0.10	0.10	2.30	0.00	0.80	0.01	0.00	0.08	0.00	0.03
BL20 – COMS=20	1.64	1.34	0.68	−0.18	0.05	−0.19	0.37	4.30	0.40	0.00	0.40	1.90	0.35	0.02	0.00	0.03	0.10
BL30 – COMS=30	0.30	11.71	−0.82	−0.23	0.84	1.07	−1.31	1.10	0.10	1.60	2.70	4.30	0.06	0.00	0.06	0.10	0.15
BL40 – COMS=40	1.73	1.22	−0.54	0.23	−0.06	0.00	−0.20	2.80	0.70	0.10	0.00	0.60	0.24	0.04	0.00	0.00	0.03
Cumulated								8.40	1.30	4.00	3.20	7.50					
39, COMR		[BM]															
BM10 – COMR=10	2.68	0.44	0.05	0.05	0.14	0.14	−0.21	0.00	0.00	0.40	0.40	1.00	0.01	0.01	0.04	0.05	0.10
BM20 – COMR=20	0.17	21.25	0.40	0.01	−1.20	0.06	0.07	0.20	0.00	1.90	0.00	0.00	0.01	0.00	0.07	0.00	0.00
BM30 – COMR=30	0.43	7.90	0.19	−0.17	−0.46	0.12	1.14	0.10	0.10	0.70	0.00	4.70	0.00	0.00	0.03	0.00	0.17
BM40 – COMR=40	0.56	5.85	−0.49	−0.10	0.08	−0.78	0.11	0.80	0.00	0.00	2.70	0.10	0.04	0.00	0.00	0.11	0.00
Cumulated								1.00	0.20	3.00	3.20	5.70					
40, MIFR		[BN]															
BN10 – MIFR=10	1.99	0.93	0.17	0.04	0.11	0.04	0.52	0.30	0.00	0.20	0.00	4.50	0.03	0.00	0.01	0.00	0.29
BN20 – MIFR=20	1.12	2.42	−0.18	0.60	−0.13	−0.18	−0.43	0.20	2.90	0.10	0.30	1.70	0.01	0.15	0.01	0.01	0.08
BN30 – MIFR=30	0.43	7.90	−0.05	−0.55	−0.03	1.17	−0.90	0.00	1.00	0.00	4.60	2.90	0.00	0.04	0.00	0.17	0.10
BN40 – MIFR=40	0.17	21.25	−0.82	−1.61	−0.69	−1.48	−0.84	0.60	3.30	0.60	3.00	1.00	0.03	0.12	0.02	0.10	0.03

BN50 – MIFR=50	0.13	28.67	0.18	−1.79	0.51	−0.88	−0.15	0.00	3.10	0.30	0.80	0.00	0.00	0.11	0.01	0.03	0.00
Cumulated																	
41, IFR		[BO]															
BO10 – IFR=10	1.04	2.71	0.72	0.17	0.30	0.36	−0.30	3.00	0.20	0.70	1.10	0.80	0.19	0.01	0.03	0.05	0.03
BO20 – IFR=20	0.82	3.68	−0.25	0.61	−0.07	−0.21	0.28	0.30	2.30	0.00	0.30	0.50	0.02	0.10	0.00	0.01	0.02
BO30 – IFR=30	0.73	4.24	−0.29	0.39	−0.53	0.35	−0.10	0.30	0.80	1.60	0.70	0.10	0.02	0.04	0.07	0.03	0.00
BO40 – IFR=40	1.04	2.71	−0.43	−0.54	0.46	−0.33	0.13	1.10	2.20	1.70	0.90	0.20	0.07	0.11	0.08	0.04	0.01
BO50 – IFR=50	0.22	16.80	0.52	−1.85	−1.58	−0.56	0.07	0.30	5.50	4.10	0.50	0.00	0.02	0.20	0.15	0.02	0.00
Cumulated								5.10	11.00	8.20	3.50	1.50					
42, CDIN		[BP]															
BP10 – CDIN=10	0.17	21.25	−0.29	−0.41	0.04	0.70	−0.75	0.10	0.20	0.00	0.70	0.80	0.00	0.01	0.00	0.02	0.03
BP20 – CDIN=20	0.86	3.45	0.87	0.48	0.28	0.01	−0.43	3.60	1.50	0.50	0.00	1.30	0.22	0.07	0.02	0.00	0.05
BP30 – CDIN=30	2.12	0.82	−0.09	−0.24	−0.23	0.03	0.13	0.10	0.90	0.90	0.00	0.30	0.01	0.07	0.07	0.00	0.02
BP40 – CDIN=40	0.69	4.56	−0.73	0.24	0.35	−0.26	0.31	2.10	0.30	0.70	0.40	0.60	0.12	0.01	0.03	0.01	0.02
Cumulated								5.90	2.90	2.00	1.00	3.00					
43, CDMK		[BQ]															
BQ10 – CDMK=10	0.43	7.90	−0.53	0.63	−0.52	−0.53	−0.32	0.70	1.30	0.90	0.90	0.40	0.04	0.05	0.03	0.03	0.01
BQ20 – CDMK=20	0.43	7.90	1.31	−0.57	0.19	−0.64	−0.68	4.20	1.10	0.10	1.40	1.60	0.22	0.04	0.00	0.05	0.06
BQ30 – CDMK=30	2.03	0.89	0.01	0.11	−0.07	0.34	−0.12	0.00	0.20	0.10	1.80	0.20	0.00	0.01	0.01	0.13	0.02
BQ40 – CDMK=40	0.95	3.05	−0.37	−0.27	0.30	−0.20	0.71	0.70	0.50	0.60	0.30	4.00	0.05	0.02	0.03	0.01	0.17
								5.60	3.00	1.70	4.50	6.20					

both directly (DEMP), and indirectly, that is by considering the resulting shortages in specific job profiles (EMPS) and its eventual evolution into new start-ups (SPIN). Although they possibly have other implications, also the maturity of the firm ICT technologies (YINF) and its strategies of horizontal integration (INTH) can be considered among the determinants and the effects of relevant changes in the labour market of the firm. Accordingly, the third axis could be used to build up a meta-variable of the 'employment dynamics' of the firm.

Coming to the fourth axis, the dynamic capabilities of the firm with respect to changes in the market fundamentals (CDMK) is among the variables whose contribution to it is the greatest. Similarly to the dynamic capabilities (CDIN) of the first axis, also in the present case dynamic capabilities come along with other variables of a relational nature, although this time of an organizational kind: the relationships through which the firms interact with their suppliers – depending on them being suppliers or subcontractors (SUPK) – and customers – being general or purchasers (CUSK); the collaborations they manage to have with their competitors (COMR); the organizational linkages they establish through both strategies of outsourcing (OUTS) and delocalization (LOCD). Because of this important association, the fourth axis can be used as a meta-variable of 'organizational arrangements'. Table 1.4 sums up the composition of the four meta-variables that have been identified above.

1.5.4 Associations among categories: characterizing pro-active and reactive firms

Given that it is based on a distributive kind of distance, in MCA closeness among points can be directly read as a measurement of association among categories. Accordingly, we can use their plot on the three systems of axis which is possible to build up by combining the four axes, in order to identify some distinguishing characteristics of pro-active and reactive firms. In drawing these plots we have retained only those categories whose absolute contribution is greater than the average (i.e. 1/106=0.9%), but left out those whose absolute contribution is due to rare frequencies and which are thus affected by large distortions (Table 1.3).

Considering the first couple of axes (Figure 1.1), a first expected association concerns the innovative performances of the two identified groups of firms: pro-active firms appear associated to cases of high (radical) innovativeness

Table 1.4 Semantic interpretations of the axes: relevant contributors (*ac* > 5 per cent)

Factor no.	*Meta-variable*	*Contributors*
1	Relationship extension	CDIN, GRUP, DEXP, DINF, WEB, INNO, SUPS, CUSS, COMS
2	Settling capacity	MIFR, IFR, COST, CAPR, INTV, DINV
3	Employment dynamics	DEMP, EMPS, SPIN, YINF, INTH
4	Organizational arrangements	CDMK, OUTS, LOCD, SUPK, CUSK, COMR

(INNO =10), while reactive ones to rare innovations of incremental nature (INNO =40). Quite interestingly, this innovative gap is accompanied by different associations in terms of settling capacities of the two kinds of firms. Reactive ones are associated with a non-satisfactory placement in their material (MIFR=10) and immaterial (IFR=10) infrastructural set-up: a result which is possibly reflected into an only moderate utilization of their production capacity (CAPR=30) and, above all, into a decreasing trend in their production investments (DINV=20 and DINV=30). Pro-active firms, instead, seem to benefit from a virtuous placement into their system of material infrastructures (MIFR=20) and, even more, into that of immaterial ones (IFR=20 and IFR=30): quite interestingly, although their associated utilization of production capacity is not high (CAPR=20), their investment trend is the most increasing (DINV=50). In our framework of analysis, this first set of associations is extremely relevant. According to the basic insights of the literature on systems of innovation (e.g. Edquist, 1997), the firm institutional and infrastructural environment crucially affects the learning processes which occurs within the firm, both in its innovative and production activities.

Further elements of differentiation between pro-active and reactive firms are provided by two other kinds of associations. On the one hand, unlike reactive ones, pro-reactive firms are associated to a business environment with a high degree of internationalization – both as far as competitors (COMS=40) and customers (CUSS=30) are concerned – and with suppliers which are also based outside Treviso (SUPS=20). On the other hand, unlike the pro-active ones, reactive firms are closer to cases of poor, if not even absent, informatisation (DINF=40) and of limited diffusion of net-technologies (WEB=20). Also this second set of associations, therefore, points to the interaction between intra-organizational and

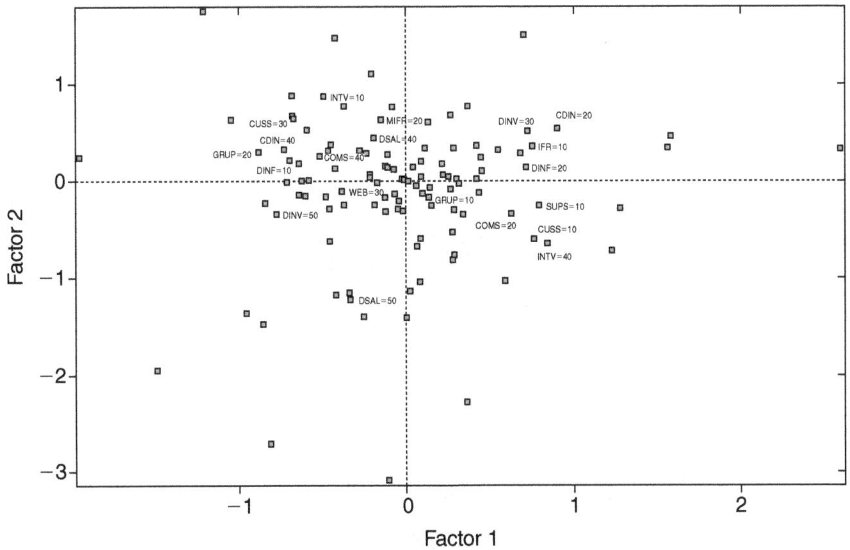

Figure 1.1 Association among categories: factor 1 and factor 2.

inter-organizational factors in driving dynamic capabilities. Indeed, pro-activeness seems to require an active involvement in the international arena, along with a qualified development of office automation and ICT technologies. Although empirical tests on this hypothesis do not yield robust results (e.g. Masini, 2004), a certain confirmation seems to come from the negative trends in exports (DEXP=30) to which the reactive firms, unlike the pro-active ones, are closely associated.

The participation to a group (in the form of parent company (GRUP=20)) and the resort to vertical integration (namely upward (INTV=10)) add two further exclusive associations to the pro-active firms: this time of organizational nature. Those formal kinds of organizational relationships through which groups are set up and managed, and through which vertical integration strategies are implemented, appear in fact more conducive of dynamic capabilities than those informal ones which pervade loosely integrated and participated companies.

Further interesting associations can be found by plotting the first axis against the third one, and thus looking at the employment dynamics of the firms (Figure 1.2). As expected, pro-reactive firms turn out to be associated with a more positive employment dynamic (DEMP=40), while reactive ones are closer to firms which just manage to keep their employment level at most unchanged (DEMP=30). Dynamic capabilities in front of innovation thus seem to result in a more sustained growth (at least in terms of employment), while simple 'reactiveness' just prevents firms from declining (still in terms of employment). This higher employment dynamic possibly demands more frequent job turnovers in pro-active firms than in reactive ones. Accordingly, although apparently counterintuitive, shortages of qualified workers are associated to a greater extent to the former than to the latter. For the reactive firms the associated employment shortage is in fact only in core

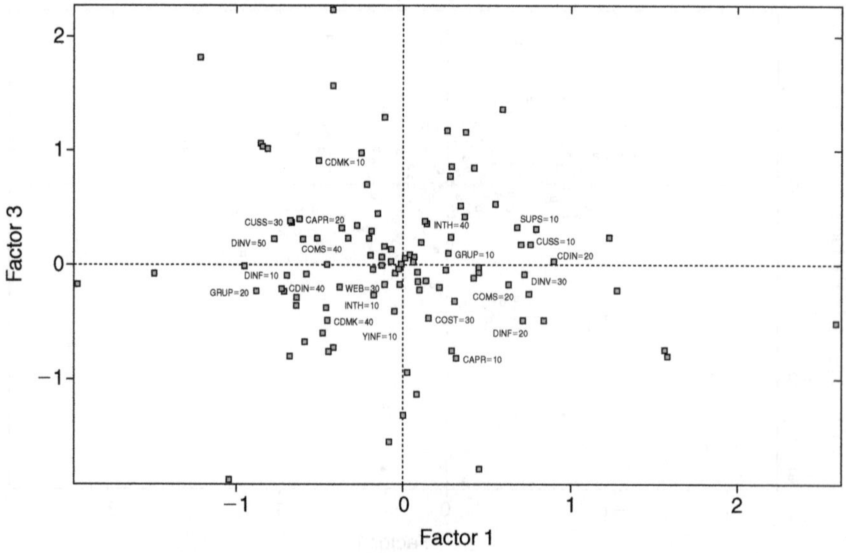

Figure 1.2 Association among categories: factor 1 and factor 3.

activities (EMPS=10), while for the pro-active ones it is in both core and auxiliary ones (EMPS=30).

Quite interestingly, the analysis of the third axis shows that dynamic capabilities are associated to the presence of diversification strategies (INTH=10). The notable debate between polarized and diffused specialization patterns appears relevant in this last respect. Indeed, the Schumpeterian idea, according to which those firms that better anticipate innovation and market change have distributed, rather than concentrated capabilities, could be invoked in interpreting this result. Let us observe that the present plot also 'qualifies' the association between pro-active firms and ICT diffusion (DINF=10) with an early adoption date for them (YINF=10): conversely, the reactive firms seem to discount the effects of a late adoption (YINF=30). Finally, also the interpretation we have put forward about the extension of the firm relationships finds a certain qualification. Purely reactive firms (CDIN=20) reveal a certain proximity with the categories denoting relationships which do not overcome the national boundaries: both as far as their competitors (COMS=20) and their customers (CUSS=20) are concerned. As several studies on local systems of production have pointed out (e.g. Chiarvesio *et al.*, 2003), the internationalization of the firm production relationships, rather than that of the firm market, could have very much to say about the development of strong dynamic capabilities.

Let us conclude our analysis of the categories association by considering the first and the fourth axis, thus recovering some other variables about the firm organizational arrangements (Figure 1.3). At the outset, pro-activeness in terms of innovation is associated to pro-activeness in terms of marketing (CDMK=40), while reactive innovative firms turn out associable to adaptive marketing ones (CDMK=30), although less closely. This fact points to an interesting complementary relationship: an active behaviour in front of a technological shock seems to require a pro-active attitude to changes in consumer preferences, and vice versa. In turn, both kinds of dynamic capabilities appear associated to collaboration relationships with the competitors, but with a different rationale in the two cases. Indeed, reactive firms coordinate with competitors mainly in order to reduce costs (COMR=30), while pro-reactive ones for reasons which are neither cost reduction, nor capabilities acquisition (COMR=40). Apparently, this latter association points the important role of learning-by-interacting in shaping dynamic capabilities themselves.

The present couple of axes also tells us something about the way the business environment of the two groups of firms is organized. First of all, reactive firms are associated to the outsourcing of auxiliary activities (OUTS=20), while pro-reactive firms are associated to a complete absence of it (OUTS=40). A 'weak' version of the strategic idea of Prahalad and Hamel (1990), according to which the outsourcing of certain activities (in the strong version, the core activities) might make the firm lose its dynamic capabilities, could be invoked in this last respect.

Let us observe that reactive firms are associated to the absence of delocalization strategies (LOCD=40), which appears consistent with the local scale of their associations with both customers (CUSS=10) and suppliers (SUPS=10).

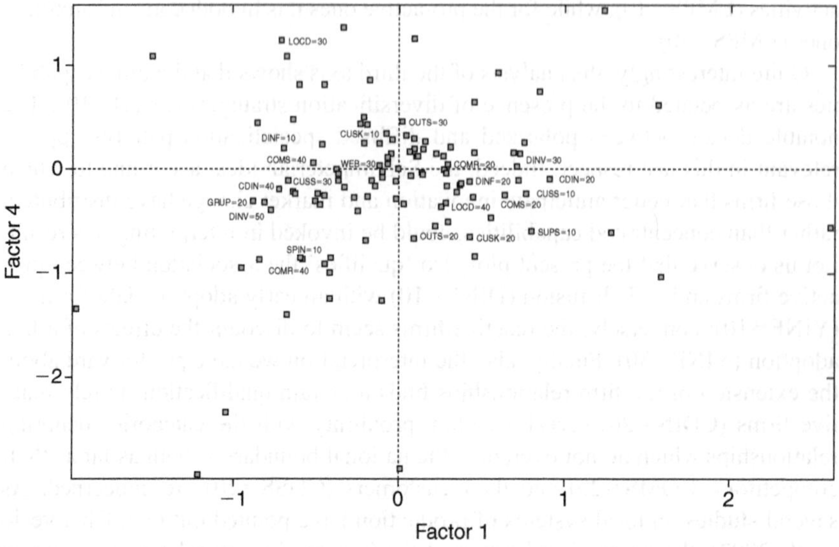

Figure 1.3 Association among categories: factor 1 and factor 4.

Finally, their closeness to customers working on commission (CUSK=20) is another feature that appears consistent with their local profile.

1.5.5 Active vs. supplementary variables

The characterization of the firm categories we have identified can be further refined by inserting in the MCA analysis some illustrative or supplementary variables. As is usually the case, we have decided to illustrate our results by referring to some of the structural variables of the dataset: the age of the firms (AGE), their location in our enlarged Pavitt taxonomy (PAV), their size in terms of both employment (EMP) and class of revenues (SALE).

Given that these variables do not enter in the identification of the factors, in the following we will reproduce the systems of axes of the previous section and report on them, along with the CDIN categories we are interested in (CDIN=20 and CDIN=40), only those illustrative categories which are significantly correlated with each couple of factors.[19,20] The two series of figures have thus to be read simultaneously.

Starting from the plot of the first two axes (Figure 1.4), the pro-active firms add to the previous associations (see Figure 1.1) close connections with the largest firms of the sample: both in terms of employment (EMP=50) and of revenues (SALE=50). That dynamic capabilities are more promptly developed by firms with both a complex organization and a wide market volume is nothing but a tentative interpretation. However, it is somehow reinforced by the fact that reactive firms are here associated with smaller classes of revenues (SALE=20 and SALE=10) and a smaller size in terms of employment (EMPS=10). Let us

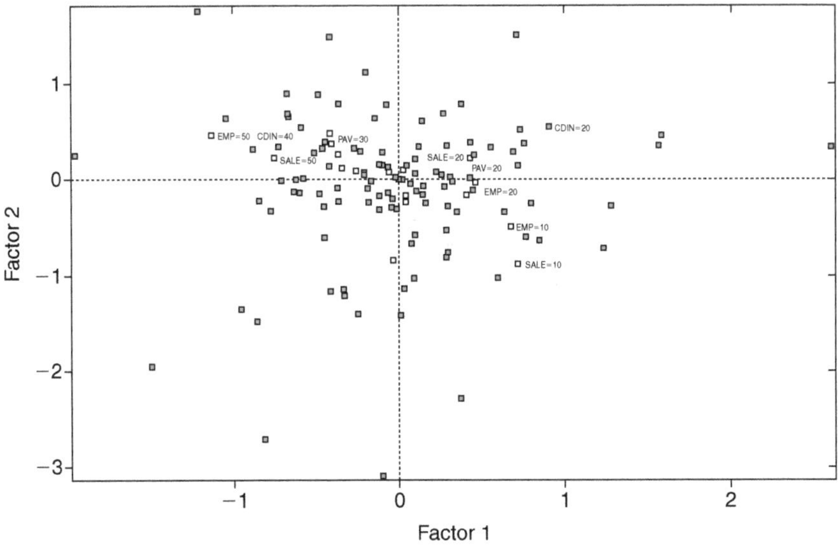

Figure 1.4 Active versus supplementary variables: factor 1 and factor 2.

observe that the same illustrative categories appear consistent with the other active categories which have been identified on the same axes (see Figure 1.1): particularly, a superior internationalization degree and a group structure.

A further important qualification comes from the sectoral illustrative variables. Quite interestingly, operating with large economies of scale or with natural resources (PAV=20), rather than in traditional sectors, is associated with at least a certain (that is reactive) level of capabilities to deal with technological change. On the other hand, a pro-active behaviour is associated, rather than with science-based firms, with those firms which in the present local system of production typically have the most satisfactory performances, that is specialized supplier firms (PAV=30). Rather than having an ideal sectoral structure, dynamic capabilities thus seems to show different specifications in different productive contexts.

Crossing factor 1 with factor 3 (Figure 1.5), the association between the two relevant CDIN categories and the firm size get confirmed. Furthermore, the same illustrative size categories fit the other active categories associated with the pro-active and reactive firms quite well: the latter, in particular, associates the local scale of their operations with a size which is at most medium. Further confirmations come from the last plot (Figure 1.6). In particular, those organizational arrangements that in the previous correspondent factorial space had been related to the pro-active firms (see Figure 1.3), are here qualified with a significant association to the specialized supplier firms of the sample (PAV=30). On the other hand, the outsourcing and the delocalization strategies that had been associated to the reactive ones are specified mainly with the association to scale and resource intensive sectors of activities (PAV=20).

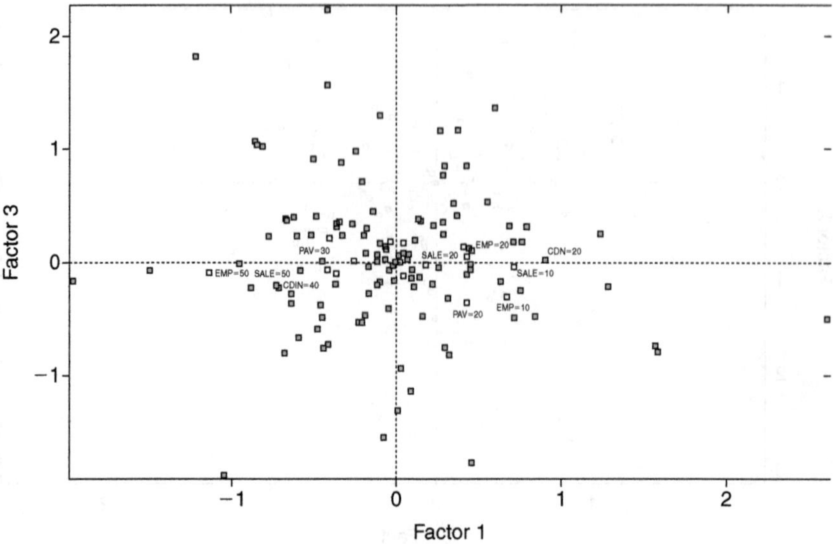

Figure 1.5 Active versus supplementary variables: factor 1 and factor 3.

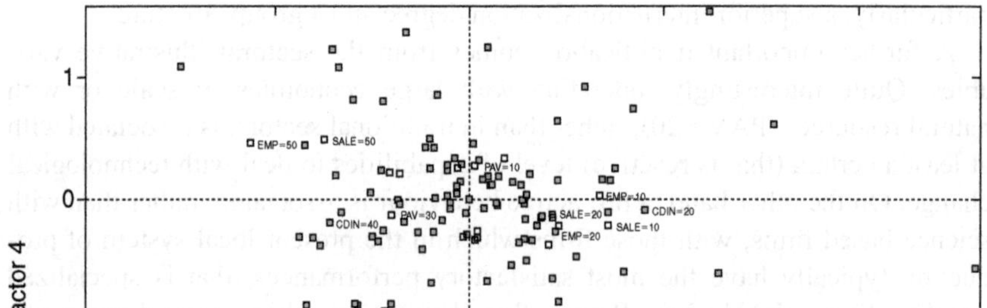

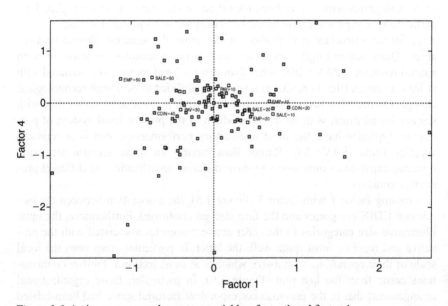

Figure 1.6 Active versus supplementary variables: factor 1 and factor 4.

1.6 Conclusions

The aim of this chapter is to explore the role of dynamic capabilities in explaining the relationship between learning and firm dynamics. From a theoretical point of view, as we have already argued elsewhere (Leoncini *et al.*, 2006), there is a need to take into account two dimensions of dynamic capabilities: one organizational and one environmental. This results from the view of the firm as an open system, whose dynamics depend on the intercourse between the internal production of disorder and the exportation of it towards the environment. The entropy exchange with the environment is at the origin of non-linear dynamics that can be analysed by referring to firms as complex adaptive systems, for which it is possible to envisage a complex process of co-evolution with the environment. It is therefore important to stress how the firm performance is the result of a dynamic exchange of flows with the outer environment, and that an order can be maintained only dynamically by balancing the export and import of disorder.

An empirical application has been performed on a set of Italian firms located in the province of Treviso by means of a very detailed questionnaire produced at the University of Padua. The province of Treviso is interesting for several reasons. In particular, it must be stressed that many characteristics (the process of internationalisation based on delocalisation of production rather than on export, the presence of industrial districts, etc.) are quite suitable to the scope of our analysis. The resulting dataset is then analysed with multiple correspondence analysis, with which it is possible to take into consideration answers to multiple choices questions.

The main results of this application refer, first of all, to the close interaction between organizational and environmental elements in determining firm dynamic capabilities. The empirical analysis in fact produces quite clear evidence about the need of building up linkages in order to benefit from the virtuous interactions offered by the industrial model existing in the province of Treviso. Indeed, a meta variable emerges about the relationships extension of the firms considered, which depends heavily on environmental variables. Another crucial meta variable seems to relate the dynamic capabilities of the firm to more generic capabilities to face market changes: in turn, both are associated to qualified organizational arrangements.

By analysing the associations among categories we have obtained more refined information. Two different profiles of firms in the area considered in fact emerge: pro-active firms (related to firms with a high level of dynamic capabilities) and reactive ones (related to low levels of dynamic capabilities). A set of further variables better qualify these two groups. As expected, the more dynamic group results are to be associated (among the others) to more developed ICT, a better placement in the infrastructural set-up, the participation to a group with an important role, the presence of diversification strategies and cooperation with competitors. The less dynamic one has instead (among the others) local kind of linkages, both with suppliers and customers, based on informal group relations, and is associated to the outsourcing of auxiliary activities rather than core ones.

Appendices

Table 1.A1 The structure of the dataset

Variables		*Label*	*Categories*				
No.	*Subject*		*10*	*20*	*30*	*40*	*50*
Structure							
1	Set-up year	AGE	1920/1969	1970/1979	1980/1989	1990/1999	2000/2002
2	Pavitt sector (enlarged taxonomy)	PAV	Supplier dominated	Scale intensive and resource based	Specialized suppliers	Science-based and services	
3	Employment class (no. of employees)	EMP	<20	[20; 49]	[50: 99]	[100; 249]	>249
4	Revenues by class (millions of euros)	SALE	<2.5	[2.1; 5.5]	[5.51; 12.5]	[12.51; 25]	>25
Employment dynamics							
5	Employment trend (yearly rate of change in the last three years)	DEMP	–10%	[–3%; –10%]	[–2.9%; +2.9%]	[+3%; +10%]	+10%
6	Employment shortage (in which activities)	EMPS	Core	Auxiliary	Both	None	Missing
Production efficiency							
7	Costs incidence (on revenues)	COST	[0; 20%]	(20%; 50%]	(50%; 70%]	missing	
8	Productive capacity (average rate of utilization)	CAPR	[0%; 70%]	(70%; 80%]	(80%; 90%]	(90%; 100%]	

Investments							
9	Fixed investments (on total investments)	INFI	[0%; 10%]	(10%; 50%]	(50%; 70%]	(70%; 100%]	missing
10	R&D investments (on total investments)	INRS	[0%; 10%]	(10%; 50%]	(50%; 70%]	(70%; 100%]	missing
11	Human capital investments (on total investments)	INHC	[0%; 10%]	(10%; 50%]	(50%; 70%]	(70%; 100%]	missing
12	Marketing investments (on total investments)	INMK	[0%; 10%]	(10%; 50%]	(50%; 70%]	(70%; 100%]	missing
13	ICT investments (on total investments)	INCT	[0%; 10%]	(10%; 50%]	(50%; 70%]	(70%; 100%]	missing
14	Investments trend (yearly rate of change in the last three years)	DINV	–10%	[–3%; –10%]	[–2.9%; +2.9%]	[+3%; +10%]	+10%
Information-automation							
15	Informatization year	YINF	pre-1980	1980–1990	1991–1995	1996–2000	2000–2002
16	Informatization diffusion (missing in which activities?)	DINF	None	Core	Auxiliary	Both	
17	Web-site (function)	WEB	Absent	Window	Window + B2		
18	Automation (percentage of the machinery park)	HTMA	[0%; 10%]	(10%; 30%]	(30%; 50%]	(50%; 80%]	(80%; 100%]
Product							
19	Product techn. content (level)	HTPR	Low	Medium-low	Medium-high	High	
20	Product price elasticity (level)	ELPR	Low	Medium	High		

continued

Table 1.A1 continued

Variables		*Label*	*Categories*				
No.	*Subject*		*10*	*20*	*30*	*40*	*50*
Innovation							
21	Innovativeness (kind of product/process innovations)	INNO	High (rad/rad)	Medium-high (rad/inc – inc/rad)	Medium (inc/inc)	Medium-low (inc/no – no/inc)	Low (no/no)
22	Patents (actions in the last three years)	PAT	Registred	Sold	Bought	Both	None
Organization							
23	Group position	GRUP	No group	Parent	Subsidiary	Missing	
24	Vertical integration (recent strategies)	INTV	Upward	Downward	Both	None	
25	Horizontal integration (recent strategies)	INTH	Diversified	Specialized	Both	None	
26	Outsourcing (of which activities?)	OUTS	Core	Auxiliary	Both	None	Missing
27	Delocalization (mainly where?)	LOCD	Local	Rest of Italy	Abroad	Absent	
28	Spin-offs (of which kind?)	SPIN	Outward	Inward	Both	None	
Relationships							
29	Number of suppliers	SUPN	[1; 3]	[4; 10]	>10		
30	Kind of suppliers (mainly)	SUPK	suppliers	sub-suppliers	Both	Missing	
31	Suppliers location (mainly)	SUPS	local	Rest of Italy	abroad		

32	Number of customers	CUS	[1; 10]	[11; 50]	>50		
33	Kind of customers (mainly)	CUSK	Standard	Commission	Both	Missing	
34	Customers location (mainly)	CUSS	Local	Rest of Italy	Abroad		
35	Number of competitors	COM	[0; 3]	[4; 10]	>10		
36	Competitors' location (mainly)	COMS	Local	Rest of Italy (alone or also)	Abroad (alone or also)	Rest of Italy and abroad (alone and also)	
37	Competitors' collaboration (main reason)	COMR	Absent	Capabilities acquisition	Cost reduction	Other reasons	missing
38	Exports trend (yearly rate of change in the last three years)	DEXP	–10%	[–3%; –10%]	[–2.9%; +2.9%]	[+3%; +10%]	+10%
Environment							
39	Placing in material infrastructure (perceived)	MIFR	Bad	Good enough	Good	Very good	Missing
40	Placing in immaterial infrastructure (perceived)	IFR	Bad	Good enough	Good	Very good	Missing
Capabilities							
41	Innovation capabilities (response in front of TC)	CDIN	Absent	Substitutive	Adaptive	Dynamic	
42	Market capabilities (response in front of prefered change)	CDMK	Absent	Substitutive	Adaptive	Dynamic	

Table 1.A2 Active and supplementary variables

No.	*Subject*	*Lable*
Active variables		
5	Employment trend (yearly rate of change in the last three years)	DEMP
6	Employment shortage (in which activities)	EMPS
8	Productive capacity (average rate of utilization)	CAPR
9	Investments trend (yearly rate of change in the last three years)	DINV
14	Costs incidence (on revenues)	COST
15	Informatization year	YINF
16	Informatization lock	DINF
17	Web-site (function)	WEB
21	Innovativeness (kind of product/process innovations)	INNO
23	Group (position)	GRUP
24	Vertical integration (recent strategies)	INTV
25	Horizontal integration (recent strategies)	INTH
26	Outsourcing (of which activities?)	OUTS
27	Delocalization (mainly where?)	LOCD
28	Spin-offs (of which kind?)	SPIN
30	Kind of suppliers (mainly)	SUPK
31	Suppliers location (mainly)	SUPS
33	Kind of customers (mainly)	CUSK
34	Customers location (mainly)	CUSS
36	Competitors location (mainly)	COMS
37	Competitors collaboration (main reason)	COMR
38	Exports trend (yearly rate of change in the last three years)	DEXP
39	Placing in material infrastructure (perceived)	MIFR
40	Placing in material infrastructure (perceived)	IFR
41	Innovation capabilities (response in front of TC)	CDIN
42	Market capabilities (response in front of prefered change)	CDMK
Supplementary variables		
1	Set-up year	AGE
2	Pavitt sector (enlarged taxonomy)	PAV
3	Employment class (no. of employees)	EMP
4	Revenues by class (milions of euros)	SALE

Although it has to be further tested, the MCA analysis also suggests that pro-active firms are associated to more dynamic performances in terms of both sales and employment. Dynamic capabilities do really seem to matter.

Notes

1 Not to say of the related strategies, especially in the process of feeding policy-makers up (Godin, 2003, pp. 18–20).

2 This section draws substantially on Leoncini *et al.* (2006).
3 It is worth noting in passing that this is the original meaning of the Latin word from which complex is derived.
4 But for our sake, we will see that the relevant flows are constituted by information.
5 Typical examples are related to bandwagon effects, self-fulfilling prophecies, network externalities. The most celebrated (and controversial, see Liebowitz and Margolis, 1990) is the QWERTY effect by David (1985).
6 It is impossible (and not very rational) to search the whole space of alternatives. That is, the search is usually local, so that the agent is more likely to benefit from the previous knowledge of the neighbourhoods, and thus can conduct a more effective and 'efficient' kind of search. This is the reason why if organizations are pushed too far from the pre-existing equilibrium they are likely to disappear.
7 Suffice to think, for instance, to the process depicted by Hughes (1989), in which large technical systems progressively incorporate chunks of the environment in order to keep their 'balance' between growth and governance right. However, as will be pointed out in the following, there is an inner element in processes like these, which relates to the fact that it is not possible to expand the system indefinitely and at request, since as the environment shrinks, the possibility of exporting entropy radically decreases.
8 For example, widely developed capital markets supply a series of information from which organizations can benefit until very high costs are reached. On the contrary, if they must do by themselves, the high costs might forbid a strategy focused on growth.
9 In Iansiti and Clark (1994), for example, the dynamic capabilities of the investigated firms in the automobiles and mainframe computers sectors turn out to be affected by their 'technology integration capacity' (Iansiti and Clark, 1994, p. 571). This refers to an ability to 'pick-up' those pieces of the technical knowledge evolving around the firm, which are more suitable to be linked with the existing knowledge base of the firm, and to actually implement this linkage.
10 In Brioschi *et al.* (2002), for example, the analysis of the dynamic performances of some traditional districts in Emilia Romagna is informed by the structure of the firms' ownership and by the organizational relationships they establish by constituting formal business groups.
11 For a detailed analysis of these indicators see Amaturo (1989) and Bouroche and Saporta (1980).
12 The variable about the firm outsourcing, for example, originally referred to each of the activities of the firm (R&D, production, marketing, etc.) as a dichotomic variable (present/absent), has been referred to the firm as a whole as a variable with five categories, depending on the kind of activities the firm has actually outsourced (Appendix 1, OUTS).
13 The question about the actual value of the firm revenues, for example, has been transformed by introducing five classes of values (Appendix 1, SALE).
14 The question about the economic sector of the firm, for example, originally distributed on the eigh digit of the standard ATECO classification, has been transformed into a variable which just comprehends four categories of an adjusted Pavitt taxonomy (Appendix 1, PAV).
15 This is the case, for example, of the variables about the number of suppliers (Appendix 1, SUPN) and of competitors (Appendix 1, COM), originally defined on ranges of values with different boundaries.
16 More precisely, the categories of these variables have been obtained by analysing the different answers the firms have given to a numerous set of detailed questions in which they have been asked to consider a large set of both material (e.g. roads, railroads, etc.) and immaterial (e.g. universities, chambers of commerce, etc.) infrastructures as either a strength or a weakness for their business.
17 In MCA the axes are identified by the eigen-values of the matrix of data which collects the relevant categories, called the Burt matrix.

18 Categories are the more significant, the higher their masses are and the lower their distortions are. Although somehow arbitrary, categories are conventionally dropped when their masses and distortions are, respectively, so low and so high to appear outlayers. Usually this reflects in factor coordinates close to the origin.

19 In order to detect significant correlations with the factorial axes, MCA uses test values for each active and illustrative variable/category. In particular, in investigating the role of illustrative variables/categories, these values are to be read with respect to the standard normal distribution of *t*, so that those coefficients whose absolute value is higher than 2 are significant with a 5 per cent probability level.

20 The diagnositic of these correlations is available from the authors at request.

Bibliographical references

Amaturo, F. 1989, *Analyse des Données & Analisi dei Dati nelle Scienze Sociali*, Turin: Centro Scientifico Editore.

Anastasia, B. and Corò, G. 1993, *I Distretti Industriali in Veneto*, Nuova Dimensione-Ediciclo, Portogruaro.

Anderson, P.W., Arrow, K.J. and Pines, D. (eds) 1988, *The Economy as an Evolving Complex System*, Redwood City: Addison Wesley.

Antonelli, C. 1987, L'impresa rete: cambiamento tecnologico, internazionalizzazione e appropriazione delle quasi rendite, *Annali dell'Impresa*, Fondazione Assi, no. 3.

Aydalot, P. 1986, Presentation, in Aydalot, P. (ed.) *Milieux innovateurs in Europe*, Paris: Gremi, pp. 9–14.

Barkley Rosser, J. 1999, On the complexities of complex economic dynamics, *Journal of Economic Perspectives*, 13: 169–192.

Baron, J.N., Hannon, M.T. and Burton, M.D. 1999, Building the iron cage: determinants of managerial intensity in the early years of organizations, *American Sociological Review*, 64: 527–547.

Barr, P.S., Stimpert, J.L. and Huff, A.S. 1992, Cognitive change, strategic action, and organizational renewal, *Strategic Management Journal*, 13: 15–36.

Becattini, G. 1979, Dal 'settore' industriale al 'distretto' industriale. Alcune considerazioni sull'unità di indagine dell'economia industriale, *Rivista di Economia e Politica Industriale*, 5: 7–21.

Becattini, G. (ed.) 1987, *Mercato e forze locali: il distretto industriale*, Bologna: Il Mulino.

Becattini, G. 1990, The Marshallian industrial district as a socio-economic notion, in Pyke, F., Becattini, G. and Sengenberger, W. (eds) *Industrial Districts and Inter-Firm Co-operation in Italy*, Geneva: ILO.

Bellandi, M. 2001, Local development and embedded large firms, *Entrepreneurship and Regional Development*, 13: 189–210.

Belussi, F. and Gottardi, G. (eds) 2000, *Evolutionary Patterns of Local Industrial Systems. Towards a Cognitive Approach to the Industrial District*, Aldershot: Ashgate.

Benzécri, J.P. 1973, *L'Analyse des Données. Tome II. L'Analyse des Corrispondances*, Paris: Dunod.

Berle, A.A. and Means, G.C. 1932, *The Modern Corporation and Private Property*, New York: Harcourt, Brace & World.

Bouroche, J.M. and Saporta, G. 1980, *L'Analyse des Données*, Paris: Universitaires de France.

Braczyk, H.-J., Cooke, P. and Heidenreich, M. 1998, *Regional Innovation Systems*, London: UCL Press.

Breschi, S., Malerba, F. and Orsenigo, L. 2000, Technological regimes and Schumpeterian patterns of innovation, *Economic Journal*, 110(463) (April): 388–410.

Breschi, S. and Malerba, F. 1997, Sectoral innovation systems: technological regimes, Schumpeterian dynamics, and spatial boundaries, in Edquist, C. and McKelvey, M. (eds) *Systems of Innovation: Growth, Competitiveness and Employment*, vol. 1. Elgar Reference Collection, Cheltenham: Edward Elgar, pp. 261–287.

Bresolin, F. and Biscaro, Q. 2001, Problematiche di internazionalizzazione dei distretti industriali della provincia di Treviso, mimeo, Camera di Commercio Industria Artigianato Agricoltura di Treviso.

Brioschi F., Brioschi, M.S. and Cainelli, G. 2004, Ownership linkages and business groups in industrial districts. The case of Emilia Romagna, in Cainelli G. and Zoboli, R. (eds) *The Evolution of Industrial Districts. Changing Governance, Innovation and Internationalisation of Local Capitalism in Italy*, Heidelberg: Physica Verlag, pp. 155–175.

Brioschi, F., Brioschi, M.S. and Cainelli, G. 2002, From the industrial district to the district group. An insight into the evolution of local capitalism in Italy, *Regional Studies*, 36: 1037–1052.

Camagni, R. (ed.) 1991a, *Innovation Networks. Spatial Perspectives*, London: Belhaven Press.

Camagni, R. 1991b, Local 'milieu', uncertainty and innovation networks: towards a new dynamic theory of economic space, in Camagni, R. (ed.) *Innovation Networks: Spatial Perspective*, London and New York: Belhaven Press, 121–144.

Chandler, A.D. 1962, *Strategy and Structure: Chapters in the History of the Industrial Enterprise*, Cambridge: MIT Press.

Chell, E. and Baines, S. 2000, Networking, entrepreneurship and microbusiness behaviour, *Entrepreneurship and Regional Development*, 12: 195–215.

Chiarvesio, M., Di Maria, E. and Micelli, S. 2003, Innovation and internationalisation of Italian districts: exploitation of global competencies or transfer of local knowledge?, Paper presented at the 2003 Regional Studies Association International Conference, 'Reinventing Regions in the Global Economy'.

Clark, N. 1991, Organization and information in the evolution of economic systems, in Saviotti, P. and Metcalfe, S. (eds) *Evolutionary Theories of Economic and Technological Change*, Chur: Harwood Academic Publishers.

Coase, R.N. 1937, The nature of the firm, *Economica*, 4: 386–405.

Cole, R.E. 1999, *Managing Quality Fads: How American Business Learned to Play the Quality Game*, New York: Oxford University Press.

Collis, D.J. 1994 How valuable are organizational capabilities?, *Strategic Management Journal*, 15: 143–152.

Cooke, P. 2001, Regional innovation systems, clusters, and the knowledge economy, *Industrial and Corporate Change*, 10: 945–974.

Cooke, P., Uranga, M.G. and Etxebarria, G. 1998, Regional systems of innovation: an evolutionary perspective, *Environment and Planning A*, 30: 1521–1714.

Crevoisier, O. 2001, L'approche par les milieurs innovateurs: État des lieux et perspective, *Revue d'Économie Régionale et Urbaine*, 0: 153–166.

Cyert, R.M. and March, J.G. 1963, *A Behavioral Theory of the Firm*, Englewood Cliffs, NJ: Prentice-Hall.

David, P. 1985, Clio and the economics of QWERTY, *American Economic Review, Papers and Proceedings*, 75: 332–337.

David, P. and Foray, D. 1995, Assessing and expanding the science and technology knowledge vase, *STI Review*, 16: 13–68.

Dierickx, I. and Cool, K. 1989, Asset stock accumulation and sustainability of competitive advantage, *Management Science*, 35: 1504–1511.

Doloreux, D. 2002, What we should know about regional systems of innovation, *Technology and Society*, 24: 243–263.

Dosi, G., Nelson, R.R. and Winter, S.G. 2000, Introduction, in Dosi, G., Nelson, R.R., and Winter, S.G. (eds) *The Nature and Dynamics of Organizational Capabilities*, Oxford: Oxford University Press, pp. 1–22.

Edquist, C. 1997, Systems of innovation approaches – their emergence and characteristics, in Edquist, C. (ed.) *Systems of Innovation. Technologies, Institutions and Organisations*, London: Pinter Publishers, pp. 1–35.

Eisenhardt, K.M. and Martin, J.A. 2000, Dynamic capabilities: What are they?, *Strategic Management Journal*, 21: 1105–1121.

Ferrucci, L. and Varaldo, R. 1993, La natura e la dinamica dell'impresa distrettuale, *Economia e Politica Industriale*, 80: 73–97.

Foray, D. 1997, Generation and distribution of technological knowledge: incentives, norms, and institutions, in Edquist, C. (ed.) *Systems of Innovation. Technologies, Institutions and Organizations*, London and Washington, DC: Pinter, pp. 64–82.

Foray, D. and Lundvall, B.-Å. 1996, The knowledge-based economy: from the economics of knowledge to the learning economy, in OECD, *Employment and Growth in the Knowledge-Based Economy*, Paris: OECD, pp. 11–32.

Foss, N.J. 1997, The resource-based perspective: an assessment and diagnosis of problems, DRUID Working Paper, No. 97–1.

Foster, J. 1993, Economics and the self-organisation approach: Alfred Marshall revisited? *Economic Journal*, 103: 975–991.

Freeman, C. 1987, *Technology Policy and Economic Performance: Lesson from Japan*, London: Pinter.

Fuller, T. and Moran, P. 2000, Complexity as a social science methodology in understanding the impact of exogenous systemic change on small business, Paper presented at the International Conference on Complex Systems, Nashua, NH, 21–26 May 2000.

Fuller, T. and Moran, P. 2001, Small enterprises as complex adaptive systems: a methodological question, *Entrepreneurship and Regional Development*, 13: 47–63.

Garrido, N. 2004, The desirable organizational structure for evolutionary firms in static landscapes, *Metroeconomica*, 55: 318–331.

Garud, R. and Rappa, M.A. 1994, A socio-cognitive model of technology evolution: the case of cochlear implants, *Organization Science*, 5: 344–362.

Gavetti, G. and Levinthal, D. 2000, Looking forward and looking backward: cognitive and experiental search, *Administrative Science Quarterly*, 45: 113–137.

Gay, C. and Picard, F. 2001, Innovation, agglomération et espace. Une mise en perspective de la littérature, *Économie et Sociétés*, 35: 679–716.

Gilbert, R.J. and Newberry, D.M. 1982, Preemptive patenting and the persistence of monopoly, *American Economic Review*, 72: 514–526.

Godin, B. 2003, The knowledge-based economy: conceptual framework or buzzword? Canadian Science and Innovation Indicators Consortium, Project on the History and Sociology of S&T Statistics, Working Paper, No. 24.

Grant, R.M. 1996, Towards a knowledge-based theory of the firm, *Strategic Management Journal*, 17: 109–122.

Henderson, R. 1993, Underinvestment and incompetence as responses to radical innovation: evidence from the photolithographic alignment equipment industry, *RAND Journal of Economics*, 24: 248–270.

Henderson, R.M. and Clark, K.B. 1990, Architectural innovation: the reconfiguration of existing product technologies and the failure of established firms, *Administrative Science Quarterly*, 35: 9–30.

Hodgson, G.M. 1988, *Economics and Institutions. A Manifesto for a Modern Institutional Economics*, Philadelphia, PA: University of Pennsylvania Press.

Howells, J. 1999, Regional systems of innovation?, in Archibugi, D., Howells, J. and Michie, J. (eds) *Innovation Policy in a Global Economy*, Cambridge: Cambridge University Press, pp. 67–93.

Hughes, T. 1987, Evolution of large technological systems, in Bijker, W., Hughes, T. and Pinch, T. (eds) *Social Construction of Technological Systems: New Directions in the Sociology and History of Technology*, Cambridge, MA: MIT Press, pp. 51–58.

Iansiti, M. 1992, Technology integration: exploring the interaction between applied science and product development, Working Paper, No. 26, Harvard Business School.

Iansiti, M. 1995, Technology integration: managing technological evolution in a complex environment, *Research Policy*, 24: 521–542.

Iansiti, M. and Clark, K.B. 1994, Integration and dynamic capability: evidence from product development in automobiles and mainframe computers, *Industrial and Corporate Change*, 3(3): 557–606.

Johannisson, B. and Ramírez-Pasillas, M. 2002, The institutional embeddedness of local inter-firm networks: a leverage for business creation, *Entrepreneurship and Regional Development*, 14: 297–315.

Johnson, B. 1992, Institutional learning, in Lundvall, B.A. (ed.) *National Systems of Innovation. Towards a Theory of Innovation and Interactive Learning*, London: Pinter Publishers, pp. 23–44.

Jones, N. 2001, Exploring dynamic capability: a longer-term study of product development following radical technological change, R&D Working Paper, No. 2001/20/TM, INSEAD.

Kaplan, S., Murray, F. and Henderson, R. 2003, Discontinuities and senior management: assessing the role of recognition in pharmaceutical firm response to biotechnology, *Industrial and Corporate Change*, 12: 203–223.

Kauffman, S. 1995, *At Home in the Universe: The Search for Laws of Complexity*, Oxford, Oxford University Press.

Le Moigne, J.L. 1995, On theorizing the complexity of economic systems, *Journal of Socio-Economics*, 24: 477–499.

Lechner, C. and Dowling, M. 2003, Firm networks: external relationships as sources for the growth and competitiveness of entrepreneurial firms, *Entrepreneurship and Regional Development*, 15: 1–26.

Leonard-Barton, D. 1992, Core capabilities and core rigidities: a paradox in managing new product development, *Strategic Management Journal*, 12: 111–125.

Leoncini, R. 1998, The nature of long run technological change: innovation, evolution and technological systems, *Research Policy*, 27(1): 75–93.

Leoncini, R. and Montresor, S. 2003, *Technological Systems and Intersectoral Innovation Flows*, Cheltenham: Edward Elgar.

Leoncini, R., Montresor, S. and Vertova, G. 2006, Dynamic capabilities between firm organization and local development: a critical survey, *Economia Politica*, 23: 475–514.

Levinthal, D.A. 1997, Adaptation on rugged landscapes, *Management Science*, 43: 934–950.

Levitt, B. and March, J.G. 1988, Organizational learning, *Annual Review of Sociology*, 14: 319–340.

Lieberman, M.B. and Montgomery, D.B. 1988, First-mover advantages, *Strategic Management Journal*, 9: 41–58.

Liebowitz, S.J. and Margolis, S.E. 1990, The fable of the keys, *Journal of Law and Economics*, 33: 1–25.

Lipparini, A. 1995, *Imprese, relazioni tra imprese e posizionamento competitivo*, Milan: Etas.

Lipparini, A. 1998, Aspetti relazionali per lo sviluppo e l'integrazione delle competenze, in Lipparini, A. (ed.) *Le Competenze Organizzative: Sviluppo, Condivisione, Trasferimento*, Roma: Carocci, pp. 225–254.

Lipparini, A. and Lorenzoni, G. 1996, Le organizzazioni ad alta intensità relazionale. Riflessioni sui meccanismi di 'learning-by-interacting' nelle aree ad alta concentrazione di imprese, *L'Industria*, 4: 111–119.

Lundvall, B.-Å. and Borras, S. 1997, *The Globalising Learning Economy: Implications for Innovation Policy*, Brussels: DG XII.

Lundvall, B.-Å. (ed.) 1992, *National Systems of Innovation. Towards a Theory of Innovation and Interactive Learning*, London: Pinter.

Lundvall, B.-Å. 1996, The social dimension of the learning economy, DRUID Working Paper, No. 1, April, Department of Business Studies, Aalborg University.

Lundvall, B.-Å. 1997, Development strategies in the learning economy, STEPI's 10th Anniversary Conference, Seoul, 26–29 May 1997.

Lundvall, B.-Å. 1998, The learning economy – challenges to economic theory and policy, in Johnson, B. and Nielsen, K. (eds) *Institutions and Economic Change*, Bath: Edward Elgar.

Lundvall, B.-Å. and Johnson, B. 1994, The learning economy, *Journal of Industry Studies*, 2: 23–42.

Lundvall, B.-Å. and Nielsen, P. 1999, Competition and transformation in the learning economy illustrated by the Danish case, *Revue d'Economie Industrielle*, 88: 67–90.

Maillat, D. 1995, Territorial dynamic, innovative milieus and regional policy, *Entrepreneurship and Regional Development*, 7: 157–165.

Malerba, F. and Orsenigo, L. 1997, Technological regimes and sectoral patterns of innovative activities, *Industrial and Corporate Change*, 6(1): 83–117.

Marangoni, G., Nicolis, O. and Solari, S. 2003, Dynamic capabilities and economic relations, in Teixeira, J.R. (ed.) *Proceedings of the IV International Colloquium – Globalisation, New Technologies and Economic Relations*, Universidade de Brasilia, pp. 161–182.

March, J.G. 1991, Exploration and exploitation in organizational learning, *Organization Science*, 2: 71–87.

March, J.G. and Simon, H.A. 1958, *Organizations*, New York: John Wiley & Co.

Marshall, A. 1890, *Principles of Economics*, London: Macmillan.

McKelvey, B. 2004, Toward a complexity science of entrepreneurship, *Journal of Business Venturing*, 19: 313–341.

Medio, A. 1992, *Chaotic Dynamics. Theory and Applications to Economics*, Cambridge: Cambridge University Press.

Metcalfe, J.S. 1995, Technology systems and technology policy in an evolutionary framework, *Cambridge Journal of Economics*, 19: 25–46.

Mitleton-Kelly, E. 1997, Organisations a co-evolving complex adaptive systems, BPRC, http://bprc.warwick.ac.uk/eve.html.

Monks, R.A.G. 1998, The Emperor's nightingale: restoring the integrity of the corporation, Oxford: Capston Publishing Limited.

Montresor, S. and Romagnoli, A. 2004, Modelling the firm from a system perspective: some methodological insights, *Institutions and Local Development*, 2: 105–140.

Nelson, R.R. (ed.) 1993, *National Innovation Systems. A Comparative Analysis*, Oxford: Oxford University Press.

Nelson, R.R. and Winter, S.G. 1982, *An Evolutionary Theory of Economic Change*, Cambridge, MA: Harvard University Press.

Nonaka, I. 1994, A dynamic theory of organizational knowledge creation, *Organization Science*, 5: 14–37.

Nonaka, I. and Takeuchi, H. 1997, *The Knowledge Creating Company*, Milan: Guerini.e. Associati.

Orton, J.D. and Weick, K.E. 1990, Loosely coupled systems: a reconceptualization, *The Academy of Management Review*, 15( ): 20–22.

Osservatorio Unioncamere di Treviso 2004, Company groups in Treviso: holding companies or receivership enterprises in Province, mimeo, Unioncamere di Treviso.

Piore, M. and Sabel, C. 1984, *The Second Industrial Divide*, New York: Basic Books.

Polanyi, M. 1958/1978, *Personal Knowledge*, London: Routledge and Kegan.

Porter, M. 1990, *The Competitive Advantage of Nations*, London: Pinter.

Porter, M.E. 1980, *Competitive Strategy: Techniques for Analyzing Industries and Competitors*, New York: Free Press.

Prahalad, C.K. and Bettis, R.A. 1986, The dominant logic: a new linkage between diversity and performance, *Strategic Management Journal*, 7: 485–501.

Prahalad, C.K. and Hamel, G. 1990, The core competence of the corporation, *Harvard Business Review*, May: 79–91.

Prigogine I. 1976, Order through fluctuation: self-organization and social system, in Jantsch, E. and Waddington, C. (eds) *Evolution and Consciousness: Human Systems in Transition*, Reading: Addison Wesley, pp. 93–133.

Reinganum, J.F. 1989, The timing of innovation: research, development and diffusion, in Schmalensee, R. and Willig, R. (eds) *Handbook of Industrial Organization*, vol. I, Amsterdam: North-Holland, pp. 849–908.

Reinganum, J.F. 1983, Uncertain innovation and the persistence of monopoly, *American Economic Review*, 73: 741–748.

Sanchez, R. and Mahoney, J.T. 1996, Modularity, flexibility, and knowledge management in product and organization design, *Strategic Management Journal*, 17(Winter): 6–76.

Scott, A. 1988, *New Industrial Spaces*, London: Pion Limited.

Scott, A. 1992, The Roepke lecture in economic geography: the collective order of flexible production agglomerations: lessons for local economic development policy and strategic choice, *Economic Geography*, 68: 219–233.

Simon, H.A. 1955, A behavioral model of rational choice, *The Quarterly Journal of Economics*, 69(1) (February): 99–118.

Smith, K. 1997, Economic infrastructures and innovation systems, in Edquist, C. (ed.) *Systems of Innovation. Technologies, Institutions and Organizations*, London and Washington, DC: Pinter, pp. 86–106.

Storper, M. 1999, The resurgence of regional economics, in Barnes, T. and Gertler, M. (eds) *The New Industrial Geography*, London and New York: Routledge, pp. 23–53.

Storper, M. and Walker, R. 1983, The theory of labour and the theory of location, *International Journal of Urban and Regional Research*, 7: 1–43.

Taylor, M. 1999, The small firm as a temporary coalition, *Entrepreneurship and Regional Development*, 11: 1–19.

Teece, D.J. and Pisano, G. 1994, The dynamic capabilities of the firms: an introduction, *Industrial and Corporate Change*, 3: 537–556.

Teece, D.J., Pisano, G. and Shuen, A. 1997, Dynamic capabilities and strategic management, *Strategic Management Journal*, 18: 509–533.

Tripsas, M. and Gavetti, G. 2000, Capabilities, cognition and inertia: evidence from digital imaging, *Strategic Management Journal*, 21: 1147–1161.

Tushman, M.L. and Anderson, P. 1986, Technological discontinuities and organizational environments, *Administrative Science Quarterly*, 31: 439–465.

Tushman, M.L. and Rosenkopf, L. 1992, Organizational determinants of technological change: toward a sociology of technological evolution, *Research in Organizational Behavior*, 14: 311–317.

Vincenti, W.G. 1994, The retractable airplane landing gear and the Northrop anomaly, *Technology and Culture*, 5(1): 1–33.

Waldrop, M. 1992, *Complexity: The Emerging Science at the Edge of Order and Chaos*, Harmondsworth: Penguin.

Witford, J. 2001, The decline of a model? Challenge and response in the Italian industrial districts, *Economy and Society*, 30: 38–65.

Zollo, M. and Winter, S.G. 1999, From organizational routines to dynamic capabilities, R&D Working Paper, No. 99/48/SM, INSEAD.

Zollo, M. and Winter, S.G. 2002, Deliberate learning and the evolution of dynamic capabilities, *Organization Science*, 13: 339–351.

Zott, C. 2002, Dynamic capabilities and the emergence of intraindustry differential firm performance: insights from a simulation study, *Strategic Management Journal*, 24: 97–125.

2 Dynamic capabilities and entrepreneurial team development in SMEs

Donato Iacobucci

2.1 Introduction

Dynamic capabilities (DC) have been claimed to be an emerging new paradigm in the field of strategic management (Teece *et al.*, 1997). They have also attracted the attention of researchers interested in firm organization and behaviour (Dosi *et al.*, 2000).

Capabilities refer to what an organization can do, i.e. knowing what to do and how to do it. The original meaning of the term implies possibility and potentiality combined with talent and ability. Capabilities and resources are sometimes used synonymously (Helfat, 2000). It is more difficult to assess their meaning when they are given the 'dynamic' attribute. While all would agree that it implies change, the concept is interpreted differently in the literature.

Some see DC as the firm's ability to integrate, build and reconfigure internal and external firm-specific competences to address changing environments (Teece *et al.*, 1997). In this interpretation DC are seen as particularly important for firms competing in rapidly changing environments (high tech industries). To be successful in these environments firms must demonstrate 'timely responsiveness and rapid and flexible product innovation, coupled with the management capability to effectively coordinate and redeploy internal and external competences' (Teece *et al.*, 1997, p. 515). DC are defined according to their function:

> The term "dynamic" refers to the capacity to renew competences so as to achieve congruence with the changing business environment; ... The term "capabilities" emphasizes the key role of strategic management in appropriately adapting, integrating, and reconfiguring internal and external organizational skills, resources, and functional competences to match the requirements of a changing environment.
>
> (Teece *et al.*, 1997, p. 515)

On the other hand DC can also be seen as specific routines that enable firms to cope with fast changing ('high velocity') markets. Operational routines are regarded as automatic or quasi-automatic responses to environmental changes. DC are those 'constant dispositions and strategic heuristics that shape the approach of a firm to the non-routine problems it faces' (Nelson and Winter, 1982). There are two different ways of conceiving DC within an evolutionary perspective. DC can be associated with routines or processes devoted to managing change: R&D activity, new product development, etc. (Eisenhardt and Martin, 2000), or can be seen as the ability of the firm to change existing routines and processes. In the latter case they are closely associated with the process of organizational learning.[1]

Another difference in the conceptualization of DC lies in whether the focus is on the internal organization of firms or on the influence of the external environment on organizational changes. The DC literature refers almost exclusively to large firms and for this reason it emphasizes the internal perspective. In studying the small firm sector it seems obvious to give more importance to the influence of the external environment. Lorenzoni and Lipparini (1999) do this by stressing the relevance of inter-firm relationships, while Leoncini *et al.* (2006) analyse the consequences of belonging to specialized local clusters.

These approaches to dynamic capabilities have spurred a large number of theoretical and empirical studies. However, some issues still remain to be investigated more deeply: first, the relationships between the type of DC and the degree of change in the organization; second, the literature on DC emphasizes 'adaptation' to environmental changes, undervaluing the role of proactivity in firms' behaviour.

This chapter proposes a classification of DC based on the degree of change implied in firms' organizational processes and resources, and the passive or proactive nature of their relationships with the external environment. Using this classification and building on recent strands of the entrepreneurship literature the aim is to identify factors affecting the ability of small- and medium-sized firms (SMEs) to innovate and grow (i.e. to identify the factors affecting DC). We explore the idea that in SMEs: (i) the role of the entrepreneur is fundamental; and (ii) innovation and growth are associated with the capabilities of entrepreneurs to exploit new business opportunities. We demonstrate that these business opportunities depend, among other things, on the ability to manipulate the governance structures (i.e. the structure of ownership and control) of new ventures. In the case of SMEs this is often achieved by giving the new venture legal autonomy (setting up a new company) and by extending involvement in the entrepreneurial role. We refer to this as entrepreneurial team development. We discuss how these processes result in the formation of business groups and analyse the basic mechanisms used by entrepreneurs to enlarge the entrepreneurial team. We use the results of a qualitative study based on in-depth interviews with entrepreneurs.

The chapter is organized as follows: section 2.2 proposes a framework for classifying DC and discusses its implications for the way in which DC are identified and conceptualized; section 2.3 examines the role and characteristics of new venture creation in SMEs and the problems this process poses for entrepreneurs; section 2.4 presents the results of the qualitative empirical study and suggests an interpretation of business groups designed to enhance entrepreneurs' capabilities to exploit new business opportunities; section 2.5 presents the conclusions.

2.2 Dynamic capabilities, degree of organizational change, and proactivity

In this section we propose a way to classify DC based on the degree of change they imply in firm organization and on the nature – passive or proactive – of the relationship with the external environment. Overlooking the importance of these dimensions can have major consequences for the way DC are conceptualized and empirically identified; it can also obscure factors on which DC depend and the ways in which they can be enhanced. Figure 2.1 presents a diagrammatic classification of DC based on these dimensions; for simplicity they are represented as discrete while in reality they vary in a continuum. The figure also highlights the fact that the two dimensions are correlated: adaptations requiring a low degree of change in existing resources (e.g. quantitative adjustments to existing production) can be managed through automated processes, while the acquisition and organization of new resources in order to exploit business opportunities are among the less automated processes and require entrepreneurs to be proactive.

In discussing the implications of the proposed classification we are interested specifically in the conceptualization and identification of DC in SMEs. The competitive advantage of SMEs, especially those belonging to local clusters, has often been associated with their flexibility in adapting to environmental changes (Brusco, 1982; Storper and Harrison, 1991; Storey, 1994). The use of the term 'adapt', common in the literature, suggests that the relationship between the firm and the economic environment is passive in nature: i.e. it implies the ability to respond to external changes rather than to anticipate them. Specifically, SMEs

Degree of change	Relationship with the environment	Type of activity	Main processes involved
Low	Passive (adaptation)	Quantitative adjustment to existing production	Re-deployment of existing resources (automatic)
↓	↓	Product/process development (differentation)	New combination of (mainly) existing resources to address market or technological change (semi automatic)
High	Proactive (shaping)	Exploitation of new business opportunities (new venture creation)	Attraction and combination of (mainly) new resources to exploit business opportunities (non-automatic)

Figure 2.1 Nature of change in existing organization and type of relationship with external environment.

are considered to be more efficient than larger firms in adapting to quantitative changes of the existing production. This flexibility can be seen as a quality of all SMEs, given their lower degree of organizational rigidity, or as a property of a cluster of SMEs. In local clusters (such as industrial districts) flexibility results from the high level of specialization of firms along the production chain (low level of vertical integration). The flexibility of SMEs in local clusters is also associated with their superior product innovation ability, especially in terms of upgrading existing products to meet the changing requirements of customers. In fact, product innovation within local clusters of SMEs is generally incremental in nature rather then the result of systematic investment in R&D (Cainelli and De Liso, 2004). In terms of both flexibility in quantitative adjustment and incremental product innovation, adaptation to environmental change is pre-eminent.

In contrast, the role of proactivity, i.e. acting in anticipation of future problems or needs, is fundamental to the exploitation of new business opportunities (new venture creation). The creation of a new venture, whatever the degree of novelty of the product/market combination, cannot be reduced to the mere 'exploitation' of a given (in the sense of objectively observable) market and/or technology opportunity. Nor can it be achieved through 'automatic' or codified processes. It is an exploration process, which implies the gradual discovery of market and technology conditions and entails a large degree of discretion on the part of the entrepreneur in interpreting environmental data and establishing business policies.

The literature on DC has not always recognized the differences in the degrees of change observed in a firm's organization or in the passive or proactive nature of these changes. One of the ways to assess the degree of proactivity implied by the different types of changes in an organization's processes and resources is to observe the degree of automation in their management. In the case of quantitative adjustment to existing products, the process can be almost completely automated allowing the system to respond to external demand in a timely and efficient way. Enterprise Resource Planning (ERP) systems facilitate this efficient response to environmental changes by codifying the processes and specifying the resources needed to accomplish specific tasks (Masini *et al.*, 2003).

New product development entails less structured processes; its aim is to allow firms to capture market needs and/or leverage existing technological knowledge to up-grade existing products or to propose new products. Most of the processes involved in new product development within existing lines of business can be (and often are) partially codified in specific routines within the organization. For a firm in the fashion industry, for example, the continual changes to products (according to seasons) are accomplished as a routine process. In most large firms, the R&D activity devoted to new product development is based on partially codified processes and specific methodologies that have been elaborated to enhance efficiency and effectiveness through the codification of processes and information (Tidd *et al.*, 2001). However, in new product development (and innovation in general) these processes cannot be completely automated and imply a certain degree of discretion to be exercised by the people responsible for their management.[2]

New venture creation is the least structured activity of the three examined. It entails two fundamental processes: (a) opportunity perception (or recognition); (b) resource attraction and coordination, normally through new rather than already existing patterns. These two processes are associated with the role (function) of the entrepreneur. Both processes require a high degree of proactivity rather than adaptation or reaction to environmental changes.[3] In the case of opportunity recognition, recent studies have stressed that the entrepreneur's role involves not just the ability to 'recognize' existing opportunities, as if they were objectively present in the environment waiting only for someone to grasp them. On the contrary, their recognition implies a creative way of organizing the abundant and disparate information from the environment to build new business opportunities (Baron, 2004; Ward, 2004). Thus, what is critical in new venture creation is not opportunity recognition but rather the development of opportunities. This view is effectively synthesized by Ardichvili *et al.* (2003, p. 113) according to whom: 'While elements of opportunities may be "recognized", opportunities are made, not found'.

The literature on DC has only recently begun to analyse the process of new venture creation, implying major changes in a firm's internal resources and market position (Eisenhardt and Martin, 2000; Katzy *et al.*, 2001). This literature has studied how firms have managed to implement these changes and how existing resources and capabilities facilitate or curb them. Because of the magnitude of change implied by new venture creation the role of top management has proved to be fundamental. Its success depends on the cognitive and learning processes of top management (Tripsas and Gavetti, 2000).[4] One of the limitations of this literature (in the context of our study) is that it refers to large firms. We are interested in analysing the relevance of new venture creation in SMEs and the role of entrepreneurs in this process, the subject of the next section.

2.3 New venture creation in SMEs: the role of entrepreneurs and entrepreneurial team development

The relevance of new venture creation in SMEs has been somewhat overlooked by research. It is usual to think of SMEs as organizations devoted to a specific product/market combination. Coherent with this view, the growth of SMEs is also normally associated with the expansion of activities within the same business, i.e. the accumulation of resources to enlarge production in the established business. Thus, the main obstacles to SME growth have usually been associated with the attraction of resources or the coordination of those resources as size increases.[5] Therefore, entering into new businesses in order to grow is excluded almost by definition.

However, recent empirical research has demonstrated that entering into new businesses in order to pursue growth is very important for SMEs as they often operate in sectors characterized by high market segmentation. This poses the question of how to measure the degree of diversity of the successive activities developed by an entrepreneur. Diversification is a very elusive and complex concept and it is difficult to measure it empirically.[6] Traditional measures of diversification, based on classification codes of business activities, underestimate the degree of diversity of new businesses even when they appear closely connected to the existing ones (Iacobucci and Rosa, 2005). This is due to the high segmentation of markets served by SMEs and to the increasing differentiation in the technology needed to serve them.

When SMEs enter new businesses, whatever the degree of diversification from established activities, the role of the entrepreneur is crucial. It is even more important than that of top management in larger firms. Indeed, in SMEs the entrepreneur (especially the founding entrepreneur) retains key positions in the ownership, control and direction of the firm.[7] While in the case of the first two types of change depicted in Figure 2.1 the entrepreneur can delegate management to the organization, the development of a new business is a process that directly involves him/her. Any analysis of the capabilities of SMEs to develop new business as a way of exploiting new opportunities must take into account the active role of the entrepreneur in this process.

Following a few path-breaking articles (MacMillan, 1986; Starr and Bygrave, 1991; Scott and Rosa, 1996) the most recent literature has increasingly focused on the factors explaining the abilities of entrepreneurs in extending their original businesses through the creation of new ventures. Entrepreneurs who have started more than one venture in the course of their career are generally referred to as 'habitual entrepreneurs'. Habitual entrepreneurs fall into two main categories: serial entrepreneurs and portfolio entrepreneurs. A serial entrepreneur will start more than one business, but sells the established business before creating the new one; a portfolio entrepreneur retains the original business while establishing or purchasing another one (Westhead and Wright, 1998). The entrepreneurship literature has debated at length whether habitual entrepreneurs (either serial or portfolio) have advantages over novice entrepreneurs in starting or acquiring new businesses (Birley and Westhead, 1993; Wright *et al.*, 1997; Alsos and Kolvereid, 1998; Westhead and Wright, 1998; Ucbasaran *et al.*, 2003b, 2006). Although no definitive conclusion has been reached, it is generally recognized that the most successful entrepreneurs are those that are capable of creating and developing more than one venture during their career. If the ability to recognize and exploit new business opportunities is fundamental to the success of entrepreneurs and the growth of SMEs, it would be interesting to analyse what factors influence this ability. These factors can certainly be considered as DC as they allow SMEs to capture opportunities arising from environmental changes.

The literature on habitual entrepreneurs has concentrated on the entrepreneur's learning process. The theoretical approach most often used in this literature is that of human capital. Human capital is a somewhat loose concept that encompasses the practical knowledge, acquired skills and learned abilities of an individual that make him/her potentially productive in some activities. In the case of habitual entrepreneurs, the knowledge, skills and abilities are those required for the start-up of new firms: i.e. the recognition and exploitation of new business opportunities. Strictly speaking the human capital concept is somewhat inappropriate in this context; human capital is normally thought of as the result of explicit 'investments' in education and training (hence the word capital). In the case of habitual entrepreneurs such accumulation is the involuntary result of an activity (the start-up of businesses) that has been carried out for reasons other than the accumulation of knowledge and skills. The improvement (accumulation) of entrepreneurs' human capital is the result of two distinct mechanisms: learning and experience (Iacobucci and Rosa, 2004). There is an important difference between the two mechanisms: while the learning process about how to start a business is general and for this reason should be applicable to any subsequent start-up, experience appears to be more 'localized' in terms of sectors and geographical areas.

A different justification for the presence of habitual entrepreneurs is that of individual specialization. The basic idea behind this argument is that individuals differ in their abilities and attitudes to risk; as a result some are more able (and prefer) to undertake managerial tasks while others prefer the entrepreneurial role (Alsos and Kolvereid, 1998). Economists have proposed several models of entrepreneurship based on individual specialization (Kihlstrom and Laffont, 1979; Holmes and Schmitz, 1990). Holmes and Schmitz (1990) developed a model that justifies the presence of serial entrepreneurs based on differences in individual abilities to develop business opportunities (start-ups). When entrepreneurial abilities are not evenly distributed among the population it pays for some individuals to specialize in developing new businesses and others to specialize in managing already established businesses. Those that specialize in entrepreneurial activity (entrepreneurs) will thus be involved in successive start-ups. The model assumes that each individual is endowed with an indivisible time unit in each period so that she/he has to choose whether to spend this time managing a previously established business or starting a new one. If the latter course of action is decided on, the entrepreneur must discontinue (close) or sell the previous business (i.e. the model allows for serial, but not portfolio entrepreneurs).

The Holmes and Schmitz (1990) model explicitly recognizes one of the most important resources of entrepreneurs: i.e. their time. This factor is sometimes referred to in discussions of the phenomenon (Rosa, 1998), but has been substantially overlooked by much of the literature on habitual entrepreneurship. The problem of allocating time between alternative tasks is particularly important in the case of portfolio entrepreneurs; they have to decide how to share their time between the managing of established businesses and the setting-up of new ones. The literature on habitual entrepreneurs generally does not consider this problem, assuming the time available to entrepreneurs is unlimited, or that there are no agency costs in delegating the running of established businesses to hired managers. In a previous study we hypothesized that in order to overcome this problem entrepreneurs can follow two (not necessarily alternative) paths: to delegate the management of established businesses in order to concentrate on the new ones (thus becoming a simple shareholder); and to enlarge the entrepreneurial team (Iacobucci and Rosa, 2004). By entrepreneurial team we mean a group of people who share the ownership and control of a venture (Kamm and Nurick, 1993; Watson *et al.*, 1995).

The allocation of time by entrepreneurs is critical to the development of new ventures, which involves a high degree of proactivity and cannot easily be delegated or routinized (as discussed in the previous section). It must be done by the entrepreneur him/herself or by persons with a similar entrepreneurial attitude who are trusted by the entrepreneur and who are given an entrepreneurial role, i.e. they participate in the ownership and control of the new venture, thereby enlarging the entrepreneurial team. The alternative to developing an entrepreneurial team would be to develop a managerial structure to control old and new businesses. We suggest that this is not generally possible as the exploitation of new business opportunities increasingly poses not just organizational problems – problems of specialization and coordination – but also governance problems: i.e. problems of ownership and control.[8] The need to involve other people in the ownership and control of the new venture (that is, to enlarge the entrepreneurial team) is one of the reasons why established entrepreneurs prefer to set up a new legal unit to exploit a new business opportunity, thus resulting in the formation of a business group. In fact, recent empirical evidence has demonstrated that business groups are widespread among SMEs and that the business group is the organizational form normally adopted by entrepreneurs when expanding the activities under their control (Rosa and Scott, 1999; Loiseau, 2001; Iacobucci, 2002). This motivates empirical analysis of the formation of business groups in SMEs, the results of which are discussed in the following section.

2.4 The business group as a device for new venture creation

2.4.1 Data and methods

The empirical part of this study is based on the application of qualitative techniques. The choice of qualitative methods was determined by the exploratory nature of the study and by its aims: to understand the role of entrepreneurial processes and capabilities in new venture creation in established SMEs. As is common in qualitative analysis, purposive rather than statistical sampling was used (Silverman, 2000; Bryman, 2001). The study was based on in-depth interviews with entrepreneurs who had developed manufacturing business groups (see Table 2.1). Interviewees were chosen from the population (about 100) of small- and medium-sized manufacturing groups located in the Marche region (Italy). From these we selected the cases that were most relevant to the aims of the study. The selection criteria used were: (a) the group is still controlled by the founder entrepreneur; (b) the group includes more than two manufacturing companies, providing a sufficiently rich context for analysing the development process; (c) most of the companies were new ventures rather than acquired businesses. These selection criteria identified about 15 groups. The results reported here refer to the nine groups whose entrepreneurs agreed to be interviewed (see Table 2.1).

The aim of the interviews was to collect data about the process of group formation and entrepreneurs' reasons for setting up new companies. The interviews

Table 2.1 Characteristics of the groups interviewed

Case	*Original activity*	*Main direction of expansion*	*Companies in 2003*	*Domestic production on companies**	*Overall employees*
1	Paper rolls for printers and calculators	Several segments of paper roll market Design and production of cash registers and other small electric household appliances	7	3	222
2	Batteries for motor vehicles	Several segments of the battery market Electric vehicles (scooter, cars, etc.)	9	2	154
3	Footwear soles	Several segments of footwear soles (leather and synthetic) Vertical integration in compound production for synthetic soles	3	3	293
4	Chemical treatment of metals	Printed circuits Assembly of electronic components Systems for car safety	4	2	142
5	Paper sacks (for industrial use)	Several types of paper sacks (for industrial use) and paper bags	8	3	210
6	Industrial electric systems	Industrial automation systems for household appliances, automotive and aerospace industries	3	2	205
7	Publishing	Printing industry Cartoon industry Products and services for the printing industry	7	5	216
8	Industrial automation for metal working	Complete range of activities for the design of automation systems in manufacturing plants	5	2	244
9	Printed circuits	Several types of multilayer printed circuits Other products and activities related to the main business (rapid prototyping, membrane keyboards, etc.)	6	3	223

Note
*Excluding the original company and the acquired companies.

were based on a semi-structured questionnaire. Table 2.1 presents some general characteristics of the groups interviewed.

2.4.2 Results

Data collected on large samples show that the companies belonging to business groups can be broadly divided into three categories (Iacobucci, 2002): foreign companies (when present); financial companies (holding companies, property companies, etc.); domestic production companies. Foreign-based companies are not of interest to this study given that by definition they must be managed as independent legal units, and financial companies are normally set up for fiscal or other financial advantages. For these reasons we concentrated our attention on domestic production companies. Apart from representing the main companies in terms of employees and sales, they are of interest for understanding the reasons why entrepreneurs set up new legal units rather than develop new ventures within established companies. We will use the term 'new company' (unless otherwise specified) to refer to a domestic production company.

Why did respondents set up new companies rather than manage the new activities through specialized divisions within the same company? This may depend on how we consider the relationship between diversification and business group formation. This differs according to whether we focus on the initial development of new activities (new venture creation) rather than the management of these activities at a later stage. All the interviewed entrepreneurs stressed the importance of setting up a new company for the initial development of a new business. When the business is consolidated there are other organizational forms that can be used to efficiently manage the bundle of resulting activities. Business groups are dynamic devices that are expanded or contracted by entrepreneurs depending on the development stage of the new venture. Indeed, in two of the cases examined (case 3 and case 8) after having set up a group of several companies, these entrepreneurs decided to merge most of the production companies to form a multidivisional company. This confirms that the degree of diversification of new businesses from the established ones does not capture per se the specific problems posed by the initial development of new businesses; the problems that demand entrepreneurial action.

In section 2.2 we suggested that enlargement of the entrepreneurial team in order to exploit new business opportunities might be an actor in why business groups are formed. This hypothesis is confirmed by the qualitative study. Three different patterns of this process emerged from the case studies (see Table 2.2). The first is when other established entrepreneurs are involved in the development of new ventures. This occurs in order to raise capital for the initial investment, to secure demand for the new product and, to some extent, to spread the risk.

The other two patterns are more interesting for our study as they more evidently represent the phenomenon of entrepreneurial team enlargement. Moreover, they have received little attention in the literature.

The second pattern is when the entrepreneur gives a stake in the new

Table 2.2 Production domestic companies set-up by entrepreneurs in business groups

Case no.	*Companies established by entrepreneurial team development*				*Production domestic companies (b)*	*(a)/(b) (%)*
	Joint venture with established entrepreneurs	*'Employee involvement'*	*Intrapreneurship*	*Total (a)*		
1	1	1		2	*3*	*67*
2	1			1	*2*	*50*
3		2	1	3	*3*	*100*
4	1		1	2	*2*	*100*
5					*3*	
6	1			1	*2*	*100*
7	2	2	1	5	*5*	*100*
8		1		1	*2*	*50*
9		1	1	2	*3*	*67*
Total	6	7	4	17	*25*	*68*

Notes
(a) (b) Excluding the original company and the acquired companies.

company to an employee to secure his/her involvement in the development of the new business; a process we will refer to as 'employee involvement' in which a former employee changes status to become part-owner in the new venture. The third pattern is when the new business is established as the result of an idea from an employee who subsequently is involved in the business (a phenomenon similar to 'intrapreneurship' in larger firms).

Pattern two is the most interesting, both in terms of quantitative importance (see Table 2.2) and for the aim of our study. The employee does not participate in the opportunity discovery phase, but only in the new venture development. The involvement of an existing employee in the new company responds to several, sometimes overlapping needs. The first and most important is to overcome the entrepreneur's limits in terms of developing new businesses while still controlling older ones. The respondents tended to feel that just installing a manager was not enough, as the initial development of a new venture requires special levels of motivation, interest and dedication. In the third pattern the new venture arises from the activities of an 'intrapreneurial' employee. In this pattern, the former employee actively participates in the new business from the opportunity discovery phase. In this case the dominant entrepreneur plays a supporting role (in terms of financial resources, market credibility, network relationships, etc.) in the development of the new business.

Whatever the nature of the associated entrepreneur – established entrepreneurs or former employees – the development of an entrepreneurial team to exploit new business opportunities is one of the most important aspects associated with the setting up of a business group in SMEs. When the enlargement of the entrepreneurial team involves a former employee, two different abilities are exploited by the established entrepreneur. In the first pattern (employee upgrading) the entrepreneur uses his/her capability to recognize and enhance the entrepreneurial attitudes of the employee to manage the new venture creation phase. In the second pattern (intrapreneurship) the capability needed is to accommodate the intrapreneur's project within the group. In both cases a resource-dependence view is implicit, as the enlargement of the entrepreneurial team is aimed at filling gaps in the human capital needed to pursue the exploitation and development of new ventures (Kamm and Nurick, 1993; Larson and Starr, 1993; Ucbasaran *et al.*, 2003a). At the same time, the choice of a former employee seems to indicate the importance of relational trust and personal similarity in the formation of the entrepreneurial team (Forbes *et al.*, 2006; Zahra *et al.*, 2006). The length of the employee relationship allows the entrepreneur to evaluate the competences and entrepreneurial attitude of employee and develop the trust relationship needed for him/her to become part of the entrepreneurial team.[9]

In both cases the setting up of new companies, and the involvement of other people in the entrepreneurial team, is especially vital during the new venture creation phase. Once the ventures have been developed, rationalization of managing existing activities takes over.

2.5 Conclusions

This chapter aimed to identify the capabilities that allow SMEs to exploit new business opportunities as a way to innovate and grow and discusses the role of entrepreneurs in managing these processes. We hypothesized that the capability to enlarge the entrepreneurial team by manipulating the ownership and control structure of new ventures, is important for entrepreneurs to pursue growth and innovation. We have developed a first analysis of this capability based on a qualitative study of a small sample of entrepreneurs who built groups of firms. We suggest that the development of a business group is one of the mechanisms adopted by entrepreneurs to overcome the problems associated with new venture development.

Recent empirical investigations into groups of SMEs show that the setting up of new companies by established entrepreneurs (resulting in the formation of a business group) is associated with the need to diversify established activities. Using conventional measures, the degree of diversification between the new and the established businesses is small. Moreover, these measures (based on classification of economic activities) undervalue the degree of diversity in technology and marketing when entering different segments of the same sector or when exploiting technology or market synergies in related sectors. We also suggest that the recent literature on growth and innovation in SMEs undervalues the role of new venture creation and the problems it involves. The process implies not only the recognition by entrepreneurs of market opportunities, but also their continuous and proactive role in structuring the new business and attracting and coordinating new resources in order to develop it. Established entrepreneurs should have the advantage over novices in pursuing new business opportunities because of the human capital they have accumulated in new venture creation (based on learning and experience). However, they face problems in relation to allocating time and attention between the established and the new businesses. This time allocation problem is highlighted by the model of entrepreneurial specialization, which hypothesizes that entrepreneurs dismiss (close or sell) the established business before starting a new one (serial entrepreneurship). However, this behaviour is not common in practice. Entrepreneurs tend to retain ownership and control of established businesses while developing new ones. One way of overcoming the time allocation problem is to enlarge the entrepreneurial team by involving other people in the ownership and control of the new business. This is even more necessary when the new venture presents a high degree of diversity with the established business(es) because the founder entrepreneur might lack some of the specific knowledge and cognitive models needed for the new activities.

The empirical evidence from in-depth case studies of medium-sized business groups shows that in most cases the entrepreneurs involved in the development of new ventures were former employees of the founder entrepreneur. Two different patterns emerged from the case studies: 'employee involvement' and 'intrapreneurship'. In the first case the established entrepreneur boosts the employee's capabilities to enhance his/her capacity to create a new venture. Entrepreneurial attitudes in employees are identified and exploited to enlarge the entrepreneurial team. The recognition of initial opportunities underlying the new venture remains the responsibility of the established entrepreneur. In the case of intrapreneurship, the entrepreneur is able to accommodate employees who want to develop their own business ideas. We suggest that the ability to enlarge the entrepreneurial team by manipulating the ownership and control structure of new ventures is an important capability of entrepreneurs for exploiting new business opportunities, thus fostering growth and innovation in established firms. The preference accorded to former employees demonstrates the importance of trust relationships in team development, although the enlargement of the team is a choice that is mainly justified by the need to overcome the founder entrepreneur's lack of time and competences.

This study is exploratory in nature and suggests several issues that need further development at both a theoretical and empirical level. At a theoretical level one of the main issues is related to the specific nature of the entrepreneurial activity needed in the early phases of new venture development. On the positive side this should help to clarify the reasons for entrepreneurial team enlargement; on the normative side it will suggest some criteria for the identification and selection of new members. A second issue is whether the development of a business group is an efficient solution to the problem of new venture exploitation or whether there are other, perhaps more efficient, organizational answers. First, it would be useful to analyse why entrepreneurs prefer 'business groups' to alternative organizational structures. Second, it would be useful to assess the factors on which the capability to enlarge the entrepreneurial team depend. Specifically it would be interesting to assess the roles played by the entrepreneur's personal attributes, and such structural variables as the sector of activity, the size of the organization, etc.

From an empirical point of view it would be interesting to analyse to what extent the performance of groups (in terms of growth and innovation) depends on the ability of the entrepreneur to enlarge the entrepreneurial team.

Notes

1 See the review on antecedents and definitions of DC by Marangoni and Solari (2007).

2 The DC literature has analysed at length the processes of new product development (Helfat and Raubitschek, 2000; Finkle and Deeds, 2001; Verona and Ravasi, 2003).

3 Proactivity is stressed by the Knightian and Shumpeterian view of entrepreneurship. The Austrian view considers business opportunities as performed objectively in the environment and stresses the role of opportunity recognition by entrepreneurs (Kirzner, 1985). The importance of proactivity in entrepreneurship behaviour is emphasized by the theory of 'effectuation' (Sarasvathy, 2001, 2003).

4 There is a close link between this literature and the vast amount of literature on corporate entrepreneurship (Burgelman, 1983; Burgelman and Sayles, 1986; Zahra *et al.*, 1999a, 1999b).

5 There is an abundant literature on the finance gap (see the *Journal of Banking and Finance* special issue on the Economics of Small Business Finance, vol. 22, nos 6–8

and *Economic Journal* special issue, vol. 112, no. 477) and on the organizational problems associated with growth (Greiner, 1974; Churchill and Lewis, 1983).

6 There are extensive reviews of the literature on diversification and its relationship with firms' performance (Ramanujam and Varadarajan, 1989; Montgomery, 1994; Sambharya, 2000). Unfortunately, almost all of this literature refers to large firms.

7 Firm founders also play a significant role in establishing beliefs and cognitive models that strongly influence the subsequent development path of firms (Baron *et al.*, 1999; Tripsas and Gavetti, 2000; Baron, 2004). We do not consider cognitive aspects in this study, but focus on the availability of time and competences of founding entrepreneurs.

8 Recent literature demonstrates that this is an increasing problem, not only in SMEs, but also in large firms, as a result of the increasing role of human capital and other intangible factors as opposed to physical capital (Rajan and Zingales, 2000; Zingales, 2000).

9 It is interesting to note that in no case were new companies set up to involve members of the entrepreneur's family. This suggests that the resource-seeking aspect is pre-eminent, transcending interpersonal trust and attraction.

References

Alsos, G. A. and L. Kolvereid. (1998), 'The business gestation process of novice, serial and parallel business founders', *Entrepreneurship Theory and Practice*, 22 (4), 101–114.

Ardichvili, A., R. Cardozo and S. Ray. (2003), 'A theory of entrepreneurial opportunity identification and development', *Journal of Business Venturing*, 18 (1), 105–123.

Baron, J. N., M. T. Hannan and M. D. Burton. (1999), 'Building the iron cage: determinants of managerial intensity in the early years of organizations', *American Sociological Review*, 64 (4), 527–547.

Baron, R. A. (2004), 'The cognitive perspective: a valuable tool for answering entrepreneurship's basic "why" questions', *Journal Of Business Venturing*, 19 (2), 221–239.

Birley, S. and P. Westhead. (1993), 'A comparison of new businesses established by `novice' and `habitual' founders in Great Britain', *International Small Business Journal*, 12 (1), 38.

Brusco, S. (1982), 'The Emilian Model: productive decentralization and social integration', *Cambridge Journal of Economics*, 6, 167–184.

Bryman, A. (2001), *Social Research Methods*, Oxford: Oxford University Press.

Burgelman, R. A. (1983), 'A process model of internal corporate venturing in the diversified major firm', *Administrative Science Quarterly*, 28, 223–244.

Burgelman, R. A. and L. R. Sayles. (1986), *Inside Corporate Innovation: Strategy, Structure, and Managerial Skills*, New York: Free Press.

Cainelli, G. and N. De Liso (2004), 'Can a marshallian industrial district be innovative? The case of Italy'. In G. Cainelli and R. Zoboli (eds), *The Evolution of Industrial Districts. Changing Governance, Innovation and Internationalization of Local Capitalism in Italy*, Heidelberg: Physica-Verlag, pp. 243–256.

Churchill, N. and V. Lewis. (1983), 'The five stages of small firm growth', *Harvard Business Review* (May–June), 30–50.

Dosi, G., R. R. Nelson and S. G. Winter. (2000), *The Nature and Dynamics of Organizational Capabilities*, New York: Oxford University Press.

Eisenhardt, K. M. and J. A. Martin. (2000), 'Dynamic Capabilities: What Are They?', *Strategic Management Journal*, 21 (10/11), 1105–1122.

Finkle, T. A. and D. Deeds. (2001), 'Trends in the market for entrepreneurship faculty, 1989–1998', *Journal of Business Venturing*, 16, 613–630.

Forbes, D. P., P. S. Borchert, M. E. Zellmer-Bruhn and H. J. Sapienza. (2006), 'Entrepreneurial team formation: an exploration of new member addition', *Entrepreneurship Theory and* Practice, 30 (2), 225–248.

Greiner, L. (1974), 'Evolution and revolution as organizations grow', *Harvard Business Review* (July–August), 37–46.

Helfat, C. E. (2000), 'The evolution of firm capabilities', *Strategic Management Journal*, 21 (10/11), 955–960.

Helfat, C. E. and R. S. Raubitschek. (2000), 'Product sequencing: co-evolution of knowledge, capabilities and products', *Strategic Management Journal*, 21 (10/11), 961–980.

Holmes, T. J. and J. A. Schmitz. (1990), 'A theory of entrepreneurship and its application to the study of business transfer', *Journal of Political Economy*, 98 (2), 265–294.

Iacobucci, D. (2002), 'Explaining business groups started by habitual entrepreneurs in the Italian manufacturing sector', *Entrepreneurship and Regional Development*, 14 (1), 31–48.

Iacobucci, D. and P. Rosa. (2004). 'Habitual entrepreneurs, entrepreneurial team development and business group formation'. Paper presented at the RENT XVIII, Copenhagen.

Iacobucci, D. and P. Rosa. (2005), 'Growth, diversification and business group formation in entrepreneurial firms', *Small Business Economics*, 25 (1), 65–82.

Kamm, J. B. and A. J. Nurick. (1993), 'The stages of team venture formation: a decision-making model', *Entrepreneurship Theory and Practice*, 17 (2), 17.

Katzy, B., M. Dissel and F. Blindow. (2001), 'Dynamic capabilities for entrepreneurial venturing – the Siemens ICE case'. Paper presented at the Management of technology, Lausanne, Switzerland, March.

Kihlstrom, R. E. and J.-J. Laffont. (1979), 'A general equilibrium entrepreneurial theory of firm formation based on risk aversion', *Journal of Political Economy*, 87 (4), 719–748.

Kirzner, I. M. (1985), *Discovery and the Capitalist Process*, Chicago, IL: University of Chicago Press.

Larson, A. and J. Starr. (1993), 'A network model of organization formation', *Entrepreneurship Theory and Practice*, 17 (2), 5–15.

Leoncini, R., S. Montresor and G. Vertova. (2006), 'Dynamic capabilities between firm organization and local development: a critical survey', *Economia Politica*, 23 (3), 475–502.

Loiseau, H. (2001), *Des groupes de la taille d'une PME. Un phenomen en plein essor*. Paris: INSEE.

Lorenzoni, G. and A. Lipparini. (1999), 'The leveraging of interfirm relationships as a distinctive organizational capability: a longitudinal study', *Strategic Management Journal*, 20, 317–338.

MacMillan, I. (1986), 'To really learn about entrepreneurship, let us study habitual entrepreneurs', *Journal of Business Venturing*, 1, 241–243.

Marangoni G. and Solari S. (2007), 'Group dynamics and growth strategies'. In R. Leoncini and S. Montresor (eds), *Dynamic Capabilities Between Firm Organization and Local Systems of Production*, London: Routledge, pp. 91–106.

Masini, A., L. N. Van Wassenhove and M. Zollo. (2003), 'The impact of IT adoption on the genesis and dynamic capabilities'. Paper presented at 'I PRIN Workshop "Capabilities dinamiche tra organizzazione d'impresa e sistemi locali di produzione"', Bologna.

Montgomery, C. A. (1994), 'Corporate diversification', *Journal of Economic Perspectives*, 8 (3), 163.

Nelson, R. and S. Winter. (1982), *An Evolutionary Theory of Economic Change*, Cambridge, MA: Harvard University Press.

Rajan, R. G. and L. Zingales. (2000), 'The governance of the new enterprise', NBER Working Paper 7958.

Ramanujam, V. and P. Varadarajan. (1989), 'Research on corporate diversification: a synthesis', *Strategic Management Journal*, 10, 523–551.

Rosa, P. (1998), 'Entrepreneurial processes of business cluster formation and growth by 'habitual' entrepreneurs', *Entrepreneurship Theory and Practice*, 22 (4), 43–62.

Rosa, P. and M. Scott. (1999), 'The prevalence of multiple owners and directors in the SME sector: implications for our understanding of start-up and growth', *Entrepreneurship and Regional Development*, 11 (1), 21–38.

Sambharya, R. B. (2000), 'Assessing the construct validity of strategic and SIC-based measures of corporate diversification', *British Journal of Management*, 11 (2), 163–174.

Sarasvathy, S. D. (2001), 'Causation and effectuation: toward a theoretical shift from economic inevitability to entrepreneurial contingency', *Academy of Management Review*, 26 (2), 243–263.

Sarasvathy, S. D. (2003), 'Entrepreneurship as a science of the artificial', *Journal of Economic Psychology*, 24 (2), 203–220.

Scott, M. and P. Rosa. (1996), 'Has firm level analysis reached its limits? Time for a rethink', *International Small Business Journal*, 14 (4), 81–89.

Silverman, D. (2000), *Doing Qualitative Research. A Practical Handbook*, London: SAGE Publications.

Starr, J. and W. Bygrave (1991), 'The assets and liabilities of prior start-up experience: an exploratory study of multiple venture entrepreneurs'. In N. C. Churchill, W. D. Bygrave, J. G. Covin, D. L. Sexton, D. P. Slevin, K. H. Vesper and W. E. Wetzel (eds), *Frontiers of Entrepreneurship Research* Wellesley, MA: Babson College, pp. 213–227.

Storey, D. J. (1994), *Understanding the Small Business Sector*, London and New York: Routledge.

Storper, M. J. and B. Harrison. (1991), 'Flexibility, hierarchy and regional development: the changing structure of industrial production systems and their forms of governance in the 1990s', *Research Policy*, 20, 407–422.

Teece, D. J., G. Pisano and A. Shuen. (1997), 'Dynamic capabilities and strategic management', *Strategic Management Journal*, 18 (7), 509–533.

Tidd, J., J. R. Bessant and K. Pavitt. (2001), *Managing Innovation: Integrating Technological, Market and Organizational Change* (2nd edn), Chichester, UK and New York: John Wiley.

Tripsas, M. and G. Gavetti. (2000), 'Capabilities, cognition, and inertia: evidence from digital imaging', *Strategic Management Journal*, 21 (10–11), 1147–1161.

Ucbasaran, D., A. Lockett, M. Wright and P. Westhead. (2003a), 'Entrepreneurial founder teams: factors associated with member entry and exit', *Entrepreneurship Theory and Practice*, 28 (2), 107–128.

Ucbasaran, D., P. Westhead and M. Wright. (2006), *Habitual Entrepreneurs*, Cheltenham, UK: Edward Elgar.

Ucbasaran, D., M. Wright and P. Westhead. (2003b), 'A longitudinal study of habitual entrepreneurs: starters and acquirers', *Entrepreneurship and Regional Development*, 15 (3), 207–228.

Verona, G. and D. Ravasi. (2003), 'Unbundling dynamic capabilities: an exploratory study of continuous product innovation', *Industrial and Corporate Change*, 12 (3), 577–606.

Ward, T. B. (2004), 'Cognition, creativity, and entrepreneurship', *Journal of Business Venturing*, 19 (2), 173–188.

Watson, W. E., L. D. Ponthieu and J. W. Critelli. (1995), 'Team interpersonal process effectiveness in venture partnerships and its connection to perceived success', *Journal of Business Venturing*, 10 (5), 393.

Westhead, P. and M. Wright. (1998), 'Novice, portfolio, and serial founders: Are they different?', *Journal of Business Venturing*, 13 (3), 173–204.

Wright, M., K. Robbie and C. Ennew. (1997), 'Venture capitalists and serial entrepreneurs', *Journal of Business Venturing*, 12 (3), 227–249.

Zahra, S. A., D. F. Jennings and D. F. Kuratko. (1999a), 'The antecedents and consequences of firm-level entrepreneurship: the state of the field', *Entrepreneurship Theory and Practice*, 24 (2), 45–66.

Zahra, S. A., D. F. Kuratko and D. F. Jennings. (1999b), 'Entrepreneurship and the acquisition of dynamic organizational capabilities', *Entrepreneurship Theory and Practice*, 23 (3), 5–10.

Zahra, S. A., R. I. Yavuz and D. Ucbasaran. (2006), 'How Much Do You Trust Me? The Dark Side of Relational Trust in New Business Creation in Established Companies', *Entrepreneurship Theory and Practice*, Vol. 30, 541–559.

Zingales, L. (2000), 'In search of new foundations', *The Journal of Finance*, 55 (4), 1623–1653.

3 Group dynamics and growth strategies[1]

GianDemetrio Marangoni and Stefano Solari

3.1 Dynamic capabilities and business groups

The object of this study is to analyse the particular evolutionary pattern of growth of many small- and medium-sized enterprises (SMEs) towards the formation of business groups.[2] Such organisational forms are rapidly spreading in many areas characterised by high concentrations of SMEs.[3] Most of the literature on business groups focuses on their role in the economic growth of emerging economies and their coordinating function as an alternative to both state and market (Khanna, 2000). Here, instead, the aim is to read this process through the lens of the dynamic capabilities approach and to relate it to the specific economic and social context. The particular relationship between inter-organisational links and the growth of SME business groups will be explored using a contingency analysis applied to data extracted from formal groups of northeastern Italy.

The departure point concerns the growth strategy of SMEs. The capability approach may provide answers relevant to why many SMEs prefer to grow by multiplying production units instead of becoming large organisations. However, the literature on capabilities has focused mainly on large companies.[4] Concepts such as *organisational routines* and *dynamic capabilities* are difficult to apply to small production units managed personally by entrepreneurs. In fact, in such firms organisation is minimal and owners control all the firm's activities directly. As a consequence, the capability approach has to be re-interpreted in order to apply it to organisational change occurring when SMEs grow.

The capability approach assumes that the division of labour encourages the development of differentiated knowledge and skills, which must be coordinated (Loasby, 1998). Sometimes the best way to organise such capabilities is neither the market nor hierarchy. Mathews (2002, 2003) has focused attention on capabilities of externally oriented firms. In fact, SMEs rely greatly on external relationships for acquisition of the knowledge resources they need. In this case, the capabilities of firms may take the form of the aptitude to relate to and coordinate partners' competences to increase the joint ability to create value. That is to say, *specific capabilities* are best produced in specialised firms and *relational capabilities* may help coordinate such knowledge to produce further advantages for a set of business enterprises. From this perspective, groups may be understood as an organisational form oriented to manage a variety of competences best elaborated in small business units.

Another issue to be considered is the persistence of the entrepreneur, and of the family firm also, within business groups. Langlois (1998), by referring to Schumpeter and Knight, has explained the reason why *charismatic entrepreneurs* may still be relevant to present-day capitalism. In his continuous attempt to bridge the capability and transaction cost theories, he has introduced the concept of *dynamic transaction costs* (costs of coordinating a major recombination of economic capabilities). He argues that in a situation of high *dynamic transaction costs*, personal authority and leadership may be convenient and the holder of the residual rights of control is best empowered to redirect the cooperating parties.

Our point of view is different and focuses on the accumulation of specific kinds of core competences of firms. We maintain that the patterns of growth of SMEs reflect the organisational form with which entrepreneurs are confident and are driven by entrepreneurs' unwillingness to change structures which have provided success in the past.[5] The success achieved by personally recombining capabilities in small firms may encourage entrepreneurs to avoid delegation of management and consequent loss of control. In the case of business groups, *charismatic entrepreneurs* may apply their managing capabilities at a higher level in coordinating the business group where single units are relatively small and transparent.

As a consequence, when SMEs grow, the organisational form is best defined as the result of incremental steps producing a path-dependent process where the crucial variable is *institutional confidence*.[6] Entrepreneurs tend to reproduce the conditions of their success and to expand structures maintaining the form they are used to. In fact, SMEs are often organised according to paternalistic patterns and the entrepreneur manages the firm personally. The growth of the firm does not necessarily mean a loss of control, even if it does necessarily imply the need to delegate some powers to managers.[7]

Below, we will first describe the context of newly industrialised areas and the logic of paternalistic organisations. Then the problem of dynamic capabilities will be discussed in relation to SMEs, showing the rationale for group formation. Finally, we will propose our interpretation and show the results of the empirical inquiry.

3.2 The resurgence of *classical capitalism*

The study of systems of SMEs has been mainly oriented to industrial districts as the typical example of external economies. However, external economies are not limited to such areas. They are, in general, associated with recently industrialised areas based on a strong concentration of small activities (not necessarily enjoying a strict business correlation).

Such developments arose in many industrialised countries after the so-called *second industrial divide* (Piore and Sabel, 1984). This was the case of the *Third*

Italy described in 1982 by Bagnasco and in particular the northeast region which represented an example of *flexible specialisation.*

The peculiarity of this form of development is that it has constituted a kind of *resurgence* of *classical capitalism*. In fact, it was based on the rise of many new entrepreneurs, mainly investing their own resources without recourse to financial markets.[8] Such an economic process can be interpreted as *Schumpeterian Mark I*[9] economic dynamics characterised by high technological opportunities, high entry rates and innovation. It resulted in an elevated social mobility leading to a new emerging middle class of entrepreneurs, but it never developed a solid techno-structure.

Seen through the lens of Chandler (1962, 1977, 1990) or Lazonick (1991, 2002), this resurgence of classical capitalism may paradoxically be interpreted as regressive. In fact, such small firms are able neither to exploit economies of scale nor invest in new knowledge to produce major innovations. However, the formation of small business groups is a structural development occurring in that context, which can be explained using the theoretical tools of the resource-based approach and the notion of *organisational capability* of Chandler (1992). In fact, the accumulation of quite specific organisational capabilities may be understood as being at the roots of a distinctive development pattern.

From an institutional point of view, areas such as the northeast of Italy are characterised by a paternalistic culture. As a consequence paternalism also permeates the organisation and governance of firms, and gives rise to a concentration of decision-making and responsibility. The entrepreneur controls every single aspect of the firm's activity thanks to a very short hierarchy. There are no predetermined positions, roles, or incentives; they are strictly personally assigned by the entrepreneur, whose informal, discretionary and benevolent allocation of rewards demands, in exchange, responsibility, commitment, flexibility and active participation.

Employees are expected to pursue the success of the firm as if it were their own. The company is seen as a large family and there are strong non-economic ties between the entrepreneur and his employees. As a consequence, the labour contract is based on and regulated by moral obligations in the style of communitarian culture. On the other hand, what is good for the firm is felt to be good for the whole employee body.[10]

This kind of relationship, which may appear outdated,[11] characterises most SMEs in the northeast of Italy, even if the degree of legitimisation of such a style among the population varies from place to place.[12] Such an organisational style works well and is capable of obtaining good performance from labour when firms are small and embedded in the appropriate social institutions. The personal qualities of the entrepreneur plays a central role and the development of the firm depends mainly on his or her competences and ability to motivate labour. Such a charismatic figure may, as Langlois (1998) stated, obtain particular success in times of rapid change when business intuition serves to develop new trajectories.[13]

Problems emerge when the enterprise achieves success and grows in size. The competences of the entrepreneur often do not allow direct management of a large organisation.[14] A problem of information processing arises, disconnecting doers from decision-makers, which requires a more sophisticated form of organisation. Consequently, the organisation of a growing firm requires delegation of responsibility, specialisation of roles and formal coordination and control. The personal nature of the company exposes it to many dangers as suggested by Schulze *et al.* (2001).[15] Personal ties are often at odds with efficient organisation. Nonetheless, as firms become larger, the delegation of decision-making is inevitable and managers increase in importance relative to owners. However, in family firms managers tend to be judged according to the extent to which they achieve owners' interests (including extra business) rather than by simple market performance. They therefore tend to develop a *fidelity to the master* which distorts management decisions made on purely economic grounds.[16]

The problems experienced by many growing firms today are somewhat similar to those which led to the development of financial capitalism at the beginning of the twentieth century in most industrialised countries. Obviously, the external conditions and the whole context of the problem are different. In particular, the critical issue is not achievement of economies of scale in an early phase of industrialisation. The economic challenges mostly relate to the openness of the economy and to the instability of demand due to rapidly evolving global competition. This is a crucial point in the pattern of development of an industrial system which demands different solutions depending on many factors. The direction taken by growing firms today appears quite different from those at the beginning of the twentieth century. Only a few companies have chosen to be quoted on the stock exchange and, above all, to develop a new class of independent managers. Most of the growing firms have preferred to form business groups.[17] This means that they have chosen to keep several manageable units connected by proprietary ties, hence the basic paternalistic structure is reproduced and multiplied.

3.3 Dynamic capabilities in SMEs

The theory of dynamic capabilities has been conceived in the context of large concerns, where the managerial activity is embedded and finds expression in a structure of routines. The concept loses most of its significance when firms are small, that is to say, when organisation is minimal or it is centred on the entrepreneur. However, environments characterised by small dynamic firms, such as those forming *Schumpeterian Mark I* patterns of development, are not at odds with the concept of capability and with the problem of acquiring and structuring new knowledge. The entrepreneur's organisational capabilities are the fundamental element of success. In this case, external relations are the primary expression of the ability to organise and coordinate knowledge.[18] The ability to mobilise and coordinate suppliers, clients, consultants, financing partners, etc. is the basic source of competitiveness. It is often acquired collectively and the competitiveness of a firm depends mainly on its ability to exploit various kinds of externalities. This outward orientation in the capability theory of the firm was first proposed by Mathews (2001, 2002, 2003). He argued that "capabilities are derivable from the way firms choose and activate their resources, through their development of routines and through their choice of linkages with other firms" (Mathews, 2001: 87).

In a dynamic environment characterised by positive externalities, the most convenient form of organisation may be the network form, which is often informal but may also assume a formal status. In this way, small business units may attain a consistent *resource leverage* (Prahalad and Hamel, 1990) allowing them to achieve results not proportionate to their size. The dynamic aspect of this organisational form is due to the possibility of rapid reconnection of the different resources of the single business units. In fact, as expressed by Mathews (2001), firms may share resources, activities, or even routines.

Teece and Pisano (1994, p. 545) defined the firm's position as "its location at any point of time with respect to its business assets". These include technological assets, complementary assets, financial assets and location assets. To this list, we add *relational assets* allowing exploitation of external resources, that is to say, relevant and relatively stable business connections and information channels defining the firm's position in the production system. These determine development paths because "the firm's resources set limits to what the company can do" (Mathews, 2002, p. 32).

The firm's strategy is supported and limited by existing resources. Consequently, the firm's change in resources, routines and relations tend to follow path-dependent processes of development. The key factors guiding such processes are the elements included in the core competences.

Dynamic capabilities are defined as the ability to direct such a process of resource accumulation by means of an adaptation of the organisational configuration. Our thesis is that, in such an environment, the change in external linkages and relational assets is equivalent to the re-configuration of internal routines in larger concerns. Consequently, for SMEs where internal organisation is fairly simple, most of the dynamic capabilities are concerned with the ability to modify external relationships in order to attain and exploit useful resources to best advantage.

3.4 Business groups: structure without bureaucracy

The process of dynamic reconfiguration of internal routines is often considered as a precondition to changes in external connections. However, in particular situations, growing firms may keep their internal organisation relatively unchanged, adapting to the new context mainly by varying their *external routines*. Such may be the case when entrepreneurs, facing growth of their firm, prefer to multiply the number of directly manageable units, inter-connecting them in a group. Thus, the basic organisational form is not modified to fit the increasing size of the firm; on the contrary, the basic organisational pattern is replicated both in the individual units and in the general management of the group of business units. We assume that faith in the effectiveness of personal management and paternalistic organisation is the driving force in such a form of development.

Industrial organisation clearly changes when single units form a group, which is a specific organisational form characterised by a higher degree of coordination than the market. Such business groups may be formal or informal. Informal groups are very common. When the firm grows, it may have an incentive to outsource or subcontract some specific activities, which are not conveniently coordinated internally. The reason is that the costs of greater organisation exceed the benefits. Frequently, certain specific activities do not reach saturation or are not strategic in the long run. In general, use of small contractors improves efficiency: they are easier to coordinate, management costs are reduced, and the prices for their services are more easily curbed. This arises when resources owned and coordinated by subcontractors are not strategic and therefore simple contractual arrangements are sufficient to connect the main firm with its partners (often suppliers). Another example of grouping without property linkages is the business association oriented towards development of specific resources.

When some strategic resources are implied, proprietary connections between firms become more frequent. Monteverde and Teece (1982) considered the case of vertical quasi-integration, when firms hold the property of strategic assets, even if they are used by subcontractors. More frequently, groups[19] may be constituted along the value chain to form some vertically integrated organisations (Blois, 1972)[20] or they may grow horizontally by the exploitation of capabilities in different markets. In fact, many growing companies, unwilling to achieve a single complex organisation, may prefer to place the management of a specific strategic resource in a subsidiary to make it responsible for exploitation of particular assets without losing its control. Production is modularised according to the opportunities that the specific productive resources may enjoy as a single business. Once productive resources are separated, they can be exploited in a more strategic way in a higher number of markets. They continue to be recombined in the main business line but, at the same time, there may be differentiated opportunities for exploitation. When a firm grows by diversification and co-specialisation of assets (Teece, 1992), often the management of some of the complementary assets may be difficult to achieve and it may be dangerous to leave their management to different people. Therefore, personal responsibility for each unit and proprietary control of the strategic assets, in accordance with the model of paternalistic management, can be highly effective. Such a process of diversification, co-specialisation, fragmentation and reconnection becomes a way of deploying dynamic capabilities in a paternalistic environment.

A further point, worth considering, is the extent to which the attempt of owners to keep control of their firms, if growing through group-formation, may be penalising economic performance – the alternative being expansion of property and establishment of independent management, with a more sophisticated organisation design (as most economists demand). Therefore, the question is whether or not this form of development is leading the industrial system into a *cul de sac*.

3.5 The inquiry: the *charismatic* entrepreneur

In order to find some evidence on the insights of our theoretical approach and obtain further answers to the question about how industrial organisation is currently changing, we conducted an investigation into the formal business groups in the most industrialised provinces of northeastern Italy.[21] We considered all industrial companies presenting a consolidated balance sheet in 2002 and 2003. As far as the year 2002 is concerned, only companies holding formal control (51 per cent of voting rights) wrote a consolidated balance. In 2003 the law extended such duty to all companies exercising de facto control over other firms. Out of this population of more than 300 companies[22] we selected industrial companies announcing less than €50 million sales. We excluded explicit financial holdings and building societies. A questionnaire was submitted to all the 105 remaining companies, but only 55 agreed to answer our questions (Table 3.1).[23]

Controlling companies have, on average, 219 employees and an average turnover of €43 million. Complete groups average 555 employees and €101 million turnover.

The trend towards group formation is confirmed by the fact that the majority of them were formed after 1990 and 20 per cent of them in the last four years.

The first question concerned the overall structure of the group (Table 3.2). 29.1 per cent of companies declare their group to be mainly vertically integrated along the value chain. In this case, the group is a more flexible alternative to a large firm. The majority of groups (58.2 per cent), however, have no direct serial connections and have been created to horizontally exploit certain competences in differentiated markets. A further 12.7 per cent of controlling companies (six firms) declare no direct productive or commercial relationships between the

Table 3.1 Sample

Industry	*Sample*	*Answers*	*Answers (%)*	*Weight sample (%)*	*Weight answers (%)*
Food and beverages	7	4	57	6.7	7.3
Textiles, clothes, and shoes	16	8	50	15.2	14.5
Glass, ceramics	9	5	56	8.6	9.1
Metal and mechanics	13	9	69	12.4	16.4
Machinery	29	15	52	27.6	27.3
Plastics	8	5	63	7.6	9.1
Sports and toys	6	1	17	5.7	1.8
Electronic appliances	4	2	50	3.8	3.6
Paper	3	2	67	2.9	3.6
Furniture	6	3	50	5.7	5.5
Transport	1	0	0	1.0	0.0
Chemicals	3	1	33	2.9	1.8
Total	105	55	52	100	100

Table 3.2 Reasons for group formation

	%
Expanding commercial opportunities	67.3
Ease of managing small organisations	45.5
Optimisation of financial resources	34.5
Technological development opportunities	29.1
Diversification and reduction of risk	21.8
Access to costly resources	10.9
Family patrimonial issues	3.6

group's firms. Such groups of firms represent simple assets for the organisation which owns them and, indirectly, for a single family, but without there being a formal financial holding company.[24]

Eighty per cent of companies belong to a single family and 81.8 per cent of all groups are managed by one or few owner-entrepreneurs. Only 18.2 per cent of such groups are managed by independent managers. Moreover, 72.7 per cent of companies affirm that the personal ability of the entrepreneur explains the firm's growth better than the particular design of its organisation. As a consequence, we have a clear picture of a new generation of *family capitalism*, where companies based on a technostructure tend to remain a small minority.

Companies indicate their financial soundness as the most important factor permitting growth. Technology and commercial capabilities are important for 45.5 per cent of groups. External economies, understood as relational capabilities allowing exploitation of suppliers' resources, are perceived to be important by only 27.3 per cent of companies.

The establishment of the group was the result of the association of independent firms in 9.1 per cent of cases only. 52.7 per cent of groups were developed via the creation of new firms by the controlling company and in 47.3 per cent of cases by the acquisition of other existing companies. Finally, 29.1 per cent of firms answer that the group is due to some fragmentation of previously integrated activities.

The main motivations for constituting a group (Table 3.2) are the expansion of commercial opportunities (67.3 per cent) and the effectiveness of management of smaller business units (45.5 per cent). This confirms our hypothesis about the motivations of group formation. However, the optimisation of financial resources was also indicated as a relevant source of motivation (34.5 per cent), especially by owner-managers. This source of motivation was more frequently chosen than the (similar) "diversification of risk" (21.8 per cent). The improvement of technological development opportunities was highlighted by 29.1 per cent of firms only. More abstract options such as "access to costly resources" were chosen by a very small number of firms (10.9 per cent).

In general, firms within groups are specialised according to technical and production principles (85.5 per cent) but segmentation in response to markets is also relevant (47.3 per cent). Although organised in a diversified group, a significant number of companies claim to maintain relevant business relations with other firms. Trading agreements are the most frequent form of relationship (38.2 per cent). Associations of firms oriented to specific types of business are relevant to 23.6 per cent of companies while 21.8 per cent use other informal agreements with suppliers or clients. The result of common R&D initiatives and combined exploitation of patents is somewhat disappointing (10.9 per cent) – but is not unexpected. Innovation and technological development are perceived either as strategic – to be managed inside groups – or not important, according to the category of firms. Only 10.9 per cent of companies claim an absence of ICT in business interaction. However, 60 per cent use ICT only inside the group.

Finally, despite the current economic crisis, only 18.2 per cent of companies declare a reduced turnover in the last three years (2001–2004). 30.9 per cent declare a robust rise in sales.

The picture provided by these simple statistics confirms, in general, the idea of a *new classic capitalism* with entrepreneurs managing their own companies. Entrepreneurial experience and preferences for ease of management tend to remain the main criteria for firms' development. The perspective revealed appears dominated by a view of the firm as the entrepreneur's personal asset rather than as a complex organisation. The multiplication of business units is not due to sophisticated economic calculation. The valorisation of resources and capabilities is obtained, as expected, by proliferating manageable business units and not by the articulation of a complex dynamic organisation. Commercial success and achievement of sound trading results remains the major challenge for this kind of company and most group strategy is determined by this. However, the analysis of differences among these firms and of diverging patterns of change is important as a means of identifying the effective trends in the evolution of industrial organisation.

3.6 Dynamic capabilities in the second generation of family capitalism

The results of the investigation provide a rather homogeneous set of answers independent of the characteristics of firms and the forms of groups. However, we have singled out some asymmetries between the variables using a set of contingency tables which may help to detect some further features of business groups.[25] In Tables 3.3–3.7 we report some of the statistically relevant results; we also include some non-statistically relevant results when absolute frequencies (cases) offer interesting information. Tables 3.3–3.7 can be read as follows: "var1" and "var2" are the related variables; "rel." is the sign of the relationship; "cases" indicates the number of cases of "var2" out of "var1"; "χ^2" is Pearson's test; "sign." is the standard statistical significance of the contingence relationship.[26]

We first looked at whether groups showing a network form (vertically integrated) relate to some specific characteristics (Table 3.3). These groups frequently affirm that the advantage on which their growth has been based is financial soundness (or good access to credit) and not technological or commercial know-how. In this case, the process of group formation is more often obtained by purchasing new firms or spin-off and less by hiving off previously integrated activities. It is also less frequently associated with the exploitation of intra-group ICT. This is also the most recently formed category of groups. The opposite holds for vertically integrated groups (var1 is dichotomic).

The second step (Table 3.4) finds some connections between the kind of management (owner-entrepreneurs and, symmetrically, the opposite results hold for independent manager-driven companies) and the growth of groups. We find an obvious negative correlation between firms personally managed by owners and both property fragmentation and the value of organisational structure on the growth of the group. Owner-managers develop groups to optimise financial resources and to diversify risk more frequently than professional management. On the other hand, in contrast to manager-run firms, they tend less to exploit the commercial opportunities of the group structure. That is to say, they base organisational change decisions on *personal property logic*, not *intrinsic performance logic*. Moreover, in the case of owner-led groups, single units are more separate and therefore the group organisational structure is less sophisticated: they tend to share resources less and display fewer common activities; conversely, groups led by professional managers are based on more sophisticated forms of resource or activity sharing.

Table 3.3 Group configuration (network versus vertically integrated)

Var1	*Rel.*	*Var2*	*Cases*	χ^2	*Sign.*
Network form	+	Financial competitive advantage	20 (32)	0.019	**
Network form	–	Formation by hiving off activities	6 (32)	0.046	**
Network form	–	Use of intra–group ICT	23 (32)	0.092	*
Network form	+	Recent group formation	20 (32)	0.087	*

Table 3.4 Relevance of owner management (versus professional management) in growth

Var1	*Rel.*	*Var2*	*Cases*	χ^2	*Sign.*
Owner manager	–	Dispersed ownership of shares	41 (45)	0.000	***
Owner manager	+	Charismatic leadership	37 (45)	0.001	***
Owner manager	+	Optimisation of financial resources as group formation motivation	18 (45)	0.071	*
Owner manager	–	Expanding commercial opportunities as group formation motivation	17 (45)	0.090	*
Owner manager	+	Risk diversification as group formation motivation	12 (45)	0.065	**
Owner manager	–	Sharing resources between group units	24 (45)	0.056	*
Owner manager	–	Common activities between group units	18 (45)	0.022	**

Table 3.5 Entrepreneur leadership (versus organisation), importance for growth

Var1	*Rel.*	*Var2*	*Cases*	χ^2	*Sign.*
Char. entrepreneur	–	Expanding commercial opportunities as group formation motivation	6 (40)	0.001	***
Char. entrepreneur	+	Optimisation of financial resources as group formation motivation	17 (40)	0.043	**

Table 3.6 Strategic assets and patterns of group formation

Var1	*Rel.*	*Var2*	*Cases*	χ^2	*Sign.*
Technological advantage	+	Formation by spin-off from mother company	16 (25)	0.126	–
Technological advantage	+	Risk diversification as group formation motivation	8 (25)	0.095	*
Commercial advantage	+	Expanding commercial opportunities as group formation motivation	16 (25)	0.023	**

Table 3.7 Process and aim of group formation

Var1	*Rel.*	*Var2*	*Cases*	χ^2	*Sign.*
Acquisition of firms	+	Technological development opportunities	11 (26)	0.041	**
Ease of management	+	Turnover growth	19 (25)	0.027	**
Ease of management	+	Recent group formation	17 (25)	0.038	**
Technological specification	–	Turnover growth	26 (47)	0.086	*

The third set of contingencies (Table 3.5) involves *charismatic leadership* as the main factor of competitiveness (as opposed to good organisation design). These charismatic entrepreneurs conceive organisational change as a way to achieve financial optimisation more often than groups enjoying a good organisational form. Moreover, they seek commercial opportunities through group formation to a much lesser extent (six firms only). However, there appears to be no correlation between group form and owner-management, on the one hand, and between group form and growth in turnover on the other. As a consequence, we cannot say much about the economic efficiency of paternalism or connect paternalism with specific organisational forms.

Some interesting facts appear when we compare factors assuring competitive advantage to groups (Table 3.6) with other variables concerning the outcomes expected from development of the group and the way it is achieved. First of all, firms enjoying technological advantages frequently spin off new firms (see the frequency) to reduce risk.[27] On the other hand, firms enjoying commercial advantages also tend to deepen their advantage by basing group formation on opportunities to expand commercial opportunities. Therefore, in this specific context, the present picture does not support the oft-advanced idea that large organisations can enjoy some advantage by internalising R&D activities. Here, companies with technological advantages tend to fragment their unitary status to reduce risk.

Further evidence concerns the process of group formation by purchase of firms and the aim of developing technological opportunities (Table 3.7). The commonly assumed positive relationship between these variables is confirmed. An important issue according to our theorisation is the aim of maintaining ease of management when forming a group. There is a positive relation between this variable and growth of sales, particularly in the most recently formed groups. Conversely, there is a negative correlation between technological specialisation and growth in sales.

3.7 Conclusions

Industrial groups have been interpreted in this article as arising from organisational changes designed to adapt firms to the varying environment while keeping production units small, generally in line with the *flexible specialisation* model. Often the motivation is preservation of the control of family capitalism over the firms. We have argued that as SMEs tend to adapt to changes improving their external connections rather than internal organisation, group formation constitutes a good response to the problem of firm growth. Enterprises exploit their competences, but without visible change in organisational configuration. They tend instead to reconnect to other production units and this is a form of application of dynamic capabilities. Groups, therefore, may be seen as an attempt to maintain the capability to adapt to context change without restructuring the firm's organisation. It is a different way of obtaining flexibility, adaptation and competence enhancement.

The study suggests that *charismatic entrepreneurs* are alive and kicking; there is no sign of their firms having significant difficulties in comparison with professionally managed companies. Business groups and, in particular, network groups have proliferated in recent years. The effectiveness of management of single firms tends to be a motivation for group creation and it emerges as related to good performance. The establishment or purchase of firms is the main way in which network groups grow. By comparison, vertically integrated groups are often the result of hiving off some of their activities. In general, groups are the result of the attempt to exploit capabilities in different markets while keeping control of strategic resources.

However, even if there are no differences in performance, groups headed by charismatic entrepreneurs display relatively less sophisticated patterns of organisation and are relatively less oriented to the increase of technological opportunities. They also tend to produce organisational change according to a *financial property perspective*, rather than seeking specific technological or commercial strategies. Professionally managed groups display more articulate strategies and organisational patterns in the division of competences. Effectiveness of management emerges as the criterion adopted in all configurations as the best way to exploit resources. We find in this result a confirmation of the hypothesis that paternalistic core organisational competences determine this kind of path-dependence. As a consequence, there is no sign that the non-delegation of management of companies is penalising the industrial development of flexible specialisation areas or that it is leading industry structure into a *cul de sac*. It remains difficult to discern to what extent family ownership is unfavourable to best organisational choices in times of economic crisis.

Notes

1 The authors would like to thank Caroline and Nigel Webb for advice on the wording of the text.
2 See Iacobucci (2002); Iacobucci *et al.* (2004a, b); Cainelli *et al.* (2004a, b); Brioschi *et al.* (2002).
3 The Italian Statistical Office (ISTAT, 2005) has published statistics on business firms in the Italian economy, stating that SME groups account for almost a quarter of total employment.
4 See Teece *et al.* (1994, 1997).
5 In fact, as pointed out by Montresor (2004), there are some epistemological diversities between the transaction cost and the competence approaches to the firm. Our aim is to adopt only the latter theory.
6 On institutional confidence, see Mistri and Solari (2003). In this case, it concerns experimental ways of organising business based on past experience. Since organisational methods are not all equally well-defined and well-tried, entrepreneurs tend to rely on the approaches they are used to.
7 The literature on agency has undervalued the problem of organisation size when studying the connection between agency costs and family firms or owner-managed firms. In fact, Schulze *et al.* (2001) argue how family firms may experience relevant agency costs when growing, because private ownership weakens the institutional safeguards that help protect public firms from many forms of adverse selection and opportunism.
8 Obviously, financing was supplied by banks.
9 In the sense that it looks like the one described by Schumpeter (1912 [1974]) in *The Theory of Economic Development.*
10 It evolves out of patronage, but it is a contractual exchange agreement. It is part of the federalist culture.
11 Actually, it is not necessarily outdated, but it effectively tends to vanish as soon as the economic and social structure evolves.
12 It is often typical of non-urban peripheral areas.
13 Obviously, we should consider dynamic transaction costs as subjective to firms and not objective properties of the environment. This problem may again highlight the epistemological difficulties of connecting transaction cost and capability theories, as Montresor (2004) clearly argued.
14 This is especially true if he continues to presume that his employees have some moral duties to respect.
15 Schulze *et al.* (2001) affirm that not all the institutional organisations designed to obtain efficiency of corporations work. Recruitment may involve a poor selection

process (resulting in loyal rather than competent personnel). Non-economic factors may affect economic decisions leading the corporation astray. These are indeed exactly the kinds of problem from which family capitalism suffers.

16 Moreover, the second generation entrepreneur may not have the qualities and the experience of the original founder and the personal style of management may thus fail.

17 Recently, the practice of buying money-losing firms to avoid taxation has come to a stop. Some fiscal advantages of groups still exist in any case.

18 See Gambarotto and Solari (2006) and Rangone and Solari (2005) for attempts to empirically evaluate such inter-firm relationships.

19 Also the – most studied – cases of joint ventures, alliances and stable partnerships are included in this category, but are not of interest here.

20 On the emergence of *visible hands* in district areas see Lombardi (2003).

21 The provinces of the so-called "Venetian plan" are Vicenza, Padova, Treviso, Pordenone and Udine.

22 Data have been provided by *Infocamere* (Chambers of Commerce).

23 Questionnaires have been distributed and collected by AES, Analisi Economiche e Sociali (Mestre VE).

24 The controlling firm is an industrial company.

25 Data are qualitative.

26 Since "var1" is a dichotomic variable, the opposite-sign relationship is valid for the complementary value (i.e. valid also for network vs. vertical integration).

27 They also frequently tend to hive off some previously integrated activity (not reported in tables).

References

Blois K. J. (1972) "Vertical Quasi-Integration", *Journal of Industrial Economics*, 20, pp. 253–272.

Brioschi F., M. S. Brioschi and G. Cainelli (2002) "From the Industrial District to the District Group: An Insight to the Evolution of Local Capitalism in Italy", *Regional Studies*, 36(9), pp. 1037–1052.

Cainelli G., D. Iacobucci and E. Morganti (2004a) "Spatial Agglomeration and Business Groups: New Evidence from Italian Industrial Districts", WP 1/2004 PRIN Capabilities dinamiche d'impresa e sistemi locali di produzione.

Cainelli G., D. Iacobucci and E. Morganti (2004b) "Diffusione e specificità organizzativa dei gruppi d'impresa nei distretti industriali italiani", WP 6/2004 PRIN Capabilities dinamiche d'impresa e sistemi locali di produzione.

Chandler A. D. Jr. (1962) *Strategy and Structure: Chapters in the History of the Industrial Enterprise*, Cambridge, MIT Press.

Chandler A. D. Jr. (1977) *The Visible Hand: the Managerial Revolution in American Business*, Cambridge, The Belknap Press.

Chandler A. D. Jr. (1990) *Scale and Scope: The Dynamics of Industrial Capitalism*, Cambridge, The Belknap Press.

Chandler A. D. Jr. (1992) "Organizational Capabilities and the Economic History of the Industrial Enterprise", *Journal of Economic Perspectives*, 6 (3), pp. 79–100.

Gambarotto F. and S. Solari (2006) "The Role of Reconnection of Competences and Institutions in the Collective Learning Process", forthcoming.

Iacobucci D. (2002) "Explaining Business Groups Started by Habitual Entrepreneurs in the Italian Manufacturing Sector", *Entrepreneurship and Regional Development*, 14(1), pp. 31–48.

Iacobucci D. and P. Rosa (2004a) "Habitual Entrepreneurs, Entrepreneurial Team Development and Business Group Formation", WP 2/2004 PRIN Capabilities dinamiche d'impresa e sistemi locali di produzione.

Iacobucci D. and P. Rosa (2004b) "Business Groups as Evolutionary Entrepreneurial Systems", WP 7/2004 PRIN Capabilities dinamiche d'impresa e sistemi locali di produzione.

ISTAT (2005) *I Gruppi d'Imprese in Italia – Anno 2002*, Statistiche in breve, April 21.

Khanna T. (2000) "Business Groups and Social Welfare in Emerging Markets: Existing Evidence and Unanswered Questions", *European Economic Review*, 44, pp. 748–761.

Langlois R. N. (1998) "Personal Capitalism as Charismatic Authority: the Organizational Economics of a Weberian Concept", *Industrial and Corporate Change*, 7, pp. 195–214.

Lazonick W. (1991) *Business Organization and the Myth of the Market Economy*, New York, Cambridge University Press.

Lazonick W. (2002) "Innovative Enterprise and Historical Transformation", *Enterprise and Society*, 3, pp. 3–47.

Loasby B. (1998) "The Organisation of Capabilities", *Journal of Economic Behavior and Organization*, 35, pp. 139–160.

Lombardi M. (2003) "The Evolution of Local Production Systems: the Emergence of the Invisible Mind and the Evolutionary Pressures towards more Visible Minds", *Research Policy*, 32, pp. 1443–1462.

Mathews J. A. (2001) "Competitive Interfirm Dynamics within an Industrial Market System", *Industry and Innovation*, 8(1), pp. 79–107.

Mathews J. A. (2002) "A Resource-Based View of Schumpeterian Economic Dynamics", *Journal of Evolutionary Economics*, 12, pp. 29–54.

Mathews J. A. (2003) "Competitive Dynamics and Economic Learning: An Extended Resource-Based View", *Industrial and Corporate Change*, 12(1), pp. 115–145.

Mistri M. and S. Solari (2003) "Behavioural rules in industrial districts: loyalty, trust and reputation" in F. Belussi, G. Gottardo, E. Rullani (eds) *The Technological Evolution of Industrial Districts*, Boston, MA, Kluwer, pp. 245–266.

Monteverde K. and D. J. Teece (1982) "Appropriable Rents and Quasi-Vertical Integration", *Journal of Law and Economics*, 25, pp. 321–329.

Montresor S. (2004) "Resources, capabilities, competences and the theory of the firm", *Journal of Economic Studies*, 31(5), 409–434.

Piore, M. J. and C. F. Sabel (1984) *The Second Industrial Divide. Possibilities for Prosperity*, New York, Basic Books.

Prahalad C. K., G. Hamel (1990) "The Core Competence of the Corporation", *Harvard Business Review*, pp. 79–91.

Rangone M. and S. Solari (2005) "Dynamic Capabilities and Interfirm Relationships: An Empirically Oriented View of Collective Learning in Local Production Systems", WP PRIN 2003.

Schulze W. S., M. H. Lubatkin, R. N. Dino and A. K. Buchholtz (2001) "Agency Relationship in Family Firms: Theory and Evidence", *Organization Science*, 12(2), pp. 96–116.

Schumpeter J. A. (1912 [1974]) *The Theory of Economic Development*, London, Oxford University Press.

Teece D. J. (1992) "Competition, Cooperation, and Innovation: Organizational Arrangements for Regimes of Rapid Technological Progress", *Journal of Economic Behavior and Organization*, 18, pp. 1–25.

Teece D. and G. Pisano (1994), "The Dynamic Capabilities of Firms: An Introduction", *Industrial and Corporate Change*, 3, pp. 537–556.

Teece D., G. Pisano and A. Shuen (1997) "Dynamic Capabilities and Strategic Management", *Strategic Management Journal*, 18, pp. 509–533.

4 Demand for skilled labour services, job design and the 'revealed learning function'[1]

Gilberto Antonelli and Mario Nosvelli

4.1 Introduction

In the last four decades economists have been increasingly concerned with the study of the nature, determinants and effects of the knowledge acquired by employees over the span of their lives. Moreover, in the last decade or so, due to the widening of the 'mismatch' and 'skill shortage' phenomena, economic research has been more and more entrusted with exploring the skill needs of the firms, particularly in countries such as Italy, where a high and persistent unemployment coexists with such phenomena.

This evolution can be very beneficial, also because it helps to limit the unbalanced expansion of studies conceived only in a labour supply perspective. From 1997, in Italy, a very detailed data base was available, the *Sistema Informativo Excelsior* (Unioncamere, Ministero del Lavoro e della Previdenza Sociale, 1997/1999), which allows us to explore, in a labour demand perspective, the nature of different kinds of skills demanded by the firms, their learning patterns and the interactions among them.

In the present work, we are willing to offer some original contributions referring both to the theoretical and methodological approach chosen.

A first contribution refers to the analysis of the cumulative effects arising from education and work based learning. That is, to the 'external organization' of knowledge in the economic system.[2] The combination of different learning patterns comes out as beneficial in favouring a better characterization of the set of workers capabilities and in increasing the chances that labour supply has to match the demand for skills. In particular, it seems quite important to further investigate whether we should continue to consider education and work-based learning as totally autonomous components of the individual knowledge or whether they should be jointly designed in a harmonized development of the human capital stock over the life cycle.

A second contribution refers to the profiles of knowledge formation and to the 'internal organization' of knowledge in the firm. In particular we look at the role of tenure in creating a favourable environment for transferring skills and generating new knowledge through firm's internal learning.

A third contribution refers to the original application adopted in this chapter of the learning function model. Its utilization in the empirical analysis of planned labour demand by firms makes it possible to investigate the contribution of the diverse learning types and processes on the construction of the different types of trades.

The ordered logit regression method has been used in this work because it can be considered a very effective econometric tool in the estimation of the influence of the diverse learning types and processes in the different trades.

This chapter is structured into seven sections. After this introduction, the section 4.2 reviews the basic economic concepts and models employed in the analysis of the relationship between job design, learning and skills formation.

Section 4.3 outlines the basic characteristics of the main analytical tool used in this work – the learning function model – and provides the specification to be tested. Section 4.4 describes the data set and the logic path followed in the construction of the variables employed in our analysis. Section 4.5 provides a synthetic overview of the econometric techniques used. Section 4.6 presents the main results achieved. The concluding section proposes a synthesis of the main findings and highlights some reasonable policy implications.

4.2 The theoretical setting

Learning can be defined as a process of gaining understanding that leads to the modification of performance, attitudes and behaviours through the acquisition of knowledge, skills and values, through study and experience.

As a result of this, learning can take place both in households and specialized agencies, like schools and universities, as well as, very often in the form of joint product, in firms, spin-offs and R&D laboratories.[3] This means that the actors involved in learning activities can be found both on the supply and the demand side of the labour markets.

These actors can play independently, share the result of their choices (benefits) and constraints (costs),[4] and jointly participate in the actions needed for improving their understanding (learning by doing, by using, by interacting).

Learning can consist of the acquisition of information, education, training (both on and off the job) and experience. Also migration and geographical mobility can be powerful vehicles of learning, acting both on the supply and demand side of the labour markets.

A variety of learning types can crop up. Among them the main categories are: general learning, vocational and specific learning, learning to learn.

The economic interpretation (Rosenberg, 1982), which contrasts the assimilation of knowledge to information, defines technology as an organized stock of knowledge and innovation as new knowledge introduced in the economic sphere. The latter is viewed as a learning process, which sees the firm as the key actor. Scope and limits of this learning process are underlined, taking into account the localized character of knowledge, together with its tacit, or non-codified components, its cumulative and irreversible nature and the difficulties faced in storing it (Antonelli, 2003).

The very nature of the firm is seen in its capability to coordinate learning processes.[5] This view is based on five postulates:

1. the key resource is knowledge;
2. the key productive process is learning;
3. learning-by-interacting (Lundvall, 1992) becomes crucial, side by side with the traditional forms of formal and informal learning;
4. learning is a process embedded in the social and institutional context;
5. knowledge bits are incorporated both in individual and collective agents.

The organizational structure of the learning processes in the firm mirrors two kinds of trade-off:

a. between the internal and external capability to acquire new knowledge;
b. between the capabilities to explore, carry out research and select new opportunities and the capability to deepen the specialization in already familiar trajectories.

The availability of employees endowed with the appropriate education and competences plays a crucial role in both trade-offs.

On the edge of the labour market theories, a paradigm consistent with this view can be found in the 'job-competition model'.

> In the job competition model, instead of competing against one another based on the wages that they are willing to accept, individuals compete against one another for job opportunities based on their relative costs of being trained to fill whatever job is being considered.
>
> (Thurow, 1976, p. 75)

Contrary to the suggestions of the standard 'wage competition model':

> the labor market is not a market where fully developed skills bid for jobs. Rather, it is primarily a market where supplies of trainable labor are matched with training opportunities that are in turn directly associated with the number of job openings that exist. Training opportunities only occur when there is a job opening that creates the demand for the skills in question.
>
> (Thurow, 1976, p. 79)

In this model, labour market equilibrium is determined by the modifications in job characteristics settled by the firms and by the amount of training they implement. Marginal product depends on the job design and organization processes in which the individual works, rather than on the individual itself.

If fully developed skills are not available to the individuals before entering the labour market, nevertheless each one of them is endowed with specific background characteristics. They concern ascriptive as well as affective and cognitive characteristics.

However, employers do not possess direct information on training costs of each potential worker. Therefore, they attribute an average ranking for each background class. The average attribute refers both to the fact that: 'this ranking is a composite of the rankings of each individual employer' (Thurow, 1976, p. 91) and to the fact that the training strategies are based on learning processes regarded as effective for the average potential worker.

A particular vector of training costs is therefore associated to each individual, which allows him to be employed in a usually limited array of jobs. The task of the firm is to choose and train the potential workers able to generate the expected productivity with the minimum investment in training costs.

For the new workers and job openings, background characteristics are the unique selection criteria.

Firms are interested to find out the background characteristics, which can serve as reliable predictors of differentials in the potential training costs. This is why educational attainment and performance become critical characteristics.

> Education is a form of training. The ability to absorb one type of training probably indicates something about the ability to absorb another type of training . . . . Through education one learns how to be trained or exhibits that one is trainable.
>
> (Thurow, 1976, p. 88)

If, as we have seen, in this model no significant competence (general or specific) can be acquired by the new workers before their access to the jobs, work-based learning is a decisive process in forming their competences (Green *et al.*, 2001). The job design carried out by the firms determines the competences needed. Training programmes are the common tools the firms use in order to adapt the heterogeneous background characteristics of the individuals to the need of competences. In doing so, the firms try to minimize the expected training costs attached to the enrolment of each new employee, looking for the individuals with the best suited background characteristics.

In this respect, their training strategies are based on optimization. And if we observe their planned labour demands, which incorporate their strategies, also the implicit learning function, which is 'revealed' by them, is an average of optimal individual choices.

In this framework, the learning function can be conceived as a simulation tool (implicitly) used by the firms in order to estimate the impact of different learning patterns on skill formation. Therefore, planned labour demands are in some way the revealed part of an overall firm's strategy.

The labour-training market is so structured in order to maximize the willingness of employees to transmit their knowledge to new workers and to minimize every worker's resistance to acquiring new skills and accepting new technology (Thurow, 1976, p. 81).

On the edge of the theories of the firm, a consistent paradigm can be found in the 'RCC approach'. In this view the firm can be conceived as a set of resources, capabilities and idiosyncratic competences. Learning processes are crucial in facing the production – transaction dichotomy and, more important, two of the channels through which 'information is interpreted, understood and turned into knowledge on a subjective basis' (Montresor, 2004, p. 413) are job design and training of employees. Following this edge, a possible line of research is spelled out in earlier chapter in the present volume.[6]

In the last four decades economists have been increasingly concerned with the study of the nature, determinants and effects of the knowledge acquired by employees over the span of their lives. The main theoretical achievement, conceived in a long-term labour supply framework, has been the human capital theory (Becker, 1964). This theory is based on the assumption that decreasing returns to investment in human capital prevail. This means that, according to this theory, which appears to be consistent with many empirical studies based on international comparisons (Psacharopoulos and Patrinos, 2004), investments in human capital in the early years of the life cycle are more fruitful – both in terms of labour productivity and wages – than the late ones.

However, in the last decade, economic research has been more and more entrusted with exploring the skill needs of the firms – the demand side of the story. And, the basic postulate of the human capital theory has been questioned by some recent evidence showing that trained workers are on average more educated than those who decide not to obtain further training after school education (Denny and Harmon, 2000; Arulampalam and Booth, 1998; Nosvelli, 2002). This evidence is consistent with two opposite viewpoints. On the one hand it could witness the existence of decreasing returns, inasmuch as further training could hamper the de-valuation of previous human capital investments. On the other hand, this finding could stress the cumulative effect of further training, which gives proportionally higher returns only if combined with a robust educational basis.

Other theoretical and empirical analyses suggest different interpretations of the positive relationship between education and training. A first important explanation can come from the consideration of the unobservable factors stemming from the heterogeneity of individuals.[7] A second explanation focuses on labour market segmentation, claiming that training is allowable just for those segments of the labour market that present some favourable conditions for being trained (Ashton and Green, 1996).

An important theoretical underpinning comes from the approach that relates the origins of skills to the learning processes enhanced by organizational and productive innovations (Green, 1998; Felstead and Ashton, 2000; Green *et al.*, 2001). The main result highlights the link between the development of new skills and the prevalence of innovative and participative management styles.[8]

New management styles make it possible for workers to acquire new skills and to combine the different components of knowledge that have been stored in the past. New skills derive from the introduction of new technologies and from a more intensive use of organizational practices such as: problem solving, team working, systems of support and reward of learning (Bresnahan *et al.*, 1999). Knowledge combination and reorganization stem from the ability to communicate effectively with colleagues and customers and especially from the capacity of interacting with those who have already mastered the trade (Stasz, 1997; Eraut *et al.*, 1996).

Two further very relevant implications are emphasized in this strand of literature. The first one stresses the importance of work-based learning, both as a source of skill creation and as a way to apply knowledge to production processes.[9] The second implication points out the crucial role assumed in learning processes by contextual/tacit knowledge, i.e. knowledge created in the workplace, typical of local production systems and transferable only through imitation.[10]

The last crucial point, stressed by several different approaches, which confirm the early Thurow perception, concerns the role of tenure. It is only with long-term contracts that both firms and workers are more likely to invest in skill 'generation and re-generation'.[11] In particular, tenure can foster tacit knowledge transfer and assimilation, since one can properly learn this kind of knowledge only through a lasting relationship with other workers and with the whole firm organization. Moreover, long-term employment contracts give more chances to transfer high-level skills, which are the most relevant for innovation and competitiveness (Green *et al.*, 2001). This explains why a labour organization grounded on long-term contracts is more likely to achieve 'innovative flexibility' (Antonelli, 1998, 2002, 2004; Pini, 2000).[12]

4.3 The learning function model

The starting point for our analysis can be found in the definition of educational production function. As Hanushek (1979) has explained in his original model, this is a tool for measuring students' achievement as a function of a given set of educational inputs. In this methodology the key agents are the individuals while they are making decisions on the formation of their knowledge to be spent subsequently on the supply side of the labour markets.

At this stage, we are faced with two alternative paths. If we adopt a 'wage competition' model, individuals are capable to spend their knowledge on the labour markets, as their skills are fully developed before entering any job. Labour markets are then able to allocate jobs and to simultaneously determine the equilibrium wages. However, if we adopt a 'job competition' model, only the matching between an individual and a job is able to generate skills or competences and the labour markets have the only function to allocate jobs.

In this second alternative, we need therefore to investigate more thoroughly patterns and processes of learning and, in this perspective, the 'job analysis' becomes important. Its main objective is to examine the 'job relatedness' of employment procedures such as education and training (Green, 1998; Primoff and Fine, 1998). In other words, job analysis determines the specific requirements needed for deploying the tasks related to each job.[13]

Since we prefer the second alternative, the closer reference to our idea of learning function can be found in the way Green *et al.* (2001) model the determinants of skills production.

In the basic function each skill depends upon prior inputs:

$$S_{it} = \alpha_1 ED_{it} + \alpha_2 WBL_{it} + \varepsilon_i + u_{it} \tag{1}$$

S_{it} measures the skill of individual job i at time t; ED_{it} is a vector of education inputs which influence the job i at time t; WBL_{it} is a vector of inputs related to work-based learning which influence the job i at time t; ε_i is a fixed level of skill naturally possessed by the worker independently of education or work; u_{it} is a random error term.

Much like job analysis, our learning function tries to measure the knowledge content needed for matching specific professional requirements. Although in our work the reference unit is not the individual, but the job itself.

In fact, the learning function implemented in our paper, presents three important peculiarities, which, all the same, are coherent with the theoretical basis from which we start.

A first peculiarity concerns the fact that our analysis is based on observations pertaining to the labour demand and not to the labour supply. We consider the labour demand side very revealing, given that employers' point of view takes into account not only the present relevance of the skills required, but also their evolution in the short/medium term, which is linked to the development of the firm organization. Moreover, as previously suggested, their choices in the field of job design can be considered as solutions to optimization problems in the framework of job competition.

A second peculiarity, strictly connected to the first one, is that we refer to the future labour demand, since the dependent variables derive from employers' forecasts on hiring decisions in the subsequent year. This means that the actual target of our econometric estimate is not the effective labour demand, but the potential one. This does not compromise at all the data set reliability, since the one-year forecasts of potential demand result very close (or equal) to ex-post evolution of effective demand.[14]

A third peculiarity concerns the fact that the dependent variables, as already noted, refer to the skill pertaining to each job and not to each employee. In our chapter the notion of trade level or 'professional level' is a crucial one, and it could be envisaged as a box, which contains a mix of different skills and is the outcome of job design by the employers. While this box remains unchanged – i.e. the definition of professional level is not modified over time – the skill mix can vary over time, entailing the need of different combinations of learning processes. A clear-cut consequence of this last peculiarity, is that we do not take into account personal characteristics of the workers, because they cannot be inferred from the available data. In other words, in our analysis heterogeneity due to genetic ability or to other sources not pertaining to the job sphere cannot be detected.

The basic form of the learning function used in our work is the following:

$$FP_{it} = ED_{it} + WBL_{it} + COMPO_{it} + u_{it} \tag{2}$$

where: FP_{it} represents the professional level i at time t. The independent variables are classified in three sets of vectors: education (ED), work-based learning (WBL) and COMPO, which represents a particular combination of the first two.[15]

Subsequently, we disaggregate each set of vectors in order to estimate the specific impact of different components of the main learning patterns. We adopt, therefore, the following specification:

$$\begin{aligned} FP_{it} = {} & a_0 + a_1 IST_{it} + a_2 IST_{it}^{\,2} + a_3 CL_{it} + a_4 CI_{it} + a_5 FT_{it} + a_6 PT_{it} + a_7 EXP_{it} \\ & + a_8 TP_{it} + a_{9c} COMPO_{it} + u_{it} \end{aligned} \tag{3}$$

The first set (ED) contains variables, which try to capture the impact of different types of formal education on skills. The variable IST is the most important of the educational variables and it is measured in terms of years of schooling required to carry on each profession. The expected sign, according to the prevalent theories, is always positive. In any case, IST is very relevant because education, in comparison with the alternative learning patterns considered, absorbs the longest fraction of the life span.

The variable IST is important also because it gives us, through its squared value, the chance to evaluate the relevance of a cumulative character of human capital. A negative and statistically significant coefficient of IST^2 in an earning function is coherent with the basic conjectures of the human capital theory (Mincer, 1993), whereas a positive coefficient of IST^2 tends to support the relevance of a cumulative character of continuing education, as recent empirical evidence indicates (De Grip and Hoevenberg, 1996; Burdett and Cunningham, 1998).

Two further variables deal with important components of education: knowledge of foreign languages (CL) and computer skills (CI). These two components have been estimated separately since they represent a specific and increasingly important ingredient of skill demand, which integrates the value of general education (IST and IST^2), especially in a more and more globalized economy.

The second set of variables refers to the components of work-based learning (WBL), a mix of learning patterns, which are usually considered very relevant by employers in the definition and completion of required skills.

A first variable considered is formal training (FT) – carried out both on and off the job – which is meant to measure the impact of training by courses.

A second variable is practical training (PT), which identifies a kind of learning based on a concrete labour experience, acquired through working side-by-side with skilled workers.

A third variable (EXP) measures the past experience of the employee, which represents both the practical knowledge in the worker's heritage and defines some consolidated skills.

The last variable belonging to this set is strongly related to firm organization: we refer to tenure (TP), measured in terms of the share of permanent contracts. This is a very useful proxy for capturing the attitude of the firm towards 'flexibility'. If the sign of the tenure coefficient is positive and statistically significant one can infer an orientation to create skills relevant for the firms' long-term development. If the tenure is relevant, in other words, this means that the trade and its knowledge contents are considered of key importance for the firm in a long-term perspective.

Along with the separate effects of ED and WBL, the learning function is also targeted to analyse any possible joint effect.

The variable COMPO – whose construction will be described in section 4.4 – portrays the most efficient combination of the whole set of vectors described above. A positive sign of its coefficient may suggest the existence of complementarity among the different learning components. In our view this is a crucial variable since it helps to clarify if learning can be better defined as an 'integrated' or a 'fragmented' set of knowledge modules. However, we are well aware that it is not an easy task to find a way of measuring complementarity, which is exempted from distortions. For this reason, we suggest high caution in the interpretation of the estimates, and this is particularly true as far as policy implications are concerned.

The process of skills formation is investigated taking into account the characteristics of the 'productive environment'. Therefore we will explicitly consider differences both in the productive sector and the firm dimension,[16] which could have very significant impact on the shape of the learning function.[17]

4.4 Data set and variables construction

The data set *Sistema Informativo Excelsior* (Unioncamere, 1997/1999) provides the statistical information needed for the estimation of the learning equation, since it measures and quantifies the professional skills each employer plans to demand by one year. This data set is the result of the submission of a questionnaire to a representative stratified sample drawn from a universe obtained by the integration of different administrative data sources: Registro Camerale, INPS, INAIL, Ministero dell'Economia.

As it is required in equations (2) and (3) the Excelsior data set surveys professions as boxes collecting skill contents. The professions in the *Sistema Informativo Excelsior* are articulated in a taxonomy, which assembles 2.400 fine occupations, collected in a standard codification defined by ISTAT in 1991. Since the definition of professions has been constant in all versions of *Sistema Informativo Excelsior*, it is possible to analyse and compare the skill contents of each profession in 1996 and 1999. Consequently, due to the impossibility to build a unique database, we carried out our econometric analysis on a different data set for each year, comparing the results relative to homogeneous professions.

Table 4.1 Values assigned to the dependent variable

Description	*Values assigned*
Senior officials and managers	8
Professionals	7
Technicians and associate professions	6
Clerks	5
Service workers, shop and market sales workers	4
Craft and skilled workers	3
Plant and machine operators and assemblers	2
Elementary occupations	1

Source: Unioncamere (1997/1999).

The dependent variable (FP) adopted in this chapter is partitioned in the following eight professional levels as they have been defined within the Excelsior data set (Table 4.1).

This taxonomy defines standard and wide professional categories[18] that are particularly suitable to the econometric analysis undertaken in section 4.6. For these professions the data set defines, in a homogeneous way, both the tasks they deploy and the firm division where they are carried on.

The values associated with each profession, ordered in terms of skill contents, are also the values used for the econometric estimation.

The distribution of the professions in the data set is shown in Table 4.2. Data on the manufacturing sector are presented and analysed in three different steps. In a first step, manufacturing is taken as a whole; in a second step, only small manufacturing firms (1 to 9 employees) are considered; in a third step, only large manufacturing firms (more than 250 employees) are taken into account. The last row shows the distribution of professions in the service sector, made up by the following sub-sectors: trade and repairs, hotels and restaurants, transportation, credit and insurance.

Table 4.2 Distribution of FP within the sample used (%)

Sector/Dimension	*FP1*	*FP2*	*FP3*	*FP4*	*FP5*	*FP6*	*FP7*	*FP8*
Manufacturing 1996	3.0	30.0	21.7	2.6	8.1	24.4	8.3	2.1
Manufacturing 1999	5.4	27.9	20.1	0.9	10.0	25.5	7.1	3.2
Manufactuing SF 1996*	2.2	26.6	32.2	3.7	10.2	19.5	5.4	0.3
Manufacturing SF 1999*	5.5	31.1	30.9	0.5	13.8	16.0	1.8	0.4
Manufacturing LF 1996**	4.5	26.7	12.5	2.8	5.3	31.3	12.0	5.0
Manufacturing LF 1999**	2.4	19.4	10.7	0.6	6.1	38.6	14.6	7.6
Services 1996	2.1	7.3	7.7	27.1	17.9	26.5	9.0	2.5
Services 1999	5.4	6.7	8.0	24.6	21.5	22.0	7.9	3.8

Source: Unioncamere (1997/1999).

Notes

* SF: Small firms ** LF: Large firms.

The distribution of the professions by sector reveals that in the manufacturing industry the highest percentages of professions are concentrated in FP2 (plant and machine operators and assemblers) and FP3 (craft and related workers). The service sector presents a different concentration of professions, since FP4 (service workers and shop and market sales workers), FP5 (clerks) and FP6 (technicians and associate professions) are predominant. This depends on well-known productive and organizational differences between these two sectors, whose implications on learning will be analysed below.

The IST variable is measured in terms of years of education needed for completing the course required by each profession. As already noted, the square of IST is used for exploring the cumulative effects of education.

All the other variables included in ED and WBL have been collected dichotomously, since they derive from questions in which the employer is supposed to assess whether a certain kind of knowledge should be required or not in order to fulfil a given profession.

The tenure variable (TP) is measured by the share of permanent contracts to the total number of employees, which are foreseen in each profession. The result of this ratio is then dichotomized by setting the variable equal to 0 if the result is less than 0.5, and equal to 1 if the result is higher than 0.5.

The variable COMPO is defined through the method of principal components. The first principal component – the best linear combination between ED and WBL variables – has been dichotomized, just as in the previous case, by setting the variable equal to 0 or 1 depending on whether the result is less or more than 0.5. This method seems particularly effective because it allows for the identification of a new variable, which is the best synthetic representation of both ED, and WBL variables. In this way, this new variable helps to analyse the complementarity among different components of ED and WBL.

A last remark about the data set must be made. The data set concerns the region of Lombardy, in which, according to 2001 Census data (ISTAT, 2006), the largest number of firms (18.4 per cent) and of employees (23.7 per cent) are located (a fifth of the total of 20 Italian regions). Moreover, Lombardy shows a high variety of firms, in terms of both dimensions and sectors, and a good representation of all different productive contexts we could find in Italy. In fact, in Lombardy both manufacturing and services are well diffused. In manufacturing we can find a high incidence either of small firms – 21 industrial districts – or of big firms (34.5 per cent of firms with more than 1,000 employees). Finally, limiting the investigation to just one region, we can control to some extent for the heterogeneity in the governance of education and training systems as well as in the institutional context in which firms operate.[19]

4.5 The ordered logit technique

In this section we outline in a very synthetic way the ordered logit technique we employ and its suitability with respect to the objective of our work.

The specific advantage of ordinal regression models is that they allow for the analysis of different categories of the dependent variable, ranked from low to high values. In this case, the additional information, which is taken into account, is the order of the categories of the dependent variables (see Table 4.1). In this case it seems very relevant to be able to estimate the specific effect of the learning function for each single professional level.

Moreover, in the last decade logit and probit techniques have been widely applied in the analysis of skill and training, because they give the chance to estimate properly many qualitative items (Arulampalam and Booth, 1997; Green and Montgomery, 1998; Green *et al.*, 2002). In particular, many studies focused on the impact of different human capital contents in labour market evolution (Felstead *et al.*, 2000; Marcus and Green, 1985).

In ordered logit the observed variable is thought to give only imperfect information about an underlying latent variable. In fact, the basic idea is that it is possible to calculate the distribution of the unobserved variable through the probabilities of distribution of the observed variable between thresholds or cut points.

In general, the probability of any observed $y=m$, returns a vector $\mathbf{x}$ of independent variables and is calculated with the following formula (Long, 1997, p. 121):

$$\Pr(y_i = m | x_i) = F(\tau_m - \mathbf{x}_i\beta) - F(\tau_{m-1} - \mathbf{x}_i\beta)$$

Where τ_m and β represent respectively the *cut point* and the vector of coefficient, while F, the cumulative density function, is a logistic with $\mathrm{Var}(\varepsilon) = \pi^3/3$.

The interpretation of ordered logit should be carefully approached. In fact high coefficients only signal an increase in the probability that the variable is positioned in the highest categories. In order to simplify the interpretation of the variable, we use the average absolute change described by Long and Freese (2001).

In our case, $J=8$, i.e. the number of professions considered. The absolute value is needed because,

$$\bar{\Delta}_k = \frac{1}{j} \sum_{j=1}^{J} \left| \frac{\Delta \Pr(y=j|\bar{\mathbf{x}})}{\Delta x_k} \right|$$

otherwise, the sum of changes would add up to zero.

The average absolute change permits the identification of a synthetic measure of the effect of each variable in the change of probabilities. For continuous variables we have chosen the change of a standard deviation around the mean, while for binary variables we have used the one relative to the change from 0 to 1.

In order to interpret even more clearly the estimation results, we added the use of predicted probabilities, which are useful in describing the probability of happen for each category. As Long put it: ‘predicted probabilities … show the relationships between the independent variables and the dependent categories’ (Long, 1997, p. 130). The predicted probabilities of each variable are calculated holding constant the remaining variables at the average value.

4.6 Results

The results obtained from the estimation of the learning function on the Lombardy data set are divided into four sub-paragraphs. The first three deal with manufacturing: the entire sector is analysed in the first sub-paragraph, then the focus switches to the learning function behaviour in small and medium firms in the second and third sub-paragraphs. The fourth sub-paragraph deals with the learning function behaviour in the service sector. An important aim of this section is thus to offer a clearer illustration of the relevant differences arising from the sectoral and dimensional characteristics of the firms in the sample.

In order to ease the interpretation, graphs are plotted on the predicted probabilities related to each professional level (see the Appendix). In particular, we plot predicted probabilities of minimum (IST-MIN) and maximum (IST-MAX) levels of education required for each professional level. Given the space constraints, the objective is to capture the effects on the two most relevant variables, as indicated in the literature, at least for schooling. The main purpose is to achieve a more fine-tuned econometric estimation, which differentiates professional levels, as well as, educational requirements.

Finally, some notations on the model's robustness and on its explanatory power are presented.

Looking at values of Likelihood Ratio χ^2 test, shown in estimations tables, it could be claimed that high χ^2 depends on the number of observations. However, the proof that the model is really robust can be obtained through the comparison of the probability of each observation conditional on the estimate – i.e. EXP(–11233/7896)=0.241 for the first case analysed – with the theoretical average probability of each one of the eight categories – i.e. 1/8=0.125. If, as it happens in this example, the former is larger it means that the model actually has explanatory power.

The possible emergence of collinearity has been checked both with the analysis of the χ^2 test and with the Tschuprov coefficient. Neither the first nor the second test reveals any collinearity problem, even though it could be expected from the density of dichotomic variables.

Finally, it is necessary to add a last important point, which helps to remove any doubt on the possible existence of reverse causality. A time difference is introduced as the dependent variables are related to the foreseen demand for professions in the following year rather than in the current year. This is supposed to rule out any risk of reverse causality.

4.6.1 Skill creation in the manufacturing sector

The estimation of the learning function for the entire manufacturing sector in Lombardy, in terms of average discrete change, gives the following main results (Table 4.3).

Education (ED) increases its aggregate effect – the sum of the effects of all ED variables shown within the square inside each table – from 0.137 in 1996 to

Table 4.3 Learning function application to Lombardy manufacturing system

Variables	*Coefficients (1996)*	*Z*	*P > |Z|*	*Δ**	*Coefficients (1999)*	*Z*	*P > |Z|*	*Δ**
IST	0.3371611	14.76	0.000	0.065	0.645283	28.93	0.000	0.119
IST^2	0.007522	3.52	0.000	0.014	–0.0057201	–2.89	0.004	0.010
CL	0.4352805	5.25	0.000	0.027	0.1485893	2.77	0.006	0.009
CI	0.493852	7.25	0.000	0.031	0.1644362	2.64	0.008	0.010
FT	–0.9154481	–19.26	0.000	0.056	–0.2904943	–7.49	0.000	0.018
EXP	0.2724682	6.21	0.000	0.017	0.4393347	12.91	0.000	0.027
PT	–0.3392599	–5.23	0.000	0.021	–0.2938893	–7.42	0.000	0.018
TP	0.0622048	1.33	0.185	0.004	0.0870511	2.53	0.011	0.018
COMPO	0.3478611	3.30	0.001	0.022	0.7923367	8.70	0.000	0.049
Cut point				*Aggregate Δ**	*Cut point*			*Aggregate Δ**
cut1	–3.159773		ED	0.137	–1.931222		ED	0.148
cut2	0.0122912		WBL	0.094	0.729953		WBL	0.063
cut3	1.386492		TP	n.s.**	2.42457		TP	0.018
cut4	1.577713		COMPO	0.022	2.525509		COMPO	0.049
cut5	2.161598				3.572923			
cut6	4.509106				6.480454			
cut7	6.630833				8.203291			
Number of obs	7,896				13,341			
LR $\chi^2(9)$	4,792.90				12,603.75			
Prob > χ^2	0.0000				0.0000			
Log likelihood	–11,233.559				–17,107.421			
Pseudo R^2	0.1758				0.2692			

Notes
* Δ: average absolute discrete change is calculated on the deviation standard around the mean; z is the *z-test* of β.
** n.s.: not significant.

0.148 in 1999, while the aggregate effect of WBL variables decreases from 0.094 to 0.063.

Among the variables that compose ED we find that IST presents the most relevant effect, particularly in the 1999 survey. IST^2 shows a moderate effect in both surveys. The negative sign in 1999 proves the possible occurrence of negative marginal effect. Finally, it is important to stress that both in 1996 and particularly in 1999 the effect either of language or of informatics knowledge is low.

Among the WBL variables, the sign of FT and PT is negative in both estimates. This shows that these two variables have a greater impact in the low segment of FP. In 1996 FT presents the second greater impact after education. The impact of experience (EXP) is relevant with reference to WBL, especially in 1999.

Tenure (TP) is significant only in the 1999 estimates and, finally, complementarity (COMPO) shows a relevant average discrete change, particularly in 1999.

A first synthetic outcome of this investigation suggests that although the role of education is always decisive for the learning process, it needs to be integrated with other kinds of knowledge derived from experience. This could be explained, in other words, as increased demand for assembling and re-organizing the learning patterns for generating the demanded skills.

Looking at the predicted probabilities (Figure A1 and Figure A2 in the Appendix) for any single professional level, differences emerge quite clearly among learning processes relative to low professional levels (FP1 to FP4) and high professional levels (FP5 to FP8).

A first counterintuitive result shows higher predicted probabilities for lower level professions; the whole set of learning patterns seem to be more relevant in the determination of professions positioned in levels 2 and 3. Of course this does not mean that learning contents are ineffective for higher level professional skills. However, they are crucial for entering the labour market for some specific professions. In other words, firms are able to identify more precisely the skills demanded for some professions: plant and machine operators and assemblers and crafts and related workers for the lower scale, and intermediate and scientific for the upper scale.

A second very clear result is the behaviour of IST-MAX, which is completely different from that of the other learning patterns. It shows that high levels of schooling are very effective just for higher level professions; education, in other words, could be a selection device for getting jobs.

A third final point signals the effectiveness of the composition effect (COMPO), even holding caution in the interpretation of this variable as it has been previously pointed out. As the graphs show, all the learning patterns are very similar and move simultaneously, confirming the value of complementarity for manufacturing professions.

At the end of this presentation of the first part of the estimation results, some general findings should be outlined both on the empirical and the theoretical grounds.

A progressive reduction of the very relevant components of skill creation emerges. The increasing importance of education – and in particular of schooling especially for higher levels of FP – shows that this constitutes, even more than in the past, a crucial pattern for skill creation. The negative impact of different kinds of training seems to signal that they are not essential, at least as conditions for entering the labour market. However, complementarity among different aspects of knowledge seems to be increasingly important. In fact, it seems that the selection of the learning patterns emerging above could be associated with complementarity, which means that the relevant skill creation patterns must be adequately mixed in order to match labour demand. Additionally, skill selection also indicates that there is a clearer perception of the kind of skills to be demanded for some professions. Finally, the scarce relevance of tenure, as an internal training resource for firms, clearly highlights the presence of some critical problems in the knowledge creation process within firms.

4.6.2 Skill creation in small manufacturing firms

The results deriving from the application of the learning function to data on small manufacturing firms, presented in Table 4.4, confirms some aspects already identified in the previous section.

In aggregate terms the effect of education (ED) and that of WBL are both smoother in 1999 in respect to 1996.

Disaggregating discrete change results, we find that IST, once again, shows the greater average discrete change. The effect of IST^2 is positive, particularly in 1999, opening the way to a conjecture in favour of increasing returns. The CL exhibits quite remarkable results, particularly in 1996, while CI shows a very relevant average discrete change, particularly in 1999 where it is almost as effective as education.

Among WBL components in 1996 FT plays a leading role, while in 1999 the most effective variable is PT. Tenure (TP) and COMPO are not significant; here high labour turnover and skills substitutability seem to prevail.

Other interesting outcomes come from the analysis of predicted probabilities of each FP as illustrated in Figure B1 and Figure B2 in the Appendix.

Excluding some items already discussed above for the manufacturing sector as a whole, here predicted probabilities clearly show the great relevance of higher schooling for upper-scale professions. Within small firms the demand for well educated executives seems to be crucial, even if, as for the manufacturing sector, learning patterns are far better defined for low level professions.

Predicted probabilities confirm the strong impact of specific knowledge components such as CL and CI, particularly for FP5 and FP6, with a different impact in 1996 and 1999. This signals that new knowledge contents are relevant for small organizations for granting their competitive advantage both in the present and for pushing their development in the future.

Table 4.4 Learning function application to Lombardy manufacturing system. Small firms (1–9 employees)

Variables	*Coefficients (1996)*	*Z*	*P > |Z|*	*Δ**	*Coefficients (1999)*	*Z*	*P > |Z|*	*Δ**
IST	0.4639619	7.40	0.000	0.068	0.4035176	6.57	0.000	0.049
IST^2	0.0117843	1.76	0.078	0.013	0.0336137	4.32	0.000	0.026
CL	0.6163134	4.54	0.000	0.037	0.2413969	1.99	0.047	0.013
CI	0.4004216	3.38	0.001	0.024	0.8260793	6.46	0.000	0.046
FT	–0.2559238	–2.37	0.018	0.015	–0.3531149	–3.87	0.000	0.018
EXP	0.3315886	3.88	0.000	0.020	0.2110413	3.09	0.002	0.011
PT	–0.4443095	–3.40	0.001	0.027	–0.2207249	–2.50	0.013	0.011
TP	0.0167286	0.19	0.851	0.001	0.0887954	1.29	0.196	0.005
COMPO	–0.1600014	–0.80	0.422	0.009	–0.2730802	–1.33	0.184	0.014
Cut point				*Aggregate Δ**	*Cut point*			*Aggregate Δ**
cut1	–3.369512		Education	0.129	–2.313477		Education	0.121
cut2	–0.2547624		WBL	0.062	0.1833259		WBL	0.040
cut3	1.699398		TP	n.s.**	2.07556		TP	n.s.**
cut4	1.976451		COMPO	n.s.**	2.118048		COMPO	n.s.**
cut5	2.77391				3.436322			
cut6	5.210313				6.689566			
cut7	8.73046				9.141597			
Number of obs	1,956				3,138			
LR $\chi^2(9)$	1,068.79				1,724.88			
Prob > χ^2	0.0000				0.0000			
Log likelihood	–2,690.209				–4,069.3784			
Pseudo R^2	0.1657				0.1749			

Notes

* Δ: average absolute discrete change is calculated on the deviation standard around the mean; z is the *z-test* of β.

** n.s.: not significant.

All this gives quite a clear picture of how the learning function is shaped in small manufacturing firms. Increasing returns and cumulativeness of further education signal how the contribution of different knowledge components could be relevant for these firms. As it happens for the whole manufacturing sector, no kind of training is required as a condition for being hired in small firms. Indeed, within these particular productive organizations, it is more difficult to identify standard learning processes since the composition of the learning patterns demanded changes over time. Patterns different from schooling are becoming very important since skills content is less standardized for these firms. But also among WBL there is no unique knowledge framework, but a selection of learning modules is required in order to match firms' requirements. Nevertheless, according to these results, small firms seem to be prone to learning processes grounded on the variety, fragmentation and substitutability of skills.

4.6.3 Skill creation in large manufacturing firms

The learning function estimation of the sub-set of large manufacturing firms (more than 250 employees) shows the following results in terms of absolute discrete change (Table 4.5).

In aggregate terms the effect of ED seems to increase (from 0.124 to 0.229) while WBL decreases (from 0.224 to 0.07). The effect of IST increases and its square presents a positive sign. The CL effect is quite relevant in 1996 but is rather low in 1999. CI is significant, but its absolute discrete change is very low in both years. FT presents a very high absolute discrete change in both years, even if the coefficient is always negative. Remaining WBL vectors – EXP and PT – are not statistically significant in 1996 while they give a positive contribution in 1999. TP is not significant while COMPO is relevant, particularly in 1996.

The predicted probability analysis, illustrated in Figure C1 and Figure C2 of the Appendix, shows a very different picture from those shown previously: in fact, higher probabilities for high levels professions with reference both to ED and WBL. Within large firms, high and low professional levels are thus dissimilar not only in qualitative terms – they need different skills – but also in quantitative terms – the same skills need stronger investments in higher level profession.

Predicted probabilities reveal a very particular shape of IST-MIN and IST-MAX in 1999; this could be a warning sign that learning patterns for low and high professional levels are increasingly diverging.

In both years the complementarity presents a significant impact; this could indicate that, at least for large firms, integration between education and WBL is required. This is quite a relevant peculiarity of large firms, where complementarity is reinforced by the selection of the required skills. In this case – among all the skills considered – education and experience are signalled as the most relevant in firm demand.

Table 4.5 Learning function application to Lombardy manufacturing sector. Large firms (more than 250 employees)

Variables	*Coefficients (1996)*	*Z*	*P > /Z/*	*Δ**	*Coefficients (1999)*	*Z*	*P > /Z/*	*Δ**
IST	0.189947	3.59	0.000	0.042	0.8194366	17.56	0.000	0.145
IST^2	0.0095214	2.06	0.039	0.023	–0.0253762	–6.87	0.000	0.053
CL	0.9695823	5.89	0.000	0.059	0.1816675	1.55	0.012	0.010
CI	0.1597855	1.02	0.307	0.010	0.3622979	3.03	0.002	0.021
FT	–5.792102	–13.57	0.000	0.224	–0.3576359	–4.58	0.000	0.020
EXP	0.1722275	1.41	0.160	0.011	0.7867494	9.80	0.000	0.045
PT	0.1086094	0.79	0.429	0.007	–0.3813762	–4.80	0.000	0.022
TP	0.1767781	1.51	0.131	0.011	0.1078371	1.44	0.149	0.006
COMPO	0.7096827	3.92	0.000	0.043	0.383694	2.59	0.010	0.022
Cut point				*Aggregate Δ**	*Cut point*			*Aggregate Δ**
cut1	–7.182603		Education	0.124	–2.136948		Education	0.229
cut2	–4.417454		WBL	0.224	1.260506		WBL	0.087
cut3	–3.517102		TP	n.s.**	2.557604		TP	n.s.**
cut4	–3.308599		COMPO	0.043	2.633534		COMPO	0.022
cut5	–2.914212				3.297185			
cut6	–0.292488				6.427399			
cut7	2.824392				8.078197			
Number of obs	1,600				2,833			
LR $\chi^2(9)$	1,366.05				2,749.48			
Prob > χ^2	0.0000				0.0000			
Log likelihood	–2,156.1245				–3,424.0397			
Pseudo R^2	0.2406				0.2865			

Notes

* Δ: average absolute discrete change is calculated on the deviation standard around the mean; *z* is the *z-test* of *β*.

** n.s.: not significant.

It should be stressed that, even if training is significant, a negative impact in its contribution to skill creation is confirmed. WBL shows to be effective for what concern experience. This indicates that also large firms prefer this kind of learning in creating required skills.

It seems that two main phenomena characterize large manufacturing firms: the amplification of learning patterns differentiation, with the clear prevalence of high professional levels, and the clearer complementarity of learning patterns in the definition of the required skills. In general terms, skills homogeneity seems to emerge within professional levels, and skills heterogeneity among professional levels.

4.6.4 Skill creation in the service sector

The following results emerge from the estimation of the learning function for the service sector (Table 4.6).

In aggregate terms both education and WBL show very low effects since the first set of variables modifies its value from 0.122 to 0.150 and the second from a not significant value to 0.033.

IST represents the highest impact in both estimates, while its square (IST^2) shows a positive and increasing effect. CL is not significant in 1996, while it shows a positive, although small, effect in 1999. CI signals a very relevant absolute discrete change, which is the highest after that of education. In 1999 the effect of COMPO variable is very relevant, whereas in 1996 it is not significant. Also TP presents a significant negative impact only in 1999.

The analysis of predicted probabilities for professional levels (Figure D1 and Figure D2 in the Appendix) suggests two main points. First, the predicted probabilities of learning patterns are particularly concentrated in the middle level professions (FP4-5-6). This means that in this sector firm demand concentrates particularly in the types of skills needed by service workers and shop and market sales workers, clerks and technicians and associate professions. Second, the impact of schooling comes out as decisive for all professional levels, as IST-MAX and IST-MIN show. The service sector shows a quite stable shape of learning patterns within the period analysed, meaning a clear focus of firms on skill requirements.

The clear-cut prevalence of educational variables among other formative patterns, and in particular the relevance of computer skills, could be interpreted as a direct consequence of the innovation that permeates this sector. This could suggest that the influence of the internet and the 'new economy' could call for learning patterns based mostly on education.

Both formal and practical training are not required, proving once again the way firms perceive this kind of learning and perhaps its need of reforms.

The role of complementarity in 1999 seems to suggest that this sector, non only is better focusing on the relevant skills, particularly among educational variables, but also uses them in combination. A change in human resource strategies driven by innovation could be under way.

Table 4.6 Learning function application to Lombardy service sector

Variables	*Coefficients (1996)*	*Z*	*P > /Z/*	*Δ**	*Coefficients (1999)*	*Z*	*P > /Z/*	*Δ**
IST	0.2779569	7.77	0.000	0.054	0.3603823	13.54	0.000	0.067
IST^2	0.0095719	2.92	0.003	0.019	0.0130545	5.12	0.000	0.022
CL	–0.0599967	–0.63	0.529	0.004	–0.2559814	–4.03	0.000	0.015
CI	0.8197054	7.51	0.000	0.049	0.7975828	11.17	0.000	0.046
FT	–0.0189199	–0.24	0.813	0.001	–0.2027698	–3.31	0.001	0.012
EXP	0.0909038	1.28	0.202	0.005	0.0468653	0.91	0.364	0.003
PT	0.0084042	0.08	0.932	0.001	–0.2097112	–3.42	0.001	0.013
TP	–0.0523383	–0.71	0.477	0.003	–0.1326012	–2.57	0.010	0.008
COMPO	0.2106564	1.48	0.140	0.013	0.6693538	6.90	0.000	0.039
Cut point				*Aggregate Δ**	*Cut point*			*Aggregate Δ**
cut1	–2.790718		Education	0.122	–1.974583		Education	0.150
cut2	–1.095773		WBL	n.s.**	–0.9828447		WBL	0.025
cut3	–0.268627		TP	n.s.**	–0.2193254		TP	0.008
cut4	1.538546		COMPO	n.s.**	1.563354		COMPO	0.039
cut5	2.611649				3.125965			
cut6	4.869324				5.33073			
cut7	6.774361				6.962543			
Number of obs	2,968				5,988			
LR $\chi^2(9)$	1,594.64				4,536.88			
Prob > χ^2	0.0000				0.0000			
Log likelihood	–4,513.7026				–8,964.0633			
Pseudo R^2	0.1501				0.2020			

Notes

* Δ: average absolute discrete change is calculated on the deviation standard around the mean; *z* is the *z-test* of *β*.

** n.s.: not significant.

The negative impact of tenure corroborates the idea that this sector is progressively based on skills acquired outside the firm, within the educational system.

4.7 Conclusion

The application of an original specification of the learning function to the data set provided by *Sistema Informativo Excelsior* on labour demand in Lombardy shows a clear picture both of the relevant learning patterns and of their interactions. The order logit technique allows us to focus the analysis on different professional levels with their distinct quantitative and qualitative knowledge contents.

In the analysis of the manufacturing sector as a whole a selection of available learning patterns emerges and, especially for high level professions, complementarity among education and training components seems to prevail.

Rather different attitudes towards learning arise from the comparison between small and large manufacturing firms. In small firms, skill creation and learning patterns are more varied, fragmented and inter-changeable. In large firms we can note the prevalence of a small number of selected learning patterns that are integrated with each other. In the first case substitutability prevails, while in the second, complementarity seems to prevail.

As far as education is concerned, formal work experience, on the one side, seems quite relevant. On the other, formal and practical training does not show any significant impact for the learning processes, signalling a big area of vacuum. This could be ascribed either to a scarce knowledge by the firms on the potential of the training system or to a still limited diffusion of training among young people. Tenure labour contract is significant in a few cases, and exhibits a small impact. This seems to confirm the evidence that firms are not inclined to invest in internal training. As a consequence, this would confirm the prevailing tendency of outsourcing and searching for the needed skills in the labour market (Vitale, 2002). This could give rise both to labour poaching and to the worsening of mismatch problems.

These results have several implications for the theoretical and policy debate.

From the theoretical point of view, the results of this chapter suggest that more attention should be devoted to processes of skill creation and composition. Since complex interactions between skills seem to emerge, it could be shortsighted to concentrate the analysis exclusively on the returns of education, taking the learning process as homogeneous and exogenously determined. A more careful evaluation of the qualitative and cumulative elements that come into play could help to clarify the way in which investment decisions in education and training are changing.

In a policy perspective a greater effort to obtain an effective integration of training and education seems desirable. The possibility to plan career patterns with more flexible – whenever a new skill need emerges – and persistent – not just at the beginning of the career – opportunities combining education and training should be planned for all workers.

The last requirement derives from the evidence that education, and particularly training systems, do not seem adequately prepared to face a demand for increasing complex skills. Particularly for the training needs, a more composite and effective institutional framework must be implemented, where schools should be more coordinated with other learning agents. In this way more appropriate and articulated learning patterns could be offered and a more effective support to young people in their formative choices could be guaranteed.

Appendix

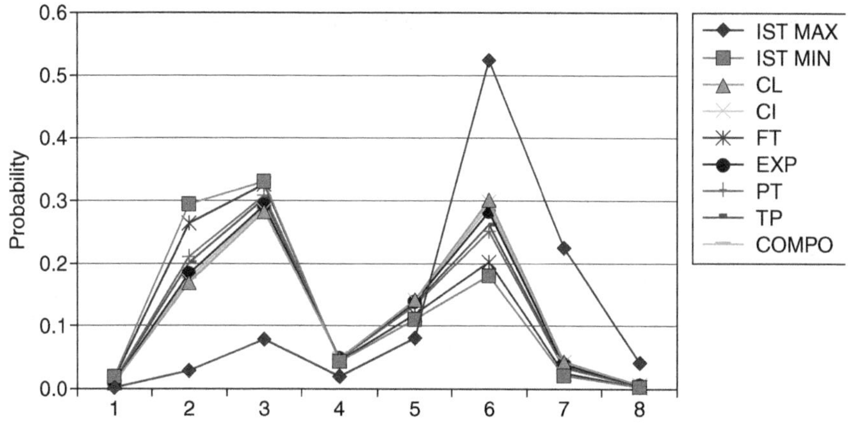

Figure 4.A1 Predicted probability of manufacturing, 1996.

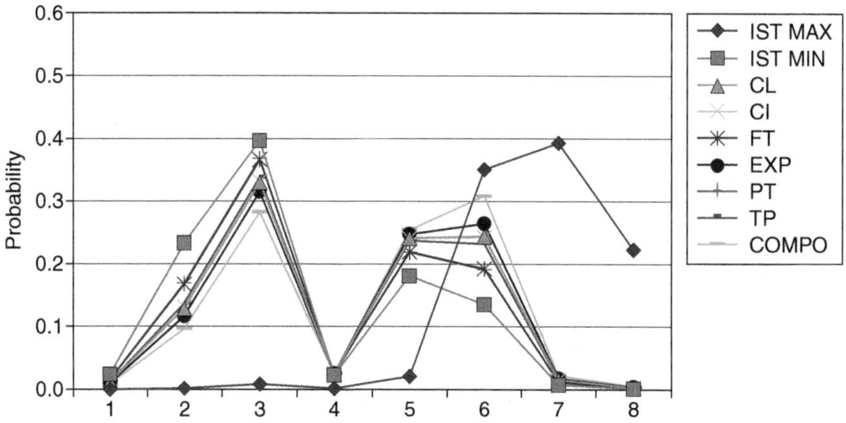

Figure 4.A2 Predicted probability of manufacturing, 1999.

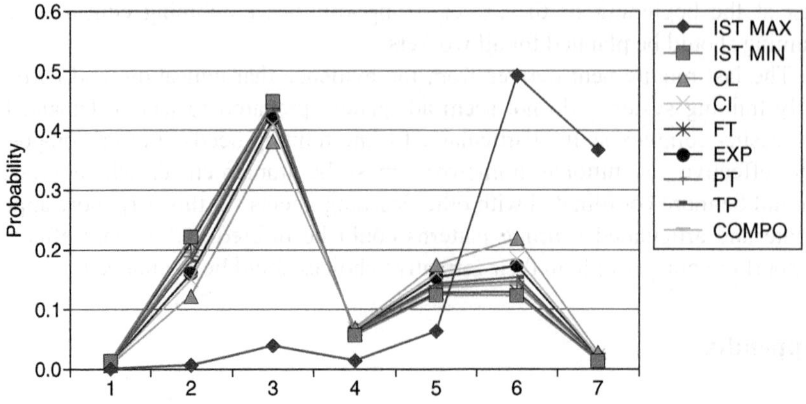

Figure 4.B1 Predicted probability of manufacturing small firms, 1996.

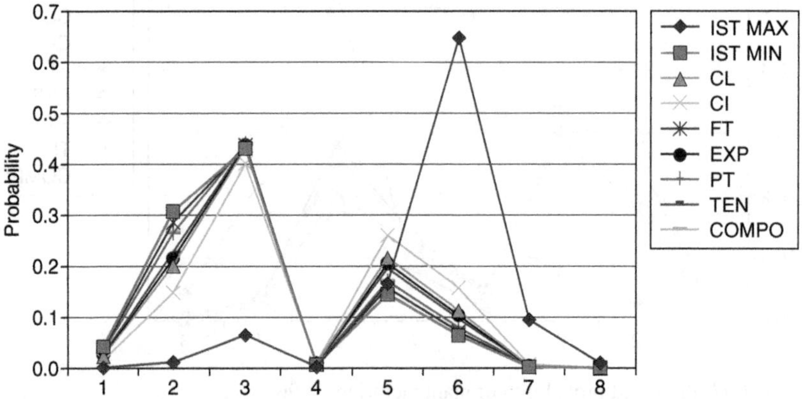

Figure 4.B2 Predicted probability of manufacturing small firms, 1999.

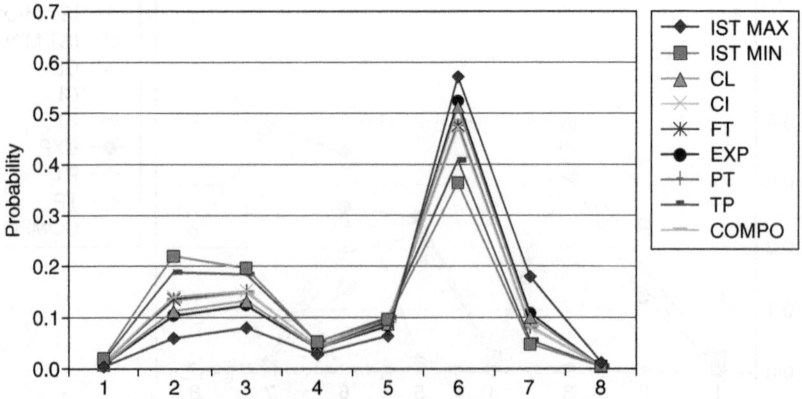

Figure 4.C1 Predicted probability of manufacturing big firms, 1996.

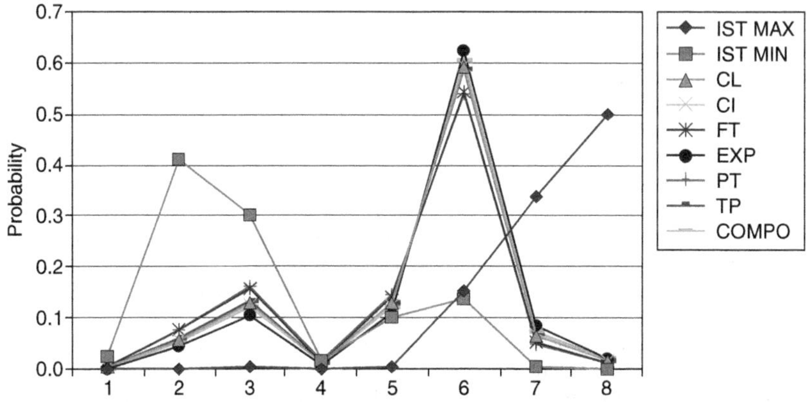

Figure 4.C2 Predicted probability of manufacturing big firms, 1999.

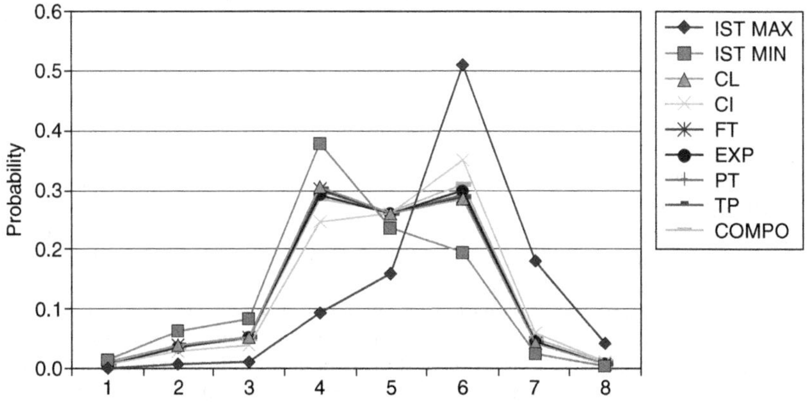

Figure 4.D1 Predicted probability of service sector firms, 1996.

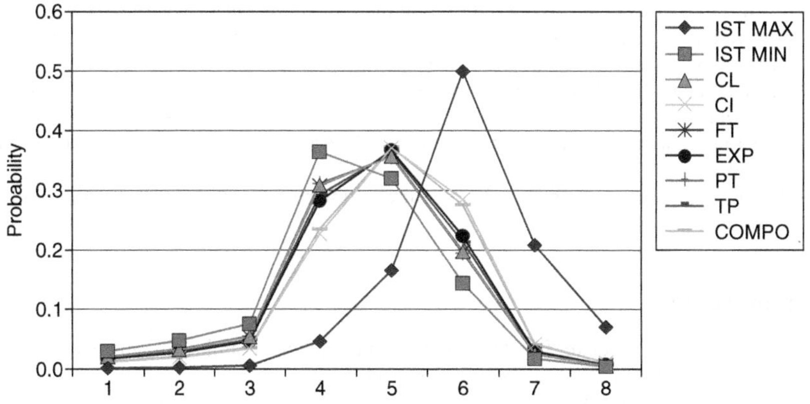

Figure 4.D2 Predicted probability of service sector firms, 1999.

Notes

1 The authors thank all the participants to the PRIN seminars and workshops held in the various universities of the network, with the usual disclaimer.
2 For a definition of 'internal organization' and of 'external organization' reference is made to Chapter 1 of the present volume.
3 It is interesting to note that, if we adopt a view in which households are both producing units and consumers, learning can be conceived as a joint product in households as well as in firms.
4 It is also interesting to note that outsourcing of the learning function is a usual phenomenon. For instance, a study from IDC estimated the US learning outsourcing market alone to be approximately US$1.3 billion in 2005, which represents 7 per cent of the entire learning market (McStravick, 2005).
5 A straightforward discussion of this view can be found in Antonelli and Leoni (1997).
6 Reference is made to Chapter 1.
7 Unobservable factors widely tested in the literature are typically social background, parents education and family income.
8 See, in particular, Green *et al.*, 2001.
9 As in a large part of the cited literature, in this chapter the term knowledge is preferred to human capital, because it clearly represents the complex link between firm organization and workers characteristics.
10 Two significant definitions of tacit knowledge are from Polanyi (1966, p. 4) 'we know more than we can tell' and from Howells (1995, p. 2) 'non codified, disembodied know-how that is acquired via the informal take-up of learned behaviour and procedures'.
11 In many articles Mincer finds a positive relation between tenure and training, with further positive effects on wages (Mincer, 1988, 1989).
12 'Flexible labour market means one in which workers are able to adapt to changing demands by firms for skills by training and retraining as necessary over their working lives' (Arulampalam and Booth, 1998, p. 2).
13 In job analysis terms 'job is a set of tasks and duties executed, or meant to be executed by one person' and 'skill is defined as the ability to carry out the tasks and duties of a given job'. Operationally, four levels of skill are defined, entirely in terms of 'achieved education' (Commission on Behavioural Social Science and Education, 1999, p. 329).
14 Data on potential demand are monitored in the subsequent year with a new questionnaire and data collection.
15 See section 4.4.
16 Firm dimension is considered only in the manufacturing sector where we can analyse differences between industrial districts formed by small firms and other productive contexts where medium and large firms prevail.
17 Arulampalam and Booth (1998), for example, show that larger firms are more likely to train their workers.
18 See International Labour Office (1990) for International Standard Classification of Occupation.
19 Regional governments in Italy control the major part of competences in the field of training policies.

Bibliography

Acemoglu D. and Pischke J.S. (1999): Beyond Becker: Training in imperfect labour markets, *The Economic Journal*, 109 (453), 112–142.

Antonelli G. (1998): Il problema della disoccupazione in Italia: come evitare impostazioni unilaterali, *Economia Politica*, XV (2), 191–207.

Antonelli G. (2002): Flessibilità e nuova economia reale, in G. Antonelli and M. Nosvelli (eds), *Monitoraggio e valutazione delle politiche del lavoro per una nuova economia*, Bologna, Il Mulino, pp. 7–20.

Antonelli G. (2003): Introduzione, in G. Antonelli (ed.), *Istruzione, economia e istituzioni*, Bologna, Il Mulino, pp. 7–21.

Antonelli G. (2004): Structural policies for structural change in Italy and European Union, in G. Antonelli and N. De Liso (eds), *European Economic Integration and Italian Labour Policies*, Aldershot, Ashgate, pp. 297–320.

Antonelli G. and Leoni R. (1997): Cambiamento tecnologico e capitale umano, *Economia & Lavoro*, XXI (3–4), 5–24.

Antonelli G. and Maggioni M.A. (1997): Formazione, competenze e lavoro in contesti economici in rapida evoluzione, in P. Terna (ed.), *La formazione e il lavoro al tempo delle reti telematiche*, Torino, Rosenberg & Sellier, pp. 91–125.

Antonelli G., Leoncini R. and Nosvelli M. (1998): Sistema formativo e crescita economica; un'analisi empirica del sistema italiano, *Economia & Lavoro*, XXXII (1), 9–53.

Antonelli G., Guidetti G., Leoncini R., Nosvelli M., Pombeni M. and Zamparini L. (1998): *Apertura dei mercati locali del lavoro e fabbisogni di risorse umane da parte delle imprese: risultati di un'indagine campionaria nella provincia di Forlì-Cesena*, Milano, Franco Angeli.

Arulampalam W. and Booth A.L. (1997): Training and labour market flexibility: is there a trade off?, Paper presented at the British Association for the Advancement of Science Meeting, Leeds.

Arulampalam W. and Booth A.L. (1998): Learning and earning: do multiple training events pay?, Paper presented at the 1996 Australian Labour Market Research Conference.

Ashton D.N. and Felstead A. (1998): Organisational characteristics and skill formation in Britain: is there a link?, Working Paper no. 22, Leicester, CLMS Press.

Ashton D. and Green F. (1996): *Education, Training and the Global Economy*, Cheltenham, Edward Elgar.

Becker G.S. (1964): *Human Capital*, New York, National Bureau of Economic Research.

Bresnahan T.F., Brynjolfsson E. and Hitt M.L. (1999): Information technology, workplace organization and the demand for skilled labor: firm-level evidence, Working Paper no. 7136, National Bureau of Economic Research.

Burdett K. and Cunningham E.J. (1998): Toward a theory of vacancies, *Journal of Labor Economics*, (3), 445–478.

Commission on Behavioural and Social Science and Education (1999): *The Changing Nature of Work: Implications for Occupational Analysis*, Washington DC, National Academy Press.

De Grip A. and Hoevenberg J. (1996): Upgrading in the European Union, Memorandum no. 1996/3E, Research Centre for Education and the Labour Market (ROA), Maastricht, Research.

Denny K. and Harmon C., (2000): The impact of education and training on the labour market experience of young adults, Working Paper no. 00/08, The Institute for Fiscal Studies.

Eraut M., Alderton J., Cole G. and Senker P. (1998): Learning from other people at work, in F. Coffield (ed.), *Learning at Work*, Bristol, Policy Press, pp. 37–48.

Felstead A. and Ashton D. (2000): Tracing the link: organisational structure and skill demands, *Human Resource Management Journal*, 10, 5–20.

Felstead A., Green F., Mayhews K. and Pack A. (2000): The impact on training on labour mobility, *British Journal of Industrial Relations*, (38), 261–275.

Green F. (1998): The value of skills, Discussion Paper no. 19, University of Kent at Canterbury, Department of Economics.

Green F. and Montgomery S.M. (1998): The quality of skill acquisition in young workers' first job, *Labour*, 12 (3) (September), 473–487.

Green F., Ashton D. and Felstead A. (2001): Estimating the determinants of supply of computing, problem-solving, communication, social and teamworking skills, *Oxford Economic Papers*, 53 (3), 406–433.

Green F., Felstead A. and Gallie D. (2002): Computers and the changing skill intensity of jobs, *Applied Economics*, 35 (14), 1561–1576.

Hanushek E.A., (1979): Conceptual and empirical issues in the estimation of educational production function, *The Journal of Human Resources*, 14 (3) (summer), 351–388.

Howells J. (1995): Tacit knowledge and technology transfer, Working Paper no.16, ESRC Centre for Business Research, University of Cambridge.

International Labour Office (1990), *International Standard Classification of Occupations: ISCO-88*, Geneva, ILO, www.ilo.org/public/english/bureau/stat/isco/index.htm.

ISTAT (2006): Censimento dell'industria e dei servizi (2001), www.istat.it.

Long J.S. (1997): *Regression Models for Categorical and Limited Dependent Variables*, London: Sage Publications.

Long J.S. and Cheng S. (2004): Regression models for categorical outcomes, in M. Hardy and A. Bruman (eds), *Handbook of Data Analysis*, London, Sage Publications, pp. 259–284.

Long J.S. and Freese J. (2001): *Regression Models for Categorical Dependent Variables Using Data*, College Station, Stata Press.

Lundvall B.A. (ed.) (1992): *National Systems of Innovation. Towards a Theory of Innovation and Interactive Learning*, London, Pinter Publishers.

Marcus A. and Green W. (1985): The determinants of rating assignment and performance, Working Paper CRC528, Center for Naval Analyses.

McStravick P. (2005): U.S. Training Outsourcing Services 2005–2009 Forecast: Demystifying Training BPO, no. 33451, IDC Market Analysis, May.

Mincer J. (1988): Job training, wage growth, and labor turnover, NBER Working Paper no. 2690.

Mincer J. (1989): Job training, costs, returns, and wage profile, NBER Working Paper no. 3208.

Mincer J. (1993): *Studies in Human Capital*, Aldershot, Elgar.

Montresor S. (2004): Resources, capabilities and the theory of the firm, *Journal of Economic Studies*, 31 (5), 409–434.

Nosvelli M. (2002): Politiche formative e inserimento lavorativo: La valutazione degli esiti in Emilia Romagna, in G. Antonelli and M. Nosvelli (eds), *Monitoraggio e valutazione delle politiche del lavoro per una nuova economia*, Bologna, Il Mulino, pp. 204–236.

Pini P. (2000): Retribuzioni flessibili e partecipazione all'impresa. Note al margine di un confronto, Università di Ferrara, Quaderni del Dipartimento di Economia, Istituzioni, Territorio, no. 14.

Polanyi M. (1966): *The Tacit Dimension*, New York, Doubleday.

Primoff E. and Fine S. (1988): A history of job analysis, in S. Gael (ed.), *The Job Analysis Handbook for Business, Industry, and Government*, New York, John Wiley & Sons.

Psacharopuolos G. and Patrinos H.A. (2004): Human capital and rates of return, in G. Johmes and J. Johnes (eds), *International Handbook of the Economics of Education*, Cheltenham, Edward Elgar, pp. 1–57.

Rosenberg N. (1982): *Inside the Black Box: Technology and Economics*, Cambridge, Cambridge University Press.

Stasz C. (1997): Do employers need the skills they want? Evidence from technical work, *Journal of Education and Work*, (10), 205–223.

Thurow L.C. (1976), *Generating Inequality*, London, Macmillan Press.

Unioncamere, Ministero del Lavoro e della Previdenza Sociale (1997/1999): *Sistema Informativo Excelsior*, Roma, Unioncamere.

Vitale L. (2002): Le imprese si sfidano sui talenti, *Il Sole 24 ore*, 8 June, p. 16.

Part II

Local and mesoeconomic level

5 A morphogenetic approach to the evolution of technological capabilities

Mauro Lombardi

5.1 Introduction

Decades after seminal works by Coase and Hayek there is neither a unified theory which is able to give an universally accepted definition of firm, nor individual and collective (firms, organizations) capabilities and competencies which are univocally defined. Thus, it is not surprising the conclusion by Garrouste and Saussier (2005), in treating main themes tackled by the more recent theories of firms,[1] that the question "What is a firm?" is still a theoretical challenge, while the research agenda is full of topics to be sharpened.

If it is true that firm is the *primum mobile* of modern capitalist economies, a set of fundamental problems remain unsolved: why do they exist and how do they develop (Stam and Garney, 2005)? What type of coordination mechanisms does prevail in different contexts where competencies and capabilities (technological and organizational) are formed and take different configurations?

The persistence of the foregoing interrogatives does not indicate a blocked situation; on the contrary, the debate is very rich, as very interesting topics have been analysed in important essays.

For example, the theoretical approach developed by Radner (1992, 1996) and van Zandt (1998) has closely examined the firm as information processor, first of all by focusing on problems relating to the costs of acquisition, storage and transmission of information, either from an individual (Radner, 2000) or organizational point of view (van Zandt, 1998). Garricano (2000) has developed a research line centred on the role of knowledge production through hierarchical organization in solving problems.

More recently Aoki (2004), Aoki and Takizawa (2002) have analysed basic aspects of information structure and incentive schemes, which are particularly significant within production systems like the "Silicon Valley model". They did that by focusing on information, role of agents and different types of information task.

A relevant component of the evolutionary approach has emphasised the concept of dynamic capabilities,[2] which synthesizes three basic elements: interaction among competencies, changing environments, strategic elaboration able to generate either adaptive or anticipating answers to changes occurring at different levels of the economic system.

In this theoretical perspective firms are conceived as "repositories of knowledge to a large extent embodied in their operational routines, and modified through times by their 'higher level' rules of behaviour and strategies" (Coriat and Dosi, 1999, p. 104), while "competencies are the collective property of the routines of an organization".

Coriat and Dosi are right in recognizing that evolutionary literature has partially neglected the double nature of firms and routines (problem solving skills and mechanisms of governance),[3] but we think that there are still a lot of aspects to be sharpened through the analysis of competencies, capabilities and their evolution. To this end we leave aside the incentive problem and focus on the production processes in terms of information and knowledge, starting from a precise statement: "The economy as an adaptive evolving system … comprising of multiple agents diverse in abilities and capabilities, interacting, adapting, reacting, and constantly modifying the patterns and structure that they help to create" (Metcalfe and De Fonseca, 2001).

The aim of this chapter is to suggest a theoretical framework and a research programme in order to analyse the evolution of competencies and capabilities.

In this perspective we lay out the cognitive foundations for analysing the dynamics for technological regimes, which are defined as macro-properties or patterns. Following a cognitive approach the latter are based on a grammar and rules, which were in turn created and evolve during techno-productive problem solving activity. The arrival point of the analysis is a tentative explanation of the evolution of socio-technical systems according to the dynamic matching of multiple elements, which act at different dimensions (micro, meso and macro). The research line is developed by embedding some suggestions drawn on the morphogenetic approach, as defined by Archer (1995). In order to escape from the quagmire caused by the dichotomy micro/macro and the respective risks of "downwards conflation" (individualism) and "upwards conflation" (holistic view of a social whole), we take up an approach aiming at discussing the linkages between structure and agency. It is worth highlighting that "the morph element is an acknowledgement that society has not a pre-set form or preferred state; the 'genetic' part is a recognition that it takes its shape from, and is formed by, agents, originating from the intended and unintended consequences of their activities" (Archer, 1995, p. 5). By adopting this theoretical perspective interdependencies and interplay between interacting elements become central units of analysis. Then, how interactions and structures of interactions shape socio-economic phenomena is our field of inquiry. The adopted approach allows us to describe and explain emergent properties as "relational, arising out of combinations" (Archer, 1995, p. 9). In this way micro- and macro-phenomena are subsumed within the development of nexus, which consequently appears as concretions at different levels of the dynamic processes. The morphogenetic approach seems particularly fruitful in analysing the evolution of competencies and capabilities, because interactions and interdependencies among elements belonging either to different theoretical spaces or to socio-economic fields are unavoidable ingredients of real processes.

In applying the suggested approach the analysis develops step by step (or according to a precise sequence).

The first step is the definition of the "elementary particles", which are the starting point for analysing the cognitive process of competencies building up. So in section 5.2 the basic concepts are defined as interactors, structures of interactions, and connective geometry, starting from the previous definition of economy as an adaptive evolving system. In section 5.3, we treat the problem solving activity in the new product development process as multiple search within a combinatorial design space.

The second step is the development of a micro-perspective, that is, to study how knowledge spaces are created and evolve. Indeed in section 5.4, the analysis is sharpened by developing a particular kind of micro-perspective, in the sense that constraints and degrees of freedom are discussed as they unfold in exploring activity of different "knowledge spaces". Thus the concepts of rules and grammar are put forward.

The third step is deepened in section 5.5, where a meso-perspective is suggested as competencies and capabilities are formed through combining rule-set and grammar, in other words by combining packages of information processing mechanisms or cognitive modules.

With the last step we enter a macro-level perspective[4] (section 5.6) by analysing the linkages between different techno-economic fields, involved in the technological dynamics. From this point of view the role of socio-technical systems is discussed in order to explain two seemingly contradictory properties: stability and evolvability of technological processes. Section 5.7 concludes.

5.2 Basic concepts: population of interactors and structure of interactions

Tightly connected to the concept of the economy as an adaptive evolving system, is the assumption that it is composed of interacting agents.

The adopted point of view is centred on the idea that dynamics and extension of interactions constitute the fundamental mechanism which feeds the economic evolution.

Four elements must be emphasized. (1) The dynamics and the structure of interactions can produce conflicting pressures on the one hand towards uniform rules, behaviour and strategies, and on the other, towards the creation of novelties to the extent that new combinations of pre-existing elements can be created. That means that the heterogeneity of agents is a fundamental property of our field of inquiry.[5] (2) This property and the centrality of interaction mechanisms lead us to conceive a population composed of agents viewed as interactors, which can exist at different levels: individual (Devezas and Corredine, 2002), information exchanging firms (Hodgson and Knudsen, 2004), organizations and structures. In other words, there are aggregates of individuals, among which interlocking relationships may develop until consolidated structures emerge, which in turn can appear in very different forms. (3) The connective geometry among agents-interactors (Potts, 2000; Loasby, 2001) becomes a fundamental field of inquiry, as information exchanges and processes of communication are tightly interdependent (Sorenson, 2003).[6] Thanks to diversity generators, which are endogenous to the economic system, a relational topology develops that is characterized by global or local topological constraints, which limit the diffusion process of novelties and the techno-productive research. Indeed the degrees of freedom allowed by the relational topology are the basic elements of various organizational forms (integrated models, loosely coupled systems, multiple forms of networks).[7] (4) An adaptive economic system, composed of populations of heterogeneous interactors, has as basic ingredients information and knowledge flows. In fact, within economic systems *teleonomic* processes prevail (Mayr, 1992),[8] that is the development and the diffusion of goal-seeking and "programme-based" behaviours. This characterization of decision units implies that techno-economic processes are fundamentally affected by unceasing elaboration of information, beyond matter and energy flows. Within social systems interactions are primarily informational and information flows continuously generate processes and phenomena leading to situations characterized by cognitive and relational complexity (Boisot and Child, 1999).

In the adopted perspective the distinction between data, information and knowledge becomes crucial.

Data are thing-like and are "discernible differences in physical states of the world" (Boisot and Canals, 2004, p. 46), while "information is relational and consists of regularities extracted from the data by mapping events or states of the world. Finally knowledge is information elaborated within a shared context, thus anchored to beliefs, expectations, strategies" (Boisot and Canals, 2004; Lombardi, 2003a, and cited bibliography).

Thanks to the aforementioned concepts (heterogeneity of agents-interactors, connective geometry, distinction between information and knowledge) we have a theoretical framework which allows us to deepen the main topic of our chapter: what mechanisms and forms occur and act within the evolution of capabilities at different levels of the economic system.

5.3 Building competencies and capabilities

Let us start from an abstract situation: an individual or a collective entity (group of individuals) singles out an unsatisfied need, then they perceive a business opportunity, to the extent that can be translated into a potential product space, that is in a new idea space for commodities.

By taking up a previously introduced distinction (data, information and knowledge), this happens if differences in the states of the world relating to requirements and consumers (i.e. data) are transformed in regularities (i.e. information) and when it is possible to map singled out opportunities into accessible options. In other words, it is possible to define something able to satisfy needs (i.e. knowledge).

These elements are the starting point of a potential path, the arrival point of which is the collocation of goods on the market.

In this perspective it seems clear that the decision unit must tackle a complex problem: to conceive a matching map from components of the need for space to the production potentialities. In order to define these latter the analysis has to start from this point: to create the hypothesized matching means to execute problem solving and goal-oriented activities.

Unless conceiving agents who freely draw on an unbounded set of all abstractly conceivable ideas, in fact they enjoy a many fewer degrees of freedom. In order to avoid combinatorial explosion, interactors have to start with sufficiently sound assumptions about how a product can be technically realized, how production activities have to be done and organized (Krishan and Ulrich, 2001). The picture is more complicated when we have to think not only about improvements and refinements of products, but also about new conceptualizations of techno-productive processes (Veryzer, 1998), that is radical discontinuities within the production systems. The latter are the unforeseeable results of "diversity generators", which are endogenous to the economic system.

Thus, it is necessary to examine and tackle two problems: (1) How to avoid the combinatorial explosion? (2) How does the endogenous generative power unfold and produce novelties?

As for the first of these, we shall see that the combinatorial explosion is avoided thanks to the goal-oriented nature of the production activity, as it unfolds like directed research and focused trials.

As for the second problem we shall see that precisely the dynamics of interactions constitute a kind of "potential of action" inside the economic system. In general terms, as a product development process, it can be defined as a sequence of steps able to realize the congruence/mapping from a set of techno-scientific principles and methods to a vector of attributes (product specifics), through component and phase specifications.

So there is a multiplicity of research spaces, which can unfold at different levels. The realization of a viable final vector of attributes requires the choices in each field of inquiry to be congruent with each other.

Combinatorial problems often arise in design and production activity, as "the design space is not Euclidean but a large, discrete configuration space" (Cooper, 2000) and problems are ill-defined, because there is a non complete and perfectly known space, within which to explore and verify every conceivable solution on the basis of well accepted criteria.

In many sistuations, above all during more intense transformation phases, a product development process cannot be executed "sequentially through strategic planning and concept generation, pre-technical evaluation, technical development and commercialization" (Veryzer, 1998, p. 308). On the contrary, it is essentially based on various overlapping phases, which must be recognized and managed. The picture is still more complex if economic growth is conceived as "driven by a succession of General Purpose Technologies sometimes overlapping and sometimes discretely separated by long periods when only small incremental changes are being made in well established General Purpose Technologies" (Carlaw and Lipsey, 2002, pp. 1305–1306).

Static and dynamic externalities, spillover effects, technological complementarities can spread within the techno-economic landscape, characterized by the abrupt emergence of new technologies. In this way multiple search spaces are periodically updated and changed depending on changes of fundamental coordinates, which affect problem solving activities and research trajectories in every economic unit.

Thus three basic cognitive requirements arise: (1) to analyse how to stir the congruence between components belonging to multiple search spaces, (2) to describe the protagonists of congruence processes, (3) to point out the fundamental mechanisms within cognitive processes and organizational dynamics.

The suggested morphogenetic approach can help us to understand that the evolution of capabilities at different levels (individual and collective) are the crux of the matter.

5.4 A micro-perspective:[9] constraints and degrees of freedom

The starting point is the following statement: first of all when there are multiple spaces the problem solving activity cannot be purely random, that is based on disordered accumulation of chunks of knowledge. Indeed technical problem solving often is a "constructive synthetic activity" as the human brain "is [an] adjuster, not [a] calculator" (Margolis, 1987) and human beings are "patterns seeking", whose evolutionary bases leads them to "seeing something, rather than nothing" (Margolis, 1987, p. 39). If knowledge is "the capacity to extrapolate patterns" by recognizing similarity and "relating them to a learnt tacit background" (Nightingale, 1998), the cognitive processes are founded on the activities of "tuning of patterns and cues" (Margolis, 1987, p. 71). Analogously, within economic processes populated by heterogeneous interactors, knowledge is developed through n-entities continually trying to tune decision-making patterns with patterns of exogenous impulses.

In order to avoid that the search activity develops as shapeless accumulation of information and knowledge, constraints are created which reduce the degrees of freedom in exploring the combinatorial space of potential solutions. What are these constraints and how do they appear?

"All organisms are subject to constraints" (Maynard Smith *et al.*, 1985) and, in general, complex systems are characterized by different types of constraints, which are biases affecting their potential for variation.[10] So, constraints, first of all, have different sources (cognitive, social, organizational) and essentially consist of general guidelines which define the inquiry field. Constraints can pertain either to individuals and groups, or to different spheres (cognitive, practical behaviour, cultural).

From the adopted point of view it must be emphasized that the degrees of freedom are reduced by introducing constraints which differ in strength and level at which they are introduced.

Let us limit the treatment of possible combinations of constraints to two basic dichotomic components: theoretical/practical, individual/collective.

Following a theoretical framework suggested by Commons, Kaufmann (2003, p. 82) states that "the fundamental unit in an economy is not a firm but a plant, or what might be referred to more generically as a 'production unit' "; thus the traditional view of alternative forms of economic organization ("market vs firms") is "only partially correct". "The two end-points in economic organization are an economy composed of N single person production units" (or "firms in the case of legally organized sole proprietorship") and one giant production unit (possibly a "firm") in which all the nation's "GDP is produced".

Thus there is a virtual universe composed of a variety of potential models of production units: from N individual producers through an entity alone. The choice of one of them depends on the exploration of multiple research spaces and then on the changing constraints which affect the inquiry.

Reciprocal influences from individual research to inquiring activity within more complex entities come to the fore and lead us to look at the structures of interactions.

Thus the analysis of the evolution of capabilities must focus on the feedback loops, which can occur at different levels of iterative procedures, which develop by combining and melting pre-existing pieces of information, so that new knowledge is produced or the old is spread. Alternatively, the evolutionary emergence of results stemming from relational forms stirs and feeds explorative activity. The morphogenetic approach aims just at capturing this type of dynamics, as interaction processes generate constraints and regularities, either in cognition or behaviour for individuals and organizations.

Once more we have to tackle questions pertaining to the basic dichotomic components: theoretical/practical, individual/collective.

First of all let us look into the product development process. Products consist of problem solving activities, which are developed by drawing on a set of available knowledge, which can be synthesized through the concept of technology. We define technology as

> a means to fulfil a purpose. Such a means may be instantiated as a physical device, or a method, or an industrial process, or an algorithm. Each technology executes at least one function and in this sense we can call it an executable. All technologies are put together or constructed from components (at least one), or assemblies, or subroutines, or stages. But each component or subsystem also has a function or assignment to carry out; each component therefore is an object with a purpose – and is also an executable. A technology therefore is an executable that is a combination of executables. Thus a given technology – think of an aircraft gas-turbine powerplant, for

> example – can be broken out into its component building blocks and these remain technologies – or executables. In this sense a technology is recursive in structure.
>
> (Arthur and Pollak, 2004)

Technology as a combination of executables has a recursive structure, in the sense that it is composed of elements which are in turn further decomposable in building blocks. The essence of these latter, be they either artefacts or conceptual devices, consists of information packages, which are worth examining. Where do information packages come from and how are they generated?

Let us discuss the genetic process of a given technology within a horizon characterized by multiple search spaces. The starting point is the statement that there is an idea space, which is the "universal set of all possible technological ideas in the past, in the present and in the future" (Olsson, 2000, p. 40). Within this space a distance metric can be defined (Olsson, 2000; Kauffman *et al.*, 2000) and inner sub-sets are "infinite, closed, and bounded"[11] (Olsson, 2005). Let us call the idea space *Ω-space*.

Within it, a set of knowledge can be produced relating to natural regularities. Let us call this type of knowledge propositional knowledge (Mokyr, 2000, 2005), which constitutes the epistemic base (*K-space*), enabling human beings to direct the searching process for solutions to problems. In this way principles can be defined that act as a set of constraints able to reduce the high dimensionality of the search spaces otherwise short of regularities and patterns, whereby it could expand everywhere.

Two points must be underlined. First of all such constraints are not fixed, to the extent that they are synthetic representations of an incompletely known world. Thus the epistemic base is subject to changes depending on the information accumulated, produced by enrichment processes and changes of inputs relating to physical states of the world.

The second point to be underlined relates to the information exchanges among agents, which are once again interactors (see section 5.1): the enlargement and the restructuring of the epistemic base is not the unavoidable result of a public process of communication of information and knowledge. Indeed the fundamental mechanism is the intermingling of private information processing and continuous exchange.

Propositional knowledge is a set of ordering principles of a search process which otherwise would be an unbounded branching tree and first of all short of cues or clues on how to extract operational solutions from changing stacks of knowledge.

In other terms, propositional knowledge shapes the surrounding world precisely during problem solving activity, by fixing biases in information processing.

These ordering principles can change owing to different information and knowledge processes. The epistemic base is a fundamental building block within the recursive structure of technology, which we view as a *λ-space*, composed of recurrent regularities within the world around us (let us call it *ρ-subspace*) and of prescriptive knowledge or techniques (*τ-subspace*) (Mokyr, 2005), "a set of instructions on how to produce goods and services".

Both sub-sets (recurrent phenomena and set of instructions) are "useful knowledge", because they allow us to find different ways of satisfying human needs and they are the result of an unceasing mapping from *Ω-space* to *λ-space*. The map correlating varying components of the two spaces is not one-to-one, but it could be – in certain historical circumstances – many-to-one in both directions, while in other contingencies it could be one-to-one.

It is particularly important to be aware that the *τ-subspace* is the set of feasible techniques relating to the epistemic base: this means that further constraints are introduced, which affect the activity – productive and explorative at the same time – as propositional knowledge and prescriptive knowledge must be understood, learned and interpreted in the light of the task environment. For example, it is fundamental to know chemical laws and those relating to the effects of combination of substances, but this knowledge must be continuously enriched by information packages generated by acting at the shop level within a given factory.

In this view the recursive structure of technology is the representation of an unceasing evolutionary mapping from sub-spaces belonging to multiple search spaces. It is clear from the picture that there is a generative power endogenous to the dynamics of cognitive processes, to the extent that raw ingredients, i.e. data on physical states of the world, are combined and elaborated so that ordering principles (*K-space*) are produced. In turn these are the core of a combinatorial activity which maps from sub-spaces of the *Ω-space* to sub-sets belonging to the high-dimensional space of the all possible solutions to problems. In order to obtain a set of feasible techniques, some procedures are considered admissible and others are excluded, i.e. mappings that beget executable functions are synthesized by means of the arrangements of components, which we call rules.

Here we find strong conceptual similarities with Chomsky's model of language faculty in human beings. In developing a research programme aiming at finding highly restrictive principles which should reduce the set of admissible grammars and at the same time sufficiently open to enrichment on the basis of experience (Chomsky, 1980), Chomsky's model (Chomsky, 2000) postulates two components: (1) general principles of language faculty, like universal properties, and (2) parameters, which mean open choices resulting from interactions with different contexts.

Analogously, propositional knowledge is the set of ordering principles which limit the search space for problem solving activities, whose parameters change depending on the task environment. So we have dynamics inside different spaces and a given technology emerges as the mapping between different spaces and sub-spaces acquire relative stability. In this perspective we can hypothesize arrangements of components and combinations of significant chunks of information and segment of knowledge sets.[12] Technology is therefore a combinatorial activity and at the same time the changing result of it within a kind of global workspace, within which feedback loops and recursive structures are fundamental.

The unceasing evolution of mapping raises some questions: (1) How is it possible that such different sources of information and knowledge are coordinated in order to produce coherent conceptual products and real objects? (2) How can we give an "explanation of principle" (von Hayek, 1964)[13] of two seemingly contradictory properties of technological processes: stability and, at the same, time evolvability?

In order to answer the two questions we have to look into the problem solving activity.

5.5 What are the competencies: a meso-level analysis

We take up a research programme developed by Vanberg and Vromen on the basis of seminal works by Mayr and Popper. Following Mayr's distinction between teleomatic and teleonomic processes (see note 8), the adaptive economic system is above all characterized by the presence of multiple teleonomic processes, in other words by entities with purposeful behaviour based on programmes. These latter are pre-arranged information, or conjectural knowledge about the world (Vanberg, 2002, p. 15),[14] which is unceasingly changed depending on encoding information acquired by interacting with the environment. Lessons from experience and processed information are stored in forms of instructions (conscious or unconscious "*if . . . then*" rules), which are used in ever changing problem solving activities and thus are subject to unforeseeable transformations, on the basis of decoding activity,[15] performed either by the same agents or by whatever other interactor.

In this way the sequences of encoding, based on feedback processes, and decoding, centred on applying elements of a repertoire of programmes, are the gist of the adaptive dynamics and the adaptedness property of human behaviour, as successful programmes or set of rules are retained while those totally or partially failed lead to changes or neglect.

According to this view "the notion of programme or conjecture-based behaviour allows one to include the study of conscious rational choice in a broader theoretical framework" (Vanberg, 2002, p. 27). At the same time the past experience – synthesized in recipes, rules or programmes – constitutes the fundamental ingredient of a problem-solving activity, viewed as unceasing search for similarities between past situations and the actual task environment. Even more the human mind is an "adaptive system" that "chooses behaviour in the light of its goals and as appropriated to the particular context it is working" (Simon, 1998, p. 15). In this way

> in complex adaptive behaviour the link between goals and environment is mediated by strategies and knowledge discovered and learned by the actor. The human mind can acquire an enormous variety of different skills, behavioural patterns, problem solving repertoires, and perceptual habits; which of

> these it will acquire in any particular case is function of what it has been taught and what is experienced.
>
> (Simon, 1979, p. 81)

In this perspective, Vromen's idea that programmes are "information processing devices, in the human mind, that enact capacities or competencies" it is a useful suggestion. Such programmes are the underlying competencies, which "are activated and run unconsciously" (Vromen, 2004a, p. 15).

This research line generates a well-founded definition of competencies, either the individual or collective view (firms, organization): competencies are packages of information processing devices or cognitive modules[16] (Vromen, 2004b), which are formed, grouped and decomposed according to the evolution of information and knowledge at different levels. In fact, the preceding treatment of competencies constitutes a meso-level analysis compared to the micro-level, previously developed (sections 5.3, 5.4), that is the aforementioned dynamics and mapping between different spaces and sub-spaces, in the form of arrangements of components and combinations of chunks of information.

The general picture is sufficiently defined: technological evolution is fed with a mapping from Ω-space to λ-space in the techno-productive problem-solving activity. We have defined rules as the outcomes of these mappings, which are embedded in productive routines and at the same time are characterized by these properties: (1) they evolve, depending on the mix of exploitation and exploration strategies performed by agents (changes in connections between components of Ω-space and elements of λ-space; recombination of pre-existing entities). (2) They compete, as they produce solutions with different degrees of success in manipulating inputs so as to have goods and services. (3) They are selected, as the micro-diversity is continually threatened by the process of leaving aside less preferred solutions. Macro-dynamics of general patterns tend to emerge, until new drivers of variety appear (ideas, mappings, recombinations, and so on) (Bargigli and Lombardi, 2006).

5.6 The macro-perspective: technological regime as macro-property

Rules and set of rules allow to lay out general patterns in order to find solutions to techno-productive problems. If a changing mix of exploration and exploitation (March, 1991, 1994) is an essential characteristic of every human activity, refinement, enrichment, improvement and adaptation are components of problem solving activities, when mapping from some sub-spaces to others must be translated in vectors of attributes. A generative power is endogenous to technological dynamics as multiple combinations of information processing devices (programmes) evolve through exchanges of information, which can be generated everywhere.

Thus sequences of mapping and matching activities can be characterized by different degrees of complexity, to the extent that it develops at different levels and matching problems can trigger (as often happens) an enlargement of the search activity. Alternatively, the development of an exploration activity, which modifies the extension and the relevance of sub-spaces belonging to different sets, occurs within an essentially combinatorial space, as chunks of information and programs or competencies are continuously updated, upgraded or eventually destroyed.

If technical problem solving "is predominantly (through not exclusively) a constructive/synthetic activity" (Stankiewicz, 2000, p. 236), how can regularities and stable configurations emerge? The theoretical perspective here suggested can help to understand two different and seemingly contradictory properties such as stability and transformation.

In fact the exploration activity does not unfold in every dimension: rules and grammar (see sections 5.4, 5.5) contain ordering principles and at the same time parameters, that is an open choice for changes according to incoming information. Technical problem solving develops within a design space, which is "a combinatorial space generated by a set of operants – for example, components, unit operations and routines", or "heterogeneous information packages" (Stankiewicz, 2000, p. 236).

The design spaces evolve through the addition of other components or the restructuring of those existing. So different patterns emerge as design spaces evolve according to the type of knowledge processed. In analysing the generative mechanisms acting within the evolution of design, research in the design science stresses the fundamental importance of knowledge and first of all the role of technological rule, defined as "a chunk of general knowledge linking an intervention or artefact with an expected outcome or performance in a certain field of application" (van Aken, 2004a, p. 6).[17] The same author distinguishes between "algorithmic rules", which have a general format ("if you want to achieve Y in situation Z, then perform action X"), and "heuristic rule", which appears in this format: "if you want to achieve Y in situation Z, then perform something like action X". In the new product development process rules are applied and changed as field-tested and grounded solution concepts[18] are found, so that distinct patterns of technological evolution emerge.

From the point of view here adopted, the essence of a technological regime is "the rule-set or grammar embedded in complex engineering practices, production process technologies, product characteristics, skill and procedures, ways of defining problems" (Rip and Kemp, quoted in Geels, 2002).

Stankiewicz (2000) distinguishes four technological regimes: (1) the craft regime, first of all based on experiential learning and gradual accumulation of knowledge. (2) The engineering regime, centred on the massive use of symbolic representation of knowledge and a large use of analytical devices. (3) The architectural regime, composed of multifunctional systems, that are developed on the basis of particular activities: "Architect-designers specialise in reading/anticipating user needs and designing complex systems which mobilise the existing technological resources to meet those needs"

(Stankiewicz, 2000, p. 240). (4) The research regime, that is the context where experimental learning[19] and the role of science becomes a fundamental ingredient of technological dynamics.

Technological regimes are not islands within a sea, but they are elements of socio-technical regime, viewed as a "semi-coherent set of rules carried by different social groups from socio-technical regimes. By providing orientation and co-ordination to the activity of relevant actor groups, socio-technical regimes account for the stability of socio-technical configurations" (Geels, 2002, p. 1260).

So mutual adaptation between different social groups and the structures of interactions among them lead to the formation of socio-technical regimes, that "can be understood as the deep structure or grammar of socio-technical systems" (Geels, 2004, p. 2004).

5.7 Conclusions

The end point of our thesis is clear: bounded information, feedback loops and recursiveness are basic elements which unceasingly feed information and knowledge flows, the formation of rules, competencies, technological regimes and socio-technical systems. On the basis of this, it is not surprising that techno-economic dynamics show stability and evolution at the same time; on the contrary, evolutionary forms of technological capabilities unceasingly oscillate between the two macro-properties. Changes at multiple levels can trigger smaller and bigger transformations, depending on the unforeseeable intermingling of individuals and systemic evolutionary paths.

Chunks of information, bounding/ordering principles, rules, grammar and technological regimes are the multiple drivers of the dynamics of competencies and capabilities.

In this chapter we have proposed a particular theoretical framework and research line, aimed at reconstructing how from "elementary particles", like chunks of information, competencies and capabilities are built up and transformed within technological evolution.

The analysis has focused on the evolution of knowledge through the combining and re-combining of information chunks into rules, which stem from mapping from one knowledge space to another during problem solving activities in the product development process. In order to avoid the combinatorial explosion of search space, "developmental constraints" are generated thanks to information exchanges between agents-interactors. The structure of interactions allows us to explain the formation of constraints at different levels of complex entities. In other words, we have the formation of technical regimes and socio-technical systems.

A future research line will focus on probing sound and robust simulation models able to represent and explain the dynamics of relationships in the mapping between multiple knowledge and production spaces, populated by interactors which execute a variable mix of local and global search.[20]

Notes

1 Garrouste and Saussier (2005) discuss different approaches to two fundamental problems: What is a firm and what are its boundaries? They consider either the view of the firm as collection of assets and internal incentive mechanisms, and that of it as collection of historical constructed capabilities. It is also relevant their treatment of the firm on the basis of concepts of authority, hierarchy, communication and dispersion of knowledge.

2 "Dynamic capabilities are the ability to reconfigure, redirect, transform and appropriately shape and integrate existing core competencies with external resources and strategic and complementary assets to meet the challenges of a time-pressured, rapidly changing Schumpeterian world of competition and imitation", (Teece *et al.*, 2000, p. 339).

3 For an analysis of competence perspective and governance theory in the analysis of firms see Nooteboom (2004), Nooteboom and Gilsing (2004).

4 It must be emphasized that the distinction micro- meso- and macro- is related to the proposed cognitive approach and thus is different from the accepted meaning within the standard economic literature (see note 9).

5 Witt (2004) discusses several important questions about the linkages between novelty, heterogeneity of economic agents and multi-level evolutionary process.

6 If human beings are rule-making and rule-using (cognitive rules for agents, blueprint rules for organization) (Dopfer, 2004), the economy can be viewed as a "complex structure of rules" (Dopfer *et al.*, 2005). In this chapter we try to sharpen the notion of rule and to demonstrate that it is a kind of "elementary particle" of a deep structure of economic processes. Constant II (2002, p. 1243) sees the selection environment of economic process as composed of "vehicles or interactors which can be artefacts, firms, or markets".

7 Abrahamson and Rosenkopf (1997) show the importance of different network structures in affecting how innovation processes unfold.

8 *Teleomatic* processes "indicate that they are automatically achieved" (Mayr, 1992, p. 125). "A teleonomic process or behaviour is one that owes its goal-directedness to the operation of a program" and "program might be defined as coded or prearranged information that controls a process (or behaviour) leading toward a goal" (Mayr, 1992, pp. 127–128).

9 The distinction between micro- meso- and macro-perspective has strong similarities with the view proposed by Dopfer *et al.* (2005), where the micro-perspective pertains to the analysis of "rule carriers and how they interact", the meso- concerns populations of rules, and the macro- consists of systems of rule-populations.

10 The concept of *developmental constraints* which bound the complex web of relationships between genotype and phenotype has been analysed by Smith *et al.* (1985) and Walsh (2001).

11 Each "technological" subset is infinite as "the number of ideas" contained in it is always infinite, closed because it includes "all its boundary points", bounded as it contains the technological frontier (its boundary points) (Olsson, 2005, pp. 40–42). For an analysis of the standard "state-space" model of knowledge see Samuelson (2004).

12 Segments can be defined as combinations of different ideas which produce useful knowledge.

13 Explanation of principle means to point out patterns of phenomena and the spectrum of their potential variations, while the actual realizations depend on specific circumstances and factors, which cannot be known in advance. Those patterns are denied by defining abstract "properties" (Hayek, 1964).

14 "If … then rules which may reach considerable degrees of complexity" (Vanberg, 2002, p. 16). For an analysis of the connections between rules and learning see

Lazaric (2000), while a selection model of routines within hierarchies, characterized by different degrees of pressure, is discussed in Lazaric and Raybaut (2005).

15 "Decoding is about how programs are implemented in, or applied to, particular choice situations" (Vanberg, 2002, p. 16).

16 The theory of morphological evolution (Eble, 2003) conceives modules as cohesive units, which are able to keep stability and at the same time to change. In the organization theory (Aoki and Takizawa, 2002; Aoki, 2004) "a module is a unit of a system within which elements are strongly interrelated to one another, but across modules they are relatively independent". In the view here suggested they are adaptive entities, comprised of bundles of rules and bonded by constraints arising in problem solving activities.

17 "'General' in this definition means that it is not a specific solution for a specific situation, but a general solution for a type of problem. (On the other hand, a technological rule is a mid-range theory, whose validity is limited to a certain application domain)" (van Aken, 2004b).

18 If a rule is "field-tested" this means it is tested in its intended field of application. If it is "grounded" this means it is known why the intervention or artefact gives the desired performance (van Aken, 2004b, pp. 10–11).

19 Amesse and Cohendet (2001, p. 1466) distinguish between experential learning, that is "based on learning processes that are routine adaptation procedures and leave no room for programming experiments during economic activity", and experimental learning, that "consists of deliberate experimentation during production process".

20 For a first trial in this direction see Bargigli and Lombardi (2006).

References

Abrahamson E. and Rosenkopf L. (1997), Social network effects on the extent of innovation diffusion: a computer simulation, *Organization Science*, 8 (3), 289–309.

Amesse F. and Cohendet P. (2001), Technology transfer revisited from the perspective of the knowledge-based economy, *Research Policy*, 30, 1459–1478.

Aoki M. (2004), An organizational architecture of T-form: Silicon Valley clustering and its institutional coherence, *Industrial and Corporate Change*, 13 (6), 967–981.

Aoki M. and Takizawa H. (2002), Information, incentives and option value: the Silicon Valley model, *Journal of Comparative Economics*, 30, 759–786.

Archer M.S. (1995), *Realist Social Theory: The Morphogenetic Approach*, Cambridge, Cambridge University Press.

Arthur W.B. and Pollak W. (2004), *The Evolution of Technology within a Simple Computer Model*, Working Paper, no. 042, Santa Fe.

Bargigli L. and Lombardi M. (2006), Information flows, embedded coordination, and competence building networks: an explorative model, Paper to be presented at the Schumpeter Conference, Nice, June.

Boisot M. and Child J. (1999), Organization as adaptive systems in complex environments: the case of China, *Organization Science*, 10 (3), 237–252.

Boisot M. and Canals A. (2004), Data, information and knowledge: Have we got it right?, *Journal of Evolutionary Economics*, 14, 43–67.

Carlaw K.I. and Lipsey R.G. (2002), Externalities, technological complementarities and sustained economic growth, *Research Policy*, 31, 1305–1315.

Chomsky N. (1980), *Rules and Representations*, Oxford, Blackwell.

Chomsky N. (2000), *New Horizons in the Study of Language and Mind*, Cambridge, Cambridge University Press.

Constant II E.W. (2002), Why evolution is a theory about stability: constraint, causation, and ecology in technological change, *Research Policy*, 31, 1241–1256.

Cooper B. (200), Modelling research and development: How do firms solve design problems?, *Journal of Evolutionary Economics*, 10, 395–413.

Coriat B. and Dosi G. (1999), Learning how to govern and learning how to solve problems: on the co-evolution of competencies, conflicts and organizational routines, in Chandler A.D. Jr, Hagström P. and Sölvell O. (eds), *The Dynamic Firm*, Oxford, Oxford University Press, pp. 103–133.

Devezas T.C. and Corredine J.C. (2002), The nonlinear dynamics of techno-economic systems: an informational interpretation, *Technological Forecasting and Social Change*, 69, 317–357.

Dopfer K. (2004), The economic agent as rule maker and rule user: *Homo Sapiens Oeconomicus*, *Journal of Evolutionary Economics*, 14, 177–195.

Dopfer K., Foster J. and Potts J. (2005), Micro-meso-macro, *Journal of Evolutionary Economics*, 14, 263–279.

Eble G.J. (2003), *Morphological Modularity and Macroevolution: Conceptual and Empirical Aspects*, in Callebaut W. and Rasskin-Gutman D. (eds): *Modularity: Understanding the Development and Evolution of Complex Natural Systems.* Cambridge, MA, MIT Press, pp. 221–238.

Garricano L. (2000), Hierarchies and the organization of knowledge in production, *Journal of Political Economy*, 108 (5), 874–904.

Garrouste P. and Saussier S. (2005), Looking for a theory of the firm: future challenges, *Journal of Economic Behaviour and Organization*, 58, 178–199.

Geels F.W. (2002), Technological transitions as evolutionary reconfiguration processes: a multi-level perspective and a case study, *Research Policy*, 31, 1257–1274.

Geels F.W. (2004), From sectoral systems of innovation to socio-technical systems. Insights about dynamics and change from sociology and institutional theory, *Research Policy*, 33, 897–920.

Hayek F. (1964), The theory of complex phenomena, in Bunge M. (ed), *The Critical Approach to Science and Philosophy*, London, Collier-Macmillan, pp. 332–349.

Hodgson G.M. and Knudsen T. (2004), The firm as an interactor: firms as vehicles for habits and routines, *Journal of Evolutionary Economics*, 14, 281–307.

Kauffman S., Lobo J. and Macready W.G. (2000), Optimal search on a technological landscape, *Journal of Economic Behaviour and Organisation*, 43, 141–166.

Kaufman B.E. (2003), The organization of economic activity: insights from the institutional theory of John R. Commons, *Journal of Economic Behaviour and Organization*, 52, 71–96.

Krishan V. and Ulrich K.T. (2001), Product development decisions: a review of the literature, *Management Science*, 47 (1), 1–21.

Lazaric N. (2000), The role of routines, rules and habits in collective learning: some epistemological and ontological considerations, *European Journal of Economic and Social Systems*, 14 (2), 157–171.

Lazaric N. and Raybaut A. (2005), Knowledge, hierarchy and the selection of routines: an interpretative model with group interactions, *Journal of Evolutionary Economics*, 15, 393–421.

Loasby B. (2001), Time, knowledge and evolutionary dynamics: why connections matter, *Journal of Evolutionary Economics*, 11, 393–412.

Lombardi M. (2003), Cognitive models, efficiency, and discontinuities in the evolution of Italian industrial districts and local production systems, in Belussi F., Gottardi G. and

Rullani E. (eds), *The Technological Evolution of Industrial Districts*, Dordrecht, Kluwer, pp. 109–138.

March J.G. (1991), Exploration and exploration in organizational learning, *Organization Science*, 2 (1), 71–87.

March J.G. (1994), *A Primer on Decision Making*, New York, The Free Press.

Margolis H. (1987), *Patterns, Thinking, and Cognition*, Chicago, IL, Chicago University Press.

Maynard Smith J., Burian R., Kauffman S., Alberch P., Campbell J., Goodwin B., Lande R., Raup D. and Wolpert L. (1985), Developmental constraints and evolution, *The Quarterly Review of Biology*, 60 (3), 265–287.

Mayr E. (1992), The idea of teleology, *Journal of History of Ideas*, 53 (1), 117–135.

Metcalfe J.S. and De Fonseca M.D. (2001), Innovation, growth and competition: evolving complexity and complex evolution, Discussion Paper, no. 41, Centre for Research on Innovation and Competition (CRIC).

Mokyr J. (2000), Evolutionary phenomena in technical change, in Ziman J. (ed.), *Technological Innovation as an Evolutionary Process*, Cambridge, Cambridge University Press, pp. 52–65.

Mokyr J. (2005), Long-term economic growth and the history of technology, in Aghion P. and Durlauf S. (eds), *Handbook of Economic Growth*, North-Holland, Elsevier, pp. 1113–1180.

Nightingale, P. (1998), A cognitive model of innovation, *Research Policy*, 29, 819–831.

Nooteboom B. (2004), Governance and competence: How can they be combined?, *Cambridge Journal of Economics*, 28, 505–525.

Nooteboom B. and Gilsing V.A. (2004), Density and strength of ties in innovation networks: a competence and governance view, Working Paper, no. 01.01, Eindhoven Centre for Innovation Studies.

Olsson O. (2000), Knowledge as a set in idea space: an epistemological view on growth, *Journal of Economic Growth*, 5, 253–275.

Olsson O. (2005), Technology opportunity and growth, *Journal of Economic Growth*, 10, 35–37.

Potts J. (2000), *The New Evolutionary Microeconomics*, Cheltenham, Edward Elgar.

Radner R. (1992), Hierarchy: the economics of managing, *Journal of Economic Literature*, 3, 1382–1411.

Radner R. (1996), Bounded rationality, indeterminacy and the theory of the firm, *Economic Journal*, September: 1360–1373.

Radner R. (2000), Costly and bounded rationality in individual and team decision-making, *Industrial and Corporate Change*, 9 (4), 623–658.

Samuelson L. (2004), Modeling knowledge in economic analysis, *Journal of Economic Literature*, XLII, 367–403.

Simon H.A. (1979), From substantive to procedural rationality, in Hahn F. and Hollis M. (eds), *Philosophy and Economic Theory*, Oxford, Oxford University Press, pp. 65–86.

Simon H.A. (1998), What is an "explanation" of behavior, in Thagard P. (ed.), *Mind Readings – Introductory Selections on Cognitive Science*, London and Cambridge, MA, MIT Press, pp. 1–28.

Sorenson O. (2003), Social network and industrial geography, *Journal of Evolutionary Economics*, 13, 513–527.

Stam E. and Garney E. (2005), New firms evolving in the knowledge economy: problems and solutions around turning points, Working Papers, no. 0505, Max Plank Institute.

Stankiewicz R. (2000), The concept of "design space", in Ziman J. (ed.), *Technological Innovation as an Evolutionary Process*, Cambridge, Cambridge University Press, pp. 234–247.

Teece D.J., Pisano G. and Shuen A. (2000), *Dynamic Capabilities and Strategic Management*, in Dosi, G., Nelson R. and Winter S.G., (eds), *The Nature and Dynamic of Organizational Capabilities*, Oxford and New York, Oxford University Press, pp. 334–362.

van Aken J.E. (2004a), The field-tested and grounded technological rule as product of mode 2 management research, Working Paper, no. 04.10, Eindhoven Centre for Innovation Studies, The Netherlands.

van Aken J.E. (2004b), Valid knowledge for the professional design of large and complex design, Working Paper, no. 04.11, Eindhoven Centre for Innovation Studies, The Netherlands.

Vanberg. V.J. (2002), Rational choice vs program-based behaviour, *Rationality and Society*, 14 (1): 7–54.

van Zandt T. (1998), Organizations with an endogenous number of information processing agents, in Majumdar M. (ed.), *Organizations with Incomplete Information*, Cambridge, Cambridge University Press, pp. 239–305.

Veryzer R. (1998), Discontinous innovation and the new development product process, *Journal of Product Innovation Management*, 15, 304–321.

von Hayek F.A. (1964), The theory of complex phenomena, in von Hayek F.A., *Studies in Philosophy, Politics and Economics*, London, Routledge & Kegan Paul, pp. 22–43.

Vromen J. (2004a), Conjectural revisionary economic ontology: outline of an ambitious research agenda for evolutionary economics, *Journal of Economic Methodology*, 11 (2), 213–247.

Vromen J. (2004b), Routines, genes and program-based behaviour, Working Papers, no. 0420, Max Plank Institute.

Walsh D.M. (2001), The causes of adaptation and the unity of biology, *Science*, first draft.

Witt U. (2004), On novelty and heterogeneity, Working Papers, no. 0405, Max Plank Institute.

6 Global value chains and technological capabilities

A framework to study industrial innovation in developing countries[1]

Andrea Morrison, Carlo Pietrobelli and Roberta Rabellotti

6.1 Introduction

In these days nobody would resist the contention that learning and innovation are key determinants of competitiveness and growth of nations, regions, clusters and firms. Sometimes, more refined observers would stress that competitiveness is affected by firm-specific attitudes and actions and also by the industrial, organizational, meso- and macroeconomic contexts in which firms are inserted. Yet, these ideas need to be integrated and encompassed in a consistent fashion, this has been achieved only occasionally, and perhaps more effectively by business scholars than by conventional economists.

In developing countries (LDCs), following an established line of thought on the international sources of development – e.g. learning by exporting, FDI spillovers – the Global Value Chain (GVC) approach has recently shown how international linkages play a crucial role to access technological knowledge and enhance learning and innovation (Gereffi, 1994, 1999; Kaplinsky, 2000; Humphrey and Schmitz, 2002a, b). Within this framework, several empirical studies have shown that the interaction between global buyers and local producers in LDCs may generate learning and innovation activities (Nadvi and Schmitz, 1999; Schmitz and Knorringa, 2000; Gereffi *et al.*, 2005; Giuliani *et al.*, 2005). In this respect, the GVC literature has focused on how different patterns of governance may enhance or hinder different types (i.e. process, product or functional) of firms upgrading, that are themselves the result of learning and innovation activities. However, as partly recognized by some scholars (Bell and Albu, 1999; Caniëls and Romijn, 2003; Schmitz, 2004), most of the studies within the GVC approach do not explicitly study how upgrading occurs at the firm-level through the external linkages taking place within value chains (i.e. the pre-conditions, the mechanics, the investments and the strategic behaviour required).

At the same time however, technological change and innovation at the firm-level in developing countries have been the focus of a very fruitful school of thought developed around the concept of "Technological Capabilities" (TCs) (Bell and Pavitt, 1992; Dahlman *et al.*, 1987; Katz, 1987; Lall, 1987, 1992, 2001; Pack and Westphal, 1986). Drawing upon the evolutionary approach of Nelson and Winter (1982), the TCs approach claims that technological change is the result of purposeful investments undertaken by firms, and that therefore technology transfers are effective insofar as they also include elements of capability building.

In this chapter introducing an analytical framework based on the TCs approach, we review how some selected GVC studies address issues of learning and innovation. We argue that, despite its widespread use, the concept of upgrading and its mechanisms within global value chains are still ambiguous. On the one hand, they suggest the idea that entering GVCs causes a sharp and automatic positive impact on local producers, neglecting that local actors have to invest in learning and building technological capability to effectively upgrade. On the other hand, shifting the research agenda on how local firms can join value chains and on the governance structure better suited for upgrading, produces a harmful neglect of the analysis of the detailed mechanisms linking value chain with learning and TCs development.

In this study we propose a shift in the research agenda at the theoretical and empirical level. First of all, we argue that research should focus on the endogenous process of TCs development, on the specific firm-level efforts, and on the contextual factors enhancing and/or hindering the process. Second, we claim that it is necessary to study the mechanisms allowing knowledge to flow *within* and *between* different global value chains, which in turn will make it easier to unravel why some firms and/or clusters benefit more or less from being part of the GVCs. Third, innovation theories and the study of the features of knowledge in the mechanisms described above may substantially contribute to improve our understanding of these complex and multidimensional phenomena. Different degrees of complexity, tacitness and appropriability of knowledge affect the GVC governance structure, the opportunity and speed of upgrading and its intensity and direction. In particular we suggest to pay attention to chain leaders' appropriability strategies and to their effect on producers' learning activities. Incidentally, these strategies can increase the private returns of individual producers who join value chains, but they can also hinder collective learning processes and have negative social effects on the cluster producers belong to.

The chapter is organized as follows. In the next two sections we present a brief survey of the GVC literature and of the TCs approach. Section 6.4 is a critical review of how some selected GVC studies analyse learning, innovation and knowledge diffusion. In this section, we outline a framework of analysis by bringing explicitly the TCs framework into the GVC approach. Section 6.5 summarizes and concludes.

6.2 The global value chain approach

As initially defined by international business scholars, a value-added chain is:

> the process by which technology is combined with material and labor inputs and then processed inputs are assembled, marketed and distributed. A single

> firm may consist of only one link in this process, or it may be extensively vertically integrated ....
>
> (Kogut, 1985)

In this literature, the key issues regard which activities and technologies a firm keeps in-house and which are outsourced to other firms, and where the various activities are located.

More recently, Gereffi (1994, 1999) and other scholars (Gereffi and Kaplinsky, 2001; Humphrey and Schmitz, 2002a, b; Kaplinsky, 2000; Kaplinsky and Morris, 2001) developed a framework that tied the concept of value-added chain directly to the globalization of industries with a focus on developing countries, stressing the growing importance of global buyers and producers as key drivers in the formation of globally dispersed and organizationally fragmented production and distribution networks.

From an analytical point of view, the value chain perspective is useful because the focus moves from manufacturing only to the other activities involved in the supply of goods and services, including distribution and marketing (Kaplinsky, 2000). All these activities contribute to add value. Moreover, the ability to identify the activities providing higher returns along the value chain is key to understand the global appropriation of the returns to economic activities.

Value chain research focuses on the nature of the relationships among the various actors involved in the chain, and on their implications for development (Humphrey and Schmitz, 2002b). The concept of "governance" is central to the analysis. At any point in the chain, some degree of governance is required in order to take decisions not only on "what" or "how" a good/service should be produced but sometimes also "when", "how much" and even "at what price". This literature deems necessary to write of governance, rather than only coordination, as the proactive involvement and participation of all the actors within the value chain is crucial. Governance may occur through arm's-length market linkages or non-market relationships. In the latter case, Humphrey and Schmitz (2000) distinguish three possible types of governance: a) *network* implying co-operation between firms of more or less equal power which share their competencies within the chain; b) *quasi-hierarchy* involving relationships between legally independent firms in which one is subordinated to the other, with a leader in the chain defining the rules to which the rest of the actors have to comply with and c) *hierarchy* when a firm is owned by an external firm.

This literature also stresses the role played by the GVC leaders, particularly by the buyers, in transferring knowledge along the chains. For small firms in less developed countries, participation in value chains is a way to obtain information on the need and mode to gain access to global markets and, more generally, to upgrade.

Upgrading is here intended as a strategy to augment per-unit value of products (product upgrading) or to increase the efficiency of production processes (process upgrading). More sophisticated strategies of upgrading concern the implementation of new functions in the chain (e.g. the transition from pure assembling to design activities, i.e. "functional upgrading") or the entry into new sectors (i.e. inter-sectoral upgrading). Humphrey and Schmitz (2000) discuss the relationship between upgrading and the different patterns of GVC governance, and suggest that global buyers tend to hinder the two latter forms of upgrading. This appears to be confirmed by the evidence presented by Giuliani *et al.*, 2005. Global buyers have indeed a clear incentive to keep their suppliers dependent on them and not to disclose their core competencies, and accordingly to discourage their attempts at developing strategic competencies, in particular those concerning design and marketing (Schmitz and Knorringa, 2000; Bazan and Navas-Aleman, 2004).

Humphrey and Schmitz (2000) conclude that insertion in a quasi-hierarchical chain offers very favorable conditions for process and product upgrading, but hinders functional upgrading. Networks chains also offer ideal upgrading conditions, but they are the least likely to occur in developing countries. In addition, a more dynamic approach suggests that chain governance is not given forever and may change because (Humphrey and Schmitz, 2002b): (a) power relationships may evolve when existing producers, or their spin-offs, acquire new capabilities; (b) establishing and maintaining quasi-hierarchical governance is costly for the lead firm and heads to inflexibility because of transaction specific investments; and (c) firms and clusters often do not operate only in one chain but simultaneously in several types of chains, and they may apply competencies learned in one chain to supply other chains. In sum, upgrading of firms participating in a value chain depends on the nature of the relationships (governance patterns and power asymmetries) among the various actors within the chain.

Notwithstanding its important advances, in this literature there are a number of issues that need to be further addressed. Let us see them in a sequence. First of all, the concept of upgrading is rather fuzzy: is it a synonym for innovation or rather the result of it? Although "at first glance the issue of upgrading appears to be straightforward enough. For a firm, upgrading means getting better – i.e. producing better products and producing them in a more efficient way. However, things are more difficult than that" (Meyer-Stamer *et al.*, 2004: 328). Thus, the GVC literature has "to rethink the concept of upgrading and acknowledge that it must be a relational category" (p. 330).

In international trade theory the concept of "upgrading" is frequently used in studies on the dynamics of countries' specialization, where upgrading is meant to represent a shift towards a specialization in higher value-added goods *within the same sector*. This is different from diversification, i.e. specialization in new areas of comparative advantage *in different sectors* (Guerrieri *et al.*, 2001). However, this notion hardly translates into a useful definition at the firm-level, and it does not reflect the current use of this term in most economics and management literature.

Indeed, in many empirical studies of upgrading we perceive a strong temptation of mixing causes and effects. Although some recent contributions advocate that upgrading needs investments and efforts at firm level (Kishimoto, 2004; Schmitz and Knorringa, 2000; Schmitz, 2004), most of the empirical analyses still lack a systematic attempt to investigate learning and innovation at the firm and cluster level.

For instance, when authors detect the occurrence of upgrading, they tend to invariably associate this outcome to some activity aimed at building capacity; yet this activity is at best only mentioned but not fully examined. Moreover, we claim that such an attitude impedes to provide any analytical treatment of the concept and may lead to misleading policy suggestions, as it assumes the presence of upgrading whenever a "good" outcome emerges from a buyer–producer interaction.

Moreover, if upgrading is crudely defined as an increase in per-unit value of products, then it may be the result of various forms of innovation but also of squeezing wages, itself a short-term strategy insofar as lower-wage firms and countries continuously emerge in international markets. In light of all these considerations, we argue that it is advisable to stick to the concept of innovation, whenever it produces an increase in the value added. The study of innovation in LDCs has been at the centre of a stream of literature focused around the concept of TCs. According to this approach, which is spelled out in the next section, it is indeed the level and depth of TCs that determine local firms' industrial and innovation performance; therefore TCs and their determinants should be the explicit object of analysis.

Second, a more explicit and thoroughly spelled out reference to innovation is useful in drawing the attention to some key knowledge features such as codificability and complexity. Only very recently some studies (Gereffi *et al.*, 2005; Giuliani *et al.*, 2005) drawing on innovation theories, have stressed that differences in knowledge may crucially help to elaborate a theory of value chain governance. Along these lines, learning hindrances are also generated by specific knowledge characteristics, such as complexity and tacitness, which in turn influence knowledge transferability with effects on the balance of power. This implies that local producers have to face several obstacles, besides power asymmetries, when dealing with external knowledge. Although this latter point has been partly recognized by the GVC literature, we claim that it requires further investigation. First, because it may be that most of the upgrading activities supported by buyers are more related to their appropriability strategies (e.g. to reduce leakages and to speed up process or product development) rather than to provide innovation opportunities to local producers. Second, because the nature of knowledge changes along the value chain, hence absorption capabilities of local producers need to change accordingly.

Our third concern claims that the GVC literature pays little attention to linkages established between producers joining global networks and other clustered firms. Thus, any proposition stating that *any* form and extent of firms' insertion into global value chain is beneficial to *all* the other clustered firms implicitly assumes that knowledge can be freely acquired by other clusters' members. This assumption produces rather undesirable implications, as already pointed out by recent studies on proximity and knowledge flows in local innovations systems that focus on the suboptimal incentive to innovate in a framework of free appropriability of knowledge (Breschi and Lissoni, 2001). Moreover, knowledge does *not* freely flow within a cluster, it is not evenly distributed therein and some (local) actors may enjoy locational or other advantages to get access, absorb, and use knowledge (Giuliani, 2005).

In order to address these critical issues in the GVC literature, we suggest to consider the well-established tradition of studies on Technological Capabilities in developing countries. We claim that this may help to move forward the GVC research agenda and to reach a more comprehensive and integrated approach for explaining industrial development and innovation in emerging countries.

6.3 Technological capabilities in developing countries

The TCs approach represents a radical alternative to the neoclassical approach, that rests on a particular conceptualization of technology at the enterprise level. It assumes that technology is freely available from a known "shelf" on which there is full information. Firms optimize by choosing from this shelf according to their factor and product prices. Any intervention is necessarily distorting resource allocation. The selected technology is absorbed costlessly and risklessly by the enterprise and used at efficient ("best practice") levels. As a necessary consequence, no learning is required and the underlying assumption is that any observed industrial inefficiency is due to government interventions.

In contrast, the technological capabilities literature draws upon the evolutionary approach of Nelson and Winter (1982), and locates learning in markets prone to imperfections, satisfying behaviour and widespread failures.[2] Moreover, the TCs approach intentionally looks at developing countries, formulating a theory of innovation and learning.

Technological capabilities are the skills – technical, managerial or organizational – that firms need in order to utilize efficiently the hardware (equipment) and software (information) of technology, and to accomplish any process of technological change. Capabilities are firm-specific, institutional knowledge made up of individual skills and experience accumulated over time. Technological change is the result of purposeful activities undertaken by firms ("Technological Efforts"). It is neither exogenous nor automatic. Individual effort is required to make the many tacit elements of technology explicit, and most technological effort does not take place at the frontier of technology at all. It covers a much broader range of effort that every enterprise must undertake to access, implement, absorb and build upon the knowledge required in production.

Technology cannot simply be transferred to a firm like a physical product: its effective implantation has to include important elements of capability building. Simply providing equipment and operating instructions, patents, designs or blueprints does not ensure that the technology will be effectively utilized. Substantial efforts to improve technical skills, acquire the necessary equipment and relevant knowledge are continuously needed. Learning plays a central role in this approach, and its success depends on the efficacy with which markets and institutions function, uncertainty is coped with, externalities tapped, and coordination achieved. If the learning period, costs, uncertainties and leakages are very high, coordination with other firms in the supply chain exceptionally difficult, or information, labour and capital markets particularly unresponsive, "difficult" knowledge may not be absorbed – even where it would be efficient to do so.

Following Lall (1990, 1992, 2001) a useful categorization of TCs considers the functions they perform and the degree of complexity as the two classificatory principles.[3] Thus, it is possible to single out "investment", "production" and "linkage" capabilities. When industries are started, many of the TCs necessary at the firm-level are absent. These missing TCs may be temporarily obtained at home or imported in an "unbundled" form, but some "core" capabilities have to be developed by firms and expanded over time. Moreover, many of these TCs are inter-related and partly over-lapping, and there is often strong inter-dependence among them.

Investment capabilities refer to all the skills required before the investment is undertaken and needed to carry it out. They include the capabilities to assess the feasibility and profitability of a project, to define its detailed specification, the technology required and the selection of its best sourcing, the negotiations of the purchase (cost and terms), the skills to erect the civil constructions and the equipment, to draw its detailed engineering, to recruit and train the skilled personnel required, and eventually to design the basic process and supply the equipment.

Production capabilities include the skills necessary for the efficient operation of a plant with a given technology, and its improvement over time. Process, product and industrial engineering capabilities are part of this subset. Among the infinite number of operations that require adequate skills are: the assimilation of process and of product technology, their adaptation and improvement, troubleshooting, quality control, equipment stretching, work-flow scheduling, inventory control, monitoring productivity and coordination of different production stages and departments, finally process and product innovations following basic research activity.

Linkage capabilities are required because of high transaction costs; in narrow and inefficient markets, the setting up of extra-market linkages often corresponds to an efficient and rational strategy. Therefore, special skills are needed to establish technology linkages among enterprises, between them and service suppliers, and with the science and technology infrastructures.

In each group there are TCs with different degrees of technological complexity. These are used for "routine", "adaptive and replicative", or "innovative and risky" activities. Different levels and depth of TCs indeed explain different levels of industrial performance across countries (Lall, 1990; Pietrobelli, 1998). However, the approach does not presume that all firms will necessarily build up capabilities in a linear sequenced process, neither does it imply that firms will start and end at the same stages (Figueiredo, 2006).

The policy implications of this approach are straightforward: policies need to adopt a firm-level focus, and must target the building and strengthening of TCs. Clusters, (global) value chains, production networks or other forms of industrial organization may contribute to a different extent in different circumstances, but firm-level efforts to build and improve TCs are the *sine qua non* of industrial development (Lall, 2001).

6.4 Learning and upgrading in GVC: a critical review of selected empirical studies

In this section we adopt an analytical framework based on TCs to study technology and innovation in a GVC context. Indeed, the original contribution of this chapter is to reconsider the GVC literature in order to investigate how knowledge generation, diffusion processes and building up of TCs occur in GVCs. This effort explicitly hinges on the TCs literature, and Table 6.1 sketches the main categories and issues we intend to analyse within the GVC context. These cover all the relevant dimensions outlined by the evolutionary and TCs literature on innovation and learning at the firm level.

The role played by "indigenous technological effort in mastering new technologies, adapting them to local conditions, improving upon them, diffusing them within the economy and exploiting them overseas by manufactured export growth and diversification and by exporting technologies themselves" (Lall, 1992: 166) is central. All these processes (e.g. mastering, adapting, diffusing) to some extent vary according to GVC features, but also and more importantly according to firm, sectoral and technological idiosyncrasies. Thus, the properties of knowledge (e.g. complexity, cumulativeness, appropriability), the channels of technology transmission (e.g. technical assistance; labour mobility; licenses; turn-key plants) and the firms' differences in absorptive capacity influence the path, speed and direction of learning and innovation (Cohen and Levinthal, 1990; Breschi *et al.*, 2000; Nelson and Winter, 1982).

All these elements have deep implications not only for firms' upgrading but also, in turn, affect GVCs governance and strategies. In other words, the direction of causality is two-way. Thus, for example, we may expect that a higher (lower) degree of knowledge complexity will induce global buyers to establish

Table 6.1 The framework of analysis

Key issues in the TC approach	*Implications for* governance and upgrading in the GVC
1 Knowledge features relevant for transfer (i.e. complexity, tacitness appropriability) 2 Nature of TCs in firms (i.e. investment, production and linkage capabilities) 3 Firms efforts and acquisition of TCs in firms (internal and external sources and channels of knowledge)	Different degrees of complexity and tacitness of knowledge, combined with different TCs and different sources of technological knowledge affect: • the GVC governance structure (relational vs. captive governance) • the opportunity/speed of upgrading (localised learning; absorptive capacity) • the intensiveness/direction of upgrading (active vs. passive learning).

closer (more distant) relationships with local producers, and consequently contribute to the emergence of specific modes of governance (more relational or more captive). Similarly, the absorptive capacity of local producers may affect GVCs opportunities to convey information and knowledge. In other words, different degrees of absorptive capacity allow firms to identify and explore close/distant knowledge and technological channels to a different extent. In turn, this contributes to explain why firms embedded in similar GVC may upgrade at different rates or following different patterns. Table 6.1 summarizes the conceptual framework we adopt for the analysis of the studies selected.

Given that the GVC literature encompasses a wide range of issues and disciplines rooted in rather different theoretical backgrounds, we have conducted our analysis on some selected papers within this burgeoning literature. These include the most influential contributions on GVCs in developing countries focused on firms upgrading, that is explicitly investigating to what extent different GVCs affect upgrading processes in firms.[4] Before discussing the results of our analysis we present the main features of the empirical contributions selected.

All the studies under analysis interpret the concept of *upgrading* in terms of improvements in either products, processes or functions. In general, what is termed *upgrading* is the outcome of an innovation process. However, the two concepts, upgrading and innovation, frequently overlap and are used as synonymous, although the analysis of the innovation process itself never appears as a core issue in this literature.[5]

The *governance* of the value chain is always central to the analysis. A key question is to what extent different patterns of governance contribute to reinforce, or conversely hamper, upgrading in firms or clusters. The studies share some consensus on the effect that different modes of governance would have on upgrading, but it is unclear why some modes are considered inherently superior to others.

In terms of the *unit of analysis* adopted, the studies differ to a large extent, ranging from clusters to industries and nations. The individual firm is never the central focus, although the majority of studies implicitly incorporate this dimension into the analysis.

From a *geographical* point of view, the studies cover a wide and differentiated set of experiences of GVC in developing countries. Some focus on Newly Industrializing Countries (NICs), such as Taiwan, Brazil and Mexico (Bair and Gereffi, 2001; Gereffi, 1999; Kishimoto, 2004; Quadros, 2004), others are more concerned with countries at a lower stage of development (Barnes and Kaplinsky, 2000; Gibbon, 2003; Nadvi, 2004). Most of the case studies focus on traditional industries (e.g. garment, furniture) inserted in quasi-hierarchical value chains (Bazan and Navas-Aleman, 2004; Kaplinsky *et al.*, 2002; Kaplinsky and Readman, 2005; Schmitz and Knorringa, 2000).

Based on the main focus of analysis of these papers, their theoretical background and their methodology, we identify two different "schools" or approaches within the broad GVC literature (Table 6.2): the *internationalist* approach, which includes the North American school on GVCs, well represented by Gereffi and

Table 6.2 Different GVC schools

	Internationalists	*Industrialists*
Main focus	GVCs governance and upgrading mainly in LDCs	Upgrading and GVCs mainly in LDCs
Methodology	Macro approach Industry level data/trade data	Micro approach Case-study, qualitative data
Policy focus	International division of labour role of bilateral/multilateral trade agreements, FDI	Competitiveness of firms and clusters Local development policies
Theoretical background	International economics Political economy; TNCs theory	Industry studies Local development studies

colleagues, and scholars like Kaplinsky, Gibbon and colleagues at the Danish Centre for Development Research, and the *industrialist* approach, represented by Humphrey, Schmitz and their colleagues at the Institute of Development Studies, at the University of Sussex. The labels proposed – *internationalist* and *industrialist* – roughly identify the early background and/or the methodology of research prevalent in each approach: *internationalists* privilege a macro perspective, both in terms of level of analysis and in terms of policy focus; conversely the *industrialists* adopt a micro-founded framework of analysis with a policy focus oriented towards issues of local and cluster development.

This classification is helpful to highlight diversities between groups and similarities within each class, although we are aware that differences can be found within each of them and that the two approaches overlap in some instances given that scholars of both schools substantially share similar thinking and frequently interact among each other, as exemplified by several co-authored papers. Thus, it is worth stressing that boundaries between these groups are indeed quite loose, and the grouping we propose mainly serves the purpose of an expositional device. Nevertheless, what clearly marks the difference between them is the method of inquiry: the *internationalists* mostly concentrate on the industry as a whole, while the *industrialists* mainly investigate specific clusters, and adopt case-study methodology.

6.4.1 Knowledge features and transfers in GVCs

Most of the studies considered admit the existence of factors binding the spread of knowledge within GVCs and influencing their pattern of governance. In particular, the studies within the *industrialist* approach often mention the presence of hampering factors like the power asymmetries emerging out of buyer-driven relationships: "power asymmetry is central to value chain governance. That is, there are key actors in the chain who take responsibility for the inter-firm division of labour, and for the capacities of particular participants to upgrade their activities" (Kaplinsky and Morris, 2001: 29). Chain leaders are those who coordinate and govern the GVC,[6] whose members, in many respects, depend upon them for setting up their own strategies. GVCs are shaped by governance structures (e.g. arm's length relations, quasi-hierarchy, networks), which define how local producers participate to the distribution of rents produced in the value chain.

From the available empirical studies it appears that "buyers do not always provide support for this upgrading" (Humphrey and Schmitz, 2004: 358), due to the asymmetry of power between them and local producers. In another empirical work Schmitz and Knorringa (2000) stress the links between GVC leaders and upgrading, looking at the obstacles and enabling conditions affecting the buyer–producer relation in the shoe sector in different countries. They note that "the problem is that marketing and often design, are part of the buyers' own guarded core competence" so, they conclude that "there is conflict", and this is particularly evident in non production activities, where "one would therefore not expect the lead firm to share their core competence with others in the value chain" (p. 197).

In the same vein, Bazan and Navas-Aleman (2004), studying the shoe cluster of Sinos Valley in Brazil, observe that "buyers are the undisputed leaders in the chain, exerting control over intermediaries, local producers and often input suppliers as well" (p. 115). Furthermore, the authors write that "buyers have resisted sharing their knowledge on higher valued added activities such as design, branding, marketing and chain coordination" (p. 115).

In other studies, the crucial role played by leaders in transferring knowledge and information is emphasized. For example, in a study on the Taiwanese ICT industry, Poon (2004) looks at the relationships between global leaders and first-tier suppliers, and notes that: "Taiwanese suppliers gradually upgraded their technological capabilities through technology transfer and knowledge diffusion (by playing the OEM/OBM role for network flagships)" (p. 134). Further on this point, she argues that knowledge spillovers have been quite pervasive in the industry as a whole, in fact "various types and levels of technological knowledge and skills absorbed from network flagships by the first tier (...) were then diffused to smaller firms, resulting in the upgrading of all manufacturers operating within the IT Global Production Network" (p. 134). Similar patterns of diffusion have also been envisaged by Gereffi in his seminal work on Asian countries (Gereffi, 1994).

The evidence presented above is useful to single out the main regularities in GVCs' modes of governance, but it should not be given a normative meaning or even used (or misused) to draw policy implications. That is, it cannot be assumed that the specific governance structure is the only determinant of the leaders' inherent ability or interest to convey (or not to convey) knowledge to local producers. Nevertheless, and with a high dose of determinism, in the literature it is sometimes argued that network-based chains "support an open-ended upgrading path" (Humphrey and Schmitz, 2004: 354). Although less frequent in LDCs, network-based chains would be more beneficial for upgrading than quasi-hierarchical value chains, which in turn are better than market-based relationships in fostering process and product upgrading. Central to this line of reasoning there is the idea that knowledge transfers and upgrading are influenced mainly by the institutional settings, with GVC structures and chain leaders' strategies setting the pace and direction of knowledge flows and upgrading (either in favour or against the interest of local producers). Little or no regard is explicitly given to other issues like sectoral specificity and knowledge features, and to the consequences of these for local firms' upgrading.

In sum, whatever the role played by leaders (i.e. supporters or obstacles to technology transfer), technology and knowledge transmission – and their effectiveness – often appear as exogenous to the local firms involved. That is, they would be either determined by the leader strategy (i.e. GVC governance) or by other forces like, for example, clusters' external economies and collective efficiency. Yet, as discussed in section 6.3, knowledge features and firms TC-building strategies affect the pace and direction of learning and knowledge absorption. Innovation theory in the Schumpeterian tradition taught us that different technological regimes showing different combinations of complexity and appropriability of knowledge, set the conditions in which firms can absorb and transfer it (Malerba and Orsenigo, 1993). Thus, for example, we may claim that the higher the complexity of knowledge, the greater the need for integrated forms of governance/interaction. On the other hand, simple technology may be easily transferred/absorbed through market-based relationships (see below on absorptive capacity).

It is worth pointing out that we do not underplay the importance of "conflicts", power asymmetries and GVC governance in knowledge transfers. All these elements should be combined within a framework where technological regimes are also included in order to explain how within GVCs knowledge is transfered and how it can be used.

In the next subsection we focus on the role of firms' efforts in building technological capabilities, i.e. the strategies and tools needed to absorb external knowledge and to effectively employ and implement it in order to upgrade successfully.[7]

6.4.2 GVCs and technological capabilities: nature and modes of acquisition

TCs, although often cited as important, do not constitute a core issue in the GVC studies we are reviewing. Most papers mention them but do not address the details of their nature, of their dynamics, and of their acquisition. Thus for example, in summing up the main results of an extensive research project on upgrading in clusters, Schmitz (2004) stresses that upgrading "requires continuous investment by the local firms themselves in people, organisation and equipments" (Schmitz, 2004: 356), probably having in mind some notion of technological capabilities. Along the same lines, Kishimoto (2004) points out the importance of pre-existing capabilities in sustaining functional upgrading in the Taiwanese computer industry. He observes that: "Taiwanese producers already possessed basic production skills and some design capabilities" and that "holding enough technological capability is a necessary condition for getting orders" (Kishimoto, 2004: 247).

The issue of capability is somehow implicit also in the early *internationalists* studies on GVC, for example, Gereffi argues that East Asian countries, after entering GVC as first-tier suppliers of large international buyers, became full-package suppliers and "thereby forged an innovative entrepreneurial capability that involved the coordination of complex production, trade and financial networks" (Gereffi, 1999: 55). According to Gereffi, the transition from OEM (Original Equipment Manufacturer) to OBM (Original Brand Manufacturer) in East Asian countries was made possible by the extensive organizational learning occurring at the firm level, and prompted by the insertion in GVCs. In a recent analysis about the de-commoditization process occurring in the coffee industry, Kaplinsky and Fitter (2004: 20) claim that the "more durable and substantial way of enhancing producers incomes lies in the systematic application of knowledge to the coffee value chain", and that firms need to enhance their "branding" and "blending" capabilities – that is they have to learn how "to promote the virtues of location-specific 'images' and tastes" (Kaplinsky and Fitter, 2004: 18).

The above examples hint that although in GVC studies there is the clear perception of the strategic relationship between upgrading and technological capabilities, they generally lack an explicit and detailed focus on TCs. In what follows, we analyse them through the lenses of Lall's categorization of technological capabilities (Lall, 1992, 2001), addressing two interrelated issues: the *nature* of capabilities, as outlined by Lall (1992) and the *acquisition* of capabilities, which can be either internal or external (Romijn, 1999; Bell and Albu, 1999).

6.4.2.1 The nature of technological capabilities

Overall, the studies reviewed do not explicitly explore the nature of firms' capabilities in terms of the differences between investment, production, and linkage capabilities. They mainly refer to investments undertaken in the production process, or generally refer to "capabilities" without further categorizations and details. A partial exception is Kishimoto (2004), who explicitly accounts for the importance of capabilities and considers the different forms they may take for the upgrading trajectory in the Taiwanese personal computer value chain. In his chapter, Kishimoto presents some empirical evidence on the *linkage capabilities* accumulated by local manufacturers through intensive collaboration with IBM and other TNCs. The recruitment of experienced engineers trained by multinationals is one of the main mechanisms of interaction he mentions. Quoting Ernst *et al.* (1998), Kishimoto also stresses the role of technological and managerial assistance provided by TNCs in improving *production capabilities*, both in the form of skill upgrading and by forcing subcontractors to upgrade product quality (Kishimoto, 2004: 243).

Moreover, some studies on the adoption of international standards by local producers in LDCs (Ponte and Gibbon, 2005; Nadvi, 2004; Nadvi and Waltring, 2004; Quadros, 2004), also explore the issue of capabilities. Most notably, Quadros (2004) provides detailed evidence on how producers intervene in the production and design phases in order both to accomplish with standards' requirements and to collaborate with international buyers. By investigating the organizational setting of the design and engineering phases, he also explains why suppliers have developed rather low capabilities in planning and design, and how this restrained their chances to acquire new technologies from outside.

However, apart from Kishimoto and some works on global standards, most other studies only mention the issue, quoting it in their introductory section, or eventually providing some evidence on how chain leaders assist local producers in upgrading (Gibbon, 2003; Barnes and Kaplinsky, 2000; Kaplinsky *et al.*, 2002; Meyer-Stamer *et al.*, 2004; Schmitz and Knorringa, 2000).

To a lesser extent, the *internationalist* approach provides some evidence of *linkage capabilities*. This can be somehow envisaged in Gereffi's analysis of the "triangle manufacturing" system developed by the Taiwanese firms in the 1990s in order to cope with decreasing profits and pressures from foreign buyers on reducing delivery time (Gereffi, 1994, 1999). This system, as also stressed by Kishimoto (2004), enhances firms capability of coordinating, searching and procuring external goods and services.

However, none of the above studies makes explicit reference and explores the vertical dimension of capabilities. Lall (1992) rightly reminds us that this is a key element for classifying and assessing the nature of the mechanisms to build capabilities, since it allows us to rank them according to their degree of complexity. The perception that the GVC framework considers certain types of capabilities intrinsically superior to others since they allow firms to climb upstream on the value added ladder (e.g. from production to design) is left implicit.

This is inherently related to the notion of "upgrading" that is often used in the GVC approach. A vivid way to illustrate this concept has led several authors to write that upgrading within a value chain implies "going up the value ladder", moving away from activities in which competition is of the "low road" type and entry barriers are low. However, although this description is certainly stunning and eye-catching, and offers some advantages, it is not very accurate. First of all, GVCs are hardly as linear as they are often described. Indeed, this assumed linearity – often for the sake of simplifying their description – drives the attention away from all the detailed and equally important efforts to build and deepen TCs *at the same stage* of the value chain. We argue that the key issue is not always "functionally upgrading" and moving to more advanced functions "along the value chain", but often deepening the specific capabilities required to explore new opportunities offered "on the side" of the stage of the value chain where the firm is currently engaged. Moving from natural resources to their exploitation, manufacturing, packaging, distribution and branding is indeed very important, and would be described as somehow "climbing the ladder". But deepening capabilities to explore new original features and varieties *at each stage of the GVC* (e.g. from new flower varieties via biotechnological research to new packages with original highly-valued characteristics) is indeed also important, and clearly requires creation and deepening of higher skills and more complex TCs.

This view is consistent and provides a microeconomic ground for the newly-emerging approach that describes economic development as a process of "self-discovery" (Hausmann and Rodrik, 2003), where the diversification of the productive structure through a process of discovery – often supported by new forms of industrial policy – plays a central role.

As said before, the studies reviewed say little or nothing about the vertical dimension of TCs and their different levels of complexity: they do not analyse whether the new capabilities are either routine, basic capabilities or rather of higher, innovative and advanced order. Without any clear distinction between the degree of innovativeness of capabilities, that is between the *knowledge using* and *knowledge changing* elements in capabilities (Bell and Albu, 1999), little can be said about the dynamics of the system (i.e. GVC), and similarly about the contribution of the chain leaders to strengthening local producers' capabilities. In addition, in order to explore the dynamics of learning and accumulation, it would be desirable to introduce a time dimension, and consequently to conduct longitudinal analyses of these capability building processes.[8]

6.4.2.2 Firms' efforts and acquisition of technological capabilities

Firms acquire technological capabilities getting access to technological knowledge from a variety of possible sources (e.g. FDI, joint ventures, licensing, imported equipment), and integrating it with in-house efforts and costly investments in learning, R&D and technical assistance. Strategies may differ but need to be internally consistent.[9] Although external sources of knowledge are essential, the creation and improvement of technological capabilities essentially require some previous accumulation of skills, coupled with substantial firm-level efforts.

In the empirical GVC literature, the idea that "technological change is the result of purposeful, well-directed effort conducted inside the firm" (Pietrobelli, 1997: 4) is often implicit in theoretical discussions, but nearly absent in most of the empirical analyses. In most of these studies it is hardly explored what occurs within firms, what makes firms differ even if they belong to the same sector or the same cluster, and how firm-level efforts to develop TCs have added to (or compensated for the lack of) the opportunities offered by GVCs.

In spite of this weakness however, we have found some indirect and sketchy discussion over the role of specific actors (mostly GVC leaders) in sustaining local producers' upgrading at the cluster or at the industry level. However, we claim that some studies put an excessive emphasis on the role of external actors. Of course this is partially a consequence of the research agenda set by this literature, which by definition focuses on global actors, but this focus ends up neglecting more careful analyses of in-house domestic technological and learning activities, that in the end substantially explain inter-firm differences in performance.

Thus, some studies notice the importance of learning within domestic markets, in particular for functional upgrading, and outline the viability of a strategy based on "prior apprenticeship in the national market and ... operating in several chains simultaneously" (Bazan and Navas-Aleman, 2004: 136). Others stress the role of industry associations and technical schools in enhancing skills and more broadly local capabilities (Meyer-Stamer, 1998; Meyer-Stamer *et al.*, 2004). Overall, these latter contributions – and with them others in the "*industrialist*" group – pay attention to local sources and in particular to collective actions developed in clusters for sustaining firms' efforts to develop TCs and achieve competitiveness. Nevertheless, none of these authors clearly focuses on the firm-level dynamics leading to TC development.

In the *internationalist* approach detailed references on local actors and their role for upgrading and TC development are indeed less frequent. This is clear in Gereffi (1999: 38), who investigates how GVCs contributed to upgrading processes in the East Asian apparel industry and argues that leading firms (i.e. international buyers) play a prominent role: "they are the primary sources of material input, technology transfer and knowledge in these organisational networks". Similarly, other studies pay attention to the role of international buyers, retailers, branded marketers and intermediaries, but say little on domestic actors, and less about TCs development *within* firms' boundaries (Kaplinsky, 2004; Palpacuer *et al.*, 2005).

Local actors may supposedly play a minor role, but still their analysis would help understand how firms acquire technology from outside, and if and how they are supported in their efforts to develop TCs. Thus, it would be useful to know which actors – firms or science and technology institutions – are involved, how they do master and adapt foreign technologies, how they influence the level and direction of investments in TCs, and so forth.

In other words indigenous learning, and the firms' activities related to it, should be more explicitly observed and studied – and policies should inevitably focus on them. Differences in inter-firm (and inter-cluster) performance are, in fact, strictly related to their ability to build internal domestic knowledge bases, which in turn allows them to access external sources of knowledge, and to exploit them efficiently. Foreign sources of technology are clearly strategic and essential sources of technological knowledge for firms in developing countries – and this makes openness desirable (Bell and Albu, 1999, Giuliani *et al.*, 2005). However, it is necessary to stress once again that selection, adaptation and improvements are not mechanical, straightforward processes, but they require specific activities and investments.

The evidence discussed so far suggests that the processes that lead to the creation of TCs, and its microeconomic foundations, have not been duly taken into account in the GVC framework, which is still far from presenting a micro analysis of the nature of knowledge, the capacity building mechanisms and efforts conducted by local manufacturers and international buyers. A more comprehensive approach should encompass the analysis of in-house activities, and integrate the process of transfer and acquisition of technologies with the in-house efforts of local producers. In this chapter, we show that the TCs approach might powerfully help to better explain upgrading and performance in GVCs.

6.5 Conclusions

Global value chains represent a new form of industrial organization that is widely prevailing in many industries across countries. Therefore, an analysis of its potential implications and consequences for firms in developing countries is of utmost relevance. However, recent research efforts in this direction have not fully clarified how global value chains foster upgrading processes in developing countries' firms. On the one hand, it has often been hinted that entering GVCs causes a sharp and automatic positive impact on local producers, in a deterministic fashion. On the other hand, the research agenda has shifted to the analysis of how local firms can join value chains, and, on the influence of governance, structures on upgrading. All this produces a harmful neglect of the analysis of the detailed mechanisms linking value chains with local firms' learning and innovation.

It is obviously false that entering global value chains – by itself – will lead to upgrading and better industrial performance in developing countries. This is not a mechanistic and risk-less process, and local firms need to invest in learning and building technological capabilities to effectively upgrade. The direction and extent of these investments may also vary in relation to features of knowledge such as its degree of complexity, tacitness and appropriability, and this has been insufficiently studied so far.

The insights offered by the TCs approach, discussed at length in this chapter, may usefully integrate the GVC approach, providing original conceptual insights to study technology and innovation in a GVC context. This has also potential implications for the definition of upgrading itself, and leads us to question whether this is the relevant concept to apply. A renovated approach may have implications for future research questions and strategies, and we propose that GVC research should more carefully study the details of the learning and innovation processes within firms in developing countries, and that TC theories may offer useful tools and concepts to this aim.

Appendix

Appendix 6.A1 The GVC studies reviewed

Authors and studies	*Main focus and results*	*Extent/depth of analysis of*	
		*Knowledge features**	*TCs, nature and acquisition**
L. Bazan and L. Navas-Aleman (2004) Footwear industry in the Sinos Valley cluster (Brazil)	Cluster study: clusters' insertion into GVC and upgrading strategies. Functional upgrading prevails in market based value chains. Process and product upgrading are supported by quasi-hierarchical value chains.	LOW	MED-LOW
C. Kishimoto (2004) Computer industry, Taipei and Hsinchu area (Taiwan)	Cluster study: it adopts an historical perspective to study the upgrading process in the industry. There is an explicit distinction between production and knowledge systems. Product and functional upgrading are widely diffused in the cluster.	MED-LOW	MEDIUM
J. Meyer-Stamner *et al.* (2004) Tile industry, clusters in Italy, Spain, Brazil	Cluster study:analysis of the insertion of clusters into GVC and its effect on local collective action. Besides cluster and GVC approaches, it highlights the importance of sectoral factors.	LOW	MED-LOW
R. Quadros (2004) Automobile component industry, San Paolo (Brazil)	Cluster study: role of global quality standards for the upgrading strategies of local manufacturers and their effects on local and international linkages. Diffusion of global standard has improved local suppliers production processes but not engineering capabilities.	LOW	MEDIUM
K. Nadvi (2004) Surgical instrumental industry, Sialkot (Pakistan)	Cluster study: analysis of the adoption of global standards by local producers. Quality standards favoured upgrading but did not extend to subcontractors. Besides, they seem to have weakened relationships with global buyers.	MED-LOW	MED-LOW

H. Schmitz and P. Knorringa (2000) Footwear industry in China, India Brazil, Italy	Industry study: empirical analysis from a buyer perspective. It examines the role of buyers in fostering/hindering learning opportunities of producers. Buyers do not search only price competitiveness, but also quality, flexibility etc.	LOW	MED-LOW
T. Shuk-Ching Poon (2004) ICT industry in Taiwan	Industry study: analysis of GVC as channels of knowledge and sources of upgrading. There is substantial evidence of upgrading fostered by GVC. Local capability is a precondition for industrial upgrading.	LOW	MEDIUM
R. Kaplinsky (2004) Canned deciduous fruit and car component sector, South Africa	Industry study: analyses of the dynamics of rents distribution along the GVC in different sectors. GVC approach allows to identify the main drivers governing these chains and who accrue major benefits from them.	LOW	LOW
J. Barnes and R. Kaplinsky (2000) Car component sector, South Africa	Industry study: it examines how local component producers respond to increasing external competition. MNC increasingly integrated their local subsidiaries, reducing the space for locally owned suppliers.	LOW	MED-LOW
R. Kaplinsky and R. Fitter (2004) Horticulture and coffee sectors in LDCs.	Industry study: it examines how LDCs can exploit changes in global market by entering new phases of the GVCs. Investing in knowledge is a winning strategy to accrue innovation rents.	LOW	MED-LOW
R. Kaplinsky *et al.* (2002) Furniture industry, South Africa	Industry study: role of buyers in fostering upgrading for their local suppliers. Production capabilities are increasingly widespread while buyers erect entry barriers for high value added activities.	LOW	MED-LOW
R. Kaplinsky and J. Readman (2005) Furniture sector, comparative study	Industry study: measurement of comparative performance of several countries using data on unit prices and market share. Analysis of upgrading and downgrading trends.	LOW	LOW
G. Gereffi (1999) Apparel industry, East Asia	Industry study: analysis of the insertion and evolution of East Asian countries in GVC. Theoretical distinction between different chains (buyer vs. producers driven). Core-periphery patterns emerges in the US apparel suppliers system.	LOW	LOW

continued

Appendix 6.A1 continued

Authors and studies	*Main focus and results*	*Extent/Depth of analysis of*	
		*Knowledge features**	*TCs, nature and acquisition**
G. Gereffi *et al.* (2005) Apparel, bicycle, electronics and fresh vegetables industries. LDCs	Industry study: governance patterns differ according to three main theoretical perspectives: transaction costs; production networks; technological capabilities. Three factors allows to build a GVC theory: complexity of knowledge; codificability knowledge; capabilities of suppliers.	MEDIUM	MEDIUM
J. Bair and G. Gereffi (2001) Apparel sector, Mexico	Clusters study: role of GVC in sustaining local upgrading. The arrival of global buyers has prompted local upgrading at industry and firm level. Institutional failures impeded further spillovers.	LOW	MED-LOW
P. Gibbon (2001) Primary sector, Tanzania	Industry study: upgrading in primary sector GVC. It suggests a new agenda for upgrading strategies and policy intervention.	LOW	MED-LOW
P. Gibbon (2003) Clothing sector, sub-Saharan Africa	Industry study: response of clothing sector to new trade agreements (African Growth and Opportunity Act) and upgrading consequences for local producers.	LOW	LOW
F. Palpacuer *et al.* (2005) Clothing sector in European countries	Industry study: to what extent clothing GVCs offer upgrading opportunities for DCs. Analysis of the buyers strategies. They raise doubts about the worthiness of entering GVCs for DCs.	LOW	MED-LOW

Notes
* High: fully examined; Medium: partially examined; Med-Low: mentioned and sketchily analysed; Low: only mentioned or not taken into account at all.

Notes

1 Preliminary drafts of this chapter were presented at the PRIN "Dynamic Capabilities Between Firm Organization and Local Systems of Production" final conference in Bologna, at SPRU, University of Sussex and at Globelics India 2006. We wish to thank Martin Bell, Riccardo Leoncini and Sandro Montresor for their useful comments.
2 Among the main contributions to this approach, see Bell and Pavitt, 1992, 1995; Dahlman *et al.*, 1987; Enos, 1991; Fransman and King, 1984; Figueiredo, 2001; Katz, 1987; Lall, 1992, 1993, 2001; Pack and Westphal, 1986; Pietrobelli, 1994, 1997, 1998; Wignaraja, 1998.
3 The complexity and the variety of TCs do not pretend to be portrayed exhaustively here. Other categorizations have been proposed by Bell and Pavitt, 1995; Dahlman *et al.*, 1987; Enos and Park, 1988; Figueiredo, 2002; Katz, 1987.
4 The complete list of all the studies analysed is presented in the Appendix.
5 An exception is Kaplinsky and Morris (2001), in their view: "the concept of upgrading (as distinct from innovation) explicitly recognizes relative endowments, and hence the existence of rent (…). Thus innovation has to be placed in a relative context – how fast compared to competitors – and this is a process, which can be referred to as one of upgrading" (p. 37).
6 Kaplinsky and Morris argue that different actors are engaged in the coordination and management of the value chains. These nodal points may change over time, and the power over the chain can be exercised in different ways: those who are "ensuring consequences along the chain" can be different from those who are "actively managing or coordinating the operations" (2001: 29–30).
7 Gereffi *et al.* (2005) start to recognize the importance of knowledge features and incorporate them in their theoretical framework. We will further discuss this issue later.
8 Notable efforts in this sense were made, for example, by Figueiredo (2001, 2002) and Katz (1987).
9 See Lall (1996) on the different strategies followed by different Asian countries to get access to technology and develop technological capabilities. On this see also Pietrobelli (2000).

References

Bair J. and Gereffi G. (2001), "Local clusters in global chains: the causes and consequences of export dynamism in Torreon's blue jeans industry", *World Development*, 29 (11): 1885–1903.

Barnes J. and Kaplinsky R. (2000), "Globalization and the death of the local firm? The automobile components sector in South Africa", *Regional Studies*, 34 (9): 797–812.

Bazan L. and Navas-Aleman L. (2004), "The underground revolution in the Sinos Valley: a comparison of upgrading in global and national value chains", in H. Schmitz (ed.), *Local Enterprises in the Global Economy*, Cheltenham: Edward Elgar, pp. 110–139.

Bell M.R. and Albu M. (1999), "Knowledge systems and technological dynamism in industrial clusters in developing countries", *World Development*, 27 (9): 1715–1734.

Bell M.R. and Pavitt K. (1992), "Technological accumulation and industrial growth: contrasts between developed and developing countries", *Industrial and Corporate Change*, 2 (2): 157–210.

Bell M.R. and Pavitt K. (1995), "The development of technological capabilities", in I.U. Haque, *Trade, Technology and International Competitiveness*, Washington, DC, EDI Development Studies, The World Bank, pp. 69–101.

Breschi S. and Lissoni F. (2001), "Knowledge spillovers and local innovation systems: a critical survey", *Industrial and Corporate Change*, 10 (4): 975–1005.

Breschi S., Malerba F. and Orsenigo L. (2000), "Technological regimes and the Schumpeterian patterns of innovation", *The Economic Journal*, 110: 388–410.

Caniëls M. and Romijn H.A. (2003), "Firm-level knowledge accumulation and regional dynamics", *Industrial and Corporate Change*, 12 (6): 1253–1278.

Cohen W.M. and Levinthal D.A. (1990), "Absorptive capacity: a new perspective on learning and innovation", *Administrative Science Quarterly*, 35: 128–153.

Dahlman C., Ross-Larson B. and Westphal L.E. (1987), "Managing technological development: lessons from newly industrializing countries", *World Development*, 15 (6): 759–775.

Enos J. (1991), *The Creation of Technological Capability in Developing Countries*, London: Pinter.

Enos J. and Park W.H. (1988), *The Adoption and Diffusion of Imported Technology: The Case of Korea*, London: Croom Helm.

Ernst D., Ganiatsos T. and Mytleka L. (eds) (1998), *Technological Capabilities and Export Performance: Lessons from East Asia*, Cambridge: Cambridge University Press.

Figueiredo P.N. (2001), *Technological Learning and Competitive Performance*, Cheltenham: Edward Elgar.

Figueiredo P.N. (2002), "Does technological learning pay off? Inter-firm differences in technological capability-accumulation paths and operational performance improvement", *Research Policy*, 31: 73–94.

Figueiredo P.N. (2006), "Introduction", Special Issue on Technological Capabilities in Developing Countries, *International Journal of Technology Management*, 36 (1/2/3): 1–13.

Fransman M. and King K. (eds) (1984), *Technological Capability in the Third World*, London: Macmillan.

Gereffi G. (1994), "The organization of buyer-driven global commodity chains: how U.S. retailers shape overseas production networks", in G. Gereffi and M. Korzeniewicz (eds), *Commodity Chains and Global Capitalism*, London: Praeger, pp. 95–122.

Gereffi G. (1999), "International trade and industrial upgrading in the apparel commodity chain", *Journal of International Economics*, 48: 37–70.

Gereffi G. and Kaplinsky R. (eds) (2001), "The value of value chains: spreading the gains of globalisation", Special issue, *IDS Bulletin*, 32 (3).

Gereffi G., Humphrey J., Sturgeon T. (2005), "The governance of global value chains", *Review of International Political Economy*, 12 (1): 78–104.

Gibbon P. (2001), "Upgrading primary products: a global value chain approach", *World Development*, 29 (2): 345–363.

Gibbon P. (2003), "The African growth and opportunity act and the global commodity chain for clothing", *World Development*, 31 (11): 1809–1827.

Giuliani E. (2005), *When the Micro Shapes the Meso: Learning and Innovation in Wine Clusters*, Dphil thesis, SPRU, University of Sussex, Brighton.

Giuliani E., Pietrobelli C. and Rabellotti R. (2005), "Upgrading in global value chains: lessons from Latin America clusters", *World Development*, 33, 4: 549–573.

Guerrieri P., Iammarino S. and Pietrobelli C. (2001), *The Global Challenge to Industrial Districts: SMEs in Italy and Taiwan*, Cheltenham, UK and Lyme, US: Edward Elgar.

Hausmann R. and Rodrik D. (2003), "Economic development as self-discovery", *Journal of Development Economics*, 72 (2): 603–633.

Humphrey J. and Schmitz H. (2000) "Governance and upgrading: linking industrial cluster and global value chain research", IDS Working Paper, No. 120, Institute of Development Studies, University of Sussex, Brighton.

Humphrey J. and Schmitz H. (2002a), "How does insertion in global value chains affect upgrading industrial clusters?", *Regional Studies*, 36 (9): 1017–1027.

Humphrey J. and Schmitz H. (2002b), "Developing country firms in the world economy: governance and upgrading in global value chains", INEF Report, No. 61, University of Duisburg, Duisburg.

Humphrey J. and Schmitz H. (2004), "Globalized localities: introduction", in H. Schmitz (ed.), *Local Enterprises in the Global Economy*, Cheltenham and Northampton: Edward Elgar, pp. 1–21.

Kaplinsky R. (2000). "Globalisation and unequalisation: What can be learned from value chain analysis?", *Journal of Development Studies*, 37 (2): 117–146.

Kaplinsky R. (2004), "Spreading the gains form globalization: What can be learned form value chain analysis", *Problems of Economic Transition*, 47 (2): 74–115.

Kaplinsky R. and Morris M. (2001), "A handbook for value chain research", Institute of Development Studies, University of Sussex and School of Development Studies, University of Natal, (www.ids.ac.uk/global, and www.nu.ac.za/csds).

Kaplinsky R. and Fitter R. (2004), "Technology and globalisation: Who gains when commodities are de-commodified?", *International Journal of Technology and Globalisation*, 1 (1): 5–28.

Kaplinsky R. and Readman J. (2005), "Globalisation and upgrading: What can be (and cannot) learnt from international trade statistics in the wood furniture sector?", *Industrial and Corporate Change,* 14 (4): 679–703.

Kaplinsky R., Morris, M. and Readman ?. (2002), "The globalisation of product markets and immiserising growth: lessons from the South African furniture industry", *World Development*, 30 (7): 1159–1177.

Katz J. (ed.) (1987), *Technology Generation in Latin American Manufacturing Industry*, London: Macmillan.

Kishimoto C. (2004), "Clustering and upgrading in global value chains: the Taiwanese personal computer industry", in H. Schmitz (ed.), *Local Enterprises in the Global Economy*, Cheltenham: Edward Elgar, pp. 233–264.

Kogut B. (1985), "Designing global strategies: comparative and competitive value-added chains", *Sloan Management Review*, 2 (4): 15–28.

Lall S. (1987), *Learning to Industrialize: The Acquisition of Technological Capability by India*, London: Macmillan.

Lall S. (1990), *Building Industrial Competitiveness: New Technologies and Capabilities in Developing Countries*, Paris: OECD Development Centre.

Lall S. (1992), "Technological capabilities and industrialization", *World Development*, 20 (2): 165–186.

Lall S. (1993), "Understanding technology development", *Development and Change*, 24 (4): 719–753.

Lall S. (1996), *Learning from the Tigers*, London: Macmillan.

Lall S. (2001), *Competitiveness, Technology and Skills*, Cheltenham: Edward Elgar.

Malerba F. and Orsenigo L. (1993), "Technological regimes and firm behavior", *Industrial and Corporate Change*, 2: 45–71.

Meyer-Stamer J. (1998), "Path dependence in regional development: persistence and change in three industrial clusters in Santa Catarina, Brazil", *World Development*, 26 (8): 1495–1511.

Meyer-Stamer J., Maggi C. and Siebel S. (2004), "Upgrading in the tile industry of Italy, Spain and Brazil: insights from cluster and value chain analysis", in H. Schmitz (ed.), *Local Enterprises in the Global Economy*, Cheltenham: Edward Elgar, pp. 174–199.

Nadvi K. (2004), "The effect of global standards on local producers: a Pakistani case study", in H. Schmitz (ed.), *Local Enterprises in the Global Economy*, Cheltenham: Edward Elgar, pp. 297–325.

Nadvi K. and Schmitz H. (eds) (1999), "Clustering and industrialization: introduction", Special Issue, *World Development*, 27 (9): 1503–1514.

Nadvi K. and Waltring F. (2004), "Making sense of global standards", in H. Schmitz (ed.), *Local Enterprises in the Global Economy*, Cheltenham: Edward Elgar, pp. 53–94.

Nelson R. and Winter S. (1982), *An Evolutionary Theory of Economic Change*, Cambridge, MA: The Belknap Press, Harvard University Press.

Pack H. and Westphal L.E. (1986), "Industrial strategy and technological change", *Journal of Development Economics*, 22 (1): 87–128.

Palpacuer F., Gibbon P. and Thomsen L. (2005), "New challenges for developing country suppliers in global clothing chains: a comparative European perspective", *World Development*, 33 (3): 409–430.

Pietrobelli C. (1994), "Technological capabilities at the national level: an international comparison of manufacturing export performance", *Development Policy Review*, 12 (2): 115–148.

Pietrobelli C. (1997), "On the theory of technological capabilities and developing countries' dynamic comparative advantage in manufactures", *Rivista Internazionale di Scienze Economiche e Commerciali*, XLIV (2, June): 313–318.

Pietrobelli C. (1998), *Industry, Competitiveness and Technological Capabilities in Chile. A New Tiger from Latin America?*, London and New York: Macmillan and St. Martin's.

Pietrobelli C. (2000), "The role of international technology transfer in the industrialisation of developing countries", in M. Elena and D. Schroeer (eds) *Technology Transfer*, Aldershot, UK and Burlington, USA: Ashgate.

Ponte S. and Gibbon P. (2005), "Quality standards, conventions and the governance of global value chains", *Economy and Society*, 34 (1): 1–31.

Poon T. Shuk-Ching (2004), "Beyond the global production networks: a case of further upgrading of Taiwan's information technology industry", *International Journal of Technology and Globalisation (IJTG)*, 1 (1): 130–144.

Quadros R. (2004), "Global quality standards and technological upgrading in the Brazilian auto-components industry", in H. Schmitz (ed.), *Local Enterprises in the Global Economy*, Cheltenham: Edward Elgar, pp. 265–298.

Romijn, H. (1999), *Acquisition of Technological Capability in Small Firms in Developing Countries*, London: Macmillan.

Schmitz H. (ed.) (2004), *Local Enterprises in the Global Economy*, Cheltenham: Edward Elgar.

Schmitz H. and Knorringa P. (2000), "Learning from global buyers", *Journal of Development Studies*, 37 (2): 177–205.

Wignaraja G. (1998), *Trade Liberalization in Sri Lanka: Exports, Technology and Industrial Policy*, London: Macmillan and New York: St. Martin's.

7 Learning at the boundaries for industrial districts between exploitation of local resources and the exploration of global knowledge flows[1]

Fiorenza Belussi, Luciano Pilotti and Silvia Rita Sedita

7.1 Introduction

In this chapter we develop an integrated view on how knowledge is developed in localised systems of specialised firms (industrial districts – IDs), through informal social networks (communities of practice – CoPs), and firms networks, in an osmotic process between the internal to the district knowledge and the external to the district knowledge. Contrary to consolidated tradition, which is based on Marshall's early writings, we describe the functioning of the modern industrial district emphasising not just the role of the local "industrial atmosphere" but the modern aspect of "learning at the boundaries", where local actors mix sources of knowledge located inside the district with external sources (Bathelt *et al.*, 2002). Starting from the concept of knowledge (Nonaka and Takeuchi, 1995), the purpose of this work is to understand how CoPs, a new concept that arose from the management field, can be useful for deepening the process of knowledge creation, absorption, and sharing of IDs. This chapter is organised as follows. Section 7.2 provides some notes on the evolution of capabilities in social systems. Section 7.3 offers a unified view of the contemporary phenomenon of industrial clustering. Section 7.4 offers a new approach to the learning process in social systems (IDs, CoPs), based on individual and collective capabilities. Section 7.5 illustrates an interpretative framework of learning activities by: (1) classifying two types of knowledge management at the firm level and the ID level: gardening activities and investments in capabilities; (2) identifying the importance of internal/external switchers for learning at the boundaries. Section 7.6 proposes some empirical evidence, illustrating three case studies. The objective is to measure the relative capacity of a single industrial district to "cultivate" the growth process of local knowledge and to face effectively the challenges of the globalisation process, being able to learn at the boundaries. In Section 7.7 some conclusive remarks are drawn.

7.2 The evolution of capabilities in social systems

Mainstream economics describes capital stock and natural resources as strategic factors for organisations. In his "Wealth of Nations" (1776), Adam Smith underlined the effects of both specialisation and technical change on the economic growth. Marshall (1920), Chamberlin (1933), and Nelson and Winter (1982), following the Schumpeterian legacy, added the power of innovation. Nonaka and Takeuchi (1995) developed some thorough insights on the importance of knowledge creation. As Teece (1998), Lundvall (1988) and others have argued, producer learning is one of the factors driving the increasing returns phenomenon (Arthur, 1994), together with network externalities. How can an organisation learn? How does it access knowledge "repositories"? What are the institutions that might aid organisations to recognise and enhance its resources?

In order to explore the ways through which an organisation, a community, or an industrial district learn we must discuss the way in which individuals absorb and possess new pieces of knowledge. The fundamental assumption adopted here concerns the individual-based approach to knowledge transfer and learning activities. This approach stresses the diverse combinations of knowledge possessed by individuals (Foss and Foss, 2003, p. 5):

> Knowledge still ultimately resides in the heads of individuals; however, when this knowledge is combined and "aggregated" in certain ways, it means that considered as a system, a set of agents possesses knowledge that they do not possess if separated.

Knowledge possessed by individuals is further extracted in firms and organisations.

Therefore the competitive advantage of firms in today's economy stems not just from market position, but from difficult to replicate knowledge assets and the manner in which they are deployed (Teece, 1998). While the production of "commodities" plays a marginal role, competition appears to be based on knowledge assets, and firm-processing information has become more strategically relevant than manufacturing activities per se (Castells, 1996, 2000). Knowledge assets are the result of a complex process of interpretation of information obtained by data elaboration.

Knowledge can be obtained from information by an individual who processes information. Data can be defined as "observations of states of the world" (Davenport and Prusak, 1997). Peter Drucker (1988) defined information as "data endowed with relevance and purpose", stressing the crucial existence of the human mediation occurring during the phase of data elaboration. Databases can be easily organised to answer many queries, thanks to the possibility of crossing different data-matrixes, through a connecting key-code. ICT tools allow us to "manage data" and to extrapolate information from them. The absorption of information by the human mind also includes contextualisation, validation, reflection and synthesis.

Individuals and organisations can shift from data to knowledge articulating a fluid mix of framed experience, values, contextual information, and expert insight. In this manner they provide a framework for evaluating and incorporating new experiences and information (Davenport and Prusak, 2000, p. 5). In organisations, knowledge is embedded not only in documents or repositories but also in organisational routines (Nelson and Winter, 1982) building a collective intelligence (Lévy, 2002), which ultimately leads to organisational wisdom (Pór and Molloy, 2000). Collective intelligence represents the evolution of knowledge from a "property" of individuals to a "resource" of social organisms (Pór, 1995). This process implies a progressive empowerment of the organisation.

The capabilities to acquire new pieces of knowledge or to re-use an old knowledge base in an innovative way implies the existence of learning processes.

Starting from the assumption that individual knowledge is scarce and incomplete, intelligent organisations should be able to valorise employees' diversity, encouraging processes of learning by interaction (Laszlo and Laszlo, 2002). Nonaka and Takeuchi (1995), drawing on the Polanyi notion of tacit knowledge, suggests the identification of two types of knowledge: tacit (not codified, not easily transferable) and explicit (codified, easily transferable). Within firms, the conversion of tacit to explicit knowledge, and vice-versa, gives rise to a four-phase learning process (Nonaka and Toyama, 2002):

a Socialisation → learning as knowledge transfer from one agent to another, sharing and creating tacit knowledge through direct experience (tacit to tacit knowledge);
b Externalisation → learning as the capability to produce new relevant pieces of knowledge, articulating tacit knowledge through dialogue and reflection (tacit knowledge to explicit knowledge);
c (Re-)Combination → learning as knowledge improvement, systemising and applying explicit knowledge and information (tacit plus explicit knowledge into new tacit knowledge);
d Internalisation → learning as absorption capability, acquiring new tacit knowledge in practice (explicit knowledge to tacit knowledge, but also absorption of tacit knowledge from outside).

The presence of tacit knowledge in individuals and organisational routines explains why knowledge maintains a high degree of subjectivity, influencing the evolution of capability, and supporting the various modes of learning in social contexts. Capabilities evolve in firms because processes of knowledge creation are at work. The "evolutionary view" of capabilities has two quite distinct "progenitors": Edith Penrose (1959) and Nelson and Winter (1982), whose works have been slowly integrated in a converging approach where firms can be described as coordinators of "organised" and "collective" specific knowledge.

Nelson and Winter interpreted capabilities as "the nature and sources of continuity in the behavioural patterns of an individual organisation" (p. 96), in other words as a "routine" or "program" which refer to a repetitive pattern. In their conceptualisation routines are organisational memory: a set of skills that a particular member of the organisation can perform in some appropriate environment. Routines are a *repertoire* where knowledge resides, and where organisational knowledge is stored. It is also a matter of knowing what routine to perform, and when to perform it. Thus, tasks are typically complex and composed of various abilities. Productive capabilities include the "ability to operate plants and equipments". Organisations do not become capable of a productive performance merely by acquiring all the necessary "ingredients" (inputs, like technology or capital). They must have the "recipe" (prescriptive instructions on the use of resources), and the ability to perform it based on a fine-tuning of complex activities of coordination. "Blueprints" are only a small part of what is needed to be stored in the organisational memory of a firm, in order to reproduce and replicate a task effectively. Routines, and therefore capabilities, change when the process of searching and exploring ends up with an innovation. The menu of routines in firms is not broad but narrow and idiosyncratic: routines in organisations are equalised to genes. The important consideration captured by this model is that "imitation, though costly and imperfect, is a powerful mechanism by which new routines come to organise a larger fraction of the total activity of the system" (p. 135). A similar analysis has been provided by Penrose[2] (1959). A firm may be regarded as a "repository of assets", a pool of resources, the utilisation of which is organised in an "administrative framework" (p. 149). Capabilities are a collection of physical and human resources, which may be developed in a variety of ways to provide a variety of services. As commented by Loasby (1999, p. 49), Penrose avoided the term "factors of production" because she did not want to obscure the difference between resources and the services that they yield when they are oriented. Penrose's definition of the firm fits with the Marshallian tradition where firms are organisations which develop knowledge (Loasby, 1999).

It can be argued that "routine" is an ambiguous surrogate for capabilities, because an executable program for repeated performance is something different from the organisational knowledge that lies behind the execution of a performance. However, these two conceptualisations share a mutual understanding, and the contemporary evolutionary literature generally refers to both (Loasby, 1999). It must be mentioned that after its introduction in 1959, the term capability was subsequently discussed by Richardson (1972), in a seminal paper in which he sets down the criteria on the basis on which, in the industrial organisation, an extensive cooperation emerges in the market. Activities in firms are carried out by organisations with "appropriate capabilities, or, in other words, with appropriate knowledge, experience and skills" (p. 888). The emergence of a complex web of cooperation is explained by the need to combine closely, complementary but dissimilar activities that in certain circumstances cannot be allocated either straightforwardly to the market (because of the existing complementarities with firm assets), or to the firm itself (because it lacks the required capabilities). So, the capability view explains the distribution of economic activities between firms in competitive markets and the ways in which these activities are coordinated through indirect and direct forms of cooperation. Firms exist as independent actors from the enlarged mechanism of atomistic exchange in the market because they possess "distinctive" capabilities, which markets, in their pure form, do not have. Capabilities influence the way in which firms choose to coordinate their resources. Richardson's contribution of 1972 can be considered the necessary complementary explanation for Coase's motivation of the existence of the firm as a separate agent in the markets. Markets lack strategic behaviour and imagination. Firms are guided by strategic behaviour and entrepreneurial imagination (Witt, 1996). Capabilities are directly related to the technological activity of firms and share a cumulative nature, being path-dependent. Firms may be victims of their past history, experimenting lock-in effects (a successful organisation will tend to conserve its capability even if the context would require some adjustment or replacement as in the examples cited by Fransman, 1994).

In order to develop their capabilities – as underlined by the business literature working on firm "competitive strategies" (Porter, 1980), core competences (Prahalad and Hamel, 1990),[3] "dynamic organisational capabilities" (Grant, 1996; Zollo and Winter, 2002), and organisational learning (Argyris and Schön, 1978) – firms invest in knowledge creation and acquisition through in-house R&D and new knowledge absorption through search processes (Cohen and Levinthal, 1990). Firms, here in this vision, become "assemblers of specific competences" (Nelson, 1992, 1994; Foss and Loasby, 1998) and related complementarities (Teece, 1987), basing their existence on a chain of articulated knowledge, learning, innovation, and experience, knowledge exploration and exploitation (March, 1991) and efficient relations with suppliers and sub-contractors, marketing and after-sales services (Wernerfelt, 1984; Teece *et al.*, 1997). In this context numerous channels, to absorb information, can be organised by individual firms (meetings, participation in fairs), which can blend internal knowledge with the external experience localised in universities, consultants, strategic alliances, and so forth.

7.3 Industrial districts as spatial knowledge repositories

Knowledge does not only reside in individuals and organisations, but is also localised in hybrid organisational forms (networks and districts), thus, it is concentrated in specific local systems.[4]

Becattini (1979) defines an industrial district, in a neo-marshallian perspective, as a local agglomeration of small and medium enterprises, all of them involved in the same productive process, but where everyone is specialised in a particular phase, everyone is independent of each other, but it lies in a local network of geographic and productive relationships with the others. As a result, an integrated industrial area arises, which produces economies that are external to the single firm, but internal to the localised thickening of intra-inter industrial and social relationships. The ID is the extreme synthesis of the social-economic interactions between the mechanism of light industrialisation and the embedded territory or institutional space (Maskell and Malmberg, 1999; Storper, 1997; Amin, 1993; Belussi, 2006). Now, at the beginning of the twenty-first century, the idea of the localisation of the economic development in specific places and its organisation in clusters has become a widespread convention (Rullani, 2000).

One of the sources of competitive advantage of local systems lies in the capability to share tacit knowledge between all the nodes of what may be called a "Multilevel Neural Network" (Pilotti, 1999).

The neoclassical approach, as argued by Tsoukas (1996), which sees firms as black boxes, characterised by input–output regularities and predictable behaviour, clearly does not take two important factors into account: time and space, which make every kind of organisation and every environment rather unique. This uniqueness is one of the roots of the success of IDs, which were born and grew in specific spaces, developing local specific knowledge, and whose evolution is often dominated by the innovations (most incremental) they are capable to create and to adopt during time. Sticky, non-articulated, tacit forms of knowledge (see also Von Hippel, 1998)[5] are among the most relevant drivers of innovations for firms located in an ID. Firms' histories, their lived experiences, the routinisation of the production activities, the amount of relationships they are able to build up, and the common sharing of the same "norms and rules" are the main sources of tacit knowledge (Belussi and Caldari, 2003). These relationships characterise what is called social capital (Jacobs, 1961; Bourdieu, 1985; Coleman, 1988; Putnam, 1993, 1995),[6] which, in fact, contributes to shape tacit and contextual knowledge, embedded in individuals belonging to a community. Furthermore, groups of locally situated firms naturally benefit from this embeddedness that allows substantial reductions in the costs of accessing this type of knowledge (Cainelli and De Liso, 2004).

However, the understanding of ID evolution might become even more complicated if we consider the process of globalisation that has opened up the district borders, fragmenting at international level the sources of subcontracting and the entire global value chains (Belussi and Sammarra, 2005). In fact, thanks to the recent development and diffusion of ICT the access to resources becomes potentially ubiquitous (Castells, 1996, 2000), and time is compressed and de-sequenced (time sometimes tends to zero in on on-line transactions). Many virtual connections overtake the role of geographically bounded social interactions.

Building new "pipelines" (Bathelt *et al.*, 2002) induces firms to sustain huge investments that might be perceived either as sunk costs or as knowledge channels. Industrial districts are experiencing a period of transition where the neo-Marshallian nodes (closed local networks) are immersed in global networks (Amin and Thrift, 1992). Closed systems are no longer representatives of the huge variety of existing organisational models (Belussi *et al.*, 2003; Giuliani *et al.*, 2005; Iammarino and McCann, 2005; Zucchella, 2006). While some districts during the last decades have suffered from a lock-in mechanism, which did not allow IDs to grow and take advantage of potential external sources of knowledge, others have evidenced a striking capability to build global supply chains (Coró and Grandinetti, 1999; Belussi and Sammarra, 2005). This "opening" process, obviously, occurs at different levels, but we mean to strike here the arising consciousness of the potential advantages, achievable from the exploitation of new communication channels, through which new resources, competences, and knowledge can be absorbed. In order to maintain their competitiveness, and to introduce complex innovation, IDs must be able to develop strategic relations with external service providers (KIBS – Knowledge Intensive Business Services), in fields where the internal competences are difficult to develop (Camuffo and Grandinetti, 2005), such as information technology, quality management, marketing, communication, R&D activity, and so forth.

Bathelt *et al.* (2002) have emphasised in their theoretical work the duality that characterises the process of local learning in districts, facilitated both by local "buzz" and "global pipelines". These two modalities are strictly connected. On the one hand, some learning stems from the district model of organisation, which takes advantage of the embeddedness, and on the other hand some useful knowledge is exchanged and absorbed through long distance channels. This becomes possible thanks to the "absorptive capacity" of local firms (Cohen and Levinthal, 1990). With this term Aage (2001) addressed the districtual firms' capability of achieving external knowledge, which is re-processed inside the system, through a boundary spanning mechanism (direct peer or gatekeeper). The latter alludes to paths of "internalisation" within firms of the competences acquired (Aage, 2005). The recent "openness" of the Italian IDs is partially due to the use of new ICT tools (Belussi, 2005a). This process is not to be viewed as a "killer" of the competitive advantage derived from the sharing of tacit knowledge among actors belonging to the "small community" of the industrial district (Chiarvesio *et al.*, 2004). Many economists (Cooke, 2001; Biggiero, 2002, Morrison, 2004; Brenner, 2004) have argued that knowledge embedded in local communities, firms, and specific networks, remains relevant also during the process of globalisation, and it helps to "lubricate" the efficacy of international relationships, allowing the enlargement of the whole system through the creation of new nodes, maybe new "growth poles" (Perroux, 1955). The new challenge is to establish to what extent this "contamination" of new knowledge might be profitable for the ID, considering the price of obtaining it (because of the great degree of uncertainty that is involved in building new partnerships with distant – not direct observable actors).

Geographical proximity has allowed so far the growth of reciprocal trust (personal capital, or self-interested trust) among the actors of the district, derived from repeated exchanges and from the sense of belonging to the same community[7] (collective capital, or social-oriented trust) as discussed by Dei Ottati (2001), Lyons and Mehta (1997), and Mistri and Solari (2003). Trust can "survive" and be built also in a virtual network, where the advantage of proximity no longer exists. Network externalities[8] can be localised or not, and they depend on the shape of the network (Wasserman and Faust, 1994).[9] Networked agents, covering the position of structural holes, develop more power than others operating in densely distributed networks (Burt, 1992). Similarly, different advantages from knowledge replication are reached in various networks. In the local environment of an ID, an agent's behaviour is pushed by reputation-saving constraints, fearing a possible exclusion from local transactions. Nevertheless, if trust is strictly connected with the sense of belonging to a community, and it is not based on individual experience, we can accept the hypothesis that it can exist in a virtual community (Orléan, 1994). In this way, future cyber-marketplace might be an efficient solution for the connection of agents over long distances. Information and communication technologies allow the matching of the benefits of physical proximity with those depending on institutional and organisational proximity (Gallaud and Torre, 2005).

Most agent interactions occurring inside the local network are spontaneous. Economic order is reached without any deliberate planning, because IDs are flexible self-organised systems (Pilotti, 2000). Can this random process of interactions also survive in the tough times of globalisation? A higher level of firm hierarchisation is observed in many Italian IDs (Cainelli *et al.*, 2006; Belussi, 2005b). High fashion global brands (and large international Italian firms) now orchestrate the production of many districtual firms, for instance in the Veneto region or in Tuscany (Amighini and Rabellotti, 2006; Rabellotti, 2004; Bacci, 2004). Thus, global leaders have emerged in the last decades (for instance: Geox in Montebelluna, Luxottica in Belluno, Prada and Gucci in Florence, Callegaris in Manzano, and Dideco in Mirandola). This is clearly forcing the delicate districtual dynamics, changing the district flows of communication, knowledge, and productive transactions.

For firms based in western countries' IDs, the possibility to have access to low-cost labour forces in developing countries has given rise to the creation of global nets of international suppliers for the production of the more labour-intensive components. Firm networks, in Italian IDs specialised in mature sectors (clothing-textile-footwear), are often long-distance networks. With time, practical know-how and codified knowledge incorporated in new machinery tend to go beyond the boundaries of the districts (for instance in Italy the new clients of ID suppliers are actually located in developing countries, like China or Romania). The diffusion of know-how takes time, but it is an unavailable process developed in parallel with the internalisation of the supply chains. The recourse to KIBS and to new linkages related to R&D cooperative agreements shows also for the firms localised in IDs the crucial role that the process of knowledge offshoring deserves in modern times. While the Marshallian IDs were described as closed systems, where knowledge mainly spilled over around, in modern IDs knowledge spreads inwards and outwards within districts in different ways, and through multiple channels: personal relationships, firm-to-firm transactions, institution-to-firm (or to individual) relationships, new start-ups (where prior acquired practical knowledge is applied to new business ideas) or entry from outside, in and out labour market mobility, and so on.

Local learning and global learning tend to coalesce. Thus, the strong embeddedness of the social interactions co-exist with processes of knowledge exchanges external to the district.

7.4 Knowledge in social networks: the role of CoPs

The ID has been described as a local system dense with social relations: a community of firms and a population of individuals tied by bonds of solidarity and cooperation (Becattini, 1979, 1990). However, following the Marshallian tradition, while the role of external economies has been deeply analysed, the specific social mechanism through which knowledge in individuals and organisations is "put in practice" and further developed has been quite obscured. On the one hand, the geographers of innovation have assumed that spatial proximity per se plays the role of knowledge diffusion, because knowledge spillovers are activated quite in automatism (Audretsch and Feldman, 1996). On the other hand, it has been argued that in IDs and in clusters knowledge diffusion is selective and not pervasive (Giuliani, 2005). As regards knowledge creation and diffusion in IDs we encounter here a problematic dichotomy of over socialisation or under socialisation. Is knowledge belonging to individual and firms free to move within IDs? Can we better describe under which conditions the existing social networks do play a role? In order to improve our understanding of the mechanism of knowledge creation and diffusion we have to turn to the concept of CoPs.

Lave and Wenger (1991, p. 98) first introduced the concept of CoP in 1991, underlining the importance of sharing practice in the process of learning in large corporations. They describe a CoP as: "a set of relations among persons, activity, and world, over time and in relation with other tangential and overlapping CoPs". And also: "an intrinsic condition for the existence of knowledge".

The CoP is an organism constituted by a group of professionals, informally bound together, who, guided by a common purpose, share their distinctive capabilities to solve organizational problems. They could be, for example, engineers engaged in deep-water drilling, or consultants specialised in strategic marketing, or reps offering technical support (Brown and Duguid, 1991). One of the most important features that characterises the existence of a CoP is its organic, spontaneous, and informal nature. The member's attitude of giving their own contribution to the problem-solving process is reinforced by the self-selected membership mechanism of participation. The CoP main purpose is to develop members' capabilities and build forms of knowledge exchange. This quality marks the difference from other forms of aggregation, such as a formal working group or a "team". The latter, for example, is normally formed by a group of workers built to accomplish a specific task – as described by Nonaka (1991) – and further refined by him using the Japanese concept of "ba"[10] – and exists until the project has been completed. In a different way, CoPs, as Wenger and Snyder (2000) explain, have the property of lasting for a long time, thus allowing the sedimentation of a social capital. In fact, the CoP strength is self-perpetuating (Wenger, 2000). This tacit and common sharing of knowledge enhances over time the potentialities of the community and its ability to solve problems (Lesser and Everest, 2001).

Although CoPs are fundamentally informal and self-organised, they need to be "cultivated" (Wenger *et al.*, 2002). Wenger and Snyder (2000) use a nice metaphor to illustrate their dynamics. They compare them to gardens, which give the best results if someone takes care of them, without forcing the natural and biological rhythm of "reproduction". In firms, managers must identify potential communities, providing the support-infrastructure, and using non-traditional methods to measure their value. But, if CoPs are completely absorbed into the organisational task they decay (Thompson, 2005).

CoPs play a key role in the process of organisational learning, mostly if we look at learning from a social perspective (Wenger, 1999). Under this view, learning takes place thanks to the interplay between competences defined in a social community and personal experience. Moreover, a community of practice can be analysed as a social container of heterogeneous but complementary competences. There are, in particular, three ways of experimenting social learning, through:

- Engagement → doing things together, everyday routine, face-to-face contacts;
- Imagination → creating an imagine of yourself and your community, self-consciousness, identity;
- Alignment → sharing experience with others that can contribute with their efforts.

One mode can dominate the others, giving different qualities to different social structures. For example, a nation is a community based on imagination; a community of practice at work is based on engagement. Going further, two strategic issues arise. They are the following: "learning at the boundaries" and "identity". Let us start from the first: the existence of a CoP implies the existence of a boundary, as Wenger (2000, p.) writes: "shared practice by its very nature creates boundaries". The boundary divides what is the core experience of the CoP from external competences that can be useful to create new opportunities for enhancing the competitive advantage of the whole organisation (as illustrated in Figure 7.1). Boundaries are both sources of new opportunities and potential difficulties, according to the cognitive distance between the CoP's own experience and the external competences (Figure 7.2).

The interaction with new CoPs can be worthy if their competences are sufficiently different; at the same time, if they are too dissimilar, the inter-community learning will cease. In other words, learning, both in firms and in districts, is possible only if the cognitive distance is neither too short, nor too large (Nooteboom, 2000, 2002).

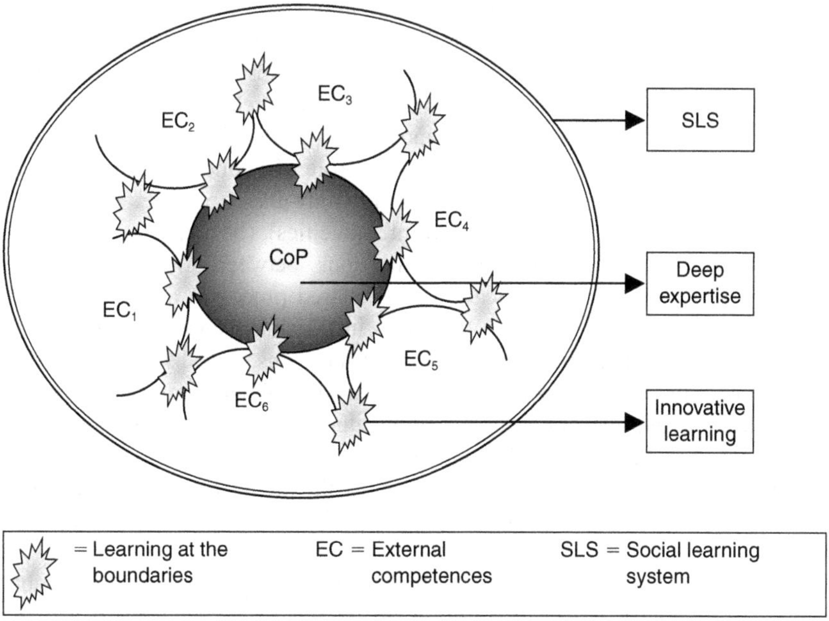

Figure 7.1 The process of learning at the boundaries.

Furthermore Wenger (2000) discusses three dimensions of the boundary effects:

- Transparency → to make the access to the boundary easier;
- Negotiability → to find an equilibrium between the powers of the actors involved;
- Coordination → to discriminate what is really useful to the organisation.

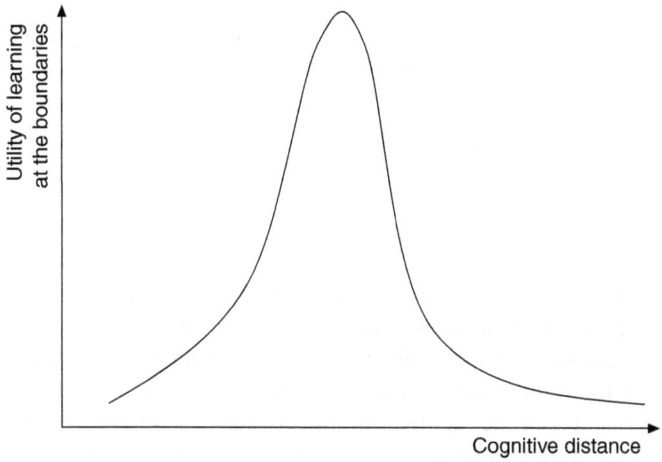

Figure 7.2 The utility function of learning at the boundaries.

The act of crossing the boundaries can be improved by the existence of intermediaries, which work as links for the dissemination of knowledge and trust (Granovetter, 1973). Coordination implies that some bridges have to be built to activate the connection within the boundaries and in relation to learning at the boundaries. Again, Wenger (2000) proposes four kinds of bridges: (a) brokering between communities (where actors play the role of boundary spanners, create connections that move knowledge by going from place to place, activate personal relationships, and capture "forefront" novelties), (b) boundary objects (we are referring to tools supporting connections between different practices, common language to communicate easily, shared processes and routine, artefacts, documents or models), (c) boundary interactions (related to practices of encountering, through visits and common discussions, and distant connections through fairs or use of websites), and (d) cross-disciplinary projects (combining knowledge of multiple practices or establishing learning loops through project teams – as argued also by McDermott (1999)).

The strength of a CoP is also determined by the members' sense of belonging to a unifying identity: "Knowing is an act of belonging, then our identities are a key structuring element of how we know" (Wenger, 2000, p. 238).

In the case of CoPs, identity involves also the concept of "multi-membership". Individuals have the opportunity to belong simultaneously to different communities (i.e. the community of workers, friends, neighbours, relatives, etc.) and to switch from one to another, without losing personal identity. Similarly, members of a specific CoP can share some information with another community, involving a natural process of learning at the boundaries through networks of CoPs (both physical and virtual (Ward, 2000)).

7.5 The evolution of IDs' capabilities between the exploitation of local resources and the exploration of global knowledge flows

In our analysis the evolution of capabilities in IDs appears to be related to two main processes activated by the principal ID actors – local firms and district institutions: the direct and indirect investment in augmenting local capabilities.

We are referring here mainly to two forms of knowledge management in IDs:

- Gardening;
- Investing in capabilities.

Gardening is a form of indirect investment in capabilities. Several researchers have used the gardening metaphor to describe the way in which organisations, managers, and coordinators can act to develop a community (Brown and Duguid, 2000; Schlager and Fusco, 2004; Wenger *et al.*, 2002). Indeed, the concept can be applied to understand an alternative way to develop local capabilities in an ID (i.e. a community of firms and persons). The theoretical base of this concept is rooted in the ecological view of the economy (Arthur, 1995), where the complexity of human interactions and the multiple ways of combining different subjective beliefs can neither be formally driven, nor perfectly ruled. According to the evolutionary and complex approach of the Santa Fe Institute (Anderson *et al.*, 1988; Arthur *et al.*, 1997), an industrial district can be seen as an evolving complex system, formed by an evolving network of heterogeneous, localised and functionally integrated interacting firms (Boero and Squazzoni, 2002). The system governance is based on self-organising dynamics, developed from long-term interactions and vertical and horizontal complex connections among spatially located firms (Biggiero, 1999). Typically top down interventions are not suitable for enhancing the capabilities of the district, which benefits, instead, from a local activity of gardening, i.e. of nurturing the internal dynamics by promoting specific initiatives.

In relation to "gardening" we suppose the existence of an actor that "takes care" of the knowledge flows, somehow enhancing the capabilities of "absorbing" new knowledge and transforming it into tools useful to the wealth of the organisation/district. Firms and institutions (spontaneous or designed for *ad hoc* purposes) as highlighted in Table 7.1 are responsible for this function.

The concept of gardening is strictly connected to the activity of direct investment in capabilities. Clearly this last function too is very important. Managers/entrepreneurs empower firms' capabilities accumulating R&D investments, adopting new technologies, and developing training activities. This creates the firm's knowledge reservoir (Argote and Ingram, 2000). The term "reservoir" derives from the French "réserver", meaning "to keep for future use", giving the idea that knowledge can be used again (see the debate around the re-use of knowledge (Langlois, 1999)). In aggregate the accumulated knowledge existing in the district represents a multiple reservoir, which, as discussed by Argote and Ingram, is composed of human resources, tools (machineries, documents, hardware, and software), and tasks (organisational practices, goals,

Table 7.1 Gardening and investing in capabilities at the firm level and the ID level

	Actors	*Gardening*	*Investing in capabilities*
Firm level	Manager Entrepreneur	CoPs cultivation	R&D investments Venture capital
ID level	Institutions	CoPs cultivation	Physical and ICT infrastructure
	Meta-organisers	Trust diffusion Cooperation incentives Providing support to create external links Guiding processes of firms modernisation Improving business strategies	Training and education KIBS

and purposes). Knowledge is transferred in the combination between them. Moving people is one of the easiest ways to transfer knowledge (embedded knowledge transfer). The investment in capabilities is also organised through the activity of the district meta-organisers which promote training activity, collective R&D investments, and other initiatives. Pilotti identifies meta-organisers as peculiar subjects in a local system with the specific function of connecting the multiplicity of technologies, the heterogeneity of organisations, and the internal market transactions, achieved through cooperation and competition (Albertini and Pilotti, 1996; Pilotti, 2000). These operators could be innovative firms as well as local institutions, which are in charge of integrating different flows of resources in a horizontal dimension. The result of their efforts is the promotion and diffusion of a generative learning, rooted in the capability to mix effectively tacit and explicit knowledge. The meta-organiser promotes initiatives that work as an occasion of cooperation and joint activities for the local firms, involving also local research centres and universities, following a "triple helix" model of local development (Etzkowitz and Leydesdorff, 2000).

The ID's capabilities can be detected not only through the aggregation of the capabilities of all local firms but also through the activity of the meta-organiser, which develops the district public goods, like physical and ICT infrastructure, training and education activities, foundation of research centres, and activation of KIBS.

It is important to stress that co-location per se is not enough to guarantee knowledge transfer between firms and what matters is being connected either locally or non-locally (Boschma and ter Wal, 2006). Therefore, the institutional setting, the implementation of specific policies and the individual engagement in learning activities occurring in an ID constitute the determinants of higher firms' performance and innovative activities, as far as the process of establishing external knowledge channels and boundary objects as shown in Figure 7.3.

The existence of direct investments in new knowledge acquisition and the constitution of CoPs reinforces the individual capabilities through social participation and knowledge sharing within a pool of practitioners. However, these individuals may suffer from lock-in and path dependency, provoking the asphyxiation and decline of the pool of district knowledge. Therefore, they need access to external relations by means of boundary spanning mechanisms and

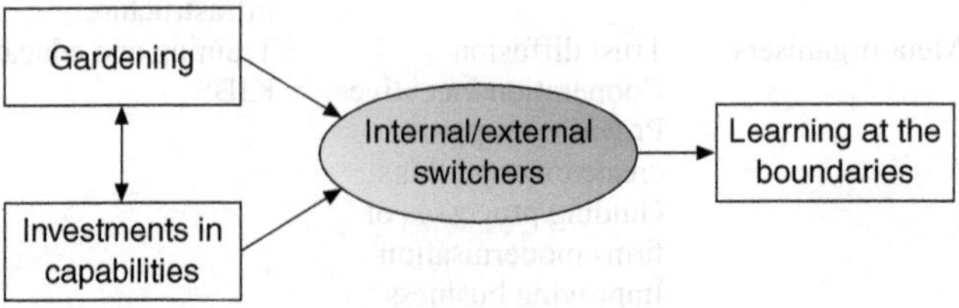

Figure 7.3 The role of internal/external switchers for learning at the boundaries.

boundary objects, facing the chance to integrate the district capabilities with other external competences and favouring a larger knowledge circulation.

However, in IDs, problems of coordination arise.

The activity of the manager/entrepreneur and of the meta-organiser gives rise to a complex form of learning that we have called "learning at the boundaries". On the one hand, this concept identifies the way through which different local CoPs interact, on the other hand, it sums up the process of exploration, selection, activation, monitoring, and nurturing of knowledge through production networks outside the boundaries of the district through "internal/external switchers" (Amin and Cohendet, 1999). One of the most important tools for guaranteeing the effectiveness of the use of external knowledge is the capacity of selection. Simon (2002) faces the problem of the over-abundance of information that needs to be filtered to contrast the scarcity of attention that characterises modern life. What we really need, he says, is not to increase the number of accesses to information, but the quality of the information selected, suggesting the need for some information processors, which are able to justify (Nonaka and Toyama, 2002) the cost of achieving a new piece of information. This implies a constant analysis of the "state of the art" of the held resources and a possible matching between "old" and "new" inputs. Often a single small firm is not able to sustain these costs of judgement. Firms located in IDs might avoid this type of sunk-cost allowing the constitution of "*ad hoc*" observatories, which might spread around information useful for the whole system.

Cohen and Levinthal (1990) speak about "gatekeepers", or "boundary spanners", referring to members of an organisation that are able to "translate" strategic external information into opportunities for improving the ongoing activities. At the same time, they point out that background knowledge is necessary for the success of the transmission, arguing that, without it, even with the presence of a highly capable gatekeeper, knowledge short-circuits are not avoided. Similarly, the meta-organiser in an ID can work as an interface between the local firms/actors and the external (extra-district/extra-region/global) environment, allowing not only the diffusion of the tacit knowledge embedded into the elements of a local system, but also the selection of the external knowledge that could be absorbed. Visits, labour mobility, fairs, virtual marketplaces, and other activities can be viewed as internal/external switchers for knowledge exchanges. These activities aid the process of building pipelines between internal and external actors (both to the firm and/or to the district).

7.6 The mechanism of knowledge creation in industrial districts: some empirical evidence

In this section we shall discuss the application of the analytical framework proposed to the evidence emerging from the analysis of three Italian industrial districts, where, in relation to the aspect of exploitation of local resources, the investment (both direct and indirect) of firms in augmenting their capabilities is juxtaposed to the activity organised by the district meta-organisers of cultivating local resources; furthermore, in relation to the exploration of global knowledge, internal/external switchers allow the exploration of global knowledge flows. It is a process that combines forms of localised learning with learning at the boundaries, through the access to pipelines (FDI, firms networks, distant KIBS) and boundary spanning actors (external CoPs).

7.6.1 The Montebelluna district[11]

The Montebelluna district is localised in the central area of the Veneto region, under the province of Treviso. The whole area of the district is composed of the following municipalities, which include both the "historical part of the district" (Caerano, Cornuda, Crocetta, Pederobba, Montebelluna, Maser, Nervesa, Trevignano, Volpago, and Giavera) and the "fringe area" of the adjacent external municipalities, populated by new firms (Altivole, Arcade, Asolo, Castelcucco, Castello di Godego, Cavaso del Tomba, Fonte, Monfumo, Povegliano, Riese Pio X, and Vedelago).

It is formed by about 400 firms (300 producers of footwear and 100 producers of clothing) that employ about 8,000 workers (6,000 units in footwear and 2,000 in clothing) (see Table 7.2 for details).

Table 7.2 The productive filière

	Firms a.v.	*Employees a.v.*
Accessory manufacturing companies	10	84
Materials coupling companies	7	201
Assembly and fitting companies	29	362
Trading companies	12	201
Die-cutting companies	4	54
Shoe string manufacturing companies	4	29
Patternmaking	2	8
Clothing manufacturing companies	12	439
Footwear manufacturing companies	104	2,979
Clothing and footwear companies	21	1,777
Machinery manufacturing companies	16	117
Services	2	48
Die-sinking	23	509
Die-sinkers?	11	153
Design studios	27	112
Sole makers	6	197
Cutters	28	72
Upper makers	51	224
Others	22	310
Total	391	7,876

Source: OSEM Report 2005.

Note

a.v. = absolute value.

Montebelluna is the world leader in technical sports shoes, ski and trekking boots, motorcycle boots and bicycle shoes. The dominant strategies of the districts' firms are: (1) openness to the international business; and (2) strong propensity towards innovation. The district is formed by a combination of a good number of mid-size family-owned firms and few important local larger companies. The latter derive from the original nucleus of the first founders, who established an enterprise at the end of the nineteenth century and during the first decades of the twentieth (Tecnica, Caberlotto, Calzaturificio Alpina, Dolomite, Munari, and Nordica). Half of them remained successfully active on the market place even after the third generation. Some international companies settled down in the district during the 1990s, through acquisitions.

7.6.1.1 History

Originally the district's first specialisation was the mountain boot (made in leather). At the beginning of the twentieth century, we witnessed the birth of the first examples of the industrialisation of ski boot production, through the factory system. It is in these years that Tecnica (1890), Dolomite (1897), Alpina and Munari (1908), Pivetta and Vendramin (1919), and Nordica (1926) were born. Most of these firms are still active (and they have become, over time, the leading firms in the area), or the brand name is still used. In 1937 Vitali Bramani (from Turin) introduced the Vibram sole, made of rubber, a waterproof material, particularly resistant for walking in the mountains. This innovation was promptly adopted and adapted in Montebelluna by local entrepreneurs.

After the Second World War, during the 1960s the entrepreneurs of Montebelluna started to modify the ski boot, rendering it more stable on the ski, and more robust. They introduced a steel plate on the sole and a new system of blockage. In 1962, the boot with the metal lever was applied by the district firms for the first time, it was a minor innovation, which offered a better closure compared to the traditional shoe-laces. In the same period, the vulcanisation of the sole, a method that allows the sole to be joined to the upper part of the boot, was introduced. Subsequently the PVC injection method, a much more rapid system was applied. It was in this period that the producers sponsored a wide product standardisation of both components and ski bindings. In 1967 Montebelluna experimented the first models of boots with plastic-covered leather, an innovation that was not very successful and was not widely adopted.

The real big technological revolution, with the creation of a new technological system, occurred with the exploitation of the patent registered by Lange in 1964 in Colorado. Lange, which presented its first exemplar of plastic boot in a US exhibition, was not able to produce a really workable boot, ready to be manufactured for the mass market. On the contrary, Montebelluna entrepreneurs, after participating in the exhibition, promptly decided to use and to improve Mr Lange's invention. His invention was in fact perfected by Nordica, which substituted Lange's fusion with the injection method, using some competences developed by a firm situated in Padua (the Lorenzin firm). After a while,

Lange himself opened a factory in Italy near Montebelluna, in order to have access to the modified technology and to the local well-experienced suppliers of technology. During the 1960s and 1970s we have the stable growth of the firms in the district; the production of ski boots shifted from 180,000 in 1963 to 1,000,000 in 1970 and to 4,100,000 in 1979. Many of the historical firms adopted the new technology (Dolomite, Munari, S. Giorgio, and Tecnica), many others, which did not believe in these novelties (or that did not have the necessary funds to reorganise the productive cycle), started to diversify into new products (sport shoes, leisure shoes, etc.). This radical change also produced a new district division of labour between the final firms, the subcontractors for the more simple tasks, and the producers of technology (specialised suppliers).

The second relevant diversification was the introduction of the after-ski boot in plastic material. The first model was the Moon Boot by Tecnica (1970) which was inspired by the astronauts that flew to the moon. In a few years the production of after-ski items took off. At the end of the 1970s Montebelluna was producing about 7.5–8.0 million pairs of this new product.

The third diversification was quite parallel, and was in the field of sport footwear like jogging shoes, ice and roller skates, basketball, football, motocross, dancing, cycling, tennis, and leisure shoes. The over-production of the 1980s created a typical firm shake-out, with the permanence of some important producers from the district, but new products (with the fourth productive diversification) substituted the decline of the demand for the more traditional production.

During the 1990s, new products like trekking, snowboards, in-line skates, football shoes, and sport shoes for walking (city-shoes), were created. During the 1990s two local leading firms emerged: Geox and Stonefly, which applied the district technological competence on technical shoes to walking shoes. These two firms were able to "stabilise" the whole output of the district.

Between the beginning of the 1980s and the end of the 1990s, Montebelluna became an area of extraordinary international concentration of competences and production capabilities: a globally specialised area, which directly or indirectly produces a large share of the total worldwide output of a distinct range of products. In the mid 1990s the Montebelluna district was already very open to international markets. About 70–80 per cent of ski boots production was exported. At the end of the 1990s, considering all the diversified range of products, half of its total production (600 million euro)[12] was exported to EU countries (such as Germany, France, Spain, and the UK), the US, and Japan. Many large local companies had opened commercial offices abroad, and local firms exhibited an intense exchange of information on the fashion trends with external international organisations (Aage, 2001). After the important date of 1989, the East European countries provided a unique opportunity to develop international supply chains, based on the manufacturing of simple phases, like shoe assembling (Belussi, 2005b).

As a result, the openness of the district, given by the internationalisation of firms, works as a knowledge switcher, activating learning at the boundaries activities.

7.6.1.2 Investing in capabilities

The historical evolution of the district is largely influenced by individual firms' investment in enlarging internal capabilities, as it appears by looking at the R&D investment in innovation. For instance, a recent survey (Belussi, 2005b) reported that, in 2001, out of 30 firms interviewed, 22 were organised with internal R&D departments, and 19 firms out of 30 held international patents. The study also reported a total value of R&D expenditures of about 27 billion euro, 127 patents registered by district firms, and a number of employees in R&D activities of 329 (about 10 per cent of total employment). Clearly, this information supports the idea that investment in capabilities by individual firms (direct investment) increases the local learning abilities.

Other types of investment in capabilities occur at the district level, mainly through the work as a meta-organiser of a very active local institution: the Foundation "Museo dello Scarpone di Montebelluna". It was established in 1992 and it has always played the role of a catalytic organiser of entrepreneurs for many projects (training, information, and knowledge diffusion). Another important meta-organiser is the centre "Tecnologia & Design", established in 1998, with the aim of diffusing the application of CAD-CAM technologies for more rapid prototyping. It provides training courses for technicians operating within the district, playing an important role in the innovation process. An important role has been played also by the local Chamber of Commerce, which in Italy is a public institution, whose management is left to the members of the local productive associations (entrepreneurs and trade unions). The most important firms in the district can easily benefit from the activities of the Chamber of Commerce, which sponsors the participation in fairs, finances the activity of local institutions for the promotion of training and technology transfer, and for other interesting new activities like the just implemented "Osservatorio Internazionale sulla Moda" – an observatory on fashion trends.

7.6.1.3 Gardening

Gardening activities are registered mainly at the district level, well rooted in the historical local social tissue. At the origin of the district, in fact, there was the presence of a community of very integrated people, which developed strong social and civic relationships. All this represents an important aspect for the development of the subcontracting nets, because all local economic relations are based on trust developed within relational networking. The high level of division of labour among firms created, over time, a group of mid-size family-owned businesses linked in the subcontracting of special components and activities. The presence of a strong economic community is traceable, above all, in the periods in which the district suffered from economic difficulties and firm crises. Then, local entrepreneurs intervened directly in the district to avoid local bankruptcies, and they worked together in order to "save" the district firms suffering from economic difficulties (a famous case is that of the saving of Lotto). Many observers have underlined the strong propensity for cooperation among people living in Treviso. Also public bodies work "in team" with the local economic community and share a "team spirit".[13]

The social environment allows personal and professional relationships to take place and to be easily nurtured. It is the case of the project "E-KM-DI.CA.MO". (sistema di E-Knowledge Management per il DIstretto CAlzaturiero di MOntebelluna), a virtual platform developed by the Treviso Chamber of Commerce, for the creation and promotion of an on-line community of designers (www.tytecnologia.it/Innovazione/dettagliEKMDicamo.asp). It counted 83 designers in the year 2004, and has now risen to 226 professionals (including designers). The gardening activity is carried out by a pool of local institutions (including TeDIS – Centre for Studies on Technologies in Distributed Intelligence Systems), working on a project coordinated by Treviso Tecnologia.[14] Veneto Region and the Chamber of Commerce of Treviso, in fact, co-financed a project called "Ekmdicamo" (Italian acronym for electronic knowledge management in sportswear industrial district of Montebelluna). The project aims at developing and consolidating a community of designers and creative people within the province of Treviso and within the sportswear district of Montebelluna. In particular, "ekmdicamo" aims to foster the aggregation of designers and creative people and increase the visibility of these professional figures both at local and national/international level. A Web portal has been developed in order to make it easier for designers to meet each other and exchange experience and knowledge. Moreover, the portal aims to be the place where designers have the opportunity to post their works and portfolios and establish connections with local enterprises. The website plays the role of both local and global knowledge switchers, allowing processes of learning at the boundaries.

7.6.2 The Matera sofa district[15]

The district, located in South Italy between the Provinces of Bari and Matera, is specialised in the production of leather sofas. Today 55 per cent of the Italian production of upholstered furniture is made in the Matera district, accounting for about 11 per cent of the world market in the sector. Of this, 80 per cent of local production is destined for international markets. The district evolved during the 1980s from a bunch of craft firms endowed with manufacturing skills in the upholstery of chairs and couches. Three main entrepreneurs founded the focal firms of the district: Natuzzi, Nicoletti, and Calia Italia. The main municipalities of the district are three: Altamura with 271 firms (37 per cent), Santeramo with 88 firms (12 per cent) and Matera with 96 firms (13 per cent). Santeramo is the headquarters, since the biggest firm of the district is located there (Natuzzi), while in Matera are located the other two leading firms (Nicoletti and Calia Italia). Table 7.3 shows some information on the structure of the district and its productive filière.

Table 7.3 The productive filière

	Firms a.v.	*Employees a.v.*
Sofa components	106	929
Transformation of polyurethane	36	838
Packaging	12	92
Sofa external covering	183	590
Finished product	380	13,521
Prototype	2	2
Mattress	19	500
Services	2	316
Total	738	16,786

Source: our elaborations on Inps and Cerved.

Note
a.v. = absolute value.

7.6.2.1 History

The history of this productive district began at the end of the 1950s. During those years a first nucleus of small artisan enterprises specialised in carpentry and upholstery was formed, producing upholstered furniture in small series, destined above all for the Lucania and Puglia market, which were part of the lowest economic market band. Around this small but well-established centre of productive activity the first shoots of industrial initiatives began to emerge. A number of artisans, on the crest of a wave of success for their products, began to develop the first production lines in series, exploiting a number of positive local traditions, above all in the leather-working sector. This trend continued up to the 1960s and 1970s, when some local entrepreneurs paved the way to a progressive transformation of the productive system. Natuzzi, today the leading world producer of leather sofas with about 7,000 employees, imported into the area some new methods of assembling inspired by the Mercedes' assembly line for car seats that he had seen in operation in Germany during the 1970s. Over time he built a continuous process of upgrading technologies, inventing numerous new machineries for the process of sofa assembling. His relationship with some ex-Italian immigrants in the US helped him to penetrate the US market with his low-cost production. He played the role of internal/external switcher of technical and market knowledge for the district firms. Natuzzi is nowadays the only firm which invests strongly in R&D activity in the district, while the other firms, using some common specialised suppliers and subcontractors, can easily have access to the new knowledge created. For example, Natuzzi has recently set up a research centre for testing raw materials and sofa components as well as for looking for new technology aimed at increasing production performance. While in Montebelluna many local agents build their external pipelines for acquiring new knowledge and new ideas on fashion trends, in the Matera sofa district it is the leading local firm which is playing the role of boundary spanning. Integrating the overall production process, Natuzzi directly controls purchasing, leather tanning, polyurethane transformation, assembly, logistics, production development and marketing activities. This has allowed new approaches to innovation, for example by improving the quality of the most strategic raw materials: leather and polyurethane.

During the 1980s, the district faced the great leap towards international markets, being able to offer good quality products at very competitive prices. At the head were a number of firms: Natuzzi, but also Calia Italia and Nicoletti.

In the last twenty years the firms grew from 88 in 1981 to 738 in 2002, and employment reached about 17,000 employees. The evolutionary trend occurred thanks to a threefold mechanism: decentralisation of production, firms specialisation within an inter-firm division of labour, and a growing technical capability related to the numerous incremental innovations introduced by the leading local firms. In the district we find a large variation of products, firms, specialised skills, and suppliers. This area represents a truly Marshallian district because there is a high level of cooperation between final firms, specialised suppliers and sub-contractors, as emerged from a recent survey, reported in Belussi and Caldari (2003), and here below in Table 7.4.

The survey, based on 100 interviews with local entrepreneurs, informs us of the great propensity of the district's actors to trust each other. Almost 60 per cent of the respondents, in fact, say they have good relations with buyers/suppliers, based on reciprocal trust.

Indeed, imitation has taken place both in terms of firm strategies and product design. An all-round innovative process, touching on processing technologies, product design, and above all, organisational and managerial aspects, is in place. An almost total standardisation of products has been achieved: different phases of work were delegated to external contractors; the wooden frames for sofas were produced by specialised firms, upholstering by others, dressing and leather-cutting by others. The mother firm could therefore proceed directly to the assembly of the sofas, using productive systems in series, not unlike those used in the vehicle industry.

Table 7.4 Trust diffusion among local actors in Matera

Type of firm	*In a district everybody trusts each other*	*Generally I trust people*	*I have good relations based on reciprocal trust*	*I don't trust people easily*	*I don't trust anybody*	*Total*
Final firm	12.5	3.1	68.8	15.6	0.0	100.0
Supplier	7.4	7.4	51.9	22.2	11.1	100.0
Specialised supplier	7.7	7.7	61.5	15.4	7.7	100.0
Total	9.5	5.4	59.5	17.6	5.4	100.0

Sources: Belussi and Caldari (2003).

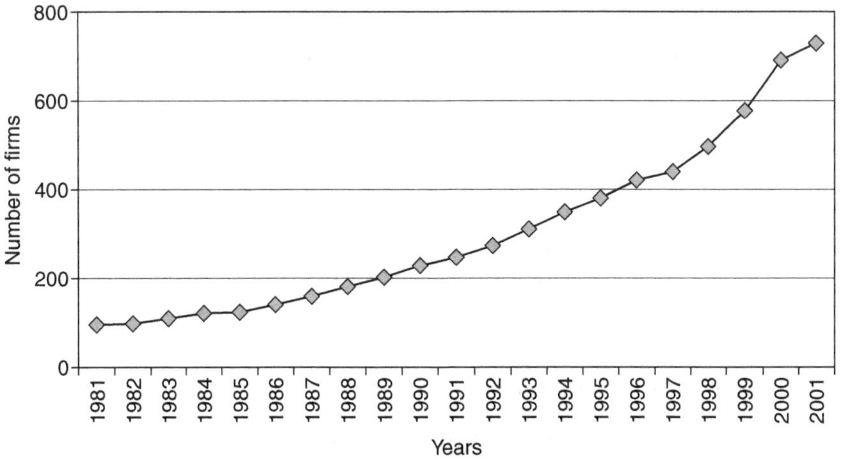

Figure 7.4 The Matera district's firm dynamics, 1981–2001 (source: our elaborations on Inps and Cerved).

During the time a mechanism of firm-scission has increased the local firms population (firm's birth and start-up), as emerges from Figure 7.4.

It was only starting from 2001 that a slowing down in this development began, caused by the international crisis and the currently unfavourable euro/dollar exchange rate. Therefore a process has begun to review marketing targets through a gradual move towards the medium-high market bands, on which the entrepreneurs of the Matera district are counting to re-launch their firms.

7.6.2.2 Investing in capabilities

Traditionally the district has been marked by the huge innovative activities of the leading firms, such as Natuzzi, Calia Italia, and Nicoletti. Therefore the technological development of the district firms relies on the local leading largest ones, rather than organised international relationships with external R&D centres. Investing in capabilities is not a diffuse activity among the district firms. Few pipelines characterise the structure of external relationships, which are strong only in the relation with export flows. Nowadays only 380 final producers have external relations with the market, while the others work with the local market for intermediate products and activities.

Meta-organisers in the district are quite weak if not absent. The district lacks infrastructures, and collective investments. Schiuma *et al.* (2003) clearly stressed in their report the lack of human resources training and education programmes in the district, where only 9 per cent of firms hold specific training courses for their employees upgrading. Mainly large leading firms invest in human capital development, the remainder apply forms of learning by doing mechanisms, where learning takes place prevalently on the job.

7.6.2.3 Gardening

The collective identity and the entrepreneurial culture, although very strong, are not supported by local organisations. CoPs are not very well developed, and learning at the boundaries through networking is very scarce. The existence of a district web-site is not a sufficient condition to stimulate interactions between the members of the district community. In the case of Montebelluna a specific project realised a web-site oriented to activate local communities in a global network, on the contrary, the Matera district website is poorly suited to perform the same function. The latter, in fact, neither offers any possibility to contact local firms, nor promotes any local initiative of aggregation for professionals.

7.6.3 The Riviera del Brenta district[16]

The Riviera del Brenta is one of the oldest Italian industrial districts, specialised in high-fashion women's footwear production, located in the Veneto region. In 2000, 88 per cent of the shoes produced in the area were medium-high price women's shoes, with an average ex-factory price of 58 euro (Rabellotti, 2004).

The district covers geographically the province of Padua and Venice. A synthesis of information about firms and employees in the Brenta productive filière is provided in Table 7.5.

7.6.3.1 History

The origins of the Riviera del Brenta district date back to the year 1898, when Giovanni Luigi Voltan founded the first footwear firm (*Calzaturificio Voltan*) around Stra (a village situated in the province of Venice). The founding of the first district firm is related to the application of Fordist methods to the craft production of shoes. Voltan learned these methods when he emigrated to the US and, on returning to his native village, he employed these new techniques in his factory. The district emerged when the best blue-collar workers of Voltan decided to set up a factory, giving rise to flows of start-ups. No real original innovations were introduced by the district firms during the expansion of the

Table 7.5 The productive filière[17]

	Firms a.v.	*Employees a.v.*
Footwear companies	315	7,568
Accessory manufacturing companies	359	2,923
Shoe designers	68	224
Trading companies	44	261
Total	806	10,976

Source: ACRIB (2005).

Note
a.v. = absolute value.

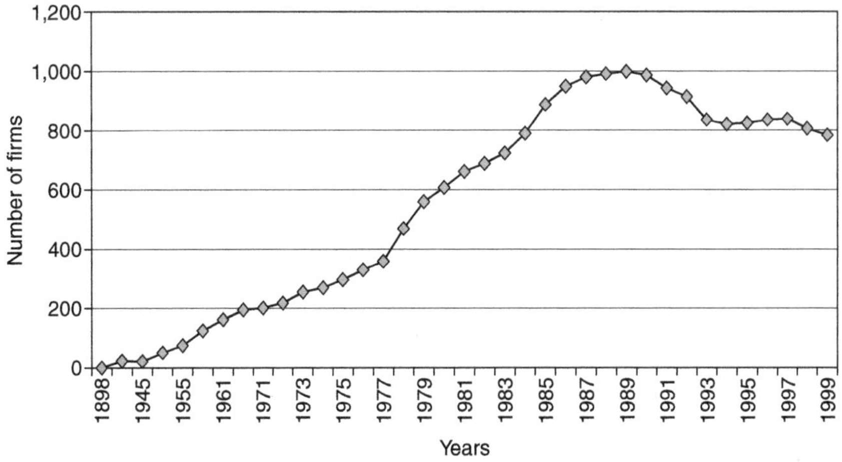

Figure 7.5 The Riviera del Brenta district's firm dynamics, 1898–1999 (source: our elaboration on Cerved and ISTAT).

Riviera del Brenta footwear system. Competition was exerted through a continuous process of cost cutting reached through firm fragmentation and decreasing of administrative costs (through the prevalent small size), and productive gains reached by the inter-firm division of labour and specialisation. The building of internal capabilities of firms was realised through a continuous upgrading of the product, firms investment in up-to-date-technologies, and improvements of selling abilities (during the 1960s some local entrepreneurs started to participate in foreign exhibitions, in Germany). Thus the firms in the district were able to specialise in the upper segments of the market, starting to export their production to the German market. The district faced a large expansion during the 1980s, as we can see from Figure 7.5, when firms shifted their production upwards, in market niches (*haute-couture* and *prêt-a-porter* collections). The proliferation tendency stops during the years 1989–1990, when a declining path characterises the local firms.

Within the district, a co-evolution of firms and institutions growth may be seen. Along with the development of the district, we may observe the constitution of many specific "district institutions", which have been created during time: a type of problem-solving institution that has played the role of enforcing innovation diffusion among local firms and fostering the local collective learning mechanism (Table 7.6).

These institutions were: training centres for the development of critical technological competencies and skills, centres for the organisation of commercial missions, institutions devolved to organise the interests of local entrepreneurs (ACRIB), and to provide them with *ad hoc* services (for instance on the evolution of market demand in various countries, and a data bank on the reliability of national and international clients, based on insolvency payments). In recent years, the collective agents operating in the district (local trade unions,

Table 7.6 The evolution of institutions in the Riviera del Brenta district in the period 1989–2000

The institutional set up of the Riviera del Brenta industrial district	
1923	Foundation of the design school O.T. Fava
1955	First exhibition of shoes produced in Riviera del Brenta organised by a group of small local entrepreneurs
1962	Birth of the local Association of Entrepreneurs ACRIB
1976	Foundation of the Consorzio Maestri Calzaturieri
1986	Foundation of Centro Veneto Calzaturiero
1999	Patto territoriale (collective agreement between trade unions, entrepreneurial associations and municipalities for actions of local policies)

Source: Fontana (1998) and Belussi (2000).

ACRIB, on behalf of the national association of entrepreneurs, and many public institutions and local municipalities) signed an agreement (*patto territoriale*), which designates a series of measures needed for the further development of the local system.

The positive effect of the existence of these institutions is powered by the local social environment, built on diffuse trust, as we can appreciate in Table 7.7. The table shows some of the results obtained by a survey conducted on 100 enterprises in the district, reported more extensively in Belussi and Caldari (2003).

7.6.3.2 Investing in capabilities

Investing in capabilities is an activity mainly provided by the local association of entrepreneurs (ACRIB) and by the local municipality, which, for instance, financed a renewed training school for pattern makers and designers. Over time ACRIB also began to provide some services to firms (economic advice, support for the adoption of new technology, adaptation of CAD technologies to the needs of the small local firms, financial and commercial support for fair participation,

Table 7.7 Trust diffusion among local actors in the Riviera del Brenta district

Type of firm	*In a district everybody trust each other*	*Generally I trust people*	*I have good relations based on reciprocal trust*	*Normally I don't trust people easily*	*I don't trust anybody*	*Total*
Final firm	14.3	4.8	66.7	14.3	0.0	100.0
Supplier	5.6	0.0	77.8	5.6	11.1	100.0
Specialised supplier	8.6	8.6	68.6	11.4	2.9	100.0
Total	10.3	5.2	68.0	11.3	3.1	100.0

Source: Belussi and Caldari (2003).

and so on). The association of entrepreneurs also created some important selling points in strategic foreign markets (New York, Tokyo, etc.), working as a knowledge switcher.

New internal/external switchers are actually playing an important role in the recent district restructuring. Because of the district reputation in high quality shoes, a large number of local final firms are now working for the most important international stylists and high fashion *Haute Couture*: Prada, Valentino, Gucci, Chanel, Christian Dior, Ungaro, Etro, Guess, Iceberg, Louis Vuitton, Miu Miu, Ralph Lauren, LVMH, etc. In some cases, this has implied that final firms have lost their distributive channels and agents, in others, like in the case of Rossi Moda, a joint venture has been set up with a prestigious French group, for the production and distribution of branded high fashion shoes. Interactions with distant high fashion distributive firms and stylists open new informative pipelines to the advantage of local firms, activating the learning at the boundaries mechanism.

7.6.3.3 Gardening

In the Riviera del Brenta district we witness spontaneous mechanisms of CoPs setting, not properly guided or supported by any institutional intervention. The interviews conducted on the 100 firms informed us of the existence of a local community of designers, which designated a local bar as a meeting point for information and knowledge exchanges on recent trends of the market and technicalities. The community is entirely spontaneous, and is driven by the local proximities of firms and the light boundary existing between work and leisure time, typical of an industrial district. No gardening activities of the community are in place. The Montebelluna project could be a good inspiration for future development policies of the district.

7.6.4 A comparative framework

In the cases presented above, we see that industrial districts are characterised by weak or strong capabilities, and by few or many internal/external switchers. The Matera district is characterised by a significant absence of global pipelines, and it also lacks collective efforts in gardening. Investment in capabilities at the firm level touches mainly the largest leader firm, and few others. On the contrary the Montebelluna district is associated with a high level of global interactions together with a significant presence of gardening and investment in local capabilities. The Riviera del Brenta district does not exhibit a high level of investment in capabilities, but the role of local institutions in gardening is very important. Here many external channels are created by the interactions with external high fashion distributors and stylists.

A synthesis of the three cases, focused on the role of direct and indirect investments in capabilities and of the number of internal/external switchers of the ID, is graphically represented in Figure 7.6.

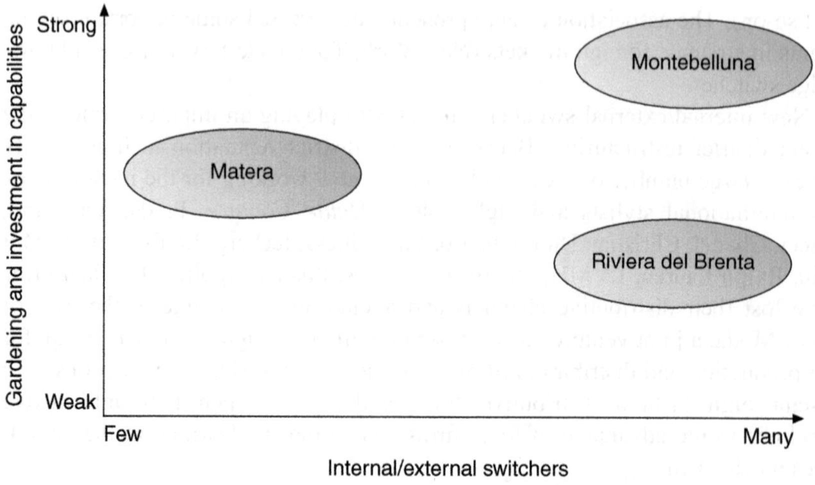

Figure 7.6 An interpretative framework for the "learning at the boundary dimension" of IDs using some empirical cases.

7.7 Some conclusive remarks

This work explored the possibility, offered by the ideas connected to the concept of CoPs and capabilities, of finding new keys to analyse the process of knowledge creation and sharing within an ID. In a world dominated by high degrees of uncertainty, deriving from growing global competition, the process of creation and transfer of knowledge holds a strategic role.

Having defined the relation between the concepts of knowledge, capabilities, CoPs and ID, the attention has been shifted towards an integrated view of the ID model, in which learning at the boundaries appears to be a crucial aspect of firm competitiveness. In the end, the application of the CoPs concept to the IDs helps to measure the "evolutionary attitude" of these territorial organisations. The existence of internal/external switchers, both coming from gardening activity and direct investment in capabilities, generates a process of learning at the boundaries, which increases the ID competitiveness in a global market. Our empirical work has shown that, while some districts are only able to exploit local resources, developing inner learning activity, others also build long bridges towards the exploration of new external sources of knowledge, using internal/external switchers (i.e. leading firms, local meta-organisers, institutions, networks of communities).

To conclude, in order to study the development of IDs, we complemented the Marshallian tradition, by adding a new focus on ID global learning. Alongside this more complex theoretical view, the concepts of CoPs, capabilities, and gardening offer a new approach to the study of IDs, escaping the "Marshallian trap" of looking at them as closed systems, where the analysis of social interactions is limited to the well-known metaphor of the "industrial atmosphere".

Notes

1 This chapter benefited greatly from comments and suggestions by Peter Maskell. We also wish to thank participants in the Danish Research Unit for Industrial Dynamics (DRUID) Winter Conference in Aalborg, Denmark, 16–18 January 2003 for comments on an earlier version of this work. The usual disclaimer applies.
2 Nelson and Winter (1982) make a singular comment on Penrose's work "Though she was apparently unaware of Coase's (1937) transaction costs approach to the nature of the firm, her analysis is largely consistent with it".
3 Core competences allow firms ample access to the market (for instance, competences in display systems enable a company to participate in such diverse business as calculators, miniature RV sets, monitors for laptop computers, and automotive dashboards, pp. 83–84); in addition, competences are difficult to imitate because they show an important tacit dimension.
4 The key assumption here is the existence of an intermediate form of knowledge appropriability, something in the middle between the modality of private knowledge (firms and individuals that protect their knowledge through secrets, internal know-how, and patents), and public knowledge (a public good, exogenously given). On the existence of different regimes of appropriability see Antonelli (2000) and Belussi (2003).
5 The author refers to the concept of stickiness of a given unit of information, in a given instance, as the incremental expenditure required to transfer it into a form usable by a given information seeker. When this cost is low, information stickiness is low; when it is high, stickiness is high.
6 For a comparison between Bourdieu's and Putnam's concepts of social capital, see M. Siisiäinen (2000), for a contribution focused on trust, see Belussi (2002).
7 For the definition of an industrial district as a community see the works of Becattini (1990) and Dei Ottati (1995).
8 The concept of network externalities (or network effects) is rooted in Metcalfe's Law (Shapiro and Varian, 1998). This law is based on a natural observation: if a net is formed by n units and the value that every one of them gives to the net is proportionate to the number of other units in the net, then the global value of the net (the value assigned by all the units) is proportionate to $n*(n-1) = n^2 - n$. Substantially, it states that the value of a network increases with the square of the number of members of the network, showing a form of increasing returns or positive feedback to network size.
9 As Arthur (2000) points out in his dissertation about myths and realities of the high-tech economy, we should, more precisely, pay attention to the type of network we are dealing with. In a radial network, where members are connected with a common node, but not with each other, for instance, benefits from network effects could not occur or could be very weak. In a combinatorial network (combination between people), a community can be formed and it can exhibit network effects.
10 The concept has been proposed originally by the Japanese philosopher Nishida and (afterwards) Shimizu and it is close to the English word "place". It refers to organisational contexts within which individuals interact at a specific time and place over a certain time period, a kind of shared space for emerging relationships, as has been described by Pilotti (2000).
11 Based on Belussi (2005b).
12 Data provided by the Chamber of Commerce of Treviso.
13 For example, recently, the association of local entrepreneurs founded an "innovation club", with a modest membership fee of 250 euro, to promote innovation among their member firms.
14 Treviso Tecnologia is a company created by the Chamber of Commerce of Treviso in 1989. It is a KIB providing services for the territory and its firms, specifically oriented to technological innovation.

15 Based on Belussi and Caldari (2003).
16 Based on Belussi (2000).
17 Data refer to firms and employment operating in the footwear production in the whole provinces of Venice and Padua.

References

Aage T. (2001), External relations and industrial districts. Paper presented at the DRUID Nelson and Winter Summer Conference. http://www.druid.dk/conference/nw/paper1/aage.pdf.

Aage T. (2005), Boundary spanning strategies of industrial districts: the impact of absorptive capacity, in Belussi F. and Sammarra A. (eds) *Industrial Districts, Relocation, and the Governance of the Global Value Chain*, Padua: Cleup.

Albertini S. and Pilotti L. (1996), *Reti di reti. Apprendimento, comunicazione e cooperazione nel Nordest*, Padua: CEDAM.

Amighini A. and Rabellotti R. (2006), How do Italian footwear industrial districts face globalization?, *European Planning Studies*, 14 (4): 485–502.

Amin A. (1993), The difficult transition from informal to Marshallian district, mimeo, University of Newcastle upon Tyne.

Amin A. and Cohendet P. (1999), Learning and adaptation in decentralised business networks, *Environment and Planning D: Society and Space*, 17: 87–104.

Amin A. and Thrift N. (1992), Neo-Marshallian nodes in global networks, *International Journal of Urban and Regional Research*, 16: 571–587.

Anderson P.W., Arrow K., and Pines D. (eds) (1988), *The Economy as an Evolving Complex System*, Santa Fe, NM: Santa Fe Institute on the Sciences of Complexity, Addison-Wesley.

Antonelli C. (2000), Collective knowledge, communication and innovation: the evidence of technological districts, *Regional Studies*, 34: 535–547.

Argote L. and Ingram P. (2000), Knowledge transfer: a basis for competitive advantage in firms, *Organisational Behavior and Human Decision Processes*, 82 (1): 150–169.

Argyris C. and Schön D. (1978), *Organisational Learning*, Reading, MA: Addison-Wesley.

Arthur B. (1994), *Increasing Returns and Path Dependence in the Economy*, Ann Arbor, MI: University of Michigan Press.

Arthur B. (1995), Complexity in economic and financial markets, *Complexity*, 1: 20–25.

Arthur B. (2000), Myths and Realities of the High-Tech Economy, Talk given at Credit Suisse First Boston Thought Leader Forum, 10 September 2000.

Arthur B.W., Durlauf S.N., and Lane D. (eds) (1997), *The Economy as an Evolving Complex System II*, Santa Fe, NM: Santa Fe Institute on the Sciences of Complexity, Addison-Wesley.

Audretsch D. and Feldman M. (1996), R&D spillovers and the geography of innovation and production, *The American Economic Review*, 86 (3): 630–640.

Bacci L. (2004), (ed.), *Distretti e imprese leader nel sistema moda della Toscana*, Milan: FAE.

Bathelt H., Malmberg A., and Maskell P. (2002), Cluster and knowledge: local buzz, global pipeline and the process of knowledge creation, DRUID Working Paper. www.druid.dk/wp/pdf_files/02–12.pdf.

Becattini G. (1979), Dal settore industriale al distretto industriale: alla ricerca dell'unità di indagine della economia industriale, in *Rivista di Economia e Politica Industriale*, n.1 (now in Id. (2000), *Il distretto industriale*, Turin: Rosenberg & Sellier).

Becattini G. (1990), The industrial district as a socio-economic notion, in Pyke F., Becattini G., and Sengerberger W. (eds), *Industrial Districts and Inter-firms Cooperation in Italy*, Geneva: International Institute for Labour Studies, pp. 37–51.

Belussi F. (2000), (a cura di), *Tacchi a spillo*, Cleup, Padua.

Belussi F. (2002), Fiducia e capitale sociale nelle reti di impresa, paper presented at the seminar: "Il valore economico delle relazioni interpersonali", University of Milano Bicocca, 24 September 2002.

Belussi F. (2003), The Italian system of innovation: the gradual transition from a weak mission-oriented system to a regionalised learning system, in Borras S. and Biegelbauer P. (eds), *Innovation Policies in Europe and the US: The New Agenda*, Aldershot: Ashgate, pp. 233–252.

Belussi F. (2005a), Are industrial districts formed by networks without technologies? The diffusion of Internet applications in three Italian clusters, July, *European Urban and Regional* Studies, 12 (3): 247–268.

Belussi F. (2005b), The evolution of a western consolidated industrial district through the mechanism of knowledge creation, ICT adoption, and the tapping into the international commercial nets: the case of Montebelluna sportswear district, in Belussi F. and Samarra A. (eds), *Industrial Districts, Relocation, and the Governance of the Global Value Chain*, Padua: Cleup, pp. 227–275.

Belussi F. (2006), In search of a theory of spatial clustering: agglomeration versus active clustering, in Asheim B., Cooke, P., and Martin, R. (eds), *Clusters and Regional Development*, London: Routledge.

Belussi F. and Caldari K. (2003), Fiducia e cooperazione nei processi di distrettualizzzione, *Sviluppo Locale*, Numero Monografico: capitale sociale e relazioni di fiducia, (23–24): 52–81.

Belussi F. and Sammarra A. (2005), (eds) *Industrial Districts, Relocation, and the Governance of the Global Value chain*, Cleup, Padua.

Belussi F., Gottardi G., and Rullani E. (eds) (2003), *The Technological Evolution of Industrial Districts*, Boston, MA: Kluwer.

Biggiero L. (1999). Markets, hierarchies, networks, districts: a cybernetic approach, *Human Systems Management*, 18: 1–16.

Biggiero L. (2002), The location of multinationals in industrial districts: knowledge transfer in biomedicals, *Journal of Technology Transfer*, 27: 111–122.

Boero R. and Squazzoni F. (2002), Economic performance, inter-firm relations and local institutional engineering in a computational prototype of industrial districts, *Journal of Artificial Societies and Social Simulation* 5 (1): http://jasss.soc.surrey.ac.uk/5/1/1.html.

Boschma R.A. and ter Wal A.L.J. (2006), Knowledge networks and innovative performance in an industrial district. The case of a footwear district in the South of Italy, Papers in Evolutionary Economic Geography (PEEG) 0601, Utrecht University, Section of Economic Geography.

Bourdieu P. (1985), The forms of capital, in Richardson J.C. (ed.), *Handbook of Theory and Research for the Sociology of Education*, Westport, CT: Greenwood Press, Chapter 9, pp. 241–258.

Brenner T. (2004), *Industrial Clusters. Existence, Emergence, and Evolution*, London and New York: Routledge.

Brown J.S. and Duguid P. (1991), Organizational learning and communities-of-practice: towards a unified view of working, learning, and innovation, *Organization Science*, 2 (1): 40–57.

Brown J.S. and Duguid P. (2000), *The Social Life of Information*, Boston, MA: Harvard Business School Press.

Burt R. (1992), *Structural Holes. The Social Structure of Competitiveness*, Harvard, MA: Cambridge University Press.

Cainelli G. and De Liso N. (2004), Can Marshallian industrial districts be innovative? The case of Italy, in Cainelli G. and Zoboli R. (eds), *The Evolution of Industrial Districts*, Heidelberg: Physica-Verlag, pp. 243–256.

Cainelli G., Iacobucci D. and Morganti E. (2006) Spatial agglomeration and business groups: New evidence from Italian industrial districts, *Regional Studies*, 40 (5): 507–518.

Camuffo A. and Grandinetti R. (2005), Distretti industriali in evoluzione, il ruolo dei knowledge business services, Paper presented at the Meeting in Urbino, "L'internazionalizzazione delle imprese e dei distretti industriali", 14 April.

Castells M. (1996), *The Rise of the Network Society*, Oxford: Blackwell.

Castells M. (2000), Materials for exploratory theory of the network society, *British Journal of Sociology*, 51 (1) (January/March): 5–24.

Chamberlin E.H. (1933), *The Theory of Monopolistic Competition*, Cambridge, MA: Harvard University Press.

Chiarvesio M., Di Maria E., and Micelli S. (2004), From local networks of SMEs to virtual districts? Evidence from recent trends in Italy, *Research Policy*, 33 (10): 509–528.

Coase R. (1937), The nature of the firm, *Economica*, (4): 386–405.

Cohen W.M. and Levinthal D.A. (1990), Absorptive capacity: a new perspective on learning and innovation, *Administrative Science Quarterly*, 35 (1): 128–152.

Coleman J. (1988), Social capital in the creation of human capital, *American Journal of Sociology*, 94 (supplement): s95–s120.

Cooke P. (2001), Regional innovation systems, clusters, and the knowledge economy, *Industrial and Corporate Change*, 10: 945–974.

Coró G. and Grandinetti R. (1999), Evolutionary patterns of Italian industrial districts, *Human Systems Management*, 18: 117–129.

Davenport T.H. and Prusak L. (1997), *Information Ecology. Mastering the Information and Knowledge Environment*, Oxford: Oxford University Press.

Davenport T.H. and Prusak L. (2000), *Working Knowledge*, Boston, MA: Harvard Business School Press.

Dei Ottati G. (1995), *Tra mercato e comunità: aspetti concettuali.e. ricerche empiriche sul distretto industriale*, Milan: Franco Angeli.

Dei Ottati G. (2001), Concertazione e sviluppo nei distretti industriali, in Ninni A., Silva F. and Vaccà S. (eds), *Evoluzione del lavoro, crisi del sindacato e sviluppo del paese*, Milan, Franco Angeli, pp. 163–195.

Drucker P. (1988), The coming of new organization, *Harvard Business Review*, 66 (January, February): 45–53.

Etzkowitz H. and Leydesdorff L. (2000), The dynamics of innovation: from National Systems and "Mode 2" to a Triple Helix of university–industry–government relations, *Research Policy* 29, 109–123.

Foss N. and Foss K. (2003), Authority in the context of distributed knowledge, DRUID Working Paper No. 03–08. www.druid.dk/wp/pdf_files/03–08.pdf.

Foss N. and Loasby B. (1998), Introduction, in Foss N. and Loasby B. (eds), *Economic Organisation, Capabilities and Co-ordination*, London: Routledge.

Fransman M. (1994), Information, knowledge, vision and theories of the firm, *Industrial and Corporate Change*, 3 (3): 713–757.

Gallaud D. and Torre A. (2005), Geographical proximity and circulation of knowledge through inter-firm cooperation, *Scienze Regionali*, 4 (2): 5–25.

Giuliani E. (2005), The structure of cluster knowledge networks: uneven and selective, not pervasive and collective, DRUID Working Papers, 5–11.

Giuliani E., Rabellotti R. and van Dijk M.P. (2005), *Cluster Facing Competition: The Importance of External Linkages*, Abingdon: Ashgate.

Granovetter M.S. (1973), The strength of weak ties, *American Journal of Sociology*, 78: 1360–1380.

Grant R. (1996), Prospering in dynamically-competitive environments: organisational capabilities as knowledge integration, *Organisation Science*, 7 (4): 375–387.

Iammarino S. and McCann P. (2005), The structure and evolution of industrial clusters: transactions, technology and knowledge spillovers, SPRU Electronic Working Paper Series no. 138.

Jacobs J. (1961), *Death and Life of Great American Cities*, New York: Random House.

Langlois R. (1999), Scale, scope, and the reuse of knowledge, in Dow S.C. and Earl E.P. (eds), *Economic Organization and Economic Knowledge: Essays in Honour of Brian J. Loasby*, Cheltenham: Edward Elgar, pp. 239–254.

Laszlo K.C. and Laszlo A. (2002), Evolving knowledge for development: the role of knowledge management in a changing world, *Journal of Knowledge Management*, 6 (4): 400–412.

Lave J. and Wenger E. (1991), *Situated Learning. Legitimate Peripheral Participation*, Cambridge: Cambridge University Press.

Lesser E. and Everest K. (2001), Using communities of practices to manage intellectual capital, *Ivey Business Journal*, March–April: 37–41.

Lévy P. (2002), *L'intelligenza collettiva*, Milan: Feltrinelli.

Loasby B. (1999), *Knowledge, Institutions, and Evolution in Economics*, London: Routledge.

Lundvall B. (1988), Innovation as an interactive process – from user-producer interaction to national system of innovation, in Dosi G., Freeman C., Nelson R., Silverberg G. and Soete L. (eds), *Technical Change and Economic Theory*, London: Pinter Publisher.

Lyons B. and Mehta J. (1997), Contracts, opportunism and trust: self-interested and social orientation, *Cambridge Journal of Economics*, 21: 239–257.

March J. (1991), Exploration and exploitation in organisational learning, *Organisation Science*, 2: 71–87.

Marshall A. (1920), *Principles of Economics*, 8th edn, Philadelphia, PA: Porcupine Press.

Maskell P. and Malmberg A. (1999), Localised learning and industrial competitiveness, *Cambridge Journal of Economics*, 23: 167–185.

McDermott R. (1999), Learning across teams: how to build communities of practice in team-based organizations, *Knowledge Management Review*, 8 (May–June): 32–36.

Mistri M. and Solari S. (2003), Behavioural roules in industrial districts: loyalty, trust, and reputation, in Belussi F., Gottardi G., and Rullani E. (eds), *The Technological Evolution of Industrial Districts*, Boston, MA: Kluwer, pp. 245–268.

Morrison A. (2004), Gatekeepers of knowledge within industrial clusters. Who they are, and how they interact, Paper presented at the Schumpeter Society Conference, Milan, 9–12 June.

Nelson R. (1992), The roles of firms in technical advance: a perspective from evolutionary theory, in Dosi G., Giannettini R., and Toninelli P. (eds), *Technology and Enterprises in an Historical Perspective*, Oxford: Oxford University Press.

Nelson R. (1994), The coevolution of technologies and institutions, in England R. (ed.), *Evolutionary Concepts in Contemporary Economics*, Ann Arbor, MI: University of Michigan Press.

Nelson R. and Winter S. (1982), *An Evolutionary Theory of Economic Change*, Cambridge, MA: Harvard University Press.

Nonaka I. (1991), The knowledge-creating company, *Harvard Business Review*, November–December: 96–104.

Nonaka I. and Takeuchi H. (1995), *The Knowledge Creating Company*, New York: Oxford University Press.

Nonaka I. and Toyama R. (2002), A firm as a dialectical being: towards a dynamic theory of a firm, *Industrial and Corporate Change*, 11 (5): 995–1009.

Nooteboom B. (2000), *Learning and Innovation in Organisations and Economics*, Oxford: Oxford Univiversity Press.

Nooteboom B. (2002), *Trust: Foundations, Functions, Failures and Figures*, Cheltenham: Elgar.

Orléan A. (1994), Sur le rôle respectif de la confiance et de l'intérêt dans la construction de l'ordre marchand, *Revue du Mauss*, 4: 17–36.

Penrose E. (1959), *The Theory of the Growth of the Firm*, Oxford: Oxford University Press.

Perroux F. (1955), Note sur la notion de pôle de croissance, *Economie Appliquée*, (1–2): 307–320.

Pilotti L. (1999), Evolutionary and adaptive local systems in north east Italy, *Human Systems Management*, (18): 87–105.

Pilotti L. (2000), Networking, strategic positioning and creative knowledge in industrial districts, *Human Systems Management*, (19): 121–133.

Pór G. (1995), The quest for collective intelligence, in AAVV, *Community Building: Renewing Spirit and Learning in Business*, Pleasanton, CA: New Leaders Press.

Pór G. and Molloy J. (2000), Nurturing systemic wisdom through knowledge ecology, *The Systems Thinker*, 11 (8): 1–5.

Porter M. (1980), *Competitive Strategy*, New York: Free Press.

Prahalad C. and Hamel G. (1990), The core competence of the corporation, *Harvard Business Review*, May, 79–91.

Putnam R. (1993), *Making Democracy Work: Civic Traditions in Modern Italy*, Princeton, NJ: Princeton Press.

Putnam R. (1995), Bowling alone: America's declining social capital, *Journal of Democracy*, 6 (1) (January): 65–78.

Rabellotti, R. (2004), How globalisation affects Italian industrial districts: the case of Brenta, in Schmitz H. (ed.), *Local Enterprises in the Global Economy: Issues of Governance and Upgrading*, Cheltenham: Edward Elgar Publishers.

Richardson G. (1972), The organisation of industry, *Economic Journal*, 82: 883–896.

Rullani E. (2000), Enhancing the competitiveness of SMEs in the global economy: the strategies and policies, Bologna 2000 SME Conference, June.

Schiuma G., Lerro A., Di Giuseppe M., Carlucci D., Linzalone R., Morelli G., Glionna S. and De Leonardis D. (eds) (2003), L.I.E.G., Dimensioni di competitività del distretto industriale murgiano del mobile imbottito, research report presented to the workshop: Competitività e sviluppo strategico del distretto del mobile imbottito di Matera, Matera.

Schlager M.S. and Fusco J. (2004), Teacher professional development, technology, and communities of practice: Are we putting the cart before the horse?, in Barab S., Kling R., and Gray J. (eds), *Designing Virtual Communities in the Service of Learning*, Cambridge, MA: Cambridge University Press, pp. 120–153.

Shapiro C. and Varian H. (1998), *Information Rules: A Strategic Guide to The Network Economy*, Boston, MA: Harvard Business School Press.

Siisiäinen M. (2000), Two concepts of social capital: Bourdieu vs. Putnam, Paper presented at ISTR Fourth International Conference: "The Third Sector: For What and for Whom?" Trinity College, Dublin, Ireland, 5–8 July 2000, http://www.jhu.edu/~istr/conferences/dublin/workingpapers/siisiainen.pdf.

Simon H.A. (2002), Organizing and coordinating talk and silence in organization, *Industrial and Corporate Change*, 11 (3): 611–618.

Smith A. (1776), *An Inquiry into the Nature and Causes of the Wealth of Nations*, London: Strahan and Cadell.

Storper M. (1997), Le economie locali come beni relazionali, *Sviluppo Locale*, IV (5): 5–42.

Teece D. (1987), Profiting from technological innovation: implication for integration, collaboration, licensing, and public policy, *Research Policy*, 15: 285–305.

Teece D., Pisano G., and Shuen A. (1997), Dynamic capability and strategic management, *Strategic Management Journal*, 23: 1–30.

Teece D.J. (1998), Capturing value from knowledge assets, *California Management Review*, 40 (3): 55–79.

Thompson M. (2005), Structural and epistemic parameters in communities of practice, *Organization Science*, 16 (2): 151–164.

Tsoukas H. (1996), The firm as a distributed knowledge system: a constructionist approach, *Strategic Management Journal*, 17 (Winter Special Issue): 11–25.

Von Hippel E. (1998), Economics of product development by users: the impact of "sticky" local information, *Management Science*, 44 (5): 629–644.

Ward A. (2000), Getting strategic value from constellations of communities, *Strategy and Leadership*, 28 (2): 4–9.

Wasserman S. and Faust K. (1994), *Social Network Analysis: Methods and Applications*, Cambridge: Cambridge University Press.

Wenger E.C. (1999), Learning as social participation, *Knowledge Management Review*, (6) (January–February): 30–33.

Wenger E.C. (2000), Communities of practice and social learning systems, *Organization*, 7 (2): 225–246.

Wenger E.C. and Snyder W.M. (2000), Communities of practice: the organisational frontier, *Harvard Business Review*, (January–February): 139–145.

Wenger E.C., McDermott R.A., and Snyder W.M. (2002), *Cultivating Communities of Practice: A Guide to Managing Knowledge*, Boston, MA: Harvard Business School Press.

Wernerfelt B. (1984), A resources-based view, *Strategic Management Journal*, 5: 171–180.

Witt U. (1996), Imagination and leadership – the neglected dimension of the (evolutionary) theory of the firm, *Max Planck Institute Working Papers*, no. 5.

Zollo M. and Winter S. (2002), Deliberate learning and the evolution of dynamic capabilities, *Organisation Science*, 13: 339–351.

Zucchella A. (2006), Local clusters dynamics: trajectories of mature industrial districts between decline and multiple embeddedness, *Journal of Organisation and Institutional Economics*, 2 (1): 21–44.

8 The role of agglomeration and technology in shaping firm strategy and organization

Giulio Cainelli and Donato Iacobucci

8.1 Introduction

The growing number of contributions in recent years is demonstrating that there is a significant presence of business groups, that is, sets of firms legally distinct but belonging to the same owner(s). This phenomenon is not specific to large firms or to the Italian economy, but is widespread among small- and medium-sized firms (SMEs) and other industrialized countries (Barca *et al.*, 1994; Balloni and Iacobucci, 1997; Rosa and Scott, 1999; Loiseau, 2001; Brioschi *et al.*, 2002).

From a theoretical point of view, the presence of business groups poses the question of whether it is the group or the individual legal unit that should be considered as the elementary unit in economic analysis: that is, what is generally meant in microeconomic theory by 'firm'. Recent research has shown that this question cannot be answered in a completely general way (Iacobucci, 2004). However, in most cases, the business group can be understood as a multidivisional (M-form) firm, whose central direction (the ultimate owner) is responsible for deciding the resources to be allocated to divisions (firms), and when they should be opened (set up or acquired) or closed (liquidated or sold).

In this chapter we consider the group as the appropriate unit to delimit the firm's boundary, that is, as the organizational form adopted by firms when they grow in size. Indeed, the characteristics of the legal units belonging to a group can be used to analyse some aspects of a firm's growth strategies and organization, such as specialization, spatial concentration, vertical integration, etc. Starting from this hypothesis, the main aim of this chapter is to analyse the role of structural variables, such as spatial agglomeration and technology, in determining features of business groups' strategy and organization. Specifically, the analysis concerns the presence and organizational specificity of business groups, based on their membership in industrial districts (as a proxy for spatial agglomeration), and the role of spatial agglomeration and technology in vertical integration strategies. Because business groups are complex structures, to identify their geographic location and the industry to which they belong we take the largest firm of the group as our reference. In some cases it might appear more appropriate to identify these characteristics by referring perhaps to the original firm; however, evidence shows that both reference points produce approximately the same results.

To conduct the analysis, we take advantage of a new and larger data-set at firm and business group level, recently developed by ISTAT (the Italian National Statistical Institute). The data-set, referring to 2001, covers all manufacturing firms organized as joint-stock companies.

The chapter is organized as follows. In section 8.2 we briefly discuss our choice of the business group as the firm organizational form; we examine the relationships between agglomeration, technology and firm strategy, and organization and develop the hypotheses to be empirically tested. Section 8.3 describes the characteristics of the data-set and discusses the empirical evidence of the presence and organizational specificity of business groups in industrial districts, by industries and Pavitt sectors. The econometric analysis aimed at detecting the joint impact of agglomeration and technology on vertical integration strategy is then presented. Finally, section 8.4 presents the main conclusions.

8.2 Related literature

8.2.1 Business group as a firm's organizational form

The phenomenon of business groups is not limited to particular firm sizes, industries or countries. Recent empirical literature has shown that it is the organizational form normally adopted by firms that are growing in size; that is, when entrepreneurs or managers expand their control over business activities (Barca *et al.*, 1994; Rosa and Scott, 1999; Loiseau, 2001). As a result, almost all the larger firms and a significant share of SMEs in the Italian economy are organized as business groups (Brioschi *et al.*, 2002; Iacobucci, 2002).

Given the definition of a business group as a set of legally distinct units controlled by the same owner, several classifications have been proposed, the most common being pyramidal and joint groups. The pyramidal group is similar to a multidivisional company in which there is a firm at the top and several layers of controlled companies; joint groups occur when several firms share minority crossholdings (and often some board members), which allows them to coordinate their strategies. The latter organization is particularly widespread among Japan's largest firms. However, because in this type of group it is not possible to identify a unitary control, they do not fit our definition of a business group; therefore, we focus here on pyramidal groups.

Most of the literature on business groups is devoted to justifying why pyramidal groups exist, and comparing the behaviour and performance of business groups with those of independent firms. This literature mainly focuses on financial aspects (Brioschi *et al.*, 1990; Gerlach, 1997; Almeida and Wolfenzon, 2004). The pyramidal group is regarded as a financial mechanism to minimize the amount of capital needed by the ultimate owner to control the business activities; that is, it enables control rights, concentrated in the hand of the vertex, to be separated from cash flow rights, dispersed among the minority shareholders of the companies belonging to the group.

There is an important strand of literature focussed on organizational issues in pyramidal groups (Goto, 1982; Kester, 1982). Adopting the transaction cost perspective, this literature considers the group as an organizational intermediary between the internal hierarchy and the market. The main aim of this strand of the literature is to explain why the relationships between companies belonging to business groups can be more efficient than those found in integrated firms or than market transactions between independent firms. Within this approach, business groups are assimilated to a multidivisional firm where the controlling owner's role is to allocate resources to existing firms, and to make decisions about new start ups and firm closures (Chandler, 1982).

While the financial perspective is more appropriate in the case of the largest groups, the organizational perspective appears to be more useful for explaining the existence and the characteristics of small- and medium-sized groups. Thus, in this chapter we consider the group as being the appropriate unit to delimit the firm's boundary; that is, we take business groups as the organizational form adopted by firms when they grow in size. It is worth noting that this assumption is not widely shared in the economics and management literature, where business groups are seen either as mere financial devices with no economic synergies (Penrose, 1959), or as a hybrid organizational form between the hierarchy (the integrated firm) and the market (Williamson, 1985). What these views have in common is that they identify the firm with the presence of an 'administrative co-ordination', which typically is conducted within a legal boundary.

The difficulty involved in considering the group as a firm is underlined by Penrose:

> The extensive and elusive lines of control in the modern business world … make it more difficult to decide what should be included within a given firm. The unincorporated individual proprietorship, the partnership and the small corporation without subsidiaries create in general no trouble, but the large corporation with many subsidiaries over which it exercises some degree of control does.
>
> (Penrose, 1959, p. 20)

Williamson considers the group (the holding form) to be a 'loosely' divisionalized structure that does not 'enjoy an *internal* relationships to the division' (Williamson, 1975, p. 144); again, these relationships are associated with the legal boundary of the corporation. Indeed, the transaction cost approach considers business groups as a hybrid organizational form, that lies somewhere between the market and the hierarchical (internal) form of co-ordination. Both Penrose and Williamson would exclude from their definitions of a firm those groups in which there are 'mere' financial (ownership) connections between legal units, and where there is a lack of administrative co-ordination between these legal units. Thus, the firm is typically associated with the legal unit, and the organizational architecture with its 'internal' structure.

Our assumption that business groups can be considered as firms has two bases. First, we delimit firm boundaries on the basis of ownership and control of business activities; in our definition of business groups we include only those legal units where the common owner(s) has a majority share. Second, the control of legal units exercised by the ultimate owner of the business group can be assimilated to the administrative co-ordination; indeed, in business groups this co-ordination takes the form of a centralized long-run strategy and an internal capital market (not dissimilar to an M-form organization). In addition, the formation of consolidated accounts formalizes the economic and financial relationships within the group. This appears to be particularly true in the case of small- and medium-sized groups, which abound in industrialized countries. Moreover, our focus on strategic choices, such us location, diversification and vertical integration, further justifies our use of the business group as the unit of analysis because it is at this level that these choices are typically made. To reinforce our definition of business groups as an organizational form, we excluded from our empirical analysis what we call 'pseudo groups', that is groups that are set up for purely financial reasons. Similarly, in our analysis only production companies (that is industrial, commercial and service companies) belonging to business groups are considered, which excludes holding and property companies.

8.2.2 Spatial agglomeration and business groups

Only recently have the relationships between spatial agglomeration and firm's organization attracted the attention of the economics literature. For example, Rosenthal and Strange (2003) examine how corporate organizations affect the benefits that arise from clustering within a given industry. Duranton and Puga (2003) argued that up to now little theoretical work has been done on the relationships between agglomeration forces and firms' heterogeneity. This chapter is a first attempt to make an empirical contribution to this literature, and extends an earlier study (Cainelli *et al.*, 2006).

We characterize agglomeration as membership of groups in industrial districts. In these production structures, which are particularly widespread within the Italian economy, agglomeration forces such as labour market pooling, local knowledge spillovers, face to face contact, etc. play an important role in enhancing firms' innovative activity and economic performance (Cainelli and Zoboli, 2004). Despite the importance of business groups and industrial districts in the Italian economy, until recently few studies had analysed the relationships between these phenomena (Bianchi and Gualtieri, 1990; Brusco *et al.*, 1996; Dei Ottati, 1996; Brioschi *et al.*, 2002). These contributions have two drawbacks for our analysis. First, from an empirical point of view, they refer to specific industrial districts, making it difficult to assess to what extent their results can be generalized. Second, from a theoretical point of view, they do not analyse the relationship between the nature of agglomeration forces and the presence and features of business groups.

Some more recent studies (Balloni and Iacobucci, 2001; Brioschi *et al.*, 2002; Brioschi *et al.*, 2004) have tried to systematically analyse the relationship between industrial districts and business groups, taking into account the characteristics of the latter; however, they do not develop a general framework for the possible relationship between a firm's organization and its belonging to an industrial district.

Information sharing about production technology and market needs, transmission of ideas, and speed of the imitative process are characteristic features of industrial districts and, more generally, of spatial agglomeration of production activities. It helps firms to increase efficiency and to foster product innovation and growth. Moreover, knowledge spillovers and information sharing enhanced by spatial proximity allow firms to seize business opportunities along the production chain or in related sectors (Cainelli and Leoncini, 1999). At the same time economic geography models have shown that specialization can have a negative impact on diversification of production activity (Duranton and Puga, 2001). For these reasons the growth processes of district firms normally take the form of either product differentiation within the same sector, or vertical integration. Both forms concern activities along the district production chain. Moreover, the familiarity of firms within the same district favours acquisitions from among them (Brioschi *et al.*, 2002). As a result, it is likely that the setting up of new firms or the acquisition of established ones will involve firms in the same sector of specialization, located within the same district.

From the previous discussion it emerges that spatial agglomeration forces play a role in shaping firms' growth strategies. Specifically, we can propose the following hypotheses: (i) business groups that result from a firm's growth process, are more widespread within industrial districts than outside them; (ii) business groups within industrial districts show a higher degree of specialization than groups outside them; (iii) business groups belonging to industrial districts show a higher degree of spatial concentration of their activities.

8.2.3 Agglomeration, technology and vertical integration

The second aspect investigated in this chapter concerns the influence of technology and agglomeration on vertical integration choices.

There are two main theories explaining the degree of vertical integration: transaction cost economics (TCE) and property rights theory (PRT). According to TCE (Williamson, 1985), vertical integration occurs as a result of the need to prevent *ex-post* hold-up problems resulting from transaction specific investments. The advantages of vertical integration in reducing or avoiding the costs of market transactions must be compared with the cost of producing within the firm (cost of integration). This latter depends on the ability to monitor employees and convey information within the organization.

In contrast to the TCE approach, which emphasizes *ex-post* transaction problems, PRT focuses on distortions in *ex-ante* investment. The residual rights of control, guaranteed by the ownership of assets, are particularly valuable in situations of *ex ante* incomplete contracting and *ex post* opportunist behaviour. Some of the assumptions and conclusions of the two theories are very similar. Nevertheless, it has been shown that there are differences (Whinston, 2001). PRT predictions are more difficult to empirically test than TCE theory. This is probably the reason why much of the empirical literature on vertical integration is based on TCE, and relies on single industry case studies. Only a few studies have used a cross industry approach to explore the intensity and the determinants of vertical integration (Fan and Lang, 2000; Acemoglu *et al.*, 2004).

Both approaches stress the importance of technology (as a proxy for asset specificity) in explaining the degree of firms' vertical integration. TCE also suggests a role for spatial agglomeration in vertical integration. The literature on spatial agglomeration stresses the importance of market-based relationships between firms located in agglomerated areas based on lower transaction cost levels. This is generally explained, on the one hand, by the lower level of opportunism between economic agents, and on the other, by the lack of information asymmetry. The low level of opportunism is commonly justified by the homogeneity of clusters in terms of local institutions, 'culture', social capital, language, etc. (Wood and Parr, 2005). The lack of information asymmetry is explained by spatial proximity, the frequency of face-to-face contacts and, more generally, by local knowledge spillovers (Breschi and Lissoni, 2001). The literature on industrial districts has emphasized the role of social capital and trust in shaping vertical relationships between independent agents, underlining their co-operative nature (Brusco, 1982; Becattini, 1992; Dei Ottati, 1994). For all these reasons we should expect firms located within industrial clusters to show a lower level of vertical integration than similar firms located outside them.

From a TCE perspective, the literature referred to above emphasizes the role of co-operation and the lack of opportunism in vertical relations between firms. This implies a focus on behavioural variables and, as a result, an under valuation of the role of asset specificity as a determinant of transaction costs. We do not question the suggestion that in industrial clusters the level of opportunism and information asymmetry is lower than in non-agglomerated areas. Nevertheless, from a TCE perspective the problem is not the 'intensity' of opportunism or information asymmetry, but whether or not they are present (Kreps, 1990). In fact, the TCE approach takes opportunism and the bounded rationality of agents as an *ex-ante* behavioural hypothesis and considers the level of transaction specific investments to be the main determinant of transaction costs.

The reduction of information asymmetry as a result of spatial agglomeration is well demonstrated theoretically and is empirically verified. However, its role in the degree of vertical integration is ambiguous. Some of the literature maintains that face-to-face contact, long-term supply relationships and sharing of market and technology information favours the acquisition of firms within industrial districts, substituting for hierarchical governance in transactions between independent firms (Brioschi *et al.*, 2002). At the same time there are some studies that suggest that the reduction in information asymmetry should reduce transaction costs thus favouring market-based relationships between agents (Wood and Parr, 2005). Which of these mechanisms is the most important in determining the relationship between agglomeration and vertical integration must be assessed empirically.

Claims regarding the relationships between agglomeration, technology and vertical integration are based mainly on anecdotal evidence or case studies of specific clusters (Enright, 1995). We do not know of any large-scale empirical attempts to verify these relationships.

8.3 Data and results

8.3.1 The data-set

For our empirical analysis we use two versions – a firm level and a group level – of a new and original data-set on business groups recently developed by ISTAT. The data refer to 2001. By merging information about joint stock companies drawn from the Italian Business Register, ASIA (*Archivio Statistico delle Imprese Attive*) with the first version of the firm level data-set, we were able to assess the presence of firms belonging to business groups by industry and industrial districts. The latter are identified according to the Sforzi–ISTAT procedure (ISTAT, 1997). This procedure considers the local labour systems (LLS) as the unit of analysis and identifies 199 industrial districts within the 784 LLS into which the Italian territory is divided.

We used the business group version of the data-set to study the organizational specificity and strategic choices of business groups. To compare district and non-district groups we isolated manufacturing groups, defined according to the following criteria: (i) comprising at least two production companies (we excluded financial and property companies or non-active companies), one of which is a manufacturing firm; (ii) largest company in the group is a manufacturing firm. The industry that a group belongs to is determined by the sector of its largest company. A manufacturing group is classified as belonging to a particular industrial district when its largest company is located in it, and it operates in the same sector of the district.

Based on these criteria we identified 8,861 manufacturing groups, of which 4,125 belonged to an industrial district. These business groups include 25,739 manufacturing and service firms, with an average of about three firms per group. The distribution of business groups by class of employees and number of firms is shown in Table 8.1.

It should be noted that according to other statistical sources the number of manufacturing business groups is higher than is identified using the ISTAT data-set. Also referring to 2001, Unioncamere (2004, p. 96) estimates that the manufacturing sector comprises some 16,000 groups. Both data-sets include joint stock companies and adopt the same definition of control: that is, ownership of at least 50 per cent of the shares. The discrepancy arises from the way the 'raw' data have been elaborated. In our analysis we excluded 'pseudo-groups' – that

Table 8.1 Manufacturing business groups by class of employees and number of firms

Class of employees	*Class of firms in the group*							*Total*
	2	*3*	*4–5*	*6–9*	*10–49*	*50–99*	*>99*	
1–9	732	138	24	2				896
10–19	893	234	60	8				1,195
20–49	1,604	546	196	34	9			2,389
50–99	815	461	270	63	18			1,627
100–249	542	395	337	118	42			1,434
250–499	117	123	156	110	58			564
500–999	49	45	67	77	63	3		304
>999	20	26	40	51	100	12	3	252
Total	4,772	1,968	1,150	463	290	15	3	8,661

is, groups with one production company and one or more financial companies, and groups that had only one Italian company and were composed mainly of foreign companies because the ISTAT data-set lacks information (employees, activity, etc.) about foreign companies. We also only included business groups with at least two 'active' companies.

8.3.2 The presence and organizational specificity of business groups in industrial districts

The first result of our analysis relates to the presence of business groups within Italian industrial districts. The empirical evidence shows that business groups are generally more widespread within industrial districts than outside them, thus confirming the findings of previous contributions on this issue (Brioschi *et al.*, 2002). In particular, columns 1 and 2 of Table 8.2 suggest that, passing from non-district to district LLSs, the share of firms in business groups tends to increase. In the first case, the share of total firms is equal to 21.31 per cent, whereas in the second it increases to 23.88 per cent. This finding is reinforced when we take account of only those firms specialized in the district sector. In this case the share of firms belonging to a business group is even higher at 24.11 per cent.

The greater incidence of business groups within Italian industrial districts is further confirmed by Table 8.3, where the analysis takes into account industrial districts by sector of activity. Our evidence shows that, with the exception only of districts operating in 'other sectors', the presence of business groups is always greater in district than in non-district firms. For example, in the food industry the share of firms belonging to a business group increases, passing from non-district to district firms. In the latter case the share is equal to 5.67 per cent, when measured as the ratio of all firms, and 20.61 per cent when measured with respect to joint stock companies. The findings were similar for other manufacturing sectors. In the textile and clothing sector the share goes from 3.09 per cent

Table 8.2 Percentage of firms and employees in business groups (2001)

	Firms %		*Employees*	
	(c)/(a)	*(c)/(b)*	*(c)/(a)*	*(c)/(b)*
Non-district LLSs (585)	4.63	21.31	44.94	63.47
District LLs (199)	5.87	23.88	35.39	53.05
Industrial district (199)	5.86	24.11	35.67	53.28

Notes
a All firms.
b Joint stock companies.
c Firms belonging to a business group.

for non-district firms to 5.01 per cent for district firms, while in the leather and footwear sector the share rises from 2.83 per cent to 4.06 per cent. The results are the same when the presence of business groups is measured as the ratio between firms belonging to a business group and joint stock companies.

We have shown that the presence of business groups is higher in district than in non-district areas. Next we empirically assess the existence of a link between spatial agglomeration and firm organization. In other words, we want to find whether district groups show organizational specificity with respect to business groups operating in non-district areas. To perform this analysis we calculated: (i) a specialization index; and (ii) a spatial concentration index. The index for groups' degree of specialization is computed as the ratio of the total employees in the group that belongs to the same sector as the largest firm (which in the case of the district group is the same as the district sector). Although this is not a proper index of diversification, it is appropriate for our hypothesis: that is, that groups in industrial districts tend to expand their activities in the sector characterizing the district.

Table 8.3 Business group firms by sector of activity (2001)

	District firms (%)		*Non-district firms (%)*	
	(c)/(a)	*(c)/(b)*	*(c)/(a)*	*(c)/(b)*
Food (17)	5.67	20.61	2.69	17.75
Textile and clothing (68)	5.01	21.82	3.09	17.43
Leather and footwear (28)	4.06	15.92	2.83	14.73
Furniture (39)	4.91	25.33	2.39	18.66
Mechanics (33)	7.46	25.77	5.43	22.31
Other sectors (14)	7.23	20.99	9.27	26.27

Notes
a All firms.
b Joint stock companies.
c Firms belonging to a business group.

The spatial concentration index is calculated as the ratio of total employees in the group of firms located in the same LLS.

To test the hypothesis about the organizational specificity of district groups, for both indicators we calculated *t*-tests of mean differences between district and non-district groups. The findings are presented in Tables 8.4 and 8.5. From Table 8.4 we can see that the degree of diversification, both for district and non-district groups, is very low. However, the degree of specialization of business groups located in industrial districts is significantly higher than that of groups located outside industrial districts, confirming Brioschi *et al.*'s (2002, 2004) hypothesis that in industrial districts there is a prevalence of a specific organizational form of business group, which they define as a 'district group'.

Table 8.5 shows that the degree of spatial concentration is very high for both types of groups. Also, in this case it is due to the large number of small groups,

Table 8.4 Degree of specialization of business groups

	District group		*Non-district group*		*Test of diff. of means*	
	(1)	*(2)*	*(1)*	*(2)*	t	*Sig.(1 tail)*
Food (17)	46	0.89	685	0.87	0.48	0.316
Textiles and clothing (68)	477	0.92	545	0.89	3.08***	0.001
Leather and footwear (28)	141	0.93	178	0.89	2.82***	0.003
Furniture (39)	39	0.89	82	0.83	1.76**	0.040
Mechanics (33)	826	0.92	3329	0.90	3.43***	0.001
Other sectors (14)	197	0.91	2516	0.88	2.59***	0.005

Notes
1 Number of business groups.
2 Degree of specialization of business group.
*** significant at 1%, ** significant at 5%, * significant at 10%.

Table 8.5 Degree of spatial concentration of activities of business groups

	District group		*Non-district group*		*Test of diff. of means*	
	(1)	*(2)*	*(1)*	*(2)*	t	*Sig. (1 tail)*
Food (17)	46	0.87	685	0.90	−1.51	0.066
Textiles and clothing (68)	477	0.94	545	0.91	2.88***	0.002
Leather and footwear (28)	141	0.94	178	0.93	0.71	0.241
Furniture (39)	39	0.96	82	0.92	1.52*	0.065
Mechanics (33)	826	0.92	3329	0.91	1.05	0.148
Other sectors (14)	197	0.92	2516	0.92	0.19	0.424

Notes
1 Number of business groups.
2 Degree of spatial concentration of business group.
*** significant at 1%, ** significant at 5%, * significant at 10%.

whose firms are mainly located around the largest one. With the exception of the food groups the share of employees within the same LLS is higher in district groups than in non-district ones. Nevertheless, the difference between the mean values is statistically significant only for business groups belonging to textiles and clothing districts (Table 8.5).

8.3.3 The presence of business groups by industry and Pavitt sectors

We now examine the presence of business groups by industry and Pavitt sectors. This is a preliminary to the next analysis, which uses industries as proxies for technology. Our hypothesis is that the technological regimes that characterize industries influence the organization of firms and therefore the relative presence of business groups. In order to identify those industries where this presence is higher, in Tables 8.6 and 8.7 we report the distribution of this phenomenon by industry and by class of employees. More specifically, the incidence of business groups is shown in Table 8.6 in terms of firms, and in Table 8.7 in terms of employees. The presence of business groups is particularly relevant in industries such as Chemicals and Allied Products (29.5 per cent in terms of firms and 66.3 per cent in terms of employees), Petroleum Refining and Related Industries (28.4 per cent in terms of firms and 74.9 per cent in terms of employees) and Transportation Equipment (26.5 per cent in terms of firms and 71.4 per cent in terms of employees). In other industries, such as Lumber and Wood Products, Leather and Footwear, and Miscellaneous Manufacturing Industries the presence of groups is low. It is fairly clear that the prevalence of business groups within an industry is generally

Table 8.6 Firms belonging to groups by industry and class of employees (% on total firms)

Industry	*Class of employees*				*Total*
	1–49	*50–249*	*250–999*	*1,000–*	
Food, beverages and tobacco	15.1	47.9	71.9	93.8	18.3
Textile and clothing	13.7	38.7	73.0	90.0	16.8
Leather and footwear	10.9	30.6	71.0	100.0	13.1
Lumber and wood products (Ex. Furniture)	10.4	34.9	100.0		12.3
Paper, printing and Publishing	18.6	49.7	80.6	83.3	20.9
Petroleum refining and related industries	23.9	54.8	60.0	80.0	28.4
Chemicals and allied products	24.5	47.4	80.0	82.8	29.5
Rubber and plastic products	17.8	47.2	80.4	50.0	21.7
Stone, clay, glass and concrete products	16.3	44.9	80.0	91.7	19.7
Metal products	14.7	38.9	66.3	92.9	17.2
Industrial machinery	19.0	45.5	76.1	82.4	22.6
Computer and electronics	17.2	45.9	70.6	82.9	20.4
Transportation equipment	20.2	48.6	54.3	82.1	26.5
Miscellaneous manufacturing industries	13.2	34.2	66.7	100.0	15.2
Total	16.1	42.6	72.3	84.0	19.2

Table 8.7 Firms belonging to groups by industry and class of employees (% of total employees)

Industry	*Class of employees*				*Total*
	1–49	*50–249*	*250–999*	*1,000–*	
Food, beverages and tobacco	19.7	51.8	78.8	90.9	53.1
Textile and clothing	17.4	43.6	73.9	94.8	41.4
Leather and footwear	12.7	35.7	71.7	100.0	30.1
Lumber and wood products (excl. furniture)	11.9	37.3	100.0		25.3
Paper, printing and publishing	22.7	53.8	84.2	99.9	50.2
Petroleum refining and related Industries	28.8	59.2	56.0	98.7	74.9
Chemicals and allied products	31.6	49.6	83.2	88.3	66.3
Rubber and plastic products	21.1	51.2	83.9	40.6	42.6
Stone, clay, glass and concrete products	21.0	49.5	79.9	89.1	48.9
Metal products	17.4	43.4	68.7	99.1	39.3
Industrial machinery	22.3	49.1	76.6	84.5	50.7
Computer and electronics	22.5	50.8	73.3	92.7	56.9
Transportation equipment	22.9	49.6	54.9	92.1	71.4
Miscellaneous manufacturing industries	16.0	38.9	69.8	100.0	32.5
Total	19.5	46.9	74.5	90.2	48.8

Table 8.8 Firms belonging to business groups by Pavitt sectors (2001) (% on firms)

	Class of employees				*Total*
	1–49	*50–249*	*250–999*	*1,000–*	
Supplier dominated	13.3	38.3	71.7	94.9	16.0
Scale intensive	18.1	45.6	72.6	79.6	21.4
Science based	20.2	49.1	65.9	89.1	24.2
Specialized suppliers	18.1	44.7	76.3	78.0	21.4
Total	16.1	42.6	72.3	84.0	19.2

associated with the presence of specific technological features. In other words, the evidence suggests that in high- and medium-tech sectors business groups often represent the most efficient solution to firms' organizational problems.

These findings are confirmed when we analyse the distribution of groups by class of employees. Table 8.7 illustrates the role of firm size in explaining differences in the presence of business groups. In all the industries considered the presence of groups is modest among small firms, and tends to increase with firm size. It is not chance that all large industries (units with more than 1,000 employees) show incidence of groups equal to 84 per cent in terms of firms, and 90.2 per cent in terms of employees.

Next we analyse business groups by Pavitt sectors. Again, the role of technology is clear. Tables 8.8 and 8.9 show that the presence of business groups is particularly relevant in the 'science-based' (24.2 per cent in terms of firms and

Table 8.9 Firms belonging to business groups by Pavitt sectors (2001) (% of total employees)

	Class of employees				*Total*
	1–49	*50–249*	*250–999*	*1,000–*	
Supplier dominated	16.3	43.0	73.4	94.8	39.3
Scale intensive	21.5	49.7	75.6	87.2	53.3
Science based	27.7	53.6	70.4	94.9	68.7
Specialized suppliers	21.7	48.1	76.3	88.5	49.4
Total	24.0	58.6	93.1	107.1	60.1

68.7 per cent in terms of employees) and 'scale-intensive' sectors (21.4 per cent in terms of firms and 53.3 per cent in terms of employees), and also in 'specialized suppliers' industries (21.4 per cent in terms of firms and 49.4 per cent in terms of employees). However, the presence of this organizational form in 'supplier dominated' sectors (16 per cent in terms of firms and 39.3 per cent in terms of employees) does not reach the values for the other Pavitt sectors.

8.3.4 Agglomeration, technology and vertical integration

This section focuses on an econometric analysis of the relationship that exists at the business group level between vertical integration on the one hand, and technology and spatial agglomeration, on the other.

To assess whether a diversified activity in a group can be considered to be a backward or a forward integration we use the Italian input–output tables for 2000, used to determine whether a pair of activities can be considered to be part of the same production chain. The table contains the value of intermediate exchanges between 58 branches of economic activity, 23 of which are manufacturing activities. Being $j = 1,2,\ldots,58$ the branches of economic activity, for each manufacturing industry $i = 1,2,\ldots,23$ we calculate the index b_{ij} as the share of intermediate consumption of industry i supplied by the industry j, so that for each $i \sum_j b_{ij} = 1$.

Excluding intra-industry exchanges combining the 23 manufacturing industries with the 58 potential supplier industries results in 1,311 pairs of activities. The larger the b_{ij}, the larger the share of input requirement controlled by the producer in industry i in case of integration with industry j; that is, b_{ij} is an index of the quantitative relevance of backward integration. Of the 1,311 potential backward relationships 284 are null while the others show a positive value. Of these, 287 show a value over 1 per cent and 85 a value over 5 per cent. We chose the 3 per cent value as a reasonable cut-off for discriminating significant backward vertical relationships among manufacturing industries.

In the case of forward integration, we followed a similar procedure. Given $j = 1,2,\ldots,58$ branches of potential acquirers, for each manufacturing industry

$i=1,2,\ldots,23$ we calculated the index f_{ij} as the share of intermediate sales of industry i supplied to industry j, so that for each $i \sum f_{ij} = 1$. Of the 1,311 potential pairs of activities, there are 945 with the index $f_{ij}>0$, 255 with $f_{ij} > 0.01$ and 97 with $f_{ij} > 0.03$. Again we took the 3 per cent value as the cut-off for discriminating significant forward vertical integration between pairs of industries.

On the basis of this analysis we constructed a dummy variable for each group according to the presence within the group of the pair of industries with the values b_{ij} and v_{ij} exceeding the threshold level indicated above. The dummy takes the value 0 if the group is not vertically integrated; 1 if the group is forward integrated; 2 if the group is backward integrated.

Table 8.10 presents the distribution of manufacturing groups according to type of vertical integration and number of production companies. Given the small number of cases we considered, we excluded from our analysis groups that were both forward and backward integrated.

The econometric analysis was carried out using the dummy variable defined above as the dependent variable. It is clear that this dependent variable is unordered since the numerical values associated with each vertical integration strategy are arbitrary in the sense that $0<1<2$ does not imply that outcome 1 is less than outcome 2, and so on. We assume that there are basically two explanatory variables for the vertical integration strategies of these business groups: that is, technology, captured in the following analyses by Pavitt and industry dummies, and spatial agglomeration, captured by a business group's belonging to any Italian industrial district. In the case of industrial districts, we use the overall dummy (*Dis*) for all the Italian industrial districts and specific dummies for the specific districts, such as food (*Dis_food*), textiles and clothing (*Dis_tex*), leather and footwear (*Dis_lea*) furniture (*Dis_furn*), mechanics (*Dis_mec*) and other industries (*Dis_oth*). Finally, in order to eliminate (at least partially) business groups' unobservable fixed effects we introduced two group

Table 8.10 Manufacturing groups by type of vertical integration within the manufacturing sector

Class of production companies	*Vertical integration*				*Total*
	Non vertically integrated	*Forward integrated*	*Backward integrated*	*Forward and backward integrated*	
2	5,008	287	368		5,663
3	1,270	123	188	4	1,585
4–5	591	89	139	10	829
6–9	228	53	60	16	357
10–49	103	31	52	17	203
50–	4	6	2	12	24
Total	7,204	589	809	59	8,661

size variables into our econometric specifications, captured by the natural log of the number of firms belonging to a group (*lprod*), and by the natural log of the number of groups' employees (*lsize*).

To model these three groups' vertical integration choices we used Multinomial Logit. Following Greene (2003), in this model the estimated equations provide a set of probabilities for the J choices of a decision maker – in our case, Italian business groups – with characteristics $\mathbf{x}_i$. In particular, this econometric methodology assumes that the probabilities for these J choices can be modelled as follows:

$$\mathrm{Prob}(Y_i=j)=\frac{e^{\beta'_j \mathbf{x}_i}}{\sum_{k=0}^{2} e^{\beta'_j \mathbf{x}_i}}, \qquad j=0,1,2$$

where $Y_i=0$ if the business group i is not vertically integrated, $Y_i=1$ if it is forward integrated, and $Y_i=2$ it is backward integrated.

The results of this econometric investigation are reported in Table 8.11. As far as technology is concerned, all Pavitt dummies are always statistically significant, but with different signs. In the case of forward integration they are all negative, taking the scale intensive sector as the reference, thus suggesting the importance of firm size in determining this choice. This finding is further confirmed by the positive and significant coefficients of the variables capturing group size. In other words, these findings suggest that forward integration within the manufacturing sectors is strongly associated with specific industries. For backward integration, the coefficients are positive in the case of the specialized supplier and science-based sectors, and negative in the case of the supplier-dominated sectors. This result shows that firms in supplier dominated sectors find it difficult to control backward production phases, thus confirming the role of innovative regimes in influencing backward vertical integration choices.

With regard to spatial agglomeration, the overall district dummy (*Dis*) is positive and statistically significant in the case of both forward and backward integration.[1] This means that spatial agglomeration, captured in our analysis by membership of firms in industrial districts, positively affects the vertical integration strategies adopted by Italian business groups. It is interesting to note that this result does not seem to support the hypothesis that agglomeration of economic activities should reduce the degree of vertical integration. In this sense, our evidence is not consistent with the industrial districts literature, which generally suggests a prevalence of market-based relationships among firms within these agglomerated areas.

However, analysis of a specific typology of Italian districts shows that these agglomeration effects are industry-specific. Indeed, the dummy for the mechanics district is positive and statistically significant in all the forms of vertical integration considered, while, with the exception of 'other districts' in the case of backward integration, the dummies for the remaining types of districts are never statistically significant. This result can be interpreted as evidence of asset specificity mechanisms in the mechanics district which push firms towards a higher level of vertical integration.

Table 8.11 Vertical integration, agglomeration and technology: estimates

	Multinomial logit[(a)]		*Multinomial logit*[(a)]	
	Coeff.	t *values*	*Coeff.*	t *values*
1 – Forward integration				
Specialized Supplier	–0.892**	–6.19	–0.908**	–6.27
Science based	–0.768**	–3.70	–0.768**	–3.70
Scale intensive	Ref.	Ref.	Ref.	Ref.
Supplier dominated	–0.674**	–6.82	–0.635**	–0.634
lprod	0.581**	6.70	0.585**	6.71
lsize	0.279**	8.24	0.279**	8.21
Dis	0.242**	2.71	...	...
Dis_food	...	...	0.213	0.75
Dis_tex	...	...	0.084	0.63
Dis_lea	...	...	0.104	0.42
Dis_mech	...	...	0.511**	4.29
Dis_oth	...	...	0.100	0.70
2 – Backward integration				
Specialized supplier	1.243**	13.10	1.242**	13.08
Science based	0.464**	3.03	0.462**	3.01
Scale intensive	Ref.	Ref.	Ref.	Ref.
Supplier dominated	–0.578**	–5.14	–0.556**	–4.92
lprod	0.682**	8.77	0.685**	8.82
lsize	0.269**	8.73	0.268**	8.70
Dis	0.219**	2.77	...	...
Dis_food	...	...	0.011	0.04
Dis_tex	...	...	0.136	1.14
Dis_lea	...	...	–0.142	–0.58
Dis_mech	...	...	0.337**	3.16
Dis_oth	...	...	0.278**	2.25
N.obs.	8,594	8,594		
Pseudo R^2	0.095	0.096		

Notes
a The regression also includes a constant term.
** significant at 5%; * significant at 10%.

8.4 Conclusions

This chapter set out to analyse the relationships between certain structural variables, such as spatial agglomeration and technology, and firms' strategy and organization. Despite the relevance of this line of research for understanding the behaviour of firms, only a few contributions have attempted to provide theoretical explanations and empirical evidence for these aspects.

Our work contributes to this literature in three ways. First, we show that spatial agglomeration influences the growth patterns of business groups and affects their presence in industrial districts. Second, we show that the organizational specificity of business groups partially depends on their belonging to industrial districts. Third, we show the joint influence of spatial agglomeration and technology on firms' vertical integration decisions.

More specifically, we show that the incidence of business groups in industrial districts is higher than in non-district areas and also that it is not simply belonging to an industrial district that matters, but that the 'size' of the local system and the strength of agglomeration forces are also important. We were able to identify the role of spatial concentration of production in shaping some features of firms' organization; groups belonging to industrial districts are less diversified and, in some cases, show a higher degree of spatial concentration. This means that agglomeration affects the process of growth of 'district groups' around the district's core business.

The greater incidence of business groups within the Italian industrial districts can be explained on the basis of the costs to district firms of acquiring information on the characteristics of competitors and/or suppliers. These costs are lower in industrial districts than in non-district areas, which encourages acquisition activity (Brioschi *et al.*, 2002, 2004).

The result related to the organizational specificity of district groups is interesting. This finding suggests that agglomeration forces operating in industrial districts are sector-specific, thus confirming that in these production structures, knowledge spillovers are of the intra-industry type, or '*a là* Porter' (Glaeser *et al.*, 1992; Cainelli and Leoncini, 1999). For this reason, spatial agglomeration seems to favour the processes of growth/specialization of district groups based on the district core business rather than fostering spatial concentration. Finally, we found that these results are not homogeneous across industrial districts, but are strongly affected by the industry in which the district is specialized. Specifically, the influence of agglomeration forces is particularly significant for the mechanics district, but not for districts specialized in the so called 'traditional industries'.

This last result questions the role of technology in these processes. We analysed how technology and innovation regimes influence the presence and growth strategies of business groups. Empirical evidence shows that there is a high heterogeneity in the presence of business groups by both industry and Pavitt sectors. Specifically, we found that business groups are more widespread in high- and medium-tech industries than in traditional industries. Because the group is the outcome of a growth process, the learning mechanisms and knowledge base characterizing firms in high- and medium-tech industries increase their ability to enter into new business activities.

Finally, we analysed some aspects of firms' strategy, such as the degree and direction (backward or forward) of vertical integration. Taking control over different stages of the production chain is one of the main strategic choices made by firms, and one that strongly affects their organizational structure. Our empirical evidence shows that vertical integration is conditioned by technology. We also detected the joint effect of technology and spatial agglomeration on firm's decisions to vertically integrate. Contrary to popular opinion that low transaction costs favour vertical production disintegration within industrial districts, our findings show that this is not the case, and especially in the case of mechanical districts. This suggests the importance of technology in influencing the internal organization of industrial districts.

Overall our findings can be considered as a first attempt to investigate the relationships between spatial agglomeration forces and technology in shaping firms' strategy and organization. We are aware that further refinements both at theoretical and empirical level are needed.

Note

1 As already mentioned to identify the geographic location of a business group we take the largest firm of the group as our reference. In other words, if the largest firm of a group is located within an industrial district this business group is considered to belong to this district: that is, it is a 'district group'. Even if this procedure might introduce some bias into our investigation we believe that this is not the case. Several empirical studies (Brioschi *et al.* 2002, 2004) have shown that 'district groups' are generally composed of firms specialized in one of the activities of the district production chain, and are located within the boundaries of the local system.

References

Acemoglu, D., P. Aghion, R. Griffith and F. Zilibotti (2004), 'Vertical integration and technology: theory and evidence', *NBER Working Paper Series* (WP 10997).

Almeida, H. and D. Wolfenzon (2004). *A theory of pyramidal ownership and family business groups*. Unpublished manuscript, New York.

Balloni, V. and D. Iacobucci (1997), 'Cambiamenti in atto nell'organizzazione dell'industria marchigiana', *Economia Marche, XVI* (1), 29–66.

Balloni, V. and D. Iacobucci (2001), 'Diffusione e caratteristiche dei gruppi di piccole e medie imprese nelle aree distrettuali delle Marche'. In F. Brioschi and G. Cainelli (eds), *Diffusione e caratteristiche dei gruppi di piccole e medie imprese nelle aree distrettuali* Milan: Giuffrè Editore, pp. 174–237.

Barca, F., M. Bianco, L. Cannari, R. Cesari, C. Gola, G. Manitta, G. Salvo and L.F. Signorini (1994), *Assetti proprietari e mercato delle imprese. Vol. I. Proprietà, modelli di controllo e riallocazione delle imprese industriali italiane*, Bologna: Il Mulino.

Becattini, G. (1992), 'The Marshallian industrial district as a socio-economic notion'. In F. Pyke, G. Becattini and W. Sengenberger (eds), *Industrial districts and inter-firm cooperation in Italy*, Geneva: International Institute for Labour Studies, pp. 37–51.

Bianchi, P. and G. Gualtieri (1990), 'Emilia-Romagna and its industrial districts: the evolution of a model'. In R. Leonardi and R.Y. Nannetti (eds), *The regions and European integration*, London: Pinter, pp. 83–108.

Breschi, S. and F. Lissoni (2001), 'Localised knowledge spillovers vs. innovative milieux: knowledge "tacitness" reconsidered', *Papers in Regional Science, 80* (3), 255–273.

Brioschi, F., M.S. Brioschi and G. Cainelli (2002), 'From the industrial district to the district group: an insight to the evolution of local capitalism in Italy', *Regional Studies, 36* (9), 1037–1052.

Brioschi, F., M.S. Brioschi and G. Cainelli (2004), 'Ownership linkages and business groups in industrial districts. The case of Emilia Romagna'. In G. Cainelli and R. Zoboli (eds), *The evolution of industrial districts. Changing governance, innovation and internationalization of local capitalism in Italy*, Heidelberg: Physica-Verlag, pp. 155–174.

Brioschi, F., L. Buzzacchi and M.G. Colombo (1990), *Gruppi di imprese e mercato finanziario. La struttura di potere nell'industria italiana*, Rome: La Nuova Italia Scientifica.

Brusco, S. (1982), 'The Emilian model: productive decentralization and social integration', *Cambridge Journal of Economics, 6*, 167–184.

Brusco, S., G. Cainelli, F. Forni, M. Franchi, A. Malusardi and R. Righetti (1996), 'The evolution of industrial districts in Emilia-Romagna'. In F. Cossentino, F. Pyke and W. Sengenberger (eds), *Local and regional response to global pressure: the case of Italy and its industrial districts*, Geneva: ILO, pp. 17–36.

Cainelli, G. and R. Leoncini (1999), 'Externalities and long-term local industrial development. Some empirical evidence from Italy', *Revue d'Economie Industrielle, 90*, 25–39.

Cainelli, G. and R. Zoboli (eds) (2004), *The evolution of industrial districts. Changing governance, innovation and internationalization of local capitalism in Italy*, Heidelberg: Physica-Verlag.

Cainelli, G., D. Iacobucci and E. Morganti (2006), 'Spatial agglomeration and business groups. New evidence from Italian industrial districts', *Regional Studies, 40* (5), 1–12.

Chandler, A.D. (1982), 'M-form: industrial groups, American style', *European Economic Review, 19*, 3–23.

Dei Ottati, G. (1994), 'Trust, interlinking transactions and credit in the industrial district', *Cambridge Journal of Economics, 18*, 529–546.

Dei Ottati, G. (1996), 'Economic changes in the district of Prato in the 1980s: towards it more conscious and organized industrial district', *European Planning Studies, 4* (1), 35–52.

Duranton, G. and D. Puga (2001), 'Nursery cities: urban diversity, process innovation, and the life cycle of products', *American Economic Review, 91* (5), 1454–1477.

Duranton, G. and D. Puga (2003), 'Micro-foundations of urban agglomeration economies', *NBER Working Paper Series* (WP 9931).

Enright, M.J. (1995), 'Organization and coordination in geographically concentrated industries'. In N.R. Lamoreaux and D.M.G. Raff (eds), *Coordination and information: historical perspectives on the organization of enterprise*, Chicago and London: The University of Chicago Press, pp. 103–142.

Fan, J.P.H. and L.H.P. Lang (2000), 'The measurement of relatedness: an application to corporate diversification', *Journal of Business, 73* (4), 629–660.

Gerlach, M.L. (1997), 'The organizational logic of business groups: evidence from the Zaibatsu'. In T. Shiba and M. Shimotani (eds), *Beyond the firm. Business groups in international and historical perspective*, Oxford: Oxford Univesity Press, pp. 245–273.

Glaeser, E.L., H.D. Kallal, J.A. Scheinkman and A. Shleifer (1992), 'Growth in cities', *Journal of Political Economy, 100* (6), 1126.

Goto, A. (1982), 'Business groups in a market economy', *European Economic Review, 19* (1), 53–70.

Greene, W.G. (2003), *Econometric Analysis*, Edgewood Cliffs, New Jersey: Prentice-Hall.

Iacobucci, D. (2002), 'Explaining business groups started by habitual entrepreneurs in the Italian manufacturing sector', *Entrepreneurship and Regional Development, 14* (1), 31–48.

Iacobucci, D. (2004), 'Groups of small- and medium-sized firms in industrial districts in Italy'. In G. Cainelli and R. Zoboli (eds), *The evolution of industrial districts*, Heidelberg: Physica-Verlag, pp. 128–154.

ISTAT (1997), *I sistemi locali del lavoro 1991*, Rome: ISTAT.

Kester, W.C. (1982), 'Industrial groups as systems of contractual governance', *Oxford Review of Economic Policy, 8* (3), 24–44.

Kreps, D.M. (1990), *A course in microeconomc theory*, New York: Harvester Wheatsheaf.

Loiseau, H. (2001). *Des groupes de la taille d'une PME. Un phenomen en plein essor*, Paris: INSEE.

Penrose, E. (1959), *The theory of the growth of the firm*, Oxford: Basil Blackwell.

Rosa, P. and M. Scott (1999), 'The prevalence of multiple owners and directors in the SME sector: implications for our understanding of start-up and growth', *Entrepreneurship and Regional Development, 11* (1), 21–38.

Rosenthal, S.S. and W.C. Strange (2003), 'Geography, industrial organization, and agglomeration', *Review of Economics and Statistics, 85* (2), 377–393.

Unioncamere (2004), *Rapporto Italia. L'economia reale dal punto di osservazione delle Camere di Commercio*. Rome.

Whinston, M. (2001), 'Assessing the property rights and transaction-cost theories of firm scope', *American Economic Review, Papers and Proceedings, 91* (2), 184–188.

Williamson, O.E. (1975), *Markets and hierarchies: analysis and antitrust implications*, New York: The Free Press.

Williamson, O.E. (1985), *The economic institution of capitalism: firms, markets, relational contracting*, New York, The Free Press.

Wood, G.A. and J.B. Parr (2005), 'Transaction costs, agglomeration economies, and industrial location', *Growth and Change, 36* (1), 1–15.

9 MNC-dominated clusters and the upgrading of domestic suppliers

The case of Costa Rican electronics and medical device industries[1,2]

Luciano Ciravegna and Elisa Giuliani

9.1 Introduction

Costa Rica is a small country that, unlike its Central American neighbouring countries, has managed to attract considerable *high-tech* FDI over the past decade. This has contributed to improving its export performance and terms of trade (Ciarli and Giuliani, 2005). However, very little is known of the impact that such FDI has had on the formation of well-functioning MNC-dominated clusters (Altenburg and Meyer-Stamer, 1999) and on the upgrading processes of domestic firms, which may link up to MNC located in the country. Drawing on the literature about the role of Multinational Companies and Global Value Chains (Gereffi, 1999) for development, this chapter explores the impact of foreign investors in the electronics and medical device (hereinafter EMD) industries on the learning and upgrading processes of Costa Rican firms. Moreover, this chapter explores whether these processes of knowledge transfer lead to the formation of well-functioning EMD MNC-dominated clusters in Costa Rica, as suggested by Altenburg and Meyer-Stamer (1999). These are clusters formed around the multinationals that have been attracted to invest in the Export Processing Zones (EPZ) as an explicit instrument of economic policy from the 1990s onwards. Our aim is to assess whether the inclusion of local producers into Global Value Chains lead by EMD multinationals has ignited any upgrading of their products, processes, or functions. The chapter shows that the majority of local firms has upgraded products and processes, while only a small share has upgraded their functions. Upgrading, especially of production processes, occurred to a large extent as local firms attempted to comply with the requirements of multinationals in order to become suppliers. Only in a few cases the linkages established with multinationals seem to have directly promoted upgrading. In most cases multinationals provided the demand stimulus for local firms to upgrade, but did not actively support it.

This chapter is organized as follows: in section 9.2 we provide a brief description of the FDI and exports trends recently followed by Costa Rica. Section 9.3 outlines our theoretical framework and develops the research questions. Section 9.4 explains the methodology used in our analysis, and Section 9.5 presents the empirical results. Section 9.5 is divided in two parts: the first part (subsection 9.5.1) analyses the formation of backward linkages and knowledge flows from MNC to domestic firms, drawing on statistics of MNC inputs' procurement at the local level and on survey data collected on the field. Subsection 9.5.2 explores upgrading at the micro-economic level by providing an in-depth qualitative analysis of MNC-suppliers relations on a sample of domestic suppliers. Section 9.6 concludes.

9.2 Costa Rica, FDI and MNC-clusters in electronics and medical device industries

Costa Rica has often been seen as an exception in Latin America, and especially in Central America. Unlike most other Latin American countries, it does not have an army, and it has been governed by a stable democracy for over 50 years. Partly thanks to its political stability, partly because of its social policies, Costa Rica has achieved the highest literacy rates and lowest poverty rates in Latin America. More recently, this country has also attracted the attention of academics and development practitioners for its economic policies (e.g. Ferranti *et al.*, 2002).

Since the 1980s Costa Rica has shifted away from import substitution industrialization, and pursued a policy of FDI attraction, aimed at increasing the valued added of its export base. Although Costa Rica's policies only started generating a significant increase in FDI flows towards the second half of the 1990s, FDI is generally considered to have been very successful in promoting non traditional exports and pushing a shift in the country's industrial structure (Monge-González *et al.*, 2005; Rodriguez-Clare, 2001; for a critical view see Ciarli and Giuliani, 2005). Quoting the OECD: "Costa Rica represents an outstanding success story of a small economy being able to increase and diversify its exports and attracting significant FDI inflows into its economy" (OECD, 2004, p. 68). As emphasized by the chairman of the Coalición Costarricense de Iniciativas de Desarrollo (CINDE), the local government agency specifically created to promote FDI: "not only have flows increased significantly in the past decade, but most have been new, green-field investment, in contrast with other Latin American countries, where part of the FDI has come from privatization programs" (OECD, 2004, p. 65).

A great share of the FDI that has flowed into Costa Rica since the late 1990s has been in high-tech industries (Monge-González, 2005), whereas in most of Latin America, foreign investors have targeted mainly resource-based industries and privatized utilities (Cimoli and Katz, 2001). Besides the country endowment of well-educated human resources and its economic and political stability, high-tech foreign firms have been attracted to Costa Rica by the special regimes guaranteed by the government in the so-called Export Processing Zones (EPZ). In EPZ,[3] foreign firms benefit from the same legal protection as national firms, they also do not pay any import taxes, and are exempted from income taxes for eight to 12 years. The number of companies operating in EPZ is estimated to be between 200 and 250, employing in 2002 over 35,000 people (Monge-Gonzalez *et al.*, 2005; PROCOMER, 2004). Since 1997, EPZ absorb around 45 per cent of total FDI per year, meaning that between 1997 and 2003 they have received each year an average of US$240 million of foreign direct investment. Since the second half of the 1990s, a great share of foreign direct investment has been in electronics and medical devices (Ciarli and Giuliani, 2005). This means that firms in these sectors manufacture products ranging from chirurgical tools to microprocessors or filters for mobile communication. Given the small size of the Costa Rican market, FDI in EMD is mainly export-oriented. In 2001, EMD exports amounted to 24.1 per cent of total export value (PROCOMER, 2002). More significantly, almost a quarter of Costa Rican exports are generated by EMD firms, which tend to operate in EPZ (Monge-Gonzalez, 2005). This wave of EMD FDI has generated employment opportunities for skilled labour, especially technical professionals such as engineers.

The localization of EMD multinational firms within Costa Rican territory has moreover given rise to a rather sectorally specialized industrial agglomeration, which we call here an "MNC-dominated cluster",[4] around the capital city of San Jose, where most of the industrial activities are concentrated. Within this territory there is no clear spatial border between the medical devices and electronics MNC subsidiaries that are situated within the ten EPZ existing in the country, located at a short distance from San Juan International Airport, in the Valle Central. Most of the MNC suppliers are also thereby located, specifically because the Valle Central is the business core of the country, endowed with better infrastructure, and where over 80 per cent of the Costa Rican population resides.

Overall, about 60 MNC subsidiaries were operative in 2004, and more than 80 per cent of investment was from the US (Procomer, 2004). Among the firms that have invested in Costa Rican EPZ, Intel (arrived in 1997) is certainly the most noticeable example. Intel has boosted the pace of FDI in EMD industries and has gradually increased the population of the EMD MNC-cluster, as also reported by the CINDE (2004). In a recent study, Altenburg and Meyer-Stamer (1999) found that MNC-dominated clusters in high-tech industries were a potential "growth pole" for the domestic economy in Costa Rica (see section 9.3.1). In order to explore whether this is the direction undertaken in Costa Rica, we analyse the linkages that are being formed between MNC and local firms and the impact that they have on the domestic economy.

9.3 Theoretical framework

9.3.1 MNC-dominated clusters and knowledge flows

The logic underpinning FDI attraction policies is that foreign firms can not only substitute for the scarcity of capital prevailing in developing countries, but they can also be an important driver for the development of organizational and technological capabilities of local firms.

More specifically, MNC subsidiaries are often associated with the generation of technological externalities through the "leak out" of relevant knowledge

(Blomstrom and Sjoholm, 1999), which may eventually enhance domestic firms' technological capabilities (Lall, 2001), and allow them to achieve efficiency gains. The generation of this type of externality is associated to several mechanisms. Among these, the formation of backward productive linkages with domestic firms in the host economy is considered here.[5] Backward linkages are often associated with the transfer of knowledge along the value chain (Blomstrom and Kokko, 1998). As argued by Görg and Ruane (2000), in developing countries "inter-firm linkages can have positive effects on the economy through the emergence of externalities, which result in the expansion of output of sub-supplier firms in response to the establishment of new manufacturing firms" (p. 218). In the same vein, Belderbos *et al.* (2001) stress that backward linkages "are associated with frequent information flows, which allow for quality improvements, reduced delivery times, and fast upgrading of designs in response to changing demand conditions for final products" (p. 190).[6]

The studies that consider FDI to be a source of technological externalities and a driver of industrial development are supported by empirical evidence about countries that seem to have managed a successful FDI-focused industrial development policy. Among them, Ireland, a country that Costa Rican politicians like to use as a benchmark, is one of the most cited. This is due to its success in building up a large and fast-growing Information and Communication Technologies (ICT) cluster through FDI attraction policies (White, 2004). In Ireland, MNC have been an important vehicle for the transmission of state-of-the-art technology to local firms via backward, lateral, and forward linkages (Görg and Ruane, 2000). The Irish FDI strategy is believed to have generated an ICT cluster, where the relevance and technological capability of local firms has steadily increased through time (White, 2004; Hewitt-Dundas *et al*, 2005). Besides the Irish case, there have also been successful cases of MNC-dominated clusters in the developing world, such as in Taiwan and Malaysia. In both countries, a policy of FDI attraction generated MNC-dominated clusters, where domestic firms have not only prospered, but gradually acquired complex technological capabilities and diversified into more sophisticated product lines (Lall, 2001, 1999, 1994; Contractor and Kundu, 2004; Pack, 2001; Kishimoto, 2003).

Altenburg and Meyer-Stamer (1999) provide a thorough description of MNC-dominated clusters, suggesting that EMD agglomerations in Costa Rica may be considered as such, because they show a high degree of specialization and inter-firm trade. However, they emphasize that the main weakness of MNC-dominated clusters is that, in high-tech industries, MNC operate at such a high level of technological sophistication that it generates a gap with the domestic industry, which is difficult to bridge. In other words, MNC-dominated clusters could potentially offer a great opportunity for local suppliers to access cutting edge technology, but they rarely do so. In this vein, Altenburg and Meyer-Stamer (1999) point out that in the case of the Mexican electronic cluster of Guadalajara, despite various institutional and grass root initiatives to promote a greater involvement of local suppliers, linkages seem to have remained weak and similarly poor was the generation of technological externalities.

The question for Costa Rica is whether these high-tech EPZ can become well-functioning MNC-dominated clusters, as is considered to have occurred in Ireland, Taiwan, and Malaysia, or if it will simply result in the formation of high-tech enclaves in the EPZ as in Guadalajara. More specifically, this chapter makes an attempt to follow up on Altenburg and Meyer-Stamer (1999) and addresses the following research question: Do MNC subsidiaries in the Costa Rican EMD cluster generate knowledge flows to their domestic suppliers?

9.3.2 Shifting perspective: the domestic suppliers and local cluster's upgrading

In this subsection, we shift the perspective of analysis and focus on the processes of upgrading occurring within the domestic suppliers tied to MNC companies. In fact, we believe that while it is important to analyse business linkages between MNC and local firms – measuring, for example, the amount of products and services purchased locally – it is equally valuable to look at the processes occurring within the local firms that operate in the MNC-dominated clusters (Lall, 2001). Do local firms effectively benefit from operating in MNC-dominated clusters by accessing cutting edge technology, foreign markets, information, and organizational techniques? Or do they benefit from it simply because of the business volume that MNC generate?

Among the different conceptual approaches to explore these questions, we adopt here the Global Value Chain approach (Gereffi, 1994, 1999; Humphrey and Schmitz, 2001). Scholars of GVC have been at the forefront of the research analysing the impact of globalization, or integration into Global Value Chains, on local firms and clusters. According to them, the globalization of value chains follows different logics depending on the technological and capital intensity of sectors. In sectors that are not capital and technology intensive, such as apparel, textiles, footwear, and the like, MNC tend to act as global buyers, retaining design and marketing activities, but not engaging significantly in production. These value chains are defined as *buyer-driven*. In technology and capital intensive sectors, such as the Costa Rican EMD, the decisional power concerning strategies, technology, and products is held by MNC that tend to set up plants abroad rather than simply buy from abroad, thus they are said to be operating in *producer-driven value chains* (Humphrey, 2000; Gereffi *et al.*, 2002). Producer-driven value chains are the context of analysis here. They have been considered an important vehicle of knowledge, as well as an important link to the international markets, for firms located in the developing world (Humphrey, 2000; Giuliani *et al.*, 2005). Using the GVC terminology, being integrated in a GVC, for example, by becoming a supplier within a MNC-dominated cluster, can be a key driver of industrial upgrading.

> The concept of upgrading refers to several kinds of shifts that firms or groups of firms might undertake to improve their position in global value

> chains. (…) It involves insertion into local and global value chains in such a way as to maximize value creation and learning.
>
> (Gereffi *et al.*, 2002, p. 11)

By way of its linkages to global actors, a firm may upgrade its position in the GVC by improving its product (product upgrading), and its processes (process upgrading), or by learning how to perform new functions, for example, developing product design or marketing functions (functional upgrading). However, becoming integrated in a Global Value Chain may also imply a set of limits on the strategic choices available to a firm such as the products it will develop, or the functions it decides to perform, depending on the extent to which the MNC exercises control over the chain (Gereffi, 1994, 1999; Humphrey and Schmitz, 2001).

In producer-driven value chains, MNC subsidiaries may have an interest in promoting the upgrading of their suppliers only as far as it increases the efficiency of their operations, and as far as it is not cheaper within the local trade regime to import rather than to procure locally their inputs. However, once MNC obtain processing or manufacturing efficiency along their value chain, they may not have any incentive to promote the upgrading of the functions performed by their suppliers, as shown by Bazan and Navas-Aleman (2001) and by Giuliani *et al.* (2005). If they operate in EPZ, their first choice will not be to promote the upgrading of local suppliers, but to attract "follow sourcing" – namely, FDI by their global suppliers. Follow sourcing, very diffused in high-tech EPZ, allows MNC to save not only on search costs – they do not have to look for local suppliers – but also on all of the mechanisms that regulate inter-firm relations, such as quality standards, systems of communication, etc. (Posthuma, 2001). Therefore, upgrading for local suppliers in MNC-dominated clusters is not an automatic process and, as suggested by Bell and Marin (2005), MNC should not be viewed as "leaky containers" of knowledge, generating benefits to the neighbouring firms just as a result of their localization.

As illustrated in section 9.2, FDI in EPZ in Costa Rica has initiated a process of formation of high-tech industrial agglomerations in EMD. FDI in high-tech EPZ *may* become a driver for the development of more advanced MNC-dominated clusters, not only if linkages to the domestic economy are formed, but also if they contribute to the upgrading of domestic suppliers. Otherwise, high-tech EPZ will evolve into highly efficient and technologically advanced processing zones with very few linkages with the local economy. Thus, the following research question is elaborated: What forms of upgrading are carried out by domestic suppliers of MNC in EMD? How far does upgrading (in all of its forms) result from the linkages that local firms have with MNC? This work looks at upgrading by dividing it into the categories "product, process, and functional", as suggested by the GVC framework. The aim is not only to assess whether there have been upgrading processes, but also to explore the mechanisms through which MNC subsidiaries may have promoted them.

To summarize, the chapter intends to explore the following research questions: Do MNC subsidiaries in the Costa Rican EMD cluster generate knowledge flows to their domestic suppliers? And, do local firms effectively benefit from operating in MNC-dominated clusters by accessing cutting edge technology, foreign markets, information, and organizational techniques? Or do they benefit from it simply because of the business volume that MNC generate? Finally, what forms of upgrading are carried out by domestic suppliers of MNC in EMD industries?

9.4 Methodology

The research draws on two sets of sources of firm-level data. First, we relied on the Costa Rican Foreign Trade Corporation (PROCOMER) data on the population of firms that operate in EPZ in the EMD industries. This database is primarily used here to explore the formation of backward productive linkages of foreign firms with domestic companies. The database contains information on the goods acquired by each EMD subsidiary in Costa Rica in 2001, 2002, and 2003 and the goods are classified using a six-digit level industrial classification (Harmonized Systems 1996 and 2002). Accordingly, it was possible to measure the procurement of subsidiaries and its industrial composition.[7] Drawing on Ciarli and Giuliani (2005), we use an indicator of "domestic procurement propensity" (DPP), defined as the value of goods procured in the domestic market divided by the sum of domestically procured and imported goods. Hence, DPP expresses how much of the inputs are acquired in the domestic market on the total inputs used for manufacturing. Moreover, the import and domestic procurement data have been classified according to the technological classification developed by Ferraz *et al.* (1992) for Latin American countries (Ferraz classification). As illustrated in the Appendix, this classification groups industries according to their degree of technological intensity, ranging from a minimum in the case of industrial commodities to a maximum in the case of diffusers of technical progress.

The second source of data is based on two original, separate, and sequential surveys, consistent with the double perspective of this study: first that of the multinational companies and, second, that of their suppliers. Both surveys were based on face-to-face interviews using structured questionnaires,[8] which took place between June and August 2004. In both surveys the interviews were directed at production managers or senior managers. The first survey was carried out using a sample of 26 EMD subsidiaries, drawn randomly from the population of MNC in the EMD industry in the Procomer dataset (see Table 9.1 for details). Apart from general information, a relevant aspect of the questionnaire used in this first survey concerned the collection of network data. The questionnaire adopted a roster study with a "free choice" design (Wasserman and Faust 1994) such that our respondents were asked to name the firms operating in Costa Rica, with whom they had established several types of relations.[9] In this study we use two types of relations: first the formation of backward linkages, measured by the existence of client–supplier relations, and, second, the transfer of inter-firm knowledge for the solution of technical problems related to the production process.[10]

Table 9.1 Sample features

	MNC subsidiaries (n = 26)		*Domestic suppliers (n = 20)*	
	N	*%*	*N*	*%*
No. of employees				
1–30	3	11.5	5	25
31–100	6	23	11	55
>100	17	65.5	4	20
Year of foundation				
1990 to today	16	61.5	8	40
1950–90	6	23	11	55
Before 1950	3	11.5		0
Missing	1	4	1	5
Type of activity				
Manufacturer	23	88.5	14	70
Service provider	2	8	6	30
Other	1	0.5	0	0

On the basis of this relationship, two different types of networks were constructed, which included both the EMD subsidiaries interviewed and the firms that they mentioned to have established a linkage with. For simplicity, each linkage maps the existence of a relationship, not its strength, so that all linkages have the same value across the network. Finally, the network data were pooled within two separate matrices, each corresponding to a different relationship (i.e. one for the backward linkages and another one for the knowledge flows).

The second survey was conducted to analyse the process of upgrading in domestic suppliers of EMD subsidiaries in Costa Rica. This survey sequentially followed the first one, an aspect that allowed a sample of 20 domestic firms to be randomly drawn from a list of domestic suppliers indicated by our respondents in the first survey. The sample includes domestic manufacturers of electrical equipment, precision mechanics, plastic moulds, and specific packaging material. It also includes providers of business software applications and services. The sample does not include the following type of suppliers: traders of imported goods, providers of security, legal, accounting, and transport services, suppliers of stationary, and other low value added office material and suppliers of food. Furthermore, our sample has been selected in order to have a roughly balanced representation of firms that supply MNC subsidiaries operating in electronics and medical devices. Among our sampled firms, 30 per cent are suppliers of medical devices and 40 per cent of electronics MNC, while the remaining 30 per cent supply MNC subsidiaries in both industries (for further details on the sample, see Table 9.1). Apart from general information, the questionnaire used for this second survey was designed to collect information on: (i) the development of new products (product upgrading), (ii) the modification of production processes (process upgrading), and (iii) the introduction of new functions (functional upgrading) in the last three years. We have also collected more qualitative information on the type of relationship they have with MNC subsidiaries, questioning whether the latter have promoted or hampered upgrading processes.

9.5 Empirical results

9.5.1 EMD subsidiaries, backward linkages, and knowledge flows

In this subsection, we analyse whether EMD MNC subsidiaries have generated backward linkages in the domestic economy. For this purpose, we adopt the indicator of "domestic procurement propensity" (DPP) defined in section 9.4. Table 9.2 reports the aggregate results of the propensity of EMD subsidiaries to source locally in 2001 as well as their average in the period 2001–2003, when data were available. In 2001 the value of domestically-procured goods is cumulatively of US$6.5 million and, in the same year, EMD subsidiaries have sourced locally an average of US$114,000 from an average of 45 domestic suppliers. The reported DPP in 2001 is 0.051, meaning that EMD subsidiaries sourced about 5 per cent of their intermediate inputs from domestic suppliers in 2001. Practically the same features are found on average for the 2001–2003 period, although a slight improvement of all the indicators can be observed.

Besides being limited in scale, locally procured inputs tend to be of poor technological content. Table 9.3 compares the technological content of domestically procured goods with that of imported goods. As explained in section 9.3, imported and domestically procured data have been classified using the Ferraz sectoral classification. As reported in the table, the procurement of domestic goods in 2001 has been concentrated mostly in "industrial commodities" (31.46 per cent) and "traditional sectors" (50.01 per cent), while only about 17 per cent of goods acquired on the domestic market are represented by the category of "diffusers of technical progress". Conversely, MNC imports are concentrated in those goods that are "diffusers of technical progress" (87 per cent), followed by "traditional sectors" (9.44 per cent) and "industrial commodities" (2.7 per cent).

Thus, if compared to the overall business value, EMD MNC subsidiaries in Costa Rica have rather weak backward linkages and are of poor technological content. These statistics are not entirely surprising. The literature reports many cases of "enclave" foreign direct investment, where the actual linkages established

Table 9.2 Domestic procurement of EMD MNC subsidiaries

	2001	*Average 2001–2003*
Domestic procurement (total, US$)	6,494,345	6,648,286
Domestic procurement (average per firm, US$)	113,935	122,424
Number of suppliers (average per firm)	45	54
Domestic procurement propensity	0.051	0.058

Source: Ciarli and Giuliani (2005).

Table 9.3 Technological intensity of domestic procurement and imports in 2001

Ferraz classification	*Domestic procurement (%)*	*Imports (%)*
1 (Industrial commodities)	31.46	2.70
2 (Agro-based commodities)	0.09	0.00
3 (Traditional sectors)	50.01	9.44
4 (Durable goods)	0.94	0.34
5 (Automotive sector)	0.07	0.01
6 (Diffusers of technical progress)	16.69	87.30
Missing	0.73	0.22
Total	100.00	100.00

Source: Ciarli and Giuliani (2005).

by MNC with domestic economies are weak. Remember, moreover, that these statistics do not allow domestically *manufactured* goods to be separated from the overall domestic procurement. This suggests the formation of business linkages that involve domestic manufacturers to be more limited than the one reported above.

This consideration is supported by the results of the original fieldwork, also visualised in Figure 9.1. It illustrates the backward linkages formed by MNC subsidiaries (square nodes) and domestic firms (circles). Each linkage maps the presence of a trade flow of inputs. Domestic firms are classified according to their activity, as manufacturers, traders and service providers. The figure clearly shows that only about a half of domestic suppliers are manufacturers, whereas the remaining half is composed mainly of traders of imported goods and a few service providers. Accordingly, domestic procurement of EMD multinational subsidiaries generates only a partial inclusion of the domestic manufacturing industry.

We explore now the transfer of knowledge generated by the sample MNC. As explained in section 9.3, knowledge flows are measured here by way of the informal technology of advice seeking and giving. This refers to inter-firm transfer of knowledge, done with the specific purpose of solving a problem related to the manufacturing process, or to aspects related to the business. The network of inter-firm knowledge transfer is visualized in Figure 9.2. This analysis is based on the Girvan–Newman algorithm that seeks to create clusters of nodes that are closely connected within, and less connected between clusters (Newman and Girvan, 2004).[11] As visualized in the figure, the network of knowledge transfer is characterized by the presence of four non-overlapping communities of highly connected firms. Each of these communities is highlighted in the figure by labels – i.e. Embedded, Quasi-embedded, and Enclave. These communities, three of which are linked together by a bridging domestic firm – indicated by the black circles – differ in many respects.

The largest community – the "Enclave" in Figure 9.2 – is composed mainly of foreign firms (square nodes), indicating that most of the knowledge diffused by our respondent firms flows within a restricted community of mainly multinational companies. In more detail, these are all subsidiaries of EMD companies, with manufacturing plants in Costa Rica, which have predominantly invested in

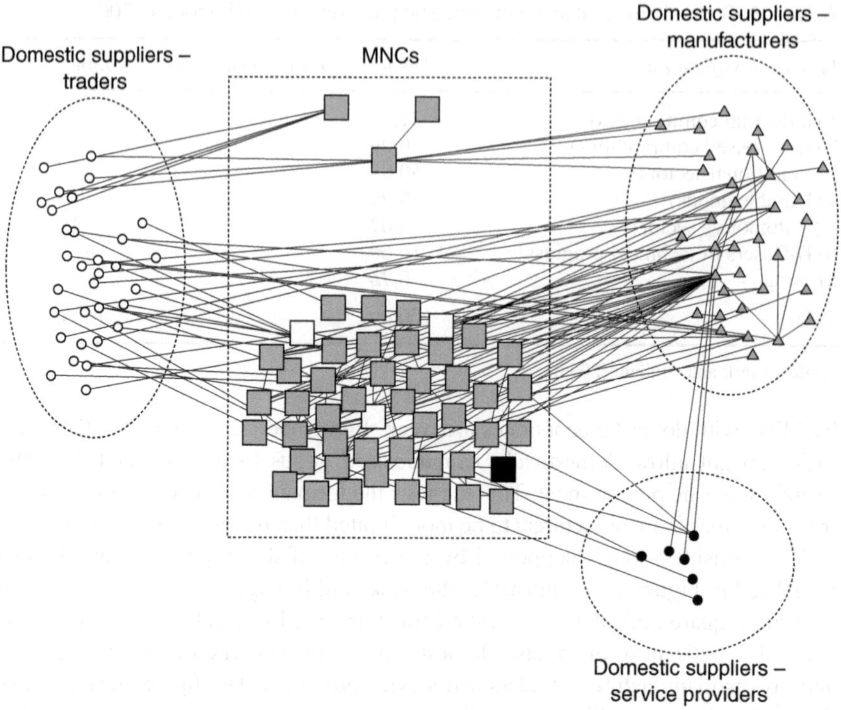

Figure 9.1 MNC backward linkages with domestic economy (source: our elaboration based on survey data using UCINET 6).

Note
Square nodes represent foreign firms, circles represent domestic firms. Grey nodes represent manufacturers, white nodes represent traders, black nodes represent

the country during the 1990s for *efficiency-seeking* purposes. The pattern observed in this group is reminiscent of what von Hippel (1987) defined as "know-how" trade. Some of the respondents in the "Enclave" group described these linkages as highly informal relationships through which information on, for example, plant maintenance, repairing, and the characteristics of domestic suppliers is exchanged. In spite of the fact that the survey was aimed at collecting network data on technical problem-solving, a lot of communication turned out to be of the type "who knows whom" or "who knows what" – i.e. of shallow technical content. However, in some cases, especially when subsidiaries share a similar technological specialization, more sophisticated technical knowledge on products and processes was transferred for problem solving purposes. Whatever the content of the knowledge flowing among EMD subsidiaries in Costa Rican EPZ, the relevant aspect here is that the subsidiaries taking part in this group have not yet created substantial knowledge linkages with the domestic economy, and are therefore still operating as a "technological enclave". This may also be due to their recent localization in Costa Rica and/or their limited overall DPP.

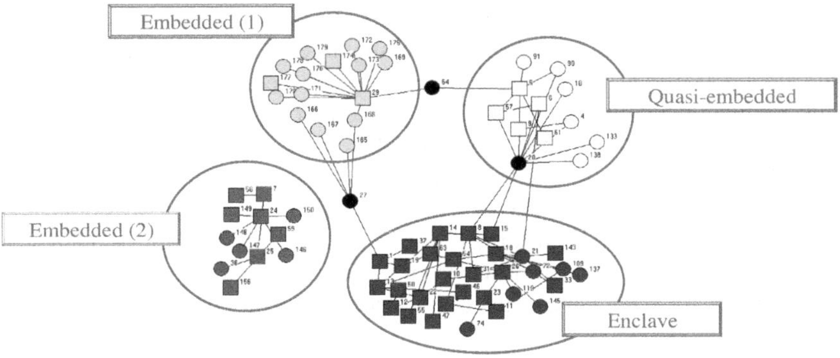

Figure 9.2 Girvan–Newman communities in the knowledge transfer network (source: our elaboration based on survey data using UCINET 6 (Borgotti *et al.*, 2002)).

Note
Different colours represent the communities of firms. Square nodes represent foreign firms, circles represent domestic firms.

A higher involvement of domestic firms in both technical advice seeking and giving is instead found in the smaller communities "Embedded (1)", "Embedded (2)" and "Quasi-Embedded". In the latter, five EMD subsidiaries have established linkages with six domestic firms, which operate mainly in the plastic industry (50 per cent), while the rest are equally divided among electronics, service, and metal-working. In the third community, "Embedded (1)", there is essentially one subsidiary, operating in the electronics industry, that operates as a hub of knowledge for the rest of the domestic firms in the subgroup. This subsidiary is a special case in this study being one of the first MNC established in the country (in 1950), following *market-seeking* purposes. Our respondent reported that in the firm there is a strong co-operative behaviour between them and their clients/suppliers in the country. However, he remarked that things have changed over time, "up until about ten to 15 years ago we had to transfer a huge amount of technical knowledge to our domestic suppliers, I was more of a 'professor' for them than for my employees. Now things have changed, in spite of the fact that we still have strong co-operative relationships with our long-standing suppliers, we do now select new suppliers on the basis of what they already are qualified to do and we are less keen to transfer technical knowledge as intensively as we used to do in the past".

A very similar case to "Embedded (1)" is found in the other embedded community ("Embedded (2)"), which is entirely disconnected from the other three groups. Here, one subsidiary, established in 1970 through the acquisition of a domestic TV producer, operates also as a hub, keeping the small groups of both foreign and domestic firms cognitively connected. More importantly, this subsidiary, now a producer of electrical switches and lamps, transfers technical knowledge mainly to its domestic suppliers of plastics, paper, and raw materials. It also visits them once a year in order to better understand their requirements and promote technical upgrading.

This empirical evidence seems to suggest that, with the exception of a few MNC – i.e. those of the "Embedded" communities – the vast majority of our surveyed EMD subsidiaries have not yet established substantial knowledge linkages with the domestic industry. On the contrary, they still seem to operate as a technological "enclave". There are, therefore, weak signs of knowledge flows being generated from MNC subsidiaries in the domestic economy, which gives a first indication of the fact that a well functioning MNC-dominated cluster has still not yet been formed in Costa Rica. This is further explored in the following section, which provides an in-depth exploration, on a number of selected domestic suppliers, of the characteristics of their upgrading processes.

9.5.2 The upgrading of domestic suppliers

The second research question – How is upgrading carried out by domestic suppliers of MNC in EMD? – is explored through a qualitative analysis of the information collected from the 20 suppliers interviewed, meant to shed light on the processes of upgrading domestic firms. Following the theoretical suggestions of Humphrey and Schmitz (Humphrey, 2000; Humphrey and Schmitz, 2002a, 2002b), we have used the concept of upgrading to highlight improvements in the quality or range of products offered by a given firm (product upgrading), improvements in the processes involved in the creation of the good or service produced, such as the adoption of new organizational structures or new machinery (process upgrading), and the diversification of the functions performed by the firm, such as the adoption of previously external design or research operations (functional upgrading).

First, we analyse patterns of product upgrading. Second, we investigate whether there has been an improvement in production processes. Finally, we explore functional upgrading, providing qualitative evidence related to the cases where it has occurred. After presenting a description of upgrading patterns, we question whether MNC have promoted it, and how they may have done so.

9.5.2.1 Product upgrading

Overall the firms in our sample seem to have been quite active in upgrading their products from 2001 to 2004. As indicated by Table 9.4, most of them (79 per cent) have introduced new products or improved their range of existing products (either increasing quality or introducing new characteristics and/or functions) since the year 2001. Seventy-three per cent of the firms, have improved the quality of their products, probably as a result of process upgrading, for example, adopting more rigorous quality control procedures or new machinery. A packaging material manufacturer, for example, introduced weather resistant labelling, and a higher range of colours for its labels, thanks to the purchase of more sophisticated machinery. The new products have been created to supply demand from MNC, but have also improved the market positioning of the local manufacturer in its local firms market: the average price per unit of packaging sold has increased as a result of better quality provided.

Table 9.4 Indicators of product upgrading

Indicators of process upgrading	*Total EMD (%)*	*Suppliers of medical devices MNC (%)*	*Suppliers of electronics MNC (%)*	*Suppliers of both electronics and medical devices MNC (%)*
New or improved products	79	50	100	85
Increase in product technological complexity	63	33	100	57
Improvement of product quality	73	50	100	70

Source: Own elaboration from the second survey.

A slightly lower percentage of firms (63 per cent) declare that their products incorporate more sophisticated technology when compared to their previous production line, indicating that there has been some improvement in the technological complexity of suppliers' products. Other suppliers, for example, a plastic mould manufacturer, affirm that the quality of their goods has increased, generally because it was required by MNC, but that the technological complexity has remained the same.

For all of the indicators of product upgrading, such as the introduction of new machinery or of new organizational structures, improvements seem to have been slightly more widespread among suppliers operating in the electronics cluster than among those operating only in the medical devices cluster.

MNC did not have to implement specific programmes to support the product upgrading of their suppliers. However, they required suppliers to improve the quality of their products in order to win new contracts. Domestic suppliers felt, and feel, a strong pressure to improve their products, as not only is there domestic competition, but the threat of "follow sourcing".[12] Thus, on the one hand, MNC provided incentives for suppliers to carry out product upgrading. On the other hand, most local firms upgraded their products autonomously, either to defend their position as suppliers, or to become suppliers in a context where MNC have no incentives to source locally.

Improvements in the quality of a firm's product often reflect both product and process upgrading. However, while, on the one hand, it is highly probable that quality improvements stem from process upgrading, process upgrading does not necessarily lead to quality improvements. Process upgrading can reduce the costs of producing a given good without actually improving its quality. Therefore, despite the strong inter-relation between product quality and production processes, it is necessary to analyse process upgrading as a different dimension of upgrading.

9.5.2.2 Process upgrading

Improvements in product quality are related to process upgrading: MNC often require their suppliers to obtain quality certifications, which imply improving

Table 9.5 Indicators of process upgrading

Indicators of process upgrading	*Total EMD (%)*	*Suppliers of medical devices MNC (%)*	*Suppliers of electronics MNC (%)*	*Suppliers of both electronics and medical devices MNC (%)*
Quality certifications obtained or pending	90	100	71	100
Adoption of quality control systems	79	83	71	83
Other organizational changes	36	0	42	66
Purchase of new machinery	61	50	100	33

Source: Own elaboration from the second survey.

the quality of the final good by implementing quality control systems throughout the whole production process. Thus, quality certifications, such as ISO 9000 or Capability Maturity Models (CMM), could be used as an indicator of process upgrading. According to this indicator, our sample of firms has performed well as 90 per cent of the firms have either already obtained quality certifications or are in the process of doing so (Table 9.5). However, firms may also implement process upgrading without applying for a certification. For this reason, we provide a summary of process upgrading by looking at certifications but also at other indicators, such as investment in new instrumental goods and adoption of new organizational techniques.[13]

In the survey we asked suppliers to indicate whether they have introduced various forms of quality control within production. Seventy-nine per cent of respondents confirmed having done so, with a lower rate of positive responses among suppliers of electronics MNC. The firms in our sample seem to have mainly carried out process upgrading in the area of quality control and certification. This stems from the fact that MNC impose strict requirements in these areas. Local firms upgraded their processes, generally without support from MNC, in order to qualify with the necessary criteria to become MNC suppliers.

A strikingly high percentage of suppliers of MNC in electronics (100 per cent) have purchased new machinery from 2001 to 2004.[14] This specific aspect of process upgrading did not result to be related to the requirements of MNC, but rather to local firms' perception of the importance of technology in their industries. As they put it: "operating in high technology, to have the most modern equipment is practically necessary to compete. You can't have less advanced equipment than your competitors, and new technology is developed everyday". (CEO and Founder, Supplier of electronics MNC, component manufacturer). Finally, only 36 per cent of firms have adopted organizational changes. Summarizing the results, MNC affected process upgrading mainly by creating a demand stimulus, and by providing specific requirements to which local firms had to comply in order to become

Table 9.6 Indicators of functional upgrading

Indicators of process upgrading	*Total EMD (%)*	*Suppliers of medical devices MNC (%)*	*Suppliers of electronics MNC (%)*	*Suppliers of both electronics and medical devices MNC (%)*
New functions	14	0	28	14
Marketing	14	0	28	14
Branding	9.3	0	14	14
Other functions	9.3	0	14	14

Source: Own elaboration from the second survey.

suppliers, especially quality certifications. MNC did not tutor their suppliers into process upgrading, nor did they finance such upgrading. The acquisition of new machinery generally resulted from local firms' will to remain competitive, rather than from the requirements of MNC, or from their direct technological assistance.

9.5.2.3 Functional upgrading

According to GCV theory, the most important form of upgrading is functional upgrading. During our interviews we asked firms to specify the functions they perform currently, and to point out whether some of these functions were acquired only recently. Very few firms seem to have acquired new functions at all (Table 9.6), and fewer firms have acquired them in the last three years. The only relevant instances of functional upgrading have been observed in three firms, two of them supplying MNC in the electronics cluster, and one supplying MNC that operate in both EMD. Interestingly enough, all of the three firms that have upgraded their functions are software producers. In order to explore the dynamics of functional upgrading, the next subsection provides a specific description of how the three domestic producers acquired new functions, and what those functions are.

9.5.2.4 Functional upgrading in the electronics cluster: positive signs from software providers

Costa Rica is endowed with a small but growing software industry. This had begun to develop before the wave of FDI, but has benefited from it, since a great share of Costa Rican software providers became suppliers of MNC. This section attempts to explain how three Costa Rican software providers have managed to upgrade their functions, and how related this process has been to the fact that they are suppliers in the EMD MNC-dominated clusters:

- Firm **A**, a corporate software producer that operates for both electronics and medical MNC devices, has recently diversified its range of products to the extent that it had to introduce whole new functions. Previously, it was only developing and selling software. Now it has installed a secure data storing system, in order to provide data management services to MNC. Performing secure data management functions has required not only the purchasing of new machinery, but acquiring expertise in managing a completely different business line, facing different competitors, and developing a different set of core strategic advantages. Thus, it has implied upgrading products, processes, and functions. The firm acquired expertise by hiring a team of external (American) consultants specialized in advising firms that provide data storage services, who had already advised various firms in India. The investment necessary to purchase machinery and acquire consulting services was realized by reinvesting profits, as in Costa Rica the financial market, which is not yet liberalized, does not offer solutions suited to the software industry, at least not in the opinion of the managers interviewed. When asked why it has diversified, considering the costs and risks involved, the CEO answered that it is in these nodes of the value chain that they foresee more potential for growth. Firm **A** has introduced new functions independently from its MNC clients. It is now in the process of negotiating new agreements as it wants to exploit its MNC client's distribution networks to sell its new data storage services. In this case being the supplier of an MNC does not seem to have been important for the upgrading process itself. The MNC did not provide incentives for its supplier to upgrade functions, nor did it promote such upgrading through technology transfers. On the contrary, it is not clear whether the MNC will let firm **A** use its distribution channels for its new services.

- Firm **B**, a software supplier of electronics MNC, has recently diversified its functions by becoming the certified franchise provider of consulting services on behalf of its MNC client in several Latin American countries, while still maintaining its core business. When asked to explain the reason for this diversification, the CEO of the company answered that these new functions are allowing the firm to have a steady income flow during the development phases of its software products, reducing risk and allowing for higher development costs and less time-constrained development periods. Firm **B** has developed as a corporate software producer, with a side business of ICT services stemming from the need to assist corporate clients. The most important MNC client, satisfied with the services provided, offered to its local supplier the opportunity to become its franchise service provider for Central American markets. Although officially it was the MNC to ask the Costa Rican firm to become its official service provider, unofficially the CEO of the local supplier had previously hinted at the idea to various top representatives of the MNC. Aggressive and risk-taking management was important for the local firm's functional upgrading. However, it was its linkage with the MNC that allowed functional upgrading to occur. The Costa Rican firm is still not providing services under its own brand, but it has benefited from functional upgrading in two different ways. First, it now has higher and more stable revenues, which have allowed it to increase its investments in R&D. Therefore, performing new servicing functions is allowing it to pursue a more aggressive technological development strategy. Second, it is acquiring expertise and know how in ICT servicing, capabilities that will not fade even if the MNC was to choose a different supplier in future.

- Firm **C**, another supplier operating only in the electronics cluster, has carried out functional upgrading, acquiring new branding and client management functions. Initially, the MNC outsourced to the local supplier certain software and IT servicing functions, which it subsequently sold, bundled with some of its products, under its brand. The MNC outsourced to its Costa Rican supplier part of the development and production processes of its value chain, while retaining all of the branding, marketing, and distribution nodes. During the last three years the supplier developed a new software and began selling it on the national market and in Mexico, without the assistance of the MNC, acquiring also branding and distribution functions. The MNC increased its interest in the product "When it saw that we could penetrate a market that is far more competitive and has far more potential than Central America" (CEO and founder of one of the top five Costa Rican software firms) and sought to acquire the technology. As a result, the MNC negotiated a different deal with its Costa Rican supplier. The MNC purchased the new technology from the local firm and began incorporating it in its products. In exchange, the MNC has gradually let the local supplier undertake all of the marketing, distribution, and client management functions for its products in Central America, stimulating a relevant process of functional diversification and learning. This amounts to an arrangement similar to a franchise, along the lines of the experience of firm **B**. The Costa Rican firm is benefiting from the MNC distribution network and brand, but is also learning how to manage a range of clients and markets with its own brand. In this case the upgrading was more significant, for the local firm managed to have its own brand recognized by the MNC rather than operate as a subcontractor – the process observed, for example, in the case of Intel with IBM and Dell. Now the local firm sells a bundled product in Central America with both its own and the MNC's brands. As a result, not only is the firm building its own brand and developing expertise in a range of functions it did not previously perform, but it is also benefiting from the credibility conferred by bundling its brand with the brand of the MNC. In this case functional upgrading resulted from the actions of both the MNC and its supplier. The Costa Rican supplier invested in R&D, developed a new technology, and attempted to sell it independently of the MNC, with the objective of shifting from being a subcontractor only to being a brand producer of ICT services. The MNC recognized the value of the technology developed, and helped the supplier upgrading its functions, by allowing it to use its distribution and marketing infrastructures. It was the MNC that proposed to the local firm to take

> responsibility for selling it together with their own solution under joint branding. The MNC, in this latter case, took an active role in promoting functional upgrading, although it possibly did so to avoid competition from its own supplier. The Costa Rican firm benefited from the partnership not only by exploiting an already established, high credibility distribution network, but also by acquiring know how in international distribution and marketing. Nonetheless, it is important to note that the MNC promoted the functional upgrading of its supplier when the latter had already began to acquire new functions. Thus, although the MNC did support and speed up functional upgrading, perhaps the Costa Rican supplier could have managed to acquire the same range of functions by itself. In this case as well, it seems that it has been the local firm's upgrading to affect its linkage with MNC rather than linkages with MNC driving upgrading processes.

Clearly, in all of the three cases that we have observed, local firms have acquired a certain degree of trust from their MNC clients, which have progressively let them perform more functions, and perform higher value added activities in the value chain. When asked about the process that lead MNC to trust them, the CEO of the three software firms answered that the most important thing is that they have proven to be reliable and to have a valid product from the technological side. However, they also all emphasized the importance of pursuing a strategy of investing in R&D, not only to develop new products, but also to explore the possibilities of process improvement and functional diversification. The CEO of firms **A**, **B** and **C** declare to invest between 3 and 5 per cent of their annual sales in R&D. However, they also emphasize that it is very difficult to define R&D expenditure, for in their industry most technicians and engineers employed are encouraged to continuously fine tune and improve the product (software applications) and processes (programming, architecture of the applications). Therefore, although there are in each firm on average 2–3 engineers specifically employed to search for product and process innovations, there are minor improvements implemented gradually along the product value chain.

9.5.2.5 What is the role of MNC subsidiaries in the upgrading of their domestic suppliers?

We have shown that in our sample the majority of firms have mainly carried out two kinds of upgrading: product upgrading, and those operations of process upgrading necessary to improve product quality. Other forms of process upgrading, such as the purchase of new machinery, or the implementation of organizational changes have been less common. We have detected signs of functional upgrading in only three software providers. In this section we try to evaluate how far the upgrading processes have been promoted – or hampered – by the MNC client in the EMD cluster. Accordingly, we have asked managers to

Table 9.7 Perceived importance of MNC for domestic suppliers' upgrading

Role of the MNC	*Irrelevant (%)*	*Little relevance (%)*	*Relevant (%)*	*Very relevant (%)*
Product upgrading	0	30	40	30
Process upgrading	0	30	45	25

Source: Own elaboration from the second survey.

evaluate the importance of MNC for upgrading processes using a 0 to 3 scale, where 0 means irrelevant, 1 means very little relevance, 2 means relevant, and 3 means very relevant. The results are reported in Table 9.7.[15]

In our sample, 70 per cent of all of the firms interviewed have considered the role of their MNC clients to be either relevant or very relevant both in the case of product and process upgrading. Only 30 per cent of the firms have considered the role of the MNC as having limited relevance, and none of the sampled suppliers regard MNC subsidiaries as totally irrelevant. Some of the firms that answered "Little relevance" explained to us that MNC did not promote or contribute to their upgrading. However, they still thought that by virtue of generating demand for their products, MNC have not been completely irrelevant. The majority of firms have evaluated MNC to have had a positive impact on those processes that GVC theory defines as product and process upgrading.

At first glance this result may seem to be striking. According to the analysis carried out in subsection 9.5.1, the transfer of knowledge from MNC subsidiaries to domestic firms is limited. However, the fact that domestic suppliers claim that MNC subsidiaries play a relevant role for both process and product upgrading does not contrast with the results of subsection 9.5.1. When asked to explain how MNC subsidiaries promoted their upgrading processes, local suppliers converged in emphasizing the role of MNC in providing incentives to upgrade. Such incentives rarely included the transfer of knowledge: local firms upgraded in order to become MNC suppliers or to expand their supply contracts. This does not necessarily imply that MNCs assisted them in their upgrading processes.

A more in-depth analysis of the product and process upgrading observed reveals that no significant upgrading occurred beyond the introduction of new products and the improvement of product quality. Although these may be important forms of upgrading, they do not necessarily imply a strong knowledge transfer from MNC. With the exception of software producers, a great share of the product upgrading and process upgrading observed has been the result of mandatory requirements that MNC have established for firms to become their suppliers. The following three quotes highlight why and how suppliers upgraded their products and processes.

> We introduced a new product line simply to adapt to our new multinational client. The new product is not necessarily any better, it is just more targeted to the client's needs, and production has been organized for higher volumes.

> Multinationals have been important for us because with them we grow much faster. For this reason we have bought new machinery.
>
> (CFO, software and service provider, supplier of electronics MNC)

> We applied ISO 9001 certification because we need it to be a supplier of firm X (a MNC operating in medical devices). After we began the process to get it, other multinationals asked us for the certification if we wanted to be their suppliers. We feel that the quality of our products was already sufficiently good before ISO, but you know, being a small firm in a developing country, you have to struggle to appear credible. Now we have also applied for another ISO certification, because it was suggested to us (by a governmental institution) as a strategy to be more competitive.
>
> (CEO, component manufacturer, supplier of medical devices MNC)

> They [MNC] gave us specifications for the part they need, and we adapted our machinery to make it. The main difference is that we get ten times the orders that we would get without them (MNC).
>
> (CEO, component manufacturer, supplier of medical devices MNC)

In most cases, new products were launched without technical support from MNC, while joint product development has been observed only in software firms. Only 35 per cent of our sampled firms have supply contracts that include technical assistance from MNC. Moreover, of those firms that do have contracts involving technical assistance, only two have effectively been assisted by their MNC clients in the adoption of new technology. Although the domestic suppliers interviewed upgraded their products as a response to demand by MNC, the latter did not take an active role in the process. The firms in our sample seem to consider MNC to be important for product upgrading because they constitute a growth factor, not because they are direct sources of knowledge that make upgrading possible.

In the case of process upgrading, MNC have required quality certifications. However, they have not provided the necessary funds or training to obtain them. Various external agents, such as the Inter-American Development Bank in the case of software producers, have provided financing for domestic firms that wish to obtain certifications. Third party consultants have been highlighted as the most common source of training used to obtain their certifications. Thus, as for product upgrading, MNC have created a stimulus for process upgrading for the suppliers interviewed, but they have not promoted it by transferring substantial knowledge and investing their own resources into it. Process upgrading did not occur through the linkages between MNC and local suppliers. The information collected during fieldwork suggests that most local firms could have upgraded their production processes without being MNC suppliers.

This evidence seems to suggest a scenario in which it is more common that linkages with MNC emerge because of upgrading, rather than the other way round: local firms upgrade so that they can try to become suppliers of MNC. Being an MNC supplier does provide advantages, but it is difficult for local firms to become a supplier in the first place, given that MNC do not have many incentives to source locally.

A final comment is given with respect to industries within the EMD MNC-dominated cluster. As a result of the second survey, we found that medical device suppliers have carried out fewer upgrading processes than the rest of the firms, and their upgrading has often been strictly related to achieving the necessary quality certifications to serve MNC. Consistent with this finding, no supplier in the medical devices cluster has found MNC to have been very important for product or process upgrading, and many – four in the case of product upgrading and three in the case of process upgrading – have deemed their role to be of little relevance. On the contrary, the suppliers operating in the electronics cluster have been the most successful in terms of upgrading. Not only have they introduced more products, but they have also purchased more machinery and acquired new functions.[16]

9.6 Conclusions

A reason why governments in developing countries make huge efforts to attract foreign investors and global buyers to operate in their countries is that foreign firms can be important drivers for the development of organizational and technological capabilities of local firms. More specifically, foreign firms are often believed to generate technological externalities in the host country through the "leak out" of relevant knowledge (Blomstrom and Sjoholm, 1999), which may eventually enhance domestic firms' technological capabilities (Lall, 2001), and allow them to reach various forms of upgrading. The literature on the impact of foreign firms on domestic suppliers is however controversial and the empirical evidence in this respect is still quite mixed (Rodrik, 1999; Görg and Strobl, 2001; Lipsey, 2002; Moran *et al.*, 2005). This chapter has made an attempt to contribute to this literature, looking at the impact of EMD multinational companies on local suppliers' upgrading.

This study sheds light on whether a well-functioning MNC-dominated cluster has developed after the successful Costa Rican attraction of EMD foreign investors. This is done with a double perspective: on the one hand, we looked at the behaviour of subsidiaries of MNC in Costa Rica and whether they produced backward linkages and knowledge flows in the domestic economy. As shown by Ciarli and Giuliani (2005), the propensity of domestic procurement was still relatively low and concentrated in low-medium technologies sectors. Moreover, we found that MNC do transfer knowledge to other firms in the country but this knowledge tends to diffuse within an enclave of foreign firms, with only a small number of domestic firms benefiting from it. On the other hand, surveying a sample of domestic suppliers of the MNC mentioned above, we found that MNC had an impact in fostering product and process upgrading in domestic firms, if not directly, indirectly generating a stimulus and a market. Consistent with Giuliani *et al.* (2005), our findings provide evidence of product upgrading and process upgrading, and very limited functional upgrading in the Costa Rican

MNC-dominated clusters. Only in the case of *software* producers, do there seem to be some promising signs of upgrading. In this sector, MNC have established a close relationship with the largest local firms. Not only have MNC invested in some of the local software producers, but in certain cases they have also assisted and promoted their upgrading of products, processes *and* functions. The three software firms that upgraded functionally are among the top five national ICT firms and were founded during the late 1980s and early 1990s. In their own words "it was the arrival of MNC that pushed our (national software developers) growth and leveraged us from the status of small software workshops". However, when MNC "arrived", there was already a small cluster of local software firms, with its own small pool of specialized workers. The MNC-dominated cluster may have boosted the learning processes of local firms and their revenues, but there also seem to be circumstances of MNC benefiting from finding a fabric of local firms that not only began operating as suppliers, but also eventually as distributors and as a training ground for the local workforce.

To conclude, we have here provided evidence that the formation of linkages between foreign investors and domestic firms is still an incipient process in Costa Rica. A certain dualism persists between the two (Ciarli and Giuliani, 2005), with the only exception being the growing domestic software industry. As a result, we could not observe a substantial conversion of EPZ into a well functioning MNC-dominated cluster, as Altenburg and Meyer-Stamer suggested in their 1999 paper. This study, however, leaves a number of interesting issues open to future investigation. First, the development of the software industry merits a more in-depth analysis, as this seems to be the most promising economic outcome associated with EMD foreign investment. Second, more accurate research should be carried out to measure the capabilities accumulated by domestic suppliers, especially in industries such as plastics and metalworking, which provide critical inputs for EMD companies. Finally, further research should shift from static analysis to dynamic analysis of networks, tracking the evolution of the linkages between foreign and domestic firms over time.

Appendix

Table 9.A1 Ferraz classification

Ferraz categories	*Illustrative 4-digit SIC industries*
Industrial Commodities	Dyeing and finishing textiles Paperboard Containers Industrial inorganic chemicals Iron And steel foundries
Agro-based Commodities	Canned, and preserved Fruits Animal fats and oils Grain mill products Sugar

continued

Table 9.A1 continued

Ferraz categories	*Illustrative 4-digit SIC industries*
Traditional Sectors	Meat products Bakery products Apparel Soap, detergents and cleaning preparations
Durable Goods	Household appliances Watches Motorcycles Bicycles and parts
The Automotive Sector	Motor vehicles Passenger car bodies Motor vehicle equipment
Diffusers of Technical Progress	Pesticides and agricultural chemicals Drugs Farm machines Machines tools Communication equipment Electrical industrial apparatus Aircraft and space vehicles

Source: Marin and Bell (2005).

Notes

1 The authors would like to thank Tommaso Ciarli for his help in the elaboration of the surveys' questionnaire and data analysis, and Alfredo del Pino for support in organizing the second part of the fieldwork. Thanks go also to Mario Cimoli, Andrea Morrison and especially to Roberta Rabellotti for their contribution at various stages of this project and for comments on a previous version of this paper. Financial support by the Inter-American Development Bank, CEPAL and IRES (Torino) is gratefully acknowledged. Thanks go also to Leiner Vargas and colleagues at CINPE Universidad Nacional de Costa Rica, to Ronal Arce Perez at Procomer, to Abraham Sanchez and the CINDE staff. Logistical support by INCAE is also gratefully acknowledged. All disclaimers apply.

2 This chapter is the result of a joint effort by the authors. However, it is possible to attribute subsection 9.5.1 to Elisa Giuliani and subsections 9.3.2. and 9.5.2 to Luciano Ciravegna. Sections 9.1, 9.2, 9.3.1, 9.4 and 9.6 can be attributed equally to the authors.

3 On the characteristics of Costa Rican EPZ see also Singa Boyenge (2003).

4 Industrial clusters have been given various definitions by the literature (see Martin and Sunley, 2003; Morosini, 2004; Giuliani *et al.*, 2005 for a review). In this chapter we use a simple definition based on pure sectoral and industrial agglomeration within a geographically bound area, consistent with Humphrey and Schimtz (1996). More specifically, MNC-dominated clusters are clusters where MNC subsidiaries dominate the value chain of the production process undertaken locally (Altenburg and Meyer-Stamer, 1999).

5 The focus here is only on backward linkages established with input suppliers. However, forward linkages are increasingly important for the development process of host countries, especially in those industries where marketing networks are crucial for

competitiveness (Gereffi and Korzeniewicz, 1994; Schmitz, 2004; Kelegama and Foley, 1999).

6 It should be noted that several studies on the impact of MNC on domestic firms for a number of advanced and industrializing countries, have produced contradictory results (Rodrik, 1999; Görg and Strobl, 2001; Lipsey, 2002; Moran *et al.*, 2005). Some have failed to find a significant effect for host countries' domestic firms (Aitken and Harrison, 1999; Javorcik and Spatareanu, 2005).

7 It should be noted that the rate of domestically procured goods is calculated on the goods that are acquired at the domestic level, but that are not necessarily manufactured in Costa Rica. For further details, see Ciarli and Giuliani (2005).

8 The questionnaires used for this analysis are available from the authors.

9 See Ciarli and Giuliani (2005).

10 In the questionnaire, respondents were asked to provide the name of the MNC subsidiary's main suppliers operating in Costa Rica and the name of the firms operating in Costa Rica to which the MNC subsidiary has transferred knowledge for the solution of technical problems.

11 The approach is that of "block modeling" (Wasserman and Faust, 1994). Rows and columns in the matrix of relations are moved to try to create "blocks" where all connections within a block are present, and all connections between blocks are absent. This matrix configuration constitutes a sort of benchmark against which the observed data are fitted. The best fit generates clusters of nodes, which describe the structural properties of the network observed.

12 The Quality Control Manager of a Costa Rican supplier described to us the threat of follow sourcing: "If we do not continuously improve our products, especially in terms of quality, our clients (MNC) may attract here their global suppliers. (…) Even if we offer better prices, these firms tend to have preferential agreements for they are suppliers of the (MNC's) headquarters, in their home-country". Quality Control Manager, Specialized packaging material producer, supplier of medical devices MNC.

13 Standard certifications may not be the best indicator of process upgrading and their importance differs from sector to sector. For example, in the ICT industry it is only recently that certifications have become an important requirement, with the diffusion of the CMM models (Capability Maturity Model for software), whereas in other sectors, such as electrical equipment manufacturing, ISO standards are an almost necessary criteria for local suppliers to be contracted by MNC.

14 Domestic firms operating in the electronics cluster may consider new machinery to be a more important form of process upgrading than other firms. However, it could also be a result of higher product clockspeed in electronics, which makes machinery obsolete faster than in other sectors.

15 We acknowledge that the analysis carried out is based on the subjective perception of entrepreneurs, which may be influenced by various factors not related to our research question, such as personal relations with MNC managers. Further research by one of the authors is currently being carried out.

16 Further research by one of the authors will explore this difference in greater detail.

References

Aitken B.J. and Harrison A.E. (1999) Do domestic firms benefit from direct foreign investment? Evidence from Venezuela, *American Economic Review*, 89(3): 605–618.

Altenburg T. and Meyer-Stamer J. (1999) How to promote clusters: policy experiences from Latin America, *World Development*, 27(9): 693–713.

Bazan L. and Navas-Aleman, L. (2001) Comparing chain governance and upgrading patterns in the Sinos Valley, Brazil, mimeo, Institute of Development Studies, Sussex, UK.

Belderbos R., Capannelli, G. and Fukao, K. (2001) Backward vertical linkages of foreign manufacturing affiliates: evidence from Japanese multinationals, *World Development*, 29(1): 189–208.

Bell M. and Marin A. (2005) The role of MNC subsidiaries in FDI-related spillovers, Paper to be presented at the International Workshop on Innovation, Multinationals and Local Development, Catania, 30 September–1 October.

Blomström M. and Kokko A. (1998) Multinational corporations and spillovers, *Journal of Economic Surveys*, 12: 247–277.

Blomström M. and Sjoholm F. (1999) Technology transfer and spillovers: Does local participation with multinationals matter? *European Economic Review*, 43(4–6): 915–923.

Borgatti S.P., Everett M.G. and Freeman L.C. (2002) *Ucinet 6 for Windows*, Harvard: Analytic Technologies.

Ciarli T. and Giuliani E. (2005) *Structural Reforms and Structural Change in Costa Rica. Industrial Dynamics, Structural Heterogeneity and Linkages: The Role of FDI*, BID-CEPAL Report, Santiago de Chile.

Cimoli M. and Katz J. (2001) Structural reforms, technological gaps and economic development: a Latin America perspective, *Industrial and Corporate Change*, 12: 387–411.

CINDE (2004) www.cinde.org.

Contractor F.J. and Kundu S. (2004) The role of export-driven entrepreneurship in economic development: A comparison of software exports from India, China, and Taiwan, *Technological Forecasting and Social Change*, 71: 799–822.

Ferranti D., Lederman D., Maloney W.F. and Perry G.E. (2002) *From Natural Resources to the Knowledge Economy*, Washington: The World Bank.

Ferraz J.C., Rush H.J. and Miles I. (1992) *Development, Technology and Flexibility: Brazil Faces the Industrial Divide*, London and New York: Routledge.

Gereffi G. (1994) The organization of buyer-driven global commodity chains: how U.S. retailers shape overseas production networks, in G. Gereffi and M. Korzeniewicz (eds), *Commodity Chains and Global Capitalism*, London: Praeger, pp. 95–122.

Gereffi G. (1999) International trade and industrial upgrading in the apparel commodity chain, *Journal of International Economics*, 48: 37–70.

Gereffi G. and Kaplinsky R. (2001) The value of value chains, Special issue of *Institute of Development Studies Bulletin*, 32, Sussex, UK.

Gereffi G. and Korzeniewicz M. (1994) *Commodity Chains and Global Capitalism*, London: Praeger.

Gereffi G., Humphrey J. and Sturgeon T. (2002) Developing a theory of global value chains: a framework document, *Global Value Chains Conference*, Rockport, Massachusetts.

Giuliani E., Pietrobelli C. and Rabellotti R. (2005) Upgrading in global value chains: lessons from Latin American clusters, *World Development*, 33(4): 549–573.

Görg H. and Ruane F. (2000) An analysis of backward linkages in the Irish electronics, *Economic and Social Review*, 31(3): 215–235.

Görg H. and Strobl E. (2001) Multinational companies and productivity spillovers: a meta-analysis, *Economic Journal*, 111(475): 723–739.

Hewitt-Dundas N., Andréosso-O'Callagan B., Creone M. and Roper S. (2005) Knowledge transfers from multinational plants in Ireland, *European Urban and Regional Studies*, 12 (12): 23–43.

Humphrey J. (2000) Governance and upgrading: linking industrial clusters and global value chain research, *Institute of Development Studies Working Papers*, no. 120, Sussex, UK.

Humphrey J. and Schmitz H. (1996) The triple C approach to local industrial policy, *World Development*, 24(12): 1859–1877.

Humphrey J. and Schmitz H. (2001) Governance in global value chains, *Institute of Development Studies Bullettin*, 32(3), Sussex, UK.

Humphrey J. and Schmitz H. (2002a) How does insertion in global value chains affect upgrading industrial clusters?, *Regional Studies*, 36(9): 1017–1027.

Humphrey J. and Schmitz H. (2002b) Developing country firms in the world economy: governance and upgrading in global value chains, *INEF Report*, no. 61, Duisburg: University of Duisburg. www.ids.ac.uk/ids/global/vwpap.html.

Javorcik B.S. and Spatareanu M. (2005) Disentangling FDI spillovers effects: What do firm perceptions tell us?, in T.H. Moran, E.M. Graham and M. Blomstrom (eds), *Does Foreign Direct Investment Promote Development? New Methods, Outcomes and Policy Approaches*, Washington: Institute for International Economics, pp. 45–72.

Kelegama S. and Foley F. (1999) Impediments to promoting backward linkages from the garment industry in Sri Lanka, *World Development*, 27(8): 1445–1460.

Kishimoto C. (2003) Upgrading the Taiwanese computer cluster: transformation of its production and knowledge systems, *Institute of Development Studies Working Papers*, no. 186, Sussex, UK.

Lall S. (1994) Industrial policy: a theoretical and empirical exposition, *Luca D'Agliano Working Papers*, no. 70, Oxford, UK.

Lall S. (1999) *Promoting Industrial Competitiveness in Developing Countries: Lessons from Asia*, London: Commonwealth Secretariat.

Lall S. (2001) *Competitiveness, Technology and Skills*, Cheltenham: Edward Elgar.

Lipsey R.E. (2002) Home and host country effects of FDI, *NBER Working Papers*, no. 9293.

Marin A. and Bell M. (2005), The local/global integration of MNC subsidiaries, their technological behaviour and FDI-related spillovers: Argentina in the late 1990s, Paper presented at Globelics Africa 2005: Innovation systems promoting economic growth, social cohesion and good governance, Tshwane (Pretoria), South Africa.

Monge-González R., Rosales-Tijerino J. and Arce- Apizar G. (2005) *Cost-Benefit Analysis of the Free Trade Zone System*, Washington: OAS, Organization of American States.

Moran T. H., Graham E.M. and Blomstrom M. (2005) *Does Foreign Direct Investment Promote Development? New Methods, Outcomes and Policy Approaches*. Washington: Institute for International Economics.

Morosini P. (2004) Industrial clusters, knowledge integration and performance, *World Development*, 32(2): 305–326.

Newman M.E.J. and Girvan M. (2004) Finding and evaluating community structure in networks, *Physical Review*, 69: 1–16.

OECD (2004) *Caribbean RIM Investment Initiative. Business Environment Report: Costa Rica*, Paris, OECD.

Pack H. (2001) The role of acquisition of foreign technology in Taiwanese growth. *Industrial and Corporate Change*, 10(3): 713–725.

Posthuma A.C. (2001) *Industrial Renewal and Inter-Firm Relations in the Supply Chain of the Brazilian Automotive Industry*, Geneva: International Labour Office.

PROCOMER (2004) *Estadisticas anuales*, www.procomer.com.

Rodríguez-Clare A. (2001) Costa Rica's development strategy based on human capital and technology: how it got there, the impact of Intel, and lessons for other countries, *Journal of Human Development*, 2(2): 311–324.

Rodrik D. (1999) *The New Global Economy and Developing Countries: Making Openness Work*. Washington: John Hopkins University Press for the Overseas Development Council.

Schmitz H. (2004) *Local Enterprises in the Global Economy Issues of Governance and Upgrading*, Cheltenham: Edward Elgar.

Singa Boyenge J.-P. (2003) *ILO Database on Export Processing Zones*, Geneva: International Labour Organization.

von Hippel E. (1987) Cooperation between rivals: informal know-how trading, *Research Policy*, 16: 291–302.

Wasserman S. and Faust K. (1994) *Social Network Analysis. Methods and Applications*. Cambridge: Cambridge University Press.

White M. (2004) Inward investment, firm embeddedness and place, *European Urban and Regional Studies*, 11(3): 243–260.

Part III

Sectoral and macroeconomical level

10 Macrodynamic capability

Concept and monetary and financial conditions[1]

Maria de Lourdes R. Mollo and Joanílio Rodolpho Teixeira

10.1 Introduction

A current assessment of the literature concerning dynamic capabilities shows an emphasis on microeconomic analysis, especially the ability of firms to implement organizational routines in pursuit of improvements and self-sustained expansion. The term dynamic capability (DC) is attributed to Teece and Pisano (1994). Notice that Teece *et al.* (1997, p. 517) define it as "the firm's ability to integrate, build and reconfigure internal and external competences to address a rapidly changing environment". In the studies above we see a preoccupation with the firm's motivation to prepare itself in terms of its knowledge base and its capacity to innovate and invest, to recombine capabilities and to develop organizational routines, in order to grow in a sustained form and in so doing to improve the economic performance. References on this matter are also found in Kogut and Zander (1992) and Zollo and Winter (2000). It means that this approach has a micro perspective, neglecting, to a large extent the macrodynamics of the system. In this sense, this analysis follows somewhat the tendency of mainstream that privileges the analysis of microeconomic aspects. Different from the mainstream, however, this approach – coherent with its Schumpeterian heritage – does not put emphasis on equilibrium.

Our chapter, however, will insist on the importance of a macroeconomic and institutional foundation linking investment, technology and the macro-management of the economy. Prosperity cannot be regarded as natural and expected as a matter of course. Nor can it be characterized by an afflux of new technology, business organization, financial flows, or whatever, unless institutional environment and historical conditions are proper. In a heterodox perspective, we will introduce and emphasize the concept of macrodynamic capacity, or macroeconomic dynamic capacity, stressing the macroeconomic foundations of the microeconomics – that is, the core and influence of the former on the latter's behaviour. To acquire this macroeconomic capacity it is necessary to prepare the macroeconomic environment, a process that we are calling macrodynamic capability (MDC).

Pavitt (1988) and Contwell (1989) seem to pioneer the extension of DC arguments to macro level, with reference to the absorption and diffusion of technology. As pointed out by Madhok and Osegowitsch (2000), significantly, they attempt to explain the international diffusion of learning through the degree of embedding of knowledge development and exploitation process in a country's institutional context. However, we argue, their task might be more problematic than may appear at first sight, since the micro-behaviours are mainly replies to the macro-environment, instead of being mere consequences of them.

Some studies of up to date mainstream economics have moved away from presumed free competitive markets, perfect information, etc. Some neoclassical authors are also giving increasing attention to incentives and to the creation of knowledge as a driving force for growth, as is the case of the papers of Aghion and Howitt (1992) and thereafter. However, they do not focus on aspects related to demand composition or monetary and financial dynamics. Furthermore, bastions of old orthodoxy are very much present in current teaching, research programmes, publications and economic policies. Instrumentalism, possessive individualism, substantive rationality, money neutrality in the short or in long term are still foundations of the neoclassical paradigm, as well as the belief in general equilibrium, provided that competition prevails. In this set up there is little room for the diversity of institutions across countries, the instabilities and inequalities related with the market process of regulation and the importance of the macroeconomic environment to improve development.

As pointed out by Basu (2003, p. 896): "But as soon as we enter the global market place, with no overarching system of law and government, we leave the textbook models behind (even the modern ones, which, though rich in other ways, are yet to properly characterize the role of power politics in the functioning of economies), and looking inadequate". Thus, there is the need for an alternative – involving a fundamental research programme different from the Walrasian economics – in order to deal with the reality of institutions and with the importance of a macroeconomic context that is not a mere aggregation of individual behaviours. Universally applicable formula on this matter is questionable, but the search for a potential contribution towards setting out a new theoretical scheme is desirable and relevant as an interpretative framework for sustained growth and fairer income distribution.

This is an ambitious objective since it not only seeks to place macrodynamic capability at the theoretical core of development strategies, but also attempts to revitalize the discussion of microdynamic capability, by calling into question its conventional framework based on a neo-classical cum neo-institutionist approach. We show that a heterodox structure may well provide a new foundation for the subject. Of course, our analytic concept of MDC needs to be further explored since it enshrines some multifaceted aspects of the political economy. Besides, there is a long journey to walk in order to establish certain mathematical and econometric relationships. Yet, we are confident that our contribution will be a positive and fresh gust of wind on the subject.

With the purpose of developing the concept of macrodynamic capability, in section 10.2 we will give an account of its definition, emphasizing its essential heterodox view and establishing some necessary conditions of macroeconomic dynamic capacity that need to be provided, by the process of macrodynamic capability. In section 10.3 we analyse, in particular, the monetary and financial aspects of macrodynamic capacity, following some lessons of five outstanding heterodox scholars, Marx, Keynes, Schumpeter, Kalecki and Minsky. Policy suggestions and concluding remarks are in section 10.4.

10.2 Macrodynamic capacity and macrodynamic capability

The preoccupation with macroeconomically-relevant aspects of capital accumulation and growth is well established in the evolution of economic ideas and contains fundamental heterodox components. Marx emphasizes the analysis of the accumulation process by appropriation of surplus and the relation between production and distribution. Schumpeter's vision is of surplus, created and destroyed in waves of technological change. Keynes insists on the importance of the aggregate demand and the liquidity preference. He also denied the possibility of the aggregation of microeconomic behaviours when discussing the "composition fallacy". Kalecki, in formal models, developed a macrodynamics of income distribution that shows the links between profits, investment and growth. Minsky, using Kalecki as a starting point, analyses the importance of financial conditions to the macroeconomic dynamic. The authors above share a heterodox view in the history of economic thought that differs from the generally accepted economic beliefs of mainstream economists, particularly, in what refers to the effects of the monetary and financial conditions, i.e. the importance of macrodynamic performance.

The orthodoxy, coherent with philosophical and methodological individualism, sustains the predominance of microeconomic behaviour in the interpretation of economics. Society is conceived as a set of individuals in the form of families and firms whose individual preferences are reflected in prices, thus conducting a collective equilibrium and justifying the market efficient allocation. On the contrary, heterodox authors conceive the microeconomic conduct of the economic agents as the consequence of a macroeconomic and institutional environment – despite the profound differences in their respective explanations.

Following Marx (1974), the economic agents behave as classes. The class behaviour is not gratuitous but it is the consequence of a macro logic of the capitalist mode of production, and depends on its profit's objective and on the origin of profit, imposing inherent laws of motion. Accordingly, the process of profit maximization is not a mere individual decision of the capitalist, but is an imposition of its role and place in society. The individual capitalist cannot, for example, satisfy himself with a determinate rate of profit, but he has to maximize it in order to sustain competition and be well placed to succeed in the accumulation of capital. The opposition between capital and labour, in the exploitation process, and the opposition among capitalists themselves are two fundamental forces to drive the movement of the socio-economic system. The investment process, or the impulse to accumulate, is inherent to the logic of capitalism. In this logic, money is particularly important as a social relation, because of the merchant character of capitalism.

Also Keynes (1936), in his General Theory and after, develops the importance of the macro context in the individual behaviour of the economic agents. It arrives when the notion of uncertainty plays its role. The economic activity is conceived as permeated by uncertainty, which explains the concept of liquidity preference and lends itself to an economic rationale. The macroeconomic conditions, in this sense, are particularly important to explain the investment decision and therefore the growth process. Even when some post-Keynesians recognize microeconomic foundations in the Keynesian conception, they sometimes fail to grasp that nothing is more heterodox in Keynes' analysis than the notion that uncertainty influences liquidity preferences. Actually, it is exactly due to the macroeconomic foundation of the explanation of microeconomic conduct that the State has an important role in the ideas of Keynes – in contrast to orthodox conceptions, in which the individual agent has fundamental importance behind the prices and the regulation presupposed by the market forces.

Kalecki (1971, and in a number of other contributions) worked out a heterodox theory of savings, investment and effective demand in which, unlike Keynes, he introduced distributive shares in income, technological progress, cyclical behaviour and degrees of monopoly. We may well consider that one of the basic differences between Kalecki and Keynes's theories is to be found in the emphasis the former gives to the role of distribution in determining expenditure and the latter accords to monetary factors. In other words, Keynes is treating distribution almost as a by-product, looking on monetary factors as part of the institutional environment for improving investment. Relevant aspects of financial considerations are less elaborated in Kalecki than in Keynes, as pointed out by Robinson (1979), although she stresses that the former emphasized the importance of the availability of finance for investment before the latter.

Schumpeter (1961) draws a clear distinction between economic growth and development. The former consists of a gradual process of expansion of output. That is, producing more of the same and using the same methods in order to do so. Economic development, in contrast, is a more dramatic and disruptive process. For him, the essential feature of economic development is not the incremental accumulation of new capital, but the mobilization of existing means of production for new uses. Credit and the presence of the entrepreneur is a *sine qua non* condition for the process to take place. By emphasizing the fundamental role of credit creation, as opposed to savings, in financing entrepreneurs, he distanced himself from the mainstream. In this heterodox phase, he is not interested in presenting the market economy as merely an equilibrating mechanism, changing only through external shocks. Instead, he seeks internal forces of the capitalist economy.

The concern with endogenous forces, inherent to the functioning of capitalism was also a characteristic of Minsky's studies (1977, 1982), when he refuses to explain its instability as a consequence of exogenous factors or errors of economic policy. For him such instability is a consequence of its financial process. The optimism in good phases of growth leads to the reduction of debt's prudence, which changes the financial structure from robust to a more fragile one. In this context, the reaction of banks with higher liquidity preference, raising the interest rate, may transform a liquidity problem in an insolvency crisis. In this vein he emphasizes the importance of liquidity conditions to avoid crisis and to improve investment, as well as the necessity of a State role of lender in last-resort and of regulator of debt's prudence.

Thus, by developing a macroeconomic perspective of dynamic capability, we are choosing a heterodox approach to analysis. We stress that it is fundamental to have a proper macroeconomic environment to sustain appropriate (productive) investment, to promote structural change, social and economic development. We also emphasize that such environment cannot be built autonomously or by the market system itself. In other words, the State needs to play its essential influence, since economic and political institutions determine the incentives and constraints in modern capitalist system-shaping processes and outcomes. Since different groups and individuals actually benefit from different socio-economic environments, there is typically a conflict over social choices, ultimately resolved in favour of groups with stronger economic and political power. It follows that the desirable way to treat this problem requires broad-based democratic institutions, with an active role for the government, empowering ordinary citizens to participate in the social decisions[2] and building a climate that facilitates investment, growth and development. The policies and practices to attain this outcome may well seem an unsolved puzzle or a daunting task, but the importance of its gains requires effort in this direction.

We call macrodynamic capacity or macroeconomic dynamic capacity, the set of characteristics that provides the possibility of a country, region or organization to grow and develop. Socio-economic initiatives, in this context, can not only be viable but have the potential to achieve much more if reinforced and surrounded by proper institutional conditions that defines macrodynamic capacity. Macrodynamic capability is thus the process of preparing or enhancing the environment of a country, region, sector or organization in the sense of stimulate and assure the macroeconomic dynamic capacity, or the possibility of investment, innovation, growth and social development, through structural changes. The macrodynamic capacity is an attribute of the economic system and depends on the ways in which the production and distribution are articulated to permit socio-economic progress. Macrodynamic capability depends on the society as a whole, but specially on the economic role of the State, since the market system is not able to guarantee this.[3]

As pointed out by Morishima (1992, p. 9): "production possibility sets are neither endowments that entrepreneurs inherited from their parents nor manna from heaven. They are produced by entrepreneurs themselves in collaboration with bankers and other financiers". So, there are necessary pre-conditions to the existence of macrodynamic capacity that have to be analysed. If DC, following a microeconomic perspective, presupposes operate routines generated and modified to pursue improvements and to achieve operational effectiveness, in our alternative approach the macrodynamic capability presupposes providing real, monetary and financial conditions to stimulate investment, innovation, growth and socio-economic development through structural change. Among the necessary conditions to be provided we can analyse, without being exhaustive: (a) the role of the State in economic regulation; (b) the conditions of demand; (c) the human learning, technological dynamics and their economic consequences; and (d) the monetary and financial conditions to improve development. The conditions (a), (b) and (c) are presented below. The condition (d), being the core of our argument, will be treated in section 10.3. All the last three conditions that define macrodynamic capacity need a State action in the process of providing macrodynamic capability.

10.2(a) The role of the state in economic regulation

Concerning the role of the State, it is necessary to mention its fundamental importance in articulating and implementing a democratic project of socio-economic development, which implies discretionary action. Public policies are important particularly in knowledge and innovation, not only as a condition directing economic forces towards productive investment, but also as a process leading to a less uneven and more socially inclusive society. The State must have a proper institutional role of listening to people and creating an efficient social network of protection. Once the development project is chosen, the role of State becomes the one of regulating and stimulating its consecution.

In this framework there are great differences between the concept of State necessary for providing macrodynamic capacity and what is known nowadays as governance, or public governance. Conceived in relation to the notion of corporate governance, the idea of public governance appears as a suggestion that the society can be run as if it were a firm, with public administrations adopting pay-per-performance programmes (Frey and Benz, 2004). It is, in this sense, a neo-liberal idea. Its general view of governance is based on general principles about choice of authority and the ability of the governments to implement an environment characterized by respect for the rule of law, accountability, democratic institutions, fairness and equity in dealing with citizens, efficient and effective services, transparent and applicable law and regulations, consistency and coherence in policy formulation and high standards of ethical behaviour. They are all principles to stimulate efficiency in governmental actions, to regulate actors in the public sphere and, hence, it is a micro principle.

The differences between public governance and the role of the State on macrodynamic capability is both of political and theoretical orders. Among the prevailing views about governance we encounter the State economic intervention in the market conceived as market-unfriendly policies (Kaufmann *et al.*, 2004) and public administration is viewed as inefficient due to rent seeking activities, in an obvious neo-liberal perception. Here, on the contrary, despite some well known operational difficulties, we stress that the State economic intervention is necessary to improve socio-economic development in capitalism and to do that it needs to induce sound reorientations in the market logic and to regulate the latter's behaviour. Legal and regulatory regimes as well as financial development are among the more important conditions in the process of resource creation.[4] Needless to say that "there is no historical case of successful late industrialization, either in the nineteenth or in the twentieth century, which did not depend upon State support in the form of promotion and protection of domestic industry", as pointed out by Bhaduri and Nayyar (1996, p. 14).

Ribeiro and Teixeira (2001) reveal, with an econometric model dealing with the private-sector investment that, apart from the positive influence of output and the negative one of uncertainty (risk), the following has been shown, among other aspects, in the case of Brazil during the 1990s: (i) the relevance of long-term credits from development banks; (ii) the predominance of a "crowding-in" effect that public investment has on private investment in the long run (with "crowding-out" in the short run). Furthermore, measures involving large devaluations of the exchange rate or cuts in public investment are detrimental to capital formation. Consequently, the conventional recommendations towards reductions of the role of the State in the allocation and creation of resources are highly questionable. Quite contrary, the revival of sustained economic growth and the establishment of sound macrodynamic capacity require the State to be recognized as a fundamental source to promote development, thus ensuring its place in the organization of the economic system.

10.2(b) The conditions of demand

Another heterodox characteristic of our conception of macrodynamic capability can be seen in our treatment of effective demand. The pace of investment depends on the demand (actual and prospective) conditions and not, as it is the vision of the orthodox thought, on the supply side. Demand plays an essential role in the formation of expectations, in the decisions to invest and in the developing pattern to be adopted. In our MDC conception there is, certainly, a potentially and advantageous role for the State in the planning and regulation of the development process, because it can influence distribution and so creating the demand conditions to enable the economy to develop. This view is quite different from mere counter cyclical intervention, despite some frustrations, distortions and troubles frequently encountered in the actual implementation of planning decisions.

According to the standard structural economic dynamic approach, technical progress (or innovation) raises the productivity and increases per capita income. But this higher purchasing power is not actually translated into a proportional increase of demand for different goods and services due to the Engel's Law. Hence, the changes in the composition of demand will give rise, in the side of production, to variations in the sectoral composition of the output and the process cannot be well conducted in distributional terms without some form of intervention in the market mechanism by an intelligent and sensitive government.

A desirable process of MDC is not a state of affairs to be reached at some future time-period but represents the system-governed part of socio-economic reality at any moment in time. As a matter of fact the short-period income elasticity of demand is different for the various types of goods, and capacity utilization will deviate in varying degrees in different sectors of production. In a growing economy, with expansion of per capita income, due to the Engel's curves, expectations held by individual agents, financial and institutional conditions, play a major role. Dealing with dynamics of prices and quantities of individual firms, Bortis (1997, p. 234) stresses some of the troubles encountered: "for instance, changing behaviour of competitors in the spheres of marketing and pricing to obtain larger market shares, unpredictable changes in consumers' behaviour, unexpected changes in government expenditures influencing short-period effective demand and so on". These changes need to be regulated and managed by economic policy.

10.2(c) The knowledge and technological structure

There is no doubt that the link between the structure of the economy, human learning and the diffusion of knowledge is an important issue. Analytical considerations on these relations can raise up interesting insights on the debate over "appropriate technology" and economic performance. Uni-sectoral and bi-sectoral models of growth cannot address the issues related to changes in preferences and different patterns of technology adoption and learning at the sectoral levels. Needless to mention that the creation of macrodynamic capacity to attain sustained development may be obstructed by the institutional structure that does not provide proper stimulus to the acquisition of knowledge and technical progress. According to Pasinetti (1993, p. 176):

> It is therefore at the stage of transmission and diffusion and acquisition of knowledge that the relations among nations must find their focal point. Those nations that remain behind have to speed up (and indeed must be helped to speed up) their processes of individual and social learning.

The same can be said about the education and knowledge conditions to the low income people and regions in a country. State needs to play a major role on this matter. That is, through the creation of a favourable structure, investing, regulating and stimulating conditions directed to the construction of its democratic project of technological and social organization.

On this structure depends the development of production, which has to be articulated with a general economic strategy and, in particular, with sectoral and regional policies. In other words, economic performance depends not only on the content on the plan chosen, but on the system of functioning and the support of society. Changes in the model of functioning is not a priori assumed to be inconsequential, nor are we assuming that macrodynamic capability is propelled exclusively by knowledge, investment and technological progress. However, it is essential, in order to stimulate the wealth of a nation and the welfare of its citizens.

Before introducing the next section, it is better to clarify a few points. First, that a planning guide focusing on the allocation of resources and directed to economic development is, to a large extent, a political problem. Marx (1978, p. 595) pointed out that: "Men make their history, but they do not make it just as they please; they do not make it under circumstances chosen by themselves, but under circumstances directly found, given and transmitted from the past". It is important, however, to insist on improving these circumstances.

Second, as a matter of fact, there are no solutions "prêt-a-porter" for the crucial problems encountered in most of the developing countries. Nevertheless, it is important not to confuse realism with pessimism. Kalecki, for instance, was a trenchant critic of governments overstepping the limits of their own ability to deliver real outcomes, but always insisted on the importance of some sort of planning. On this matter, in order to provide macrodynamic capacity, some controls that operate more directly on motivation and the conduct of society's behaviour seem to us highly recommended. To proceed in this direction, industrial, financial and fiscal policies have a central influence. Micro-goals and activities consistent with the macro-goals would reduce business uncertainty, enabling a more efficient and dynamic pattern of development. This may be achieved through strategic guidelines, increasing relevant information as well as financial support to desirable investment. The validity of such an approach depends on many points, including the impact of investment coming from demand, as indicated by Verdoorn's Law, as well as the importance of effective demand for the configuration of consumption patterns, i.e. Engel's Law.

10.3 Monetary and financial conditions of macrodynamic capacity

The heterodox foundation of the monetary conditions of macrodynamic capacity is an emphatic characteristic of this article. Contrary-wise to mainstream economics that sees money as neutral, here the neutrality of money is denied. The capital accumulation, following Marx, Schumpeter, Kalecki, Keynes and Minsky, is conceived as always preceded by money that anticipates investment, technological progress, productivity and growth, with credit amplifying it. In other words, money and finance are privileged in their analysis. The orthodoxy, in opposition, understands the economic growth as stimulated by preferences and technology that change supply and demand, and sees the credit as a mere transfer from savers to investors.

In Marx (1974, vol. I), for instance, it is money that opens the cycle of capital reproduction and closes it. Money in the hands of the capitalist allows him to buy the labour force as a commodity, and explores it, so obtaining surplus-value and profit. It is credit that amplifies the scale and the rhythm of accumulation because it anticipates the investment. Credit is also important in the reduction of circulation costs, augmenting profits and giving force to capital accumulation. Surely, credit also amplifies the contradictions inherent in capitalism, aggravating potential (and real) crises. In this framework we see the functioning of non-neutrality of money. He also stresses that by the formation of stock companies, credit leads to "an enormous expansion of the scale of production and of enterprises, that was impossible for individual capitals" (Marx, 1974, vol. III, p. 482). When analysing the relation between money-capital and real-capital he concludes that "the maximum of credit is here identical with the fullest employment of individual capital, that is the utmost exertion of its reproduction power without regard to the limits of consumption" (Marx, 1974, vol. III, p. 482).

Accordingly, the rate of interest is the fruit of competition between capitalists, where the power of establishing it varies with conjuncture or with the rhythm of affairs. The supply of credit by the financial capitalist and the demand of credit by the industrial capitalist change with the conjuncture and define the interest rate. In the beginning of a cycle the supply of credit is vast. However the interest rate increases in the process of economic growth, attaining its summit before the breakdown of business cycle, with economic agents trying to take cover behind ready cash. Marx (1974, vol. III, p. 361) points out that: "The rate of interest reaches its peak during crises, when money is wanted at any cost to meet payments". Ready cash is then desired as such, not to buy goods to be invested in productive activities, but as value *par excellence*, showing in another way the importance of money.

Sylos-Labini (1984, p. 58) argues that:

> The explanation given by Marx for the increase of what today is called liquidity-preference seems to be more adequate than that advanced by Keynes. In a nutshell, for Marx the increase in liquidity preference is typically an effect of crisis, which in its initial phase takes precisely the form of monetary crisis.

From this argument it follows that money and credit have specific roles during the different stages of innovative business activities and business cycles.

Marx conceives an endogenous notion of money that is born to satisfy both production and circulation of commodities, and its volume adjusts itself to the business needs (Mollo, 1999). He does not dissociate saving and investment reasons related to the accumulation process. Banks can exaggerate the quantity of credit supplied, what is related with the development of "fictitious capital" (De Brunhoff, 1998). Such exaggeration means a separation between production and circulation that can last for a while, but is limited. The time of duration of this separation shows, in another way, the role of credit anticipating and stimulating production, differently from the mainstream approach which views the process in real terms as mere transfers of savings to investors.

Keynes (1937a, 1937b), in his more heterodox phase, also insisted on the importance of money and credit to allow the investment's decision and the growth of production. He emphasizes this role, comparing the greater importance of liquidity in relation to saving, introducing the finance motive for demand of money. He insists that saving can exist without being transformed into investment, which can be financed without previous savings by credit created *ex nihilo* from banks. As pointed out by Chick (1994, p. 400): "The crucial element here is that banks can create money without prior saving and so reverse the causality between saving and investment". If the concession of credit is done with interest rates compatible with the return on capital, investment starts and the process of investment, via multiplier effect, guarantees the quantity of savings necessary to equal investment ex-post, after the growth of income.

The role of savings in Keynes conception also clarifies the necessary financial conditions for funding the investment. He emphasized the necessity of finance with different possibilities of placements to get compatible the different liquidity preferences of savers who will lend their funds and the time interval to completion of the investment that will be funded. What is important, in this case, is not the quantity of savings but its allocation. If the liquidity preference is high, it will inhibit investment, not only because money will not be loaned in adequate conditions, but because the savings will be placed in short-term assets and therefore long-term investment will not be viable. We see here that Marx and Keynes present substantial reasons for the importance of money.[5]

As we have mentioned in the previous section, another heterodox conception about money is that of Schumpeter. For him innovation is fundamental in the development of structural changes, but innovation needs an anticipation of credit to be viable. The entrepreneur changes the routine, introducing an innovation that needs additional money. The new production must be financed by banks' credit, created *ad hoc* without previous savings. Even the entrepreneur's imitators need new credit to attend longer delays of the new production and await its outcome. According to Schumpeter (1961, p. 107):

> [Banks] granting credit in this sense operates as an order on the economic system to accommodate itself to the purpose of the entrepreneur, as an order on goods which he needs: it means entrusting him with productive forces. It is only thus that economic development could arise, from mere equilibrium. And this function constitutes the keystone of the modern credit structure.[6]

Kalecki (1971, p. 14), following Marx, notes that there is "a close connection between the phenomenon of the business cycle and the response of the banking system to the increase in demand for money in circulation at a rate of interest which is not prohibitive to the rise in investment". It follows that the banking system holds the key to expansion in their willingness to meet the increase in transactions demand and this is clearly a "technical monetary problem".[7] Minsky, following Keynes, emphasizes bank's expectation of profits in explaining the pace and the conditions of credit. In the case of Kalecki, although he considers expectations, the main determinants of credit are in the past, and to Keynes they are, fundamentally, in what is expected in the future. In this sense, Kahn (1984, p. 159) argues that:

> Keynes' insistence on the overwhelming importance of expectations, highly subject to risk and uncertainty, was one of his biggest contributions. On the

other hand, Kalecki brought into the argument a point, which cannot be ignored in the theory of investment: the outside finance that a firm is able to obtain is largely determined by the amount of resources owned by the firm itself due to the problem of "increasing" risk.

The view that the financial sector plays an essential role in the economic process is thus shared by the five outstanding economists discussed above, and emphasizes the non-neutral character of money.[8] Marx not only defines capital as money that transforms itself in both means of production and working force that increase the value of commodities, but he also discerns that credit, as such, "potentializes" the accumulation of capital. Accordingly, the social character of capital is mediated and completely realized only by the full development of the credit and the banking system. Keynes (1937a, p. 210) observes that any investment carried out by entrepreneurs is, ex-post facto, covered by savings generated, regardless of whether there is, or there is not, the ex-ante support of previous savings. Accordingly, "it is to an important extent the 'financial' facilities which regulate the pace of new investment". According to Schumpeter (1934, p. 102), the entrepreneurs need to get purchasing power "in order to produce at all, to become an entrepreneur. He can only become an entrepreneur by previously becoming a debtor".

Morishima (1992, p. 22), however, conceives a difference between Schumpeter and Keynes, because "in the former the entrepreneurs cannot make innovation without the help of bankers..". and "in the latter the entrepreneurs can make their own decisions on investment independently of bankers". But even if the entrepreneurs can invest without borrowing, Keynes (1937b, p. 222) says that

> banks hold the key position in the transition from a lower to a higher scale of activity. If they refuse to relax, the growing congestion of the short-term loan market or the new-issue market, as the case may be, will inhibit the improvement, no matter how thrifty the public purpose to be out of their incomes.

Kalecki equations show how gross capital income is related to investment, government spending, foreign balance, consumption financed by profits and savings after income. Minsky (1977, p. 30) develops the idea of the importance of finance conditions, saying that

> in a capitalist society the terms on which bankers (broadly defined to include commercial, investment and merchant bankers) finance positions in capital assets and the production of investment output are critical determinants of system behaviour. Such financing directly affects profits and thus whether or not current income validates the inherited liability structure.

The point we would like to stress here is the centrality of monetary and financial conditions and of institutional environment in determining the core of macrodynamic capacity. This is the main reason why we emphasize the need for a coherent account of how and why money, finance and credit matter in the stimulus and viability of investment, therefore, in the innovation process. In essence, to improve organizational macro-capability means the transformation of the economic structure in order to achieve new levels of productivity, which requires higher levels of investment. We take the view that advanced economies are somewhat accurately seen as "synergetic and organic systems" in which change is cumulative, while the notion of peripheral economies itself implies a "dualistic and asymmetrical pattern".[9] The problem, then, is one of breaking out the trap into cumulative growth. Any relatively small-scale effort designed to generate gradual macrodynamic capacity will be inadequate. The actual solution lies in a critical minimum effort in which the scale of increased investment enables a country to achieve and sustain structural change. The role of money and financial conditions must be incorporated into the proper account of this dynamics.

To improve monetary and financial conditions and generate macrodynamic capacity we need, first, sufficient liquidity to finance investment in good terms relative to the expected profits. Second, that financial market development is needed to provide the funding of the investment. But to assure these two conditions, monetary policy needs to control the short-interest rate at low levels, to allow the finance loans necessary to make investment decision viable and to guarantee that the long-term interest rates are higher than the short-term rates – that is, the need for a liquidity premium to recompense the savers who decide to lend for refusing liquidity in an uncertain environment.[10] But long-term interest rates cannot be higher than the expected rate of return on investment, otherwise investment will be inhibited. It becomes evident here the role of monetary policy in macroeconomic capability of the economy.

It is important to observe, however, that the authors we have mentioned here, as our starting point, called attention not only on the positive impacts of credit amplifying and accelerating investment and production but also in relation to crisis. That is, the case with the notion of "fictitious capital" in Marx's analysis,[11] and the growth of speculation in Keynes's analysis; the same arriving in Minsky's studies of financial fragility and instability of capitalism. In all cases there is a negative effect of an excess or a speculative development of finance with the development of credit and financial system.

But the control of credit, in its turn, can also be dangerous, in terms of aggravating the difficulties of selling, reducing investment and starting a financial crisis in the economy (Minsky, 1982). It is interesting to notice that Keynes (1937a, pp. 210–211), when discussing banks' leading role, argued that "the control of finance is, indeed, a potent, though sometimes dangerous, method for regulating the rate of investment (though much more when used as a curb than as a stimulus)". Control of credit is thus more potent in order to break the investment than to stimulate it, because even when there is sufficient supply of liquidity the uncertainty about prospective earnings can reduce investment. This shows that the monetary and financial context requires the fine tuning of economic policy to improve credit without exaggerating it.

Our analysis shows the necessity of contemplating not only the positive but also the problematic impacts of finance on building an adequate financial context on MDC. This implies not only stimulating but also regulating finance. In some countries, the major problem is the high interest-rate – in particular, high short-term interest rates, as one outcome of the management of public debt. This inhibits medium- and long-term placements of savings and consequently the sustained medium- and long-term investment funding. But with the prevailing neoliberalism, especially in the last three decades, we have problems with finance all over the world. The high interest rates and the so called "financialization" of the global economy engender the gains of "financial capitalist" or "rentiers", in disfavour of productive investment.

As emphasized by Plihon (2002), a substantial part of investment, nowadays, is self-financed, which means that it is financed out of retained profits (savings) and out of new-issues in the financial market. In the present regime of finance the shareholders gain importance (in particular, the institutional funds), introducing a different logic of enterprise's management. The objective of the shareholders is to raise the firm's equity values, or raise the return on equity, objectives not always compatible with the enterprise's productive logic. Actually, what improves equity returns is a set of mergers, re-purchase of equities, and practices of management that are not actually designed to improve production. In addition, the stock-exchange market does not always bring new money to the enterprises, exactly because its gains are transformed in distributed dividends and re-purchases of equities to raise its return. This shows how Marx and Keynes can still explain today's financial practices with the notions of fictitious capital and of speculative logic, thereby showing the relative autonomy of financial capital in respect to real production.

This type of financial regime is a consequence of what Chesnais (2004) calls the "insatiability" of finance that is responsible for a desired return of shareholders that is incompatible with productive activity. This is in the origin of crises, capital's concentration, inequalities, and explains the low pace of investment and economic growth during the last decades.[12] Another negative and still more serious effect of this financial regime is on the real wages, that grow less than productivity, as a result of the small rate of investment and high unemployment. Total wages fall to compensate the rise of financial costs and to avoid reductions of profits (Plihon, 2002; Salama, 1996).

All these negative consequences of a conspicuous financial environment show once more the importance and the necessity of a State's regulation of finance and the role of economic policy in general to expand productive investment and employment, and to improve wages share, interviewing in capital–labour relations. In this respect, Minsky (1982) inspires us, with his suggestion of the role of State on Central Bank's role of lender on last resort, to abort financial crisis, and also to avoid it with prudential regulation and control. This type of role requires first of all a system of fine tuning management of monetary instruments, to feel and attend to the monetary and financial needs of the economy in relation to the macroeconomic policy in general. When money is conceived as non-neutral, it is imperative to maintain coordination and complementarity between monetary, fiscal, industrial and regional policies, looking for improvement in social and economic development (Dow, 1987; Chick, 1998; Dymski, 1993; Pollin, 1993; Wray, 1998, 2000).

In these conceptions money is endogenous in the sense of a money and credit supply reacting to the demands of economic society (business cycles and liquidity preferences), imposing a Central Bank action of listening, interpreting and sanctioning the necessities of the economy as a whole. This requires finc tuning, which is what makes the use of strict monetary rules so difficult. Similarly, the heterodox idea of a non-neutral money, influencing the economic process all the time, is what imposes the articulation of the monetary and other economic policies, denying the possibility of Central Bank independence (Carvalho, 1995–1996).

Money, whose role is more active and more necessary than can be conceived by the mainstream of economics, is what requires the relative independence of domestic monetary policy from what happens in international markets (Kregel, 1996),[13] or from the volatility of exchange-rate fluctuations and of international capital movements. It is why building macrodynamic capacity and the process of macroeconomic capability requires exchange-rate management and capital controls. With these monetary and financial instruments, it is possible to give priority to domestic objectives of growth and employment, taking into account the interest rates, in particular basic interest rates, giving rise to an adequate interest-rate hierarchy.

Of course, there have been important transformations in the economy and the capitalist society since Marx's days. New features also appeared since Schumpeter, Kalecki, Keynes and Minsky produced their seminal works. One may well argue that some of the changes were somewhat influenced by pertinent considerations expressed by them and their followers. Certainly, a number of issues they have analysed are still relevant nowadays, given the richness and profoundness of their understanding of capitalist society. Naturally, there are significant similarities as well as differences among the mentioned economists, depending on the issue to be tacked and ideological perspective. This being the case, it may sound too ambitious to provide a perfectly integrated model of their views as an alternative foundation for MDC. We do not intend to dispute this point, but to insist that the focus of our analysis is on investment decisions, innovations, finance, market power and organizational macro-environment. There is much that we can learn from their political economy which is distant from "modern" economic teaching, research programmes and economic policies.

One may consider: (a) that the present structure of capitalism, especially the activities of the public sector encircling the economic organization and institutions, has reduced the potential importance of entrepreneurs; (b) that in large corporations technical change is routinized and management is highly bureaucratized; (c) that "revolution" in Information and Communication Technologies (ICTs) is the new driving force of the capitalistic engine; (d) that credit creation, as opposed to savings in financing such activities is less important due to the fact that self financial resources based on retained profits are dominant; (e) that in the long-run the firms, sectors and countries will learn how to master ICTs and public policies are no longer welfare enhancing; (f) that well-functioning market economy, with broadly defined property rights only requires court to enforce contracts and twist claims.

Many other orthodox statements are often raised and some of them may deserve serious consideration. However, we are far from these perspectives as the major source for macro analysis. We argue that production, investment, finance, technological change, distribution of income and institutional considerations must be dealt with first at the macro level. Macrodynamic configurations cannot be ignored, since they provide the boundary conditions that allow firms and consumers to function. For instance, the liquidity preference of firms depends essentially on their state of confidence and prospective profits. The interplay of industrial firms' expectations and investment decisions with banks' conditionalities on lending determines to a large extent the level of investment, and thus productivity, technological change, level of income and employment. We stress that such complex process cannot be conducted without a proper State's participation. Adequate regulation is still more important in an environment of significant inequality of wealth and political power. This shows the importance of the State on macrodynamic capability.[14]

So far we have argued that macrodynamic capacity defined as the proper environment to stimulate productive investment, increased productivity, growth and socio-economic development is constituted of a set of institutional characteristics involving real, monetary and financial conditions. Providing these conditions are thus necessary to obtaining what we are calling the process of macrodynamic capability of a country or region. Concluding this section we represent graphically some of the major relations that we have analysed. This may stimulate subsequent research formalizing relevant aspects of these relationships. Needless to say, the conditions that define macrodynamic capacity are complex and numerous. We indicate, in Figure 10.1 below, features dealing especially with the monetary and financial elements.

Finance conditions are responsible for the pace of investment and innovation. Long-run interest rates have to be higher than short-run rates, warranting a liquidity premium to savers who choose to lend to long-term investors. But, at the same time, long-term interest rates cannot be higher than the return on capital, or it will inhibit investment. The solution of this difficulty requires a low short-run interest rate, or a low interest rate of public bonds in the market of liquid assets. This denotes appropriate conditions of finance as important conditions to stimulate innovation (1) and investment (2), thus increasing income and production (3 and 4). Even if we know that the investment and innovation can be financed out of profits, they can be augmented if the conditions of credit are improved, and regulated to inhibit speculation. Adequate financial conditions will also induce the placement of an enlarged part of savings, out of income (5), in medium- and long-term assets (6), because of a higher difference of return, inhibiting speculative finance. Such a part of savings will pay the debt of financed investment, serving to recompose the bank's liquidity (7). The other part of savings will be

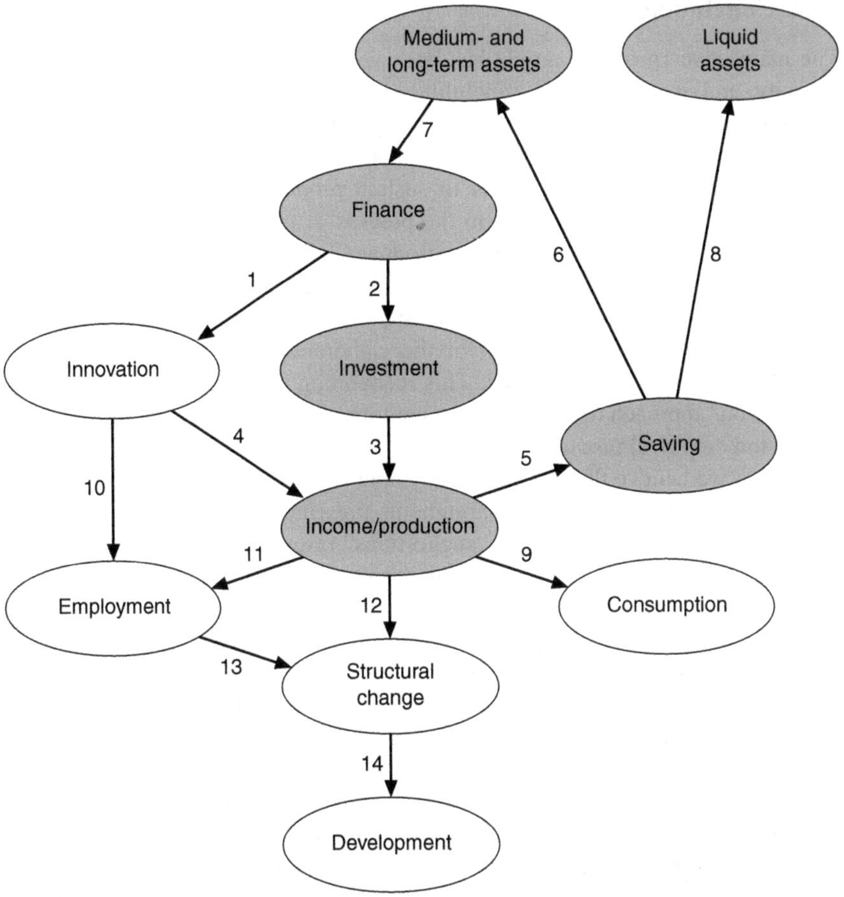

Figure 10.1 Monetary and financial aspects of macrodynamic capacity.

placed in liquid assets (money and public bonds), and will not contribute to improve investment and growth (8). To organize the financial system to these roles is a State responsibility, providing an adequate macrodynamic capability of the economy.

Low short-term interest rate is an incentive to investment and innovation and, by stimulating growth and employment, tends to improve the profit's expectation, reducing liquidity premium. Good conditions of finance can also affect consumption (9). The introduction of innovations and the rise of effective demand will improve income (3, 4). Innovation, increasing productivity and new level in production, will impact employment (10 and 11) that, depending on changes of demand and supply will lead to structural change (12 and 13). Distribution and demand and the changes in production structure will determine the pace of development (14) in terms of social inclusion.

10.4 Concluding remarks

The main concern of this article has been with the concepts of macrodynamic capacity and macrodynamic capability, instead of microdynamic capability, exploring a heterodox content whose analytical foundation is encountered in Marx, Schumpeter, Keynes, Kalecki and Minsky. In particular, we explored monetary and financial conditions to sustain productive investment and economic development as important in the process of macrodynamic capability of the economy. We are attempting to introduce a refreshing alternative that may bring new light to discussions of the creation of dynamic capability. It should also be obvious that, at the moment, we are a long way from being in a position to set out a consistent apparatus for the elaboration of operational processes towards a prospective programme. This recognition in no way reduces the relevance of our approach to MDC. On the contrary, it is a stimulus for further theoretical and empirical research.

Indeed, we believe that we are already able to provide some preliminary suggestions which follows from the arguments presented in the previous sections. Notice that we are using the term "suggestions" instead of "prescriptions", since an universally applicable macro and micro organizational formula to attain economic development is unlikely to be encountered. On the other hand, theory, if it is not to remain sterile, must prepare the terrain for policy orientation.

Some of the suggestions for improving the monetary and financial conditions of macrodynamic capacity which follows from the analysis presented in this article include: (i) an adequate structure of real interest rate to improve investment; (ii) a sustainable budget structure to stimulate growth without a burdensome debt that could affect negatively the interest rates; (iii) a restructuring of the public debt through renegotiation with reasonable discount avoiding pressure on the interest rates; (iv) a competitive and stable exchange rate; (v) a Central Bank that focuses on financial stability but is also concerned with production and employment; (vi) prudential control of the banking system so as to avoid financial fragility; and (vii) state regulation to inhibit financial supremacy over production. All these suggestions are important in giving monetary policy the necessary conditions for the macrodynamic capability of the economy, improving investment, being as independent as possible of international conditions and without surcharging interest rates with policy objectives other than improving growth and employment.

Our preoccupation in this article was mainly with the monetary and financial conditions of macrodynamic capacity, and that was the reason for the suggestions above. As we have seen in the beginning of this article, the creation of institutional conditions of demand, State regulation and learning, among others, mean macrodynamic capability of the economic system. In this sense we can propose also: (i) the enhancement of the domestic market, giving priority to economic growth with better distribution of income and wealth; (ii) the creation of employment opportunities to absorb skilled labour and, at the same time, to expand job posts directed to the absorption of the industrial reserve army of less qualified manpower; (iii) the creation of safety nets to protect the mass of the population; (iv) the reform of tax system to alleviate its incidence on the lower income groups, by the reduction of indirect taxes, which are usually highly regressive; and (v) long-term strategies to finance public investment projects especially in infrastructure, health, education and research.

The points above indicate that it is not difficult to offer propositions towards the process of MDC, but the fundamental dilemma is how to implement them. Naturally, the simultaneous pursuit of these gains requires a multiplicity of instruments. Kaldor (1985, p. 40) argues that:

> In so far as there is a conflict between the simultaneous pursuit of objectives, I think policies which strengthen the "real economy" – i.e. output, employment, capital formation and the role of economic growth – ought to be given higher weight than "monetary objectives", such as a lower rate of inflation and a stronger balance of payments. I am sceptical, however, of econometric models which aim at discovering an "optimal policy mix" on the basis of a particular model of the workings of the economy [...], in the last resort the "best" combination of policies must remain a matter of flair and insight, not susceptible to precise calculation.

This type of caution has to be present when developing econometric relations on MDC of an economy.

Notes

1 Financial support from CNPq is acknowledged. We are grateful to Adriana Amado, Philip Arestis and to Gary Dymski for useful comments. References on this chapter should be addressed to mlmollo@unb.br and joanilioteixeira@hotmail.com

2 This does not dispense with society's struggles seeking for better conditions, what it means is that governments are pressed to improve democratic institutions.

3 Even when we recognize the difficulties or impossibility of solving completely the problems and conflicts inherent to capitalism, there are some ways better than others to its functioning in terms of more democratic gains and benefits. In this sense, to promote macrodynamic capability means to prepare the macroeconomic context to stimulate fairer and enduring results of the economic process.

4 It is imperative to mention that international finance tends to show a double standard when dealing with a well-industrialized country and an emerging economy, as well as with different people in terms of income's levels in the same country (Dymski, 2005). Thus, it is indispensable to understand the particular institutional conditions of each nation before blaming it for an unsuccessful development strategy.

5 It is not by accident that Marx (1975) insisted in criticizing Ricardo for not understanding the importance of money in a commodity economy like the capitalist one, and Keynes (Moggridge, 1999) criticized the (neo)classical vision for the same reason, introducing the concept of monetary production economy.

6 Notice that according to Schumpeter, the banking system is defined as producing money and grating credit to firms, without taking part in the production of commodities. Banks create means of payments on the basis of legal tender supplied by the Central Bank. On this matter, see Graziani, 1984.

7 On this ground there are important differences between Keynes and Kalecki's approach. Both shared the view that investment preceded savings but the mechanisms underlying

their respective analysis are not the same. The treatment given by Keynes on savings does not contain references between savings out of profit and out of wages – a theme that became fundamental in the post-Keynesian literature.

8 For a comparison between orthodox concept of neutrality of money, and the idea of non-neutral money of the heterodoxy, emphasizing its theoretic consequences, see Mollo (2004).

9 As a historical and social concept, development is, by nature, an open-ended, disequilibrium path, contrary to the notion of organic development. Like Joan Robinson's elephant, socio-economic backwardness is a concept difficult to express but easy to recognize. As pointed out by Sachs (2004, p. 161): "(…) development does not yield itself to be encapsulated in simple formulas. Its multidimensionality and complexity explain its elusiveness". To some extent this also applies to macrodynamic capability.

10 Obviously, a full treatment of how uncertainty can finance the evolution of technological opportunities and to show how the macroeconomic forces (such as the rate of interest) affect investment is the subject matter of a book and not of a single article.

11 Guttmann (1994) analyses the effects of "fictitious capital" in the economy with financial globalization, in particular the case of the United States.

12 Chesnais (2004, pp. 39–40), based on OECD statistics, shows the fall of per capita income growth in the world: 1960–1973: 4.0 per cent; 1973–1980: 2.4 per cent; 1980–1993: 1.2 per cent. For the average growth rate of the world's product we have: 1963–1973: more than 7 per cent; 1973–1990: 3 per cent; and 1990–1999: 2 per cent.

13 See also Kregel (1998) for an analysis of the difficulties of coordination of the monetary policy internationally and the negative impacts of international factors on domestic demand.

14 The importance of the State on macrodynamic capability does not exclude the perception of the political role of the society conducting it in desirable directions.

References

Aghion, P. and Howitt, P. (1992) A Model of Growth Through Creative Destruction, *Econometrica*, vol. 60, no. 2, March, pp. 323–351.

Basu, K. (2003) Globalization and the Policies of International Finance: The Stiglitz Verdict, *Journal of Economic Literature*, vol. XLI, September, pp. 885–899.

Bhaduri, A. and Nayyar, D. (1996) *The Intelligent Person's Guide to Liberalization*, New Delhi: Penguin Books.

Bortis, H. (1997) *Institutions, Behaviours and Economic Theory*, Cambridge: Cambridge University Press.

Carvalho, F.C. (1995–1996) The Independence of Central Banks: A Critical Assessment of the Arguments, *Journal of Post Keynesian Economics*, vol. 18, no. 2, Winter, pp. 159–176.

Chesnais, F. (2004) Le Capital de Placement: Accumulation, Internationalization, Effets Économiques et Politiques, in F. Chesnais (ed.) *La Finance Mondialisée: Racines Sociales et Politiques, Configuration,Consequences*, Paris: La Découverte.

Chick, V. (1994) *Macroeconomics After Keynes*. Cambridge, MA: The MIT Press, Second Printing.

Chick, V. (1998) Finance and Investment in the Context of Development, in J. Halevi and J.-M. Fontaine (eds) *Restoring Demand in the World Economy – Trade, Finance and Technology*, Cheltenham, UK and Northampton, MA: Edward Elgar, pp. 95–106.

Contwell, J. (1989) *Technological Innovation and Multinational Corporation*, Oxford: Basil Blackwell.

De Brunhoff, S. (1998) Money, Interest and Finance in Marx's Capital, in R. Bellofiore (ed.) *Marxian Economics – A Reappraisal – Essays in Volume III of Capital – Method, Value and Money*, London and New York: Macmillan.

Dow, S. (1987) The Treatment of Money in Regional Economics, *Journal of Regional Science*, vol. 27, no. 1, pp. 13–24.

Dymski, G. (1993). How to Rebuild the U.S. Financial Structure: Level the Playing Field and Renew the Social Contract, in G.A. Dymski, G. Epstein and R. Pollin (eds) *Transforming the U.S. Financial System: Equity and Efficiency for the 21st Century*, Armonk, NY and London: M.E. Sharpe, pp. 101–132.

Dymski, G. (2005) Financial Globalization, Social Exclusion, and Financial Crisis, *International Review of Applied Economics*, vol. 19, no. 4, October, pp. 439–457.

Frey, B. and Benz, M. (2004) Corporate Governance: What Can We Learn from Public Governance, www.iew.uzizh.ch/home/benz/amr.pdf.

Graziani, A. (1984) The Debate on Keynes' Finance Motive, *Economic Notes*, vol. 1, pp. 5–33.

Guttmann, R. (1994) *How Credit-Money Shapes the Economy – The United States in Global System*, Armonk, NY and London: M.E. Sharpe.

Kahn, R. (1984) *The Making of Keynes' General Theory*, Cambridge: Cambridge University Press.

Kalecki, M. (1971) *Selected Essays on the Dynamics of the Capitalist Economy: 1933–1970*, Cambridge: Cambridge University Press.

Kaldor, N. (1985) Evidence to the Treasury and Civil Service Committee, July 1980, *The Scourge of Monetarism*, 2nd edn, Oxford: Oxford University Press.

Kaufmann, D. Kray, A. and Mastruzzi, M. (2004) *Governance Matters III: Governance Indicators for 1996–2002*. Washington, DC: The World Bank.

Keynes, J.M. (1936) *The General Theory of Employment, Interest and Money*. Republished in *Collected Writings*, vol. VII, London: Macmillan.

Keynes, J.M. (1937a) Alternative Theories of The Rate of Interest, *The Economic Journal*, June. Republished in *Collected Writings*, vol. XIV, London: Macmillan.

Keynes, J.M. (1937b). 'Ex Ante' Theory of the Rate of Interest, *The Economic Journal*, December. Republished in *Collected Writings*, vol. XIV, London: Macmillan.

Kogut, B. and Zander, U. (1992) Knowledge of the Firm, Combinative Capabilities and the Replication of Technology, *Organization Science*, vol. 3, no. 3, pp. 383–397.

Kregel, J.A. (1996) Risks and Implications of Financial Globalisation for National Policy Autonomy, *Conferência Internacional Macroeconomia em Face da Globalização*, mimeo, Brasília, CORECON.

Kregel, J.A. (1998) The Myth of Economic Policy Independence: Some Reflections on the Failure of Post-War Schemes for Stablization of Global Demand in Post-War Period, in J. Halevi and J.-M. Fontaine (eds) *Restoring Demand in the World Economy – Trade, Finance and Technology*, Cheltenham, UK and Northampton, MA: Edward Elgar.

Madhok, A. and Osegowitsch, T. (2000) The International Biotechnology Industry: A Dynamic Capabilities Perspective. *Journal of International Business Studies*, vol. 31, no. 2, pp. 325–335.

Marx, K. (1974) *Capital*, vols I and III, London: Lawrence & Wishart.

Marx, K. (1975) *Théories sur la Plus Value*, Paris: Editions Sociales.

Marx, K. (1978) The Eighteenth Brumaire of Luis Bonaparte, in R. Tucher (ed.) *The Marx-Engels Reader*, 2 EMBED Equation, 3rd edn, New York: N.W. Norton.

Minsky, H. (1977) The Financial-Instability Hypothesis: Capitalist Processes and the Behavior of the Economy, in E.I. Altman and J.W. Sametz (eds) *Financial Crises*, New York: John Willey & Sons.

Minsky, H. (1982) *Inflation, Recession and Economic Policy*, Armonk, NY: M.E. Sharpe, Inc.

Moggridge, D. (ed.) (1989) *The Collected Writings of John Maynard Keynes (1971–1983)*, London: Macmillan.

Mollo, M.L.R. (1999) The Endogeneity of Money: Post Keynesian and Marxian Concepts Compared, *Research in Political Economy*, vol. 18, pp. 3–26.

Mollo, M.L.R. (2004) Ortodoxia e Heterodoxia Monetárias: A Questão da Neutralidade da Moeda. *Revista de Economia Política*, vol. 24, no. 3(95), July–September, pp. 323–343.

Morishima, M. (1992). *Capital and Credit*. Cambridge: Cambridge University Press.

Pasinetti, L. (1993) *Structural Economic Dynamics*, Cambridge: Cambridge University Press.

Pavitt, K. (1988) International Patterns of Technology Accumulation, in N. Hood and J. Vahlne (eds) *Strategies in Global Competition*, New York: John Wiley.

Plihon, D. (2002) *Rentabilité et risque dans le nouveau régime de croissance*, Paris: La Documentation Française.

Pollin, R. (1993) Public Credit Allocation through the Federal Reserve: Why it is Needed, How it Should be Done, in G.A. Dymski, G. Epstein and R. Pollin (eds) *Transforming the U.S. Financial System: Equity and Efficiency for the 21st Century*, Armonk, NY: M.E. Sharpe.

Ribeiro, M. and Teixeira, J. (2001) Econometric Analysis of Private-Sector Investment in Brazil, *CEPAL Review*, vol. 74, August, pp. 153–166.

Robinson, J. (1979) *Collected Economic Papers*, vol. V, Oxford: Basil Blackwell.

Sachs, I. (2004) Inclusive Development and Decent Work for All, *International Labour Review*, vol. 143, no. 1–2, pp. 161–184.

Salama, P. (1996) La Financiarisation Excluante: les Leçons des Économies Latino-Américaines, in F. Chesnais (ed.) *La Mondialization Financière: Genèse, Coût et Enjeux*, Paris: Syros.

Schumpeter, J. (1934) *Theory of Economic Development*, Cambridge, MA: Harvard University Press.

Schumpeter, J. (1961) *The Theory of Economic Development*, New York: Oxford University Press.

Sylos-Labini, P. (1984) The Problem of Economic Growth in Marx and Schumpeter, *The Forces of Economic Growth and Decline*, Cambridge, MA: The MIT Press, chap. 2.

Teece, D. and Pisano, G. (1994) The Dynamic Capabilities of Firms: An Introduction, *Industrial and Corporate Change*, vol. 3, no. 3, pp. 537–556.

Teece, D., Pisano, G. and Shuen, A. (1997) Dynamic Capabilities and Strategic Management, *Strategic Management Journal*, vol. 18, no. 7, pp. 509–533.

Wray, R. (1998) *Understanding Modern Money – the Key to Full Employment and Price Stability*, Cheltenham, UK and Northhampton, MA: Edward Elgar.

Wray, R. (2000) *Modern Money*, in J. Smithin (ed.) *What is Money?*, London and New York: Routledge, pp. 42–67.

Zollo, M. and Winter, S. (2000) Deliberate Learning and the Evolution of Dynamic Capabilities, *Organization Science*, vol. 13, no. 3, May–June, pp. 339–351.

11 Knowledge endowment and composition as dynamic capabilities[1]

Gilberto Antonelli and Giovanni Pegoretti

11.1 Introduction

A strong disatisfaction with the conception and policy prescriptions regarding competitive advantage put forward by the mainstream approach is the general stimulus stirring the present work. Essentially, in this approach, economic policy prescriptions aiming at enhancing the competitive advantage of economic systems are mainly based on two intertwined foundations: equilibrium in a labour market shaped by wage competition and ubiquitous predominance of the comparative advantage principle. In fact, most of the liberalization and privatization strategies as well as 'structural reform' policies have been conceived and implemented within this analytic scaffold.

Whereas structural and institutional changes in the last twenty years have radically transformed the economic systems, one could be surprised to note how great, in the policy debate, has been the switch from a common conjecture according to which labour markets do not usually provide wage equilibrium to a 'residual' conjecture, widely and often implicitly accepted, in which they normally grant it.

In a parallel way, the prescriptions of the basic model of comparative advantage have been acknowledged without much questioning the impact of the deep transformations taking place in the global arena on the configuration of international competition[2] side by side with the drastic assumptions implied in the model concerning labour market equilibrium and migration.

Microeconomic behaviours and macroeconomic policies have been significantly reshaped by the opening of the markets and technological change, giving a new meaning also to the spatial dimension and, therefore, to the mobility of economic resources, including human resources. The expansion of independent labour and flexible practices in the labour markets are only the most evident consequences. However, the equilibrium conjecture seems to remain at least questionable as well as unrealistic.[3]

Moreover, also the very perception of the labour market as a wage competition mechanism can be questioned, and has been severely questioned by well-known scholars.[4]

One might think that this argument was made obsolete by the deep reorganization of the global economic structure brought about by the so-called 'new economy'.[5] However, we believe that a lot of theoretical and applied work is still needed in order to assess the real nature and functioning of the labour markets.

One of the main shortfalls is that, clever as they may be, the standard recipes usually do not pay enough attention to structural economic dynamics and its interaction with the business cycle: in other words, linkages between short-term conduct and long-term structure are crucial.

The same research line has been tackled by the authors in two previous works (Antonelli and Pegoretti, 1995; Antonelli and Pegoretti, 2005), even if in different regards. They constitute a useful reference background. However, the present chapter is completely novel and addresses one principal and three subordinate research questions.

The principal research question concerns the role of knowledge and competences in structural economic dynamics and business cycle. In particular, we will study the trade-off between the need for change, flexibility and new human resources inputs faced by the firms in the business cycle downswings and the destruction of knowledge and competences taking place in them. This question is tackled in the second part of the paper. Section 11.5 presents a stylized model, building on a model presented in a previous paper (Antonelli and Pegoretti, 2005). The model is based on a very simplified stylization of the actual working of the economic system. It offers only an aggregate view of the production process. In particular, it concentrates on the impact on firm productivity of some of its key determinants. Since the economic system is typified by a representative firm, the stress is on international competition between different economic systems, rather than on competition between different firms within each system. Given the importance of productivity dynamics, the model shows that even very simple assumptions concerning its determinants can bring about complex paths that soften usual unilateral conjectures about the causal links between productivity and employment. Different configurations of the 'competence pipeline' and the related cost functions are explored.

In sections 11.6 and 11.7 we'll try some 'mind experiments', which are based on the conceptual framework introduced with the model. Further analytical and numerical extensions – as well as solutions – are left for future work. Section 11.6 investigates the reactions of the representative firm to the different phases of the business cycle. Section 11.7 considers the effect of innovation on the firm strategy.

Instrumental in answering the principal question are the subordinate questions addressed to in the first part of the chapter. The first subordinate question is: How can we define knowledge, competence and learning relevant to innovation aimed at improving the competitive options of an economy? This question is dealt with in section 11.2 and builds on an analysis introduced in a previous paper (Antonelli and Pegoretti, 1995). The distinctions are emphasized between acquired knowledge and used knowledge, on the one side, and knowledge and competence, on the other. The significant redefinition of network boundaries in the knowledge system taking place in the last decades, due to both scientific dynamics and economic evolution, is reinterpreted as a fragmentation process going with a reconstruction process. The superior capability of the job-competition model to capture many of the important features of used knowledge is underlined.[6] Even if in a very synthetic way, we try to reflect on the fact that job-competition and wage-competition impact differently on macroeconomic performance.

The second subordinate question is: In dealing with the competitive advantage between different economic systems, can we rely only on the comparative advantage principle and forget about the absolute one? This question is tackled in section 11.3. The answer helps to stress how crucial artificial assumptions are for an appropriate implementation of the comparative advantage principle and what the implications are for the analysis if we assign a less unbalanced role to the absolute advantage principle. The organization of knowledge, internal, but also external, to the firm, maintains a pivotal role in translating the potential for growth in its actual exploitation and in balancing the relationships between innovation and the absolute advantage, and therefore competitive advantage, on the one side, and the relationships between innovation and the opportunity cost of production factors, and therefore the comparative advantage, on the other. All this helps in motivating the assumptions made in the model presented in the second part of the chapter.

The third and last subordinate question refers to the organization of knowledge[7] in the economic system. How can we conceive the interactions and trade-offs originated by the organization of knowledge, internal and external to the firm when economic responses to the needs of business cycle are required? This question is dealt with in section 11.4. The structure of the organization of knowledge, internal and external to the firm, brings us to focus our attention on three engines or paths affecting productivity increases. Changes linked to the internal organization of knowledge are better explained in the framework of the job-competition model and the notion of 'competence pipeline', previously used, can be inferred from it.

In the concluding section, the overall suggestion is drawn that a relativistic approach should be preferred when assessing the performance of economic systems with various degrees of 'flexibility' of the labour markets, whenever knowledge management is involved.

11.2 Knowledge, competence, learning

Whenever knowledge and innovation are relevant in order to improve the competitive options of an economy, a great consideration should be paid to the distinction between the formation of its growth potential and the exploitation of this potential (Abramovitz, 1989, 1991; Antonelli, 2004). The just stressed polarity has a dual in the field of the development of economically relevant knowledge. In this case we can distinguish between acquired knowledge and used knowledge.[8] We can come to accept the relevance of this distinction also starting from the recognition that complementarity among production inputs is relevant and complementarity between specific and general training is even more relevant (Acemoglu and Pischke, 1999).[9] From our standpoint the consequences are threefold (Guidetti *et al.* 2006):

i the coincidence between educational qualifications and competences falls down, with the side effect that 'the labor market is not the conventional bidding market where people meet to buy and sell existing skills' (Thurow, 1976);
ii the investment by the firm in the acquisition of general knowledge and training that increase the productivity of its employees becomes rational;
iii the return on each set of competences does not only depend on the competences themselves, but also on the complementarities between different sets of competences and productive inputs.

While the first and the third consequences entirely fit the job competition model, the second implies an updated view of the way organization of knowledge takes place in contemporary economies.

11.2.1 Acquired knowledge

Acquired knowledge is the potential outcome of both formal and informal education and training attained by the individuals and the community at large which contributes to the overall growth potential.

11.2.1.1 Individual and social capabilities

As previously argued (Antonelli and Pegoretti, 1995), mental power co-determines the formation of this potential and fosters economic competition by means of a continuous transformation of context specific knowledge, in general codified knowledge, which is then conveyed in other specific economic contexts. The aim of each economic agent, which is ultimately conditioned by path dependency, is to achieve commensurability among projects or commodities, also in order to select among different technological paths and to create the new ones.

Information is a necessary but not sufficient tool in order to exploit the opportunities of new variants of goods, services and processes, when starting from a specific context. Knowledge, experience and capabilities to extract and decode the relevant elements from the context are mostly needed.

In relatively simple contexts, in which little technological, organizational and institutional change prevail, growth potential is rather stable and uncertainty plays a minor role. Routine knowledge, relatively few stable skills and on-the-job training are sufficient to support a standardized production process. A standard method of production is obtained after a decoding process has been fully implemented, and refers to the complete array of inputs needed, including labour force endowed with the mean skill implicit in average practice techniques. In these contexts knowledge incorporated in human beings plays a minor role compared with that incorporated in machines. On the contrary, in economic contexts made more complex by persistent technological, organizational and institutional change human resources play a pivotal role. Rules help the innovation system to maintain and adapt itself in a more uncertain environment, in that they limit the range of feasible alternatives facing the agents along a given trajectory. Progress in knowledge adds an antagonist function to the conservative and adaptive one. In other words, new knowledge, on the one side, contributes to the deepening of the opportunities offered by the existing potential, on the other, tends to develop the opportunities made available by the innovation of the potential.

Today nobody disagrees with the view that knowledge plays a pivotal role also in the economic realm. However, we have still to achieve a deeper understanding of the relationship between knowledge, capabilities and competences.

Capabilities consist of 'acquired knowledge' which is economically relevant. Individual capabilities are considered when we are concerned with the internal organization of knowledge. At an aggregate level, they merge in the social capabilities, that can be considered as an infrastructure resulting from the accumulation and interaction of individual capabilities. These are relevant when we are concerned with the external organization of knowledge.

Capabilities can be defined as a mix of knowledge, experience and information needed by organizations to carry out 'the large number of activities related to the discovery and estimation of future wants, to research, development and design, to the execution and co-ordination of processes of physical transformation, the marketing of goods, and so on' (Richardson, 1972, p. 888). Capabilities are essential in explaining the development of the power to create and increase specialist competences and of the division of labour. They are endogenous and idiosyncratic (Loasby, 1998, pp. 13–14), and both the cumulativity associated to the former and the context specificity of the latter stress the importance of irreversibility in this setting. Moreover, capabilities are organized around different sets of rules in which markets also work through different channels and in different ways. In other terms they are institution specific.[10]

11.2.1.2 Knowledge dimensions relevant in the economic game

Starting from this framework, we can conceive, first of all, knowledge as a stock of results achieved by means of intentional and unintentional investments in research activity.[11] This knowledge affects future economic activity. Additional knowledge increases the stock and its economic use does not necessarily imply depletion, on the contrary it may mean accumulation through work-based learning. The main instances of this kind of knowledge are research and development and human capital accumulation through schooling, also impinging on formerly acquired knowledge.

However, this dimension of knowledge can be contrasted with the remark that knowledge cannot be easily stored[12] and recalling the Marshallian disagreement in accepting stock-based concepts related to knowledge, like the one of 'human capital'. This raises huge practical difficulties in the accumulation of knowledge.

Therefore, the more relevant the role of knowledge in the firm, the more its management is complex and the improvement of our capability to measure and account for knowledge is badly needed at all levels, from the national accounts to the corporate budget.

External as well as internal organization matters. This means that a collection of elements, some of them clearly outside the traditional 'pure theory' of production, are to be considered from the beginning in an updated theory. We refer specifically to the institutional environment including legislation, factor markets, product markets, financial markets, together with agencies providing for public services and implementing public policies. Institutional change becomes partially endogenous (North, 1990). 'Cognitive limitations cause us to rely on institutions to guide reasonable behaviour; market institutions reduce the cost of search, negotiation, and monitoring entailed in making single transactions' (Loasby, 2000, p. 297).

The complexity of the cognitive process, which asks for management policies by the firm in the field of creation, storage, organization, accountancy, use and reproduction of knowledge, involves the necessity that institutions surrounding the firms perform a role of simplifier in the path of knowledge organization useful to them. Local production systems can be considered as important knowledge reservoirs (Becattini, 2003). Knowledge and human capital, which are managed in a social environment, achieve the nature of semi public goods.

In this perspective the main issues concerning growth and employment dynamics are long-term oriented. Therefore, when we consider productivity, it is better to refer to output per worker which takes into account the effect of all production factors, including the so called 'total factor productivity'. Pushing for the progress of competitive advantage in the long run, this view promotes the role of research and development and innovation, material and immaterial infrastructures capable of strengthening local production systems, social cohesion: in a few words, 'long-term or innovative flexibility' (Killick, 1995).

However, knowledge can also be conceived as an ongoing learning process which can affect current as well as future economic activity. In this case knowledge is a flow of new ideas generating a stream of economic effects starting from the very time interval in which these ideas have been generated. We could refer to incremental innovation and organization change, as they increase productivity, but also to improvements in human resources quality through experience, off-the-job and on-the-job training, learning by doing and other forms of learning as by-products of economic activity. With notable exceptions, little attention has been paid so far to it by economic literature.

A third dimension of knowledge which can affect current as well as future economic activity is its role of filter and organizer of available information. A relevant instance of this role can be found in imitation or in the gains in productivity deriving from the improvement in the organization of information flows within a firm. We can note that in the last decades an increasing attention has been paid to it by several lines of research in economics.

11.2.1.3 Complementarity and substitutability

As far as the acquisition and/or production of knowledge is concerned, either complementarity or substitutability can play a role in the relationship between the supply of knowledge from specialized organizations (such as schools, universities, professional training) and the production within the firms of competence or skills, as joint products, which are increasingly important. However, the accumulation of knowledge maintains a social and public dimension. Put in other words, this type of accumulation is difficult outside of broader socio-economic systems (e.g. local or national) with which firms interact. They allow for the development of social and individual capabilities making firms more innovative and competitive, either informally (e.g. tacit knowledge, social capital) or formally. We can then think of organizational models based on various forms of participation or long-term contracts with workers, easing the solution of the problem. It is necessary to take into account, however, the fact that multilevel governance, by reducing the degree of protection, exposes firms to both new risks and opportunities.

11.2.1.4 Human resources at the crossroads of growth

A different series of objections derive from the multidimensional economic role of human resources which severely limit the effectiveness of human capital markets. Human resources available are the outcome of intentional as well as unintentional investments in education accomplished in the past. Education and training can be listed among the determinants which affect both the potential of growth and productivity and the actual realization of this potential. Thus the characteristics of labour supply, unemployment, migration and so on are all phenomena that facilitate or limit structural change in production, income distribution, localization, growth, in one word. This dual role of human resources does not imply that their importance is clearly perceived, also because of the systematic time lag elapsing between the making of the plans and the use of resources themselves. On the contrary a pro-cyclical visibility of the economic worth of human capital can be experienced.[13]

But an even more challenging objection can be raised taking into account some of the basic features of the new real economy (NRE).[14] Even if several features of the NRE are not yet understandable and the service sector maintains a hybrid nature, we can use some of the evidence already available to rearrange and update our understanding of the innovation process and determinants of productivity dynamics.

On the one side, the evolution of new market characteristics can be introduced in the analysis, even if in a very sketchy way, by considering the impact of aggregate demand on the adjustments in output and employment by the firms.

On the other, a very simple way of taking into account the interaction between the internal organization of the firm and its institutional environment is to consider the adjustment process related to the enrolment of workers belonging to different vintages. In some way, each vintage incorporates evolving institutional and market characteristics.

11.2.1.5 Knowledge and competence

The notion of knowledge concerns the potential of intellectual and psychological capabilities to comprehend new general principles and to develop them with the help of science, culture and other knowledge sources. In other words, it refers to the collection of information, insight and abilities achieved by means of education and experience. When knowledge is codified it is usually certified by titles and degrees validating the individual potential capabilities as they are stated by the educational system and the scientific community. From this definition a relationship between formal education and work-based learning can be derived which can stress both substitutability and complementarity.

The notion of competence, on the other side, concerns the actual capability to perform skills and the ethical beliefs assembled by individuals who involve a certain performance in a particular context: the job place. Therefore, competences are tools for the management of human resources, spanning from the hiring phase to the training and payment ones. The use of these tools implies the operation of an evaluation system by the firms. Competences do not substitute formal degrees but contain them.

This distinction can be analytically exploited in a better way differentiating acquired knowledge/skills, on the one side, from used knowledge/skills or competences, on the other.[15]

11.2.1.6 Knowledge and fragmentation

In the post modern era, according to an extremist view, attributed to the 'second' Feyerabend (1975), no privileged position should be attributed to science; 'scientific method' does not exist; scientists are 'opportunist' in spite of the rationalist prescriptions.

Even not accepting in full this extreme view, we have to admit that role and position of science have dramatically changed in the last decades. In some matters science is perceived as a routine activity (e.g. in the ICT's realm). In other matters science is assumed to play a 'back office' role (e.g. in the field of biotechnologies and genetic research). Very often the willingness to pay for it is low if short-term results cannot be anticipated (at least in terms of 'voluptuary consumption' or 'reciprocity gift').

Although the internationalization of scientific networks in most sciences is a well established phenomenon since the Middle Ages, their structure, span and frequency of contacts has been strongly influenced by the same determinant of the so-called 'economic fragmentation' (Jones and Kierzkowski, 2001). From this point of view, we can speak of fragmentation, while only a few of the national research systems, even in Europe, seem to be sustainable.

We could say that the functioning of the stocks and flows mechanism which links the different dimensions of knowledge is vital for the sustainability of a research system. The interaction between the different dimensions and forms of knowledge allows for synergy between various sources and channels of trade.

This in turn requires that the scale of activity, the diversity/sectoral differentiation of the research system and its capability to interact in a satisfactory way with economic requirements are appropriate.

The significant redefinition of network boundaries which took place in the last decades, due to both scientific dynamics and economic evolution, did not leave the situation unchanged.

Fragmentation can be a creative phase but reconstruction is subject to strong constraints. The most relevant concerns the capability of each research system: to reach an appropriate threshold level; to reach a balanced sectoral composition; to be rooted in economic activity.

11.2.2 Used knowledge

Used knowledge is the effective outcome of formal and informal education and training accessible by the economic organizations working in a given context.

The job competition model helps to capture many of its features. As Thurow (1976, pp. xii–xiii) puts it, with particular reference to the functioning of labour markets:

> If something is a market imperfection, there are always profits to be made by eliminating it. If markets are basically competitive, someone will sooner or later discover a way around the imperfection. Thus, there is a reasonably high probability that any long-lasting 'market imperfection' plays some kind of a functional role in the economy. If markets are not basically competitive, then the imperfections are permanent features of the economic game and need to be built into the distributional mechanism.

This means that: 'static inefficiencies of the present tenure system promote the dynamic efficiencies of the present system. They minimize the resistance to spreading information and job skills' (Thurow, 1976, p. 83). But, under what conditions can 'imperfections' be helpful? 'A labor-training market must be so structured as to maximize the willingness of existing laborers to transmit their knowledge to new workers and to minimize every worker's resistance to acquiring new skills and accepting new technology' (Thurow, 1976, p. 81). Therefore, 'the training function of the labor market makes the repression of direct wage competition profitable' (Thurow, 1976, p. 76).

> in a job market where no one is trained unless a job is available (this is what on-the-job training means), where strong seniority provisions limit employment insecurity to a clear minority (the newly hired), and where there is no danger that some competitor with the requisite skills is going to be allowed to bid down wages, employees are going to be willing to transmit information to new workers and to accept new techniques.
>
> (Thurow, 1976, pp. 81–82)

This is a totally different argument against excessive flexibility from the standard suggestion, derived from the human capital theory, according to which, in the absence of an adequate incentive, the provision of human capital will diminish. This suggestion deals mainly with the provision of formal education outside the firm and refers to a perfect wage competition model. While the former argument deals with the provision of on-the-job training within the firm and refers to a job competition model.

Furthermore:

> flexible wages are necessary for an economy to maximize its current production (reach its static efficiency frontier), but ... efforts to maximize current production may engender a slower future rate of growth of production (its dynamic efficiency frontier). Since the potential gains from maximizing long-run growth usually dominate the potential gains from maximizing current production, employers find it *profitable* to structure the labor market in order to maximize long-run growth at the expense of short-run output. Repressing wage and employment competition becomes a tool for increasing long-run productivity.
>
> (Thurow, 1976, pp. 84)

And 'the lack of wage and employment competition ... is not an illustration of 'market imperfection' that produces inefficiency but rather represents a functional market adjustment that produces long-run efficiency' (Thurow, 1976, p. 84–85).

> To keep the training process going, employers will not allow the unemployed to bid back into his old job at lower wages .... The net result is the formation of a series of internal labor markets with limited ports of entry. Outside of these ports of entry jobs, the supply and demand conditions on the external labor market are basically irrelevant. Because of the institutional need to facilitate informal on-the-job training, workers cannot regain employment opportunities by accepting lower wages. Technically, the individual may possess the necessary skills, but institutionally speaking he does not. His wage bid will not be accepted.
>
> (Thurow, 1976, pp. 85–86)

The attention is focused also on the impact of the business cycle on the employees career and productivity.

> In the process of normal job turnover or as the result of business cycles, individuals may acquire cognitive job skills and be unemployed, but ... even this limited supply of trained labor is restricted in its ability to bid back into their old job categories. To allow them to bid back their old job categories at lower wages would bring on-the-job training to a halt and be counterproductive in the long run.
>
> (Thurow, 1976, p. 81)

> The individual will be trained into the marginal productivity of the job he is slated to hold, but he does not have this marginal productivity independent of the job in question. This is true even if the worker has managed to acquire the necessary job skills in some exogenous manner or if he has acquired the job skills on the job and has been laid off due to fluctuations in aggregate demand.
>
> (Thurow, 1976, p. 85)

However, if it is true that the job competition model can give very significant insights with regard to the formation and role of used knowledge, still, contemporary economies, due to the very nature of structural change and the overall organization of knowledge and production, tend to develop new instruments for the formation of competences. Their incubators are not only firms through work-based learning, but also research and development laboratories and spin-offs. Moreover, a greater importance is assigned to the utilization of general knowledge, due to the role of learning to learn (Antonelli and Maggioni, 1997). Therefore, a more updated framework of analysis is required.

These considerations could refer also to the extension of the job competition model in order to include, together with training costs, hiring and firing costs. That is the costs incurred by the firm in performing all actions needed in finding, evaluating and establishing a working relationship with future employees, interns, contractors or consultants.

Yet, at this stage, we will not pursue this line of research, focusing only on training costs.

11.3 Labour markets, comparative and absolute advantage

The term fragmentation suggests the persistence in real economic systems of a pattern of 'creative destruction'. 'Breaking down the integrated process into separate stages of production opens up new possibilities for exploiting gains from specialisation' (Jones and Kierzkowski, 2001). In economic terms, globalization is characterized by increased freedom in international trade of goods and services,[16] greater mobility of financial assets, law shopping.

In a complementary way, technological change and lowered cost of services fostered a 'fragmentation of vertically integrated production processes into separate segments that may enter international trade' (Jones and Kirzkowski, 2001). This pattern is one of the most important features of market globalization.

It reduces the relevance of the national boundaries, but also of the supra-national ones when not fine-tuned with actual trends of growth.

Fragmentation can take place at different levels:

a at a macro-economic level, in international trade, national innovation systems, sectoral innovation systems;
b at a micro-economic level, in the corporate value chain (outsourcing);
c at a meso-economic level, in industrial districts and local production systems (delocalization).

A knowledge-based economy is subject to 'creative destruction' more than a traditional economy. This is why it needs more flexibility, high labour mobility, ease of forming new companies. Multilevel fragmentation implies difficulties at the different level of government to implement effective strategies and policies.

Scientific knowledge and scientific organizations have undergone the same pattern.

Even if internationalized from the origin, advances in technological change and reduction in costs of services have significantly reduced the costs of international coordination for scientific networks and changed the overall incentive structure.

If we are ready to accept that fragmentation is a theoretically as well as an empirically relevant phenomenon, we cannot accept anymore minimalistic assessments by mainstream economists according to which the competitive advantage is only relevant at the firm level, not at the overall economy level, and that only comparative advantage or absolute productivity matters.

In this line of thought, policy prescriptions are often derived using the Ricardian model, the simplest model, which shows how differences between countries give rise to trade and gains from trade. In this model, labour is the only factor of production and countries differ only in the productivity of labour in different industries. A country will export that commodity in which it has comparative (as opposed to absolute) labour productivity advantage. The distribution of the gains from trade depends on the relative prices of the goods countries produce.

Labour migration is not allowed and the labour market is in a perfectly competitive equilibrium.

Extending the one-factor, two-good model to a world of many commodities makes it possible to illustrate that transportation costs can give rise to the existence of non-traded goods.

Size effects are not seriously taken into consideration in order to incorporate in the analysis the impact of the economies of scale and complementarities that can affect international specialization when small and big countries are confronted.

Moreover, as suggested by Baldone *et al.* (2006), a basic assumption of traditional trade models is that production processes are integrated within just one country. But this assumption

> is being increasingly violated as previously integrated productive activities are segmented and spread over an international network of production sites: as a result, an increasingly large share of trade flows is made up of intermediate and unfinished goods being transferred from one country to another in order to be processed.

Among the important effects of this finding, the same authors note that: 'international disintegration of production processes leads to a lessening of the power of comparative advantages when it comes to explaining both merchandise composition and directions of trade, while it is the concept of absolute advantage to become increasingly relevant'.

Taking into consideration these conjectures, our work tries to draw the attention on the relationships link innovation to the economic performance at large. This overall linkage can be decomposed into three types of relationships.

When we refer to Type 1 Relationship (T1R), we focus on the interaction between human capital (HC) and technological change (TC), whose result is flexibility in economic production, on the one side, and innovation, on the other. This relationship is generally deemed robust in the economic literature. However, it must be stressed that it refers to potential rather than actual innovation.

As we come to consider the relationships between innovation and economic performance, we should distinguish between its impact on the absolute advantage, on the one side, and on the comparative advantage, on the other.

If we take into account the relationships between innovation and the productivity of production factors, and therefore the absolute advantage or competitive advantage, we bear in mind a Type 2 Relationship (T2R). While if we take into account the relationships between innovation and the opportunity cost of production factors, and therefore the comparative advantage, we bear in mind a Type 3 Relationship (T3R).

Of course T2R and T3R coexist, however they can assume different significance and weight in different economic systems. In our conjecture, the organization of knowledge, internal, but also external, to the firm maintains a pivotal role in translating the potential for growth in its actual exploitation and in balancing T2R and T3R.

In this framework, we are allowed to take an extreme view for the sake of theoretical precision, focusing our attention on T2R. In this respect we have to recognize from the beginning that this relationship refers to a necessary but not sufficient condition for productivity growth. This means that it is a fundamental relationship, but it is not mono-directionally linked to the T1R (Antonelli and Pegoretti, 2005).

The core mechanisms outlined here are some specific choices and trade-offs the firm is facing in deciding its policy with special reference to innovation, knowledge and training.

An example of such choices is the decision about committing internal resources to the creation of on-the-job skills and specific knowledge, when external alternatives are present, e.g. private and/or public agencies. Another example is a choice the firm faces during the slump phase of the economic cycle, namely the trade-off between cutting sharply labour-related costs, and maintaining inside the firm, knowledge and competences which have been provided (at a cost) by the firm itself and could be valuable during the recovery phase.

Such choices (together with others, related to investments in research and development, innovative equipment and intangible assets, etc.) affect the capability of the firm to react adequately during the different phases of the economic cycle and in response to waves of innovations. The firm takes the decisions, which affect its competitive advantage, in the framework of the institutional, economic and social system; these can provide a more or less adequate support to competitiveness, through mechanisms which the model takes broadly into account. The degree of 'flexibility' of the system is influenced by these choices.

11.4 Organization of knowledge

Some refinement is also required when we speak of 'organization of knowledge'. First, we should take into account that its aim is to:

i preserve and select acquired knowledge;
ii transmit, transfer, use and diffuse acquired knowledge;
iii create new knowledge.

Second, we should distinguish between the organization of new and acquired knowledge and the organization of used knowledge.

While the organization of the acquired knowledge does not pertain only to the economic realm,[17] the organization of used knowledge and learning is mostly linked to economic aims and behaviours. These, in effect, determine the very range and kind of used knowledge.

If we take into account this, we must also accept that the endowment and composition of the human capabilities or human resource base depend more heavily on the organization of used knowledge and complementarities among inputs (Guidetti *et al.*, 2006) than on the production and acquisition of new knowledge.

11.4.1 The internal organization of knowledge and the 'competences pipeline'

In our model, presented in section 11.5, we will make extensive use of the concept of 'competences pipeline'. In order to spell out this concept, tentatively outlined in a previous work of ours (Antonelli and Pegoretti, 2005), we will devote some attention to this definition and its basis in the economic analysis.

First of all, let's recall some basic features of the system we considered in the previous paper, where the concept was developed. We considered an aggregate economic system, where labour was assumed to be heterogeneous, because of differences originated by the organization of used knowledge and learning both inside and outside the firm. In this respect, the composition of the human resource base depends more heavily on the organization of used knowledge and complementarities among inputs, rather than on the acquisition of a new one. On the other side, capital goods used by different workers were assumed to be homogeneous in kind; marginal productivity for workers belonging to the same group was assumed to be the same across the group, and constant over each single period of time.

In such a framework, the permanence of the worker inside the same firm entails a learning effect, which amounts to acquiring two kinds of competences:

a competences which can be exploited only inside the specific firm;
b competences which are usable also in different firms.

As regards the former, their effect is to build up different 'vintages' of workers, according to the duration of the respective permanence inside the specific firm.

In the chapter, we portrayed this process as a kind of 'pipeline': fresh workers enter the first stage, then inside the pipeline their competences are upgraded with their 'vintage' from stage to stage (see Figure 11.1). In this representation, it was assumed that firms do not incur any costs for such improvement, which is due to accumulation of experience of the specific organizational and productive environment – in other words, learning by doing.

Each stage of the pipeline represents a level of 'competences' the workers have acquired; for the sake of simplicity, we did not consider (and we also do not in the present work) different tasks, though the firms organization can be of course articulated in a high number of them. In any case the pipeline represents the available composition of knowledge and learning. More advanced competences are assumed to make the production more efficient; we use the output/labour ratio as a measure of 'productivity'.

The pipeline is based on stable routines, which have been generated by the organization of knowledge mainly internal to the firm. The job-competition model can be useful in explaining how the competences pipeline works. However, some basic features of the model have to be taken into account. First, in this model competition takes place on the job openings and, therefore, markets adjustments refer to the quantities (number and types) of the jobs and workers involved, while the wage rates are exogenous.[18] Second, job-competition fits better to the working of internal labour markets. Third, in the job-competition

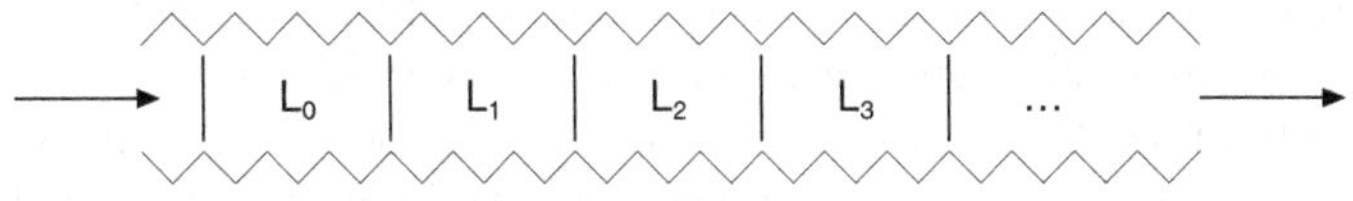

Figure 11.1 The competences 'pipeline'.

model demand and supply curves shift in the short run in order to bring about equilibrium in labour markets. Modifications in relative wages take place only after persistent phases of disequilibrium. Due to the fact that particular competences are generated only when labour demand needs them, the demand and supply curves are not independent from each other: the supply of trained labour depends on the demand of trained labour. Lastly, mobility between pipelines belonging to different firms can be determined only by firings and 'poaching'.

However, the general learning process which entails the worker with acquiring skills and competences usable in different firms is due partly to the *learning mechanisms internal to the firm* and partly to the *external educational and training sub-system* (E&T).

As regards the external educational and training system, its effects on productivity are supposed to be connected to collective and private (by households and firms) expenditure in such fields. This allows the labour supply to acquire some degrees of autonomy with respect to the demand side. In order to simplify the structure of the model, we considered training activities external or internal, other than the ones which are directed to increase firm-specific competences, to have the simple effect of up-dating workers' knowledge. Since fresh workers too are endowed by E&T with an updated knowledge, such assumption was equivalent to assuming that the only source of differentiation among workers' abilities is given by the acquisition of firm-specific competences. One consequence of this is that in such a model drop-out workers can be treated like fresh ones; in the case when one firm hires such workers, they are put at the beginning of the 'pipeline', just like fresh workers. From the whole system point of view, this entails a loss in efficiency, since the experienced workers re-entering the production process lose part of the ability they had acquired, i.e. the firm-specific competences.

In what follows, we will relax such an assumption, in order to take into account more complicated – and realistic – dynamics which affect the relationships among knowledge, competences and innovation, in the framework previously outlined.

Nonetheless, this elementary case explains in a better way the distinction we already made in the previous paper between knowledge and competences. In order to clarify it, we will distinguish between acquired and used knowledge and competences. The 'downgraded' worker, who re-enters the pipeline at a lower stage, looses the opportunity of using some of the competences he/she is endowed with.

At the same time, he/she is compelled to compete with the younger colleagues, which can reverberate itself inside the firm, as well as on the labour market, and may generate conflicts between different coalitions of interests.

To begin widening our representation, let us reconsider the case when workers move from one firm to another; this implies the loss of the firm-specific competences the moving worker had acquired while in the former firm. Nonetheless, we assume that such competences account for only a part of the knowledge/competence advantage he/she accumulated, if compared to the fresh worker. This means that the workplace change will position the worker not at the beginning, but somewhere in the middle of the pipeline. A similar case is depicted in Figure 11.2.

In this example, an experienced worker moves from firm A to firm B, where the knowledge/competence endowment he/she has acquired from the external education and training sub-system and from the internal one (to the firm) entails an advantage with respect of the fresh worker, whose endowment comes from external sources only.[19]

Since the cost of the internal training is sustained by firm A, this latter creates an externality for firm B, which gains, in the example, an L_1 level worker at no cost (except for wages, of course). This worker has been trained at the cost of an L_3 level worker, which has been sustained by Firm A. At the aggregate level, the overall productivity suffers a loss, since the more experienced worker has been 'downgraded', moving to a workplace where his/her experience is partially unusable. There takes place a process where 'preserving' the acquired knowledge does not mean using it, since a selection mechanism focuses on the subset which is usable in the new environment.

Note that, in this as well as in the previous case, the older worker competes with the younger ones, in the new firm. Since his/her experience is partly not usable, his/her knowledge/competence endowment falls in the same range of the younger colleagues: in other terms, there no more exists a precise correspondence between the 'vintage' of the worker and the stage of the pipeline.

The same applies to the case where the general (non firm-specific) learning process is different for the younger and for the older workers: for instance, we could assume that the life-long education system (which operates both inside and outside the firm) is not as efficient, in updating the workers' knowledge/competences, as the formal mechanisms which is involved in E&T of the next-to-be fresh workers. Or, simply, the learning capability of the older is less than the younger one. This involves a competition between the two categories, which can take place inside the same firm too.[20]

In the following example, such a likely outcome is represented by two features: an 'updated' pipeline, where new cohorts of workers are endowed with better knowledge, and a 'leakage' from the former pipeline to the latter, where

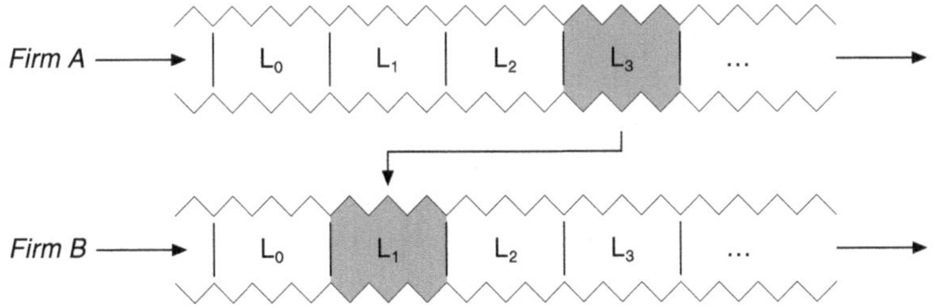

Figure 11.2 Changing job.

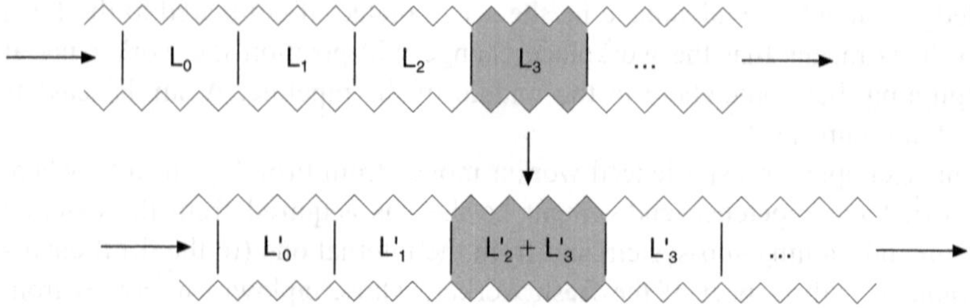

Figure 11.3 Competing cohorts.

the older worker competes with the younger (for the sake of simplicity, only one vintage, L_3, appears to have been downgraded in Figure 11.3).

Finally, we can consider the case where a sharply innovative process is introduced. Fresh workers are able to manage it, while the older ones are experienced in the obsolete process. If the two processes co-exist for a number of periods, which can happen inside the same firm too, this situation could be shown, for example, as follows (see Figure 11.4):

In this case, the system's efficiency will be increased, though the employment dynamics may evolve along different paths, depending on the labour-intensity of the new technique and the demand for the good being produced.

While the case shown in Figure 11.4 represents a technological discontinuity, Figure 11.3 describes a process which takes place continuously, even if not regularly. Nonetheless, both of them involve a series of questions, internal and external to the firm.

As regards the internal issues:

a cohorts may overlap partly, crowding some intermediate stage of the pipeline;
b while, in the adjustment phase, the upper stages may be underfed;
c a conflict may arise, between the younger and the older workers, focused on job positions and salaries;
d the firm must activate appropriate policies, which range from salaries and responsibilities rescaling, to reinforced training activities;

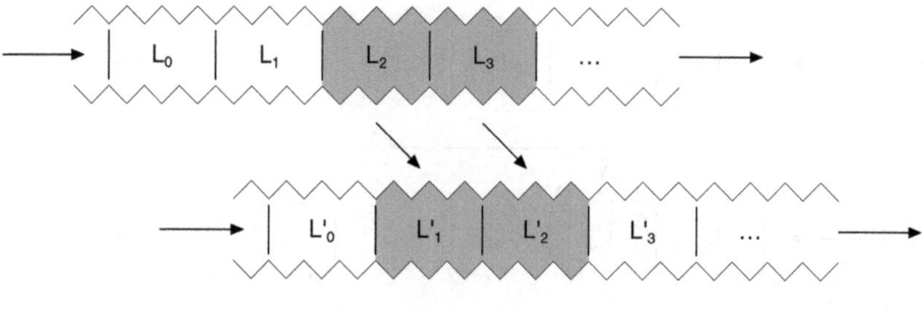

Figure 11.4 Innovating processes.

e the investment policy of the firm (both in tangible and in intangible assets) must keep pace with the changes (either progressive, or irregular) in the technological framework.

In the simplified model we will introduce, only a part of the possibilities we outlined above. Moreover, an important difference with respect to the assumptions we made in the previous work, is that we assume here that firms pay costs explicitly related to organized training activities. In other words, in this case we are considering on-the-job training. At the same time, we set aside the hypothesis that the permanence of the workers inside the same firm entails a learning effect *per se*. Though interesting, such a mechanism will be neglected here, since our focus will be on the active (and costly) training strategies that firms purposely design.

11.4.2 The external organization of knowledge and the 'engines of growth'

The working of the NRE seems to drive us to give more attention to at least two features of the relationship between labour markets and economic growth: long term is an essential time dimension; institutions, together with internal firm organization, are crucial tools in the management of knowledge that can lead to productivity increases.

In this respect, we have to stress that productivity in what follows is defined as the output labour ratio.

Our attention is focused on one main point. Given the importance of productivity dynamics, the model shows that even very simple assumptions concerning its determinants can bring about complex paths that soften usual unilateral conjectures about the causal links between productivity and employment.

Our model is based on a very simplified stylization of the actual working of the economic system. It offers only an aggregate view of the production process. In particular, it concentrates on the impact on firm productivity of some of its key determinants.

The three key 'engines', or paths, which have the effect of enhancing productivity are analysed in the framework of NRE. Knowledge is the basic production factor and its use in the production process can be channelled through three paths (see Figure 11.5):

i The first one corresponds to the work-based learning and in this case knowledge is generated as a by-product of the production process within the firms. Productivity increases from this source are not easily transferable to different firms and contexts.

ii The second engine corresponds to the general learning process which is partly internal to the firm and partly external. The external component takes place in the educational and training public/private agencies. Along this

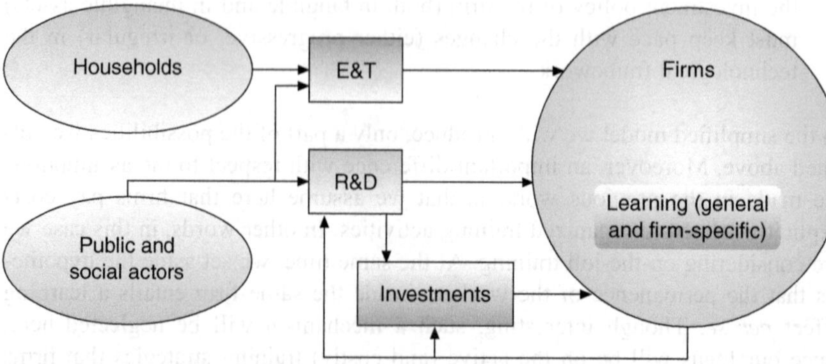

Figure 11.5 Sources of productivity increase.

path general skills and competences are acquired which are usable in different firms and in different contexts.

iii The third engine works through process innovation,[21] which is originated by investments in new capital (technological innovation) and in new organizational methods. They are favoured by research and development activities, carried out both by firms and public/private agencies.

In this way knowledge can be captured and structured by organizations which are both internal and external to the firms.

A clear-cut distinction is maintained in this framework of analysis between knowledge and competence.

As regards the system as a whole:

a the labour markets must reallocate workers which were dropped out, as a result of the overcrowding of some stages of the pipeline;
b E&T shall provide new and old workers the skills/competences needed in the technologically updated framework;
c the research and development sub-system (R&D) will provide the flows of innovations which are included in the firm investments.

Such processes appear to be more complicated when we take into account the aggregate demand along the business cycle. In some phases a number of workers will be dropped out as a consequence of a lack of demand; which stages of the pipeline will be mainly hit depends on a number of factors, like for instance productivity, salary schemes, institutional arrangements, norms and incentives for retiring, and many others. In some other phases, a shortage will emerge, in some stages of the pipeline. This depends crucially on two elements:

A the policy previously adopted by the firms in making some stages of the pipeline thin;

B the capabilities of E&T, which is in charge for providing the required skills/competences.

11.5 A stylized model

The simple model we are going to introduce here aims at highlighting some key relationships between economic system dynamics, human resources, knowledge, flexibility and competitive advantage. We will make use of the conceptual framework developed in the preceding sections, though in a simplified way: in particular, the model does not take into account the competition among firms inside the same economic system, while concentrating on the role of a 'representative' firm, which exemplifies the average competitive position of the home system in terms of absolute advantage. Nor does it investigate deeper the competition among workers inside and across the pipelines. The core mechanisms of the model refer to the ways the firm acts internally, and interacts with the wide (socio-economic) system, in order to incorporate, use and improve the knowledge made available through E&T, R&D and investments. To this purpose, we'll introduce some cost functions, which can help in showing the dynamic effects, on the firm performance, of non-regular (non-predictable) events, such as the cyclical variability of the economic activity and the spurts of innovations.

The following assumptions are made.

a Only one good is produced in the system and is utilized as 'numéraire'. The good being produced by different firms is supposed to be homogeneous, being thus entitled a unique price.

b We take a constant coefficient production function, which emphasizes the complementarity relationship between the factors of production.

c The goods market is assumed to be not perfectly competitive, so firms can gain an extra profit. This comes from the firm ability to select and train the best employees for the job it offers.

d The initial knowledge endowment is supposed to be the same for all workers, as provided by E&T. A minimum endowment is required, in order to operate the production process. More advanced technical processes require higher initial endowments.[22]

e The firm picks the workers from a labour market ruled by a 'job competition' mechanism. On the one hand, workers compete for a job paid initially at an entry wage rate; on the other, the firm selects the workers it believes best suited to be trained for enhancing their productivity, on the basis of their individual characteristics.

f The internal training provided by the firm is mainly, but not only, firm-specific.

Being mainly interested in the competitive advantage at the system level, we do not pay attention here to the competition in the home market. Though we consider each firm in this market to be different in principle from the others (e.g. as regards entrepreneurial capacity and experience, organization and forecasting ability), the firm we explicitly consider here will be treated as a kind of 'representative' firm. What is important, in our perspective, is to show how the firm behaviour and its chances to compete are heavily affected by the national system capacities, through its norms, institutions and specific sub-systems – like the ones we have introduced before.

Thus, while assumptions (a) and (c) depict a system with a multiplicity of firms, we will not consider the market relationships among them. In particular, while concentrating upon the competitive position and the strategies of the average, representative firm, we rule out some interrelations – like, for instance, the mobility of trained workers between firms, with the associated externality effects – which broadly cancel out in the average. In similar ways, possible shortages or excess supply of workers pertaining to a specific stage of the pipeline, cannot be eliminated at the system level by moving workers from a firm to another one. The 'average' firm is representative of this situation, where the availability of workers with the proper training depends on the system mechanisms (e.g. the initial knowledge endowments) and on the firm capacity to forecast, and to plan and operate the necessary training policies.

In such a framework, therefore, the competitive advantage derives from the firm organizational capacity, together with the social capabilities, in particular, the ones which are related to the creation of knowledge, innovation and to the working of E&T. This latter plays a crucial role, since the firm can improve the performance of the employees through (expensive) internal training, but the initial level is given by the knowledge endowment each worker received from E&T. Moreover, not all employees are suitable to be trained properly up to a certain degree inside the firm: this is the reason why each stage of the pipeline may be less populated than the previous one.

The firm incurs some costs in order to train the employees, with the aim of increasing their efficiency. On the other hand, such training increases the employees' efficiency and raises the workers' marginal product. An extra profit arises when such a marginal product overrides the marginal cost, taking also into account the higher wage paid to trained workers. It is implicitly assumed that workers accept to be trained and thus forwarded in the pipeline, because they deem the marginal disutility of their work with the new competencies to be less than the utility brought about by new wages.[23] In this situation, the difference between the marginal product and the latter can give rise to an extra profit and constitute the margin for increasing the firm competitive advantage.

The structure of production costs will derive from a simple fixed coefficient production function, where:

a_t is the variable capital input coefficient at time t

l_t^j is the labour input coefficient of j type at time t, where "j type" refers to the stage in the pipeline and hence to the attached labour efficiency

k_t is the fixed capital[24] depreciation coefficient at time t

The unit cost of production at time t is then:

$$UC_t = a_t + k_t + \sum_{j=1}^{n} w_j x_t^j l_t^j$$

where w_j is the unit wage, measured in terms of the numéraire, for the labour of kind j, x_t^j is the share of total product produced by workers belonging to the same stage j of the pipeline at time t, and n is the number of stages in the pipeline.

Consider now the relationship between the internal training activity and the increase in labour productivity. Being that the trained labour is more efficient, the firm would like to use as much as possible of it, provided that the training costs and the extra-wage do not exceed the benefits in terms of productivity. But, at any time t, the availability of trained labour depends on the training activity which has been carried out in the past. In other terms:

$$L_t^j = L_{t-1}^j + \hat{L}_{t-1}^j - \hat{L}_{t-1}^{j+1}, \quad j = 2, \ldots, n-1$$

where L_{t-1}^j represents the *stock* of labour of kind j available in the period $t-1$, $L^{\wedge j}_{t-1}$ the number of workers upgraded to the stage j of the pipeline during the same period, and $L^{\wedge j+1}_{t-1}$ represents the number of workers passed from the stage j to the stage $j+1$, plus the j-stage workers who left the firm for whatever reason. The hypothesis is made, that the time necessary to upgrade workers from one stage to another of the pipeline coincides with the production period.[25] As we pointed out, not all the workers are necessarily involved in a training process, due to a selection operated by the firm on the basis of the single worker's characteristics. The above relation holds recursively, so the firm faces a dynamic optimization problem, which, starting from the demand forecast for the product, involves the investment in fixed capital (i.e. the choice of technology and productive capacity) and the decision on how to implement the pipeline over the time. The latter is not a trivial aspect of the problem, since the stock of each kind of labour is subject to depletion due to a series of reasons:[26]

a the transition of upgraded workers, who leave the previous stage of the pipeline;
b the retirement of older workers;
c the tear-off of workers during the negative phases of the business cycle.

Note that the last two processes cause a loss of acquired knowledge. Since its acquisition by part of the workers was costly to the firm, it is reasonable to suppose that the retirement age had been one of the variables it considered while making its decisions. On the other hand, this is not the case for workers dropped out during a slump: in such cases, part of their training costs becomes a sunk cost for the firm.

What is the nature of the training cost for the firm? It cannot be assimilated to a part of the wage, since it is not correlated to the labour services. It must be seen instead as an investment cost, since its purpose is to set up a stock of incorporated knowledge, which the firm can use in the future as long as the trained workers remain employees. Thus the fixed capital coefficient is made of two parts: k_t and $\sum_{j=2}^{n}\omega_t^j$.

Where k_t is the coefficient of physical capital depreciation, and ω_t^j represents the period amortization share of the training costs paid in the past in order to train workers from the $j-1$ to the j stage. This is worth a deeper explanation. Firms usually recover such costs in the same period they pay for them, though their effects will span over a number of future periods. Nonetheless, only along a steady state path would it be correct to attach ω_t^j such meaning, since in such a case the balance in each period is obviously the same and the cash flow generated will cover all the costs and allow for the (extra) profit at a constant rate.

The unit production cost is thus given by:

$$UC_t=a_t+k_t+\sum_{j=1}^{n}\omega_t^j+\sum_{j=1}^{n}w_jx_t^jl_t^j$$

and the marginal cost:

$$MC_t=a_t+\sum_{j=1}^{n}w_jx_t^jl_t^j$$

The firm is interested in activating the training process which will upgrade a worker from the stage $j-1$ to the stage j of the pipeline, at the cost φ_j, if:

$$\varphi_j\leq\sum_{t=1}^{m}\frac{1}{(1+r)^t}\left[\left(\frac{1}{l_t^j}-w_j\right)-\left(\frac{1}{l_t^{j-1}}-w_{j-1}\right)\right]$$

that is, if the increase in labour efficiency overrides the training cost and the extra wage (m being the planned periods of activity of the trained workers). In the last expression, as well as in the following, the time subscript could be omitted for the technical coefficients (physical and variable capital, and labour of type j), if they are supposed not to vary over time.

Different labour efficiencies could bring about different consumption of variable capital, which would give rise to a specific variable capital coefficient a_t^j. For the sake of simplicity, we will not consider here such possibility. For the same reason, we assume that using different kinds of labour will not affect the duration of the physical capital.

In the short period, the firm's interest to stay in the business depends on the possibility of covering at least the variable costs:

$$1\geq a_t+\sum_{j=1}^{n}w_jx_t^jl_t^j$$

But in general the firm will aim at maximizing its profit over a number of periods, which could be related, for instance, to the time horizon of the investment in physical capital. It is reasonable to suppose that the length of the pipeline be less than the duration of the physical capital.[27] Thus, taking the length of h periods for the latter, we have the following problem:

$$\max \sum_{t=0}^{h-1} \frac{1}{(1+r)^t} \left[1 - \left(a_t + k_t + \sum_{j=0}^{n} \omega_t^j + \sum_{j=0}^{n} w_j x_t^j l_t^j \right) \right] Q_t$$

subject to

$$\begin{cases} L_t^j = L_{t-1}^j + \hat{L}_{t-1}^j - \hat{L}_{t-1}^{j+1}, \quad t=1,\dots,h, j=1,\dots,n-1 \\ \sum_{j=1}^{n} L_t^j / l_t^j \geq Q_t \end{cases}$$

where Q_t is the total quantity to be produced in the period t.

Merging the two constraints, we have:

$$\sum_{j=1}^{n} (L_{t-1}^j + \hat{L}_{t-1}^j - \hat{L}_{t-1}^{j+1}) / l_t^j \geq Q_t, \quad t=1,\dots,h$$

Since the stocks of trained workers are given in each period, the firm can only increase its production, if the demand requires it, by hiring fresh workers (of the kind L_1), whose efficiency is lower.

The stylized model above represents the problem the firm faces while planning its activities; the system described can show a very complex dynamics. We are not interested here in a solution (either analytical, or numerical) of the model, but we simply want to emphasize some relationships between the firm and the economic and institutional framework and discuss how such relationships may affect the firm strategy.

The firm tries to identify an optimal path (capital investment, training activities, production) starting from such data as the forecasts about future demand, the firm organization capacity, the labour market supply (also with regard to the individual characteristic of workers), the base wage, the wage differentials for different levels of efficiency, which are presumably subject to bargaining between the firm and its employees.

Then, due to a number of reasons, the real path may diverge from the optimal one. In such circumstances, the firm faces the necessity of taking some decisions, which are mainly of two kinds:

i Reshape the optimal trajectory, adapting it to the changed framework; this is a long-run planning decision and has to be taken when the change is supposed to be definitive, or persistent along a considerable number of periods at least.

ii Correct the path along the present trajectory, in order to optimize the transition to the new one (or to the old one in the case where the perturbation is perceived as transitory); this is a short-term decision.

Both of them depend not only on the internal organization of knowledge, but also – and often considerably – on the external one, notably on the working of the sub-systems we mentioned before. The interactions of such elements with the firm decisions affect its competitive advantage in the short as well as in the long run, though in different ways.

In order to give an illustration of this, we focus on some events which change the framework the firm observed when designing its strategy: notably, the effects of the working of the business cycle and of the introduction of an innovative production process.

In performing this analysis, we make a 'qualitative' use of the model, which is neither solved, nor simulated here. Some dynamics were simulated for a simpler environment, in a previous paper:[28] the model we introduced there was quite simple, but nevertheless it showed that the kind of interactions between the actors we are considering in the present work can represent crucial mechanisms.

Thus, in the following two sections we will not trace the firms behaviour out of the model, but we will show some possible strategies and consequences, using the relations we drew as a logical framework for mind experiments. Such experiments will be extended to analytical and numerical tests in a future work.

11.6 The business cycle – flexibility vs. rigidity

Though the business cycle is a well observed (and studied) phenomenon, its timing and phasing are unpredictable in the medium to long term, which is the planning horizon for the firm. When the actual business diverges from the planned one, the firm has to take some decisions. Take, for instance, the case where the demand is higher than the level predicted. In such a case, the firm can react promptly, by hiring new workers on the labour market.[29] Being the fresh workers less efficient than the trained ones, the unit cost of production will increase:[30] the component of the cost given by

$$\sum_{j=0}^{n} w_j x_t^j l_t^j$$

will become greater, due to the increasing weight of the workers belonging to the initial stage of the pipeline.

If, after adjusting its forecasts the firm believes that the demand change will last for a sufficient number of periods, it will adjust its training plans, gradually increasing the pipeline capacity: an upsurge in the production cost will then be followed by a progressive fall, provided that the firm training and organization capacities are adequate.

The opposite case, when the cycle enters a slowdown phase, is more interesting, since it involves a greater variety of phenomena and the working of various mechanisms. When the demand decreases, the firm faces a situation where its stocks of trained workers become partly redundant.

If the slowdown is deemed to be transitory, the firm will probably keep the workers, thus facing an increase in the production cost, since part of them will be not- or under-utilized. Since the wages are to be paid to all employees, the unit labour cost will increase, as if each active worker would be paid more, or if the labour coefficients increased.[31] The firm will maintain for a short time a reservoir of non-active workers, in the perspective of a future increase in the demand, which will probably pick from the lower stages of the pipeline (representing lower degrees of labour efficiency).

But what if the slowdown is perceived to be not just a short-run phenomenon? Here the firm strategy will depend on its evaluation of a number of long-run factors. In particular, the various alternatives will be evaluated also taking into account the necessity to reach the upturn in competitive conditions. A crucial decision refers to the opportunity to dismiss part of the labour force employed. In this way the firm could ease its situation on the cost side; on the other hand such a decision would imply the non-utilization – and practically the removal from the firm endowment – of the knowledge acquired by the workers being dropped out. This could result in damage when the firm tries to keep pace with the future business expansion. While considering this kind of decision, the firm takes into account some external elements – deriving partly from governmental policies – such as, for instance, the existence of incentives to dismiss specific categories of workers (e.g. the more aged ones), and the capacity of the system to provide competitive boosts in the following phases of the cycle. This involves, in particular, the working of R&D and E&T.

Let us imagine the demand falls in the period t_1 and the firm forecasts place the recovery after *s* periods. If we suppose that the external framework will not change as regards technology and E&T performance, the firm will consider the initial (i.e. before the demand slump) unit cost to be restored at the end of the transition period. Then the alternative strategies the firm can devise – which involve interactions with the external system – turn out to be different cost trajectories.

In order to give a simplified graphic representation, let us assume, for a moment, that the original long-term plan of the firm identified a unit cost *constant* over time, at the level UC_0. Therefore, this will also be the target cost at the end of the transition period.

Consider the following graph (Figure 11.6), which shows possible dynamics of the unit cost of production.

The initial slump will cause an increase in the unit cost (UC_1), since the firm would probably not react instantaneously to the new situation. After that, the firm strategy will determine the cost dynamics. Let us consider here two opposite strategies.

In the first one, the firm aims at reducing the cost during the transition period, and in order to do so, it dismisses part of the labour force; in this way, it follows a path like the one going from UC_1 to UC_A.

With the second strategy, the firm maintains the whole (or the main part) of the labour force, thus accepting an increase in cost, like moving UC_1 to UC_C.

What are the long-term consequences of the two alternatives? If we suppose that the firm will dismiss, in the first hypothesis, also part of the trained workers,[32] it will loose a stock of acquired knowledge; moreover, the firm could decide, in order to reduce the costs, to shrink or suspend the training pro-

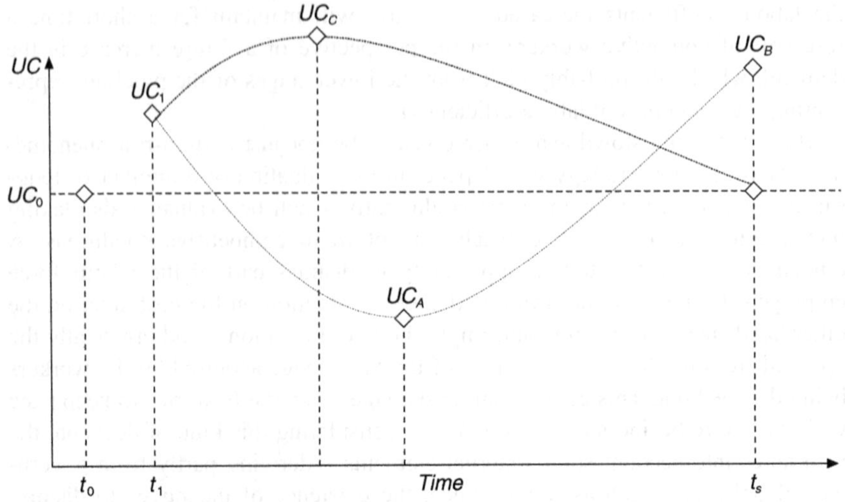

Figure 11.6 Conjectural paths for cost dynamics.

grammes. In the upswing, therefore, such stock will have to be rebuilt, and the firm will start the new cycle with a half-empty pipeline, thus producing at higher costs. The pipeline will be filled gradually, affecting the ability of the firm to compete for a number of periods. By adopting the second strategy, the firm will find itself at the end with the pipeline in full operation. In the recovery phase its cost will drop down to the initial one, and the competitiveness conditions will be restored.

Of course, such strategies are only sketched here, since the firm faces a variety of alternatives as regards the training policy and the choice of the degree to which the pipeline should be implemented during the transitory phase. Nonetheless, they give a clear view of the problem and its implications. If we further remove the assumption of a constant target cost (which is neither implied in, nor can probably result from the dynamic optimization process), the decision process turns out to be more complicated, but still hinges on the same factors.

Which strategy will be chosen depends on a number of factors, among which the most relevant are:

i The length of the transition phase, which affects the capability of the firm to sustain extra costs.
ii The social adaptation capacity, with particular reference to the allowed alternatives regarding the labour utilization: norms, contracts, social habits and industrial relations, for instance, influence the range of options open to the firm in dismissing part of the labour force.
iii The system's social capabilities, which can be more or less adequate in supporting the firm in the recovery phase. Note, in particular, that dismissing

labour force in excess supply will often determine a loss of acquired knowledge. Such loss can be compensated if R&D and E&T are able to provide adequate competences to be transferred into the firm (if not, a possible outcome is a path like the one from UC_A to UC_B).

Some simulation exercises carried out on a simplified model in a previous paper[33] have shown that the organization of knowledge external to the firm can play (through the 'engines' we mentioned above) a decisive role in compensating the loss of acquired knowledge which takes place in a 'flexible' system.

11.7 Innovation and its effects on the firm's strategies

Let us turn now to a different kind of event, such as the introduction of an innovative production process for producing the same good, which can therefore be produced at a lower cost. As we have seen before (see Figure 11.4), an aspect of this phenomenon can be represented by a shift of the pipeline. Now the firm faces two problems: (a) how to adapt its long-period strategy and to plan a new optimal path, and (b) how to manage the transition phase, during which the two techniques (the old and the innovative one) may co-exist. Since the old technique entails higher production costs, the firm will try to get rid of it as soon as possible. Possible obstacles in this direction are:

a The path of acquisition of the new technique takes time, since it requires adapting the organization, the fixed capital and the training process, and also allowing the latter the time to fill in the new pipeline.
b It is not possible – or is too expensive – to convert part of the employees to the new technique, since the knowledge requirement is different from the old technique, and the firm cannot dismiss them, due to various possible reasons.

Anyway, the old technique will be dismissed abruptly (and the firm will probably get out of the market, if it cannot quickly implement the new one) if the costs entailed are too high, compared with the new (lower) price of the good. If not, the firm can gain a low profit rate by operating it during the transition phase.[34]

Let us suppose the two techniques coexist for a number of periods. In the transition phase, some of the workers could be moved from the old process to the new one. This change could entail a different use of their competences: in particular, there will be a loss of acquired knowledge and the 'old' workers will be subject to a new training scheme, at least partially. The shift in the pipeline means that they will be 'downgraded', passing to a lower stage in the new pipeline. The firm will sustain a new training cost (after paying for the 'old' training) and moreover, in some cases (depending on the contractual mechanisms) such workers could possibly maintain a higher wage, related to their past efficiency, which could potentially trigger a conflict among workers. Thus the transition phase is rather critical, since the long-run decision the firm must take is intertwined with the short-run constraints. If the firm cannot utilize, in the new process, the existing labour force, or cannot hire a new labour force to replace it, this will result in a slower transition to the new technique.

But, even more important, every time an innovation is introduced the firms need people endowed with the necessary capacities to run it. This means that E&T must work synchronically with R&D, in order to make the new technique operable, by providing workers endowed with adequate knowledge, suitable for further training inside the firm.

The residual life of the old technique (and hence the time required to substitute it entirely with the new one) will thus depend on the following determinants.

i The cost advantage of the innovative process, i.e. the efficiency gradient with the old one.
ii The technological 'distance' between the two techniques,[35] which affects the possibility of utilizing – at least partially – with the new process the competences created for the old one.
iii The 'flexibility' in the utilization of the labour force, depending mainly on normative and contractual arrangements.
iv The capability of R&D and E&T to provide, in due time, technological support and adequately trained people needed to operate the new technique. The latter issue relates both to the training of new workers which will be further trained inside the firm, and to the ability of converting the 'old' workers (life-long education system), making them acquire the necessary knowledge.

If the firm does not implement a training activity for the old process any more, though, continuing to utilize it for a while, the cost attained will progressively increase, since the gradual retirement of the older workers will involve also the workers belonging to the upper stages of the pipeline, thus decreasing the average efficiency.

We can portray such a situation in a graph based on the simplifying assumptions that both the average (planned) cost for the old and for the new process are constant over time.

Let UC_a be the unit cost relative to the old technique, and UC_b the unit cost relative to the new one.

The progressive increase of the cost related to the old process would bring it towards the price ceiling (i.e. 1), for instance, along the path passing through the points B and A. In A, the old process would be deactivated (also possibly below A), and the workers involved in it would be dismissed. Such an outcome could be partially changed if the interaction between the firm and the system (i.e. norms, institutions, markets, R&D and E&T) produces a different framework.

For instance, an effective long-life learning policy could deviate the path from B-A to B-C, by easing the transition of the 'old' workers to the new process and by making the old process to be dropped early. On the contrary,

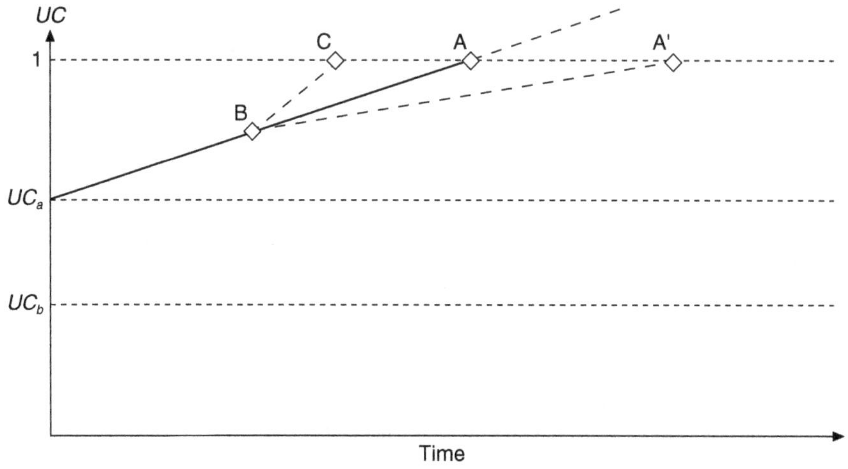

Figure 11.7 Cost dynamics: two techniques.

the existence of 'exit costs' or some other kind of disincentives for the firm to dismiss workers could make convenient to prolong the life of the old process, thus moving along the path B-A. In the meantime, however, the firm would suffer a loss in its competitive advantage, due to the higher production cost.

The relationships between social capabilities and flexibility is, therefore, complex, and different combinations may result in different profiles of competitive advantage. But it is also important to take into consideration the costs which are partly external to the firm: mainly the cost of knowledge, on the one hand, and the social costs of flexibility on the other.

11.8 Conclusions

The knowledge endowment of an economic system depends on the existence of a coherent and balanced mechanism for the creation and management of potential/acquired knowledge, on the one side, and actual/used knowledge, on the other. It is the final outcome, measurable by means of its different dimensions considered in this work, of the external and internal organization of knowledge each system has been capable to develop over time. Both apparatus function as focusing devices as well as rewind structures. They converge in the formation of the competencies pipelines, which can be considered as reservoirs for used knowledge. Their size and composition are long-term assets crucial for the competitive advantage of the economy.

The conclusion we can learn from the investigation carried out in the present work is very simple. A proper evaluation of the costs and benefits of flexibility/rigidity in the labour markets in terms of competitive advantage cannot be confined to their obvious short-term effects on the firm budget associated with variously conditioned utilizations of a productive factor.

A systemic and dynamic view is required. In this framework, what really matters is the brand of the overall interaction of the firm with the other component of the economic system, and particularly with the components which influence the organization of creation and use of knowledge in the economic arena.

Differences in the performance of these components can drastically influence the competitive position of a country. Therefore the competitive advantage should be considered as the final outcome of the degree of flexibility/rigidity side by side with the social capabilities available in the system.

Notes

1 The authors thank all the participants to the PRIN seminars and workshops held in the various universities of the network, with the usual disclaimer.
2 Reference can be made, for instance, to Kaplinsky (2005) and Baldone *et al.* (2006).
3 To the best of our knowledge, no exhaustive and general empirical evidence in favour of the wage equilibrium conjecture has been provided, making acceptable the above mentioned shift.
4 Among them we can mention Doeringer and Piore (1971) and Thurow (1976). But, more recently, also Green *et al.* (2001) seemed to share some of the views of the preceding authors.
5 An instance of an applied point of view along these lines can be find in Soete (2005).
6 For clarifications on the 'wage competition model', reference is made to section 2 in Antonelli, Nosvelli (2007), Chapter 4 in the present volume.
7 That is, making knowledge relevant for economic utilisation.
8 A similar distinction is made between skill acquired and skill used by Guidetti *et al.* (2006).
9 The notion of 'competences pipeline' tries to capture both forms of complementarity (Antonelli and Pegoretti, 2005).
10 Different models of capitalism are associated with different mechanisms for the generation of capabilities.
11 E.g. principles, formulas, patents, algorithms, prototypes.
12 This refers to tacit knowledge, but also to codified knowledge that overtime depreciates and even get lost. On the problem of knowledge storability see Michellone and Zollo (2000).
13 See, for instance, Antonelli and Leoncini (1994).
14 See, for instance, Antonelli and Pegoretti (1995), Antonelli (2002).
15 Apart from Antonelli and Pegoretti (2005) and Antonelli (2003), see again Guidetti *et al.* (2006).
16 Meaning that the acquisition of productive factors can take place wherever they cost less on a global scale.
17 Think, for instance, of the autonomous role of universities, science academies and cultural foundations.
18 E.g. wages can be determined by the bargaining process.
19 While considering different firms, the hypothesis of an aggregate system is conveniently replaced by the assumption that a single good is produced, which is the same for each firm; workers' productivities across the different firms are thus comparable.
20 In a post-industrial society, this effect can possibly become more important than the decline in efficiency in the manual work brought about by the age.
21 Product innovation is also important, but in the present context it is not relevant to

distinguish between different kinds of innovation, since we are focusing on the aggregate output. Moreover the demand for goods is assumed to be exogenous and cannot be stimulated by competition on quality.

22 This simplifying assumption in no way is intended to minimize the importance of the external E&T, which plays a vital role. It just allows us to get rid of any initial 'gradient' of knowledge endowment, and thus to focus on the internal training process (i.e. the new workers enter the pipeline at the level 1). The effects of the existence of different entry conditions for the individual workers is treated exhaustively by Thurow (1976).

23 The new wage level is determined by internal bargaining.

24 The hypothesis of one single good implies that the two capital coefficients are physically homogeneous. We assume here that the part of the capital we call 'fixed' consists of a portion of the good which takes a specific form and can be used only in the production process, where it is subject to depletion. We skip here the many interesting problems which arose in relation to this and were discussed in the literature on the theory of capital. We also assume that, given the initial investment made in accordance with the desired productive capacity, small adjustments in the capital endowment can be made in the short run (e.g. by buying additional machinery, or selling some pieces of it). In this way, the fixed capital coefficient can be seen as constant *vis à vis* changes in the production level. In this way, we can concentrate our attention on the role of labour (see below).

25 This is, of course, a simplifying, not necessary, hypothesis.

26 In addition, workers' efficiency may be affected by their age. In this respect, we could superimpose an 'efficiency decline' curve to the efficiency dynamics described by the upgrading of workers from one stage to another in the pipeline. But, since we did not suppose that all the workers pass through all the stages of the pipeline, the age distribution of workers may not be related to their distribution along the pipeline. In that case, such a curve could be seen as a 'background noise', not correlated with the functioning of the pipeline.

27 Since the new physical capital often (if not always) incorporates some kind of innovation, it would not make sense to train workers to make a better use of a capital that will be dropped out before the training process will be completed.

28 See Antonelli and Pegoretti (2005).

29 Let's suppose the level of unemployment is sufficient to prevent an increase in the wage rate. This hypothesis is made in order to isolate the mechanisms affecting the competitive advantage which we described above. A more complete description of the labour market could only, in this framework, add complexity without contributing to clarify the mechanisms we want to enlighten.

30 Since we are using a fixed coefficients production function, the unit cost for the physical capital will not benefit from the increase in production (as we pointed out above – see note 20 – we allow for a certain degree of flexibility in the supply of fixed capital). Otherwise, the greater share of non-trained workers would cause either an increase in the unit cost of production, or a smaller decrease, depending on the ratio between the increase in the labour cost and decrease in the (unit) fixed capital cost.

31 Similar effects would modify the capital coefficients, but since we focus in this chapter on the labour factor, we 'sterilize' this aspect – see notes 24 and 30.

32 This consequence might also be boosted by the incentives for the aged workers to retire.

33 See Antonelli and Pegoretti (2005).

34 On the transition between techniques, see also Pegoretti (1997).

35 For an analytical definition, see Pegoretti (1990).

References

Abramovitz M. (1989) *Thinking about growth*, Cambridge: Cambridge University Press.

Abramovitz M. (1991) The elements of social capability, Paper presented at the International Conference on 'Economic Development of LDC's', Seoul, Korea Development Institute, July, mimeo.

Acemoglu D. and Pischke J.S. (1999) Beyond Becker: training in imperfect labour markets, *The Economic Journal* 109 (453): 112–142.

Antonelli G. (1998) Il problema della disoccupazione in Italia: come evitare impostazioni unilaterali, *Economia Politica* XV (2): 191–207.

Antonelli G. (2002) Flessibilità e nuova economia reale, in G. Antonelli and M. Nosvelli (eds) *Monitoraggio e valutazione delle politiche del lavoro per una nuova economia*, Bologna: Il Mulino, pp. 7–20.

Antonelli G. (2003) Introduzione, in G. Antonelli (ed.) *Istruzione, economia e istituzioni*, Bologna: Il Mulino, pp. 7–21.

Antonelli G. (2004): Structural policies for structural change in Italy and European Union, in G. Antonelli and N. De Liso (eds) *European Economic Integration and Italian Labour Policies*, Aldershot: Ashgate, pp. 297–320.

Antonelli G. and Leoncini R. (1994) Creation and destruction of human resources in the process of economic growth: some thoughts on the Italian experience, *International Journal of Technology Management*, Special Issue on Technology, Human Resources and Growth 9 (3/4): 367–393.

Antonelli G. and Maggioni M.A. (1997) Formazione, competenze e lavoro in contesti economici in rapida evoluzione, in P. Terna (ed.) *La formazione e il lavoro al tempo delle reti telematiche*, Torino: Rosemberg & Sellier, pp. 91–125.

Antonelli G. and Nosvelli M. (2007) Demand for skilled labour services, job design and the 'revealed learning function', in R. Leoncini and S. Montresor (eds) *Dynamic capabilities between firm organization and local systems of production*, London: Routledge, pp. 107–135.

Antonelli G. and Pegoretti G. (1995) Paths of technological change, markets for production factors and the social cost of knowledge, *Dynamis – Quaderni IDSE*, Working paper no. 6.

Antonelli G. and Pegoretti G. (2005) Economic structure, organisation of knowledge, productivity, in G. Huber, H. Krämer and H.D. Kurz (eds) *Einkommensverteilung, technischer Fortschritt und struktureller Wandel*, Marburg: Metropolis Verlag, pp. 209–235.

Baldone S., Sdogati F. and Tajoli L. (2006) On some effects of international fragmentation of production on comparative advantages, trade flows, and the income of countries, Department of Management, Economics and Industrial Engineering, Politecnico di Milano, mimeo, May.

Becattini G. (2003) Nuovi orientamenti nello studio del pensiero di Alfred Marshall, *Rivista Italiana degli Economisti* (1): 3–20.

Doeringer P.B. and Piore M.J. (1971) *Internal labor markets and manpower analysis*, Lexington, MA: D.C. Heath.

Feyerabend P.K. (1975) *Against method. Outline of an anarchist theary of knowledge*, London: Verso.

Green F., Ashton D. and Felstead A. (2001) Estimating the determinants of supply of computing, problem-solving, communication, social and teamworking skills, *Oxford Economic Papers* 53 (3): 406–433.

Guidetti G., Mancinelli S. and Mazzanti M. (2006) Complementarity in training practices. Methodological notes and empirical evidence for a local economic system in Emilia-Romagna, Dipartimento di Economia Istituzioni Territorio, University of Ferrara, Working paper no. 5, April.

Jones R.W. and Kierzkowski H. (2001) A framework for fragmentation, in S. Arndt and H. Kierzkowski (eds) *Fragmentation: New Production and Trade Patterns in the World Economy*, Oxford: Oxford University Press, pp. 17–34.

Kaplinsky R. (2005) *Globalisation, poverty and inequality*, Cambridge: Polity Press.

Killick T. (1995) Relevance, meaning and determinants of flexibility, in T. Killick (ed.) *The flexible economy*, London: Routledge, pp. 1–33.

Loasby B.J. (1998) On the definition and organisation of capabilities, *Revue Internationale de Systémique*, 12 (1): 13–26.

Loasby B.J. (2000) Market institutions and economic evolution, *Journal of Evolutionary Economics*, 10 (3): 297–309.

Michellone G.C. and Zollo G. (2000) Competences management in knowledge-based firms, *International Journal of Manufacturing, Technology and Management* 1 (1): 20–41.

North D.C. (1990) *Institutions, institutional change and economic performance*, Cambridge: Cambridge University Press.

Pegoretti G. (1990) Offerta di risorse non riproducibili, scelta della tecnica e struttura produttiva, in A. Quadrio Curzio and R. Scazzieri (eds) *Dinamica economica strutturale*, Bologna: Il Mulino, pp. 81–121.

Pegoretti G. (1997) Sentieri di sviluppo tecnologico, mercati dei fattori.e. irreversibilità, *Economia e Lavoro*, XXXI (3–4): 243–257.

Richardson G.B. (1972) The organisation of industry, *Economic Journal*, 82: 883–896.

Soete L. (2005) Activating knowledge, United Nations University, Maastricht (mimeo).

Thurow L.C. (1976) *Generating inequality*, London: The Macmillan Press.

12 Vertical and horizontal patterns of intra-industry trade between EU and candidate countries

Hubert Gabrisch and Maria Luigia Segnana

Introduction

Trade flows are usually identified as being of inter-industry or intra-industry type. Inter-industry trade takes place when countries export and import goods produced by different industries. This type of specialization can be explained by factor endowment differences between the countries. The similarity of the countries generates a different type of trade flow, that is, intra-industry trade (IIT) or trade in similar goods.

The models produced by early IIT research (the "first generation") assumed it to be characterized by the exchange of varieties of the same quality backed by the same technologies; but in recent years one of the issues addressed by IIT is the distinction between horizontal and vertical product differentiation. The "second generation" of IIT models distinguishes two different flows of IIT: trade in varieties of similar qualities (horizontal or HIIT), and trade in different qualities (vertical or VIIT), which is explained by different determinants. This distinction means that industry or country characteristics of IIT may differ according to the type of product differentiation. Moreover, this distinction has certain implications for the welfare analysis of economic integration (Facchini and Segnana, 2003).

The importance of VIIT was first apparent in North–South trade, but it has recently attracted attention in regard to trade among members of regions with far-reaching trade liberalization, for example, the EU countries,[1] and particularly EU trade with Central and East European countries which are or have been candidate countries (CCs) for EU entry.[2] Empirical research on factors determining this structure within a EU-CC framework may be of specific interest in light of the rapid liberalization of trade between 1993 and 2000,[3] but it lags behind theoretical and empirical research on horizontal and vertical trade in other regions of the world. The literature on EU-CC trade patterns is often overwhelmingly descriptive, or has tenuous relations to trade theory. One of the few empirical studies on the subject pertains rather to industrial economics (Aturupane *et al.*, 1999) and has tested VIIT and HIIT separately by industry specific effects. However, in the international literature, the empirical tests of country-specific models seem to perform better than do those of industry-specific models.

The importance of VIIT in EU-CC trade flows can be explained by drawing on the "second generation" IIT literature, after full recognition, that different factors account for horizontal and vertical IIT. The explanation of IIT by means of a "horizontal" model may yield inconclusive results when IIT is overwhelmingly vertical, as it is the case of EU-CC trade flows. This highlights the importance of the VIIT models developed by Falvey and Kierzkowski (1987) and Flam and Helpman (1987), which were largely neglected in the earlier empirical IIT literature. Both models belong to a class where endowment or technological differences are combined with differences in consumers' preferences. In both of them, income inequality differences play a leading role in explaining demand by households for the differentiated goods. The models differ in one important respect: the source of quality differentiation.

The Falvey-Kierzkowski model (1987) derives from the traditional Heckscher-Ohlin framework with perfect competition, and explains VIIT by factor endowment differences (which correspond to per capita income differences in the context of the model) between countries. Thus, VIIT will be greater, the greater the differences in relative factor endowments, but the model also suggests that VIIT is positively correlated with differences in the pattern of income distribution between countries.

The Flam-Helpman model (1987) assumes monopolistic competition in a Ricardian framework and adds income distribution among households to the usual determinants of intra-industry flows. VIIT is explained by differences in technology, income, and income distribution. The source of quality differentiation is not the amount of capital used to produce the good, as in Falvey and Kierzkowski (1987), but the technology used.

The aim of this chapter is to examine the relationship between the pattern of IIT and its determinants, with the focus on VIIT. We apply the framework developed by the literature on vertically differentiated products to EU-CC trade patterns and utilize an empirical strategy to estimate the Flam-Helpman model's predictions. In this case, unlike in the Falvey and Kierzkowski approach, a product-quality cycle with vertical intra-industry trade can be set in motion. This cycle associated with technological and income distribution differences manifested by an increasing share of VIIT in total trade.

The chapter is organized as follows. Section 12.1 provides stylized facts on the emergence of different types of trade between EU and CCs. It illustrates how intra-industry trade flows come about and vertically differentiated products gain momentum. Section 12.2 shows how the link between the increasing share of VIIT and the product quality cycle comes into play in the IIT literature. Section 12.3 defines the model used and the reasons why specific determinants of VIIT can be associated with the product quality cycle, being explained by improvements in technology and in physical and human capital, and by income redistribution Section 12.4 tests the model with two specifications and EU-CC data, using regressions with OLS and fixed effects. Section 12.5 concludes.

12.1 Intra-industry trade between EU and CCs: stylized patterns

Overall IIT is conventionally calculated using the Grubel and Lloyd index and then dividing it into horizontal and vertical components on the basis of the unit values of exports and imports. This method has been used in the past decade to assess the product quality in trade data, and it has become widely employed to separate HIIT and VIIT.

In order to measure IIT, we use adjusted Grubel-Lloyd indices that correct for overall trade imbalances, given that balanced trade is a basic assumption of all models explaining IIT:[4]

$$GL = \frac{\sum_{i=1}^{n}(X_i+M_i) - \sum_{i=1}^{n}|X_i-M_i|}{\sum_{i=1}^{n}(X_i+M_i) - \left|\sum_{i=1}^{n}X_i - \sum_{i=1}^{n}M_i\right|} \qquad (1)$$

where GL is the adjusted share of intra-industry trade in the total trade of n industries, X_i and M_i are the exports and imports of the individual industry i. The second element in the denominator is the factor correcting for the overall trade imbalance. According to equation (1), inter-industry trade is the remainder: $1-GL$.

The indices are calculated for 778 industries throughout Chapters 3 to 8 (manufacturing industries) of the Comext Database for the years 1993[5] and 2000 (Combined Nomenclature). These industries accounted for 80 per cent of aggregate EU trade with 11 CCs[6] in 2000 (see Table 12.A1 in the Annex). The choice of the disaggregation level has a significant impact on the measured size of intra-industry trade.[7] We selected the four-digit level, because it best corresponds to the industry concept, while the two-digit level instead stands for sectors, and lower levels for products.

Our first finding is that trade among EU countries is of the intra-industry type, while EU trade with CCs is of the inter-industry type, measured at the chosen four-digit level of disaggregation (Table 12.1). While about 65 per cent of trade among the EU countries is IIT (unweighted mean), more than 60 per

Table 12.1 Intra-industry trade indices in intra-EU trade[a] and EU trade with candidate countries[b] (unweighted means), 1993 and 2000

	GL index (adjusted)	
Year	1993	2000
Intra-EU	0.637	0.649
Trade with candidate countries	0.342	0.391

Source: Own calculations based on Eurostat, 2002; see Annex Table 12.A2 and 12.A3.

Notes

a Individual EU countries against all other EU countries.

b Total EU with individual candidate countries.

cent is still inter-industry trade when we consider trade flows between EU and CCs. Trade liberalization caused the IIT share to increase between 1993 and 2000: The mean value of intra-industry trade shares in EU relations with CCs amounted to about 39 per cent of total trade in 2000, after being 34 per cent in 1993, reporting an appropriate decrease in inter-industry trade shares. The share of IIT was higher in EU trade with the Czech Republic, Poland, Hungary, and Slovenia (Annex Table 12.A3). The lowest share was to be found in trade with the Baltic countries (Latvia, Estonia, and Lithuania). In three cases – Bulgaria, Estonia, and Hungary – the IIT shares decreased between 1993 and 2000.

Our second finding is that IIT is more vertical in trade between EU and CCs than it is in trade among EU countries. The structure of IIT can be identified by applying the standard procedure for decomposing[8] VIIT and HIIT, that is, by using unit values (UV). A UV is defined as the turnover in exports or imports in ECU per metric ton. A relative unit value (RUV) outside the range selected – in this case, 15 per cent on either side of unity – qualifies the traded item as belonging to vertical intra-industry trade:[9]

$$\text{GLviit, if } 1.15 < \left(RUV_i = \frac{UVX_i}{UVM_i} \right) < 0.85 \qquad (2)$$

where *UVX* stands for the UV in exports, and *UVM* for the UV in imports of a single item. If $RUV > 1.15$, the aggregate index is often seen to be "high-quality VIIT" of the exporting country, assuming that the higher "price" that the export industry may obtain corresponds to a higher quality. If $RUV < 0.85$, a "high-quality VIIT" of the importing country is assumed.

The results of this calculation are illustrated in Figures 12.1 and 12.2.[10] The *X*-axis measures the share of IIT in total trade, and the *Y*-axis measures the share of VIIT in IIT. If a region or country is in one of the left quadrants, inter-industry trade is predominant. Horizontal intra-industry trade dominates in the lower right quadrant. This application confirms the inter-industry structure of aggregate EU trade with individual CCs in 1993 and still in 2000, and the IIT type flows in trade among the EU countries. The share of VIIT in IIT was 83 per cent in 1993 as well as in 2000. While trade with CCs moved towards the IIT type, it remained more or less unchanged in the VIIT quadrant.

EU trade pattern with four CCs – the Czech Republic, Hungary, Poland, and Slovenia – were in the upper right quadrant in 2000, indicating that trade was intra-industry dominated, and that among IIT it was VIIT dominated (Figure 12.2).

Our third finding concerns the quality split between EU and CCs. The term "vertical" implies that one member of each country pair has a quality advantage in the industry considered. When the export price of an EU industry exceeds the import price in this industry by more than 15 per cent, we assume that the EU has an advantage in quality in this industry. Mirror-inverted, the industry of a CC has a quality advantage over the respective EU industry when the EU's import price is at least 15 per cent less than the export price On isolating industries with a RUV higher than 1.15 and lower than 0.85, we

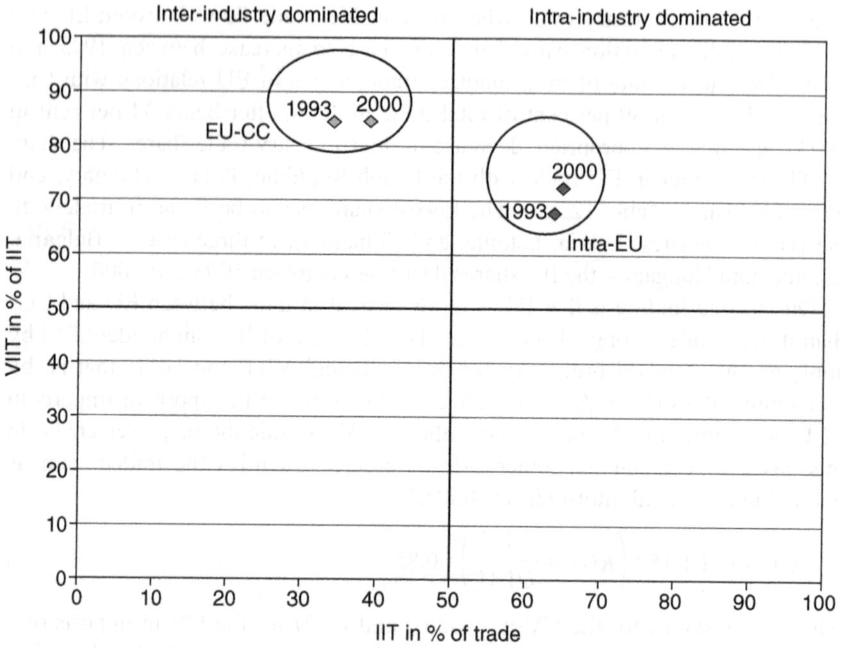

Figure 12.1 Types of EU trade flows, 1993 and 2000, adjusted Grubel–Lloyd Indices (unweighted means) (source: own calculations based on Eurostat, 2002. See also Tables 12.A2 and 12.A3 for Grubel–Lloyd indices).

found that the CCs had more quality advantages in vertical trade with the EU in 1993, but fewer such advantages in 2000. The quality advantage of the EU has increased significantly since trade has been liberalized (Table 12.2). The distribution of EU trade with individual CCs is illustrated by Figure 12.3: the most significant shift towards higher quality has occurred in trade with the Czech Republic and Poland, while in the case of trade with Romania, Bulgaria, and Estonia, the quality advantage of the EU has slightly diminished.

In light of these three findings, the emerging patterns of trade between the EU and the CCs can be characterized as follows:

- increased intra-industry trade;
- the dominance of vertically differentiated flows;
- the dominance of high and low quality differences in VIIT.

This predominantly vertical structure with quality advantage for the EU and less quality advantage for the CCs can be straightforwardly construed in terms of a product-quality cycle in which firms find it profitable to produce at the low end of the quality spectrum in a CC and at the high end in a EU country.

In order to explain this pattern, in what follows we identify the role played by product quality cycle in vertical trade flows.

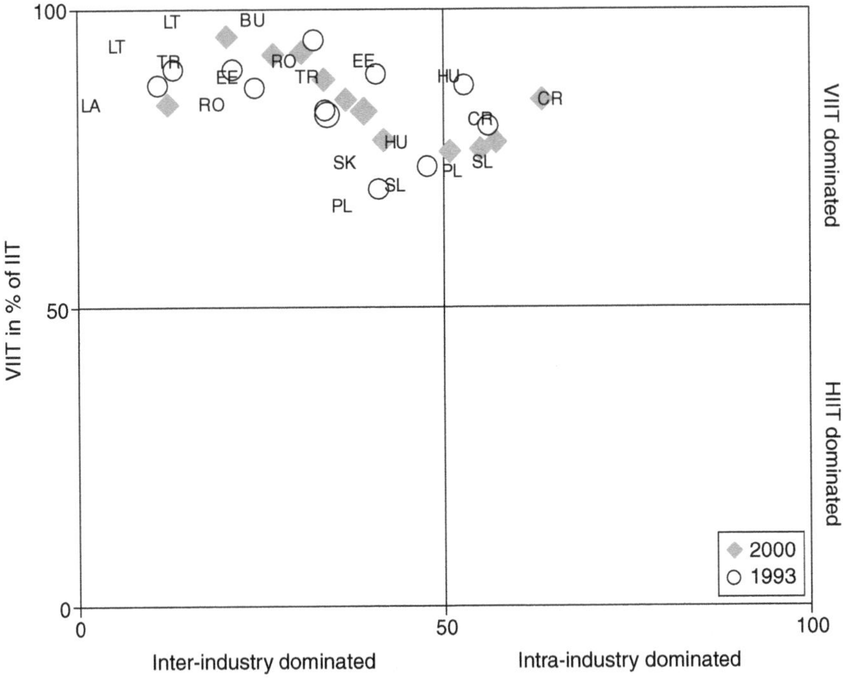

Figure 12.2 Types of EU trade flows with individual CC, 1993 and 2000, adjusted Grubel–Lloyd Indices (unweighted means).

Notes

BU: Bulgaria, CR: The Czech Republic, EE: Estonia, HU: Hungary, LA: Lithuania, LT: Latvia, PL: Poland, RO: Romania, SK: Slovakia, SL: Slovenia, TR: Turkey.

Table 12.2 High-quality VIIT[a] in percentage of total VIIT in EU trade with individual candidate countries, 2000 (unweighted means)

Year	*Total VIIT*	*EU HQ-VIIT*		*Candidate countries HQ-VIIT*	
	Adjusted GL-indices	*Adjusted GL-indices*	*in % of total VIIT*	*Adjusted GL-indices*	*in % of total VIIT*
1993	0.284	0.136	47.9	0.148	52.1
2000	0.324	0.213	65.7	0.110	34.0

Source: Own calculations based on Eurostat, 2002. See also Table 12.A4.

Note

a Ruv>1.15.

12.2 Theory and empirics of intra-industry trade: an overview

There is an abundant literature on the relationship between IIT flows and country and/or industry characteristics. These studies typically construct an index of intra-industry trade and investigate correlates of the index with country

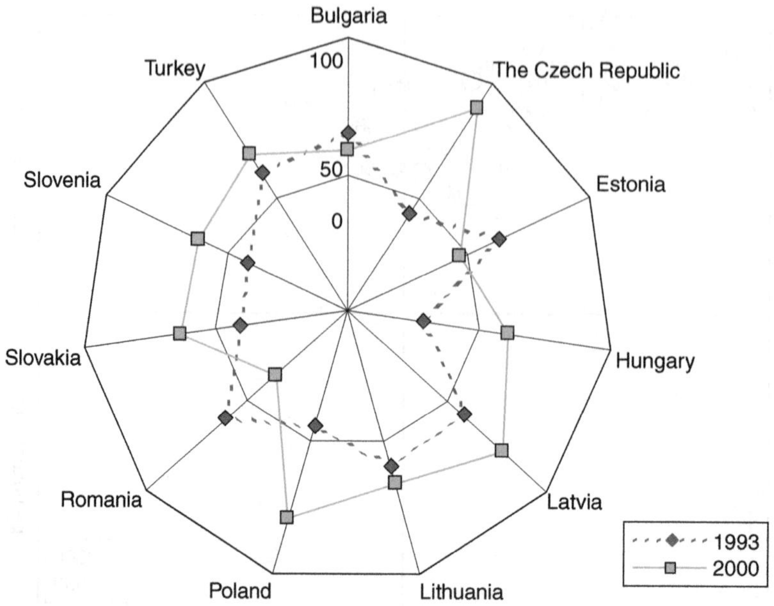

Figure 12.3 High quality VIIT[a] in percentage of total VIIT of EU in trade with individual CCs, 1993 and 2000 (source: own calculations based on Eurostat, 2002. See also Table 12.A4).

or industry determinants. While these studies are certainly interesting, their relationship to the theory of international trade is often tenuous and debatable.[11] An important exception is Helpman (1987), who developed some simple country models of monopolistic competition and tested the hypotheses that the theory "suggests",[12] using OECD data spanning from 1956 to 1981. His first empirical test concerned the volume of trade in a model in which all trade is, by assumption, intra-industry trade. His other tests were based on a model in which some trade is intra-industry and some trade is endowments-based. Helpman's theoretical model implied that intra-industry trade increases with similarity. He found that the theory is supported in that both the volume of trade and the measure of size similarity increase over time. The selected measure for intra-industry trade was regressed on per capita income differences and the minimum and maximum size of GDP, and it was found that intra-industry trade and per capita income differences were negatively related. The results supported the theoretical predictions. The inclusion of income differences was robust to several specifications; but the minimum and maximum GDP variables were less so.[13] Helpman's second test separated GDP size from GDP similarity; the results confirmed that both seem to contribute positively to intra-industry trade. Helpman concluded that the theory of monopolistic competition finds some support in the data.

Hummels and Levinsohn (1995) drew on Helpman's paper for their empirical analysis but they questioned the apparent empirical success of monopolistic competition models. They found a *negative* relationship between per capita GDP and the share of IIT in OLS regression, but they found a *positive* relationship in panel regression controlling for country-specific fixed effects.

Hummels and Levinsohn used country-pairs instead of the entire OECD, from 1962 to 1983, and instead of estimating each year as a separate regression, they employed standard panel data econometric techniques (fixed and random effects for country pairs). They found support for a negative relationship between similarity and trade volumes in both an OECD data set with similar countries and a data set comprising a random selection of developed and less developed countries distributed around the globe. They concluded that perhaps something other than monopolistic competition accounted for the empirical success of the estimating equation. An additional finding was that the estimating equation in which the share of intra-industry trade was explained by the differences in the log per capita GDP was less robust to standard panel data estimation. For example, evidence of a negative relationship between differences in GDP per capita and IIT shares in OLS regressions turned out to be rather weak. When the explanatory power of their regressions was improved by applying fixed effects, the sign of the coefficient turned positive and remained significant. Hummels and Levinsohn attributed this result to the fact that the fixed effects regressions control for the differences in distance and land endowments, which affect the share of intra-industry trade, so that the distance effect[14] seems to be much stronger. They concluded in their "in-conclusions" that "we find, at best, very mixed empirical support for the theory. Most of the variation in intra-industry trade is explained by factors idiosyncratic to country pair" (Hummels and Levinsohn, 1995, p. 828).

Several researchers have been prompted by these anomalous results to challenge the optimistic interpretation of earlier results considering the important distinction between horizontally and vertically differentiated products. Greenaway *et al.* (1994, 1995) separate the determinants of HIIT and VIIT in a cross-section study, finding per capita GDP differences negatively correlated to the shares of both VIIT and HIIT. Durkin and Kryiger (2000) found a negative sign for horizontal flows and a negative one for vertical IIT, the latter being confirmed by the analysis of Martin-Montaner and Orts Rios (2002).

Within VII, if attention is focused upon the importance of quality differentiation, two models usually neglected in the earlier empirical IIT literature come into play: the Falvey and Kierzkowski (1987, or FK) and Flam and Helpman (1987, or FH) models, both of which combine factor endowment or technological differences with differences in consumers' preferences in order to explain vertically differentiated trade. The models differ because in FK the reason for quality differentiation is the amount of capital used to produce the good, while in FH it is the technology used. In both models, income inequality in countries play a leading role in explaining the demand by households for differentiated goods.

In the FH model of vertically differentiated products, trade is determined by differences in technology, income and income distribution. There are two countries, one factor and two goods, but one good is homogeneous and the other one is quality differentiated. Both countries have the same unit labour requirements for the homogeneous good, but labour input per unit of output of the quality differentiated products differs between countries where quality is a positive function of the labour input. The home country has an absolute advantage in production of all qualities while the foreign country may have a comparative advantage in low quality variety. Demand for varieties arises from variation in income across consumers, which is a specific quality reflecting their preferences and income constraint. Higher effective labour endowments (implying higher income) demand the higher quality good. Therefore the home country specializes in the differentiated product of high quality and the foreign country exports the homogeneous and the differentiated good of low quality. On assuming an overlap of income distribution, VIIT appears. The prediction is that greater bilateral technological differences give rise to higher share of VIIT.

12.3 The product-quality cycle model for vertical intra-industry trade

It is possible to apply the framework of vertically differentiated goods to the EU-CC relations.

Assume that the less advanced country, say, the CC, produces a homogenous good and the low-quality variety of the differentiated product, while the developed country, the EU in this case, produces the high-quality variety. On the production side, both countries have the same unit labour requirements to produce the homogeneous good but different unit labour requirements to produce one unit of the differentiated good with quality level q. Labour input requirements – $a(q)$ for the EU and $a^*(q)$ for the CCs – are increasing and convex in the quality level. Their ratio $Z=a^*(q)/a(q)$ is assumed to increase in q since the EU has an absolute advantage in producing all quality levels (as in Figure 12.7). The reason why the EU does not produce the entire range of the differentiated product is the possible comparative advantage of the CC in producing part of the low quality variety. The problem is to identify the split between the two regions of the "chain" of comparative advantages defined by quality levels with a continuum of varieties q of the differentiated commodity. The model provides a solution based on changes in the relative wage (due to productivity and quality changes), on population growth, and on changes in income distribution.

The demand for a specific variety is associated with different income levels of consumers. Those with higher effective labour endowments earn higher incomes and demand higher quality varieties of the differentiated good. It is possible to describe the distribution of income across households by two density functions: g for the EU, and g^* for the CCs. These functions also denote the density of the distribution of effective labour endowments across households.

There is a "dividing income" level at which consumers are indifferent towards a marginal change of quality but respond to changes in the relative price of varieties. These consumers demand a quality q_d. Consumers/households with higher incomes purchase high-quality varieties, *gh*, and those with lower incomes purchase low-quality ones, *ql*. Assuming balanced trade, the model can be solved for the "dividing" income class. The dividing income class determines not only the split in the demand for quality in both countries, but also the relative wage per effective labour unit $\omega = w/w^*$ and a pattern of specialization typical of Ricardian models with a continuum of goods.

The explicit expression for the share of VIIT in total trade according to FH is

$$S = \frac{\alpha+\gamma}{\alpha+\gamma^*} \frac{wL}{w^*L^*} \frac{F(h_d)}{1-F^*(h_d^*)} \tag{3}$$

where α is a parameter for consumer preferences (equal in both countries) and γ, γ^* describe the comparative advantage in the unit labour input functions. $F(.)$ and $F^*(.)$ are the cumulative distribution functions in the EU and in the CCs up to the consumer with the dividing income level, which is in the interval $h,h^* = [0,...h,h^*_d,...1]$. The wage rate and the labour supply are defined by w and w^*, and L and L^*, respectively. All EU households in the interval $h, = [1,h_d]$ spend a share $\frac{\alpha}{\alpha+\gamma^*}$ of their income wL on the imported low-quality variety. All households in CCs in the interval $h^*, = [h^*_d,1]$ spend a share $\frac{\alpha}{\alpha+\gamma}$ of their income w^*L^* on the high-quality variety produced in the EU country.[15]

The income of the consumers/households which are indifferent towards quality is the product of the wage ratio and the amount of effective labour supplied by these households. As shown by Figure 12.4, with density functions g for EU and g^* for CCs, for an arbitrary relative wage ω, the CC exports the quality variety between ql and q_d, whereas the EU country produces and exports the quality variety between q_d and q_h. Equation (3) describes how changes in the relative wage level, the labour supply, and the dividing income class influence the share of (vertical) intra-industry trade in total trade. The most interesting determinants are the changes in the relative wage and in income distribution.

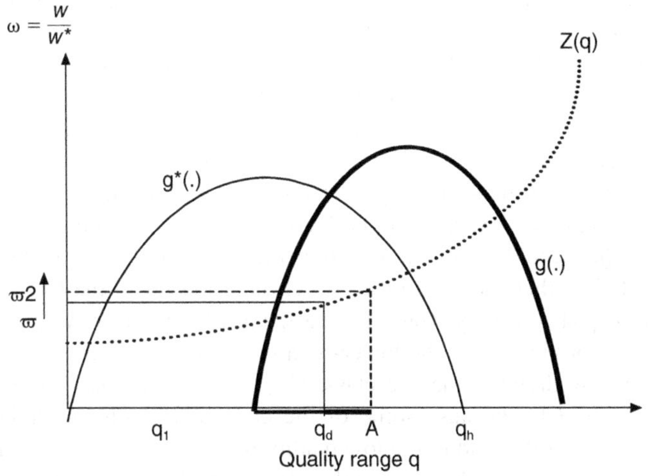

Figure 12.4 The quality split.

Assuming that (case 1) the EU country improves technology, or increases physical capital and human capital in its high-quality goods industry, the prices of all qualities in the range q_d and q_h will fall. With increasing demand for these qualities, demand for labour will increase, and so will the EU wage rate w and the relative wage rate ω with labour supply given. The demand for the low quality range, produced in the CC, will decline. For EU producers, it becomes profitable to abandon the lower section of the quality range and shift it to the CCs, where cheap labour is available. As can be seen in Figure 12.4, the range of q_h, produced in the EU, has narrowed; and for q_l, produced in the CCs, it has broadened. On the demand side, the income of households up to the dividing income increases due to the higher wage rate. These households start additionally to consume precisely the variety of the differentiated good that was formerly produced in the EU and has been shifted to the CCs. There emerges a quality-based product cycle that finds expression in an increasing share of VIIT in total trade. In equation (3), the numerator increases due to the wage increase. The wage rate of the CCs w^* may have increased (and so the denominator), but it has done so to a lesser extent than in the EU country. The shift of the lower-quality section of the differentiated good from the EU country has added some level of higher productivity to the quality-range in the CCs, but this productivity level is considerably lower than the productivity level of the high-quality range in the EU country.

When productivity and ω increase, the bold section A on the quality range will shift from the EU to the CCs. With a given income distribution (density functions), a given labour supply, and a dividing income, this additional part will be produced and exported by the CCs, and consumed by the EU country.

Some of the factors which affect the relative wage, ω, may exert indirect effects on S via a change in the dividing income level (case 2). In the case considered here, the falling price for the high-quality version would induce households with the dividing income and indifferent to quality to demand the higher quality. The dividing household income h_d would fall, and so would $F(h_d)$, with the effect of reducing VIIT. The same may happen in the CCs, only that $1 - F^*(h_d)$ would increase, and so too would total trade (in the denominator). This, however, is an effect that cannot compensate completely for its cause.

Let us now assume (case 3) that, in the CCs, income distribution becomes more unequal, to the detriment of the poorer households, and that demand for imported goods increases. Consumers in both countries now face a higher price level for q_h. EU households with the dividing income would react to higher prices for q_h and shift their demand to q_l, which is produced in the CCs. The price of the lower quality variety would increase, and EU producers would find it profitable to shift production of the lower-section of the high-quality range to the CCs. With a new dividing income class, $F(h_d)$ would increase. The same would happen in the CCs because some of the consumers with the dividing income would shift their demand to the low quality product. Again, the dividing income would increase, and $F^*(h^*_d)$ would follow suit. According to (4), the share of VIIT in total trade would turn out to be higher.

In the former case (case 1), the cause of all changes was an improvement in technology and physical and human capital which increased the comparative advantage of the EU country. The intermediate result (case 2) was an increase in productivity that may give rise to a change in the dividing income class. In the latter case (case 3), the cause was income redistribution.

In cases 1 and 3, there is a product cycle based upon a shift of the lower end of the quality range in the EU country to the upper end of the quality range in the CCs. The productivity gap in both cases is not closed. The productivity increase in the poorer country needs to be decisively higher than in the rich country if it is to compensate for the comparative advantage in producing higher quality. Only then does the share of VIIT fall (and the share of HIIT increase) as in case 1 or turn out to be higher as in case 3. But this higher productivity cannot be achieved simply by shifting the lower end of the EU quality range to the CCs (through foreign direct investment, for example) because the links with changing income distribution must be taken into account as well.

12.4 Estimations and results for EU trade with CCs

Equation (3) may be a good candidate for disentangling the different determinants of both HIIT and VIIT in the context of EU-CCs, where the EU represents a region of more developed countries and the CCs a region of less developed ones. The framework of vertically differentiated flows predicts that the volume and share of VIIT between two countries will be positively related to the difference between their wage rates and to domestic income distribution. Following Durkin and Kryieger (2000), the empirical form of equation (3) takes the following form:

$$\begin{aligned}\ln s_{jk,t} = {} & \beta_0 + \beta_1 \ln \left| \mathrm{GDPC}_{j,t} - \mathrm{GDPC}_{k,t} \right| + \beta_2 \mathrm{MIN}(\ln \mathrm{GDP}_{j,t}, \ln \mathrm{GDP}_{k,t}) \\ & + \beta_3 \mathrm{MAX}(\ln \mathrm{GDP}_{j,t}, \ln \mathrm{GDP}_{k,t}) + \beta_4 \mathrm{DISTANCE}_{jk} + \beta_5 \mathrm{INDIS}_{jk} \\ & + \mu_{jk} + \mu_{jk,t} \end{aligned} \quad (4)$$

where s_{jk} is the share of intra-industry trade flow in total trade. The bilateral shares ($14 \times 11 \times 2 = 308$ observations) are calculated for the years 1993 and 2000 as total IIT, HIIT, and VIIT according to adjusted Grubel-Lloyd indices, where j refers to trade flows of the EU country to and from its CC counterpart k. The first explanatory variable $\ln \left| \mathrm{GDPC}_{j,t} - \mathrm{GDPC}_{k,t} \right|$ depicts the relative wage difference between a pair of countries, where GDPC is the GDP per capita as a proxy for the wage rate. In an IIT model which consists entirely of horizontal IIT, the variable should have a negative sign (or turn out to be insignificant). If it explains vertical IIT, it should have a positive sign, either reflecting factor endowment differences according to the FK model or differences in technology according to the FH model. For the sake of brevity, we shall call this variable RELGDPC in all estimations.

The MIN and MAX variables are proxies for size in terms of total income (GDP). In most, but not all, cases MIN(ln GDP) stands for the CC, and MAX(ln GDP) for the EU country. We abbreviate the former as MINGDP, and the latter as MAXGDP. We expected a negative impact on VIIT if the developed country was significantly smaller than the less advanced country ($\beta_2 < 0$), and a positive impact if the developed country was larger than the less advanced country (β_3). GDP data were in US dollar terms based on the average exchange rate[16]

DISTANCE measures the time-invariant distance between the capitals of each country pair in kilometres. The inclusion of distance augments the model so as to capture transport costs and brings it closer to standard gravity models in international trade. The expected direction of the sign is negative: the trade volume declines with increasing distance.

INDIS represents differences in income distribution between each pair of countries, and changes in it approximate shifts in the dividing income. We calculated the variable as the ratio of the share of the lowest quintile in an EU country to the share of the highest quintile in the CC (using income in US dollar exchange rate terms). Data were taken from the World Bank (2001) (Table 12.A5). However, this comparison should be viewed with caution: first, the country data were from different years (for example, Austria 1987 and Estonia 1998). Second, data for some countries (Hungary, Lithuania, Poland, and Turkey) reported household expenditure and not income.[17] Third, the data may not be harmonized (World Bank data on high-income economies – EU countries – were taken from Luxembourg Income Study database (LIS, 2001), data on CCs from government statistical agencies). These are the usual statistical flaws and drawbacks of household income data (see Atkinson and Brandolini, 2001).

In pooled OLS regressions, the error term μ may include time-invariant effects (either random or fixed). Therefore, μ_{jk} stands for country-pair specific factors. The Hausman test was applied to check whether random or fixed effects should be used. Further, the Redundant Fixed Effects tests were used to decide as to the relevance of pooled vs. fixed effects regressions.

The empirical strategy was to utilize equation (4) in two different specifications in order to check:

- first whether the Hummels and Levinshon country approach was empirically significant (the results of specification 1 in what follows) and
- second whether the positive link between vertically differentiated products and technological and income distribution differences was empirically confirmed (the results of specification 2 in what follows).

In the first specification, we estimated a set of equations excluding income distribution and distance, and compared the results with those that Hummels and Levinsohn obtained for total IIT with the same specifications (OLS and fixed effects). The Hausman test suggests the superiority of the fixed effects model. In principle, we found similar results for OLS and fixed effects regressions (Table 12.3) with a significant improvement in the explanatory power of the VIIT specification with fixed effects. The most important result was that, in OLS regressions, RELGDP did not obtain the predicted sign for IIT, it was insignificant for HIIT, and it was

Table 12.3 Specification 1 – regression results, 308 observations

	Dependent variables					
	OLS (pooled data)[a]			*Fixed effects*		
	(1)	*(2)*	*(3)*	*(4)*	*(5)*	*(6)*
Explanatory variables	IIT	HIIT	VIIT	IIT	HIIT	VIIT
C	−14.024***	−26.342***	−13.788***	−13.519***	−33.056***	−12.223***
MAXGDP	0.379***	0.927***	0.327***	0.241	1.160*	0.130
MINGDP	0.328***	0.766***	0.294***	0.326***	0.722***	0.285***
RELGDP	0.434***	0.261	0.488***	0.484***	0.272	0.502***
Adjusted R^2	0.26	0.21	0.31	0.46	0.36	0.48
FE significance	–	–	–	Yes	Yes	Yes

Note
Significance levels: * 10%, ** 5%, *** 1%.

significant and with the predicted sign for VIIT. Hummels and Levinsohn obtained a negative sign for the coefficient of this variable in explaining IIT, and a positive sign in fixed effects regressions. They concluded that their mixed empirical results stood for country-pair specific effects (for example distance) in explaining IIT, and not for factor endowment differences. Our results are plausible in a case where about 85 per cent of IIT is vertical. The insignificance of RELGDP in explaining HIIT is predicted and confirms the specific role of this variable in explaining intra-industry trade.

A second important result is that MINGDP does not obtain the predicted negative sign. This result is not surprising in view of the few EU countries with a GDP smaller than that of any CC. We conclude that this confirms the hypothesis that relative GDP per capita explains VIIT and even total IIT, in so far as the latter is overwhelmingly vertical. We further conclude that the fixed effects specification gives better results than pooled estimations, because the Redundant Fixed Effects test signals superiority, and all country fixed effects are significant at the 1 per cent level.

In the second specification we fully tested equation (4). We followed Durkin and Krygier (2000), who used distance and income distribution as explicit country-pair specific fixed effects. The first OLS result (Table 12.4, columns 1 to 3) shows that RELGDP is negative and insignificant for HIIT (and IIT), but significant and positive in explaining VIIT as predicted by VIIT theory. Furthermore, in all specifications we found DISTANCE to be highly significant and had the expected sign. The third finding was that differences in income distribution yield the expected signs (negative for HIIT and positive for VIIT) when they are handled as time-invariant country-pair specific factors. Inclusion of the two new variables significantly increased the explanatory power of the models compared to OLS estimates of the previous specification.

Table 12.4 Specification 2 – regression results, 308 observations

	Dependent variables					
	OLS (pooled data)[a]			*Fixed effects*		
	(1)	*(2)*	*(3)*	*(4)*	*(5)*	*(6)*
Explanatory variables	IIT	HIIT	VIIT	IIT	HIIT	VIIT
C	−5.252***	−14.796***	−5.547***	−4.171	−18.863**	−2.681
MAXGDP	0.422***	1.022***	0.367***	0.013	1.251	−0.165
MINGDP	0.415***	0.881***	0.375***	0.406***	0.772***	0.382***
RELGDP	−0.042	−0.249	0.060	0.148	−0.114	0.211*
DISTANCE	−0.429***	−0.796***	−0.419***	−0.357***	−0.725***	−0.374***
INDIS	1.702***	−0.796***	1.608***	1.453***	1.489*	1.482***
Adjusted R^2	0.35	0.33	0.42	0.48	0.44	0.54
FE significance	–	–	–	No	Yes	No

Note
Significance levels: * 10%, ** 5%, *** 1%.

The explicit inclusion of time-invariant country-pair specifics in the OLS model may still leave room for general country specifics. We, therefore, again discriminated between random and fixed effects and found the fixed effects specification to be superior. The first result of the fixed effects regressions was that RELGDP again had the predicted signs for HIIT and/VIIT, although at a lower significance level than in simple OLS estimations. Secondly, MINGDP became insignificant, which is explained by the small number of observations. Thirdly, income distribution was significant and positive in all specifications, including HIIT, which was contrary to the prediction. However, we found country-fixed effects not to be significant in IIT and VIIT estimates. Although the Redundant Fixed Effects tests signalled the superiority of fixed effects specification, we reject this model in explaining VIIT and assume that the OLS specification includes sufficiently relevant country-pair specific and time-invariant factors.

The results indicate important differences methods to detect the determinants of horizontal and vertical IIT.

The focus on VIIT between EU and CCs shows it as being due to three factors: first, the per capita income differences; second, the size differences between them; and third, the inequalities in income distribution among households. Among these three factors, the two most important results give not only significant support for the country rather than the industry specific explanation of vertical intraindustry flows (shown by the positive role of per capita income differences), but also support for a significant role of income distribution differences (shown by the positive role of differences in income distribution). The first result is able to proxy the crucial role of technology differences (as in Flam and Helpman, 1987), while the second shows that income distribution differences do play a leading role in explaining the high share of VIIT. Taken together, they suggest that a product quality cycle within vertical trade may have taken place in the period considered, with a shift of the lower end of the EU quality range to the CC.

When these conclusions on determinants of VIIT are associated with the EU-CC quality split of trade flows during the 1990s (the third finding identified in section 12.1), we can conclude that the differences in technology as well as the changes in income distribution were responsible for the asymmetric distribution of quality advantages in vertical trade flows.

More recently, the tendencies have probably changed: recent observations on the diminishing technology gap and the shift of the CCs' income distribution towards equality, may be more recent causes of the diminishing vertical and increasing horizontal shares of trade.

12.5 Concluding remarks

After a period of trade liberalization, the pattern of trade between the EU and the CCs reflects a dominance of vertical trade, together with a specialization in low and high quality goods with dominant quality advantages for EU firms. Having identified these stylized facts, the first empirical result of this chapter is that there are important differences in methods to detect the determinants of horizontal and vertical IIT, in that the two types of trade are explained by different factors. These differences are evident in the second result, where technology size and inequalities in income distribution among households are shown to play a significant role in explaining the share of vertically differentiated trade flows between EU and CCs during the 1990s.

These results support an explanation of VIIT in line with the results of recent studies that have found more support for country rather than industry-specific explanations. They also show that technological as well as income distribution differences play the expected positive role in explanation of vertically differentiated trade.

It has been shown that, during a relatively short period of trade liberalization, technological and income differences did affect the pattern of trade between the EU and the CCs, which was predominantly vertical. The increasing importance of vertically differentiated goods reflects a product-quality cycle in low and high quality goods: in EU-CC vertical trade, firms find it profitable to produce the low end of the quality spectrum in CCs, and the high end of the spectrum in an EU country, evincing a product cycle or a division of labour between the low/high ends of the product-quality spectrum.

A product-quality cycle has been in operation behind the main features of VIIT: a suggestion supported by the distribution of the quality advantages of trade flows between the two sets of countries with dominant quality advantages for the EU firms.

These results open the way for discussion of the role of increasing VIIT and the associated product-quality cycle as important outcomes of technology transfer processes. Both can dynamically give rise either to product upgrading along the quality spectrum or to a quality technology trap, as the alternative results of technology transfers. On the one hand, the product-quality trade cycle incorporates very different channels of potential technology transfers at the country level with distributional and geographical consequences: for instance, the relocation of stages of production processes across countries, the increasing trade in parts and components associated with the reduction in trade barriers/costs, the spatial (re)distribution of economic activity induced by trade integration. All these channels have important distributional implications associated, for instance, with the relocation of economic activity or, more generally, with the significantly higher costs of adjustments of vertically differentiated trade.[18]

In the presence of these distributional and geographical consequences, trade policy will not yield the desired benefits unless there are parallel efforts to address the redistribution of the gains from trade in favour of skill creation and learning activities able to prevent occurrence of the quality technological trap.

On the other hand, product-cycle trade does not in itself necessarily lead CCs into a quality technological trap. The product cycle includes the transfer of technology, capital, and human capital, and it may foster skill upgrading in the host country.[19] These opportunities need only to be exploited. Economic policy can mobilize resources to support catching-up in quality, productivity, and per capita income when they concentrate on domestic sources of skill upgrading in local firms in CCs.

The final result between technology trap and upgrading crucially depends on the interaction between firms' dynamic capabilities to upgrade along the quality spectrum and the effectiveness with which the economic system addresses firms' learning processes.

Annex

Table 12.A1 Trade turnover (exports + imports) of individual EU countries with 11 candidate countries, 2000

	Total trade	*Trade in the panel of selected industries*	
	mn ECU	*mn ECU*	*in % of total trade*
Austria	19,619	15,102	77.0
Belux	11,305	8,761	77.5
Denmark	4,308	2,915	67.7
Finland	62,890	5,568	88.5
France	22,769	19,864	87.2
Germany	107,086	88,750	82.9
Greece	3,486	2,590	74.3
Ireland	2,339	2,028	86.7
Italy	32,359	27,566	85.2
Netherlands	14,380	9,598	66.7
Portugal	1,175	1,001	85.2
Spain	8,278	6,740	81.4

continued

Table 12.A1 continued

	Total trade	Trade in the panel of selected industries	
	mn ECU	*mn ECU*	*in % of total trade*
Sweden	8,673	6,653	76.7
United Kingdom	17,954	15,378	85.7
Total	260,021	212,515	81.7
Mean	–	–	80.2

Source: Own calculations based on Eurostat, 2002.

Table 12.A2 Adjusted Grubel–Lloyd Indices: intra–EU trade, 1993 and 2000

EU country against all others	*1993*			*2000*		
	IIT	*HIIT*	*VIIT*	*IIT*	*HIIT*	*VIIT*
Austria	0.700	0.219	0.481	0.731	0.177	0.554
Belgium and Luxembourg	0.750	0.370	0.380	0.799	0.384	0.415
Denmark	0.673	0.187	0.486	0.738	0.004	0.734
Finland	0.440	0.104	0.336	0.395	0.097	0.298
France	0.834	0.479	0.355	0.844	0.469	0.375
Germany	0.817	0.405	0.412	0.864	0.457	0.407
Greece	0.405	0.059	0.345	0.512	0.021	0.490
Ireland	0.495	0.063	0.432	0.572	0.044	0.528
Italy	0.613	0.163	0.450	0.596	0.213	0.383
Netherlands	0.741	0.343	0.398	0.790	0.333	0.457
Portugal	0.395	0.130	0.265	0.569	0.120	0.449
Spain	0.695	0.172	0.523	0.772	0.202	0.570
Sweden	0.602	0.175	0.426	0.624	0.234	0.390
United Kingdom	0.764	0.201	0.563	0.276	0.016	0.260
Mean	*0.637*	*0.219*	*0.418*	*0.649*	*0.198*	*0.451*

Source: Own calculations based on Eurostat, 2002.

Table 12.A3 Adjusted Grubel–Lloyd Indices: EU trade with 11 candidate countries, 1993 and 2000

Candidate country with all EU countries	*1993*			*2000*		
	IIT	*HIIT*	*VIIT*	*IIT*	*HIIT*	*VIIT*
Bulgaria	0.325	0.018	0.307	0.308	0.022	0.285
Czech Republic	0.563	0.110	0.452	0.637	0.097	0.540
Estonia	0.411	0.045	0.366	0.267	0.020	0.247
Hungary	0.529	0.068	0.461	0.509	0.121	0.389
Latvia	0.111	0.014	0.097	0.124	0.020	0.104

continued

Table 12.A3 continued

Candidate country with all EU countries	*1993*			*2000*		
	IIT	*HIIT*	*VIIT*	*IIT*	*HIIT*	*VIIT*
Lithuania	0.131	0.013	0.118	0.206	0.009	0.196
Poland	0.414	0.125	0.288	0.551	0.130	0.421
Romania	0.243	0.032	0.211	0.337	0.040	0.297
Slovakia	0.342	0.061	0.281	0.418	0.092	0.326
Slovenia	0.478	0.127	0.351	0.574	0.127	0.446
Turkey	0.213	0.022	0.191	0.367	0.055	0.312
Mean	*0.342*	*0.058*	*0.284*	*0.391*	*0.067*	*0.324*

Source: Own calculations based on Eurostat, Comext databank, 2002.

Table 12.A4 Adjusted Grubel–Lloyd Indices: extra-EU trade: high-quality (HQ-)VIIT, 1993 and 2000

	1993			*2000*		
	VIIT	*'HQ'-VIIT EU 1.15<RUV*	*'HQ'-VIIT CC 0.85 > RUV*	*VIIT*	*'HQ'-VIIT EU 1.15<RUV*	*'HQ'-VIIT CC 0.85 > RUV*
Bulgaria	0.307	0.199	0.108	0.285	0.167	0.118
Czech Republic	0.452	0.189	0.263	0.540	0.481	0.059
Estonia	0.366	0.228	0.138	0.247	0.116	0.130
Hungary	0.461	0.132	0.329	0.389	0.239	0.150
Latvia	0.097	0.056	0.041	0.104	0.081	0.023
Lithuania	0.118	0.069	0.049	0.196	0.129	0.067
Poland	0.288	0.127	0.162	0.421	0.333	0.087
Romania	0.211	0.129	0.082	0.297	0.107	0.190
Slovakia	0.281	0.114	0.167	0.326	0.207	0.119
Slovenia	0.351	0.145	0.206	0.446	0.276	0.171
Turkey	0.191	0.114	0.077	0.312	0.212	0.100
Mean	*0.284*	*0.136*	*0.148*	*0.324*	*0.213*	*0.110*

Source: Own calculations based on Eurostat, 2002.

Table 12.A5 Distribution of income or consumption

EU country	*Survey years*	*Gini*	*Percentage share of income or consumption*				
			Lowest 20%	*Second 20%*	*Third 20%*	*Fourth 20%*	*Highest 20%*
Austria	1987	23.1	10.4	14.8	18.5	22.9	33.3
Belgium	1992	25.0	9.5	14.6	18.4	23.0	34.5

continued

Table 12.A5 continued

EU country	*Survey years*	*Gini*	*Percentage share of income or consumption*				
			Lowest 20%	*Second 20%*	*Third 20%*	*Fourth 20%*	*Highest 20%*
Denmark	1992	24.7	9.6	14.9	18.3	22.7	34.5
Finland	1991	25.6	10.0	14.2	17.6	22.3	35.8
France	1995	32.7	7.2	12.6	17.2	22.8	40.2
Germany	1994	30.0	8.2	13.2	17.5	22.7	38.5
Greece	1993	32.7	7.5	12.4	16.9	22.8	40.3
Ireland	1987	35.9	6.7	11.6	16.4	22.4	42.9
Italy	1995	27.3	8.7	14.0	18.1	22.9	36.3
Luxembourg	1994	26.9	9.4	13.8	17.7	22.6	36.5
Netherland	1994	32.6	7.3	12.7	17.2	22.8	40.1
Portugal	1994–1995	35.6	7.3	11.6	15.9	21.8	43.4
Spain	1990	32.5	7.5	12.6	17.0	22.6	40.3
Sweden	1992	25.0	9.6	14.5	18.1	23.2	34.5
UK	1991	36.1	6.6	11.5	16.3	22.7	43.0
	Mean	**29.7**	**8.4**	**13.3**	**17.4**	**22.7**	**38.3**
	St.Dev.	4.4	1.2	1.2	0.8	0.3	3.3
Bulgaria	1997	26.4	10.1	13.9	17.4	21.9	36.8
Czech Rep	1996	25.4	10.3	14.5	17.7	21.7	35.9
Estonia	1998	37.6	7.0	11.0	15.3	21.6	45.1
Hungary	1998	24.4	10.0	14.7	18.3	22.7	34.4
Latvia	1998	32.4	7.6	11.4	15.3	20.8	45.0
Lithuania	1996	32.4	7.8	12.6	16.8	22.4	40.3
Poland	1998	31.6	7.8	12.8	17.1	22.6	39.7
Romania	1994	28.2	8.9	13.6	17.6	22.6	37.3
Slovakia	1992	19.5	11.9	15.8	18.8	22.2	37.7
Slovenia	1998	28.4	9.1	13.4	17.3	22.5	37.7
Turkey	1994	41.5	5.8	10.2	14.8	21.6	47.7
	Mean	**28.2**	**8.1**	**13.1**	**16.9**	**22.1**	**39.8**
	St. Dev.	5.9	1.7	1.6	1.2	0.6	4.1

Source: World Bank 2001, World Development Indicators.

Notes

1 See Fontagné *et al.* (1998); Díaz Mora (2002).
2 See Burgstaller and Landesmann (1997); Aturupane *et al.* (1999); Rosati (1998); Gabrisch and Werner (1998); Thom (1999); Gabrisch and Segnana (2001).
3 Liberalization had already started in 1990. In 1993, the EU signed the first free trade agreements with the transition countries, and liberalization gained pace. By 2000, a free trade area had been almost completely established for manufacturing.
4 There is a large body of literature on the flaws in the unadjusted Grubel-Lloyd index, and it suggests various alternatives. For an overview, see Vona (1991).
5 Data for Austria, Finland, and Sweden are for 1995.

6 Bulgaria, the Czech Republic, Estonia, Hungary, Latvia, Lithuania, Poland, Romania, Slovakia, Slovenia, and Turkey.
7 For a critical review, see Gullstrand (2002).
8 The procedure was first developed by Abd-El-Rahman (1984). Since Greenaway *et al.* (1994), examples of application of this methodology abound.
9 Alternatively, a dispersion factor of 25 per cent is used in empirical applications. In Aturpane *et al.* (1999) the shift from the 15 to the 25 per cent specification lets the differences in the value of the coefficients of HIIT and VIIT disappear (signs and significances remained unchanged).
10 The scheme has been proposed by Dìaz Mora (2002).
11 For a survey, see Leamer and Levinsohn (1995).
12 Helpman (1987) does not derive a structural equation from the theory.
13 See Leamer and Levinsohn, 1995, p. 1380.
14 The empirical success of the gravity models is well known.
15 The ratio between the two shares yields the parameter term in expression (3).
16 GDP and population data were taken from OECD (2001).
17 Average income-based estimates of the Gini coefficient were up to 6.6 percentage points higher than those based on expenditure (see Atkinson and Brandolini, 2001).
18 Implying even negative welfare effects if higher quality products completely displace lower quality ones.
19 See the results of the effect of the product cycles on skill upgrading in Chun-Zhu (2005).

References

Abd-El-Rahman, Kamal (1984) "Firms' Competitive and National Comparative Advantage as Joint Determinants of Trade Composition", *Weltwirtschafliches Archiv* 127, 1: 83–97.

Atkinson, Anthony and Andrea Brandolini (2001) "Promise and Pitfalls in the Use of 'Secondary' Data-Sets: Income Inequality in OECD Countries as a Case Study", *Journal of Economic Literature* XXXIX, 3: 771–800.

Aturupane, Chonira, Simeon Djankov, and Bernard Hoeckman (1999) "Horizontal and Vertical Intra-Industry Trade Between Eastern Europe and the European Union", *Weltwirtschfliches Archiv* 135, 1: 62–81.

Burgstaller, Johann and Michael Landesmann (1997) "Vertical Product Differentiation in EU Markets: The Relative Position of East European Producers", Research Reports No. 234, Vienna, WIIW.

Chun-Zhu, Susan (2005) "Can Produce Cycles Explain Skill Upgrading?", *Journal of International Economics* 66: 131–155.

Díaz Mora, Carmen (2002) "The Role of Comparative Advantage in Trade Within Industries: A Panel Data Approach for the European Union", *Weltwirtschaftliches Archiv* 138, 2: 291–317.

Durkin, John T. and Markus Krygier (2000) "Differences in GDP Per Capita and the Share of Intraindustry Trade: The Role of Vertically Differentiated Trade", *Review of International Economics* 8, 4: 760–774.

EUROSTAT (2002) *Comext Database. Intra- and Extra-EU Trade*, Luxembourg, European Community.

Facchini, Giovanni and Maria Luigia Segnana (2003) "Growth at the EU Periphery: The Next Enlargement", *Quarterly Review of Economics and Finance* 43: 827–862.

Falvey, Rodney E. and Henryk Kierzkowski (1987) "Product Quality, Intra-Industry

Trade and (Im)Perfect Competition", in Henryk Kierzkowski (ed.) *Protection and Competition in International Trade*, Oxford: Basil Blackwell, pp. 143–161.

Flam, Harry and Elhanan Helpman (1987) "Vertical Product Differentiation and North–South Trade", *American Economic Review* 76, 5: 810–822.

Fontagné Lione, Michael Freudenberg, and Nicolas Péridy (1998) "Intra-Industry Trade and the Single Market: Quality Matters", CEPR, Discussion paper no. 1959.

Gabrisch, Hubert and Klaus Werner (1998), Advantages and drawbacks of EU membership – the structural dimension, *Comparative Economic Studies*, XXX (3): 79–103.

Gabrisch, Hubert and Maria L. Segnana (2001) "Trade Structure and Trade Liberalization: The Emerging Pattern Between the EU and Transition Countries", *MOCT-MOST* 11, 1: 27–44.

Greenaway, David, Robert Hine and Cris Milner (1994) "Country Specific Factors and the Patterns of Horizontal and Vertical Intra-industry Trade in the UK", *Weltwirtschafliches Archiv* 130, 1: 77–99.

Greenaway, David, Robert Hine and Cris Milner (1995) "Vertical and Horizontal Intraindustry Trade: A Cross-Industry Analysis for the United Kingdom", *Economic Journal* 105, November: 1505–1518.

Gullstrand, Joakim (2002) "Does the Measurement of Intra-Industry Trade Matter?", *Weltwirtschaftliches Archiv* 138, 2: 317–340.

Helpman, Elhanan (1987) "Imperfect Competition and International Trade: Evidence from Fourteen Industrial Countries", *Journal of the Japanese and International Economies* 1: 62–81.

Hummels, David and James Levinsohn (1995) "Monopolistic Competition and International Trade: Reconsidering the Evidence", *Quarterly Journal of Economics*, 110, August: 799–836.

Leamer, Edward E. and James Levinsohn (1995) "International Trade Theory: The Evidence", in Gene Grossman and Kenneth Rogoff (eds) *Handbook of International Economics*, Amsterdam, Elsevier, Science B.V., Vol. III, pp. 1339–1394.

LIS (Luxemburg Income Studies) (2001) Unpublished series, data available on request.

Martin-Montaner, J.A. and V. Orts Rios (2002) "Vertical Specialisation and Intra-Industry Trade: The Role of Factor Endowments", *Welwirthschaftliches Archiv* 138, 2: 340–365.

OECD (2001) OECD Statistical Compendium, edition 01#2001 (maxdata).

Rosati, Dariusz (1998) "Emerging Trade Patterns of Transition Countries: Some Observations from the Analysis of 'Unit Values' ", *MOCT-MOST*, 8, 2: 51–67.

Thom, Rodney (1999) "The Structure of EC-CEE Intraindustry Trade", Working paper no. 1, Dublin: Centre for Economic Research, January.

Vona, Stefano (1991) "On the Measurement of Intra-Industry Trade: Some Further Thoughts", *Weltwirtschaftliches Archiv*, 127, 4: 678–700.

World Bank (2001) *World Development Report 2001*. Washington, DC.

13 ICTs and the *digital* division of labour

Nicola De Liso

13.1 Introduction

Information and communication technologies (ICTs) and the *digital* basis they share have been at centre stage at least since the 1980s. In the mid-1970s clear signs of heavy restructuring processes became visible in what used to be called industrialised countries. Restructuring meant deindustrialisation-cum-tertiarisation, while tertiarisation is often associated with digital technologies. Structural change was leading towards a new techno-economic paradigm whose core technologies are those of the computer industry, by which we mean hardware, software and the combination of the two which led to the creation of the present networks which include firms, governments, universities and consumers.

The transition from the old industrial to the new ICT-dominated tertiarised economy is well illustrated by the restless structural change which has concerned employment. In the United States in 1960 civilian employment in industry amounted to 33.4 per cent of total employment, while services accounted for 58.1 per cent; in 2005 the figures are 19.8 per cent and 78.6 per cent, respectively; in the United Kingdom industry shrank from 46.1 per cent in 1960 to 21.7 per cent in 2005, while services have expanded from 49.2 per cent to 77 per cent (US-DL, 2006). Countries such as Japan and Italy in 1960 were characterised by an *agricultural* sector which accounted for 30.2 per cent and 32.6 per cent of civilian employment, respectively (OECD, 1999). In 2005 in the European Union 69.5 per cent of total employment is in the service sector, 26.8 per cent in industry and the remaining 3.7 per cent in agriculture (Banca d'Italia, 2006).

The process of digitisation of the economies has affected the division of labour in all of its micro and macro dimensions, that is, inside firms, between firms, sectors and nations. New sectors and services have emerged and new markets created.

What we have just said would lead one to think that a clear-cut revolution has occurred; indeed a revolution has occurred, but one which was not easy to understand, particularly in the 1980s and early 1990s. Internet, the computerised economy and ICTs in general have put a strain on economists' categories of thought. During the last 25 years we have been through various waves of pessimism and euphoria.

The 1980s were characterised by many studies dealing with a crisis in productivity, the mantra – usually referred to as Solow's paradox – being that computers and the consequences of them being adopted could be seen everywhere except in the field of productivity statistics; restless structural economic dynamics was leading towards more and more tertiarised economies affected by a *cost disease* – at least that was the vision.

By the mid-1990s the climate changed radically, at first in the United States, followed by Europe and then the rest of the rich world: the catchword became *new economy*. The party had continued for a long time, particularly in the United States – whereas in Europe the Maastricht criteria, aimed at creating the conditions which would enable the common currency to be introduced, meant tight fiscal and monetary policies. In the United States, productivity and overall economic growth were increasing and could match the golden age of the 1960s; inflation was no longer an issue, while employment in the service sector was growing continuously. With regard to the latter, 12 million jobs were created in the United States between 1990 and 2000, and nearly 10 million in Europe in the six-year period 1995–2000.

Then, in 2000 things started to go wrong; the turning point was the downfall of all of the world stock exchanges; people realised that no profits were earned by the large majority of dotcoms, many of which went bust. Americans, in particular, found themselves worse off than expected. The worldwide spending spree on ICTs, and in general the long honeymoon with the new economy, was over. Looking at growth data, in the years 2002–2006 the picture we have is blurred. European economies have experienced a long period of stagnation, with rates of growth close to zero (0.9 per cent and 0.7 per cent in 2002 and 2003, respectively, in the euro area); in 2006 the euro area should experience a 2.2 per cent rate of growth. On the other hand, the United States has shown a different trend with 4.2 per cent and 3.5 per cent rates of growth in 2004 and 2005.

When we look around us we see that microchips, computers and networks are now everywhere, and have become part of our everyday life. Our way of producing commodities, delivering services, exchanging information, consuming and so on, has evolved. To see this let us just provide two more introductory data, on Internet users and e-commerce: according to ITU (2006) in the United States there are 185 million Internet users out of a population of 293.6 million; in Italy 28.8 million out of a population of 58 million; in Sweden 6.8 million out of 9 million total population (data refers to 2004) – we have chosen three countries which differ widely between them; the second datum we want to stress concerns the United States' retail e-commerce which, in the first quarter of 2006, amounts to 2.6 per cent of total sales – it was 0.8 per cent at the beginning of the year 2000; the series shows an increasing trend throughout the overall seven-year period (US-CB, 2006).

All of this makes it sufficiently clear that the pervasiveness of digital technologies means that we must modernise one of the most celebrated principles of economics, i.e. the Smithian principle of the division of labour, which must be updated and be preceded by the adjective *digital*. The chapter is organised as follows: section 13.2 provides a short résumé of the early analyses concerned with the division of labour; section 13.3 reconsiders the evolution of the digitisation of our economies; section 13.4 illustrates some data which, in turn, gives an account of the pervasiveness on ICTs; section 13.5 is concerned with some dimensions of the *digital* division of labour; section 13.6 is devoted to the legal foundations of digital capitalism; finally, the section 13.7 contains the conclusions.

13.2 The division of labour

The phrase *division of labour* has been made famous by Adam Smith who opened his inquiry into the nature and causes of the wealth of nations by pointing out that "The greatest improvement in the productive powers of labour, and the greater part of the skill, dexterity, and judgment with which it is any where directed, or applied, seem to have been the effects of the division of labour" (Smith, 1776, p. 13). The division of labour takes place in different forms, which require different degrees of co-operation and co-ordination. Technological and economic determinants affect the way in which the division of labour evolves; in particular, about the economic determinants Smith wrote that "the division of labour is limited by the extent of the market".

Before we go on with a short illustration of some dimensions of the division of labour it is worthwhile remembering that according to Shackle the division of labour represents a rare example of a substantive – as distinct from logical – *principle* in economics[1] (Shackle, 1992, p. 116).

The most celebrated form of division of labour is that illustrated by Smith himself by means of the example of the manufacture of pins in which pin-making becomes a sequence of 17 workers working under the same roof. This sort of division of labour has been given different names by different scholars: Groenewegen (1987) uses the phrase *manufacturing* division of labour, Leijonhufvud (1986) speaks of vertical division of labour, Bücher (1907) calls it subdivision of labour.

Other forms are considered by Smith, starting from what can be called the *social* division of labour, that is the division into occupations and professions which we observe within society. Each occupation or profession may lend itself to *specialisation*: for instance, within the legal profession we find the civil lawyer, the criminal lawyer or the expert in taxation law – another form of division of labour.

We can speak of a *sectoral* division of labour, from macrosectors such as agriculture, industry and services, to sub-sectors such as the computer industry or machinery building. Another dimension is that of the *international* division of labour to which a lot of attention has been dedicated since David Ricardo (1817) conceived his theorem of comparative advantage.

Various refinements and complementary concepts have been introduced by economists and technologists: Charles Babbage referred to the process of the mental division of labour which led to the calculation of logarithms from 1 to 200,000; also, he clarified that

> in every manufacture which is conducted upon the principle of the division of labour ... [w]hen the number of processes into which it is most advantageous to divide it, and the number of individuals to be employed in it, are ascertained, then all factories which do not employ a direct multiple of this latter number, will produce the article at a greater cost.
>
> (Babbage, 1835, p. 212)

John Stuart Mill, making use of the work by Edward Gibbons Wakefield,[2] pointed out that a more fundamental principle lies beneath that of the division of labour, and comprehends it, namely the *principle of co-operation*. The latter may be divided into *simple* and *complex* co-operation. As examples of simple co-operation Wakefield recalls a vast number of simple operations performed by human exertion: in the lifting of heavy weights two men working together can do much more than two individuals. Complex co-operation arises, for instance, when

> one body of men having combined their labour to raise more food than they require, another body of men are induced to combine their labour for the purpose of producing more clothes than they require, and with those surplus clothes buying the surplus food of the other body of labourers.
>
> (Mill, 1871, p. 117)

Karl Marx participated in the development of the concept in different ways, starting from the analysis of the dual origin of manufactures, which have emerged (i) by the assembling together in one workshop of workers belonging to various independent handicrafts or (ii) by the assembling together of craftsmen who all do the same kind of work (Marx, 1867, p. 457). Marx also refers to the two fundamental forms of manufacture which he calls *heterogeneous* and *organic*:

> This double character arises from the nature of the article produced, which either results from the merely mechanical assembling of partial products made independently [heterogeneous manufacture], or owes its completed shape to a series of connected processes and manipulations [organic manufacture].
>
> (Marx, 1867, p. 461)

One more dimension with which economists are familiar which deserves attention is the division of labour between firms on the one hand, and markets on the other hand – this debate was started in 1937 by Coase's pathbreaking article on the nature of the firm.

These concepts have been re-elaborated up until the present day: one just has to think of the flow-funds model proposed by Georgescu-Roegen (1971), of Richardson's analysis of economic organisation (Richardson, 1998) or the models and empirical studies which tackle the sectoral and the international division of labour (UNCTAD, 2004). To conclude this section we stress the fact that whatever dimension of the division of labour we have in mind – be it within the firm, between firms, occupations, sub-sectors, and so on – ICTs affect it.

13.3 Digitisation: from manufacturing to the information society

The *information society* is arising from the convergence of information technology, telecommunications and media sectors (EC, 1997). This process is having a revolutionary impact on the organisation of many human activities, whether in the private, public or professional spheres. The development of this infrastructure is producing economies of scale and economies of scope; it has already begun to modify production processes, consumer behaviour and social and institutional rules.

Some clarifications would be needed in order to clarify what is meant by digital technology, ICTs and the Internet. In a minimal view, electronic binary coded decimal computers synthesise these three points. Definitions abound, but, given the complexities of the technologies involved, together with the way in which societies and individuals internalise the use of these technologies, the same words seem to mean different things to different people. On the other hand, a common view emerges which gives people the sensation of sharing a common certainty.[3]

The way in which we perceive and internalise economic evolution is necessarily affected by a sort of "technological average". In 1829 Thomas Carlyle wrote in his *Signs of the Times* that "Were we required to characterise this age of ours by any single epithet, we should be tempted to call it ... the Mechanical Age". Incidentally, this explains why Charles Babbage in the 1820s and 1830s called his (never-completed) computers the difference engine and the analytical engine – the key word, in this case, being *engine*. As for the early part of the twenty-first century the epithet seems to be "the age of the Internet".

The above-mentioned process of convergence is based on computerised binary digital technologies, which have made it possible for certain sectors that were once distinct to become compatible and *convergent*.

When we discuss the current applications of digital technology we usually think about the tertiary sector. It is, however, important to point out that the process of mass digitisation of the economy also began with the informatisation of certain *old economy* productive processes. Excellent examples are numerically controlled machine tools and flexible manufacturing systems. Three key steps concerning the early phases of the digitisation process are briefly reviewed here.

i A first step was the creation of the first numerically controlled machine tool – a milling machine – built between 1949 and 1952 within the framework of a project promoted by the United States Department of Defence. The goal was to create a flexible, precise and fully automated machine that could cut metal in order to produce the wings of military aircrafts. The machine was first used in 1952 (Reintjes, 1991). Numerical control spread rapidly in civilian production through the 1960s, and became the *dominant* technology in the 1970s.[4] The introduction of flexible manufacturing systems, which automatised whole work processes, was the "natural" development of numerical control. Put another way, local networks of interacting computers were a reality in the second half of the 1970s.

ii The second step concerns the use of powerful computers – although not connected through a network – in the management and administration of various ministries, or the use of mainframes with great calculation capabilities in universities. The computerised management of many administrative functions and the use of mainframes accessible through terminals was already a routine practice in many American and British ministries and universities in the 1960s.

iii The third step concerns the widespread use of computers in private firms, both in the manufacturing and tertiary sectors. Schiller (1999) points out that as early as the mid-1960s, about 35,000 computerised work stations were in use in the United States, two-thirds of which were used by manufacturing firms, banks, insurance companies and private businesses; the ways in which these work stations could be used kept growing, and local networks of computers that could communicate with each other began to emerge.

If these steps point to the continuities, one important discontinuity has to be stressed. In the 1960s, in fact, computers began to experience that change of nature which has led to the diffusion of the Internet. Computers were being changed from machines used to store, update and process data and to govern work processes into machines used to exchange communication, the object thus being active interaction between people through machines. This passage is made quite clear in an astonishing paper by Licklider and Taylor (1968).[5]

13.4 The pervasiveness of ICTs and sectoral dynamics

"Computers fly our airliners and run most of the world's banking, communications, retail and manufacturing systems" (Jackson, 2006). As we will see in Table 13.3 in this section, in 2000 in the United States ICTs represented 9.38 per cent of the GDP – and 6.64 per cent in 2005. The most advanced economies have become more and more computer-dependent and tertiarised: in 2005, in the United States, 78.6 out of 100 employees have a job in the service sector, while the average in the European Union is nearly 70 per cent. The complementary process that must be stressed concerns the transition from *industrial* society to *information* society. Both tertiarisation and informatisation have been characterised by a continuous reshaping of the division of labour which has affected, and has been affected by, technological dynamics.

The processes leading towards a service-dominated information society have not been painless; these processes have heavily affected the existing capabilities and the way they have been organised within the firm, besides the division of labour between firms, local and national systems of production. On the other hand, many new opportunities have been created for all of the actors involved in this restless dynamics, from individual workers to firms and countries.

Sectoral dynamics plays a fundamental role. The recent and past histories of our economies have seen the rise and relative domination of certain sectors over others, but always for a limited period of time: one only has to think of the decline of the automotive industry in recent years. For over 60 years the car industry spearheaded the manufacturing division of labour, the re-composition of the production process through flexible manufacturing systems, and the introduction of new materials such as plastics and ceramics. However, when one thinks today of the key sectors of advanced economies, the automotive sector is hardly mentioned.

The above explains why many authors rely less and less on macro-aggregate data and rely more on sectoral data in order to study growth rates. Put another way, aggregate data and average productivity of labour are of little use in understanding the dynamics of growth.

The ICTs "sector" has jumped to everyone's attention in recent years as one of the most dynamic and important sectors. The reason we put the term *sector* in inverted commas is that this is a broad and heterogeneous sector whose boundaries change according to the source. According to the definitions given by the *European Information Technology Observatory* (EITO, 2006) ICTs include all hardware, software and related services as well as everything related to telecommunications, both in terms of equipment and services. One should try not to overlook what these definitions include,[6] as for instance *office equipment* such as old typewriters are considered as ICTs.

Despite some OECD efforts to establish a widely accepted definition of the ICT sector, definitions are not yet consistently applied (OECD, 2002, 2006a). This explains why a high variability of data, and consequently results, can be found according to the source one refers to – EITO, OECD, ITU, etc. For instance, the worldwide ICTs market for 2005 is valued at US$2,963.5 billion by the OECD and at US$2,417.3 billion by EITO – i.e. there is a difference of 546.2 billion (OECD, 2006a, p. 44; EITO, 2006, p. 190).[7] Big differences may even be found in "simple" indicators such as the internet users as a percentage of population: for instance the data for Germany and Spain for 2004 are 42.7 per cent and 33.2 per cent according to ITU (2006), while they are 57.6 per cent and 44.4 per cent according to EITO (2005), that is, there exists a difference of nearly 15 percentage points in the case of Germany and 11.2 percentage points in the case of Spain. One more difficulty is given by the fact that the borders of the European Union have changed radically through time in recent years.[8]

The data in the tables below refers to the categories proposed by EITO. Table 13.1 shows the value of the global ICT market in the year 2005. The data is subdivided into Europe (European Union – except Cyprus and Malta – plus Bulgaria, Norway, Romania and Switzerland), the United States, Japan, and the Rest of the World.

As one can see, Europe has the greatest world share of the ICTs market value (33.8 per cent), followed by the United States (28 per cent) and Japan

Table 13.1 Global ICT market and relative importance of geographic areas, 2005 (values in billions of euro-2004)

	Year 2005	*Value as % of total*
Europe*	659	33.8
USA	545	28.0
Japan	287	14.7
Rest of the world	457	23.5
Total	1,949	100.0

Source: Eito, 2006, p. 43.

Note

* Includes: Austria, Belgium, Bulgaria, the Czech Republic, Denmark, Estonia, Finland, France, Germany, Greece, Hungary, Ireland, Italy, Latvia, Lithuania, Luxembourg, the Netherlands, Norway, Poland, Portugal, Romania, Slovakia, Slovenia, Spain, Sweden, Switzerland, the UK (Cyprus and Malta are not included).

(14.7 per cent). It is worth noting that the overall population of Europe as defined to obtain those statistics is about 500 million people, while the US population does not reach 300 million.

It is also useful to refer to a series of indicators which show the spread of information technology (IT) in selected countries. IT is the subset of ICTs which contains the combined industries of hardware for office machines, data processing equipment, data communication equipment, software and all related services (EITO, 2006, p. 251).

Table 13.2 considers, for a selection of countries, four indicators: the IT/GDP ratio, the per capita spending on IT, the number of available computers in the workplace per 100 of white-collar workers, and the number of available computers per 100 of population. Data refers to 2004 unless otherwise stated.

With regards to the IT/GDP ratio, the United States shows a higher percentage with respect to both the EU-15 and Japan: in fact, in the US this ratio amounts to 4.02 per cent to be compared with 3.05 per cent in the EU-15; within the latter, the only countries that match the US are Sweden (4.39 per cent), the United Kingdom (4.22 per cent) and the Netherlands (3.82 per cent). If one considers per capita expenditure, one finds that the US is far ahead of the EU-15 (1,058 euro vs. 719).

A stronger dominance of the Unites States is found by looking at the data on the number of personal computers available for every 100 of white collar workers or for 100 citizens. In the US there are 148 computers per 100 of white collar workers, to be compared with 97 in the EU-15. European countries in which this ratio reaches or exceeds 1:1 are Ireland (not shown in table, 195 computers per 100 of white collars),[9] Norway (176), Switzerland (139), Sweden (120), the UK (107), the Netherlands (101) and Denmark (100).

An even stronger dominance of the United States over Europe and Japan emerges in the number of personal computers available per 100 citizens, which in the United States is 77, in the EU-15 is 33 and in Japan 43.

Table 13.2 IT diffusion in selected countries, 2004

	IT/GDP	*IT spending per-capita (euro)*	*No. of personal computers in the workplace per 100 "white collar" workers**	*No. of personal computers per 100 citizens*
Italy	1.94	426	97	21
Denmark	3.46	1,226	100	57
Finland	3.63	950	92	41
France	3.31	843	97	33
Germany	3.06	776	87	37
Netherlands	3.82	988	101	50
United Kingdom	4.22	1,023	107	41
Sweden	4.39	1,211	120	59
*EU-15***	*3.05*	*719*	*97*	*33*
Switzerland	4.20	1,464	139	54
Norway	3.27	1,199	176	59
USA	*4.02*	*1,058*	*148*	*77*
Japan	3.40	986	54	43

Source: Eito, 2006, p. 68.

Notes

* Data of this column are taken from Eito, 2005, p. 59 and refer to 2003.

** Includes: Austria, Belgium, Denmark, Finland, France, Germany, Greece, Ireland, Italy, Luxembourg, the Netherlands, Portugal, Spain, Sweden and the UK.

Finally, let us briefly look at the overall ICTs expenditure as a percentage of GDP (Table 13.3) between 2000 and 2005. The first comment concerns the United States in which in 2000 the weight of ICTs on the GDP amounted to 9.38 per cent – and such a high percentage explains the importance of the ICT sector for the overall economy; in the same year, in Western Europe (that is EU-15 plus Norway and Switzerland) the figure is 7 per cent, which, even though is not as impressive as America's, it does represent an important share of the economy. After the crisis of 2000 one sees a reduction in the share of ICTs which is more

Table 13.3 ICTs as a percentage of GDP

	2000	*2001*	*2002*	*2003*	*2004*	*2005*
Western Europe*	7.00	6.90	6.59	6.43	6.40	6.40
USA	9.38	8.63	8.11	7.07	6.81	6.64
Diff. (%) US–West Eur	*2.38*	*1.73*	*1.52*	*0.64*	*0.41*	*0.24*
Japan	7.14	7.41	7.77	7.53	7.59	7.65

Source: data for 2000 and 2001 is from Eito, 2004, p. 314; data for 2002–2005 is from Eito, 2006, p. 244.

Note

Includes: EU-15, Switzerland and Norway.

marked in the Unites States than in Western Europe – from 9.38 in 2000 to 6.64 in 2005 for the United States and from 7.0 to 6.4 for Western Europe. Japan, instead, has actually experienced an increase in the percentage from 7.14 to 7.65. The gap between the United States and Western Europe in the ICT/GDP ratio has narrowed from 2.38 per cent in 2000 to 0.24 per cent in 2005. The fact that Japan has shown the highest percentage for the last three years is worth stressing.

13.5 The *digital* division of labour

From the previous two sections the importance of digital technologies clearly emerges. ICTs are general-purpose technologies which are now everywhere. Today, we can well say that there is no sector or business – in manufacturing, services and even agriculture and mining – in which ICTs are not important. Services are ICT intensive merely by definition, but many other activities now depend heavily on ICTs which govern processes of production or provide information and monitoring.

At whatever scale we look at the economy, macro or micro, ICTs have had an impact on the way in which production takes place as well as on productivity (OECD, 2004; Brynjolfsson and Hitt, 2003). The various stages and phases – e.g. design, manufacturing and marketing of cars – in which production and sale of goods can be divided has been affected by the adoption and diffusion of ICTs. ICTs have also reduced some of those which Coase defined transaction costs. In the end, ICTs reduce both co-ordination and transaction costs and usually alter the existing hierarchy and market relationships.

Thus, following Varian *et al.* (2004) we see that information technology besides transaction costs, affects pricing, switching costs, scale economies and system co-ordination. We cannot review all of these items in detail, and we concentrate on some specific points, starting from the creation of the hardware sector.

13.5.1 Hardware

The history of the birth of the first electronic calculators, between 1936 and 1945, is well-known,[10] and is closely tied to strategic and military needs, such as designing aircrafts, calculating bomb trajectories, or deciphering codes. However there were already significant needs for powerful calculators in the civilian sphere as well, for example, for dealing with census data, or for the needs of private firms (such as actuarial calculus). The post-Second World War period saw a slow development of competition in the computer sector. A dominant player has always been IBM; however, its dominant position was not easy to defend: in the 1950s Remington Rand had become a major computer supplier for many departments of the United States government, while by the end of the 1950s there were at least a dozen firms producing computers in the United States.

The hardware sector goes beyond the computer and its key components: it includes all the other hardware, such as telephone networks, modems, routers, fibre-optic cables, antennas and even satellites, upon which the physical network that gave birth to the world wide web (www) was founded and developed.

It is interesting to note how the web was created and developed using "old" copper telephone cables and "old" telephone lines. Using such telephone lines to connect computers with each other was far from easy: this process required the creation of modems, which can transform digital outputs in analog signals and vice versa. The need to translate such signals gave birth to the development of an entirely new sector, characterised by innovative dynamics spurred by both purely technological aspects and by economic concerns. In particular, the need to transfer ever-growing quantities of data through cables led to the development of broadband modems, which multiplied data-transfer capabilities starting in the mid-1990s. Not surprisingly, these developments took place while Internet connections were growing at an exponential rate.

Routers and switches equipment – which are used to regulate the traffic of data – also played a key role. This type of hardware is manufactured by a limited number of producers, dominated by Cisco Systems. The routers and switches equipment market has experienced a long period of growth, the crisis hitting this market only in late 2002 and 2003. Cisco Systems' net sales of routers and switches amounted to US$16.1 billion in 2001, 13.1 billion in 2002, 12.6 billion in 2003 and back to 16.9 billion in 2006.[11] Looking at the technological side, at least three generations of this type of equipment have followed one another since 1986. As usual, the technology has evolved towards higher speed, better data routing efficiency, versatility, the possibility of operating in parallel and the capability of interconnecting different standards.

New developments in the fibre-optics sectors are another important step. This sector is not new – the first commercial applications were developed in the second half of the 1970s – but the last few years have seen some very important technological and economic development, which have led to a much greater diffusion. Just as the data transfer capabilities of copper cables have grown, so have those of fibre optics. Many technical problems have been overcome: joining loose cables together was a serious problem until recently, as was having to bend cables in tight spaces, such as in small offices or around the desks on which computers rest. Furthermore, prices for fibre-optic cables are falling, and are starting to become competitive with those of copper cables if one considers performance (Hecht, 1999). Once again, one sees the *sailing-ship effect* at work, which leads to a dramatic improvement in the efficiency of the old copper cable technology once it is subjected to competition from the new, fibre-optics technology.

Hardware also includes the entire wireless transmission network, which includes signal-emitting stations as well as receiving sets and the network of antennas. This ensemble includes all of the infrastructure necessary for mobile telephone communication along with satellite technology, which since the second half of the twentieth century has played an increasingly important role in signal diffusion.

The sub-system called "end user communication equipment" is worth a closer look. It includes fixed telephones, mobile telephones and other communication hardware, such as fax machines. Cellular telephones play an important role in this sub-sector in terms of both volume and value.

The overall technological and economic evolution of the hardware sub-sector is well illustrated by the following data, taken from Jorgenson (2001). Memory microchip prices have *fallen* by almost 41 per cent *annually* for the timespan between 1974 and 1996 while the GDP implicit deflator rose by 4.6 per cent annually; prices of logic chips, available only starting in 1985, fell by 54.1 per cent annually; finally, the fall in micro-processor prices in the second half of the 1990s accelerated even more, surpassing 90 per cent; at the same time as the semiconductor industry cycle becoming shorter, going from three years to two years. A similar, albeit slower process, is taking place with regards to computer prices[12] (Jorgenson, 2001).

The exponential growth in computer performance, along with the price dynamics described above, have made it possible – at least in the United States – for the computer sector to affect productivity indices for the entire economy, even though this sector counted for only 1.2 per cent of GDP in 1999. Gordon (1999) has shown that if the computer sector is excluded, the growth rates for the US economy in the second half of the 1990s would be lower than those of 1972–1995, which is regarded as a particularly negative period.

13.5.2 Software

In Chandler and Cortada's (2000) work on the diffusion of information tools, the authors identify patterns of continuity and discontinuity in the evolution of infrastructure for the transmission of information; the most important discontinuity has been *software*. Software is a necessary infrastructure for both single computers, and, even more, for computer networks. This infrastructure has a very particular characteristic: it is *immaterial*. The production, or *writing*, of software is one of the pillars of the digital division of labour.

While hardware was the dominant aspect in the early stages of the computer era, software is currently more and more at the centre of attention. A division of labour between hardware and software producers has arisen, and has grown especially with the explosion in the market for personal computers.

At first, hardware producers also developed the software necessary to make their machines work, or at least they controlled the firms which wrote the software. This was "natural" since computers were still seen as objects that worked in mysterious ways. However, with the enlargement of the market and with the passing of time, computer users began to acquire familiarity with the new machines and began to write and exchange application programmes; the first software houses, which produced operating systems as well as application programmes, began to appear (Fisher *et al.*, 1983, p. 54).

This last step led to the division of labour between hardware and software producers, which began to grow starting in the 1970s. This does not mean that hardware producers gave up on writing software: while Microsoft, which produces only software, is the colossus that dominates the global market, it must be stressed that IBM is the second largest producer in the world when one looks at revenue from software – 39.8 billion dollars for Microsoft and 15.7 billion for IBM in 2005.

Following Chandler and Cortada (2000), we can distinguish between three types of software: (i) operating systems and their utilities; (ii) programming languages; (iii) application software. The first allows computers to communicate with all their components and peripheral hardware; the second allows one to command a computer to do something; the third is the type of software with which computer users normally interact, from word processors to statistical packages, etc.

There have been significant developments in each of these types of software, from DOS to Windows, from Fortran to Java, from the earliest word processors to the other programs we all know. We will limit our discussion to some key steps in the development of programming languages, since they have been fundamental in the development of both stand-alone computers and, more importantly, of networks.

At least five different generations of programming languages can be identified. The first generation used only ones and zeros to "talk" to machines; the second generation began to introduce letters, which were then translated into ones and zeros that machines could understand; the third generation took an important step forward with the introduction of some brief English key words, such as "Read", "Write" or "Goto": the syntax of these languages became independent of the computers on which they ran; the fourth generation, of limited use, is restricted to data base access and the development of particularly complicated operations (*structured query language*, SQL), the fifth generation, which was originally supposed to integrate artificial intelligence with programming, blossomed with the Internet and is based on the principles of the Java language, introduced by Sun Microsystems in 1995: "write once, run everywhere" (The Economist, 2001c).

The way in which software is developed follows the "trial-and-error" path, so that first versions of programs are tested in-house, bugs are fixed, beta versions are released and some more flaws are mended and then one gets the final result – which does not necessarily mean reliability: unforeseen and unexpected problems often emerge.[13] Computer scientists are trying to produce design-checking tools, that is models or analysers which operate on *design* rather than on program code; programmers can use these software design checking tools

> to analyze and test their codings for structural and conceptual inconsistencies … [T]hese commercial and open-source design-evaluation tools are based on specialized high-level languages that researchers have developed to ease the specification, modelling and simulation of different types of software schemes.
>
> (Jackson, 2006, box on p. 64)

Other types of division of labour concerning software – which overlap with institutional aspects, especially those related to intellectual property – concern the development of *open source* programs, such as the *Linux* operating system, or the software package *Staroffice* (or *OpenOffice*), which can offer the same performance as *Windows* and *Office* respectively, but which are freely available online. This illustrates two competing visions of the software world which can be summed up as follows: one is based on closed-source and copyright protection for software, and the other on the freely available open-source development. These two visions can bring about different types of division of labour.

We also have to deal with a new aspect which has arisen with the development of the Internet, and which allows for the possibility of no longer installing software on one's computer, and instead accessing programs installed elsewhere, usually by paying a fee. From a conceptual point of view this process can be considered as a mere extension of a widely used service, namely database access; quite simply, instead of paying for accessing data, one pays to access software programs online. Another up-and-coming development concerns the possibility of using specific software to access the processors of computers connected to the Internet which are momentarily not in use, in order to boost processing power. This development might lead to the jump from the Internet to the "Grid" (The Economist, 2001b). The basic idea rests on the premise that the actual time of use of personal computers, which are almost all connected to the Internet, is relatively low. Indeed, this was the basic idea upon which Napster was originally developed.

13.5.3 Digital production, teleworking and digital consumption

The first, however obvious, distinction we have to recall is that between those who created the digital technologies and those who use them – be it for work or for leisure. About the creation of digital technologies we tend to remember companies and institutions – Bell Laboratories and transistor, IBM and computer, US Department of Defence/MIT/UCLA and ARPANET – but the role of individuals employed by them should not be overlooked. Thus, we have to stress the role of those who helped create and develop the digital industry, in terms of both hardware and software: these include qualified professionals such as information technology engineers and scientists.[14] The development of the Internet has created innumerable new activities, from web masters to network administrators, to e-commerce.

The biggest quantitative impact has been on the final users of digital technology, as demonstrated by the large-scale use of personal computers in offices and, before that by the use of mainframes, the introduction of numerically controlled machines and flexible manufacturing systems. In many countries there are now over 100 personal computers available for every 100 white-collar workers, while an increasing percentage of workers are being transformed into teleworkers (or e-workers).

The widespread use of computers has led to the *necessary* development of new skills, from the secretary that long ago had to abandon the typewriter to the researcher that posts his/her research projects online. More and more jobs make use of ICTs and the process of tertiarisation of our economies has made it easier to digitise various tasks.

More and more workers have thus become familiar with digital technologies, while the young generation is growing up with digitised habits, both for leisure and work. The emergence of reliable networks has made it possible to develop one more step, which has been called teleworking (or e-working).

As the European framework agreement on telework states, "Telework is a form of organising and/or performing work, using information technology, in the context of an employment contract/relationship, where work, which could also be performed at the employers premises, is carried out away from those premises on a regular basis". Thus, ICTs permit e-working from home or other remote locations with the positive side effects of reducing commuting and the promotion of family-friendly work practices (EC, 2003). Should one prefer specific categories, some suggestions are provided by Gillespie *et al.* (1995), who speak in terms of (i) *home telework*: the worker does his/her own work from his/her home, for all or part of the working time, being helped by information and communication technologies; (ii) *telecottages and teleservice centres*: an office is supplied with ICTs equipment for a work position that can be shared by different organisations, employees or free-lance teleworkers; (iii) *mobile teleworking*: the teleworker, equipped with portable devices, does his/her own work at home or when travelling, or at a client's premises or in the main office; (iv) *teleworking group*: this kind of activity is carried out by a number of persons, each working in a different physical place; the work at different stages is transferred from one point to another of the members' locations or it is shared on the web; (v) *call centres and remote offices*: firms can reorganise across space.[15] The more time goes by, the more categories will be added as the technological performance improves and networking costs decrease.

If in quantitative terms telework is a fairly recent phenomenon, a pioneering book published in 1990 made clear many of the opportunities which emerge from the use of information technology; indeed, the second part of the title of the volume is quite telling: *towards the elusive office* (Huws *et al.*, 1990). As is made clear, telework affects many categories of cost – e.g. office overhead costs, equipment costs, start-up costs, transportation costs, management costs, communication costs – as well as productivity and pay, besides contractual and general working relationships.

While until the mid-1990s e-work represented a small percentage of total employment, according to two reports published by the European Commission (EC, 2003, 2005) and a survey conducted by the International Telework Association and Council (ITAC, 2005) telework has become an important reality.

To avoid confusion we have to stress the fact that when we refer to teleworkers we do *not* mean that these workers *always* work from home or remote places; the figures provided hereafter refer to workers who telework fairly regularly – e.g. one day per week.

According to ITAC (2005) in the United States, out of 135.4 million workers, during the period considered by the survey, 45.1 million had done some work from home and 24.3 worked at client's or customer's place of business. Standardised data for Europe is not easy to find, but telework concerns on average at least 13 per cent of the working population, with some countries in which the percentage is much higher such as the Netherlands (26.4 per cent), Finland (21.8 per cent), Denmark (21.5 per cent) and, among the big countries, the United Kingdom (17.3 per cent) and Germany (16.6 per cent) (EC, 2003, pp. 20–21). More recent data is not systematically available; however, it is worthwhile stressing that in Sweden 37 per cent of workers took advantage of teleworking in 2004 and that in companies with 100 employees or more, at least 65 per cent of workers do make use of some form of telework (EC, 2005, p. 67).

Within teleworking one more dimension is being added: teleconferencing. The idea in itself is not new; audio conferences via the telephone have been a reality for a long time, and for a few years video conferencing systems have also been used. However, until very recently, when meetings were particularly important they had to be traditional, personal, meetings as the conferencing technology was not perfected. Typically, the images on the screen or the audio could be hazy, audio and video did not correspond so that the movement of the lips of the speaker did not match what was being heard, often a time lag made the conversation a bit difficult. Two conferencing systems, which solve all of the problems just indicated, are now available – one produced by Hewlett-Packard and the other by Cisco Systems. Both companies claim to provide a technology which redefines the experience of face-to-face communication, increases team effectiveness, provides faster decision-making capabilities and, of course, decreases the need for travel. The latter point is very important for many large companies and institutions, given their usually high travel expenses for their managers and senior officials. If the basic service consists in providing a face-to-face-like virtual meeting, the reliability of the technology and the ultra high definition of the images make it possible to foresee additional applications, from healthcare to entertainment.[16]

The digitisation process and the ever-growing use of the Internet have led to a further wave of IT knowledge diffusion among *consumers*. This aspect is very important, because certain basic principles of computer use are becoming widely known. For instance, about one of the most diffused forms of entertainment, i.e. music, although computer programs are becoming more user-friendly, listening to music on a traditional stereo set is quite different from going online, finding the websites on which music tracks are stored, downloading them and listening to them on a computer or on an iPod. Mutatis mutandis, similar processes are taking place in various types of consumption of both goods and services: examples are e-books, home banking or studying at e-universities.

With regard to Internet use, a survey conducted in 2003 by the Oxford Internet Institute shows that among Britons aged 14 and over, 59 per cent use the Internet; among those in education, aged 14 to 22, Internet users are 98 per cent – be it from home, school, the library or elsewhere; finally, the biggest difference between users and non-users is age, rather than education (OII, 2003).

In a few years a large majority of the population, of the rich countries at least, will be IT literate.

13.5.4 ICTs and the international division of labour

Digital technologies have made possible a reshaping of the international division of labour and have contributed to the process of globalisation. The most apparent change of recent years consists of the new role which is being played by China and India, but cases such as that of Finland, Ireland or the Baltic States should not be overlooked.

China and India are now numbered among the 33 countries in which the 250 largest ICTs firms are based. In particular, according to the OECD ITS database, in 2004 China has surpassed the United States as the world biggest exporter of ICT goods: in fact, in that year, China exported information technology goods worth US$180 billion, while the United States exported ICT goods worth "only" US$149 billion. At the same time China is also one of the biggest importers of ICT goods (US$150 billion), and in particular of electronic components. In 2005 a symbolic passage took place, i.e. China's Lenovo acquisition of IBM's personal computer business.

If China is emerging mainly as a hardware power, India is becoming a large producer and exporter of software and software services. In the period 1994–2002 India's export of software and software services increased from less than half a billion dollars to 9.9 billion; in 2002 software and related services accounted for 20 per cent of India's total exports (D'Costa, 2004). It is important to stress the fact that India's software industry has basically developed independently of the hardware industry and the home market. India is also gaining ground in providing ICT-enabled services.

Besides developing its own software and service industry

> India has been very successful in attracting foreign multinationals wanting to benefit from local skills and cost structures. Approximately one-third of Indian exports of IT services and two-thirds of ICT-enabled services are estimated to be generated by foreign-owned companies … Companies that locate in India's software technology parks to serve foreign markets benefit from temporally limited but generous tax exemptions and various measures for facilitating investment and businesses' daily operations.
>
> (OECD, 2006a, p. 129)

One more comment about these two countries is necessary, and concerns their population size[17] and high GDP growth: these countries are becoming not only important producers and users of ICTs, but important markets for various types of goods and services. A refrain which often applies to China is that it is the fastest growing market for something (cars, computers, mobile phones, Internet connections, and so on).

Other countries have joined the ICTs race and we can mention Finland, Ireland and the Baltic States. As far as the Baltic States are concerned, they may be small in absolute size, but Latvia shows the highest growth in reported exports of business services and computer information services between 1995 and 2004 (compound annual growth rate: 55 per cent), while Estonia (32.4 per cent) and Lithuania (28.8 per cent) come fifth and seventh, respectively. Ireland has become a success story for its capability of attracting non-European companies which use the country as an export platform to serve the European market: Ireland shows the highest share of ICT services in total business services in terms of value added (about 14 per cent) (OECD, 2006a). Finland has become an important player in ICTs because of the presence of Nokia – a world leader in telecommunication technologies.

What has been said up to now should not lead one to think that the United States and Japan have become minor players. Looking at the world top 250 ICT firms – however rough an indicator – one finds that 116 of them are based in the United States and 39 in Japan (OECD, 2006a). The three most important producers of software are based in the United States: Microsoft leads the world software industry – and, incidentally, has been among the top three companies of the world, including all sectors, in terms of market capitalisation for the last few years; when we look at companies' reports we discover that IBM, in terms of revenue, is the second largest producer of software, followed by Oracle. As for hardware, IBM and HP are world's leaders, while Intel is still the largest chip maker. Japan's Hitachi, Matsushita, Toshiba and NTT are also important world players.

Besides the aspect of the countries which have started to participate in ICTs production and development we have to consider the side of the users of digital technologies. We have already hinted in the previous section at the new possibilities which have emerged together with improved ICTs, starting from telework. However, other dimensions have to be considered, in terms of opportunities but also of threats. Easiness of communications, together with massive improvements and availability of transportation, has made the relocation of many productive activities – not just services – possible. Thus, while on the one hand new working opportunities have been created, on the other hand unequal competition between workers based in different countries has emerged. Competiton between workers is unequal because it is not possible, for instance, for a computer programmer living in the United States to compete in terms of salary with another one living in India. In many services – from call centres to banks – it is not difficult to outsource or offshore to low-wage countries part of the activities (for a thorough analysis one can refer to OECD, 2006b). ICTs have also facilitated the process of fragmentation and/or relocation of traditional manufacturing activities. In recent years a dramatic increase in the share of "parts" and "components" – as opposed to final goods – has been observed in international trade statistics. As Arndt and Kierzkowski (2001) point out, aircrafts may be designed and engineered in one country, but the parts of which an aircraft is made up of come from a dozen of other countries; the same is true for cars, watches, textiles and many other products (including computers, mobile phones and other hardware). This phenomenon is not new, but what is new is its increasing importance. Thus, the various phases of production may now be physically separated and undertaken where costs are lower; a more detailed division of labour, which in many cases implies different countries, takes place. In this sense, the international division of labour matches factor intensities of components rather than average intensity concerning the whole end product (Arndt and Kierzkowski, 2001). Producers could not take advantage of these opportunities without ICTs which allow co-ordination, communication and transfer of codified knowledge at very low cost.

13.6 The legal foundations of *digital* capitalism[18]

Digital technologies, and the Internet in particular, have put many economic, juridical and political categories under strain. Economic theory has taught us that in competitive markets price equals marginal cost, but marginal cost for many digital services is basically zero; protection of copyright in a digital world may be difficult to enforce: one just has to think of the entertainment or of the software industry, from audio CDs to DVDs and programs which are often illegally reproduced on an industrial scale; new opportunities have emerged such as the free and open source software movement and the so-called *copyleft*; in a service economy antitrust laws may need revision and new interpretations: when Microsoft added its "Internet Explorer" to Windows was it applying an anticompetitive behaviour or was it promoting a "natural" development of its operating system?; barriers to entry have a different flavour with respect to a manufacturing economy; new digital opportunities are being continuously discovered.

13.6.1 Rules of the game and the role of governments in digital development

Public institutions *invariably* play a fundamental role in shaping, pulling, limiting or encouraging technological progress. Obviously, those who lead institutions do not necessarily have access to privileged information on the state-of-the-art of a particular technology, nor do they have better instruments to predict the direction that technological change will take. Nevertheless, institutions have always played a key role in many aspects, such as setting standards, ensuring quality control, managing technologies that are tied to national security, protecting intellectual property, preventing monopolies from abusing their position, guaranteeing privacy, and so forth.

Also, government-financed R&D has often been a key structural feature of many major technological breakthroughs: one only needs to think of particle physics, nuclear energy, aviation technology, or the early development of biotechnology.

Policies concerning information technology could emerge more easily in the United States than in Europe, because that is where the largest hardware and software companies were born, often in close interaction with the public sector – and the Department of Defense in many cases. We can briefly recall the classic example of the rise of the Internet, which as is universally known was developed by the Department of Defense and a few universities in the United States.

We have already mentioned the case of the first numerically-controlled machine tool. More generally, the very emergence of the new economy in the United States is a product of the strong role played by the state and the public sector, through project financing, selection and evaluation, which implies both the will and the capacity to set a course for the economy.

A different example of institutional support is the *Internet Tax Freedom Act* passed in 1998 by the US Congress which exempted on-line transactions from any kind of taxation for three years – a measure that certainly contributed to the development of electronic commerce. The tax moratorium which was supposed to expire in October 2001 was extended to November 2003. India has also granted foreign companies tax exemptions and other measures in order to attract them.

While the European Union has often acted later than the United States, it has nevertheless tried to implement policies and programmes that could stimulate technological progress, and this holds true for digital technologies. We have already mentioned that in 1997 the European Commission published a *Green Paper* on the convergence between the telecommunications, media and information technology sectors, and on its normative implications. This was an ambitious project, as the Green Paper was to be the launching pad for an overall reference framework that could set the foundations for the development of the European information society (EC, 1997). The existing normative framework was not particularly encouraging at the time, as many of the laws had been created in previous years, when the technological context was mainly analog rather than digital, and the geo-political context still consisted of a group of nations that were not well integrated with each other. These conditions have now changed. In 2000 the Lisbon European Council set the goal for Europe to become the most competitive and dynamic knowledge-based economy in the world, while specific *Action Plans* aimed at ICTs were launched – e.g. *eEurope 2005* was launched in 2003 (EC, 2003).[19]

We cannot deal with all the aspects in which institutional influences are decisive; we will only discuss a few relevant factors. Setting standards is an enormously important problem in ICTs. A standard can emerge through competition, leadership, negotiation between firms or imposition. The first three are market options, the fourth comes from some regulatory body. The competition between videotape technologies, i.e. Betamax vs. VHS is widely known; leadership in standard often comes when one firm is far ahead of its rivals and reaches the market with a new product or technology thus imposing a de facto standard – many examples can be found, from the early machine tool industry in England to the car industry; as for negotiation, for instance in 1977 both Philips and Sony were working to develop a digital sound system making use of optical disks; in 1979 they started a co-operation which led to the establishment of the new world standard for CD audio. In these cases no regulatory body made any interference. However, while the market itself can sometimes be enough to set or select standards, at other times institutions must take the lead in setting a course: this was the case with mobile phones in Europe. This sector deals with a pervasive technology, into which several needs are now converging and will continue to do so – needs such as greater miniaturisation, data storage capabilities, longer-lasting batteries, Internet access, better signal reception and better overall management of telephone traffic.

The United States approach has been hands-off, thus letting the market select the technology with the best price/performance ratio. In the early stages such an approach led to the establishment of three different standards – TDMA, CDMA and GSM – which were only partly compatible, and which slowed the diffusion of cellular telephones, since it hampered the development of a critical mass large enough to create the necessary economies of scale in terms of both physical infrastructure and associated services.

The European approach opted for the adoption of a single *mandatory* standard, GSM. This approach has proven successful in terms of the diffusion and price dynamics of mobile telephone services. This could prove an important factor, since the very nature of the telephone has now changed: it is no longer just an instrument for voice communication, but has other functions ranging from writing and sending text messages to performing banking operations. In other words, just as computers are used for communication as well as for data processing, telephones have now evolved from voice communication instruments to data storing and processing tools.

A specific comment must be devoted to the role played by antitrust institutions which monitor the behaviour of large multinational corporations. Antitrust authorities are playing an increasingly important role, especially in those countries that are at the forefront of creating the tools of the new digital division of labour. The case brought against Microsoft by the United States Department of Justice – and later by the European Union – is perhaps the best such example: the behaviour of this industry giant impacts not only on the US economy, but the global economy as well. Furthermore, it is interesting to note that practically all the key steps in the development of the information technology sector have been punctuated by the actions of the US antitrust: the Microsoft case is the most recent; IBM was taken to court for abusing its dominant position in a case that started in 1969 and lasted for 13 years, until charges were dropped in 1982; an earlier case is that of Bell Laboratories, which was sued by the United States government in 1949 over the failure to make patents on transistors publicly available (the two parties settled the case in 1956).

13.6.2 Some legal and technological idiosyncrasies

In this section we point to some – at times controversial – digital-specific aspects which have emerged over time, and which have characterised the recent development of the ICTs. Given the vastness of the applications of digital technologies there is no pretension of exhaustiveness: simply, we want to stress some important passages.

We have already used the word *convergence*, which has also been defined as the *quadruple play* (e.g. *The Economist*, 2006), that is the combination of fixed and mobile telephony, broadband internet access and multichannel television. Convergence poses many questions, ranging from technological standards to regulation. In some countries it is now possible to watch television with a computer as well as with a mobile phone; should anyone possessing a computer or a mobile phone have to pay the annual television licence as is paid, on a mandatory basis (in many European countries), by those who possess an ordinary TV set?

We have already referred to the two different legal standards which exist for sowftware, that is proprietary on the one hand and and free open-source software on the other. Proprietary software is protected by copyright laws, but this is not the whole story. An important debate has taken place in Europe since 2002, when the European Commission proposed a directive on the *patentability* of computer-implemented inventions, where "computer-implemented invention is stated to mean any invention implemented on a computer or similar apparatus which is realised by a computer program" (CEE, 2002, p. 13); in this proposal the complementarity between patent and copyright protection is explicitly recalled, and in Europe, in some cases, patents – as distinct from copyright protection – are awarded; however this is the exception rather than the rule. In the United States, instead, patentability of software innovation is much easier (Blind *et al.*, 2005). Now, while companies, international and national institutions and regulators and their lawyers and consultants are debating these themes and while the courts are busy sorting out trials which concern the infringement of patents and copyright, the biggest proprietary software world player, Microsoft, has struck a deal with Novell, i.e. one of the leading open-source software companies.[20] The technical and business collaboration has created a technical and legal bridge which not only makes interoperability possible, but has also overcome all of the patent infringement claims between the two former enemies.

In general terms, in the digital economy the protection of intellectual property is increasingly difficult to guarantee: many firms, from the entertainment industry to software firms, see the low-cost availability of programs that allow for the duplication of any intellectual work (scanners, MP3, MP4, CD burners, etc.) as a kind of universal "photocopying machine". The importance of the role that international and national institutions play in enforcing the rules agreed upon by nearly all the world's countries is obvious.

One more peculiar legal aspect which characterises the Internet revolves around the words *privacy, censorship* and *price discrimination*, the common point being that some Big Brother is minding your business. While the early stages of the Internet's development were fundamentally anarchic and lacking any borders, recent developments have gone the other way round, i.e. limiting freedom and setting new borders. Whenever an individual surfs the web he/she leaves traces of his/her journey, so that his/her tastes, preferences or political persuasion can be monitored; moreover, often once one registers somewhere electronically sooner or later one gets plenty of spam, that is unsolicited e-mail messages which we all get, informing us that we have won a lottery or which ask co-operation in managing some million dollars. Privacy is lost.[21]

For a long time the Internet was vaunted at the land of freedom, censorship, though, has grown rapidly. Of course in some cases censorship is justified; however, the agreements signed by Yahoo in 2002 and by Google in early 2006 with the Chinese government – agreements which limit search and results on the web in such a way to avoid "harmful information" – do not seem to belong to the category of censorship which may be justified. At the origin of the development of censorship tools is the need for so-called geo-location technology. The story begins in 2000 for the following reason: France has a law that forbids Nazi memorabilia from being bought or sold; in November 2000, a French judge ordered Yahoo to find a way to prevent French citizens from buying such objects online, even if the country from which they are sold is not France. While at first Yahoo answered that it was not technically possible to identify users by country, eventually a way to do it was found.[22] Once geolocation technology allows the identification of users by geography it may be used for censorship, prosecution, political control or tax purposes. Incidentally, we can note that geolocation technologies represent a further step in the digital division of labour.

Price discrimination is the third aspect to which we want to draw attention. In 2000 Amazon was caught – by Linda Rosencrance of *Computerworld* – charging different prices to different customers for the same product; differences could be up to US$10 for the same DVD. This is hardly new for economists who have written about price discrimination for a long time,[23] what is new is the easiness with which unrestrained monopolists or technology leaders may apply such a pricing policy. Once more one has to compare what has just been written with the uncritical early view of the Internet as the great *deus ex machina* of competitive markets and defender of consumers.

The final paradoxical comment I want to make begins with the first lines of an article which appeared in the *New York Times* on 19 July 2004: "Microsoft will pay upstart Linux seller Lindows $20 million to settle a long-running trademark dispute." The reason to refer to this quotation is that things are not what they seem: in fact it was Microsoft which sued Lindows; the article goes on, the former contended the Lindows name infringed on its Windows trademark. Thus, while on the one hand Microsoft sued Lindows, on the other hand it accepted to pay Lindows 20 million dollars in an out-of-court settlement to acquire Lindow's Internet domain names.

13.7 Conclusions

Digital ICTs are among the most important technologies to have impacted the last three decades. The key word is *digital*: digitisation has led to the process of technological convergence which we have witnessed over the 1990s, and which has made it possible for us to talk about the digital economy and the birth of new forms of division of labour.

The digitisation of the economy began in the 1960s, and many of its basic impulses came not only from needs of the tertiary sector – managing large databases in ministries, universities, and the banking and insurance sectors – but also from the need to produce physical goods: one only needs to recall numerically controlled machine tools. However, one of the most surprising aspects of the digitisation process lies perhaps in the digitisation of *consumption*.

While the digitisation of productive processes, both within and outside the tertiary sector, took place over a relatively long period of time, the impact of digital technology on consumer electronics has been extremely rapid and overwhelming. One need only think of how CDs have replaced old vinyl records, which, today, are hardly available; the same process is being experienced by other products, such as DVDs which are quickly replacing videotapes. We are, therefore, witnessing, as Scientific American (2000) points out, the development of an *entertainment economy* in which there is a growing interaction between contents (video, audio, data), means of distribution (cable, CDs, wireless, Internet connections) and final consumer goods (television, personal computers, videogame consoles and even cellular phones) all of which serve the ultimate goal of entertainment.

The exponential growth of the Internet has taken place alongside the digitisation of the economy, and has involved an ever-growing number of countries, institutions, firms and individuals.

These processes have already changed work, consumption and interaction patterns, and will continue to do so. This is reflected in language: an entire new vocabulary has sprung up regarding new technologies and the Internet, from business to business – B2B, to business to consumer – B2C, or peer to peer – P2P; the possible impact of working online, which is becoming increasingly feasible, is hotly debated, and large numbers of e-workers already exist.

Many new forms of division of labour have come about as a result of the spread of digital technology. In this case we are faced with completely new technological opportunities, on the one hand, and the possibility of creating convergence processes between previously separated sectors, on the other.

The presence of digital technology has contributed to the reorganisation of firms, industries and to the re-definition of sectors and their relative importance; also, as the economies of China and India demonstrate, it has been an impetus for the modification of the international division of labour.

Notes

1 Shackle notes that in its aspiration to become a science, economics has had to turn its back on the concrete and particular arts, as distinct from abstract and general logic:

> There is one great difference between the … technologies, on the one hand, and the sciences … on the other. Technique is essentially the particularity of detail. Science is abstraction, generalness … In electing to be a science, economics was obliged to confine itself to some aspects of business which are generalizable.
>
> (Shackle, 1992, p. 116)

2 In the 1830s Wakefield edited a new edition of Smith's *Inquiry*; he made many comments to the work and it is from these comments that Mill takes the quotations above.

3 It is worth recalling that *digital* is an adjective which simply means that the variables which are being referred to are only allowed to have a discrete number of values – and thus dice, for instance, are digital computers.

4 See United Nations (1986).
5 Licklider as early as 1962 "envisioned a globally interconnected set of computers through which everyone could quickly access data and programs from any site" (Internet Society, 2003).
6 See pp. 251–259 of EITO (2006) for definitions; EITO has published an annual report since 1993.
7 EITO gives data in euro (1,949.5; the exchange rate is US$1.24 per euro); to appreciate the difference one can note that, according to EITO, Japan's market amounts to US$356.3 billion.
8 Until the end of 2003 the Union was made up of 15 countries; of these only 12 adopted the euro; in January 2004 the Union had grown in size by including ten more countries; in January 2007 two more countries – Bulgaria and Romania –joined the Union.
9 Two more countries, not shown in Table 13.2, in which the ratio is 1:1 or more are Spain (113) and Austria (110).
10 An excellent concise recap can be found in Freeman and Soete (1997, pp. 171–186); the comments that follow are inspired by this work; a thorough history can be found in Goldstine (1993).
11 Data are taken from Cisco Systems Annual Reports.
12 When technological dynamics is so rapid we are faced with serious comparability problems; Jorgenson (2001, p. 5) briefly discusses the debate on the use of *hedonic techniques* to create a series that allows for comparability over time.
13 Jackson (2006) recalls a few software failures which compromised massive investments at Denver International Airport, the US Internal Revenue Service, the Federal Bureau of Investigation and the Federal Aviation Administration; other examples could easily be added.
14 On computers, see Goldstine (1993), on fibre optics see Hecht (1999), on semiconductors see Morris (1990), on software see the *Charles Babbage Institute* web page, on the Internet see the *Internet Society* web page and the work here referred to as Internet Society (2003).
15 For a more detailed analysis see the pages written by Annaflavia Bianchi (in Antonelli and De Liso, 2004, pp. 200–207).
16 See the two companies' web pages, www.hp.com and www.cisco.com; H-P called its system "Halo Collaboration Studio" while Cisco has called it "TelePresence".
17 According to the Population Reference Bureau, the 2006 estimated population of China is 1.31 billion while India's is 1.12 billion.
18 As some readers may have noticed, the title of this section adds the adjective *digital* to the title of the book by John Commons, *Legal foundations of capitalism*, published in 1924.
19 Nearly 70 projects concerned with the various aspects of ICTs – from the opportunities for disabled people to "widening women's work in information and communication technology" – are listed in Annex 2 of the European Commission report on "Collaboration @ Work" (EC, 2003).
20 Novell and Microsoft announced their "broad collaboration on Windows and Linux interoperability and support" on 2 November 2006.
21 One aspect made possible by ICTs, in terms of ease of gathering and processing large data sets, which deserves attention, concerns the data on millions of individual consumers which many large retailers are getting through customer fidelity or loyalty cards.
22 A detailed account can be found in Goldsmith and Wu (2006); for an early report see the Economist (2001d).
23 A.C. Pigou wrote about price discrimination in the 1920s; for a recent analysis of the different types of price discrimination one can refer to Varian *et al.* (2004, pp. 13–15).

Bibliography

Antonelli G. and De Liso N. (eds) (2004), *European Economic Integration and Italian Labour Policies*, Aldershot, Ashgate.

Arndt S.W. and Kierzkowski H. (eds) (2001), *Fragmentation. New Production Patterns in the World Economy*, Oxford, Oxford University Press.

Arrow K.J. (1979), "The economics of information", in M.L. Dertouzos and J. Moses (eds), *The Computer Age: A Twenty-Year View*, Cambridge, Mass., MIT Press, pp. 307–317.

Babbage C. (1830), *Reflections on the Decline of Science in England and Some of Its Causes*, London, Fellowes.

Babbage C. (1835), *On the Economy of Machinery and Manufactures*, London, Knight [4th edn; 1st edn 1832].

Banca d'Italia (2006), *Appendice alla Relazione Annuale del Governatore sull'esercizio 2005*, Rome, Banca d'Italia.

Blind K., Edler J. and Friedewald M. (2005), *Software Patents. Economic Impacts and Policy Implications*, Cheltenham, Elgar.

Brynjolfsson E. (1993), "The productivity paradox of information technology: review and assessment"; http://ccs.mit.edu/papers/CCSWP130/cccswp130.html.

Brynjolfsson E. and Hitt L.M. (1994), "Paradox lost? Firm-level evidence of high returns to information system spending"; http://ccs.mit.edu/papers/CCSWP162/ccswp162.html.

Brynjolfsson E. and Hitt L.M. (2000), "Beyond computation: information technology, organizational transformation and business performance", *Journal of Economic Perspectives*, vol. 14, no. 4, Fall, pp. 23–48.

Brynjolfsson E. and Hitt L.M. (2003), "Computing productivity: firm-level evidence", *Review of Economics and Statistics*, vol. 85, no. 4, November, pp. 793–808.

Bücher C. (1907), *Industrial Evolution*, New York, Henry Holt & Co [translated from the 3rd German edn].

Castells M. (2000), *The Rise of the Network Society*, vol. 1, Oxford, Blackwell Publishers, 2nd edn.

Commssion of the European Communities (CEE) (2002), *Proposal for a Directive of the European Parliament and of the Council on the Patentability of Computer-Implemented Inventions*, Brussels, European Commission.

Chandler A.D. (2000), "The information age in historical perspective: introduction", in A.D. Chandler and J.W. Cortada (eds), *A Nation Transformed by Information: How Information has Shaped the United States from Colonial Times to the Present*, New York, Oxford University Press, pp. 3–37.

Chandler A.D. and Cortada J.W. (eds) (2000), *A Nation Transformed by Information*, Oxford, Oxford University Press.

Cisco Systems (2001), *The Economics of Cisco's Metro IP Solutions – White Paper*, San Jose; www.cisco.com.

D'Costa A.P. (2004), "The Indian software industry in the global division of labour", in A.P. D'Costa and E. Sridharan (eds), *India in the Global Software Industry*, Basingstoke, Palgrave Macmillan, pp. 1–26.

D'Costa A.P. and Sridharan E. (eds) (2004), *India in the Global Software Industry*, Basingstoke, Palgrave Macmillan.

De Liso N., Filatrella G. and Weaver N. (2001), "On endogenous growth and increasing returns: modeling learning-by-doing and the division of labor", *Journal of Economic Behavior and Organization*, Vol. 46, October, pp. 39–55.

De Liso N. (2006), "Charles Babbage, technological change and the national system of innovation", *Journal of Institutional and Theoretical Economics*, vol. 162, no. 3, September, pp. 470–485.

European Commission (EC) (1994), *Europe and the Global Information Society – Bangemann Report*, Brussels, European Commission.

European Commission (EC) (1997), *Green Paper on the Convergence of the Telecommunications, Media and Information Technology Sectors, and the Implications for Regulation*, Brussels, European Commission.

European Commission (EC) (2003), *Collaboration @ Work. The 2003 Report on New Working Environments and Practices*, Brussels, European Commission, October.

European Commission (EC) (2005), *Collaboration @ Work. The 2005 Report on New Working Environments and Practices*, Brussels, European Commission, October.

Economist, The (2001a), "A survey of software", vol. 359, no. 8217, 14–20 April.

Economist, The (2001b), "Computing power on tap", in *The Economist Technology Quarterly*, vol. 359, no. 8227, 23–29 June, pp. 16–20.

Economist, The (2001c), "Java or C#: which language for the Internet?", in *The Economist Technology Quarterly*, supplement to vol. 360, no. 8240, 22–28 September, pp. 14–18.

Economist, The (2001d), "The Internet's new borders", vol. 330, no. 8234, 11–17 August, pp. 9–10, 18–20.

Economist, The (2004), "E-commerce takes off", special report, vol. 371, no. 8375, 15–21 May.

Economist, The (2006), "Your television is ringing. A survey of telecoms convergence", special report, vol. 381, no. 8499, 14–20 October.

Edquist C. (2003), "The fixed Internet and mobile telecommunications sectoral system of innovation: equipment, access and content", in C. Edquist (ed.), *The Internet and Mobile Telecommunications System of Innovation*, Cheltenham, Elgar, pp. 1–39.

European Information Technology Observatory (EITO) (2003), *2003 Report*, EITO, Frankfurt [annual report; first one 1993].

European Information Technology Observatory (EITO) (2004), *2004 Report*, EITO, Frankfurt.

European Information Technology Observatory (EITO) (2005), *2005 Report*, EITO, Frankfurt.

European Information Technology Observatory (EITO) (2006), *2006 Report*, EITO, Frankfurt.

Feller J., Fitzgerald B., Hissam S.A. and Lakhani K.R. (eds) (2005), *Perspectives on Free and Open Source Software*, Cambridge, Mass., MIT Press.

Fisher F.M., McGowan J.J. and Greenwood J.E. (1983), *Folded, Spindled and Mutilated. Economic Analysis and US v. IBM*, Cambridge, Mass. , MIT Press.

Freeman C. and Soete L. (1997), *The Economics of Industrial Innovation*, London, Pinter.

Frieder L.L. and Zittrain J.L. (2006), "Spam works: evidence from stock touts and corresponding market activity", Working paper, July [internet document].

Georgescu-Roegen N. (1971), *The Entropy Law and the Economic Process*, Cambridge, Mass., Harvard University Press.

Gillespie A., Richardson R. and Cornford J. (1995), "Review of telework in Britain: implications for public policy", report for the *Parliamentary Office of Science and Technology*, London, House of Commons.

Goldsmith J. and Wu T. (2006), *Who Controls the Internet? Illusions of a Borderless World*, Oxford, Oxford University Press.

Goldstine H.H. (1993), *The Computer from Pascal to von Neumann*, Princeton, NJ, Princeton University Press, 2nd edn.

Gordon R.J. (1999), "Has the 'new economy' rendered the productivity slowdown obsolete?", Working paper, Northwestern University, mimeo.

Gordon R.J. (2003), "Five puzzles in the behavior of productivity, investment and innovation", draft of a chapter for World Economic Forum, Global Competitiveness Report, 2003–2004.

Groenewegen P. (1987), "Division of labour", in J. Eatwell, M. Milgate and P. Newman (eds), *Palgrave Dictionary*, London, Macmillan.

Hecht J. (1999), *City of Light*, New York, Oxford University Press.

Helpman E. (ed.) (1998), *General Purpose Technologies and Economic Growth*, Cambridge, Mass., MIT Press.

Huws U., Korte W.B. and Robinson S. (1990), *Telework: Towards the Elusive Office*, New York, John Wiley & Sons.

Internet Society (2003), *A Brief History of the Internet*, by B.M. Leiner, V.G. Cerf, D.D. Clark, R.E. Kahn, L. Kleinrock, D.C. Lynch, J. Postel, L.G. Roberts and S. Wolff [internet document available at www.isoc.org].

International Telework Association and Council (ITAC) (2005), *American Interactive Consumer Survey*, Scottsdale [web page: www.workingfromanywhere.org].

International Telecommunication Union (ITU) (2006), *World Telecommunication Indicators* [ITU data base, version used released in April].

Jackson D. (2006), "Dependable software by design", *Scientific American*, vol. 294, no. 6, pp. 58–65.

Jorgenson D.W. (2001), "Information technology and the US economy", *American Economic Review*, vol. 91, no. 1, March, pp. 1–32.

Landes D.S. (1969), *The Unbound Prometheus*, Cambridge, Cambridge University Press.

Leijonhufvud A. (1986), "Capitalism and the factory system", in R. Langlois (ed.), *Economics as a Process*, Cambridge, Cambridge University Press, pp. 203–223.

Licklider J.R.C. and Taylor R.W. (1968), "The computer as a communication device", *Science and Technology*, April [reprinted by the Digital Equipment Corporation, downloaded from the DEC web page].

McKnight L.W. and Bailey J.P. (eds) (1997), *Internet Economics*, Cambridge, Mass., MIT Press.

MacWilliams W.H. (1952), "Computers – past, present, and future" [unknown original reference, copy obtained as courtesy of IBM, Corporate Archives].

Marx K. (1867, English translation 1976), *Capital*, vol. I, Harmondsworth, Penguin Books.

Mill J.S. (1871), *Principles of Political Economy*, 7th edn, [1st edn 1848] London, Parker, reprint 1987, Fairfield, Augustus M. Kelley Publishers.

Mokyr J. (2002), *The Gifts of Athena. Historical Origins of the Knowledge Economy*, Princeton, NJ, Princeton University Press.

Morris P.R. (1990), *A History of the World Semiconductor Industry*, London, IEEE.

Mowery D.C. and Nelson R.R. (eds) (1999), *Sources of Industrial Leadership. Studies of Seven Industries*, Cambridge, Cambridge University Press.

OECD (1996), *The Knowledge-Based Economy*, OECD, Paris.

OECD (1999), *OECD Historical Statistics*, OECD, Paris.

OECD (2000), *OECD Information Technology Outlook. ICTs, E-commerce and the Information Economy*, OECD, Paris.

OECD (2002), *OECD Information Technology Outlook. ICTs and the Information Economy*, OECD, Paris.

OECD (2004), *The Economic Impact of ICT. Measurement, Evidence and Implications*, Paris, OECD.

OECD (2006a), *OECD Information Technology Outlook*, OECD, Paris.

OECD (2006b), *The Share of Employment Potentially Affected by Offshoring – An Empirical Investigation*, OECD, Working paper on the Information Economy, Paris.

Oxford Internet Institute (OII) (2003), *How Much is Enough for the Internet?*, Nationwide representative survey of Britons aged 14 and older [downloaded from the OII web page].

Raymond E.S. (2001), *The Cathedral and the Bazaar. Musings on Linux and Open Source by an Accidental Revolutionary*, Cambridge, Mass., O'Reilly.

Reintjes J.F. (1991), *Numerical Control. Making a New Technology*, New York, Oxford University Press.

Ricardo D. (1817), *On the Principles of Political Economy and Taxation*, [3rd edn 1821], London, John Murray.

Richardson G.B. (1998), "Some principles of economic organisation", in N.J. Foss and B.J. Loasby (eds), *Economic Organization, Capabilities and Co-ordination*, London, Routledge, pp. 44–61.

Schiller D. (1999), *Digital Capitalism*, Cambridge, Mass., MIT Press.

Schreyer P. (2000), "The contribution of information and communication technology to output growth: a study of the G7 countries", STI Working paper 2000/2, Paris, OECD.

Scientific American (2000), "The future of digital entertainment", *Scientific American*, Special report, vol. 283, no. 5, November, pp. 31–64.

Shackle G.L.S. (1992), *Epistemics and Economics*, London, Transaction Publishers [1st edn 1972, Cambridge University Press].

Shapiro C. and Varian H.R. (1999), *Information Rules*, Boston, Mass., Harvard Business School Press.

Smith A. (1776), *An Inquiry into the Nature and Causes of the Wealth of Nations*, edited by R.H. Campbell, A.S. Skinner and W.B. Todd, Oxford, Oxford University Press [1976].

Steil B., Victor D.G. and Nelson R.R. (eds) (2002), *Technological Innovation and Economic Performance*, Princeton, NJ, Princeton University Press.

UNCTAD (2004), *World Investment Report. The Shift Towards Services*, New York, United Nations.

United Nations (1986), *Recent Trends in Flexible Manufacturing*, United Nations, New York.

US-CB (2006), "United States Census Bureau News", *Quarterly Retail Trade E-Commerce Sales*, Washington DC [Internet document].

US-DC (2004), "News – retail E-commerce sales", United States Department of Commerce [web document, ORD6FEMC.htm].

US-DL (2006), *Comparative Civilian Labor Force Statistics, 10 Countries, 1960–2005*, compendium prepared by the United States Department of Labor.

Varian H.R., Farrell J. and Shapiro C. (2004), *The Economics of Information Technology*, Cambridge, Cambridge University Press.

Wu T. (2003) "Network neutrality, broadband discrimination", *Journal of Telecommunications and High Technology Law*, vol. 2, pp. 141–178.

Wu T. (2006), "The World Trade Law of Censorship and Internet Filtering" [web document].

14 Persistent seasonality of demand and local tourist market development

Anna Serena Vergori and Luca Zamparini

14.1 Introduction

The majority of tourism destinations appears to be characterized by a remarkable degree of seasonality of demand that causes several problems to local firms and administrations, as it hampers the efficient use of available facilities (mostly unused in off-peak months but whose amount must be based on peak season's demand) and the development of local capabilities and of the job market (Yacoumis, 1980; Stynes and Pigossi, 1983; Pearce, 1989; Krakover, 2000). However, seasonality of demand may not necessarily be a problem when people employed in the tourism industry have other complementary jobs (Flognfeldt, 1988; Ball, 1989; Shaw and Williams, 1994). Moreover, some economists have underlined the possible benefits linked to the existence of off-season's periods with respect to the environment and to cultural and social traditions (Mathieson and Wall, 1982; Murphy, 1985; Pearce, 1989). The wide array of issues related to seasonality of demand for tourism destinations has thus stimulated economic research, which has investigated this phenomenon both in a qualitative and in a quantitative way.

The papers that have tried to tackle this problem in a quantitative way have followed a twofold approach. On the one hand, there is a wide body of research that has tried to elicit the best statistical techniques to be used in describing seasonality. It is worth mentioning that the Gini coefficient, the Peak Season's Share and the Coefficient of Variation seem to be most widely used tools (Baum and Lundtorp, 2001; Koenig and Bischoff, 2003; Riera *et al.*, 2003). On the other hand, the econometric approach to seasonality has used the ARIMA models in order to have the possibility to forecast future developments of tourism demand (Lim and McAleer, 2000).

The present chapter aims at analysing the evolution of tourism demand in the province of Lecce (an Italian peripheral region whose tourism demand has historically been mostly related to sun-and-sand mass tourism) in order to figure out if, and to which extent, this sector can be considered as pivotal for the economic development of this region. The econometric analysis of the time series will allow to ascertain the persistency of seasonality in the Province of Lecce. The chapter is based on a time series related to monthly tourist nights and it is structured as follows. The next section provides a discussion of the economic issues related to seasonality of demand and of the role that dynamic capabilities of both firms and administrative authorities can exert in this respect. The third section introduces and comments on the data-base. The fourth section performs the unit roots tests in order to choose the appropriate forecasting model which is developed in the following section. The last section concludes.

14.2 The economic implications of seasonality of demand in tourism

The researchers that have investigated the seasonality of demand for tourism destinations have tried to figure out all the main economic issues connected to such phenomenon (see, for a review, Vergori, 2004). Baum and Lundtorp (2001) have provided a survey of all the issues related to seasonality of demand that can be summarized by the following list: (a) reduced level of activity in off-peak months; (b) need to generate a sufficient revenue in a few months; (c) under utilization of physical capital; (d) difficulty to attract investments; (e) difficulty to implement a sustainable supply chain; (f) difficulty to provide a reliable transport network throughout the year; (g) seasonal hiring of the labour force; (h) consequent difficulty to reach and maintain a good qualitative standard of the tourism services provided.

It emerges that the seasonality of demand influences both the amount of invested capital and the dynamics that characterize the labour market of this specific industry. This is due to the fact that firms are confronted with a relatively short period of intense activity during which they have to accrue sufficient profits that can alleviate the low level of (or lack of) utilization of physical capital during the off-peak period. Candela and Figini (2003) have highlighted the risks connected to periods of intense activity in terms of overcrowding, higher prices and jeopardizing of reputation for a tourism destination. This normally leads firms to choose a level of physical capital inferior to the amount needed to serve all potential demand of the peak months.

Moreover, seasonality of demand contributes, in most tourism destinations, to the establishment of a dual labour market. Applying a general framework of labour economics theory (Atkinson, 1984), it is possible to notice that, on the one hand, managers and highly skilled workers are normally employed with full time contracts and they exert a wide range of capabilities that can be improved and modified over time. On the other hand, for the most part low skilled workers are hired only for the peak season period and they are not able to develop their capabilities over time.

A similar theoretical framework, that takes into account the firm as the unit of analysis (see, for a general discussion, Doeringer and Piore, 1971 and for an application to the tourism industry, Simms *et al.*, 1988; Riley, 1991), considers the division between internal and external labour markets. In case the wage differentials are high, firms tend to hire external workers in case of short training periods. This is particularly relevant in the tourism industry in the Province of Lecce, given its remarkable seasonality (see next sections).

All the above-mentioned issues, characterizing tourism destinations with a remarkable degree of seasonality of demand, hamper the development of dynamic capabilities (Leoncini *et al.*, 2006) at the firm's level. Moreover, persistent seasonality is also an index of the fact that local administrative authorities and institutions are not able to establish good relations with tourist firms in order to help them exploit all of their competitive potential. The following sections will perform an econometric analysis related to the time series of tourist nights in the province of Lecce in order to ascertain whether the seasonality of demand in this area is marked by the tendency to be persistent over time.

14.3 The database

The empirical evidence emerging from the analysis of time series often shows that the stationarity hypothesis is not fulfilled when actual data are considered. Consequently, the original time series must be treated in order to obtain a stationary series that can be modelled.

The data considered in this chapter are related to tourist nights in the province of Lecce between January 1988 and December 2003.

Figure 14.1a and 14.1b represent the above-mentioned series. Given the remarkable seasonality, the original series (Figure 14.1a) was monotonically transformed by using natural logarithms. This allowed the heteroschedasticity of the considered sample to reduce. The following statistics, tests and econometric modelling are based on the natural logarithms of tourist nights. The statistical analysis of a previous paper by the authors Vergori and Zamparini (2005), based on the same time series, highlighted a growing trend and a marked seasonal pattern which might be linked to the non-stationarity of the considered time series.

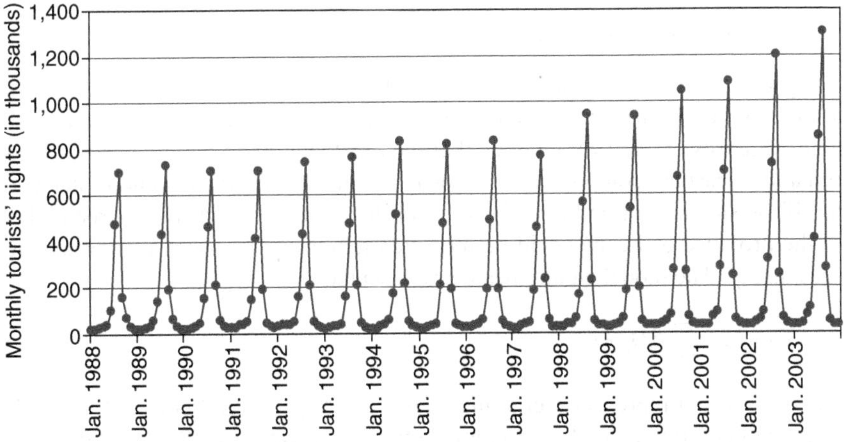

Figure 14.1a Monthly tourists' nights (in thousands).

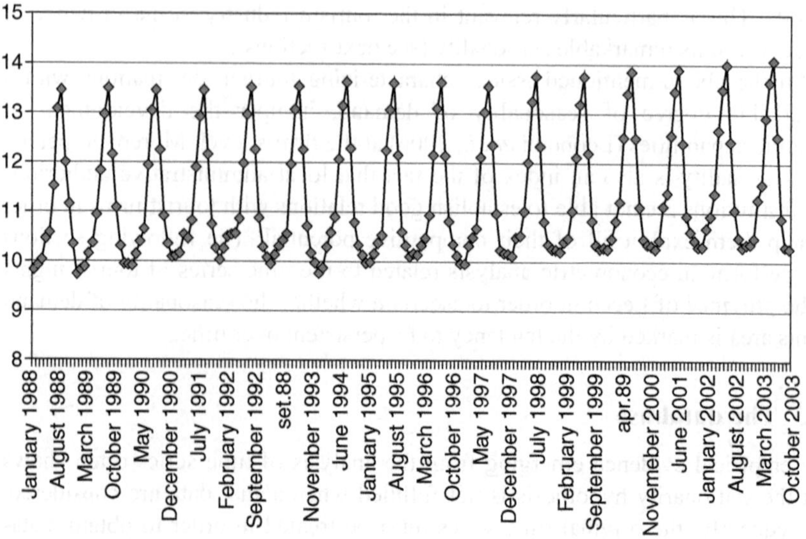

Figure 14.1b Natural logarithm of tourist nights.

In this respect, a preliminary analysis of the correlogram (Figure 14.2) detects a linear and slow reduction of autocorrelations, thus confirming the absence of stationarity in the time series.

The next subsection develops the tests of deterministic seasonality of the time series – that can be modelled by using dummy variables – coupled with a stochastic trend – which can be eliminated by differentiating (or recursively differentiating when necessary) the original series. The above-mentioned condition can only be satisfied if no seasonal unit roots exists.

14.3.1 Deterministic seasonality

The joint presence of a stochastic trend and of seasonal fluctuations which form a large share of variance is a common characteristic of several economic variables (Franses *et al.*, 1995). Given that the available time series displays a long run and a seasonal component, it seems reasonable to test if the trend is stochastic. If the stochastic trend hypothesis is fulfilled, the time series of tourist nights in the province of Lecce could be modelled taking into account a deterministic seasonality. The model would then be represented by:

$$\nabla \log X_t = \sum_{i=1}^{12} \delta_i D_{it} + \varepsilon_t \tag{1}$$

where X_t would represent tourist nights in period t, ∇ would constitute the difference operator which allows to remove the stochastic trend, D_{it} would describe the dummy variable at period t which corresponds to the ith month, δ_i are the

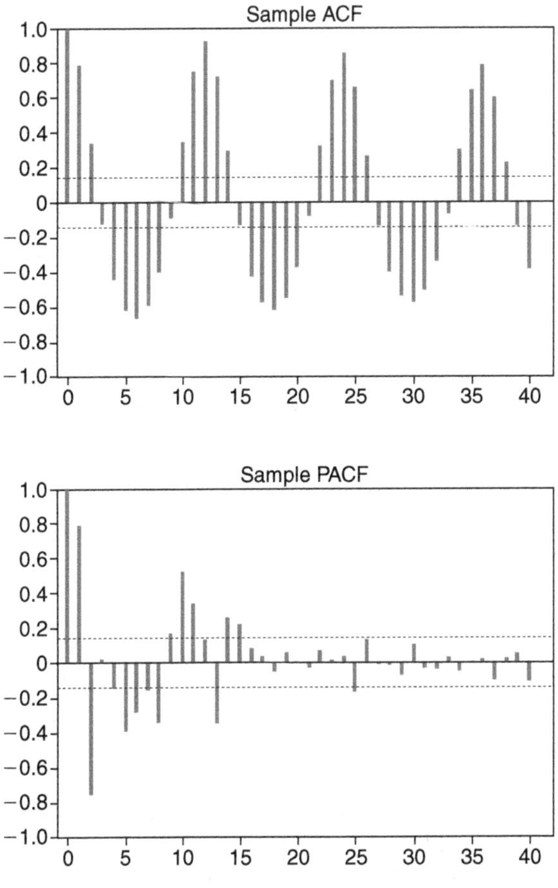

Figure 14.2 Autocorrelation and partial autocorrelation functions of the natural logarithm of tourist nights.

coefficients of the seasonal dummies which measure the growth rates of tourist nights in the *i*th month and ε_t is the error term.

The left-hand variable of equation (1) can be interpreted as the percentage variation of tourist nights at period *t*; being a difference of logarithms it represents the logarithm of the ratio between the values assumed by a determined variable at period *t* and at period $t-1$. Consequently, the coefficients δ_i represent the monthly growth rates. The results of the regression based on equation (1) are represented in Table 14.1.

The coefficients' values are coherent with the evolution of monthly tourist nights in all considered years. Positive coefficients are related to the months which constitute the upward part of Figure 14.1b. Negative values apply to the months of January, September, October, November and December. Each of

Table 14.1 Equation (1) estimation results

Variable	*Coefficient*	*Standard error*	*T-statistic*	*Probability (t)*
D1	–0.026899	0.039682	–0.677860	0.4987
D2	0.035538	0.038422	0.924932	0.3562
D3	0.236537	0.038422	6.156312	0.0000
D4	0.248018	0.038422	6.455123	0.0000
D5	0.330829	0.038422	8.610447	0.0000
D6	1.210973	0.038422	31.51784	0.0000
D7	1.023971	0.038422	26.65077	0.0000
D8	0.488823	0.038422	12.72255	0.0000
D9	–1.392516	0.038422	–36.24285	0.0000
D10	–1.378430	0.038422	–35.87623	0.0000
D11	–0.545756	0.038422	–14.20433	0.0000
D12	–0.204542	0.038422	–5.323581	0.0000
R^2	0.964415	Schwarz criterion	–0.642695	
Adjusted R^2	0.962228	F-Statistic	441.0210	
Akaike Info Criterion	–0.847027	Probability (F)	0.000000	

these months is marked by a reduction of tourist nights with respect to the preceding month. The values of most of the estimated coefficients are statistically significant; the only exceptions being represented by the months of January and February. The most relevant piece of information is represented by the R^2 value which should provide evidence about the deterministic seasonality.

The Adjusted R^2 for regression (1) – equal to 0.96 – is remarkably high and it should indicate (at least theoretically) the goodness of fit of the proposed model. However, extremely high values of the Adjusted R^2 might signal a "spurious" deterministic seasonality, following the definition by Franses *et al.* (1995). Consequently, equation (1) could be spurious, suggesting thus a stochastic seasonal trend in the time series of tourist nights in the province of Lecce. It is then necessary to test the presence of unit root that would confirm the stochastic nature of the seasonality.

14.4 The unit root tests

When time series displaying a clear seasonal evolutionary pattern are considered, it is important to check the stochastic nature of the underlying process by using unit root tests which allow to ascertain their presence at a yearly or at a seasonal frequence. In order to test for seasonal unit roots, it is necessary to factorize the seasonal difference polynomial; for monthly data, such a polynomial is defined as $\nabla_{12} = (1-B^{12})$. Factorizing it, it is possible to obtain (Banerjee *et al.*, 1993):

$$(1-B^{12})=(1-B)(1+B+B^2+\cdots+B^{11}) \quad (2)$$

that is, $(1-B^{12})$ can be decomposed as the product of the first difference operator times a filter containing eleven seasonal unit roots; this implies the presence of twelve unit roots, one of them at the zero frequency and the remaining ones at the seasonal frequencies. Box and Jenkins (1976) have proposed the joint application of the ∇ and the ∇_{12} operators, which implicitly assume the presence of thirteen unit roots, two of which at the zero frequency. The implicit risk emerging from the use of the Box and Jenkins operators lies in the over-differentiation of the series, given that the unit roots may be absent in some frequencies. It is thus important, to avoid the shortcomings connected to the Box and Jenkins procedure to ascertain the actual presence of the unit roots by using a specific test.

The HEGY test, developed by Hylleberg *et al.* (1990) for quarterly observations, was extended to monthly data by Franses (1991) and by Beaulieu and Miron (1993). The latter specification was used for the time series of tourist nights in the province of Lecce. Moreover, Taylor (1998) proposed the application of two different F-statistics which allow to obtain an overall check of the necessary integration. The Taylor statistics – indicated with $F_{1..12}$- and $F_{2..12}$-test, respectively, the presence of unit roots at all frequencies and at all seasonal frequencies (excluding, thus, the zero frequency). The related null hypotheses (tested estimating equation 3 by OLS) are: $\pi_1=\ldots=\pi_{12}=0$ and $\pi_2=\ldots=\pi_{12}=0$. The critical values of such statistics were computerized by Taylor (1998) using the Monte Carlo procedure.

The next subsection presents a HEGY test and a Taylor test, applied to monthly tourist nights in the province of Lecce in the period between January 1988 and December 2002. The available sample was reduced by one year in order to allow – once the most suitable model is chosen – "ex-post forecasts". The forecasts are related to the January 2003–December 2003 months. For this period, the actual tourist nights are known and it is then possible to compare the forecasted and the actual nights in order to evaluate the forecasting potential of the chosen model.

14.4.1 Test results

This subsection discusses the estimated values obtained both by the HEGY (as developed by Beaulieu and Miron, 1993) and by the Taylor (1998) test. Table 14.2 summarizes the results which were obtained for each test, the statistic that was used with the related critical value and the results of the autocorrelation in the residual test, which allows to choose the number of lagged values (p). In particular, the considered critical values were obtained by Beaulieu and Miron (1993) and by Franses and Hobijn (1997).

On the basis of the residual autocorrelation tests, it does not seem necessary to introduce lagged values of the dependent variables. The lagged values selection criteria are based on the LM test, on the Akaike Information Criteria (AIC) and on the Schwarz Criterion (SC). The Breusch–Godfrey LM test, based on twenty-four models, estimates the null hypothesis of lack of autocorrelation in the residuals up to the specified lag order. The estimation values differ on the basis of the chosen lags; in particular, thirteen models are considered where $p=0,\ldots,12$ and the other eleven models imply the $p=12$ lag coupled with other lags (0 and 12; 1 and 12; 1, 2 and 12; 1, 2, 3 and 12; and so on). The choice of the fittest model – among those which display residual autocorrelation – is based on the Akaike and Schwarz criteria.

According to both criteria, it does not appear necessary to introduce lagged dependent variables. For $p=0$, the LM test – computed for the first twelve and twenty-four autocorrelations in the residuals – displays values which are clearly above the 5 per cent confidence region.

In Table 14.2, such probabilities – indicated in parentheses – are associated with a LM statistic which is asymptotically distributed as a χ^2 with p degrees of freedom. Moreover, the model with $p=0$ has the lowest value of the Schwarz criterion (–0.94) and a value for the Akaike Information Criteria equal to –1.41, which is slightly higher than the value displayed by the model which considers the twelfth lag (–1.42). Despite this, it is preferable not to introduce lagged variables given that the coefficient of the twelfth lag is not statistically significant.

With respect to the unit roots, considering the Taylor (1998) tests it is possible to reject the null hypothesis of unit roots at all frequencies, given that the $F_{1..12}$ has a value which is outside the 5 per cent confidence region. Following such rejection, the $F_{2..12}$ statistic – by which the presence of unit roots at all seasonal frequencies is supposed – and the *t*-statistic computed to check the presence of unit roots at the zero frequency were estimated. The results allow to reject the null hypothesis underlying the $F_{2..12}$ statistic and they do not allow to reject the π_1 filter. In other words, the Taylor tests reject the application of the $(1-B^{12})$ filter and indicate the presence of a unit root at the zero frequency. Therefore, they suggest the use of the lag operator – which allows to take into account the stochastic trend – and they also suggest the possibility to use

Table 14.2 Hegy and Taylor tests results

t-statistic	*Estimated value*	*Critical value*
π_1	–1.56	–3.19
π_2	–3.85	–2.65
F-statistics		
π_3, π_4	14.33	6.23
π_5, π_6	18.44	6.23
π_7, π_8	6.70	6.23
π_9, π_{10}	11.18	6.23
π_{11}, π_{12}	5.31	6.23
F-statistics for taylor (1998) tests		
$\pi_1 \ldots \pi_{12}$	13.60	4.50
$\pi_2 \ldots \pi_{12}$	14.74	4.73
Lagged values (p)	*LM (12)*	*LM (24)*
0	11.30 (0.50)	24.77 (0.42)

seasonal dummy variables. It was then important to perform the HEGY test in order to check for the presence of unit roots at all possible frequencies.

The HEGY test has shown the presence of unit roots at the $\pi/6$ and at the – above mentioned – zero frequencies. The time series of monthly tourist nights in the province of Lecce might then be made stationary by applying the $(1-B)$ and $(1-\sqrt{3}B+B^2)$ filters. In order to check the robustness of the Taylor and HEGY tests, they were extended to the entire available sample (January 1988–December 2003). The same results were obtained confirming the necessity to adopt the considered filters.

However, the correlogram of the differenced time series (Figure 14.3) seems to indicate that this differenced process is also non-stationary, given that it decays very slowly. Such possibility was confirmed by a further application of the HEGY test on the differenced series. The results displayed the presence of two further unit roots at the π and $\pi/3$ frequencies. Despite the results,

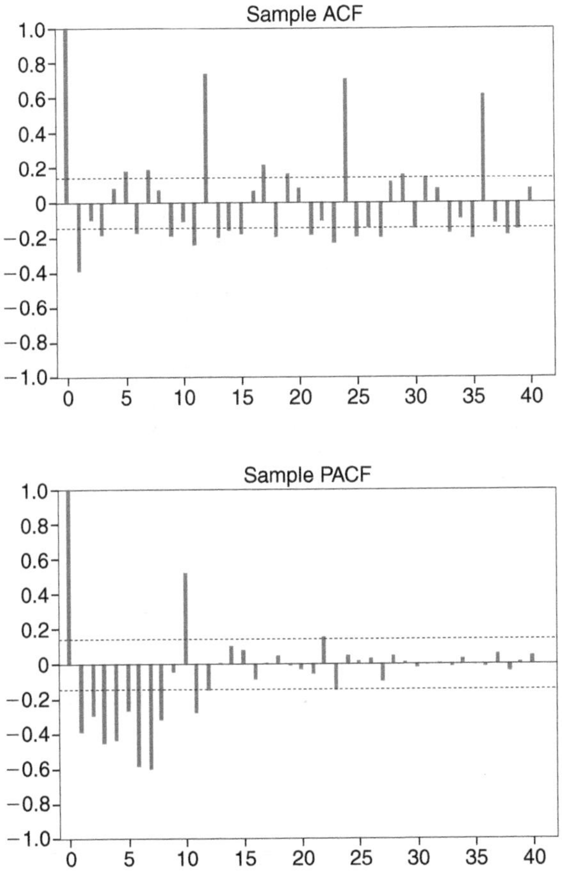

Figure 14.3 Global and partial autocorrelation functions of the differenced time series.

the first HEGY test rejects the necessity to apply the seasonal difference filter (Table 14.3), the empirical evidence for monthly tourist nights in the province of Lecce requires the application of the $(1-B^{12})$ filter.

The related differenced series is represented in Figure 14.4 while the corresponding correlogram is shown in Figure 14.5. The stationarity of such series emerges from both the correlogram and the results of the HEGY test applied to seasonal differences, which allow to reject all further unit roots.

Moreover, some researchers (Clements and Hendry, 1997; Osborn *et al.*, 1999) have shown that the application of the $(1 - B^{12})$ filter allow to obtain forecasts that have a robustness comparable to those obtained by applying the lower number of filters identified by the HEGY tests. The joint application of the $(1 - B)$ and $(1 - B^{12})$ filters (as suggested by Box and Jenkins, 1976) does not seem appropriate, given that the HEGY test on the difference of the seasonally differenced series does not display any unit root at the zero frequency. The following section aims at selecting the appropriate forecasting model on the basis of the results emerging from this section.

14.5 The forecasting model

The considerations of the preceding section suggest the application of the seasonal difference operator to the sample of monthly tourist nights in the province

Table 14.3 Estimation results of the SARIMA $(1, 0, 0)(1, 1, 0)_{12}$ model

	Coefficient	*Standard error*	*T-statistic*	*Probability*
Constant	0.033069	0.013543	2.441738	0.0158
AR	0.433695	0.073523	5.898777	0.0000
SAR	–0.378657	0.073348	–5.162498	0.0000
AIC	–1.20	JB	3.07 (0.22)	
SC	–1.14	Curtosi	3.45	
LM(12)	15.77 (0.20)	Asimmetry	0.26	

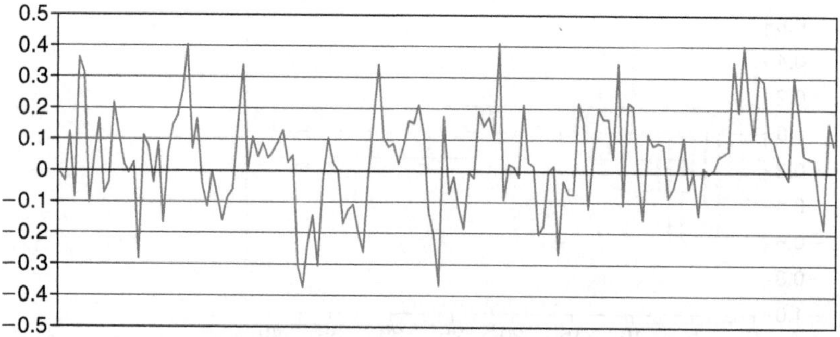

Figure 14.4 Seasonal differences of the natural logarithms of tourist nights.

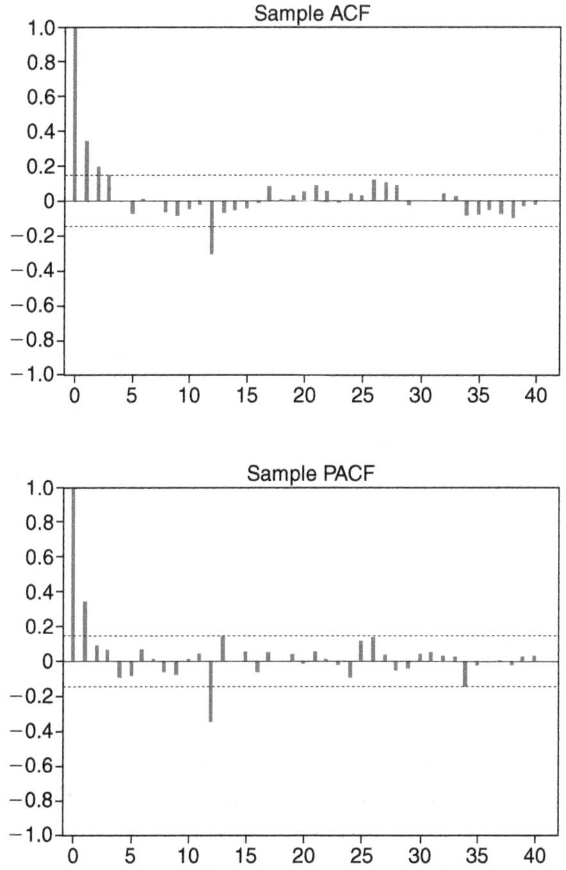

Figure 14.5 Global and partial autocorrelation functions of the seasonally differenced time series.

of Lecce in order to have a stationary time series. The next step is related to the identification of the fittest short-term forecasting model. The model is based on the observation for the January 1988–December 2002 period, while the forecasts are generated for the year 2003. The characteristics of the time series have suggested to adopt a SARIMA $(p,d,q)(P,D,Q)_s$ model. The preceding section has allowed to determine the order of integration of d and D which correspond, respectively to the month by month and to the seasonal differences. In particular, d is equal to zero while D is equal to one.

In this section, the degree of the seasonal polynomials P and Q and of the non-seasonal polynomials p and q will be determined for the Autoregressive and Moving Average components. Their identification is based on an analysis of the correlogram of the differenced series (Figure 14.5) which represents the first step in the model identification.

In particular, twenty-one different models were estimated. The selection of the fittest model was then based on the comparison of the Akaike and Schwarz criteria. Moreover, the significativeness of the estimated coefficients which correspond to the Autoregressive and to the Moving Average components was considered. The models which contained at least one coefficient which was not statistically significant (on the basis of a *t*-statistic) were discarded. Moreover, for all models, the absence of residual autocorrelation and their normal distribution were checked.

The model which displays the lowest AIC and SC values jointly with the statistical significance of coefficients, with the lack of residual autocorrelation and with their normal distribution, includes a seasonal and a non-seasonal autoregressive components. It is a SARIMA $(1,0,0)(1,1,0)_{12}$. The estimation results of the chosen model are summarized in Table 14.3.

The estimated coefficients have a high degree of significance. The LM test computed for twelve lags in the residuals allows not to discard the null hypothesis of lack of autocorrelation in the residuals. Consequently, the SARIMA $(1,0,0)(1,1,0)_{12}$ to be used for forecasting purposes is:

$$Y_t(1-0.43B)(1+0.38B^{12})=0.03+\varepsilon_t \tag{5}$$

14.5.1 Short-term forecasts and goodness of fit

The model chosen in the preceding subsection is based on the sample spanning since 1988 to 2002. Consequently, the forecasts will be related to the monthly tourist arrivals in the period January 2003–December 2003. Such ex-post forecasts allow to evaluate the forecasting potential of the model. The forecasting procedure adopted is the dynamic one (Hamilton, 1994).

Table 14.4 summarizes the forecasted values obtained for each considered month and compares them to the actual ones. The values are related to the percentage variation of tourist nights at period *t* with respect to the tourist nights at period $t-12$. For example, the value for January 2003 expresses the percentage variation of tourist nights in that month with respect to those of January 2002.

Figure 14.6 provides a graphical representation of actual and forecasted values. It can be noticed that the forecasting model underestimates two-thirds of the values and it is not able to identify the proper sign in four cases.

However, the statistical goodness of the forecasts can be evaluated by means of the Mean Squared Error (MSE) criterion which is given by the following formula:

$$\frac{1}{s}\sum_{t=1}^{s}\left(\hat{Y}_t-Y_t\right)^2 \tag{9}$$

The value of the MSE for the forecasts analysed in this section is 0.025; sufficiently small to allow to consider the forecasting model appropriate (Hamilton, 1994).

Figure 14.7 displays the actual and forecasted values in terms of monthly tourist nights. It clearly appears that the model tends to underestimate the values, especially in the peak and shoulder season (June, July and August) months.

Table 14.4 Forecasted and actual values of year by year monthly tourist nights' variations for 2003

Forecasted month	*Forecasted values*	*Actual values*
January 2003	–0.01207	0.04946
February 2003	–0.00094	0.05662
March 2003	–0.05873	–0.19835
April 2003	0.11563	0.33745
May 2003	0.04651	0.18658
June 2003	0.00880	0.25389
July 2003	0.03007	0.15112
August 2003	0.00727	0.08042
September 2003	0.32758	0.09054
October 2003	–0.00179	–0.17111
November 2003	0.08914	–0.18795
December 2003	0.09712	–0.02899
Mean Squared Error (MSE)	0.025	

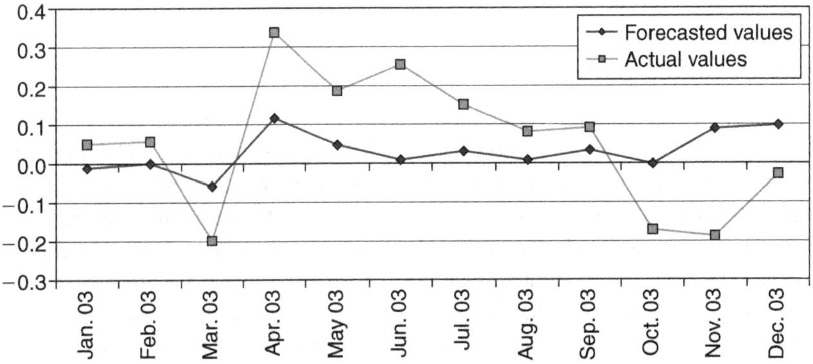

Figure 14.6 Actual and forecasted values – 2003.

This can be explained by the fact that those months polarize the most part of arrivals. Consequently, a small divergence in terms of percentage variation is reflected by a relevant difference in terms of arrivals. However, a large part of the divergence might be explained by the fact that, since 2001, the evolution of tourist arrivals in the province of Lecce (see Vergori and Zamparini, 2005) has experienced a sensible increase in its upward trend with respect to the preceding years.

It is apparent that the strong seasonality of demand in the province of Lecce tends to be persistent over time. Consequently, the implementation of policies aimed at improving the tourist supply potential of the area and at upgrading the local dynamic capabilities in this particular sector results as a key factor for the increase of the competitive power of the local firms. In this respect it would be remarkably important that local authorities foster the formation of a regional system of innovation (Cooke, 2001) that would generate the networks and

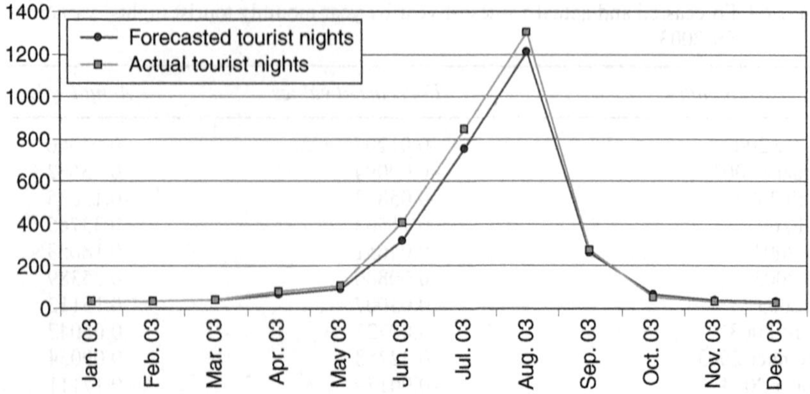

Figure 14.7 Forecasted and actual tourist nights – 2003.

interactions that are necessary to upgrade the capabilities of the local firms and to, consequently, diversify the local tourism market.

14.6 Concluding remarks

This present chapter represented an attempt to link the persistence of seasonality of tourist demand to the impossibility to take advantage of dynamic capabilities in order to increase the competitiveness of local tourist firms. It analysed the data related to tourists' arrivals to the province of Lecce on the basis of statistical and econometric techniques and related this phenomenon to the lack of sound policies aimed at exploiting the dynamic capabilities of firms. Despite the importance of this sector for the economic development of the region, the strong seasonality of demand poses problems in terms both of accommodation facilities and of employment. The strong characterization of the province as a sun-and-sand mass tourism destination tends to be persistent over time especially with respect to domestic tourists. This implies that the tourism sub-sector is probably, at the moment, mostly relevant in terms of the amount of liquidity which it can attract to this region.

It seems very important that the local administration and institutions assume a positive role in the development of dynamic capabilities that might lead to the creation of a complementary market in the off-peak season months. It appears that the only viable option to pursue this goal is a combination of investment in the upgrading of local supply in terms both of infrastructure and of capabilities of the employed workforce and of a strong and targeted marketing. The analysis of these latter issues constitute the future development of the present research.

References

Atkinson, J. (1984) *Flexibility Uncertainty and Manpower Management*, Institute of Manpower Studies, Report no. 89, Falmer, University of Sussex.

Ball, R.M. (1989) Some aspects of tourism, seasonality and local labour markets, *Area*, 21(1): 33–45.

Banerjee A., Dolado J., Galbraith, J.W. and Hendry, D.F. (1993) *Co-integration, Error-correction and the Econometric Analysis of non Stationary Data*, Oxford: Oxford University Press,

Baum, T. and Lundtorp, S. (2001) *Seasonality in Tourism*, Oxford: Pergamon.

Beaulieu, J.J. and Miron, J.A. (1993) Seasonal unit roots in aggregate U.S. data, *Journal of Econometrics*, 55(1–2): 305–328.

Box, G.E.P. and Jenkins, G.M. (1976) *Time Series Analysis: Forecasting and Control*, San Francisco: Holden Day.

Candela, G. and Figini, P. (2003) *Economia del turismo*, Milan: McGraw Hill.

Clements, M.P. and Hendry, D.F. (1997) An empirical study of seasonal unit roots in forecasting, *International Journal of Forecasting*, 13: 341–355.

Cooke, P. (2001) Regional innovation systems, clusters and the knowledge economy, *Industrial and Corporate Change*, 10: 945–974.

Doeringer, P.B. and Piore, M.J. (1971) *Internal Labour Markets and Manpower Analysis*, Lexington, MA: Lexington Books.

Flognfeldt, T. (1988) The employment paradox of seasonal tourism, Paper presented at Pre-Congress Meeting of International Geographical Union, Christchurch, New Zealand, 13–20 August.

Franses, P.H. (1991) Seasonality, non-stationarity and the forecasting of monthly time Series, *International Journal of Forecasting*, 7(2): 199–208.

Franses, P.H. and Hobijn, B. (1997), Critical values for unit root tests in seasonal time series, *Journal of Applied Statistics*, 24(1): 25–47.

Franses, P.H., Hylleberg, S. and Lee, H.S. (1995) Spurious deterministic seasonality, *Economics Letters*, 48: 249–256.

Hamilton, J.D. (1994) *Time Series Analysis*, Princeton: Princeton University Press.

Hylleberg, S., Engle, R.F., Granger, C.W.J. and Yoo, B.S. (1990) Seasonal integration and cointegration, *Journal of Econometrics*, 44(1–2): 215–238.

Koenig, N. and Bischoff, E.E. (2003) Seasonality of tourism in Wales: a comparative analysis, *Tourism Economics*, 9(3): 229–254.

Krakover, S. (2000) Partitioning seasonal employment in the hospitality industry, *Tourism Management*, 21(5) 461–471.

Leoncini, R., Montresor, S. and Vertova, G. (2006) Dynamic capabilities between firm organization and local development: a critical survey, *Economia Politica*, 23: 451–514.

Lim, C. and McAleer, M. (2000) A seasonal analysis of Asian tourist arrivals to Australia, *Applied Economics*, 32: 499–509.

Mathieson, A. and Wall, G. (1982) *Tourism: Economic, Physical and Social Impacts*, Harlow: Longman.

Murphy, P.E. (1985) *Tourism: A Community Approach*, New York: Methuen.

Osborn, D.R., Heravi, S. and Birchenhall, C.R. (1999) Seasonal unit roots and forecasts of two-digit European industrial production, *International Journal of Forecasting*, 15: 27–47.

Pearce, D.G. (1989) *Tourism Development*, Harlow: Longman Scientific and Technical.

Riera, A., Rossellò, J. and Sansò, A. (2003) *The Economic Determinants of Seasonal Patterns. Seasonality in Monthly International Tourist Arrivals to the Balearic Islands*, mimeo.

Riley, M. (1991) An analysis of hotel labour markets, in C.P. Cooper (ed.) *Progress in Tourism, Recreation and Hospitality Management*, vol. 3, London: Belhaven Press, pp. 232–246.

Shaw, G. and Williams, A.M. (1994) *Critical Issues in Tourism*, Oxford: Blackwell.

Simms, J., Hales, C. and Riley, M. (1988) Examination of the concept of internal labour markets in UK hotels, *Tourism Management*, 9: 3–12.

Stynes, D.J. and Pigossi, B.W. (1983) A tool for investigating tourism-related seasonal employment, *Journal of Travel Research*, 21(3): 19–24.

Taylor, A.M. (1998) Testing for unit roots in monthly time series, *Journal of Time Series Analysis*, 19(3): 349–368.

Vergori, A.S. (2004) Stagionalità della domanda di servizi turistici.e. sue implicazioni sull'offerta, *Istituzioni.e. Sviluppo Economico*, 2(3): 77–100.

Vergori, A.S. and Zamparini, L. (2005) Turismo e politiche di sviluppo locale: un caso di studio, in A. Lopes, M. Lorizio and F. Reganati (eds) *Istituzioni.e. Imprese nello Sviluppo Locale*, Rome: Carocci Editore, pp. 195–217.

Yacoumis, J. (1980) Tackling seasonality: the case of Sri Lanka, *Tourism Management*, 1(2): 84–98.

Author index

Subject index